JACOBEAN PAGEANT

JAMES I   1566–1625
by Daniel Mytens

JACOBEAN PAGEANT

OR

THE COURT OF KING JAMES I

———————

BY

G. P. V. AKRIGG

ILLUSTRATED

HARVARD UNIVERSITY PRESS
CAMBRIDGE MASSACHUSETTS
1963

PRINTED IN GREAT BRITAIN

TO

HELEN

FOREWORD

BEFORE listing my obligations to those who helped me while I was working on this book, I wish to acknowledge an earlier debt, that to two teachers of my undergraduate days, the late Professor G. G. Sedgewick and the late Professor Thorleif Larsen. For a generation they sought to instil into the Honours students in English at the University of British Columbia the spirit of humanism and the ethics of scholarship. I hope this book does no discredit, coming from one who is proud to have been the student of such men.

My immediate debts for counsel or assistance begin with Professor W. E. Farnham of the University of California, the director of my doctoral dissertation. To his nomination I owe the research fellowship at the Folger Shakespeare Library which in 1946 enabled me to begin work on this book. My debt to the Folger, both during my fellowship and since, has been great. I am under particular obligation to its director, Louis B. Wright, and his colleagues, James G. McManaway and Giles E. Dawson.

In 1952 I received from the University of British Columbia a grant which enabled me to study in Britain. My work there was done chiefly in the Public Record Office and the British Museum, though I used various other libraries and collections. Everywhere I was received with courtesy and co-operation. I recall with pleasure time spent in the company of Mr. John Charlton, Inspector of Ancient Monuments for the Office of Works, and his colleague, Mr. G. H. Chettle, viewing Hampton Court Palace, St. James's Palace, and the Inigo Jones chapel at Marlborough House.

Among those who have helped me with my enquiries are Mr. John Kerslake and Miss Mary Pettman of the National Portrait Gallery; Miss Madeleine Blumstein of the Victoria and Albert Museum; Sir James Mann, Master of the Armouries, The Tower of London; Sir Anthony Wagner and Mr. W. J. G. Vergo of the College of Arms; the Hon. V. Sackville-West and Mr. G. D. Squibbs. I am indebted to Mr. G. T. Kent for help in drawing the plan of Whitehall Palace. The Courtauld Institute and the Royal Academy supplied the photographs used for several of the illustrations.

Chief of my obligations is to my wife, Helen Manning Akrigg. Over the

vii

years she has been my research assistant, typist, critic and proof reader, and she has borne in addition all the tribulations of being married to a man who is writing a book. Without her, *Jacobean Pageant* could hardly have been written.

G.P.V.A.

*The University of British Columbia,
    Vancouver, Canada.*

TABLE OF CONTENTS

LIST OF ILLUSTRATIONS

PROLOGUE

'A ROYAL MAJESTY is not privilege against death.' Queen Elizabeth lay dying in Richmond Palace. Forty-five years earlier the members of her first parliament had urged her to marry and perpetuate her line, or at least to name her heir. She had put them off on both counts—she was always good at putting people off—and now she was dying with no heir officially recognized.

It had always been assumed that Elizabeth meant her distant kinsman the King of Scots to be her successor. Only recently she had told the Lord Admiral, Nottingham, that her throne had always been the throne of kings, and none but her nearest heir of blood and descent should succeed. Now that she was near the end Nottingham approached her deathbed, and in the presence of the Privy Council reminded her of her earlier words and asked just what she had meant. 'I told you,' said the dying queen with a flash of her old spirit, 'my seat has been the seat of Kings, and I will have no rascal to succeed; who should succeed me but a King?' Sir Robert Cecil, her Principal Secretary of State, put in his word gently, trying to win her to break the cautious rule of a lifetime and unequivocally name the heir. What did she mean, he asked, by 'no rascal shall succeed'? She gave her answer: 'My meaning was a King shall succeed me; and who should that be but our cousin of Scotland?' And so, with a rhetorical question, she came as near as ever she did to naming her heir. Those who were about her at the last said that, when she lay no longer capable of speech, they asked her directly if it were indeed her will that the King of Scotland should succeed, and that the dying woman touched the crown of her head in reply. The significance, said some, was that she desired to be succeeded by one who already wore a crown.

Matters of such moment as the succession of a kingdom are not left to the chance of a dying woman's gesture. For years Cecil had been secretly corresponding with King James VI of Scotland, preparing the way for his coming in. Their letters, which if discovered could have ruined Cecil, had been smuggled through in packages between the French Duke of Rohan in London and the Earl of Mar in Scotland. Other great lords in the English court had also been in touch with the Scottish king. And in Dublin there was the master of a free school, James Hamilton (in later years to become Viscount Clandeboye) and his usher James Fullerton (later Sir James Fullerton) through whom the English in Ireland could send their messages to Scotland and receive back their answers from the royal recipient.[1]

About two o'clock on the morning of March 24, 1603, the great Elizabeth surrendered her spirit to the keeping of the God with whom her relations had always been somewhat equivocal. The Privy Council ordered the court gates closed. No man was to enter; no man was to leave.

The moment of crisis lay upon England. Would there be war or peace? Would the English Catholics, still perhaps one-third of the nation, rise and put a Catholic on the throne which Elizabeth, pretending to be a Catholic, had received from a Catholic? Would the Protestant James then come storming south with an army, claiming the English crown as a great-great-grandson of Henry VII? Were the anguish and the agony of the Wars of the Roses, or of the civil war in France so lately ended, to come upon England? The messengers of the Privy Council went to direct the closing of the ports of the kingdom.

Meanwhile at Richmond Lord Hunsdon, the Lord Chamberlain, thrust his way past the palace gate. The porter dared not halt the great officer but he stopped a second man who sought to slip out in his wake. Hunsdon turned and said angrily, 'Let him out, I will answer for him,'[2] whereupon the porter stood aside. The second man was Sir Robert Carey, a brother of the Lord Chamberlain. The spotlight of history was upon him. He was a man of some forty-three years, having behind him a career of minor distinction as a soldier and a diplomat. In 1586 he had gone to Scotland as an ambassador to James VI during the delicate period following the execution by Elizabeth of his mother, Mary Queen of Scots. The following year he had returned to James as ambassador. More recently, when it had become evident that the Queen was gravely ill, he had written to James desiring him not to stir from Edinburgh for 'if of that sicknesse she should die, I would be the first man that should bring him newes of it'.[3] It was important to Carey to get past the porter at Richmond Palace gate.

As he left the palace precincts, Sir Robert had in his possession a blue ring. This ring was important too. It had just been given to him by his sister, Lady Scrope, who had received it from the Scottish king as a token to be sent him once Elizabeth was dead.

Strangely enough, Sir Robert did not depart post-haste for Scotland once he had slipped beyond the palace. Instead, he lingered some hours in London, long enough for the Council, which knew of his escape and intentions, to send the Knight Marshal with word that if he would wait a little longer they would make him their own messenger into Scotland. However, Sir William Knollys, Treasurer of the Household, whispered to the Knight Marshal that his fellow councillors were resolved to send someone else to bear the great news. When the Marshal delivered the Council's message he informed Carey of the intended double-cross. Sir Robert realized that the sands of time were running out. Some time between nine and ten o'clock in the morning, he mounted his horse and started north. The drumbeat of his horse's hooves along the Great North Road was the prelude ushering in the new reign.

Sir Robert Carey's ride is one of the often told stories of history. Riding at breakneck speed he managed to cover 162 miles that first day before he stopped for the night at Doncaster. On March 25th he covered another 136 miles to his next stopping-place, his country home at Widdrington in Northumberland. By noon of the third day he had covered about 49 miles when he was thrown by his horse. Since his head had been injured in the fall, he had to ride softly the final 50 miles to Edinburgh. Late that night he reached Holyrood Palace.

> . . . the King was newly gone to bed by the time that I knocked at the gate. I was quickly lett in, and carried up to the King's chamber. I kneeled by him, and saluted him by his title of *England*, *Scotland*, *France* and *Ireland*. Hee gave mee his hand to kisse, and bade me welcome. After hee had long discoursed of the manner of the Queen's sicknesse and of her death, he asked me what letters I had from the Councill? I told him, none: and acquainted him how narrowly I escaped from them. And yet I had brought him a blue ring from a faire lady that I hoped would give him assurance of the truth that I had reported.[4]

Chapter I

The New King

SIR ROBERT CAREY'S ride from London to Edinburgh had its parallel in another though less arduous ride thirty-seven years earlier. The day had been June 19, 1566. Between nine and ten o'clock that morning a prince had been born in Edinburgh Castle. Within two hours a messenger, Sir James Melville, was galloping southward to London and the English court. He arrived there on Sunday, June 23rd, in four and one-half days as against Carey's three. Melville's tidings came when Queen Elizabeth was dancing in great merriment after supper:

> . . . bot sa schone as the secretary Cicill roundit the newes in hir ear of the prince birth, all merines was layed asyd for that nycht; every ane that wer present marveling what mycht move sa sodane a chengement; for the Queen sat down with hir hand upon hir haffet [the side of her head]; and boursting out to some of hir ladies, how that the Queen of Scotlandis was leichter of a faire sonne, and that sche was bot a barren stok.[1]

This was the prince who stood now before Sir Robert Carey. He was a thickset man, of little more than medium height, in the robust health of maturity. His complexion was high and sanguine, his skin remarkably white and soft. His eyes were large, their look of vacant intensity giving way readily to worried gleams of apprehension, or the half-twinkle of a canny wit. Light brown hair framed a broad forehead. The King's face was full, set off by a sparse square-cut beard. It was unfortunate that his tongue was large for his mouth for it added a thickness of speech to his broad Scots accent, and made his act of drinking singularly ungraceful, 'as if eating his drinke'.[2] His muscular co-ordination was poor, so that his walk was a species of jerky shamble—'that weaknesse made him ever leaning on other mens shoulders, his walke was ever circular, his fingers ever in that walke fidling about his codpiece'.[3] Despite these minor disabilities, the King could show dignity and command of presence. One of his enemies was prepared to concede that, despite his physical handicaps, 'in the whole man he was not uncomely'.[4]

Strangers seeing James sometimes got an impression of corpulence, but this impression was faulty—they did not know that the stocky sovereign habitually wore a heavily quilted doublet for protection from the stilettoes of assassins. This was a king who lived in constant fear of murder. He had, indeed, a morbid horror of death, a feeling so intense that in later years he would be unable to bring himself to attend the funerals of either his wife or his elder son.

The quilted doublet and the unconscious fumbling with his codpiece were outward signs that the new king was one of the most complicated neurotics ever to come to the English throne. In view of his earlier years, he could hardly have been otherwise.

First of all there was the murder of David Rizzio. Three months before James's birth his mother, Mary Queen of Scots, had been restrained by force while a group of malcontent lords, headed by her wastrel husband Henry Stuart, Lord Darnley, had dragged from her presence her trusted secretary, friend and counsellor, the Italian David Rizzio, and brutally murdered him in an adjoining room. Some of King James's subjects always believed that his dread of bared weapons, so acute that he dissolved in panic when his own queen came to him, sword in hand, though only to propose a ceremony of knighting, sprang from the prenatal effects on Mary's child as she saw the swords and daggers drawn against Rizzio. In any event, the appalling story of Rizzio's end was one of the things with which the young prince had to grow up. All his days the slander was to haunt him that he was himself Rizzio's bastard.

The young prince having been born, Mary called into the lying-in room the young husband whom she scorned and hated, and exacted from him acknowledgment of his son's legitimacy. Then the young babe was carried off by direction of the Estates of Scotland to Stirling Castle, to rest in the care of the Earl of Mar. When he was baptized according to the Roman Catholic rites by the Archbishop of St. Andrews, the Protestant Earl of Bedford, proxy for Queen Elizabeth, pointedly remained outside the chapel. Mary's child was still at Stirling, a babe less than a year old, when his father was in his turn murdered. Weak, shiftless Darnley had been lying ill in Kirk o' Field, a house outside the walls of Edinburgh, when the night was rent by a terrible explosion. In the morning searchers found the body of the strangled Darnley lying in the ruins. Three months later Mary married the man whom all Scotland suspected of being her husband's murderer, James Hepburn, Earl of Bothwell. A few weeks later she was forced to abdicate. The great lords of Scotland came to Stirling; the royal regalia, 'the honours of Scotland', were brought from their places of safe-keeping; John Knox preached a sermon; and James, barely one year old, was crowned King of Scotland. The Earl of Morton and Lord Home grimly promised on his behalf that he would defend and maintain the Protestant religion.

Violence dogged the boy king. Mar guarded him vigilantly, but Mar could not anticipate every move of the turbulent Scottish lords. On the

morning of September 4, 1571, a few days after the five-year-old monarch
had made his first public appearance to open parliament at Stirling, the
Catholic Earl of Huntly and his allies the Hamiltons tried to capture both
parliament and King. The coup failed, but the little boy saw his grandfather
the Earl of Lennox, Regent of Scotland, brought mortally wounded into
the castle to die.

At Stirling the little boy grew up with a sense of loneliness. In later
years he spoke feelingly of the irony of his youth: 'I was alane, without
fader or moder, brither or sister, king of this realme, and heir apperand
of England.'[5] He was indeed without a mother. Mary, in her long English
imprisonment, might as well have never existed. He was less than a year
old when he saw her for the last time. Her place was taken to some extent
by the Countess of Mar, a stern but not unaffectionate guardian.

The young prince's education was not neglected. When he was only
three years old, the Estates chose four preceptors to take his schooling in
hand. 'They gar me speik Latin ar I could speik Scottis' was the King's
later comment. Of the four, only two were concerned with the boy's day-
by-day tuition, George Buchanan and Peter Young.

Old George Buchanan was the greatest scholar in Scotland, a man
known among the learned all over Europe. He had taught at Paris, and
Montaigne had been his pupil at Bordeaux. Later he had returned to
Scotland, turned Protestant, and been rewarded with the principalship of
St. Andrews. At first he had been one of Queen Mary's friends, but friendship had turned to hatred and now, even while he was educating Mary's
son for kingship, he published in the purest Latin the foulest slanders
against her. All his life James prided himself on being Buchanan's student.
He accepted scholarship at Buchanan's own high valuation and remained
attached not only to the name but to the substance of learning. There was
always a notable streak of pedantry in King James, and it was Buchanan
who put it there—in many ways he fitted him better for the study than
the throne room.

The boy James respected Buchanan, but he did not love him. Buchanan
was too stern a preceptor to inspire love. As the King testified in later
years, he trembled at the approach of his teacher. A significant little anecdote tells how, late in life, James was visited in a nightmare by Buchanan
'who seemed to check him severely, as he used to do',[6] turning from
him with a frowning countenance when the King sought to pacify him,
and dictating verses which the King remembered perfectly when he
awoke.

Buchanan's junior associate Peter Young, aged only twenty-five, was
just back from his own studies at Geneva. For him the boy king developed
such a liking and affection that in later years he kept him with him and

made him the tutor of his own son Charles. This Peter Young was a theologian instructed by John Calvin's close friend and successor as professor of theology at Geneva, Theodore Beza. With Young the boy king explored the whole intellectual approach to God and His universe, and became acquainted with every quiddity of the case against Catholicism. Young made him an unshakable Protestant and a part-time theologian to the end of his days.

There can be no doubt that James was an adept student. When in June 1574 the English ambassador, Killigrew, was brought to view the boy, he was amazed by his command of French; but what really dazzled him was that Buchanan and Young invited him to choose at random passages out of the Latin Bible which the eight-year-old translated *ex tempore* first into French and then into English. As the years passed the boy's studies broadened. He developed a taste for writing verse, and by the time he was eighteen had published in Edinburgh his *Essayes of a Prentise in the Divine Art of Poesie*, which was followed a few years later by *His Majesties Poeticall Exercises*.

It would have been pleasant for James if his boyhood could have been spent tranquilly with his books and sports, his languages, his theology and his poetry, but such was not to be the case. Two earls, Argyll and Atholl, came more and more to dominate the royal household. Through insinuations in the boy's ears they brought him to distrust the Earl of Morton, Regent of Scotland. At their prompting, a few months before his twelfth birthday James abolished the regency and proclaimed his own 'acceptance of the government'. The triumph was somewhat dashed for Argyll when the young Earl of Mar managed to regain control of Stirling Castle from him by a sudden coup, brought Morton before the King, and secured for the deposed regent a place on the Council. The scene was a nasty one and might have turned murderous. James was awakened from his sleep by the tumult and rose to see swords and daggers drawn, and the son of his governor, the Master of Mar, trampled to death in the mêlée. About the young King swirled the violent ambitions and passions of the great lords. He must have been sick with fear for his own safety.

Then young King James found somebody to love. In the autumn of 1579 there landed from France his cousin, Esmé Stuart, Lord of Aubigny. He was a cultivated courtier, a man of experience and breeding, sophisticated, charming, dazzling—very different from the rough, half-barbaric Scottish chieftains. He was, moreover, the King's own kinsman. The lonely uncertain boy of thirteen, without father, mother, brother or sister, welcomed the thirty-seven-year-old Aubigny with hope and joy. For him he developed the all-encompassing admiration that a schoolboy of thirteen can develop for a mature man who represents all that he himself would like to be, surer and more confident than himself in his dealings with the world. James had found the first of his favourites.

Esmé Stuart's rise was spectacular. Within a few months he had been created Earl of Lennox. Within a year he was a duke, the only duke in all Scotland. Lennox helped and guided the boy. He saw to it that for the first time there was a royal bodyguard answerable only to the King. Rewards were heaped upon rewards for Lennox. Lennox became Lord Chamberlain. Lennox became governor of the key fortress of Dumbarton. Lennox was against Morton, and so Morton went to the scaffold. Most of Morton's estate passed to Lennox, including the palace of Dalkeith. The Duke of Lennox was the man whom the King delighted to honour. Not least of the reasons was that he had listened to the boy's earnest theological reasoning and had allowed him to convert him to the Protestant faith.

For three years James was happy in the company of the Duke of Lennox and that of his lesser favourite James Stewart, Earl of Arran. Then there came utterly humiliating disaster, and the direct threat of physical violence. The day was August 22, 1582; the event was the Ruthven Raid. James, for once without either Lennox or Arran, had gone to hunt at Ruthven Castle. He awoke to find the castle surrounded by throngs of armed men. A group of unshakably Protestant lords, among them the Earl of Gowrie, the Earl of Mar and the Master of Glamis, marched into the room. They distrusted the 'conversion' of Lennox, they were jealous of the influence that he and Arran had over the King, and they feared that they would win him to Catholicism. James, affronted, turned to leave the room. One of the lords thrust his leg across the door and kept him from leaving. When the sixteen-year-old boy burst into tears of mortification, fear and anger, the Master of Glamis taunted him to his face: 'Better that bairns should weep than bearded men.'[7] There was a mocking call for a rocking-horse for the King.

The Raid was entirely successful. The young King, learning that for survival he needed the arts of dissimulation, a lesson never forgotten, put the best face he could on things. Arran was imprisoned. For Lennox's own safety James ordered him to leave Scotland. He returned to France and died there within the year. On his deathbed he professed himself a Protestant—the conversion had been genuine after all.

Less than a year after the Ruthven Raid, James escaped from custody at Falkland, and the Ruthven lords had to flee for safety to England. From that time on King James was pretty much master in his own house, except when he chose to let his ministers of state exceed their proper bounds or found it necessary to placate powerful parties temporarily. There were of course difficulties with the Kirk, but even the more arrogant of the ministers, the 'Popes of Edinburgh', learned to have respect for their King.

B*

There was attempted rebellion by the Earl of Bothwell, a kinsman of his mother's lover, but nothing came of that. At one point, however, James had a horrible fright. Entering his bedroom in his nightshirt, he found the redoubtable Bothwell kneeling on the floor, a drawn sword in his hand. (The Earl meant to signify both his power to slay and his resolve to submit, but the allegory was a bit beyond the terrified King.) Finally, there was the dark business of the Gowrie Plot.

There will always be some shadow of doubt, some unresolved curiosity, as to what really happened when King James came to the house of the Earl of Gowrie on August 5, 1600. However, the official account is probably true in the main. It goes as follows. On that day King James was at his hunting at Falkland. To him in the morning, as he prepared to join his fellow huntsmen, came handsome young Alexander Ruthven, who enjoyed the title of Master of Ruthven, and was the brother of the Earl of Gowrie. The two brothers were sons of that Earl of Gowrie who with the other Ruthven Raiders had seized the King eighteen years earlier. Pardoned for his participation in that raid, the father had nevertheless been later executed on other grounds as a traitor. This bright morning in August, the Master of Ruthven begged the King for a chance to speak a word in private. While the two walked up and down, the Master poured into the royal ear a strange story of how the evening before he had seized a suspicious figure in the fields outside Perth, and had found that under his cloak he had a pot filled with foreign gold coin. He had imprisoned the man in the great house at Perth belonging to his brother the Earl, and he urged the King to come and examine his captive and receive the gold. James proceeded to his hunting, accompanied by the Master, but at the end of the morning's chase decided to investigate this strange mystery and set forth for Perth. He took with him various of his nobles, to the annoyance of the Master who urged that in a matter so secret the King should come with only a servant or two.

The mansion of the Earl of Gowrie at Perth faced on Speygate Street with pleasant gardens behind reaching down to the River Tay. When King James arrived he was conducted to a private apartment and served dinner. His courtiers dined separately in the great hall and then went out into the gardens and killed time eating cherries while waiting for their royal master.

King James, having finished his own dinner, was impatient to see the mysterious prisoner. The Master of Ruthven, alone, led the King down various corridors, locking the doors behind them, until they reached a small chamber in a turret. In it was no bound prisoner but Andrew Henderson, the chamberlain to the Earl of Gowrie. The Master shut the door, drew the sword from Henderson's side and turning on his King declared, 'Sir, you must be my prisoner; remember my father's death.' When James began to speak, the Master cried, 'Hold your tongue, sir, or by Christ ye shall die.' The Master then declared that James must swear a promise to be proposed by his brother and, locking the door, went to fetch him. While he was gone James questioned the chamberlain who declared that he himself had been locked in the chamber like a dog, and swore that he would die before he would let Gowrie do evil to the King. At this juncture the Master returned without the Earl and, shouting, 'By God, sir, there is no remedy', sought to bind the King's hands. James struggled desperately, his back to a small window. Andrew Henderson contrived to get the window open and the King disengaged himself sufficiently from the Master to lean out and cry, 'I am murdered! Treason! My lord Mar, help, help!'

The King's outcry was heard by his lords, already a mightily perplexed and worried group of men. While they had been loitering in the gardens with the Earl, their host, there had come to them Cranstoun, Gowrie's master stabler, with word that the King had already started back to Falkland and desired them to follow swiftly. One of the lords, sensing that something was wrong, slipped away to the front gate facing on the street, and there received the assurance of the porter that the King had not departed. The Earl, coming up with the other lords, angrily rejoined that the King had left by the back gate, to which the porter, unaware how much hinged on his answer, protested that the back gate was locked and that he himself had the key to it. It was while the King's attendants stood by the gate, not knowing what was going on or whom to believe, that they saw the window above flung open and heard James's frantic cry.

First to reach the King was young Sir John Ramsay who came racing up a spiral staircase into the turret chamber. He found Henderson standing by, helpless and trembling, while the King and the Master wrestled furiously. James wrenched his mouth free from the clutching hand of the Master long enough to shout to Ramsay to strike low since the Master had a secret coat of mail under his attire. Ramsay drew his dagger and struck. The King, breaking free from the wounded man, sent him reeling down the stairs. Coming up were several more of the royal retinue, Sir Hugh Herries and Sir Thomas Erskine. Erskine's man gave another stroke at the Master who cried out, 'Alas! I had na wyte [blame] of it!' and died.

James was not yet safe. The Earl of Gowrie, calling for his men to rally to him, tried to get to the King, only to die at the sword of young Ramsay. Though the Earl fell, another Ruthven took over the leadership and the fight continued. All this while, the main body of James's courtiers, ignorant of the open access by the spiral stairs, were trying to batter down a locked door which gave access to the turret room from an upper level. They broke through to the embattled King, and James was safe at last.

Meanwhile all Perth was in turmoil. Citizens thronged the street outside the mansion gates. Their sympathies were with the Ruthven family and, remembering the old slanders about Queen Mary and Rizzio, they raised a shout to James in the turret room above, 'Come down, come down, thou son of Seigneur Davie!' Another clamour mingled with their uproar. The provost of Perth had ordered that the great bell of the city be rung to sound the alarm. Added to its clanging was the hysterical screaming of the Ruthven women that the King and his men had murdered the Earl. At last the bailie of Perth managed to clear the mob from the streets and the uproar subsided. The magistrates of Perth took over Gowrie House and ordered that the corpses of the Earl and the Master be put by for presentation before Parliament for attainder for treason. At eight o'clock that evening, the bright day having turned to rain, the shaken monarch took horse and returned to Falkland.

James never allowed the day of his escape to go unremembered. Every Tuesday for the rest of his life there was a sermon to commemorate James's escape that day. Every August 5th there was an anniversary feast at which Ramsay, the Earl of Holderness as he came in time to be, was the principal guest and had any boon he requested granted.

Startling stories grew up around the Gowrie Plot—that James was the aggressor, that he had the Master killed because he was the Queen's lover, that there was perjured evidence given to cast the blame on the King's victims. No evidence supports these tales. It is, in fact, inconceivable that James should have cut short his hunting midday to seek out his enemies among their retainers in their own house, and there to have contrived murder. The received account of the Gowrie Plot is probably true in its main outlines, though we can never know for sure what really took the King and the Master to the seclusion of the turret chamber, or whether the tragic consequence was not due to one or the other losing his head and panicking.

Not only was James repeatedly threatened by physical violence during his years in Scotland, he was menaced too, or so he believed, by malevolent supernatural powers. The King had trouble with witches. They made their great assault against him in 1590, just after his marriage to Princess Anne, the daughter of the King of Denmark. James's godmother, Queen Elizabeth, had previously recommended the Princess of Navarre as a bride for her probable heir. James however passed over the French princess in favour of Anne, who was younger and more beautiful. There was also a thrifty Scottish consideration—marriage with the Danish princess would settle in Scotland's favour a dispute with Denmark over the ownership of the Orkney Islands. Accordingly, in June 1589, the Earl Marshal of Scotland was sent in magnificent state to Denmark to make a formal proposal of marriage. The marriage was celebrated by proxy in Denmark in August and the bride sailed for Scotland in September. Unfortunately, contrary winds repeatedly drove back her ship. At length James sailed with his own fleet to bring home his queen. His Majesty's voyage was not necessarily inspired by impatience to possess his bride. James never gave any evidence of being particularly attracted by women. Before sailing for Denmark he made it plain to the Privy Council that he had married for reasons of state, chiefly to provide his kingdom with an heir—'as to my own nature, God is my witness, I could have abstained langer'.[8] James made the voyage safely and on November 24, 1589, the marriage was solemnized at Oslo. The newly married couple visited the Danish court at Copenhagen for some months, and did not sail for Scotland until April. They had a hard time getting to James's own country. Adverse winds and storms made their crossing exceptionally difficult. A little while later James discovered the apparent cause for these troubles—a covey of witches, living around North Berwick and led by the schoolmaster at Saltpans, had conspired to ruin James by their diabolical arts. The chief of the witches was Agnes Tompson. King James attended her trial in person.

> . . . she confessed that at the time when his Majestie was in Denmarke, she . . . took a Cat and christened it, and afterwards bound to each parte of that Cat the cheefeste partes of a dead man, and severall joynts of his bodie, and that in the night following the saide Cat was conveied into the midst of the sea by all these witches sayling their riddles or Cives [sieves] as is aforesaide, and so left the saide Cat right before the Towne of Lieth in Scotland: this doone, there did arise such a tempest in the Sea, as a greater hath not beene seene: which tempest was the cause of the perishing of a Boate or vessell comming over from the towne of Brunt Iland to the towne of Lieth, wherein was sundrye Jewelles and riche giftes, which should have been presented to the now Queen of Scotland, at her Majesties comming to Lieth.
>
> Againe it is confessed that the said christened Cat was the cause that the Kinges Majesties Ship at his comming foorth of Denmarke, had a contrary winde to the rest of his Ships, then being in his companye, which thing was most strange and true, as the Kings Majestie acknowledgeth, for when the rest of the Shippes had a faire and goode winde, then was the winde contrarye and altogither against his Majestie: and further the said witche declared, that his Majestie had never come safelye from the Sea, if his faith had not prevailed above their ententions.[9]

Agnes Tompson and the other accused persons gave their confessions only after appalling torture. James, however, was convinced of the truth of their testimony. Indeed, some years after his trouble with the Leith witches, he was so annoyed with the scepticism being expressed in some quarters about witchcraft that he, as an authority with first-hand experience on the subject, wrote a book, the *Daemonologie*, to acquaint the world with the nature and danger of witches. Later in England, however, he became more sceptical and took to sending suspected witches to the medical faculty at Cambridge for psychiatric study rather than burning them.[10]

*

Such, then, were some of the experiences that lay behind James Stuart as he received the homage of Sir Robert Carey and learned that Elizabeth, she who he had thought would outlive the sun and moon, was dead and that he was King now both of England and Scotland. His experiences had left him a strange and complex personality. He was both suspicious and gregarious, distrustful of men's motives yet ready to rely unwisely upon those he befriended. He was at once stubborn and indirect, thriftless and stingy, acute and negligent. He was a scholar and a pedant, but a scholar and a pedant with a homely pawky Scottish sense of humour. He was a good judge of men and affairs, yet because of inherent laziness failed again and again to enforce policies which he knew to be necessary and good. He had learned early the arts of duplicity but had come to practise them so unconsciously as to have no doubt at all of his own goodness and honesty. There was a current of geniality in him which made him like people and want to be liked by them, though he always regarded the populace with a testy impatience. His relations with the handsome young male favourites whom he found so necessary to him were at least tinged with homosexuality. His marriage with his Danish princess without quite being a failure had never quite become a success. While there was much in him that might be deprecated, there was much too that was likeable and even admirable. He tried to be just and, in an age of bigotry, he was surprisingly broadminded and tolerant. He hated physical violence and cherished peace. All things considered, he had been a successful King of Scotland. Now he stood at the threshold of a greater kingdom.

CHAPTER II

The Journey South

JAMES VI was by no means the only possible claimant to the English crown,[1] and real reasons could have been found for keeping him from the English throne. Not only had Queen Elizabeth left no document declaring him her successor, but during the reign of Edward VI, her half-brother, it had been maintained that the will of Henry VIII, properly interpreted, excluded the Scottish royal family from the English succession. Some lawyers were ready to argue that James Stuart was an alien incapable of inheriting so much as a cottage or an acre of land within England. Finally, no parliament had ever approved the passing of the crown to James. As it happened, no person of real authority in England was prepared to bring up these objections—and those who had governed England under Elizabeth had long since decided that James was the man to bring to the throne. Sir Robert Cecil, Principal Secretary of State and chief contriver of the succession, had the pleasure of seeing the new king receive the crown with the very minimum of confusion and trouble.

Elizabeth died between two and three o'clock in the morning of March 24th, her passing so imperceptible that none could fix the time exactly. Shortly after nine o'clock Sir Robert Carey started on his unauthorized journey to Scotland. Less than an hour later Cecil, attended by the heralds, the Privy Council, and various of the nobility, proclaimed at Whitehall Palace that James VI, King of Scotland, was now, by the Grace of God, also James I of England, France and Ireland.

From Whitehall the glittering retinue proceeded to the nearby City of London. At the city boundary they found Ludgate barred, the portcullis down, the city militia in arms, and the Lord Mayor and the aldermen in their scarlet gowns awaiting them. The Lord Treasurer and the Lord Keeper of the Great Seal knocked upon the gate and were told that none would be admitted unless he came to proclaim the King of Scots as King of England. When the lords replied that this was their intent, the Lord Mayor demanded a pledge that they would proclaim no other. At this the Lord Treasurer took his massy chain of state, the 'Collar of SS', from about his neck and gave it to the Lord Mayor. The pledge received, the Lord Mayor ordered the gate thrown open, and courtiers and citizens 'with most exceeding joy' went to the open space before the old Gothic cathedral of St. Paul's where at two o'clock in the afternoon King James was proclaimed within the metropolis of his new kingdom.

The proclamation of the new king was read in the other chief cities of England. Everywhere it was received with rejoicing. The celebrations at Hull were typical. 'As soon as the Proclamation was ended, the King's health was drunk, liquor given to the populace, and the whole day spent in ringing of bells, bonfires, and such other demonstrations of joy.'[2] Here and there a malcontent foolishly let his grumblings be heard above the jubilation. One Richard Carter got himself into trouble, for instance, when he shouted, 'Shamy Jamy proclaimed King!',[3] drew his dagger, and declared himself for Henry, Duke of Bourbon. From Carlisle came word that no sooner had His Majesty been proclaimed than the Scottish border-ers began making 'great incursions, burnings and spoils'.[4] Law and order were speedily restored to the Marches, however, and a great wave of joy and relief swept through England as it became apparent that James's accession was to be unquestioned and unresisted. On the day before Elizabeth's death hoarding by those who feared civil war and a contested succession had skyrocketed the price of grain to eight shillings a bushel. Two days later it dropped to four shillings four pence. From York the Lord President of the North, Burghley, wrote to his brother Sir Robert Cecil, '. . . the contentment of the people is unspeakable, seeing all things proceed so quietly, whereas they expected in the interim their houses should have been spoiled and sacked.'[5]

There was again a King of England. After forty-five years of having Queen Elizabeth for their monarch, the English found the word 'king' strange upon their lips. All eyes turned towards Edinburgh 'through a fixed and Adamantine desire to behold this 45 yeares wonder now brought forth by Tyme'.[6] Eager aspirants for the new king's favour were losing no time in ingratiating themselves with him. Among these was witty Sir John Harington, one of whose jests was the invention of the water-flush privy. A few months earlier Harington had sent James as a New Year's gift a lantern, inscribed on one side with the words of the penitent thief, 'Lord, remember me when Thou comest into Thy kingdom.' Sir John now penned a poem, 'The Welcome to the King', observing that 'God for His house a *Steward* hath provided.'[7] Others did more than send letters or gifts; they hastened to present themselves before the King. Six days after Queen Elizabeth's death, Lord Burghley wrote to Secretary Cecil from York, 'Here are numbers of gentlemen that by troops post into Scotland.' Among the gentlemen posting towards the King was one with a name fatal to his house—'Mr. Oliver Cromwell has gone towards the King.' This, however, was an uncle, not the regicide. In London, Master John Chamberlain contemptuously observed the rout of fortune-seekers posting northward and wrote to his friend Dudley Carleton:

> . . . many run thether of theyre owne errand, as yf yt were nothing els but first come first served, or that preferment were a goale to be got by foot-manship.[8]

While the Scottish court was becoming crowded with the new arrivals from the south, England itself was astir with reports of the great good to be expected from the new king. In a few years the English were to become nostalgic about the great days under Elizabeth, but now they were glad to be done with her and confidently expected all their discontents to vanish before this paragon coming from the North. Later, Bishop Goodman recalled the mood of 1603:

> . . . there was a general report throughout the whole kingdom what a good king he was, that he was the king of poor men, and would hear any man in a just cause. . . . Then for the queen she was ever hard of access, and grew to be very covetous in her old days . . . and in effect the people were very generally weary of an old woman's government.[9]

The petty poets of the time rushed to the printing houses with eulogizing verses:

> Then frolicke England, sport in lawfull games,
> Make roome to entertaine matchlesse king *James*,
> Shine bright with bonfires: let Bels ring aloude,
> And of our fortunes let us all be proude.[10]

James, meanwhile, was preparing to enter into his kingdom. Difficulties arose about finances, and Secretary Cecil received a message, one that he was to receive many many times during the years which lay ahead—James needed money.

> The King wants present [immediate] money, and therefore you shall do well to provide money to be sent forthwith, which he will take very thankfully.[11]

On Sunday, April 3rd, King James made his last public appearance in Scotland, attending divine service at St. Giles' Church in Edinburgh. After the sermon the King spoke a few words to his people of Scotland. With typical self-complacency he observed that he had settled 'both Kirk and Kingdom'; and, promising his Scots that he would ever have care for them and their good, he gave them 'a most loving and kind farewell'. They were not to see him again for sixteen years.

On April 5th King James began his journey south, leaving his wife and children to follow later. An impressive company went along with him—the Duke of Lennox (son of his early favourite), the Earl of Argyll, the Earl of Moray, the Earl of Cassillis, and a great many other lords and gentlemen. The French ambassador accompanied the King, taking along his wife, who was carried on slings by four 'pioneers or porters'.

The royal progress southwards was made at a very leisurely rate for James, with his morbid abhorrence of funerals, did not want to arrive in London until after the burial of Queen Elizabeth on April 29th. Journeying into his new realm, he was everywhere received with rapturous acclaim. Spring was coming and with the spring the new monarch. If the symbolism was not immediately apparent to James, plenty of poetasters and municipal orators were ready to point it out to him.

The King's progress into England began on April 6th at the stern frontier fortress of Berwick. On the 9th he reached Newcastle-on-Tyne, where he remained for four days, and under a general amnesty released all the prisoners except those held for treason, murder or Papistry, 'giving great summes of money for the release of many that were imprisoned for debt'. April 13th saw him at Durham, and on the 16th His Majesty entered York where a 'Conduit all the day long ran white and claret wine, every man to drinke as much as he listed.' Two days later he was on the road again, to Grimston, then on to Doncaster where for lack of better quarters he put up at the Bear Inn. He came next to Worksop where he was the guest of Gilbert Talbot, Earl of Shrewsbury, in his towering Tudor mansion rising at the top of a gentle green eminence.

On April 21st King James entered Newark-upon-Trent. Here there occurred an untoward incident:

> In this towne and in the Court, was taken a Cut-purse doing the deed: and being a base pilfering theefe, yet was all Gentleman-like, in the outside: this fellow had good store of Coyne found about him; and upon his ex-amination confessed that hee had from *Barwick* to that place, plaied the cut-purse in the Court. . . . His Majestie hearing of this nimming gallant, directed a Warrant, presently [at once] to the Recorder of *New-warke*, to have him hanged, which was accordingly executed.[12]

The new king's councillors were aghast at this hanging of a man out of hand, and intimated to James that, whatever the practice might be in Scotland, in England the sovereign left such cases to the judges and due process of law. James never committed this error a second time.

From Newark James went to Belvoir (or Bever) Castle as the guest of the Earl of Rutland. On Easter Sunday he was with Lord Burghley, Cecil's elder brother, at Burghley-by-Stamford. On the 27th he arrived at Hinchingbrooke Priory as the guest for two days of Master Oliver Cromwell. From here His Majesty's route took him to Standon and to Brockesbourne. At the border of each shire the Sheriff, the Justices of the Peace, and the principal gentlemen awaited James to escort him to the uttermost bound of their shire, where he was received in turn by the Sheriff and gentry of the next. Meanwhile the country people thronged the royal route in greater and greater numbers. The King's progress turned into a triumphal procession.

> But our King coming through the *North*, (Banquetting and Feasting by the way) the applause of the people in so obsequious and submissive a manner (still admiring *Change*) was checkt by an honest plain *Scotsman* (unused to hear such humble Acclamations) with a *Prophetical expression: This people will spoil a good King.*[13]

James had never been in England before. Everywhere there were new sights—cities, mansions, homesteads and villages, and a wealth and profusion far beyond that of barren, penurious Scotland. James rejoiced in the richness of his realm. Gone for ever were the days when as King of Scotland he had been down to two or three jewels and plate worth less than £100.

On May 3rd King James came to Theobalds, the magnificent country mansion, or rather palace, of Sir Robert Cecil, a short two hours' ride from London itself. His arrival there was really the climax of his journey. The Londoners poured forth to see their new king, clogging the roads, and setting great clouds of dust swirling into the air. So noisome indeed was the dust that a private road was hastily made by which His Majesty might arrive. To get some idea of the multitude, Master John Savile with two friends took an upstairs front window at the Bell Inn at Edmonton, set up an hourglass and began to count the travellers on the Theobalds Road below. Within less than half an hour, before abandoning the count, they had noted 309 on horse and 137 on foot. The host of the Bell assured them the traffic had been as heavy as that since four o'clock that morning, and all the day before.[14]

It was half past one in the afternoon when James arrived at Theobalds. Besides his own retinue with which he had set out from Scotland, he had with him a great many gentlemen who had attached themselves to the royal procession as it passed through the shires. An escort supplied by Sir Edward Denny, Sheriff of Essex, consisted of 150 men uniformed in red and yellow. As His Majesty came down the entrance avenue of elm and ash leading to the great house, two heralds sounded trumpets before him. At the end of the avenue his attendant lords dismounted and, bareheaded, accompanied the King, still on horse, as he rode through an ornamental gateway and entered the forecourt of Theobalds. Before him stood the entrance door of the great house, flanked by magnificent stretches of mullioned windows. On either side of the broad façade rose square towers, three storeys high, more glass than wall in their stretches of window. From each tower rose four turrets, surmounted each with a golden lion holding a golden vane shining brightly in the sun above the rich red brickwork of the building below.[15]

Clustered before this block of buildings stood a group of men resplendent in silks and satins, gold and plumes—the Privy Council of England. They were ranged about a little hunched man with a long white face, a high perplexed forehead, and fingers incredibly thin, delicate even for a woman. This was Sir Robert Cecil, the master of the house and the second son of its builder, the first Lord Burghley. He had already had a first meeting with the King at York.

James was conducted through the door into the Fountain Court which lay beyond. With his shambling walk he passed through the great halls and apartments. Here wonders were to be seen. There was a hall whose ceiling was a kind of planetarium with the signs of the zodiac, the stars shining by night, and the sun performing its course by ingenious mechanism by day. Flanking the walls were trees with natural bark attached, with birds' nests, and leaves and fruit so natural in appearance that when the steward opened the windows overlooking the pleasure gardens outside birds flew in and, perching on the trees, sang. There were galleries filled with paintings. There were prospects of all the principal cities of Christendom. There was a hall on whose walls and ceiling were blazoned the map of England, showing the cities, towns and villages, the mountains and rivers, and 'the armorial bearings and domains of every esquire, lord, knight and noble who possess lands and retainers to whatever extent'.[16] In an open loggia the history of England was pictured with its kings and battles. In the Great Gallery there were depicted the rulers, costumes and customs of every land of the world. In the Presence Chamber, Venus and Vulcan in bronze formed a magnificent chimney-piece. In the Hall a fountain soared from a base made of many-coloured stones to fall into a great basin supported by two carved savages.

James must have been dazzled by the grandeur and richness of Theobalds. The country where private citizens could afford such palaces must be rich beyond dreams. None of his Scottish subjects had ever owned anything comparable. Indeed, to be honest with himself, James had to admit that none of his own royal palaces could match it.

From the dazzling apartments James was conducted to the gardens, arbours, and walks beyond 'where hee recreated himselfe in the Meanders compact of Bayes, Rosemarie and the like'. From these pleasant retreats he was summoned by the clamour of the populace demanding to see their king. For half an hour James showed himself at a window looking down into the forecourt. Then he retired while the crowds dispersed to enjoy the hospitality of Cecil, who that day feasted even the ragged regiments of vagabonds with 'beefe, veale, mutton, bread and beere'.

Theobalds was to be important in the life of James in England. He was so captivated by it that in 1607 he secured it as a gift from Cecil, giving

QUEEN ANNE AND HER DOGS
by Paul van Somer

him in return the royal manor of Hatfield in Hertfordshire, with other property to help to pay for the building of a new mansion there. At Hatfield Cecil built the great house that stands there still, the home of his descendants, enshrining over the great fireplace in one of its chief apartments a statue of King James presented by that grateful monarch.

Theobalds suited James well. He had no great liking for the life of London and was unattracted by Whitehall Palace. He was happiest when off with chosen companions at his hunting-lodges at Royston and Newmarket. Theobalds made a handy stopping-place on the route from London northward to these retreats. When business called James from his sport he would sometimes travel as far south as Theobalds, let the ambassadors or ministers meet him there, and then head north again. Conversely, if court routine or matters of state kept him for long at Whitehall, a short ride allowed him to spend the day hunting in the park at Theobalds. One thing that James could not have guessed when he entered the magnificent manor in 1603 was that he would die there twenty-two years later.

James remained at Theobalds for four days. Then came the final stage to London. The entire route was so jammed with spectators that the King had to pause repeatedly for fear of trampling people. At Stamford Hill, three miles outside the City, the Lord Mayor of London and the aldermen awaited him, all in their scarlet robes, and with them 'five hundred Grave Cittizens, in Velvet Coates, and chaynes of golde'.[17] Here, too, were the English heralds in their resplendent tabards, and hundreds of other minor royal officers. Thus escorted, James entered the City, coming at last to the Charterhouse, the great town residence of Lord Thomas Howard. The children attached to the Charterhouse hospital sought to greet James with song but were swept away by the unruly mob fighting for places of vantage. After three days of having a mob milling around the Charterhouse, James, who loathed crowds, moved into the Tower of London for a few days and then retreated to the pleasant seclusion of the royal manor at Greenwich. His long journey was over.

James was followed from Scotland by his blonde dissatisfied queen with two of their children, Prince Henry, aged nine, and Princess Elizabeth, aged seven. The youngest child, sickly Prince Charles, remained in Scotland since the journey was considered too dangerous for his frail constitution.

James's marriage with his Danish princess had not turned out well. Anne had proved to be both dull and indolent, though showing a certain tolerant amiability so long as her whims were satisfied. She was interested in little that was more serious than matters of dress. Along with her yellow hair and fair complexion she had a good figure, and she enjoyed dressing up in rich clothes. Her chief delight lay in court balls and masques.

The English soon learned that they had 'an huntinge kinge, a dauncinge queen'.

After the first months of their marriage James and his wife settled down to a relationship something less than ideal. They were not a well-matched pair and their squabbles were frequent. James must often have found his wife tiresome with her querulous demands and her moodiness—not that he himself would ever have proved a passionate lover for any woman. However, as he had notified the Estates of Scotland, he had married to procreate, and he doggedly persevered even though a disappointing number of his queen's pregnancies ended in miscarriages. Scandal linked Anne's name with several noblemen in Scotland. The old ballad of the murder of the Earl of Moray still preserves for us an echo of at least one possible liaison:

> He was a braw gallant,
> And he played at the glove;
> And the bonny Earl of Moray,
> Oh he was the Queen's love!

Some said that the young Master of Ruthven who had perished at Perth was likewise the Queen's lover. It is hard to believe these allegations. The listless Anne was not the sort to enter into anything more than flirtations. These she may have indulged in as much to annoy her husband as anything. The same motive may not have been entirely absent from her conversion to Catholicism some time around 1600.

When James left Edinburgh for England, he expected Anne to follow three weeks later. One reason for delaying the Queen's journey was that Anne was in the midst of one of her pregnancies. Another was that the chief ladies of the English court would have to remain in London for a few weeks more to attend Queen Elizabeth's funeral before being free to meet Anne.

The Queen's departure for England, when it did come, was marked by an unseemly quarrel between her and the Earl of Mar. It had not been intended originally that Anne should bring the heir, Prince Henry, with her. She suddenly made up her mind, however, that she wanted to take the boy along and went to Stirling Castle where she tried to remove the prince from the custody of his governors, the deputies of the Earl of Mar. The Earl himself was in England with James; but to the fury of the Queen his people refused to let her have her son, saying that they were responsible to the King for his care and could not surrender him without the King's own warrant. At this point Anne wrote furious letters to the King, took a fever, and lost her baby through miscarriage. James, caught between violent charges and counter-charges, wrote Anne a letter somewhat testily declaring his love, but smacking rather more of protocol than passion:

I thank God I carie that love and respect unto you quhich, by the law of
God and nature, I ought to do to my wyfe and mother of my children, but
not for that ye are a King's dauchter, for quither ye waire a King's or a
cook's dauchter, ye must be all alike to me, being once my wyfe. For the
respect of your honorable birthe and decente I married you; but the love
and respecte I now beare you is, because that ye are my married wyfe, and
so partaker of my honoure as of my other fortunes.[18]

To patch matters up, James despatched Mar back to Scotland, and after
him he sent the Duke of Lennox with a warrant for Prince Henry to be
handed over to his mother. Two months had elapsed when Anne, only
partly placated, finally set out for England at the end of May.

James was determined that his wife should be received with due ceremony. No sooner had he crossed into his new kingdom at Berwick than he
wrote to the Privy Council ordering them to send thither in readiness for
Anne 'such Jewells and other furnyture which did appertaine to the late
Queene, as you shall thincke to be meet for her estate; and also coaches,
horses, litters, and whatsoever els you may thinck meet. . . .' When Anne
did belatedly enter England she found awaiting her not only these but a
whole company of noble lords and ladies ready to attend her southwards.
Among them was the vivacious and beautiful Lucy Russell, Countess of
Bedford, destined to become Anne's closest friend.

The Queen's itinerary south was much like her husband's. Once more
there were celebrations and civic rejoicings. At York Anne was presented
with a large silver cup filled with coin, 'fourscore angells of gold', while
Prince Henry received a smaller silver cup containing twenty pounds in
gold, and his sister a purse with twenty angels of gold in it. Nearing London, Anne and the children were entertained at Althorp, the home of the
Spencers, with a delightful little dramatic piece by Ben Jonson. It had
elves and a satyr in it, not to mention Queen Mab, who presented Anne
with a jewel. When Anne left on the following day there was 'a morrise
of the clownes thereabout' with a speech delivered by Nobody, who wore
breeches up to his neck and 'a cap drowning his face'.[19] The royal children,
at least, must have been delighted. Anne's next stopping-place was at
Easton Neston, the Northamptonshire home of Sir George Fermor and
here, on June 27th, she found King James awaiting her, ready to conduct
her to Windsor. The pestilence was raging in London and Whitehall was
best avoided.

CHAPTER III

The New Court Is Formed

A ROYAL COURT in the sixteenth and seventeenth centuries was a gigantic establishment of thousands of officers, retainers, servants and hangers-on. In 1592 the Duke of Wurtemberg, speaking of the much reduced court which accompanied Elizabeth on her summer 'progress' through the shires, mentioned that more than 300 carts were required to transport its baggage. The Court's enormous size was the consequence of at least four functions which it had to perform. The first was to minister to the needs, comfort and recreation of the sovereign, his family and his intimates. The second was to display to the world, represented chiefly by ambassadors from abroad and visiting dignitaries, the wealth and greatness of the kingdom as reflected by the magnificence which surrounded the monarch. The third was to supply posts of prestige and reward for those of his subjects whom the monarch wished to encourage or recognize or keep about him. The fourth was to supply the machinery for the central government of the nation.

At the funeral of Queen Elizabeth her chief court officers snapped in two their white rods of office. This act signified the end both of their obligation to her and of their own tenure of office. Elizabeth had chosen her officers shrewdly, and James had the good sense to reappoint most of them almost immediately to their former posts. A few were not reappointed. For example, the day after his arrival at Theobalds, no doubt after considerable discussion with Cecil, James appointed as his Lord Chamberlain Lord Thomas Howard, shortly to be created Earl of Suffolk, in place of George Carey, Lord Hunsdon. Sir Robert Carey's ride into Scotland had not saved his brother from being discarded, and he himself received but meagre rewards.

Suffolk's appointment was a key one, for the Lord Chamberlain was the principal officer of the Court. He had jurisdiction over 'the Chamber', which meant that he had under him all those whose employment brought them directly into the royal presence within doors. Assisting the Lord Chamberlain was the Vice-Chamberlain, and to this post James reappointed Sir John Stanhope, who had served well under Elizabeth.

The Chamber over which the Lord Chamberlain had jurisdiction was divided into two areas, the Outer and the Privy Chamber, each with its own staff. The Outer Chamber consisted of those parts of the palace where the King could be seen by all who were permitted access to the Court. Over the years there was some variation of establishment, but the Outer Chamber staff was generally composed of the Groom Porter, 4 Gentlemen Ushers, 4 Yeomen Ushers, 12 Grooms, 4 Pages, 4 Messengers, 2 Clerks, 4 Carvers, 4 Cupbearers, 7 Sewers, 2 Surveyors of the Dresser, 4 Esquires of the Body and the Chief Butler. Also counted as part of the Outer Chamber were the Sergeants-at-Arms, the 200 Yeomen of the Guard with their captain, standard-bearer and 'Clerk of the Cheque' (paymaster), and the 50 Gentlemen Pensioners with their captain, lieutenant, standard-bearer and clerk of the cheque; as also the Knight Harbinger with his 2 gentlemen and 4 harbingers. Separate from all these was a smaller staff which looked after the Privy Chamber, the apartments to which the King withdrew whenever he desired seclusion and where only privileged persons might see him. Here there were 48 Gentlemen,[1] 4 Gentlemen Ushers and 12 Grooms. Within the Privy Chamber establishment was an inner group of gentlemen, grooms and pages, the King's most trusted intimates and servants, known as 'the Bedchamber'.

Besides the staff required by the two divisions of the Chamber, the Lord Chamberlain had under him the personnel of seven 'standing offices' or permanent departments. These were the Great Wardrobe, the Revels, the Tents and Toils (i.e. fabrics), the Works, the Armoury, the Ordnance and the Mint. A great many other persons came under the Lord Chamberlain also. There were, for instance, the members of the Removing Wardrobe of Beds (2 Yeomen, 5 Marshals, 4 Sewers, 2 Surveyors, 2 Grooms, 2 Pages and 1 Clerk). There were the members of the Wardrobe of Robes, and of the Jewel House. There was the establishment of the Chapel Royal, which included besides the clergy (dean, sub-dean and 7 priests), 23 gentlemen of the Chapel, 12 choir children and 2 organists. Incidentally, the Court was well supplied with music, for the Lord Chamberlain had under him also the sergeant trumpeter with 16 trumpeters, 2 lute-players, 2 harpers, 8 singers, a rebeck player, 6 sackbut players, 8 players on the viol, 2 drummers, 2 flutists, and a bagpiper. To supply these there were 2 instrument makers. For other royal recreations, the Lord Chamberlain had in his establishment the Master of the Harriers, the Master of the Harthounds, the Master of the Otter Hounds, and the Hawking-Master, with their underlings. For the maintenance of the royal health there were 3 physicians, 6 surgeons, 3 apothecaries. Finally, under the Lord Chamberlain came a whole company of miscellaneous persons ranging from the Astronomer Royal to the gardeners, and from the Keeper of the Libraries to the King's Fool.

The second great court officer was the Lord Steward. If the Lord

Chamberlain presided 'above stairs', the Lord Steward presided 'below stairs'. In other words, he had charge of the provisioning, maintenance and housekeeping of the Court. For his Lord Steward King James reappointed Charles Howard, Earl of Nottingham.

Just as the Earl of Suffolk did not concern himself with the day-by-day routine administration of his department, leaving that to the Vice-Chamberlain, so the Earl of Nottingham did not concern himself with the minutiae of keeping the Court supplied with butter and eggs and paying the help. The supervision of these matters he left to no vice-steward, for there was none, but to the members of a very important small committee, known as the Board of Green Cloth. Those who sat at the daily meetings of this board, over which the Lord Steward presided at least on important occasions, were the Treasurer of the Household, the Comptroller of the Household, the Master of the Household and the Cofferer. Daily these officers scrutinized the expenditures of the royal household, arranged for the purchase of needed supplies and supervised the behaviour of the royal servants. The actual bookkeeping of the Lord Steward's department was looked after by the staff of the Counting House (i.e. Accounting Office).

An enormous staff worked under the supervision of the Lord Steward and the Board of Green Cloth. Here we find the palace porters, including the Sergeant Porter at the palace gate with his assistant yeomen porters and groom porters, the servants of the Hall (the great chamber where many of the Court received their meals), and the personnel of a great many departments concerned with the actual preparation of food. A fascinating diversity of functions and names marks these 'offices'. They were the Kitchen, the Pantry, the Buttery, the Spicery, the Wafery, the Ewery, the Larder, the Accatery, the Scalding-House, the Scullery, the Bottlery, the Bake-House, the Cellar, the Pitcher-House, the Chandlery, the Confectionery, the Laundry, the Boiling-House, the Poultery, the Pastery, and the Woodyard. Each of these had its establishment of sergeant, clerks, yeomen, grooms and pages, running anywhere from six to twenty-four persons.

Third of the great court officers, ranking with the Lord Chamberlain and the Lord Steward, was the Master of the Horse. King James reappointed Elizabeth's Master of the Horse, Edward Somerset, Earl of Worcester. If the Lord Chamberlain and the Lord Steward were thought of as having charge within doors, the Master of the Horse was thought of as the chief officer out-of-doors. Assisted by the Chief Avenor, he had charge of the royal stables and coaches, and directed the labours of more than a hundred gentlemen riders, yeomen riders, esquires, coachmen, littermen, farriers, bitmakers, granitors, and plain ordinary grooms.

A fourth important court post was that of the Earl Marshal. His duties, while carrying much prestige, were hardly exacting. Under his surveillance was the College of Arms, that is the heralds under their three 'kings', Garter, Clarenceux and Norroy. When questions of chivalry such as rights of precedence or rival claims to a particular coat of arms arose, the Earl Marshal heard the cause in his Court of Constable and Marshal. The Knight Marshal, who had charge of the policing of the Court, was at least nominally the Earl Marshal's subordinate. When King James succeeded Queen Elizabeth there was no Earl Marshal. The post belonged by tradition to the Duke of Norfolk, but there had been no Duke of Norfolk since 1572 when Queen Elizabeth had sent Thomas Howard to the block and extinguished his title. His grandson, now the nominal head of the powerful Howard family, was a coldly patrician but impoverished eighteen-year-old, Thomas Howard, Lord Maltravers. He and his unfortunate mother had endured the hostility of Queen Elizabeth ever since his father, his earldom attainted, had died in the Tower in 1595. Young Thomas Howard and his mother hoped for much from King James and they were not entirely disappointed. The new monarch gave to the young man his father's lost dignity of Earl of Arundel, and assigned to him the Crown's share in the attainted estates of his grandfather. However, he never granted Arundel his dearest wish, his own creation as Duke of Norfolk, and not until July 1621 did he confer upon him the hereditary family dignity of Earl Marshal. During the eighteen-year interim King James gave occasional special appointments to the Earl of Worcester to serve as Earl Marshal when some ceremony required the presence of one. Otherwise he entrusted the duties of the Earl Marshal to a small committee of Lord Commissioners.

The traditional right of the Dukes of Norfolk to the post of Earl Marshal had a parallel in two other hereditary offices, those of the Lord Great Chamberlain and of the Lord High Steward. These extremely honourable but completely archaic offices existed only as inherited dignities which carried with them purely ceremonial functions upon state occasions such as coronations or state trials. The Lord Great Chamberlain was the Earl of Oxford. Since the office of Lord High Steward had passed from John of Gaunt to the Crown several centuries before, James entrusted its duties on an *ad hoc* basis to temporary appointees.

It is hard to determine the size of the Jacobean court. For one thing, while most men served full-time, some were only 'quarter waiters' who gave three months' attendance at the Court each year and then were free from further duties. The Court did have a prescribed 'establishment' of a kind, but there were various 'extraordinary' appointments over and above the set complement. Moreover, since some men held more than one appointment, the number of positions can never be equated with the number of persons. Useful lists survive of the royal servants who received grants of black cloth when there were royal funerals, but these lists vary considerably over the years. Interesting but unreliable are the 'Books of Offices', small vellum-bound manuscript brochures which list in tabular form the Court establishment with the fees paid for each post. Lineal ancestors of *Whitaker's Almanac's* lists of civil servants, these books seem to have been in demand among James's courtiers—partly because of the usual human curiosity as to what the other fellow is getting, partly as a guide to one's own fortune-hunting at Court.

All things considered, it seems probable that the Lord Chamberlain had under him at least 750 persons (many employed only part-time), the Lord Steward somewhere near 250 persons (nearly all full-time), and the Master of the Horse about 140. One reason for this swollen establishment was the principle of 'limited service'. Whereas a nobleman's servant was expected to do any work assigned to him, a royal servant could only be called upon to do the work assigned to his particular office. An idle groom of the Woodyard could not be asked to lend a hand in the Boiling House. A Jacobean palace flunkey had nothing to learn from a modern trade unionist where 'limited service' was concerned.

To the Jacobeans, these eleven hundred persons would comprise only a fraction of the Court. The dichotomy so clear to us between the government of the realm and the personal household staff of the monarch was far from being plain to them. They saw nothing incongruous in the Lord Chamberlain having direction over the Royal Artillery and the Mint as well as the Royal Wardrobes and the Chapel Royal. When James's subjects spoke loosely of the 'Court', they included in it the Privy Council and the Court of Star Chamber, the Lord Chancellor, the Lord Keeper of the Great Seal, the Secretaries of State, the Masters of Requests, the Court of Exchequer, the Court of First Fruits and Tenths, the Court of Wards and Liveries, the Pipe Office, the King's Counsel at Law. Even the Courts of King's Bench, Common Pleas, and Chancery, meeting a few hundred yards from Whitehall in the precincts of the older Palace of Westminster, could be comprehended within the term 'Court' used in its very widest application.

There were, moreover, courts within the Court. The Queen had an establishment with her own council, chancellor, lord steward, lord chamberlain, master of the horse, and her own household, though this was on a much smaller scale than that of the King. We read of a lady who had offended Anne as well as James—'. . . she hath lost her favor and is forbidden her court, as also the King's'. A separate establishment was maintained for Prince Henry and his sister Princess Elizabeth, and this alone

by the end of their father's first year in England numbered 56 above stairs
and 85 below.

Peripheral to the royal court proper were a great number of gentlemen
and servants belonging to officers of the royal court or to the lords or
gentlemen in attendance on the King. When a great territorial magnate
such as the Earl of Northumberland took up his residence in one of the
riverside mansions lining the Thames from Whitehall to the City of
London, he brought with him a household of hundreds. A court officer
of any consequence occupying quarters within Whitehall had at least one
servant of his own in attendance on him. The net result of all this was that
the 'Court' came to consist of an undefinable conglomerate of thousands
of individuals all centring ultimately around the person of the King.

*

With his Queen beside him in England and his household established,
King James was ready for his coronation. Once more a Scottish king was
to sit on the ancient coronation Stone of Scone, brought south centuries
before by Edward III. On it he was to be crowned King of England.
While James had been on his journey south, the day of St. James the
Apostle (July 25th) had been set for his coronation at Westminster.

For a while it looked as if there would be no coronation that day. The
plague was raging in London. On the doors of the doomed the red plague
cross was splashed. By night the wagons gathered the dead and the victims
were hastily thrust into great common graves. In 1603 over 30,000 Londoners, one-fifth of the city's population, died of the pestilence. With the
weekly plague bills showing no abatement, James and Anne lingered at
Windsor away from the danger of their contaminated capital. Anxious
conferences were held. Should the coronation proceed or be postponed?

Finally, on July 6th a royal proclamation announced that the coronation
would be held on the day already set, but that 'all shew of State and pompe'
not essential to the ceremony would be omitted. In an endeavour to prevent the spread of the pestilence, a second proclamation sharply restricted
the number of persons allowed to gather for the occasion. Earls, instead of
their usual great retinues, were to bring only sixteen servants to Westminster with them, while bishops and barons were allowed but ten. The
hardest blow was dealt the City of London. Not only was the coronation
procession through the City indefinitely postponed, but only a handful of
Londoners (the Lord Mayor and aldermen accompanied by twelve principal citizens) were to be permitted to see the coronation.

On July 22nd the King and Queen finally arrived at the great rookery
of buildings by the Thames which was Whitehall Palace. On the 25th the
Court marched in procession from there to the Abbey. First came the

pursuivants of arms—Rose, Bluemantle, Portcullis, Rouge Dragon, Rougecroix—then the officers of the King's household, the judges, the King's councillors, the barons in their parliament robes, the bishops, and ambassadors from Wurtemberg, Brunswick, Lorraine, Denmark, and France. One earl bore the royal spurs and another the sceptre of St. Edward. Three earls walking abreast carried the three swords of state. Behind them advanced the three great ceremonial officers; the Contable of England, the Lord Great Chamberlain, and the Earl Marshal. Then came three more earls bearing the Sceptre of the Dove, the Crown, and the Orb. Two bishops bore the patina and the regale. Finally, supported by the Bishops of London and Durham and flanked by the Barons of the Cinque Ports, with his train borne by his Lord Chamberlain and his Master of the Horse, came the stocky figure of King James. There followed the gentlemen and grooms of his Privy Chamber. Then came the Queen, similarly supported by bishops, in her own procession. Her sceptre and crown were borne by earls before her. The marchionesses, countesses and baronesses of England followed, along with the ladies of the Privy Chamber.

The procession entered the Abbey by the western doors. Then, according to 'the forme sett downe in the auncient Booke kept among the Records at Westminster', the new king was anointed with the sacred oil, invested with the robes of King Edward the Confessor, and crowned with the crown of England.

Outside the rain poured down. It beat upon the unfinished scaffolds of the triumphal arches which the Londoners had begun to build for a coronation procession through their city. Once crowned, the new king and queen lost no time in withdrawing to the uninfected air of Hampton Court. That week there died of the plague in the city 1,103 persons.

Quite eclipsing the curtailed coronation was the royal procession through London which was finally held on March 15, 1604, after the plague had departed from the city. The Londoners had all in readiness when the great day arrived. Pageants and shows had all been freshly painted. The streets through which the royal procession was to pass had been railed and gravelled. Marshalled along one side of the route, from St. Mark's Lane to Fleet Street, stood the members of the city guilds in their liveries, 'the Streamers, Ensignes, and Bannerets of each particular company decently fixed'. On the opposite side the way was jammed with inferior citizenry and sightseers from all parts of England. To better enable spectators to view the show below, the houses along the route had had 'all glasse windowes taken downe, but in their places sparkled so many eyes'. To add to the general festivity, the conduits which supplied the Londoners with their drinking water ran all day with claret wine.

Shortly after eleven o'clock in the morning the King set forth from the Tower where he had taken up residence three days earlier. Before him extended an enormous procession, far far longer than that at his coronation. Practically the entire Court, judiciary, civil service and aristocracy of England, walked in it. The Lords deputed for the office of Earl Marshal had spent long hours fixing everybody's place according to precedence. Now the eldest sons of barons marched in their proper place ahead of the younger sons of earls, who were themselves followed by the eldest sons of viscounts, each group outranking that which preceded it. At last, after all the messengers of the chamber, gentlemen ushers in ordinary, clerks of the privy seal, chaplains, sergeants-at-law, knights bachelors, masters of offices, knights of the Bath, barons, bishops, earls, and a very great many other persons and personages, the cheering throngs saw King James. Flanked by his gentlemen pensioners, His Majesty rode on a white jennet under a canopy held high by eight of his Gentlemen of the Privy Chamber. After him, preceded by her vice-chamberlain and her chamberlain, came Queen Anne, riding in her 'chariot' and followed by the ladies of the Court and her maids of honour.

Spectacle and music greeted James and Anne all along the route. Barely had the King left the Tower than he was saluted with song by three hundred children of Christ's Hospital ranged on a platform in Barking churchyard. At Fenchurch Street he was greeted by the first of eight sumptuous triumphal arches, a double archway surmounted by a model of the City of London. Here the city 'Waites and Hault-boyes [oboes]' made loud music as the King approached, and the 'Genius of the City' made a speech of welcome as did 'Thamesis the River', the latter being equipped with 'an earthen pot out of which live Fishes were seene to runne forth, and play about him'.[2]

> ... the whole frame was covered with a curtaine of silke, painted like a thicke cloud, and at the approach of the K. was instantly to be drawne. The Allegorie being, that those clouds were gathered upon the face of the Citie, through their long want of his most wished sight: but now, as at the rising of the Sunne, all mistes were dispersed and fled.[3]

A second triumphal arch had been built at Gracechurch Street by the Italian colony, and here their spokesman addressed the King in Latin. At the Royal Exchange at Cornhill the Dutch merchants had set up their arch with seventeen children, representing the seventeen provinces of the Low Countries, each bearing the arms of a particular province. Again King James was received with a Latin oration.

Entering Cheapside, the great street which was the pride of all London, James encountered his fourth triumphal arch at the Great Conduit by Soper Lane. Here the Fountain of Virtue ran, let it be noted, with wine,

and here Fame, Euphrosyne and Circumspection greeted His Majesty.
At the Little Conduit was still another arch, this one representing the
Garden of Plenty, being decorated with 'pompions' and 'Cowcumbers' and
all kinds of fruit. The Nine Muses and the Seven Liberal Sciences presided and Sylvanus made a speech to the King.

His Majesty's journey brought him next to the high monument, orna-
mented with allegorical figures and surmounted by a cross, which in recent
years had replaced the old Eleanor cross on Cheapside. Here the Lord
Mayor and other civic dignitaries of London awaited him. After the
inevitable congratulatory oration from Sir Henry Montagu, the Recorder
of London, cups of gold were presented to the royal family as gifts from
their loyal city.

As James approached the old Gothic cathedral of St. Paul's, choristers
ranged along the lower battlements hailed him with an anthem. One of the
boys from the cathedral school delivered a Latin oration of welcome, and
the great procession threaded its way down Fleet Street. At the conduit
there James passed under his sixth triumphal arch. Here Zeal told him how
well all things were ordered under his government. As a special compliment to Queen Anne, the musicians played a Danish march.

At Temple Bar the Londoners had erected the last of their arches, one
dedicated to the theme, particularly dear to James, of peace. Since the
stork was a symbol of peace, perhaps because of its domesticated habit of
building its nest by chimney tops, Ben Jonson and the other contrivers of
the arch had resolutely worked in a stork motif, and the allegorical figures
here included:

> ESYCHIA or *Quiet*, the first hand-maid of peace; a woman of grave and
> venerable aspect, attyred in black, upon her head an artificiall nest, out of
> which appeared storkes heads to manifest a sweet repose.[4]

Temple Bar and his loyal City of London left behind, King James rode
along the Strand. On his left hand, bordering the Thames, stood the great
mansions of the magnates of his realm, each set deep amid its trees and
gardens—Essex House, Arundel House, Somerset House, Worcester
House, Salisbury House, Durham House, York House, Suffolk House.
One final triumphal arch had still to be endured: that of Westminster,
which exhibited the rainbow, moon, sun and the seven stars of Pleiades,
set between pyramids blazoned with the King's pedigrees in England and
in Scotland.

At Charing Cross the procession approached its end. Widening in front
of the King was a large cobbled open area. Beyond it, under the high arch
of the Holbein Gate, King's Street led to Westminster Abbey and what
remained of the old Palace of Westminster. To the left stood the great
Court Gate, leading to the newer Palace of Whitehall, a vast jumble of

buildings, courtyards and galleries, garden and orchard, extending down to where the favoured ranges of apartments and the landing-stairs looked out on the sparkling waters of the Thames. After more than six hours of spectacle, speeches and crowds, James was probably glad to dismount from his white jennet and head for the quiet of his Privy Chamber.

CHAPTER IV

A Day's Business at Winchester

ELIZABETHANS, now become Jacobeans, who looked at the court of their new king in the summer of 1603 and asked King Lear's question, 'Who loses and who wins, who's in, who's out?' had little difficulty finding the answer. The 'ins', quite obviously, were Secretary Cecil and the family of the Howards. Equally obviously, Sir Walter Raleigh was among the 'outs'. Sir Robert Cecil had gone from strength to strength since the day when he had welcomed James at Theobalds. Confirmed in office as Principal Secretary of State, he had within a few weeks entered the peerage as Lord Cecil of Essenden. The advance of the Howards had been equally plain. Lord Thomas Howard had been given the highest of all offices at court, that of Lord Chamberlain, and a month or so later been created Earl of Suffolk. Meantime his uncle, Lord Henry Howard, had been made a Privy Councillor, though almost a year was to elapse before he too received an earldom, that of Northampton.

If the advance of Cecil and the Howards was plain, the downfall of Raleigh was equally apparent. Before James completed his journey southward from Scotland he removed Raleigh from his post of Captain of the Guard, and the succeeding weeks saw Raleigh having to resign his wardenship of the Stannaries, lose his profitable patent of wine licensing, and suffer the notable humiliation of having to return his London residence, Durham House, to its former owner, the Bishop of Durham.

Early in the summer of 1603 the acute observer might have deduced that Raleigh had further trials in store, though he might not have guessed how imminent and terrible they were to prove. Certainly he could not have known that Cecil, long the apparent friend of Raleigh, had for the past two years been secretly working with Lord Henry Howard to turn the mind of the new king against him.[1]

For the beginnings of Raleigh's tragedy one must go back to the execution of the Earl of Essex after his attempt at armed rebellion in 1601. Raleigh and Cecil had been allies against Essex, but after the death of their common enemy Cecil turned against Raleigh, while keeping up every appearance of friendship. Various reasons have been suggested for Cecil's course. He may have been hurt by some lack of attention on Raleigh's part. He may have been incensed by what he felt was a lack of appreciation for

34

his good offices in the past. He may have become annoyed by Raleigh taking up with Lord Cobham, Cecil's foolish reckless brother-in-law, and thinking to rise more by his means than Cecil's. None of these reasons, however, is entirely likely. Little hunchback Cecil was a classic example of the politician who neither loves nor hates (though these cold men can turn venomous when they find that what they think is their friendship is being underprized). The main reason for Cecil turning against Raleigh was almost certainly political. Raleigh had been a favourite of Elizabeth even during Essex's time and, with Essex gone, the way was open for Raleigh to advance further. Raleigh was ambitious. He knew too well his own great gifts of intellect, imagination and resolution, to be content to be a mere decoration of the court. He wanted to be one of the framers of national policy—and his policy of continued war with Spain was not Cecil's. Cecil saw the danger of such a man—a splendid, restless, even if highly unpopular genius. Of Raleigh's unpopularity there could not be any doubt: practically all England was against him because of his arrogance and because of misconceptions about his part in bringing Essex to the block.

There is no evidence that Cecil hated Raleigh. But Cecil does seem to have reached the conclusion that in his own self-interest, and in the interest of his policies, it was necessary to break him. Lord Henry Howard hated Raleigh. He hated him with a virulent hatred which was almost obsessive. If Raleigh had any inkling of this hate (and in his splendid pride and self-sufficiency he was singularly unperceptive), he could have found little comfort in the knowledge that to be hated by a man such as Lord Henry Howard is in itself almost an honour.

Lord Henry Howard was one of the most odious and corrupt of all the sycophantic self-seekers in the court of King James. Hardly one of the chroniclers of that court has failed to register his disgust for the man. Yet he was not without his good parts. He was far from unprepossessing in appearance. In dignity and address he was a worthy representative of the 'old nobility' among the upstarts and parvenus of the Jacobean court. He possessed great learning, and had been at one time a lecturer at the University of Cambridge. He was a fluent and able speaker, 'of a subtile and fine wit' though his tortuous thinking betrayed itself in a style so complicated that even King James found it 'Asiatic'. He was a patron of literature, a collector of art, and the builder of a magnificent mansion. He was a skilful diplomat and a first-class administrator who devoted long hours to the duties of his offices. Yet for all his personal charm, taste and ability, he died at last, in S. R. Gardiner's phrase, 'unregretted by men of all classes and all parties'.[2] For this cultivated aristocrat was also a boot-licker, capable of the most nauseating flattery and sycophancy. He was an implacable enemy who would stoop to any treachery to even a score. He was

a lecher and a turncoat. He was 'of so venemous and cankered a disposition, that indeed he hated all men of noble parts, nor loved any but Flatterers, like himselfe'.[3] His principles, as far as such a man can be said to
have principles, consisted of attachment to family and a desire to restore
England to Catholicism. To the latter end he worked for peace and a
subsequent alliance with Spain. On grounds of policy as well as instinct,
he was Raleigh's utterly irreconcilable enemy.

The process by which Cecil and Howard undermined and brought to
ruin the magnificent Raleigh began in the months following the death of
Essex on the scaffold.

Essex's revolt had been a very worrying matter for James VI up in
Scotland. Essex was widely known to be pro-Scottish and a champion of
the claims of James to the English throne. Now that he had fallen, the
Queen might in her bitterness turn against James also, even though he was
not involved in Essex's treachery against her. She might cease her generally
understood acceptance of James as her successor and her councillors
might encourage if not endorse the claims of others. James decided that no
time could be lost. Not only must Queen Elizabeth be reassured, but supporters must be recruited among those in the highest positions in the
English government to prepare the way for James's own accession.

James was a shrewd politician. Making a canny appraisal of the situation, he decided that Secretary Cecil was the man who must be won if
possible. Accordingly he instructed his secret emissaries in London, the
Earl of Mar and Edward Bruce, to make overtures to 'Mr. Secretary, and
her [the Queen's] principal guiders . . . especially to Mr. Secretary who is
king there in effect.'[4] If they failed to gain Cecil's support, they were to
recruit a pro-Scottish faction among the London citizenry, cultivate the
Lieutenant of the Tower of London, secure the allegiance of the Royal
Navy through the Lord Admiral (one of the Howards), sound out various
knights and lords on the part they would be ready to play 'at the great day'
of Elizabeth's death, and arrange to arm those whom they found friendly
to James. Fortunately, Mar and Bruce found Master Secretary well disposed. The Scottish king was spared the need of mustering and arming a
faction, an attempt which would have ruined his chance of securing the
succession if the Queen had ever learned of it.

In giving his support to James, Cecil was to some extent making a virtue
of necessity. James's dynastic claims to the throne were as good as those
of any of the many possible claimants. James had already demonstrated his
ability as a sovereign in Scotland and the political advantages of a union
of the two kingdoms were immense. Moreover, if James were denied the
throne, he might invade England and seek it by force. Finally, if Cecil
proved unfriendly, there were plenty of others in England who would be

ready to give their support in expectation of the rewards to be received from the King. Cecil, for his part, had much to offer. In his hands were all the threads of the English government. He had the apparatus, the friends, and the connections. It is not surprising that he and James reached their understanding.

It was dangerous for Cecil to communicate directly with James—an intercepted letter could ruin him. (Elizabeth packed Sir William Evers off to the Tower once she found that he was corresponding with James.) Accordingly, though James and Cecil did at times write directly to each other,[5] the precaution was often taken of having Mar and Bruce write for the King and Lord Henry Howard for both Cecil and himself.

Though Mar and Bruce swore an oath by God and his angels to destroy all the letters sent to them by Lord Henry Howard, these letters have survived. They are not attractive reading. Along with the reports of Cecil's views on the courses to be followed and dangers to be avoided, there are confidential reports on the views held by this person or that in the English court. Howard had his spies, for instance, in the household of the Earl of Northumberland. As head of the powerful Percy family, a force to be reckoned with especially in the North, Northumberland might prove a key man when the succession came to be determined. Howard was able to report that Northumberland had been heard bitterly arguing with his countess, declaring that he and all his friends would die rather than see James King of England, to which his countess had made the spirited retort that rather than see someone other than James get the throne she would 'rather eat all their hearts in salt'. Unable to conceal his pride in the efficiency of his spies, Northampton could not forbear adding that at the conclusion of their argument the earl and the countess had proceeded to sexual intercourse.

Not long after their secret correspondence with James began, Howard and Cecil were cast into profound apprehension. During a brief visit to London late in 1601 the King's kinsman, the Duke of Lennox, had met with Raleigh and sought his support for James's claims to the English succession. Learning of this development, Howard wrote to the King in the strongest terms. He reminded him of his earlier warnings concerning 'the diabolical triplicity, that is Cobham, Raleigh, and Northumberland', he advised James to keep Raleigh harmlessly engaged in vain hopes, not to give any commitments or encouragement and yet not to make a dangerous enemy of him by open rejection. He ended with a most pointed declaration:

> You [Edward Bruce, to whom the letter was addressed] must persuade the King, in his next dispatch, to direct you to thank Cecil in the letter which you write to me, for the light he receives of Cobham and Raleigh by this

advertisement; and if it please his Majesty to speak of them suitably to the
concert which Cecil holds, it will be the better; for Cecil sware to me this
day, that *duo erinacii*, that is, he and they, would never live under one
apple-tree.[6]

It was as blunt as that. Cecil and Raleigh could not live under the same
patron. King James must choose. He chose Cecil. In subsequent letters
Howard continued to poison the mind of James. Little wonder that the
King came to think of Raleigh as a bloody-minded, treacherous, arrogant
trouble-maker, like those turbulent, unruly barons whom he had learned
to fear and detest in Scotland. Sir Walter Raleigh was already ruined when
James was proclaimed King of England.

Raleigh had not the slightest suspicion of the trap which was being dug
for him. He even confided in Cecil about his dealings with Lennox. Cecil
for his part sent messages of friendship to Raleigh, became his partner in
financing a privateering venture, and sent his son William on repeated
visits to Raleigh's house at Sherborne. It is unlikely that Cecil thought of
himself as treacherous or perfidious in any of this. Politically it was necessary to stop Raleigh and steps would be taken in due order to end him at
court, but in the meanwhile Cecil probably saw no reason why he should
not continue to associate with a man for whom he may well have had some
personal liking. In any case, it would be unwise to put Raleigh on his
guard.

After James had been proclaimed King of England, Cecil and his fellow
Privy Councillors failed in an attempt to keep Raleigh from meeting James
on his journey south, but the King himself made it clear to Sir Walter that
he was not a man who enjoyed the royal favour. Raleigh's office at court,
that of Captain of the Guard, was given to one of James's Scottish followers, Sir Thomas Erskine, and other losses followed. Had Raleigh known
the full truth of his situation he might have realized that his only hope lay
in complete retreat to his native Devonshire, remote from all the machinations of court intrigue. As it was, he decided to remain about the Court
though a man obviously not in favour. Then the great blow fell. One
morning in mid-July, while Raleigh was waiting on a terrace at Windsor to
follow the King when he went hunting, Cecil came to tell him he was to
attend a meeting of the Privy Council, which had some questions to ask
him. Raleigh's ruin had begun.

The Privy Council was, at the time of Raleigh's arrest, much exercised
over the discovery of a plot to kidnap the King and force him to change
both his ministers and policies. The prime mover of this plot was a
Catholic priest named William Watson. In the days before James's accession to the English throne, Watson had visited him in Scotland to learn
what treatment the Catholics in England would receive if James came to the

English throne. At the time James was out to win friends in England. The last thing he wanted was to make irreconcilable enemies out of the English Catholics. Accordingly, he spoke gently to Watson, so gently in fact that Watson came away satisfied that James would extend religious toleration to the English Catholics. Back in England Watson championed James so ardently among his co-religionists that his enemies tauntingly referred to James as 'Watson's king'.

Established on the English throne, James had to decide upon his policy in matters of religion. Hoping the Catholics would be a useful counterpoise to the Puritans, he suspended the penal laws which Elizabeth had imposed upon them. He did not, however, proceed to the open tolerance that the Catholics desired. Watson, bitterly angered, blamed the King's Anglican counsellors for his failure to keep what he considered a royal promise. Aided by a fellow priest, Clarke, he formed a plot timed for June 24, 1603. On that day a band of conspirators, dressed in the uniform of the royal guard, were to seize the King at Greenwich and take him to either the Tower of London or Dover Castle. Then James was to be required to give a general pardon to his captors, to declare toleration in matters of religion, and to replace his chief officers of state with persons chosen by the conspirators. Their choice for the new regime was a curious one. Watson had learned that the Puritans, like the Catholics, were bitter against James for not showing them more tolerance. They had expected that a king coming from Presbyterian Scotland would give them countenance and favour, and were angry at receiving not regard but rebuff. Accordingly, Watson made overtures to a rabid Puritan, young Lord Grey of Wilton, to join with him. It was proposed to declare a universal toleration and to parcel out the chief offices between the Puritans and Catholics. Watson himself was to become lord chancellor and a co-religionist, Sir Griffith Markham, principal secretary of state; on the other hand, Lord Grey was to become earl marshal and master of the horse, while a second Puritan, George Brooke, was to become lord treasurer.

Such was Watson's plot as it was revealed to the government by Watson's bitterest enemies within the Catholic camp, the Jesuits. The Privy Council at once began a series of arrests and examinations. One of those examined was George Brooke, whom the conspirators had meant to make lord treasurer. He was the brother of Lord Cobham. During examination Brooke spoke of Watson's conspiracy as the 'Bye plot'.

> Being ask'd what was meant by this Jargon, the Bye and the Main? he said, that the Lord *Cobham* told him, that *Grey* and others were in the Bye, he and *Raleigh* were on the Main.[7]

The investigations of the Privy Council swiftly extended beyond the 'Bye Plot' to what now became known as the 'Main Plot' or 'Cobham's Plot'.

Henry Brooke, eleventh Lord Cobham, Knight of the Garter, was not only the brother-in-law but a former close political ally of Secretary Cecil. With Cecil and Raleigh he had played an important part in bringing Essex to the block. A fussy, self-important man, Cobham was highly emotional and unstable. He was a fool, and an indiscreet fool. He was, moreover, in a state of near panic. One of King James's early acts had been to release from the Tower the Earl of Southampton, who had been Essex's chief ally. Cobham was terrified that the King, who regarded Essex as his martyr, would pass from favouring his friends to punishing his enemies, notable among whom were Raleigh and himself. In his fright Lord Cobham hatched a wild scheme to replace James with the royal kinswoman Lady Arbella Stuart. Making contact with the Count of Aremberg, who had recently arrived from the Archduke Albert and hoped to arrange a peace between England and the Spanish alliance, Cobham asked for 600,000 crowns with which to purchase for the projected peace a body of influential supporters in England. Actually he intended to use the money to put Arbella on the throne. While laying plans to visit both the Archduke and the King of Spain, Cobham wrote a letter to Lady Arbella asking for an interview and hinting darkly that she had enemies about the King. This letter Lady Arbella had the good sense to turn over to James. Meanwhile Cobham vapoured away about his scheme. Lady Arbella, he had decided, was to write letters promising to make peace between England and Spain, to tolerate Catholicism, and to marry according to the wishes of the Catholic rulers of Spain and Austria. Discussing this wild scheme, Cobham used Raleigh's name. Then, before his conspiracy could become more than talk, he was arrested. Summoned by Cecil, as earlier noted, Raleigh too was brought before the Council. The question was put to him: what did he know of dealings between Cobham and Aremberg? Raleigh replied that he knew nothing. He was dismissed and placed under house arrest.

Back home Raleigh decided that perhaps after all he did have evidence about Cobham and Aremberg. He had once seen Cobham, at the conclusion of a visit to himself at Durham House, proceed to the house of Lawrence Renzi, a known agent of Aremberg's. He wrote to Cecil telling him as much. Cecil confronted Cobham with this letter. The result was spectacular. Cobham became highly emotional, then in rage and terror declared that all the schemes with which he was charged had had their origin in Raleigh.

If Raleigh's letter to Cecil was a major blunder, he now capped it with one even worse. He sent his trusted servant, Keymis, to the imprisoned Cobham to tell him that he had cleared him before the Privy Council. Keymis, in addition, told Cobham to be of good cheer since a single

witness could not condemn a man of treason. The Privy Council, having
Cobham under surveillance, learned of these words. They proceeded with
their investigation, and on September 21st Sir Walter Raleigh was indicted on charges of high treason.

The date of Raleigh's trial was November 17, 1603; the place (since
London was still considered unsafe because of the plague) Winchester, in
the great hall of the Castle. Tall, lean, saturnine, with that pointed beard
that turned upward from the chin of his strangely long face, Raleigh rode
to Winchester flanked by his keepers. As his coach rolled out of London,
the populace turned out to hoot him, pelting him with 'tobacco-pipes,
stones, and mire'. For a number of reasons he had long been the most hated
man in England. There was the damnable pride and arrogance of the man.
There was the general opinion that he had as good as murdered Essex—
practically everyone believed the slander that he had taken a pipe from his
mouth and blown smoke in the face of Essex as he went to the scaffold.
There was envy at the favours he had wheedled out of the old Queen.
Some of these, his licences of wine and cloth, had been in effect unpopular
taxes levied upon the kingdom. Raleigh was an intellectual. In the philosophical speculations within his circle was to be found the most advanced
thinking of his day on matters of religion. Out of all this had come a host
of rumours about the 'diabolical atheist' Raleigh. The loathed term of
'Machiavellian' had been fastened upon him:

> The originall of ye rude rauly
> it is too base to tell
> From Italy it came to us
> to Italy from Hell.[8]

Thus, surrounded by misconception, slander, hate—in part the consequence of his own pride, greed, intemperance, and occasional sycophancy
in the past—Raleigh went to his trial. His accusers could be confident
about one thing: the country would rejoice at his downfall.

The trial opened. Presiding were the commissioners, appointed by the
Crown, who had conducted the investigation which had led up to the trial.
They played an ambiguous role, partly as judges, partly as supporters for
Attorney-General Coke when he presented the case against the accused.
Included among the commissioners were not only the Lord Chief Justice
of England and the Lord Chief Justice of Common Pleas, but also
Secretary Cecil, Lord Henry Howard (soon to become Earl of Northampton), and his nephew the recently created Earl of Suffolk. It was
not customary in trials for treason to permit the accused to have
counsel, and so Raleigh had no lawyer and had to conduct his defence
himself.

C*

The indictment was read, charging that Raleigh:

> . . . did conspire, and go about to deprive the King of his Government, to raise up Sedition within the Realm; to alter Religion, to bring in the Roman Superstition, and to procure foreign Enemies to invade the Kingdom.[9]

Raleigh entered his plea of 'Not Guilty' and Sir Edward Coke opened the case for the Crown.

By the standards of any British court today, Coke simply did not have a case against Raleigh. What followed was a sheer travesty of justice with more resemblance to the Moscow trials of the 1930's than anything seen in modern times in any Anglo-Saxon country. All that Coke could offer was an unsigned declaration, allegedly made by Cobham, incriminating Raleigh. He refused to produce Cobham himself in court. In fact, the prosecution put only one witness in the stand, a seaman named Dyer, who testified that once when he was in Portugal he had heard a Portuguese gentleman say that James would never be crowned King of England 'for Don Raleigh and Don Cobham will cut his Throat ere that Day come'. For the rest, Coke had to make what he could of Raleigh's message to Cobham that he had cleared him, and Keymis' message that Cobham need not fear anything charged by a single witness.

Coke tried, in various ways, to make up for his lack of evidence. He dragged in the whole story of the Bye Plot, though he had to admit Raleigh was right when the latter interposed: 'You, Gentlemen of the Jury, I pray remember, I am not charged with the Bye, being the Treason of the Priest.' For the rest, Coke resorted to insult, innuendo, and plain abuse of the prisoner:

> . . . I will prove you the notoriest [sic] Traitor that ever came to the Bar. . . . Thou art a Monster; thou hast an *English* Face, but a Spanish Heart. . . . We have to deal today with a Man of Wit . . . Raleigh, in his *Machiavellian* Policy, hath made a Sanctuary out of Treason. . . . Came this out of *Cobham's* quiver? No; but out of *Raleigh's Machiavellian* and devilish Policy. . . . see the most horrible Practices that ever came out of the bottomless Pit of the lowest Hell . . . thou Viper; . . . thou Traitor.[10]

Raleigh, for his part, exhibited magnificent restraint, address, and courage. Only occasionally did he allow himself a certain cold contempt towards the Attorney-General:

> *Attorney :* Thou art the most vile and execrable Traitor that ever lived.
> *Raleigh :* You speak indiscreetly, barbarously and uncivilly.
> *Attorney :* I want Words sufficient to express thy viperous Treasons.
> *Raleigh :* I think you want Words, indeede, for you have spoken one thing half a dozen Times.[11]

Coke has long been enshrined among the great champions of the English law. But despite his prodigious labours on his reports and commentaries, despite all that he strove to do later in the name of common law, he deserves only contempt for the part he played that day at Winchester.

If Coke had ever the semblance of a case against him, Raleigh demolished it. He pointed out how fantastic the charge was that he, known to be the most inveterate enemy of Spain and the Catholics, whose chief policy was active prosecution of the Spanish war, should be conspiring to end that war and aid the Catholics. He dwelt on the emotional instability of Cobham himself—'as passionate a Man as lives: for he hath not spared the best Friends he hath in *England* in his Passion'. Dealing with the charge that Cobham had mentioned him as his ally when seeking to recruit support for his plot, Raleigh made the entirely reasonable suggestion that Cobham had been making false use of his name in an attempt to muster adherents, just as Jack Straw had claimed the support of the Duke of Buckingham, and Jack Cade that of the Duke of York. As for Keymis having told Cobham not to be afraid of what could be charged on the word of a single witness, Raleigh denied having ever instructed Keymis to say anything of the sort (not that it would have been evidence of treason on Raleigh's part if he had!) Coke had made much of a treasonable manuscript which he alleged Raleigh had given Cobham. Raleigh retorted that Cobham had taken it from his table, and in any case it was one of a number of libellous works which he had received from Cecil's father, Lord Burghley, for official examination during Elizabeth's time. At this Coke sneered that Raleigh, not being a Privy Councillor, could not possibly have secured the paper in this fashion. He was wrong. Cecil himself now spoke up, declaring that Raleigh 'was not a sworn Counsellor of State, but he has been called to Consultation'. Cecil further testified that Raleigh had indeed had access to his father's study, where he claimed to have secured the manuscript in question.

Chiefly, however, Raleigh rested his defence on calling in question Cobham's testimony against him. He tried desperately to force Coke to produce Cobham in court. Surely, he argued, his prosecutors would not seek to take his life on the strength of a statement which Cobham had not even signed:

> . . . All this is but one Accusation of *Cobham*'s. I hear no other thing; to which Accusation he never subscribed nor avouched it. I beseech you, my Lords, let *Cobham* be sent for, charge him on his Soul, on his Allegiance to the King; if he affirm it, I am guilty.[12]

It was a desperate risk but Raleigh took it. Apparently he realized that his only chance of acquittal in a court such as this lay in making Cobham withdraw his charges. On and on Raleigh fought, challenging his accusers, bargaining with them, daring them to produce Cobham:

You try me by the *Spanish* Inquisition if you proceed only by the Circumstances, without two Witnesses. . . . Christ requireth it, as it appeareth,
Mat. 18. If by the Canon, Civil Law, and God's Word, it be required, that
there must be two Witnesses at the least; bear with me if I desire one. . . .
The Proof of the Common Law is by Witness and Jury; let *Cobham* be
here, let him speak it. Call my Accuser before my Face and I have done.[13]

Raleigh made his appeal to the common law in vain:

Raleigh : The common Trial of *England* is by Jury and Witnesses.
Lord Chief Justice : No, by Examination.

When Raleigh protested against hearsay evidence being admitted against
him, the Lord Chief Justice ruled that hearsay evidence was admissible.
At this, Raleigh came near to despair.

Raleigh : If this may be, you will have any Man's Life in a Week.

Now that the trial was nearing its close, Coke produced a letter written
by Cobham only the day before. In it the abject lord revealed that shortly
after he had been lodged in the Tower, an apple had been thrown through
his window bearing with it a letter from Raleigh appealing to him to withdraw his accusations. Cobham had sent such a letter but now he was making a recantation of his recantation. Raleigh had kept Cobham's first letter
all this time. It was his one trump card, though Coke had robbed it now of
half its usefulness. Nevertheless Raleigh decided to play it. The account
preserved in the volumes of *State Trials* supplies the scene for us:

Nota, Here *Raleigh* pulled a Letter out of his Pocket, which the Lord
Cobham had written to him, and desired my Lord *Cecil* to read it, because
he only knew his Hand; the effect of it was as follows:
Cobham's *Letter of Justification to* Raleigh
Seeing myself so near my End, for the discharge of my own Conscience,
and freeing myself from your Blood, which else will cry Vengeance against
me: I protest upon my Salvation I never practised with *Spain* by your
Procurement; God so comfort me in this my Affliction, as you are a true
Subject, for any thing that I know. I will say as *Daniel, Purus sum a sanguine
hujus.* So God have mercy upon my Soul, as I know no treason by you.[14]

The effect was spectacular. The court broke into general uproar. Coke was
on his feet, livid with fury, shouting that this letter had been 'politickly
and cunningly urged from the Lord Cobham'. Cecil stood silent; he knew
that of Cobham's two letters this was the truer one. Three months earlier
he had mentioned in a letter to the English ambassador in France that
Cobham was withdrawing most of the charges he had made against
Raleigh.[15]

With this last development the case was pretty well at an end. The jury
departed. Within fifteen minutes it returned with its verdict—Guilty.

Preparing to pass sentence, the Lord Chief Justice launched into a diatribe against the man standing before him: 'Two Vices have been lodged chiefly in you; one is an eager Ambition, the other corrupt Covetousness.' He noted that the world had taxed Raleigh with holding 'the most heathenish and blasphemous Opinions'. Finally, he declared judgment:

> ... since you have been found guilty of these horrible Treasons, the Judgment of the Court is, That you shall be had from hence to the Place whence you came, there to remain until the day of Execution; and from thence you shall be drawn upon a Hurdle thro' the open Streets to the Place of Execution, there to be hanged and cut down alive, and your Body shall be opened, your Heart and Bowels pluck'd out, and your Privy Members cut off, and thrown into the Fire before your Eyes; then your Head to be stricken off from your Body, and your Body shall be divided into four Quarters, to be disposed of at the King's Pleasure: And God have Mercy upon your Soul.[16]

With all its faults and abuses, the trial at least had been held publicly. The world had been given the case against Raleigh, and it had heard Raleigh's defence. Its judgment was not that of the jury—intimidated, corrupted, or partial as that jury must have been to deliver its incredible verdict. Raleigh's calm courage and cool reason in the presence of such outrage and oppression decisively turned public opinion towards him. Hatred changed suddenly to admiration and pity. For this we have the testimony of those present that day at Winchester. Dudley Carleton, who was to become ambassador successively to Holland and Venice, was present at Raleigh's trial. Writing to a friend when it was all over, he said:

> He answered with that temper, wit, learning, courage, and judgment, that, save that it went with the hazard of his life, it was the happiest day that ever he spent. And so well he shifted all advantages that were taken against him, that were not *fama malum gravius quam res*, and an ill name, half hanged, in the opinion of all men he had been acquitted.[17]

Even the men who reported to James the finding of the court were unable to withhold their admiration for Raleigh.

> The two first that brought the news to the king were Roger Ashton, and a Scotchman, whereof one affirmed that never any man spake so well in times past, nor would do in the world to come; and the other said, that whereas, when he saw him first, he was so led with the common hatred, that he would have gone a hundred miles to have seen him hanged, he would, ere he parted, have gone a thousand to have saved his life. In one word, never was a man so hated and so popular in so short a time.[18]

Twelve days after judgment was passed on Raleigh, the priests, Watson and Clarke, convicted of guilt in the Bye Plot, went to the appalling death to which Raleigh had been sentenced. Amid the horrors of their mutilation they protested their innocence. On December 6th George Brooke met his

death. Since he was a brother-in-law to Cecil, he was spared disembowl-
ment and castration and given the honourable death of beheading. He too
protested his innocence to the last, uttering a cryptic statement, 'There is
something yet hidden, which will one day appear for my justification.'
The next day King James signed warrants ordering the execution on
Friday, December 9th, of Cobham, Grey and Markham. It was generally
understood around the court that Raleigh himself was to die a few days
later.

Raleigh in his prison cell, meanwhile, had been writing to the King
imploring life. He had written also to every lord or councillor who might
aid him, begging them to intercede with James. These letters make painful
reading. Here is none of that fine manliness shown at the trial—only servile
grovelling, abject flattery, shameless self-pity. All who have known the
true greatness of Raleigh have wished that he had never written those
letters. Later he tried to assure that they would not survive him. We must,
however, forgive much to a man so trapped and hopeless as Raleigh. He
was in the fulness of mature life. He was only too conscious of his own
great powers and aspirations. Should he die, Lady Raleigh and his young
son would be left unprotected. Little wonder if he were ready to stoop to
win life. During these days he wrote other lines, ones we would not lose.
Turning to the consolations of poetry, he penned 'The Pilgrimage'. The
verses are moving, for all their quaint archaic conceits:

> Give me my scallop-shell of quiet,
>   My staff of faith to walk upon,
> My scrip of joy, immortal diet,
>   My bottle of salvation,
> My gown of glory, hopes true gage!
> And thus I'll take my pilgrimage.

Remembering the travesty of his trial, Raleigh looked forward to receiving
true justice at last in 'Heaven's bribeless hall':

> Where no corrupted voices brawl;
> No conscience molten into gold;
> No forged accuser bought or sold;
> No cause deferred, no vain spent journey;
> For there Christ is the King's Attorney. . . .

December 9th came. Sir Griffith Markham was the first to go to the
scaffold. Just as the headsman was ready to proceed, barely in time to stop
him, the Sheriff had his attention seized by the frantic signalling of a man
in the crowd. It was John Gibb, a Scottish groom of the royal chamber,
whom King James had despatched with reprieves without the knowledge
of even his most trusted councillors. Following the instructions brought
by Gibb, the Sheriff told Markham, 'You say you are ill-prepared to die;

you shall have two hours' respite.' After Markham had been removed to the adjacent hall, Lord Grey was brought to the scaffold. For the better part of an hour he and a Puritan divine offered up prayers while the spectators stood soaking in a heavy rain. When at last he was ready to put his head on the block, the Sheriff, still following closely his royal instructions, told him that the order of execution had been changed and that he was to wait until after Cobham had died. Grey then joined Markham in the hall.

The contemptible Cobham was now produced. The assurance and boldness of his manner made watchers suspect later that he had already some knowledge of what was up. In any case, he and a clergyman proceeded to pray. Cobham declared his guilt but once more put all the blame on Raleigh. Then the Sheriff intervened for the third time. He ordered Markham and Grey brought again to the scaffold and told the three men that the King in his mercy had granted them their lives.

Why this gruesome and sadistic play? James wanted proof. He wanted confessions. He hoped that at the very threshold of death these men would divulge the truth. But he learned nothing new. Raleigh hurriedly wrote to James begging that he too might be included in this 'work of so great mercy'. He was. On December 15th, Raleigh with the other three was taken to the Tower of London. He was to be a prisoner there for the next thirteen years.

How was it that Raleigh was let off at last with not too onerous an imprisonment—he had a small suite of chambers in the Tower, and the adjacent stretch of battlements is still known as Sir Walter's Walk. Various things had joined to save him. His enemies, perhaps appalled to see that their revenge was proceeding further than they had intended, had relinquished the attack; friends—and Raleigh did have some friends—were seeking to save him; public opinion had swung decisively for him, especially after the barbarous death of the priests and Brooke's disquieting charge from the scaffold. Finally, there was the conscience of the King. James was not a wicked man. He did believe that a king should be just and should temper justice with mercy. For all his fear, distrust, and suspicions where Raleigh was concerned, he had been unable to send him to his death. Perhaps he realized that all that could really be urged against Raleigh was that he had 'listened too patiently to the treasonable maunderings of a fool'.[19]

CHAPTER V

The Hungry Scots

Hark! Hark!
The dogs do bark,
The beggars have come to town.
Some in rags,
And some in tags,
And some in velvet gowns.

So RUNS the nursery-rhyme which may have started as a political libel, the beggars in velvet gowns being the Scottish courtiers who flocked southward in the wake of their James VI, eager to enjoy with him the wealth of his new kingdom. It is little wonder if the English were provoked to such derision. The Scots who swarmed about Whitehall made little secret of their hopes, and their avarice was only too apparent. Not that there was much love to be lost between the Scots and the English. Bannockburn and Flodden were in their memories, as well as the raids and burnings on the border marches. To Shakespeare they were the 'weasel Scots'. To others they were a bloody, barbarous people, for ever with knives at each other's throats. Sir Anthony Weldon, in a letter written from Leith, gives a contemporary Englishman's view of Scotland. Everywhere in Scotland he finds foul houses, foul sheets, foul dishes. He is equally appalled by the poverty of the people and their craftiness. The Scottish nobles he gives up as hopeless:

> . . . their followers are their fellowes, their wyves their slaves, their horses their masters, and their swords their judges.

The Scottish women are no more attractive than the men:

> . . . every whore in Houndsditche is a Helena, and the greasy bawdes in Turnebull-street are Greekish dames, in comparison to these.

As for Edinburgh, he scorns to dignify the Scottish capital with the name of a city:

> . . . the men of olde did no more wonder that the great Messias should be borne in so poore a Towne as Bethlem in Judea, as I do wonder that so brave a Prince as King James should be borne in so stinking a Towne as Edenborough in lousy Scotland.[1]

Much as they might dislike the change, the English had to reconcile

48

themselves to finding in their royal court a host of new faces from Scotland. Installed as Captain of the Guard was James's trusted friend, Sir Thomas Erskine. Naturalized as an Englishman and admitted to the Privy Council was Erskine's brother, the Earl of Mar. Similarly sworn in as Privy Councillors were the King's kinsman Ludovick Stuart, Duke of Lennox; James Elphinstone, Lord Balmerino; Edward Bruce, Lord of Kinloss; and Sir George Home, the future Earl of Dunbar. This Sir George Home was doing particularly well for himself, for he had also become Chancellor of the Exchequer and Master of the Wardrobe. In the latter capacity he was to make a tidy fortune disposing of the thousands of costly dresses left by the late Queen Elizabeth. There were many others. There was the noble Marquess of Hamilton, whom even the most unfriendly of the English conceded to be the 'flower of the Scottish nation'. There was that magnificent profligate Sir James Hay, in time to be created Earl of Carlisle, who was to excel in parvenu ostentation. There was Sir John Ramsay, the future Earl of Holderness, (soaking up the royal bounty. And everywhere there were Murrays. Looking after Prince Henry was Sir David Murray, soon to be enriched with monopolies on brimstone and copper pyrites, and a pension out of the taxes on Rhenish wine. Groom in the King's Bedchamber was John Murray, whose services were to be rewarded not only with estates and land, but with bonds for £8,000 (multiply by eight for modern values) due to the Exchequer. Rewarded on a less grand scale was Thomas Murray, tutor to Prince Charles. Among the recipients of 'Free Gifts . . . paid out of the Exchequer' in 1603 was Sir Patrick Murray with £300, though he was quite eclipsed by the Earl of Linlithgow who received £3,000 and the Earl of Moray who got £2,600.

As the royal bounty flowed from the seemingly inexhaustible wealth of England, James's Scots must have felt that the Golden Age had indeed returned. The story went that Sir Roger Aston, the King's master falconer, bred and raised in Scotland though born in Cheshire, when asked how he did at his first coming back into England, confided, 'Even my Lords, like a poore man wandring above forty yeares in a Wildernesse, and barren Soyle, and now arrived at the Land of Promise.'[2]

The English, especially those disappointed in their own hopes of reward and office from their new king, hardly shared the joy of the Scots at King James's generosity. There were mutterings that the Scots were

> . . . suffered like locusts to devour this Kingdom; from whence they became so rich and insolent, as nothing with any moderation could either be given or denied them.[3]

Appreciative laughter greeted the story about a happening at Theobalds. A religious fanatic, dressed like a serving-man, had got past the watch and

entered the premises. When the watch caught up with him and demanded
to know whom he served, he at once replied to them, 'The Lord Jehovah!'
At this the constable said, 'Well, let him pass; I believe it is some Scottish
Lord or other.'[4]

The undisguised hostility the English bore the Scots found expression
on the London stage in 1604. Ben Jonson, working with two fellow play-
wrights, had concocted a wonderfully funny piece entitled *Eastward Ho*.
At one point in the play a mariner, Captain Seagull, fills his hearers in a
Thameside tavern with wonder at his tales of Virginia and its wealth.
According to Seagull, the land is so rich that even the chamber-pots are
made of solid gold. Moreover, he adds, there is plenty of room for colonists
since there are only a few industrious Scots there:

> And for my own part, I would a hundred thousand of 'em were there, for
> we are all one countrymen now, ye know, and we should find ten times
> more comfort of them there than we do here.
>
> (III, iii, 57–62)

A little later in the play, as the deflated trickster Sir Petronel Flash is
lying half drowned by the river edge at Cuckold's Haven, an unidentified
gentleman crosses the stage and, in unmistakable parody of James's own
Scottish accent, says, 'I ken the man weel; he's one of my thirty pound
knights' (i.e. one of the hundreds whom King James, in his eagerness for
ready cash, was knighting to secure the thirty pounds fee). Jonson, Chapman and Marston could hardly hope to get away with this sort of stuff. A
Scottish courtier in the audience (one of the Murrays) hastened to Whitehall with news of the outrage, and Jonson and Chapman were shortly
behind bars. The word around town was that Jonson was to have his nose
slit and his ears cropped for his punishment. Fortunately he had friends
at court, and after an interval both Jonson and Chapman were released,
noses and ears still intact.

Over the years the friction between the Scots and the English went on,
generating sometimes more heat, sometimes less. In November 1605 Sir
Edward Hoby was appreciatively writing to a friend that Guy Fawkes,
after his arrest for the Gunpowder Plot, 'told some of the Scots that his
intent was to have blown them back again into Scotland'. In 1607 an M.P.
from Buckinghamshire rose in the House of Commons to declare that the
Scots were 'beggars, proud, and generally traitors and rebels to their
kings'. Informed of this by one of his Scots, King James lost his temper,
summoned the Privy Council and declared to them that he was himself a
Scot, loved Scots, and would charge his heir Prince Henry, under pain of
his curse, to love the Scots also. This outburst, however, was unusual.
Generally James was careful not to identify himself with either nation. In

this case, he saw to it that the offending M.P. made a retraction and then sent him to the Tower to think things over.

Parliament—especially when it was a matter of voting supplies—continued to be notably unenthusiastic about James's bounty to his Scots. In 1610 Master John More wrote to Winwood, the English ambassador at The Hague:

> I conceive by the common Discourse that the Parliament could be content to replenish the royall Cistern (as they call it) of his Majesty's Treasury, were they assured, that his Majestie's Largess to the Scots Prodigallity would not cause a continual and remediless Leake therein.

A real crisis between the Scots and the English came in 1612 with battle lines forming in the court, and a very real danger that attempted intimidation would mount through violence to a massacre. The first incident was at the Croydon races, where a violent flare-up occurred between the Earl of Montgomery, one of the earliest of James's English favourites, and Patrick Ramsay. The latter was brother to another of the King's minions, John Ramsay, who had been dear to James ever since he had killed the Gowries while making the famous rescue of some twelve years earlier. John Ramsay, we may note in passing, had prospered greatly since he had followed his King southward. He had married a daughter of the Earl of Sussex and had received upon that occasion a handsome annuity from the King. In 1606 James had advanced him to the dignity of Viscount Haddington in the Scottish nobility, and the next year he had paid his debts, some £10,000 for him.

As for the Earl of Montgomery, if he is remembered at all today it is because he and his brother, the Earl of Pembroke, figure as 'The Most Noble and Incomparable Paire of Brethren' in the dedication of the First Folio of Shakespeare. The brethren were hardly more than boys when James came to the English throne. The elder, aged nineteen, had already inherited the family title of Earl of Pembroke. It was, however, the eighteen-year-old Philip who particularly attracted the King's attention. The choice was a curious one. Pembroke himself, with his gentle easy temper, his aristocratic grace and elegance, would have proved to most men the more attractive. James was not unaware of the elder brother's charm. He was glad to visit him at his noble mansion at Wilton, 'an Academie, as well as Palace . . . the Apiarie, to which Men, that were excellent in Armes, and Arts, did resort, and were carress't'. In his final years, in fact, King James made Pembroke his Lord Chamberlain. It was, however, to Pembroke's younger brother that James extended his particular grace in 1603, making him the first of his favourites in England.

All that Montgomery had to commend him was his good looks, though

these had a powerful attraction for James who was more drawn to handsome men than beautiful women. For the rest he was a young boor utterly
unworthy of the uncle, Sir Philip Sidney, from whom he derived his
Christian name. His interests were hunting and hawking, the bowling alley,
the tiltyard, and the gaming table. He did not even take the trouble to
cultivate the attentions of the King, treating the royal favours with an offhand neglect even while accepting them. His furious bursts of bad temper
made him a man for whom most people had little liking, and a nasty streak
of malice and treachery added nothing to his reputation. Despite all this,
James was powerfully attracted to the young man, and poured forth his
bounty upon him. He made a great court occasion out of his marriage in
1604 to Lady Susan Vere, a daughter of the Earl of Oxford, and presented
him with lands worth £1,200 per annum. Next year, when Philip Herbert
turned twenty-one, the King created him Earl of Montgomery. In 1607
he paid out of the royal purse the debts which the loose-living and extravagant young man had accumulated. The next year he advanced him to the
honour of the Garter and made him an outright gift of £6,000 (about
£50,000 in modern values). This pretty well marked the summit of Montgomery's favour. The year that followed saw the emergence of a much more
gifted and attractive royal favourite in the young Scot, Robert Carr. In
1611 Carr was advanced to the title of Viscount Rochester, while Montgomery had the misfortune to lose his good looks through smallpox. The
succeeding year found Montgomery more than usually cantankerous and
quarrelsome. It was at this point that he was switched in the face by
Patrick Ramsay.

The scene of the quarrel between the two men was a horse race at Croydon. Many courtiers were there for the sport and standing by when
Ramsay, losing his temper, suddenly struck Montgomery in the face with
his switch. There was an electrifying pause. In view of Montgomery's
reputation, he might well have tried to kill Ramsay on the spot. Whether
from discretion or, as some maintained, simple cowardice, he did not
return the blow. The crowd, however, was thrown into an uproar and a
general attack upon the Scots appeared imminent:

> [The English] did upon this accident draw together with a resolution to
> make it a *National Quarrel*, so far as Mr. *John Pinchback*, though a maimed
> Man, having but the perfect use of two fingers, rode about with his dagger
> in his hand, crying, *Let us break our fast with them here, and dine with the
> rest at London*.[5]

It was a bad moment. All that was needed was somebody to strike the first
blow and the field would, in a few minutes, have been running with blood
and London itself swept by violence. Later the violently anti-Scottish
Osborn declared that, had that first blow been given, '. . . all after must

have proved fatal to the *Scots*, so long as any had staid in *England*; the Royal Family excepted.'

King James acted quickly and decisively. Summoning both Ramsay and Montgomery before him, he made a most thorough examination of the whole incident. Finding Ramsay the offender, he immediately committed him to the Tower of London. James's firmness and impartiality did much to ease the tension, and Henry, the Prince of Wales, seized the occasion to declare his own 'indifferent Affection to both the Nations'.

It was well that the Croydon incident was handled so firmly for soon there was another one to inflame national feeling. This was the murder of an English fencing-master, Turner, by the Scottish Lord Sanquhar. The circumstances were utterly inexcusable. Back in the summer of 1604 Sanquhar had been a house guest of Lord Norris at Rycote in Oxfordshire. Here, while practising fencing with the well-known instructor Turner, he had been accidentally struck in the eye by the latter's sword and had lost its sight. Years later Sanquhar was presented at the court of France. Henri IV enquired about the misadventure which had left him only one eye, and asked if the man who had so injured him still lived. Sanquhar took this as a reflection on his honour. Back in England, he hired two assassins to murder Turner and, when these failed, he commissioned two of his own servants, Grey and Carlyle, to kill him. Grey, horrified at his master's orders, sought to flee to Sweden but Carlyle, accompanied by a certain Irwin, went to Turner's house at Whitefriars and shot him down in cold blood. This was not the end of the matter, however. Grey, Carlyle and Irwin were apprehended and Sanquhar implicated. Arraigned before the Court of King's Bench as plain Robert Crichton—his Scottish peerage meant nothing in the eyes of the English law—Sanquhar was sentenced to die. A group of Scottish lords pleaded in vain with the King for his life. Once more James saw that strict justice was done. Sanquhar might be a nobleman and the King's compatriot, but he was hanged as a common felon. Friends who waited at the foot of the gallows received the body, had it embalmed, and returned it to Scotland.

In this same year of 1612 there came an incident which stirred violently anti-Scottish feeling among the members of the Inns of Court. These men, lawyers and young law students, formed a compact community proud of their gentility and sensitive to any affront offered them. The occasion itself was trifling, but not its consequences in a society where human lives could be sacrificed in a matter of punctilio. One of the members of the Temple was a certain Hawley, a rough roistering fellow who made himself a nuisance at Whitehall Palace during a banquet in honour of a visiting French duke and had to be removed. Unfortunately the usher who attended to his removal was a 'dogged ill-natured Scot' named Maxwell, who inflicted what was deemed an unforgivable indignity upon Hawley. It was the custom for dandies to wear an ear-ring in one ear. Maxwell, grabbing Hawley by the ear and lugging him away, ripped his ear where the ring pierced it. The next few days saw Hawley's fellow lawyers, and indeed all the English gentlemen at the court, seething with anger. As for the Scots, it was reported that they were in such fear that during the next ten days three hundred of them streamed northward to Scotland and safety. In the end the King himself intervened. He had a talk with the injured Hawley, then he had Maxwell summoned before the Privy Council where he was required to go on his knees and beg forgiveness of Hawley. James no doubt gave a sigh of relief that that fire had been put out, and reflected bitterly in his heart on the readiness of his Scottish and English followers to fly at each other's throats.

Other crises arose. There was the occasion upon which one of the Murrays murdered the sergeant whom the sheriffs of London had sent to arrest him. Plenty of the English were not ready to let such things be forgotten, and they put into circulation a jingle about the King's Scots:

> They *Beg* our *Lands*, our *Goods*, our *Lives*,
> They *Switch* our *Nobles*, and lie with their wives;
> They *Pinch* our *Gentry* and send for our *Benchers*,
> They *Stab* our *Sergeants*, and pistol our *Fencers*.[6]

To picture the Jacobean court as being in constant tension because of national enmity would, however, be wrong. Rather there was an undercurrent of feeling with occasional flare-ups. Friendships and marriages crossed the national lines. Even at the Croydon races there was one Englishman who sided with Ramsay's party. That things were not much worse must be credited to the good sense and firmness shown by the King. He made some mistakes of course. He would have done well to avoid using English titles, English estates, and English taxes when rewarding his Scots. Certainly he poured forth too much largesse upon them. On the other hand, he tried to be impartial. If he was profligate in his gifts to his Scottish followers, he was profligate too in his rewards for his favourites among the English. If he paid Ramsay's debts, he paid Montgomery's also. The royal family successfully avoided becoming identified with either faction. If Prince Henry had a Scottish tutor in Adam Newton, he had the English Sir Thomas Chaloner for his 'governor' and later chamberlain of his household. If Queen Anne had for the first lady of her bedchamber the Scottish Mistress Drummond, she had for her closest confidante Lucy Russell, the English Countess of Bedford. If the King had for his first great favourite in the English court the young Scot, Robert Carr, he later had an even greater one in the Englishman George Villiers. As for Carr, possibly at James's suggestion, he made a point of recruiting his household and party almost entirely from among the English, making it very clear that,

> . . . he did utterly dislike the bold carriage and importunity of the Scots . .
> and he did but little esteem their clamorous complaints to the King.[7]

Politically the Scottish party, if there could have been said to be such a thing, was almost negligible in its power. The real positions of political strength were held almost entirely by the English. If the Scots had any political policy which they supported as a group, it consisted of urging that the 'auld alliance' with France be preserved by marrying the heir to a French princess. They were heeded hardly at all by King James who, supported by various English advisers, for years persisted in seeking a Spanish match.

It cannot be really maintained that the Scots got more than their fair share of offices at Court. English courtiers too often forgot that since there was no longer a royal court in Scotland, the Scots were entitled to a certain number of the places about their king now that he had gone into England. The Court was the centre for a seventeenth-century aristocracy, and Scotland had lost much in giving up its court to England.

CHAPTER VI

Ambassadors from Beyond the Seas

MORE THAN aristocratic licence and royal prodigality lay behind the luxury of a seventeenth-century court. Serious statesmen approved of magnificence about the monarch and extravagance of style among his courtiers. Their reason was simple—the court being the centre of the nation's life and government, its opulence determined in good measure the prestige the nation enjoyed among its neighbours. One occasion upon which any court exerted itself to show the utmost splendour was the reception of an ambassador from abroad.

The early years of the seventeenth century saw much travelling hither and yon of ambassadors. The wars of the previous century had given way to a period of uneasy peace, and the international situation had become fluid. Soon there would come the cataclysm of the Thirty Years War, but in the interim there was constant diplomatic manœuvring. An essential role was played by the ambassadors who arrived in such state and were entertained so sumptuously.

Ambassadors were of two kinds. The ordinary resident ambassador served usually for a term of three years during which he attended to the routine of diplomacy. The special or extraordinary ambassador of ceremony was a much more notable person, and the sending of such an ambassador was a signal gesture of honour and friendship. Being usually an aristocrat of the highest rank, such an ambassador came with a retinue of hundreds. His stay was usually brief, sometimes lasting only a week. Then, his particular mission completed, he hastened home.

A chief reason for special embassies was the offering of congratulations or condolences. James's accession to the English throne brought embassies of compliment from the United Provinces, France, the Spanish Netherlands, Spain, Denmark, Venice, Florence, Poland, Savoy and Lorraine, and from a number of German states, including the Palatinate of the Rhine, Wurtemberg, Brandenburg, Brunswick and Cleves. When the King survived Cobham's Plot, and later the Gunpowder Plot, special ambassadors congratulated him upon his preservation. When Queen Anne died in 1619, special embassies arrived to condole. Among thes was one from Savoy which, coming six months after the event, embarrassed the English by arriving in full mourning after the English themselves had put away their blacks.

Negotiating a treaty or making a royal marriage almost always required special ambassadors. In 1611 a marshal of France arrived with a retinue of one hundred and twenty to take King James's oath to a league between England and France. In 1623 no less than three ambassadors extraordinary from Spain were at the English court trying to keep alive negotiations for a marriage between the Infanta and Prince Charles. Not all ambassadors of ceremony had such important missions. Some were on errands which were purely honorific. Thus, in the summer of 1605 Henricus Ramelius, principal secretary to Christian IV of Denmark, arrived as his master's proxy to be invested with the Order of the Garter. In 1613 the Duc de Bouillon arrived from France to return the Garter bestowed on the recently defunct Henri IV. A more novel use of the special ambassador came in 1610 when Contarini arrived from Venice to explain, as tactfully as possible, why the Venetian State had banned a book of which King James was the proud author.

Ambassadors were received with such elaborate protocol that the English, following the example of the French, appointed a special officer to look after these complicated matters. In 1605 Sir Lewis Lewkenor was named Master of Ceremonies and charged 'to receive and entertaine, Ambassadours, and Princes, during their abode in England: in all honorable manner as is used in France and other places'. He had, in fact, been performing these duties from the very beginning of the reign.

The reception of a special ambassador began the moment he set foot on English soil. If he were of sufficient importance, and if the court had sufficient forewarning, he landed at Dover to find the Master of Ceremonies already there to greet him. Royal coaches and wagons would be at hand to transport him and his retinue to Gravesend. Here he might well find the Lord Chamberlain and a body of courtiers with a further welcome, ready to conduct him and his retinue to the royal barges. Their journey up the Thames ended with a ceremonial landing at Tower Wharf to the accompaniment of salutes from the Tower artillery. From here the Lord Mayor and aldermen of London would escort the newcomers as they travelled in procession through the city to their lodgings. This was the first real opportunity for the members of the embassy to display their numbers and the richness of their dress. From the thronged street side the Londoners watched them, comparing their number and brilliance with that of other embassies.

The English king usually paid a daily sum for the maintenance of an ambassador of ceremony. This might range from the £10 allowed a visiting Pole in 1621 to the £300 a day granted the Spaniards who arrived to negotiate the peace treaty of 1604. Sometimes a royal house would be made available as a residence. Thus in 1622 the Emperor's ambassador

extraordinary was accommodated in Somerset House. At other times some
courtier was required to billet the distinguished visitor. In 1624 the Earl
of Suffolk had to turn over almost the whole of Suffolk House to an ambassador from France, being 'forced to a corner of his own House, which
he could not wholly leave by reason of his lingering sicknesse'.[1] The
ambassadors who occasionally arrived from Russia and Turkey were
regarded chiefly as commercial agents, and their entertainment was made
a charge upon those who might expect to benefit most, the Muscovy and
Levant merchants.

After an ambassador and his followers had settled in their quarters,
there came their first audience with the King. This great occasion usually
fell within a few days of their arrival. Setting forth in all the splendour and
state they could muster, they rode in procession to Whitehall Palace.
Careful gradations of honour were shown in their reception. The visitors
might be greeted formally first at the court gate, then by a second group
of courtiers in the centre of the first courtyard, and finally by a third group
at the Guard Chamber door, before being ushered into the royal presence.
This was the full treatment, reserved for the most august ambassadors.
Lesser ones had to be content with a mere twofold greeting, or even just
one at the court gate. In any event, having passed through the Guard
Chamber, the ambassador found himself ushered into the Presence
Chamber, a large and impressive hall, where he found James I, the British
Solomon, seated in florid majesty. The ambassador presented his creden-
tials, kissed the royal hand, and discoursed with the King. Often he pre-
sented gifts.

There was always a lively public interest in the gifts. Some ambassadors
carried their presents in display with them as they went through the
London streets to their audience at Whitehall. Such was the practice of
the Russians who in 1617 presented James with an extensive list of gifts:

> ... sable Furres, black Foxes, Ermynes, Hawkes, with their Hoods and
> Mantles (covering their backs and wings) all embroydered with Gold and
> Pearle; two lining Sables, a Persian dagger, and knife set with stones and
> Pearles, two rich Cloath of Gold Persian Horse-clothes, a Persian kettle
> Drum to lure Hawkes with &c.[2]

Comparable to these were the gifts which Sir Thomas Roe, serving as
ambassador for the Great Mogul, brought James in 1619: 'two antelopes,
a straunge and bowtifull kind of red-deare, a rich tent, rare carpets, certain ombrellaes, and such like trinckets'. The gifts were scrutinized with
critical eyes by the court, which had no hesitation about looking gift horses
(James liked receiving horses) in the mouth. A letter-writer of 1611 noted
that while the Savoy ambassador's gift horses were excellent, the 'rich
furniture' which accompanied them was 'somewhat worne'. Problems

could arise in connection with some of these gifts. A supposedly tame leopard presented by a Spanish ambassador almost killed a little white fawn which was one of the royal pets with a woman specially employed for its care.

After his audience the ambassador returned with his retinue to his lodgings, once more the cynosure of all eyes as he passed through the streets. At times there were misadventures. Pity must be felt for the unfortunate Venetians who were welcomed to court late in 1603. The day of their arrival in London was the foulest of the year as far as weather was concerned, and when they reached their lodgings they found only seven beds provided for the 140 of them. On the day of their presentation at court, the authorities requisitioned for their use all the coaches found waiting by the court gates. In these they brought the Venetians to Whitehall. No sooner had the ambassadors and their train entered the Presence Chamber, however, than the courtiers quickly repossessed their coaches and drove off, leaving most of the Venetians to tramp home on foot. Other ambassadors were dissatisfied with their audiences with the King. Some found themselves waiting an hour or so in an antechamber because the slack mismanagement of the court had brought them to Whitehall before the King was ready to see them. Sometimes the King could not be bothered to make a distasteful trip to London on their account, and ambassadors had to travel out to Theobalds to see him, or journey over appalling roads to the more remote royal hunting-lodges at Royston or Newmarket.

Their ceremonious first audience with the King completed, the ambassadors proceeded with their negotiations either with the monarch or his council, with plenty of time being taken out for entertainments, state dinners, and masques. Banquets in the Hall or the Banqueting House were prime occasions for dazzling the visitors with the wealth and magnificence of the English court. In April 1622, Swartzenberg, the Emperor's ambassador,

> ... had a banquet which in sugar-works represented a complete army of horse and foot, with drums, ensigns, &c. ... There was six cartloads of plate, brought from the Tower, at this banquet, wherewith two stately stages [sideboards] were furnished, one very large and spacious, valued at £200,000; and the other far less but valued at £500,000.[3]

There were problem cases and unfortunate accidents. Definitely a problem was the Russian ambassador who refused to stir from his lodgings all winter. When he finally desired some fresh air Sir John Finett, Lewkenor's successor as Master of Ceremonies, managed to round up four coaches and take the Muscovites out to Theobalds for an airing. Then there was the very unfortunate incident of the Venetian ambassador in 1604. He had been invited to the day-long festivities at Whitehall attendant upon the marriage of the royal favourite, Sir Philip Herbert (soon to be Earl of Montgomery) and Lady Susan Vere. During the afternoon he found it necessary to retire. Those who conducted him to the desired convenience neglected to wait to show him his way back. The result was that the forgotten envoy missed the great banquet, a thing which he took very ill, even though supplied with a private supper in Cecil's own chambers.

When an ambassador extraordinary had completed his mission, he received his last audience with the King. Once again he distributed gifts about the court; but now it was also the turn of James to become a giver. From the royal hand came gifts for both the ambassador and his retinue— gilt plate, royal portraits, diamond rings and the like. To Swartzenberg returning home went James's picture 'set in Gold richly inchaced with Diamonds, and hung at a Chaine of Diamonds, Rubies, and Pearles'. A returning French ambassador was given a diamond ring valued at £4,000. Upon at least one occasion, an ambassador made it plain that he considered the King's largesse niggardly rather than princely:

> Monsieur Beaumont the French ambassador went homeward the first of this moneth, and hath blotted his former reputation with very mecanicall [common, vulgar] tricks at parting: for having 2000 ounces of plate geven him, he cavilled for 500 more, as having seene a president [precedent] of the like, which being graunted him, he begd two horses more by name of the King, besides pictures great and small with jewells at his own appointment, and not a noble man or other of his neere acquaintance but he got horses, geldings or somewhat of him . . . as yf he made no conscience to robbe the Egiptians.[4]

Elated or disappointed at his gifts, the departing ambassador headed for the port of his embarkation. If the King was pleased with him and his mission, royal coaches and wagons again gave him transport. But if King James was offended, he was quite capable of letting the envoy make shift as best he could.

Of the special embassies of ceremony that arrived at the Jacobean court none was more splendid, or prompted the court to greater endeavours of magnificence, than the Spanish embassy of 1604. From the moment of his arrival in England James had perceived that nothing was to be gained from the hostilities with Spain which had dragged on through the last years of Elizabeth. Spain, for her part, was near exhaustion and glad to make peace on any sort of reasonable terms. Accordingly negotiations were commenced. By midsummer, 1604, the stage had been reached where a formal treaty could be signed and sworn. For the treaty-making the Spaniards sent to England a resplendent embassy headed by Juan de Velasco, Duke of Frias and Constable of Castile. Spain was already far gone in decadence. The magnificent fleets and superb regiments of Philip II were things of the past. The economic strength of the Spanish kings was

THE NEGOTIATORS OF THE SPANISH TREATY OF 1604

Attributed to Marc Gheeraedts II

dwindling, and Spain little more than a shell of her former self. Of all this the English had little inkling. To them Spain, unstripped of her possessions, was still the great power she had been in the mid-sixteenth century. With a certain awe the English court awaited the coming of the Spanish grandees. The Spaniards for their part meant to reveal no signs of need or weakness, and they began things with suitable arrogance. Forerunner of the Constable was Juan de Taxis, Count of Villa Mediana, designated as the permanent Spanish ambassador to the English court. Having arrived in England, he insisted that the only house in London sufficient for the rank and state of the coming special ambassador was Somerset House, the residence of the Queen herself. The King was taken aback but referred Villa Mediana to Her Majesty. Anne, who was consistently pro-Spanish throughout the reign, readily agreed. King James then put into the house his best furniture and richest tapestries, and assigned an extensive staff to attend the Duke and his retinue upon their arrival there.

Determined to impress the visitors by the sheer size of the English court, the Lord Chamberlain and his officers proceeded to get every possible person into royal livery. A year before, Shakespeare's company of actors had received royal patronage as the King's Company of Players and been given the more or less nominal status of grooms of the chamber. As grooms they had each received four and a half yards of red cloth to furnish them with liveries in which to march in King James's coronation procession. Now they were required to put on this livery once again and attend upon the visiting Spaniards.

Early in August the Spanish embassy arrived at Dover. When they travelled up the Thames in twenty-four covered barges on the tenth of that month, the river was almost covered with the boats of persons curious to see the Dons. Among those gawking from a disguised barge were the Queen of England herself, wearing a mask, her friend the Countess of Suffolk, the Lord High Admiral of England (Nottingham) and Secretary Cecil.

After they had settled in Somerset House, the Spanish commissioners met with the English to draft the formal treaty of peace. Marc Gheeraedt's picture has preserved the scene. Down the centre stretches the traditional long table of diplomacy, covered with a rich brocade cloth. On either side gowned, beruffed, and formal in their high-backed chairs, sit the negotiators. On the left are the Spaniards: the Constable of Castile himself, the Count of Villa Mediana, and Senator Alessandro Rovida, Professor of Law at the College of Milan. Seated beside them are the representatives of the Spanish puppet government in Brussels: Charles, Count of Aremberg, Jean Richardot, president of the privy council, and Verreyken, principal secretary. On the right sit the English representatives: the Earls of Dorset,

Nottingham, Devonshire, and Northampton, and Robert Cecil, now Viscount Cranborne. Perhaps significantly Cecil is the one with ink and papers on the table before him.

On August 19th, in the Chapel Royal at Whitehall, King James gave his oath to observe the treaty. Afterwards he entertained the commissioners in the Banqueting House at a feast which even the Spaniards found 'sumptuous and profuse'. There was protracted drinking of toasts. The English drank to the health of the King of Spain, and the Spaniards to the health of the King of England. The Constable of Castile, producing an agate cup of extraordinary beauty and richness set in diamonds and rubies, invited the King to join him in drinking a toast to Queen Anne. The cup circled the board and then the Constable ordered that it be put, as his gift, on the King's buffet. After this a herald appeared and, at the royal command, proclaimed to the accompaniment of drums and trumpets the new peace with Spain. After the herald had left to proclaim the peace in the City of London also, the Constable arose, produced 'a very beautiful dragon-shaped cup of crystal garnished with gold' and requested the Queen to join him in drinking from it a health to the King. When the toast had been completed, he ordered that it be put, as his gift, on the Queen's buffet. Toast followed toast as King James, perhaps curious to see if the Constable had any more cups to give, announced that he had his permission to drink to the health of his three children.

After the drinking there was dancing. Fifty ladies of honour 'very richly and elegantly dressed, and extremely beautiful' as a gallant Spaniard noted in his journal, joined in the ball. There were galliards and corrantoes. Young Prince Henry danced for the company, exhibiting much sprightliness and modesty as he took the floor with the lady whom the King and Queen designated for his partner. Later the company flocked to the windows to look into the palace courtyard below. Here a vast company had already assembled to watch the King's bears fight with greyhounds, and mastiffs bait a tethered bull. These delights were succeeded by tumblers on tightropes and displays of horsemanship. When all these shows had ended, the Lord Chamberlain saw the Constable and his followers to their coaches, and fifty halberdiers with torches conducted them home. The Constable may have danced a little too energetically with some of the extremely beautiful ladies, for the next day he suffered an attack of lumbago. Fortunately the attack proved only a light one, and after some days of further celebration the Spaniards started for home.

The next year saw the English sending a special embassy to return the compliment of the Constable's visit. With a retinue which some reports placed as high as six hundred, the Lord Admiral of England (the Earl of Nottingham) contrived to eclipse the splendour shown by the Spaniards the year before. Honour demanded that the King of Spain display generosity on a scale commensurate with the grandeur of the embassy. Nottingham, when he started home, found himself presented with plate, jewels and horses to the value of £20,000. This was very nice for Nottingham, but both King James and King Philip must have felt that much more diplomacy on this scale would leave them both bankrupt. This expensiveness of embassies of ceremony was, in fact, one of the reasons why in the years that lay ahead there was a perceptible tendency to dispense with them and transfer their functions to the resident ambassadors already at the various courts.

The resident or, as the seventeenth-century English called him, 'lieger' ambassador was still something of an innovation when James became King of England. Only during the previous century had the major powers, almost reluctantly, adopted the practice observed among the Italian city-states of accrediting permanent envoys to each other. During their century of existence, these resident ambassadors had won a rather bad reputation both for espionage and deception. Sir Henry Wotton, King James's witty lieger ambassador to Venice, punning upon the contemporary use of 'to lie' as a synonym for 'to reside', defined an ambassador as 'an honest man sent to lie abroad for the good of his country'. The quip did him no good with his royal master. James agreed with continental critics that it impeached his own honour and he made it plain in Wotton just how seriously he had offended.

A lieger ambassador had nothing like the status of a special ambassador of ceremony who was generally an aristocrat of high rank. The resident English ambassadors despatched to various courts constituted a small corps of career diplomats, none with a title higher than knight. In the first years of his reign, King James had for his representatives abroad: Master Ralph Winwood at The Hague, Sir Thomas Edmondes at Brussels, Sir Thomas Parry at Paris, Sir Charles Cornwallis at Madrid, and Sir Henry Wotton at Venice. Subsequent years saw the service of such men as Dudley Carleton, ambassador first to the Venetians and then to the Dutch, and Sir John Digby, who succeeded Cornwallis at Madrid. They were devoted and highly competent men who served their king well despite disheartening difficulties. Some of them worked in an atmosphere of hostility and suspicion as heretics barely tolerated in a Catholic country. Only rarely did they manage to get home for direct briefings on the policy of their government. Communications with London were tardy and unreliable. (Despatches sent from London on August 27, 1606, did not reach Sir Charles Cornwallis in Madrid until October 17th.) During the interim between his own queries and the receipt of his instructions, an ambassador might find that circumstances had changed completely. At such times he could only hope that what he did on his own initiative would keep the situation in hand without leading to his discredit and recall.

The financial rewards were not very attractive. Under a schedule adopted in June 1622 resident ambassadors received £4 *per diem*, with £400 a year added for intelligence expenses, but nothing for travel. On this sum an ambassador was expected not only to maintain an establishment worthy of the honour of the King of England but to hire, as members of his own household, embassy officials such as secretaries and cipherers. As it turned out, King James's ambassadors abroad were usually months if not years in arrears in salary, a consequence of the constant crisis in the royal exchequer. Even royal servants in attendance on the court, able to press in person for payment of their fees, often had to wait a long time for their money. The situation was worse for an ambassador hundreds of miles distant who had to rely on what the Secretaries of State could secure with the aid of the ambassador's friends at court.

At times the position of an impoverished English envoy became simply desperate. In December 1617 Isaac Wake, the English agent at Turin, wrote home that he could maintain himself no longer, observing 'it will be some dishonour to have a public minister starve in a foreign country'. Three months later in another appeal he reported, 'I am now enforced to sell the poor stuff that was in my house to buy bread.' By mid-June 1618 Wake had reached the last of expedients. 'It is now sixteen months since I have received one penny out of the Exchequer. . . . I have lived many months upon my own poor stock, and having sold and pawned all that little which I had, I do not know how to subsist any longer.'[5] The schedule of 1622 was no doubt accompanied by good intentions to prevent such incidents recurring, but within a few months of its establishment Sir Dudley Carleton, H.M. Ambassador to The Hague, learned that his London agent Thomas Locke had been informed that there just was no money to pay any of the £2,895 now owing to him. King James's ambassadors had one poor consolation—the ambassadors of most other princes were in the same boat. Gondomar, after working miracles for Spain as ambassador in London, found that he had bankrupted himself in the process. Not surprisingly, another Spaniard, De Vera, writing his treatise *El Embajador*, declared that only a man with a large personal income could keep up a major embassy.

In the face of all this, it is a little surprising that men were found to serve so well and faithfully in the embassies abroad. Some of them did finally collect all their arrears. And there were other rewards. Titles could be won—Digby in time became Earl of Bristol, and Carleton, Viscount Dorchester. The embassy abroad, moreover, could prove a stepping-stone to high office at home. Winwood was recalled from The Hague to become Secretary of State. But there was a greater attraction than this:

> The ambassador's lonely task of upholding his master's honour at a foreign court, aided by no more than his own wit, courage and eloquence, was calculated to excite the imagination of the baroque world, its taste for magnificence, its interest in extraordinary individuals, its appreciation of complicated intrigue.[6]

The duties of the resident ambassador were legion. His chief duty, of course, was to speak for his government, to ascertain the views and policies of the court to which he was accredited, and to inform his own government about these. He was expected to create a climate of feeling as favourable as possible to his nation, and to achieve this he sometimes offered pensions to useful persons in key positions. Every nation had its secret lists of pensioners in the courts of others. Today a minister's acceptance of a pension from a foreign power would be regarded as completely treasonable. Such was not the case in the seventeenth century, though even then such pensions were felt to be somewhat suspect and their payment was usually kept confidential.

Spain made particularly generous use of pensions as a means of securing for her ambassadors a sympathetic and friendly group with whom they could maintain useful connections. Among the Spanish pensioners in the English court were Secretary Cecil, the Lord Privy Seal (Northampton), the Countess of Suffolk, Queen Anne, and King James. James certainly did not regard his Spanish pension as a betrayal of his realm of England any more than as King of Scotland he had felt his pension of £4,000 from Queen Elizabeth meant that he was a traitor to Scotland. Both pensions he certainly regarded as evidences of compliment and friendliness. With his ministers it was somewhat different. There was always the temptation that, to curry favour with the pensioning power, a minister might pass beyond permissible friendliness and divulge information which should be withheld. The pensions did not mean treason but offered a temptation to treason. It was to the credit of the Earl of Suffolk, the Lord Chamberlain, that he refused a pension from Spain when offered one by the Constable of Castile in 1604.

A major duty of the resident ambassador was the collection of information useful to his government. Pensioners, anxious to show their gratitude, would let him in on a certain amount of rather confidential material. Downright bribery could secure real state secrets. Among the payments made by Gondomar, the Spanish ambassador in the later years of James's reign, were 3,000 reals to a servant of Secretary Lake who had provided summaries of despatches, 1,200 reals to a person who had provided copies

D

of treaties in the English archives, and over 4,800 reals to various palace servants.

All the ambassadors played the game of espionage. Secretary Cecil, in a letter of 1607 to the English ambassador at Madrid, demanded information about the Spanish naval forces—not mere court talk but accurate information. He rebuked him for having sent an unfounded report that 16,000 land soldiers were in readiness to embark and pointed out that, had he not secured better information, there would have been a needless alarm. Cornwallis, in his reply, could only plead the difficulty of securing reliable agents.

A constant worry for any ambassador was how to get his despatches safely through to his home government without interception. Couriers were sometimes available, but there were never enough of these, over-worked though they were. One King's Messenger, Master Dickenson, ordered back with fresh despatches to Spain the moment that he had arrived with a pouch from Madrid, '. . . lingering a day or two to kisse his wife (after so long absence) . . . received a sharpe message that the King would hange him or cut his head off yf he went not away instantly'.[7] Even when couriers were used, ambassadorial despatches were often intercepted and copied, and their crude ciphers broken. Thus, a farcical situation finally developed between England and Spain. Gondomar managed to learn through his network of spies and informants just about everything he wanted to know. He then took elaborate precautions to get his information secretly to Madrid. The English ambassador in Spain, Digby, managed however to frustrate all Gondomar's endeavours and, securing transcriptions of his despatches, sent them back to King James in England. Here, in turn, one of Gondomar's informants let him know each time that still another of his secret messages had been divulged to the English king and his Privy Council. 'This went on for years to the helpless exasperation and cynical amusement of all concerned.'[8]

Along with superintending his spies, the resident ambassador had other duties. Then, as now, he had to look after the interests of his compatriots trading or residing within his territory. He acted as an agent for the purchasing of works of art for court grandees (the English ambassadors at Venice were very useful to Buckingham, Somerset and Arundel in their collecting). He reported on the movements of disaffected English émigrés and ran counter-intelligence operations to smoke out their plots and stratagems. Cornwallis in Madrid kept Cecil posted on the moves of the Scottish Earl of Bothwell and the fugitive Irish Earls of Tyrone and Tyrconnel.

A final duty of the resident ambassador must be noted, one which he shared with the special ambassadors of ceremony—the maintenance of national prestige. This required constant alertness for every nuance in the infinitely formalized and complicated punctilio of the seventeenth-century courts. The claims and prerogatives of his royal master or state must always be jealously preserved. We have the details of scores of imbroglios that arose in this connection. One had to do with the use of chairs at the wedding of Princess Elizabeth in 1613. Chairs, with their arms and high backs, were expensive and not very common. Nevertheless, although Prince Charles himself was content to accept a stool, the ambassadors of France and Venice maintained that, since the bride and groom had chairs at the marriage banquet, they too must have chairs, being the representatives of sovereign states. There were feuds over titles. The Emperor's ambassador refused to address the Venetian envoy as 'Excellenza' since he represented only a state, not a monarch. Instead he addressed him as 'Signioria Illustrissima' and declared that if the Venetian refused to address him as 'Excellenza' he would reduce him to a bare 'Signioria'.[9]

Though these storms over protocol and precedence may today seem slightly lunatic, to seventeenth-century diplomats they were deadly serious. The struggle for primacy of place which raged between the ambassadors of France and Spain plagued the courts of Europe for over a century. In England the rivalry for precedence between the two was so tense that the court, anxious to avoid a head-on collision, decided to invite neither the French nor the Spanish ambassador to the creation of Henry as Prince of Wales in 1610. As it turned out, the French ambassador announced that being in mourning for Henri IV, recently assassinated, he could not fittingly attend, and the Spaniard was invited after all.

The real showdown between France and Spain came on Twelfth Night, 1618. The Spanish ambassador Sarmiento, shortly to be created Count of Gondomar, had been almost five years in England, but only now did he feel himself sufficiently established to strike. He let it be known that he could attend the festivities only if he were given precedence over the French ambassador. Now a favourite with King James, he was given this priority. The results were sensational. The French ambassador, Desmaretz, demanded that the ruling be reversed. When he was refused, he wrote to Paris that the honour of France demanded his recall and, if necessary, war. The French government recalled him. By adroitly exploiting a point of protocol, the Spaniard had effectively disrupted relations between England and France at a point when the two acting in conjunction could have posed a major threat to Spain.

Only the really first-class diplomats knew how to use the childish game of punctilios to serve major political ends. With most, it was simply a routine matter of always asserting the prestige of their masters. Right through the reign the game went on. At the very end, the Venetian ambassador refused to attend the funeral of King James. True, the royal officers had provided him with a suit of mourning to wear at the obsequies, but the Master of Ceremonies had neglected to send a formal invitation. The ambassador could not overlook the slight, however unintentional, to the Signory of Venice.

CHAPTER VII

Gunpowder, Treason and Plot

ON THE MORNING of November 5, 1605, Robert Winter, brother-in-law and private secretary to Lord Mounteagle, arrived at the great court gate of Whitehall Palace to find a guard refusing admission to all comers. At the Parliament House in Westminster he met other guards refusing passage. Heading homeward along the Strand, he learned why these sentinels were posted—a plot had been discovered to murder the King.

On the previous night a guard conducted by Sir Thomas Knyvett, Justice of the Peace for Westminster, had captured a desperado watching over thirty-six barrels of gunpowder hidden under piles of cordwood in a cellar under the Parliament House. The gunpowder was to have been exploded that very day when King James came with his queen and heir to open Parliament with a joint session of the Lords and Commons in the chamber above. Since early morning the Privy Council had been interrogating the captured conspirator. He had given his name as John Johnson and claimed to be a servant to Thomas Percy, constable of Alnwick Castle, a royal Gentleman Pensioner, and a cousin to the Earl of Northumberland. Having learned part at least of the news, Master Winter returned to his lodgings, took horse, and headed quietly for Worcestershire.

This Robert Winter was a stocky man in his late thirties. His life had been an eventful one. In his Protestant youth he had fought with the Dutch against the Spaniards, but subsequent conversion to Catholicism had been followed by a Holy Year pilgrimage to Rome in 1600. In 1602 he had travelled to Spain as emissary for a group of militant English Catholics, headed by his daredevil cousin Robert Catesby, who wanted Spanish money and troops to support an English rebellion. When the Spanish mission had proved fruitless, Catesby had broached to Winter early in 1604 a new scheme: to blow up King and Parliament and in the resulting chaos to seize the government of the realm. Catesby wanted to restore the Catholic religion which James, goaded by Parliament, was beginning to persecute after his first months of semi-tolerance.

Riding along the road to Worcestershire, Winter could recall how, after learning of Catesby's murderous plan, he had tried to make it unnecessary by interviewing at Brussels the Constable of Castile as he travelled on his embassy to England, and imploring him to make toleration for the English Catholics a condition for peace with Spain. His mission had proved completely unsuccessful, but on his return to England Winter had brought with him a new recruit for Catesby's plot. This was the brave and accomplished Guy Fawkes, a veteran soldier who had fought on the Continent in Sir William Stanley's regiment of Catholic émigrés serving under the Spanish as the 'English Legion'. At this moment, as 'John Johnson', Fawkes was maintaining his indomitable silence before the Privy Council.

Ahead of Winter on the Worcestershire road were fellow conspirators who had fled London earlier: Ambrose Rookwood, a wealthy young Suffolk landowner who, despite the sword engraved with Christ's Passion at his side, had been won over to the plot chiefly by the personal magnetism of Catesby; Thomas Percy, a violent and unstable man with red face and greying beard, the renegade Gentleman Pensioner who had been especially bound to defend his king; and Percy's brother-in-law, Christopher Wright.

Galloping north, Winter, Rookwood, Percy and Wright hoped to find a powerful Catholic force in the field ready to strike for the Old Religion. Their plot to murder the King might have failed, but they clung to a hope that rebellion would be successful. Complete disappointment awaited them. True, young Sir Everard Digby, a very recent recruit to their conspiracy, had assembled a company of Midland Catholic gentry, ostensibly for a day's hunting on Dunsmore Heath. But when, late on that famous November 5th, he and Catesby called upon the assembled squires to rise in rebellion in the name of the Catholic Faith, they were greeted with horrified refusals. Resort to arms, as most of the assemblage knew, would mean not only treason to the Crown but disobedience to Rome. The Pope had decided that the best policy for the English Catholics was peaceful endurance while he sought gradual amelioration of their lot, and he had declared against all use of violence. Of this ruling the gunpowder conspirators themselves were fully aware. In fact, in following the course which they had taken, these Catholics were behaving like Protestants inasmuch as they thought they knew better than the Church.

Disappointment after disappointment followed the fiasco of Dunsmore Heath. Catholic gentlemen closely related to the plotters refused to lift a finger to help them; and Father Garnet, provincial of the Jesuit order in England, from his nearby place of hiding sent a stern rebuke to Catesby and his friends for endangering the entire body of English Catholics. Meanwhile, the authorities had raised the hue and cry against the conspirators. On November 7th, travelling from Hewell Grange (home of the absent Catholic Lord Windsor, where they had helped themselves to arms but had won no recruits), Catesby and his friends found their rear shadowed by pursuers. On they pressed through the long rainy day, a forlorn little

band of some thirty-six horsemen. Among them were half-hearted sympathizers who contrived to slip away, even though four of the original
conspirators at the head of the train and four others at the rear were prepared to shoot deserters. Late that evening the little company reached
Holbeach, the home of Humphrey Littleton, a prominent Catholic.

The morrow began with a notably evil omen. Seeking to dry gunpowder
that had got wet in the previous day's downpour, Catesby and others
spread it out before a fire to dry. Suddenly a spark from the hearth ignited
it. In the resulting blast Catesby and Rookwood were badly burned, and
John Grant, Winter's brother-in-law, practically blinded. During the
morning forces loyal to King James surrounded the house. In the afternoon the assault began.

From behind the safety of a wall Sir Richard Walsh, High Sheriff of
Worcestershire, exhorted to the attack about two hundred men whom he
had organized into a *posse comitatus*. Opposed to the two hundred stood
twelve desperate men, some of whom already saw God's punishment in
the gunpowder mishap of the morning. Superstitiously they believed that
Heaven had turned against them the very means by which they had sought
to murder their king. The assault was brief but bloody. When it was over,
Catesby, first deviser of the Gunpowder Plot, lay dead. Percy and his
brothers-in-law, John and Christopher Wright, were dying of their wounds.
Rookwood and Robert Winter's brother, Thomas, were wounded prisoners. Some of the original conspirators were still loose, however, having
fled from Holbeach earlier in the day. Three of these fugitives, Digby,
Keyes, and Catesby's serving-man Bates, were rounded up in short order.
The fourth, Master Robert Winter, with whom this chapter began, escaped
capture for several months.

Events had not stood still in London while these last tragic scenes were
being enacted at Holbeach. Confronted by Fawkes' obdurate refusal to
talk, the Privy Council followed their instructions from King James:

> If he will not other wayes confesse, the gentler tortours are first to be usid
> unto him, *et sic per gradus ad ima tenditur* [and so by degrees proceeding
> to the worst].[1]

In his agony on the rack, Fawkes named his fellow conspirators and
revealed that they had planned to seize Princess Elizabeth and exercise
the royal power in her name. Meanwhile, the agents of the government
were everywhere busy seeking out witnesses, taking evidence, and making
arrests. The Earl of Northumberland was led prisoner to the Tower under
suspicion of complicity in the plot. So were three Catholic peers, Lord
Montagu, Lord Mordaunt and Lord Stourton.

Sunday, November 10th, was observed as a solemn day of national
thanksgiving for the preservation of the King. At St. Paul's Cross, in the

open yard beside the huge dilapidated Gothic cathedral, Barlow, Bishop
of Rochester, preached. His text was Psalm XVIII, verse 51: 'Great
deliverances giveth he unto his King and showeth mercy to his anointed
David and to his seed for ever.' Along with the customary Jacobean adulation of the King, the bishop included a statement of what Fawkes had revealed in the torture chamber, and he released to the Londoners the news
which the government had just received from Holbeach.[2]

King James himself, proroguing Parliament the day before, had already
revealed for the first time how the Gunpowder Plot had come to be discovered. This speech, together with an extended *Discourse of the Maner
of the Discovery of this Late Intended Treason* and the confessions of
Fawkes and Thomas Winter, was now printed in what came to be called
The King's Book.[3] The story of the detection of the plot was indeed a
marvellous one. It centred about Lord Mounteagle. William Parker, fourth
Lord Mounteagle, had been one of Catesby's closest friends a few years
earlier. With him he had been involved in Essex's revolt in 1601. With
him he had been associated in sending Robert Winter to Madrid to seek
Spanish aid for their projected Catholic revolt. However, in March 1604,
Mounteagle had written to King James assuring him of his conversion to
Protestantism. Apparently Mounteagle had convinced the King of his
worth and sincerity, for he subsequently prospered at court, even while
maintaining his connections with Catesby and the rest of his Catholic
friends and kinsmen. It was through Mounteagle, according to the government, that the Gunpowder Plot had become known.

According to the *Discourse*, the manner of the discovery was as follows.
On October 26th, ten days before Parliament was to have been blown up,
Lord Mounteagle ordered a supper prepared for him at a house in
Hoxton which he had acquired through his wife Elizabeth, one of the heirs
of the wealthy Sir Thomas Tresham. The main estate of this Sir Thomas
had passed to his son Francis, a turbulent young man who rather less than
two weeks earlier had become the last and most reluctant member of the
gunpowder conspiracy. When Lord Mounteagle was sitting down to
supper, one of his footmen sent out on an errand was accosted in the street
by an unknown man who gave him an unsigned letter for his master.
This missive, almost certainly from Francis Tresham, proved one of the
most interesting in English history.[4] It read:

> My Lord, Out of the love I beare to some of your friends, I have a care of
> your preservation. Therefore I would advise you, as you tender your life,
> to devise some excuse to shift off your attendance at this Parliament. For
> God and man have concurred to punish the wickednesse of this Time. And
> thinke not slightly of this Advertisement, but retire your selfe into your
> Countrey, where you may expect the event in safetie. For though there be

no apparence of any stirre, yet I say, they shall receive a terrible Blow this Parliament, and yet they shall not see who hurts them. This counsell is not to be contemned, because it may doe you good, and can doe you no harme; for the danger is past so soone as you have burnt the Letter. And I hope God will give you the grace to make good use of it: To whose holy protection I commend you.[5]

Having read this letter, Mounteagle, despite the lateness and darkness of the night, hastened to Whitehall Palace where he put it in the hands of Cecil. According to the official account later, Cecil showed the letter to the Lord Chamberlain (the Earl of Suffolk) and several other Privy Councillors, and they agreed to put it by until the King, who was hunting at Royston, should return to London in some five days' time. On November 1st James was shown the letter. According to *The King's Book*, His Majesty then divined that the letter, with its mention of an invisible blow, referred to a plot to blow up Parliament. When the gunpowder was discovered, the whole court rang with praises of the princely perspicacity of King James. The next year, when Parliament made November 5th an annual day of thanksgiving, their statute declared that the entire kingdom would have been ruined:

> . . . had not it pleased Almighty God, by inspiring the king's most excellent majesty with a divine spirit, to interpret some dark phrases of a letter shewed his majesty, above and beyond all ordinary construction, thereby miraculously discovering this hidden treason not many hours before the appointed time. . . .[6]

All this Jacobean rhetoric is so much poppycock. A letter survives, written by Cecil on November 9, 1605, to Sir Charles Cornwallis in Madrid, acquainting him with the plot and declaring that when he and Suffolk first saw the letter they surmised that it referred to a plot against Parliament and very likely a gunpowder plot.[7] Gunpowder plots, after all, were not unheard of. King James's own father had been the victim of one. If His Majesty really believed that he was the first to smell out the secret meaning of the letter, we can only surmise that he had failed to notice that Cecil had adroitly planted the suggestion in his mind. However, officially the King was the discoverer, and officially it had been at his insistence that a search had been made of the Parliament House, first by Suffolk and later by Knyvett.

The plot having failed, it remained to punish the conspirators. Catesby and Percy were already dead, but their heads were cut off and nailed to the gables of the Parliament House, where they became one of the sights of the town. On January 27, 1606, eight of the surviving conspirators, the Winter brothers, Grant, Fawkes, Keyes, Bates, Rookwood and Digby, stood their trial. Coke, the Attorney-General, opened the prosecution with a mighty

D*

speech about the wickedness of the accused. He exclaimed at the inconceivable sin of such an offence against such a king in such a place. The confessions of the accused were read, and they all received the same appalling sentence of hanging, castration, disembowelment and quartering, which had been passed two years earlier on Raleigh. Digby, arraigned on a separate indictment, received the same judgment. For these men there was no commutation of sentence and they all went to their ghastly death. Even some of Cecil's supporters were shocked when he ruled that the churchyard of St. Paul's Cathedral should be the scene of the mutilation and death of Sir Everard Digby and three of the other conspirators. There was more public sympathy for Digby than for any of the others. A young man of twenty-four, endowed with every worldly advantage, Digby possessed not only great wealth but an adoring wife and three small children. His splendid good looks, his skill as a rider, swordsman and musician, had made some consider him 'the goodliest man in the whole court'. He was a sober and responsible young man, and the only reason why the conspirators, bankrupt men, had brought him and Tresham into their scheme was need for their money. Only the fatal charm and self-confidence of Catesby had prevailed upon Digby to join. He was the most tragic of Catesby's victims—he, and perhaps Thomas Bates, Catesby's servant, the simple loyal yeoman who had been drawn willy-nilly into his master's crimes.

The death of the conspirators at Holbeach or on the quartering-block did not end the toll of victims. The conspiracy was a Catholic conspiracy. The plotters had taken their oath of secrecy upon the Blessed Sacrament. Their spiritual directors had been priests, members of the underground Jesuit mission to England. The government now turned their attack against the latter, seeking to shatter the strength of the Jesuits and so to inflame public feeling against them as to end all possibility of a national reconversion to Catholicism.

It was not easy for Cecil and his friends to link the Jesuits with the treason. In simple truth, no member of the order had been aware of the plot until some four months before its final failure. At that time Catesby had revealed the details when making confession to Father Tesimond at the latter's headquarters at Hindlip House, the Worcestershire home of Thomas Abington, a brother-in-law of Lord Mounteagle. Catesby had given Father Tesimond permission to acquaint Father Garnet, the head of the Jesuit order in England, with the proposed plot, but only if he did so under the seal of his own confession. Only thus did Father Garnet secure foreknowledge of the plot.

The effects of Catesby's procedure were curious and complex. He could tell himself, as he went ahead with his plot, that what he did was done

with the knowledge of his church. More important, he could say as much
to others when seeking recruits for his scheme. On the other hand, since
the Jesuits had received their knowledge in the confessional, they were
powerless to act upon it outside of the confessional. While Father Garnet
could write to Rome, as he did, imploring the Pope to promulgate a brief
against all resort to violence since His Holiness' merely reported prohibition
was proving insufficient, he could not divulge, even to Rome, the terrible
plot with which he was now acquainted. Indeed, he could not even
remonstrate directly with Catesby about it, but only with Father Tesimond
from whose own confession he himself had learned about it. Catesby had
placed the Jesuits in the paradoxical position of at the same time knowing
and not knowing about the intended treason.

Partly because of this manœuvring by Catesby, the English government
failed at first in its endeavours to tie the Gunpowder Plot to the Jesuits.
The conspirators to a man insisted, quite truthfully, that the plot had not
been conceived (as the government would have liked to establish) by the
Jesuits. They agreed, in fact, in clearing the Jesuits of all complicity.
Frustrated by their replies, the authorities might have had to accept failure
but for a piece of great good fortune—they captured Father Garnet.

The English provincial might have escaped them. Only the remarkable
persistence of Sir Henry Bromley, Justice of the Peace for the area in which
lay Hindlip House, secured this most important prisoner for Cecil and the
Council. Acting no doubt on information received, Cecil wrote to Bromley
several months after the storming of Holbeach ordering him to search
Hindlip House. On January 19th Bromley arrived with about a hundred
men and turned the great mansion inside out in his search for Jesuits.
Various secret hiding-places were discovered, but all of them were empty.
A less thorough officer would have given up, but not Bromley. Occupying
the house, he maintained unremitting surveillance. After twelve days he
secured his reward. Out of a narrow 'priest's hole' which had become
untenable with their own excrement, stumbled Father Garnet and a fellow
fugitive, Father Oldcorne.

Sir Henry treated Father Garnet with the greatest courtesy, keeping
him a guest in his house in Worcester until he was sufficiently recovered
for the long journey to London. Finally, on February 12th, he delivered
his two prisoners at the gatehouse of the Tower of London. The next day
the streets of London were jammed with people curious to see the English
provincial of the Jesuit order as he went a prisoner to Whitehall for the
first of his interrogations by the Privy Council.

Their hours of questioning yielded the Council nothing new. They put
to the torture the lay brother 'Little John' (Nicholas Owen), caught at
Hindlip also, but could wring from him nothing to incriminate his master,

At their instruction, Garnet's gaoler pretended conversion to Catholicism, thus winning the provincial's trust and becoming his messenger, but the messages thus intercepted helped them little. Finally they used another trick. After stationing two of their agents in an adjacent hollow wall where they could overhear and take notes, they moved Father Garnet to a chamber where he could speak through an opening in that wall to Father Oldcorne in the room beyond. On four different days Father Garnet, completely unsuspecting, held surreptitious conversations with his fellow prisoner. At the end, confronted with the agents' notes, he finally admitted foreknowledge of the Gunpowder Plot.

On March 28th Father Garnet stood trial at the Guildhall. The accused priest had but one defence, that what he had known was privileged by the inviolable secrecy of the confessional. This inviolability the Church of England recognized for its own followers; but the government was not prepared to allow it to the heretic Church of Rome. For Coke, the Attorney-General, Garnet's defence that he did not know as a private individual what he knew but could not communicate as a priest was just so much hellish equivocation. He said so, and the jury, agreeing with him, took less than fifteen minutes to find Father Garnet guilty. On May 3rd Father Garnet became one of the martyrs of his church on the gallows in St. Paul's churchyard. From the scaffold he declared:

> As for the treasons which are laid against me, I protest now at my death that I am not guilty of them, neither had knowledge of the Powder but in confession, and then I utterly disliked it and earnestly dissuaded it. Yea, I protest upon my soul I should have abhorred it ever, though it had succeeded. And I am sorry with all my heart that any Catholics had ever any such intention, knowing that such attempts are not allowable, and to my own knowledge contrary to the Pope's mind.[8]

Most of Father Garnet's hearers probably shrugged off his words as jesuitical lies. The nation concurred in that opinion. The Jesuit mission to England, which had once promised so well for the Church with its restoration of morale and coherence among the hundreds of thousands of English Catholics, and in the process had caused so much worry to Cecil and the other Protestant governors of England, had ended finally in utter disaster.

When all the excitement of the gunpowder treason was over, Cecil should have felt decidedly grateful to Catesby. The murderous plot had served him well. If the Cecils represented anything in the national life of England, it was the Protestant cause. Their own wealth rested upon the confiscated Catholic properties acquired by the father of the first Lord Burghley, the founder of the family's greatness. In the intensity of his Protestant convictions Burghley had been, as A. L. Rowse has quipped, an Elizabethan Gladstone. However much the son may have deviated from the father in his private morals, he was as unshakable as he in his Protestantism. At times Cecil's language had a positively Puritan ring. Speaking in Parliament he could describe England under Queen Elizabeth as 'a sanctuary for all the persecuted Saints of God'.[9] He was, indeed, not without sympathy for the Puritans and they saw him as 'a good Statesman, the onely supporter of the *Protestants* faction'.[10]

Being so completely attached to Protestantism, Cecil could not but have felt disquiet at the lenity with which King James treated the English Catholics upon his accession. Meeting a Catholic delegation at Hampton Court, James promised that so long as they remained peaceful and loyal, they need not fear the fines levied upon them by Queen Elizabeth. Deeds gave substance to his words. Whereas during the year ending in Michaelmas 1603 the Exchequer took in £7,115 in fines from recusants, in the year similarly ending in 1604 it collected only £1,414.[11] The Pope made equally conciliatory gestures, and the Nuncio at Brussels informed the English ambassador there that turbulent priests would be recalled from England and that Catholics who were wanted for treason would be surrendered to the King. Quite as pleasing to King James was the part that the Jesuits played in revealing Watson's Plot. A rapprochement appeared to be in process, one that might lead to religious toleration for the English Catholics.

If Cecil was dismayed by the turn of events, he knew better than to demand that the King change his attitude. Instead, he bided his time while he and allies did what they could by other means to hinder the burgeoning of Catholicism. Parliament, when it assembled in March 1604, displayed a notably Protestant temper and James, yielding reluctantly to it, agreed to re-enactment of the recusancy acts. The presence of the acts in the statute book was, however, no guarantee that they would be enforced. James had not yet really abandoned his conciliatory attitude to the Catholics.

The Gunpowder Plot changed everything. The King, by nature neurotically fearful, had received a scare which he would not soon forget. So, for that matter, had England. The session of Parliament which followed detection of the Plot saw King, Lords, and Commons united in passing a mass of anti-Catholic legislation. The government was empowered to confiscate two-thirds of the estate of a convicted recusant; special fines were levied against those whose servants did not attend the Church of England (a blow directed against the great Catholic households which represented strongholds of the Old Religion); and all Catholics were required to take a new oath of allegiance which declared that the Pope could not absolve them of their allegiance to the King. Catesby's plot in its final consequences had indeed served the Protestant leaders well.

In another way the Plot had proved useful to Cecil. In his secret despatches to Scotland before James came to the English throne, Cecil had
been at pains to set him against the Earl of Northumberland, who in his
own letters northward was urging James to offer religious toleration for
the English Catholics. This manœuvre of prejudicing in advance, so successful against Raleigh, had failed against Northumberland for, once in
England, James came to be friendly with the Earl. The Plot ended all
friendship there. Northumberland, it transpired, had failed as Captain of
the Band of Gentlemen Pensioners to administer to his cousin, the traitorous Thomas Percy, the Oath of Supremacy required of him as a member
of that band. Moreover, during the night of Fawkes' arrest, Percy had
visited Northumberland at the latter's mansion of Sion House. Nothing
treasonable could be proved against the Earl, but when the other lords
suspected of complicity in the Plot were released, Northumberland continued a prisoner in the Tower. Here, for the next sixteen years, the
'Wizard Earl' remained, carrying out his scientific experiments and meeting
the scholars to whom he was a generous patron. When Northumberland
was released, it was in consequence of his daughter's marriage to one of
King James's Scots, the gorgeous James Hay, Earl of Carlisle.

Observing how much Cecil benefitted from the Gunpowder Plot, some
Catholic historians have maintained that the whole thing was planned by
him and initiated by his *agents provocateurs*. There is nothing inherently
unlikely about such a charge. A Machiavellian like Cecil was quite capable
of hitting on such a device. The objection to the theory is the complete
absence of any evidence to rob Catesby of his role of inventor of the plot.
On the other hand, the obvious discrepancies between verifiable facts and
the official account as published in *The King's Book* make it plain that the
government was not entirely honest in its account of the detection of the
Gunpowder Plot.[12]

All that can be said finally of the Gunpowder Plot is that it gave King
James and his people a terrible fright, brought the Catholic cause in
England to the verge of ruin, and bequeathed to the historian some murky
problems to which he can offer only conjectural solutions.

CHAPTER VIII

The Royal Brother-in-Law

ON JULY 17, 1606, a squadron of Danish warships anchored off Tilbury. As seamen manned the sides and masts, and trumpets sounded, the King of England accompanied by his heir and Privy Council came alongside in the royal barge. On the deck of the Danish flagship King James found his brother-in-law, Christian IV, King of Denmark and Norway. The two monarchs hastened to embrace. Eager to see James's new realm, and to visit a sister for whom he felt real affection, King Christian had waited a decent interval until the royal family was settled in its new kingdom, and now had arrived for a month's visit.

Escorted by English barges, the Danish flagship carried the two kings up the river towards Greenwich while the other Danish warships and the English blockhouses guarding the lower Thames made the day thunderous with cannonades. At Greenwich was the royal palace assigned to Queen Anne as her own residence. Here she toyed away months of separation from her husband, enjoying her own mild amusements while James was hunting the deer at Royston or Newmarket.

When King Christian came forward to kiss his sister, he saw not the beautiful gold and silver little blonde who had sailed for Scotland seventeen years before, but a somewhat bony sallow woman, sharp-nosed and tight-mouthed, a discontented wife and a purposeless woman. A month before, one of her numerous pregnancies had ended with the birth of a princess. King Christian in planning his journey had hoped to see her happy with her babe, but Princess Sophia had died at the age of one day and been given solemn burial in Westminster Abbey.

The first two weeks of King Christian's visit were spent quietly with his sister at Greenwich. To the lonely Queen, the time must have seemed all too short for talk with her brother about their childhood and what had happened since. Not that all the time was given to family talk. There was hunting with King James in the morning, and drinking at night. James had a weakness for wine, especially the rich sweet wines of Greece, but he was no match for Christian and his Danes. The drinking reached a climax during a four-day visit to Theobalds where the two kings were the guests of Cecil, who for over a year had been Earl of Salisbury. The wonders to be seen at Theobalds we noted earlier. Now they were augmented by such

79

things as an artificial oak tree with leaves of taffeta, each inscribed with 'WELCOME'. After viewing these sights, Christian and his courtiers settled down to some hard drinking with their English hosts. An account of the four-day debauch which followed is preserved for us in a letter by the witty Sir John Harington who attended these besotted revels:

> I came here a day or two before the Danish King came, and from the day he did come untill this hour, I have been well nigh overwhelmed with carousal and sports of all kinds. The sports began each day in such manner and such sorte, as well nigh persuaded me of Mahomets paradise. We had women, and indeed wine too, of such plenty, as would have astonishd each sober beholder. Our feasts were magnificent, and the two royal guests did most lovingly embrace each other at table. I think the Dane hath strangely wrought on our good English nobles; for those, whom I never could get to taste good liquor, now follow the fashion, and wallow in beastly delights. The ladies abandon their sobriety, and are seen to roll about in intoxication. In good sooth, the parliament did kindly to provide his Majestie so season-ably with money, for there hath been no lack of good livinge; shews, sights, and banquetings, from morn to eve.
>
> One day, a great feast was held, and, after dinner, the representation of Solomon his Temple and the coming of the Queen of Sheba was made, or (as I may better say) was meant to have been made, before their Majesties, by device of the Earl of Salisbury and others.—But, alass! as all earthly thinges do fail to poor mortals in enjoyment, so did prove our presentment hereof. The Lady who did play the Queens part, did carry most precious gifts to both their Majesties; but, forgetting the steppes arising to the canopy, overset her caskets into his Danish Majesties lap, and fell at his feet, tho I rather think it was in his face. Much was the hurry and confusion; cloths and napkins were at hand, to make all clean. His Majesty then got up and woud dance with the Queen of Sheba; but he fell down and humbled himself before her, and was carried to an inner chamber and laid on a bed of state; which was not a little defiled with the presents of the Queen which had been bestowed on his garments; such as wine, cream, jelly, beverage, cakes, spices, and other good matters. The entertainment and show went forward, and most of the presenters went backward, or fell down; wine did so occupy their upper chambers. Now did appear, in rich dress, Hope, Faith, and Charity: Hope did assay to speak, but wine renderd her en-deavours so feeble that she withdrew, and hoped the King would excuse her brevity: Faith was then all alone, for I am certain she was not joyned with good works, and left the court in a staggering condition: Charity came to the King's feet, and seemed to cover the multitude of sins her sisters had committed; in some sorte she made obeysance and brought giftes, but said she would return home again, as there was no gift which heaven had not already given his Majesty. She then returnd to Hope and Faith, who were both sick and spewing in the lower hall.[1]

It was probably during one of these evenings of carousal at Theobalds that King Christian contrived to insult unforgivably the Lord Admiral of England, the aged but spry Earl of Nottingham. As Lord Howard of

Effingham, Nottingham had commanded the English fleet against the Spanish Armada, and he carried the prestige of his great victory with him into the reign of James I, even though it was generally known that under his slack and easy administration the navy was abominably mismanaged and riddled with graft. In September 1603, at the age of sixty-eight, he culminated a whirlwind courtship, begun during a night of dancing at Queen Anne's court at Basing, by marrying Lady Margaret Stuart, a sister of the Earl of Moray and a remote relative of the King. Plenty of jests were made about the old man's marriage, some quite unprintable. The Earl of Worcester wrote to the Earl of Shrewsbury that during the night the bride had been heard singing, but nobody knew whether she had done so to keep the old man awake or to get him asleep. The next morning, however, the old Lord Admiral boasted mightily of his exploits, and subsequently Lady Margaret bore him two sons.

In the succeeding years Nottingham shared in the general prosperity of the Howards under James. His only real disappointment came when James refused to make him a duke when he went on his embassy to Spain in 1605, complementing that of the Constable of Castile to England the year before. Now, in 1606, he was a lively oldster of seventy-one, a likeable old epicure looking very distinguished with his ruff and white forked beard but ready to join in the fun of the court and of the kings. Then came the deplorable incident. King Christian found the old admiral and his young wife amusing. Perhaps he had heard some indiscreet rumours about the countess. In any event, in drunken mirth he came to the Lord High Admiral of England and waggled his fingers at the side of his head in mockery of a cuckold's horns. Fortunately the countess was not present, but a report of what had happened soon reached her. In a letter to King Christian's secretary, she told him exactly what she thought of his master:

> I protest to yow sir, I did thinke as honourably of the king your master, as I did of my owne Prince; but now I persuade my selfe there is as much baseness in him as can bee in any man ffor although hee bee a Prince by birth, it seems not to mee that there harbours any Princely thought in his breast; for either in Prince or subject, it is the basest parte that can bee to wronge any wooman of honor and I would the King your Master should knowe that I deserve as little that name which hee gave mee, as either the mother of himselfe, or of his children.[2]

By the time that things had reached this pass, some of the English court were probably quoting Master William Shakespeare's Prince Hamlet on the drunkenness of the Danes and, having applied the 'swinish phrase' to Christian and his boozing court, wished they were on their way. Obviously some sort of decency and discipline had to be introduced among the Danes. Accordingly, King Christian appointed a special marshal to take charge of drunken members of his household, chain their thumbs together and nail the chain to a post. They were to remain thus exhibited until somebody interceded for their release and they themselves declared their hearty repentance. By measures such as this, the Danes had been brought to good behaviour when the time came for the kings to make their state visit to London.

The passage of James and Christian through the London streets was a magnificent spectacle, almost comparable to the coronation procession of two years earlier. The guns of the merchantmen in the Pool of London fired salutes as the kings came ashore from their royal barge at Tower Wharf to be greeted by Sir Leonard Hollyday, Lord Mayor of London. From here the procession started through the city. All along one side of the way the streets had been railed and decorated with cloth of Danish blue and the royal arms. Here the city companies were marshalled, each in their livery, their streamers and pennons flying. Down the route came the royal procession. Each court sought to dazzle the other with its display. Danes magnificent in blue velvet, white satin, and silver lace were matched by English in crimson and gold. King James's Gentlemen Pensioners were resplendent with yellow and red feathers and scarfs with golden lace. A company of knights were adorned with 'strange Fethers, of rich and greate esteeme: which they called *The Birdes of Paradice*. But what really stole the show was the mounted drummer who preceded the eleven trumpeters of the Danish King, 'with two Drums, one of each side the horse necke, whereon hee strooke two little mallets of wood, a thing verie admirable to the common sort, and much admired'.[3] As for the two kings, they rode side by side on matching horses, preceded by the English earls who were each paired with a Danish dignitary.

Slowly the dazzling company—marshals, heralds, bishops, nobles, guardsmen—travelled through the acclaiming crowds. Their procession broke up finally near Temple Bar as the two kings entered Denmark House (formerly Somerset House), the London residence of the Queen. Here they reposed that night.

The next day King Christian was turned over to the Lord Chamberlain for a day of strenuous sightseeing. In the best tourist tradition he viewed the tombs in old St. Paul's Cathedral, and climbed up to the steeple, where he was pleased to command that the imprint of his royal foot be marked on the lead to commemorate his visit. He took coach to Sir Thomas Gresham's Royal Exchange and walked amid the throng of merchants there. As further evidence of the wealth and importance of the London citizenry, he was shown the rich shops and elaborate houses of Goldsmiths' Row in Cheapside. Finally he went to the Tower of London where he found King James waiting to show him in person the Jewel House, the Wardrobe, the

Ordnance and the Mint. Leaving the Tower by barge, the two kings passed under the great masonry arches of London Bridge to land at last at the King's Stairs at Whitehall Palace.

The succeeding days passed pleasantly. There was hunting of the deer in St. James Park and Hyde Park. There was running at the ring in the tiltyard, with both kings distinguishing themselves in the presence of Queen Anne. There was bear-baiting and bull-baiting. James, bent on impressing his brother-in-law, took him off to see his palaces at Richmond, Hampton Court and Windsor. At Hampton Court the entertainment apparently became more intellectual with a command performance of Shakespeare's *Macbeth*.[4]

The time arrived for Christian to return to his ships and start for home. On August 9th he took his formal farewell of the English court at Greenwich 'with many rich and bountifull Rewardes to the Officers of the Kinges Household and Guarde'. James reciprocated with gifts of gilt plate to the Chancellor of Denmark, to the Admiral of Denmark and other principal Danes. To the lesser officers he presented gold chains. Next day James, Anne and Prince Henry accompanied King Christian to Rochester. Here, after divine service in the cathedral, they took to barges and reviewed the galleys, ships and pinnaces of the English navy, arriving at last at the *Elizabeth Jonas* which had been 'perfumed with sweete and pleasant Perfume, and hanged with Cloth of Golde all the sides within'.[5] Joined to this ship by a bridge two hundred feet long was the *White Bear*. Aboard the two ships tables were spread for a banquet, and at these the company seated themselves, food being despatched to them from a hulk which had been converted into a floating kitchen set midway between the two vessels.

When the banquet was completed, the kings arose from their table set under a silken tent on the deck of the *Elizabeth Jonas* and went ashore at Chatham for a panoramic view of the fleet anchored in the river, while 2,300 shots were discharged from their great guns in salute. That evening the navy gunners put on an elaborate display of fireworks.

Next day the royal party travelled to Gravesend where King Christian feasted James, Anne and Prince Henry on his flagship. Volleys from the guns on the ships and ashore accompanied the drinking of toasts. Later there was an elaborate piece of set fireworks showing the English lion holding a chain to which were fettered the eight capital Vices. Part of the effect of this moralistic display was lost since the fireworks had to be let off in bright sunlight, the English royal party being unable to wait until evening if they were to catch the tide going back to London. Three days later, tide and wind were right and Christian sailed for home, accompanied by an escort of English warships.

This was not King Christian's only visit to England. One evening late in July 1614, as Queen Anne was having her dinner privately at Denmark House, a French servant ran into the room and declared that he had just seen her brother the King of Denmark enter at the gate. Knowing that no visit by her brother had been arranged, Anne was contemptuous of the report. At that moment she was seized from behind and firmly kissed. Breaking free, the Queen found herself in her brother's embrace. Once she had regained her composure, Anne presented the Frenchman with the richest jewel she was wearing.

Christian had embarked upon this second visit to England in the greatest secrecy. Not a word of his intent had reached the English court. His own subjects believed that he was bound for Germany. Landing at Yarmouth, Christian maintained strict incognito as he hired post-horses to take him to London. Here, after dining at an ordinary inn near Aldgate, he took a hackney coach to Denmark House and walked in to surprise his sister.

This second visit of King Christian has been dismissed as a prank on the part of the monarch. It was probably more than that. Letters from Anne had made it clear that relations were far from happy between herself and her husband. She had been particularly bitter about indignities she believed to have been put upon her by some of the court, notably the Earl of Northampton. Probably pity and affection for his sister, and a hope that he could do something to help her, prompted Christian to make his trip. Actually, he arrived to find that the offending Northampton had died a month before and that James himself was out of town on a summer progress which was to take him to Rutlandshire. The latter's absence was not inopportune for it allowed the brother and sister a day or so completely to themselves.

Informed of the arrival of his royal brother-in-law, James cut short his leisurely journey through the shires and hastened back to London. There followed the usual round of royal entertainments: hunting, running at the ring, bear-baiting, fencing matches, fireworks and the like. Two state banquets were held for King Christian at Whitehall and James, remembering his Danish Majesty's taste for such things, arranged also 'a drinking feast' in his private chamber where everybody got suitably drunk.

On August 5th Christian started for home. The general feeling was that he would have liked to stay longer but had been rather hastened away by James. There was the usual lavish exchange of gifts at parting. King Christian set something of a record by suddenly presenting Prince Charles with one of the three warships with which he had come hither. Brother and sister were never to meet again. Five years later Anne was dead, her corpse lying in state for months before money could be raised for a state funeral.

Chapter IX

The Empty Exchequer

ONE OF THE LIVELIER of the anti-royalist 'secret histories' published during the Commonwealth was *The History of Great Britain, Being the Life and Reign of King James First* by the Puritan Arthur Wilson. Among Wilson's anecdotes is one, true in spirit if not in fact, of the thriftless generosity of King James. It tells how one day at Whitehall Sir Henry Rich, the handsome younger son of the Earl of Warwick, seeing three thousand pounds in coin being carried to the Keeper of the Privy Purse, whispered something to James Maxwell, a Scottish gentleman of the King's Bedchamber. King James overheard the sound and asked what had been said. He was told that Rich had wished that he had that much money. 'Marry, shalt thou Harry,' exclaimed King James, and at once ordered the bearers to carry the money to Rich's lodgings. Noting the amazed delight on the young man's face, he added, 'You think now you have a great Purchase; but I am more delighted to think how much I have pleasured you in giving this money, than you can be in receiving it.'

During his first months in England James, impressed by the apparent wealth of his new kingdom, indulged to the full his taste for lavish giving. Old friends from Scotland, new admirers in England, ambassadors from abroad, all flourished amid the golden rain of the royal bounty. After all, a king was expected to be lavish in his giving. Prestige required a certain royal generosity. As one of James's councillors observed later in a memorandum about proposed economies, '... in kinges howses some kind of prodigalitie is not so much discommendable as a little sparing'.[1] James, in the euphoria of his new English kingship, was hardly in the mood for sparing during the spring of 1603.

Disillusion soon arrived. The wealth of England, or at least that part of it the King could get his hands on, proved far from inexhaustible. By November the royal coffers were empty, the household officers unpaid, and the King's own guard ready to mutiny unless they received their money. For some time the storm signals had been flying. An estimate of the expenses for the year beginning on October 1, 1603, had given the alarming intelligence that, whereas the household expenses for the last year under Elizabeth had totalled about £47,000, for these twelve months they would probably amount to almost £93,000.

The next year brought steps to improve the royal finances. Since recent experience under Elizabeth had demonstrated that 'farmers', with the incentive of private profit, collected the customs duties much more effectively than royal officers, it was decided to abandon direct administration and return to the system under which private contractors bought up the rights of collection, reimbursing themselves out of their receipts and keeping any surplus as profit on their speculation. A new schedule of import and export duties was compiled (the first since the time of Queen Mary), and the rights to these sold *en bloc* to a syndicate of London capitalists. Not included were certain farms such as those of the customs on wines and currants which had already been leased. The 'Great Farm', which came into effect on December 24, 1604, after months of negotiating and bidding by rival groups each with their own connections at court, sold the right of collection of all import and export duties and customs, except those specifically excluded, for £112,400 annually.

In 1611 the syndicate headed by Francis Jones, Nicholas Salter and William Garway which had found the Great Farm extremely profitable, gladly renewed the lease for £136,226 per annum, and in 1614 for £140,000. In 1621, when the duties on silks, lawn and cambric were added, the lease of the Great Farm was raised to £160,000.

The attempt to secure a steady and increased income through the negotiation of the Great Farm was complemented by economies at the royal court. On July 17, 1604, King James signed a book of 'Ordinances for the Governing and Ordering of the Kings Household', clearly intended to inaugurate an era of economy and reform. To begin with, these ordinances cut sharply the number of dishes to be served in the messes maintained by the chief court officers for their subordinates. By way of setting an example, the King ordered that in the future only twenty-four dishes of meat were to be served at his table instead of the customary thirty for each meal. Unauthorized messes which had been set up at the royal expense by Sir Edward Carey, Master of the Jewel House, and Sir John Sandolan, Master of the Wardrobe, were abolished completely. Furthermore, the Sergeant of the Cellar was instructed to stop issuing sack to everybody in the household and to limit his issues to twelve gallons a day, this to be given only to noblemen and ladies who 'for their better health desire to have sacke'.[2]

Savings on the royal wine rations were not likely to achieve very much. The substantial economies effected during the early years of King James's reign were in military expenditures. Providentially Mountjoy's subjugation of Ireland was just being completed when James came to the English throne. Henceforth the King would be free from the enormous military expenditures in Ireland which had made the last years of Elizabeth one continuous financial crisis. Whereas the Irish establishment had cost Elizabeth £342,074 for the year ending at Michaelmas 1602, it cost James only £38,251 for the year similarly ending in 1607.[3] Moreover, with England and Scotland under the same sovereign, there was no longer any point in maintaining a large English garrison at Berwick. James sharply reduced the force stationed there and symbolically built a bridge across the Tweed. The signing of the peace treaty with Spain meant further savings on ships, arms and men. The effect of all these savings was that while the total expenditures of the Crown during the last five years of Elizabeth were £2,622,037, they were down to £2,102,157 for the first five years of James.[4]

With such a reduction in the total royal expenditure, the financial embarrassments of the opening year of the new reign might have been expected to be of short continuance. Such, however, was not the case. In 1604 the crisis continued, and a compulsory interest-free loan had to be levied on all persons of substance to bring in £111,891 to help the King with his needs. Other loans followed and by Michaelmas 1606 the royal debt was up to £550,331, an increase (as Professor Tawney has noted)[5] of some 30 per cent over the debt of £422,749 inherited from Queen Elizabeth. As for the conditions the next year, a sufficient sidelight is cast in a poignant letter from Sir Thomas Chaloner, governor of the household of Prince Henry, to Sir Julius Caesar, Chancellor of the Exchequer:

> And let me Intreat your favour to Mr palmer the princes Imbroderer, who is redy to perish for wante of money, all his frends and creditors having in his distresse left him: Beleeve me Sir you shal do a greate deede of charity, one fifty pounde would helpe him & his family that are ready to sterve.[6]

The reason for this sorry state of affairs was that the financial crisis which King James had inherited from Elizabeth was so fundamental that it required much more than had yet been done to relieve it. In an age of soaring inflation, the income from the royal estates had not increased proportionately, and the direct taxes, the subsidies, fifteenths and tenths voted occasionally by Parliament, were each yielding smaller and not greater returns. Unless additional sources of income could be found, the Crown's receipts and expenditures could be balanced only if the King practised the most rigid parsimony, and if the royal officers eliminated all corruption which lessened his means or swelled his expenses. Unfortunately these two conditions were equally impossible of fulfilment.

King James's prodigality is recorded in the issues made from his Exchequer. In 1603 'diverse causes and rewards' accounted for £11,741, the next year £18,510, and the year following £35,239. In 1603 the Exchequer paid out £27,270 in 'fees and annuities', in 1604 the sum was

£34,593, and in 1605 it amounted to £47,783.[7] On and on the gifts, grants and pensions continued: 'To Sir George Creighton and Sir George Howme jr. £2000', 'Mrs. Jane Drummond [a favourite of Queen Anne's] £2000', 'Jon Gib [one of the King's trusted Scottish servants] £3000'.[8] Some time around 1605 a commission reporting on the royal finances sadly informed King James:

> . . . the empty places of that glorious garland of your crown . . . cannot be repaired when the garden of your Majesties Treasure shall be made a common pasture for all that are in need or have unreasonable desires.[9]

What the commission thought of the £15,593 lavished upon Queen Anne's childbed when Princess Mary was born we do not know.

The drain put upon the King's means by the corruption of his officers at times seems limitless. This corruption was not due to any lack of administrative machinery. On the contrary, a highly organized group of 'offices', originally designed in medieval times but improved under the Tudors, provided an entirely adequate apparatus for the proper administration of the royal finances. All that was needed to make the machinery work properly was a provident king, sufficient income, and honest servants. As it happened, all three were wanting.

Centre of the complex system of royal finance was the Exchequer, managed by its Chancellor under the direction of the Lord Treasurer. The Exchequer had a twofold purpose and organization. In part it was a judicial organization with its Court of Exchequer and Revenues, presided over by the Barons of the Exchequer, who heard cases that affected the revenues of the Crown; in part it was the equivalent of a modern treasury board, receiving payments due to the Crown, making payments or assigning specific revenues to various branches of the royal household, periodically auditing their accounts, and entering them in the Pipe Office, where the Exchequer's own accounts were similarly preserved.

For insight into what went on in a department submitting accounts to the Exchequer, one may look at the Board of Green Cloth which attended to the housekeeping expenses of the court. Regulations carefully prescribed the procedure to be followed. Monies assigned to the Board were received by one of its members, the Treasurer of the Household, who was required to pay them over within six days at the Counting-House to a second officer, the Cofferer, while a third officer, the Comptroller, stood by to witness the receipt. Early each morning the Green Cloth officers (the Treasurer of the Household, Cofferer, Comptroller and the Master of the Household) met under the Lord Steward to agree upon coming expenditures and to check accounts for the previous day. Actual disbursements were made by the Cofferer, whether to pay the wages of household servants, to settle outstanding accounts, or to provide the court's purchasing agents, the 'purveyors', with money with which to buy the supplies noted on the officially approved lists given to them. The Cofferer's disbursements were all recorded for him by a Clerk of the Green Cloth. Within a set period after the end of each year the Cofferer had to send in his books to the Exchequer. Here they were audited, partly through comparison with a similar set of books submitted by the clerk comptrollers of the Counting-House. These clerk comptrollers were a very important part of a system of checks. One of their duties was to keep a close watch on the amount and quality of the provisions delivered to the court in consequence of the purveyors' purchasing. In their keeping was the cheque-roll, the official record of the establishment authorized for each of the various departments under the Lord Steward and of the emoluments due to each person listed within it. Aiding the clerk comptrollers were the avenors. The latter were charged with seeing that unauthorized persons did not frequent the offices or lodgings in the court.

Complicated checks, audits and inspections such as these should have kept the expenditures of the royal household well under control. Actually they did not. Although the senior Exchequer and Green Cloth officials, and such other officers as the Treasurer of the Chamber who was paymaster for the Lord Chamberlain's department, appear to have been in the main conscientious men doing their best, corruption lurked everywhere lower down. Inferior officers and servants constantly connived with those set to police them, or used ingenious tricks to elude them. Malfeasance and waste caused a continual drain.

For a picture of what went on one may turn to an undated report in the Public Record Office.[10] It paints a dark picture of conditions in the Court. Even the most inferior servants in the Lord Steward's departments, the grooms and 'children', have their own servants coming into the palace and secretly conveying away wood, coal, butter, fruit, spices, etc. The royal bakers are making lightweight loaves and misappropriating what they save. The pantry officers are disposing improperly both of the fine bread and the coarse. The officers of the buttery are selling the King's drink for their own profit. The cooks in the kitchen are selling the best of the meat delivered to them so that only half of that supplied is being served on the King's tables. The officers of the poultery are selling lamb, capon, and fowl intended for the use of the household. The woodyard officers are charging for wood that never arrives, and half of what does come is being stolen. The officers of the boiling house are interpreting so freely their perquisite of the 'strippings' as to leave little on the fowls served to 'the kinges poore officers'. The purveyors, happily exploiting their right to require others to sell to them at the low rates set by the Green Cloth officers, are buying much more than they should and reselling the excess for their own profit.

Malfeasance such as this was not restricted to the departments under the Lord Steward. Almost everywhere royal servants were helping themselves at the King's expense. The more one regarded the situation, the worse it looked. The King had not money enough to pay his servants promptly and keep them honest; they therefore resorted to peculation and made things that much worse. The more the King's household lacked money, the more it had to buy on credit with the inevitable result of 'yll provision at Unreasonabl rate'. The accumulating debts made it harder and harder to pay the King's servants, and gave them the more reason for resorting to graft.

King James regarded the corruption of his officers and servants sometimes with cynicism, sometimes with anger. To the Venetian ambassador he observed that were he to use the rule of Venice and execute all who defrauded the state, he would soon have no subjects left. Learning that one of the officers of his court was filled on his deathbed with remorse at having cheated his king, James sent him word that he did 'freely and lovingly forgive him', but at the same time he bitterly exclaimed, 'I wonder much that all my officers do not go mad with the like thoughts; for certainly they have as great cause as this poor man hath.'[11]

The Lord Treasurer who grappled with the multitudinous problems of King James's finances during the first years of his reign was old Thomas Sackville, Lord Buckhurst, a carry-over from the regime of Elizabeth, whom James had created Earl of Dorset. In his youth he had been a promising poet, the co-author, as the handbooks on English literature remind us, of *Gorboduc*, the first 'regular' English tragedy. He had, however, long since relinquished the Muse for money and now, in his last years, combined the traditional avarice of old age with a streak of self-righteous Puritanism. It is not impossible that Shakespeare has preserved something of the Lord Treasurer for us in the person of Polonius, who considered himself a judge in literary matters.

One day in April 1608, Dorset was sitting at the board when the Privy Council was questioning an accused man. Dramatically the old Lord Treasurer rose to his feet and declared, 'Here is that which will strike you dead.' He reached within his robe for a document and fell forward, dead. His demise was celebrated in anonymous verses which circulated about the court:

> Discourteous *Death* that wouldst not once confer,
> Or deign to parly with our Treasurer:
> Had he been Thee, or of thy fatal Tribe,
> He would have spar'd a life to gain a bribe.[12]

For his new Lord Treasurer, King James made the best possible choice
—Cecil. Grimly the little overworked man set about trying to clean the
Augean stable of the royal treasury. Working closely with Sir Julius
Caesar, the Chancellor of the Exchequer, he attacked the problem before
him. The costs of the royal household were compared with those of the
French *Maison du Roy*. The expenses of Henry VIII's children, computed
in Jacobean values, were set against those of King James's children. By
such means Cecil tried to determine the proper scale of expenditure for the
various branches of the royal establishment. The limits determined, he
laboured hard to keep the various royal offices within their allowed
budgets. When it became clear that the household of Prince Henry, after
increasing from 141 persons in 1604 to 233 at the end of 1608, was continuing to be altogether too costly, Cecil ordered an investigation which
revealed that persons were impoverishing themselves to buy posts in the
Prince's household, and then clamouring for increased wages to justify
their investment; that when Sir Thomas Chaloner, the Prince's 'governor',
refused to add unnecessary servants or officers to the staff of the boy prince,
disappointed applicants were going behind his back and procuring warrants
for their appointment from the King; that persons drawing wages in lieu
of board were still eating at the Prince's tables; and that these same tables
were 'pestered' with unauthorized persons getting free meals at the royal
expense.[13] The abuses were typical of those in the King's own household.
Gradually, against the entrenched interest of courtiers and royal officers,
Cecil achieved some degree of reform.

The new Lord Treasurer knew that for real success he had to have the
support of the King. At the outset he wrote to Sir Julius Caesar, 'How
miserable a case ours is, if he expect help from us who have no power
without his own absolute resolution to discourage all hopes for a while
from all men, of taking any thinge from him untill he be in better estate.'[14]
One way and another, Cecil tried to make James realize what his good-
natured generosity meant in terms of hard cash. One story goes that when
the King sent for a warrant for £20,000 (the sum is surely exaggerated!)
to be paid to a favourite, Cecil had the sum set out in coin in a room where
the King would pass and see just how great the sum really was. 'Thereupon
the King fell into a passion, protesting he was abused, never intending any
such gift: And casting himself upon the heap, scrabled out the quantity of
two or three hundred pounds, and swore he should have no more.'[15]

In 1610, at Cecil's prompting, the King issued a special 'Declaration
of his majesties royal pleasure in the matter of bountie.' This proclaimed:

> We doe on the one part expressely forbid all Our Servants and Subjects (of
> what condition soever they be) to propound or offer any Suites to us by
> which Our People in generall may be impoverished or oppressed. So on the

other part Wee doe likewise expressely forbid all persons whatsoever, to presume to presse Us, for any thing that may either turne to the diminution of Our Revenew and setled Receipts, or lay more charge upon Our Ordinarie.[16]

Attached to the proclamation was a schedule of permissible and impermissible suits. Among things which were not permissible were requests for rents, lands and leases in the King's possession or reversion, royal tenures, alienations, fines, recoveries, and any new pensions. Permissible suits for the royal bounty would be referred to a weekly meeting of James, Cecil, and one of the Masters of Requests.

Aware that mere economies would not suffice, Cecil set himself to augment the revenues of the Crown. The courts having ruled a few years earlier in 'Bate's Case' that the King could impose import and export taxes without parliamentary consent, Cecil brought in a whole set of new 'impositions'. He ordered that an unaccustomed rigour be shown in the collection of debts due to the Crown. When Prince Henry was knighted in 1609, Cecil saw to it that the old feudal right of collecting an 'aid' upon such an occasion was made to pay handsomely.

The Lord Treasurer, moreover, decided to sell land. The course was an extreme one—each piece sold meant a diminution of the King's future revenues. On the other hand, confronted with the mountainous debt left by Dorset, Cecil felt that the step was justified. In 1608 he ordered a great survey made of all the King's lands. On the basis of this, it was decided which of the Crown lands should be sold as being the least profitable. Then the government put on the market not only hundreds of manors and four hundred or so mills along with their lands, but also rectories, tithes, and prebends. On certain other properties, sixty-year leases were offered. The buyers were syndicates of London capitalists who bought large blocks for cash down and then very profitably resold the individual properties. By January 1610 Cecil through these drastic measures had reduced to £300,000 the debt which had stood at £597,337 when he had become Lord Treasurer in May 1608.

At a cost of £14,500 lost in annual rents from the lands which he had sold, Cecil had halved the King's debt. The basic problem remained: James was still a long way from living within his means. A new, permanent, and substantial increase in the royal revenue was imperative. Such an increase could only be secured from Parliament. Parliament, however, held by the time-honoured principle that 'the King should live of his own', a phrase which meant that the sovereign should meet the expenses not only of his own household but of the national government out of his income from the royal estates, various feudal levies upon the lords and gentry, the first fruits and tenths of the clergy, the customs levied at the ports, and certain other traditional sources. Parliament regarded its own votes of supply as extraordinary grants for special contingencies such as foreign wars. This view Cecil now sought to change by convincing Parliament that there was a principle of 'support' as well as of 'supply', and that the economic situation was such that they should grant the King a subvention of some £200,000 annually.

Appearing before a parliamentary committee early in 1610, Cecil put his case before them. On March 26th, Parliament made its counterproposal: let the King grant freedom from the irksome payments arising out of antiquated feudal rights and tenures and they would grant him £100,000 per annum. At this point bargaining began on what came to be called the 'Great Contract', a measure intended to make the King solvent and to protect his people from archaic and arbitrary levies.

By July, largely through the skilful negotiating of Cecil, the bargain was struck, though the final details of the agreement were put over until Parliament reconvened in the autumn. The King was to end the much-abused practice of purveyance. Certain of the impositions levied by Cecil were to be removed, and no new ones added. Moreover, the Court of Wards was to be abolished. This court administered the estate of any minor of gentle blood, contriving to make it a profitable source of income for itself and the King. Royal wardship, which usually meant the plundering of an administered estate, had long been one of Parliament's grievances. For these and other concessions, Parliament would pay the King an annual grant of £200,000. Cecil could congratulate himself upon the outcome of his endeavours. A precedent of annual parliamentary grants would now be set, and the royal revenue would not only be augmented but made more constant and regular.

The reopening of Parliament in November brought disaster. Its members, thinking over the agreement during their recess, had come to like it less and less and felt now that they had got the worse of the bargain. Seeing the extravagance and mismanagement which all too obviously still prevailed in King James's court, they were less and less inclined to accommodate him. The King, for his part, possibly in consequence of some statistics submitted by Sir Julius Caesar, Chancellor of the Exchequer, had decided that he was not getting compensation commensurate with the monetary value of his concessions. Determined at any rate to get his £200,000 completely clear of charge, James now demanded that Parliament pay the compensation for the officers of the Court of Wards who were now to lose their jobs. At this, a storm at once blew up. In the end James dissolved Parliament without any contract being made.

The most promising financial reform of the reign had not materialized. Because of the consequent failure to get the national finances on a sound footing, crisis after crisis would dog succeeding Lord Treasurers. Charles I would have to continue the forced loans and benevolences so unpopular in the time of his father. The failure of the Great Contract would lead at last to the catastrophe of the Civil War.

In 1611, with all hope of the Great Contract in abeyance, Cecil turned to another means of securing money—the wholesale issuance of 'Privy Seals', which were form letters printed in great numbers in a font made to look like manuscript hand. Each advised its recipient that he was required to lend the King a sum which had been written in on the blank spaces on the form. These forced loans took their name from the fact that they were issued under authority of the King's privy seal. They had already been used earlier in the reign. Cecil now issued about five thousand privy seals, ranging from £10 to £50 each. Foreign merchants in London coming out from church found royal officers waiting at the door to serve the letters upon them. By this expedient Cecil at the end of 1611 endeavoured to raise, at least for the coming year, the £200,000 he had hoped to get through the Great Contract. Six months later he was dead, and free from all further worry about King James and money.

With Cecil enjoying his eternal rest in Hatfield Church, King James was at a loss to find a new Lord Treasurer. The toadying Earl of Northampton was ambitious for the honour but James, while vulnerable to his flattery, had not enough confidence in him to make him custodian of his finances. Sir Julius Caesar had a record of faithful and efficient service since the beginning of the reign, but lacked the family connections which might have advanced him to the treasurership. In the absence of a satisfactory candidate, James appointed Northampton and his brother, the Earl of Suffolk, Sir Julius Caesar, and Lord Wotton (the Treasurer of the Household), along with Lord Zouch and the Earl of Worcester to perform, as a board, the duties of the treasurership. The new commissioners had their work cut out for them. Within a month of Cecil's death, Sir Julius Caesar advised the King that the royal debt which Cecil by one expedient or another had got down to £300,000 in 1610 had since then risen to £500,000.

The commissioners tinkered away at the problem confronting them. Caesar helpfully submitted to them a list of possible 'abatements of expense'.[17] He thought that, if no more buildings were put up, £18,000 might be saved on the Office of Works. Forty thousand pounds could be saved on pensions 'if the King grant no more nor renew old' (hardly a realistic condition). The sum of £5,000 could be saved on the Jewel House —one of James's extravagances was collecting gems. Another £100 could be saved on 'Two judges abated in Westminster hall.' This last item was followed hopefully by a further abatement: '£200 In prison, if fewer prisoners be committed.'

One of Caesar's hoped-for savings was '£10,000 by Lady Elizabeth's departure after her marriage'. Ironically, Princess Elizabeth's marriage to Frederick V, the Elector Palatine of the Rhine, was accompanied by such expenses for ceremony and display that it almost bankrupted the King. The situation was so bad that when the Elector and his bride finally left for Heidelberg, the ambassador from the rulers of the Spanish Nether-lands was taken to see 'the auncient goodly plate of the house of Burgundie', which had been pawned to Queen Elizabeth in 1578, and was told that if it was not now redeemed it would be melted down.

A month later King James, simply desperate for money, accepted a gift of £22,000 in gold from his current favourite, the Earl of Somerset. Since Somerset's spectacular advance to riches had contributed in some measure to the crisis, it was after all fitting that he should now return some of his loot. By September, the English ambassadors at The Hague and at Paris were both nine months in arrears in their salary. By December the arrear-age in the court itself was so bad that the King's guard and the messengers who rode post for him were directly petitioning him for their pay. Typi-cally, in the midst of this crisis, the King made a gift of £10,000 in jewels to Lady Frances Howard upon her marriage to Somerset. By the end of 1613 the King's debts were up to £680,000.[18]

A new parliament convened in April 1614 amid hopes that it would come to the King's rescue with substantial money votes. This, however, turned out to be the most discordant and intractable of all James's parlia-ments, so confused and undirected as to win for itself the name of the 'Addled Parliament'. It did not vote the Crown any supplies and James soon dissolved it in disgust. After this, the royal exchequer was saved from complete exhaustion only by the bishops agreeing to supply the King with a 'benevolence' in the form of the best piece of plate possessed by each. The Archbishop of Canterbury led off with a basin and ewer which he redeemed for £140, and was matched by the Bishop of Winchester. The lesser clergy were encouraged to contribute according to their means. The lay lords took up the example of the spiritual. The Lord Chamberlain sent in £200, as did Somerset and Lord Chief Justice Coke. All the officers of the court were under pressure to contribute. Were they or were they not attached to the King? Let them pay up and demonstrate their devo-tion. A judge who offered only £20 had his money contemptuously re-turned to him.

Obviously King James could not long keep going by such desperate expedients as these. On July 13, 1614, he suspended the board of commis-sioners and appointed as Lord Treasurer Thomas Howard, Earl of Suffolk, who was succeeded as Lord Chamberlain by Somerset. James could hardly have made a worse choice. 'Good Thomas,' as Queen Elizabeth

had liked to call him, was a thoroughly nice, agreeable, easy-going aristocrat with a record of gallant service at sea in his earlier years—but not the
slightest aptitude for finance. He was at this time quietly ruining himself
building an enormous mansion at Audley End. Left to his own devices
long enough as Lord Treasurer, he would probably have bankrupted his
monarch also. His wife was a notable virago, greedy and completely without principles. Partly with the unsuspecting compliance of her husband
and partly with the active help of her creature Sir John Bingley, Remembrancer of the Exchequer, she now proceeded to tap the royal revenues for
the benefit of her family. The Exchequer was hardly in a position to
support such leeches. A statement prepared when Suffolk took office
revealed that the royal debt had now gone up to £700,000.[19]

Under the charming maladministration of the Earl of Suffolk, things
went downhill fast. By January 1615 the English ambassador at Paris was
writing that he had exhausted both his funds and his credit and would have
to close the embassy unless given immediate payment on some of the
accumulating arrearages. At the same time Quester, the master of the
royal posts, although daily required to furnish messengers for the Lord
Treasurer and the Chancellor of the Exchequer, could not get a penny
from either of them towards the £600 they owed him. The next month the
royal brewer, with £16,000 unpaid to him, went bankrupt. Seven other
London brewers in turn refused 'to have theyre drincke taken to serve the
King without monie', and were imprisoned in the Marshalsea by way of
reprisal. The succeeding months saw all sorts of wild schemes to raise
money. 'Pope' Hakewill had a project to hawk general pardons at £5 each,
forgiving all offences, debts or duties to the Crown. Somebody else figured
that since 1568 the heralds had granted 7,000 coats of arms without the
concurrence of the Earl Marshal, and suggested that a fee of £20 or £30
could be collected from each of the recipients to make good the flaw in
their right. Nothing came of these sanguine ideas, and the King borrowed
£30,000 from the London merchants, kindly knighting William Garway,
chief of the syndicate farming the customs, who went security for the
repayment of the loan. The £30,000 helped, but as John Chamberlain,
the letter-writer, observed, 'What is that among so many that gape and
starve after yt?'

Bankruptcy was avoided the next year by a drastic sacrifice to secure an
immediate gain. For years the English had held and garrisoned the towns
of Flushing, Rammekins and Brill in Holland, their possession being the
security that England enjoyed for the large loans made to the Protestant
Dutch during the time of Elizabeth. Although the Dutch still owed
£618,000 on these loans, King James now returned these 'cautionary
towns' to them in return for £210,000. It was a poor bargain, but since

James had no money with which to pay his garrisons in these towns, he did not have much choice.

Obviously things could not go on this way. It was already a wry jest around the court that James might think that he was too poor to fight a war with Spain but that he could easily make the King of Spain as poor as himself—all he needed to do was to give him Suffolk for his treasurer. Things came to a head in the autumn of 1617 when James, back from his journey to Scotland, learned that his debts had now reached £726,000.[20] He liked Suffolk, but something had to be done. While leaving Suffolk in office, he turned over to the Privy Council the responsibility of reforming his finances. To the councillors he wrote urging drastic measures:

> ... Long discourses, & faire Tales will never repaire my Estate. ...
> Remember that I told yow that the Shooe muste be made for the ffoote,
> and let that be the Square of all your proceedings in this Busines: Abate
> Superfluities in all things, and Multitudes of unnecessary Officers, where
> ever they be placed; But for the Household, Wardrobe and Pensions, cutt
> and carve as many as may agree with the possibilitie of my Meanes. ... In
> this I expect no Answere in Word or Wryting, but onely the reall perform-
> ance for a beginning to releeve me out of my Miseries, ffor now the Ball is
> at your ffeete, and the world shall beare me Witnes, that I have put yow
> fairly to it: And so praying God to blesse your Labours, I byd yow heartily
> farewell.
>
> Your owne   James R.[21]

Stirred on by this and even sterner messages, the Privy Council was able to secure some real improvements in the King's finances. By the end of 1617 things were obviously taking a turn for the better.

A major part of the credit was due to the King's new favourite, George Villiers, recently created Earl of Buckingham. Buckingham had a taste for administration and some real talent where it was concerned. It was undoubtedly he who was responsible for James's keeping the Privy Council at its tedious and difficult task of investigating and reducing the royal expenditures. His task became easier after the hopelessly inept Suffolk was dismissed as Lord Treasurer in July 1618, amid charges of malfeasance, and a commission appointed to administer his office. For an incorruptible to head this new commission, James and Buckingham chose the Archbishop of Canterbury. Assisting the commissioners was Sir Lionel Cranfield, a practical business man and highly competent financial expert to whom Buckingham had previously turned for help with the chaotic royal finances.

Cranfield's career is a Jacobean success story of how a London apprentice rose to become in time Lord Treasurer of England. The first steps in that career were routine. Like many another ambitious young man, he married his master's daughter. His bride was Elizabeth Shephard,

E

child of Richard Shephard, merchant adventurer of St. Bartholomew's Lane, who promptly cancelled Cranfield's two remaining years of indentureship and paid a dowry of £800. With this money and his own shrewdness, Cranfield became a successful capitalist, trading with the Continent, speculating in various commodities, and lending money at usurious rates. In 1604 he was one of the shareholders in the great farm of the customs. Some time afterwards, learning that the Earl of Northampton wanted to purchase a small plot of land, part of a block which a syndicate to which he belonged had recently bought from the King, Cranfield persuaded his associates to make Northampton a gift of it. This judicious gift won Cranfield a useful friend. Brought into government service by Northampton, Cranfield soon showed his worth. Appointed Surveyor-General of the Customs in 1613 with surveillance over all the customs in farm, Cranfield within two years increased the King's revenues by £30,000 per annum.

After Northampton's death in 1615, Cranfield found a new patron in the rising royal favourite, Villiers. Appointed, through Villiers' good offices, one of the Masters of Requests charged with hearing petitions submitted to the King by poor men and royal servants, Cranfield so distinguished himself as to win completely the confidence of King James. Late in 1617, when it was decided as part of the new economy drive to investigate the expenses of the vast 'household' presided over by the Lord Steward, Cranfield was the logical man to head the enquiry.

With its expenditures more than twice what they had been in Queen Elizabeth's time, the household was overdue for investigation. Everywhere Cranfield and his committee found waste and graft. To take one example, using the Knight Marshal's figures, they found that 1,248 sheep and 132 oxen which had been paid for had never reached the tables of the court. This discovery provoked from Cranfield the sarcastic comment that he wondered into what corner of the palace all these lost animals had strayed. In April 1618 the committee submitted their report. They had decided that with proper management the household expenses could easily be reduced from £77,630 to £55,560 annually. Cranfield added a recommendation that in the future any officer who exceeded his allowed expenditure should either pay the extra out of his own pocket or be dismissed. Enforcement of this one rule alone, Cranfield maintained, would save the King £12,000 a year.

One of the most notoriously wasteful of the royal offices had long been the Great Wardrobe. Presided over by the prodigal Lord Hay, this department was charging a small fortune every year for the cloths, silks, velvets, furniture, saddle goods etc. which it supplied for the King. The simplest way of stopping the waste here seemed to be to install Cranfield as master. Hay was persuaded to resign in return for £20,000 paid to him out of the Exchequer, and into his place went Cranfield. As Master of the Wardrobe, Cranfield had no difficulty in making good his promise to the King to reduce to £20,000 per annum its expenses, which Hay had claimed could not be less than £28,000. Indeed, without impairing the services of the office, he made further substantial savings which, under the terms of his bargain with the King, he put into his own pocket.

Meanwhile the services of the indefatigable investigator and economizer were being used elsewhere. The corruption which had been going on in the Admiralty under the lax administration of Suffolk's kinsman the Earl of Nottingham, Lord High Admiral of England, was considered remarkable even in the graft-ridden court of King James. Bishop Goodman provides an illustrative anecdote. On a visit to Chatham, he was shown a stately row of fourteen houses and told that they were a sight worth seeing since they were all made of chips. The meaning, Goodman explains, was that the officers of the navy who had the perquisite of the chips around the dockyard 'took the best timber which came for the repairing of the navy for the building of their houses'. In his investigation of the Admiralty Cranfield was assisted by eleven fellow commissioners, mostly either businessmen or naval experts.

Appointed on June 21, 1618, the commission presented its report to the King and Privy Council at Hampton Court on September 29th. To Buckingham, at least, its findings came as no surprise. Three weeks earlier Cranfield had written to him:

> I will not trouble your lordship with the abuses which we every day discover, being such as you will hardly believe; as that when ships were to be brought up to Wollich or Debtford [sic] to be repaired, it had been better for his Majesty to have given them away at Chatham, and £300 or £400 in money, to any that would have taken them.[22]

The commissioners declared that the waste and corruption in the Admiralty were really appalling. Captains were sometimes putting to sea with only half the number of men for which they collected wages and victuals. Of the 43 ships in the Royal Navy, only 29 were fit for sea duty. Fourteen of the others were too far gone in mouldering decay for any future usefulness. As for expenses, the commissioners declared that the cost of the Admiralty could at once be reduced from £57,700 to £30,000 per annum for the next four years while new ships were being built to replace those which were hopelessly rotten. After the rebuilding, the navy should manage nicely on £20,000 a year.

In consequence of this report Nottingham resigned as Lord Admiral. The King then reappointed Cranfield's commission and charged it with implementing its own proposed reforms. This the commissioners success-fully did. In November 1619, when King James travelled to Deptford to see the first two ships built by the commissioners under their programme, he showered commendations upon them. Cranfield had already received a more substantial reward, a highly lucrative appointment as Master of the Court of Wards.

At this point Cranfield was made aware that if he hoped for further advancement a condition would have to be met—marriage to one of Buckingham's kinswomen. The favourite's domineering old mother, dedi-cated to finding husbands for her female relations, had decided that Cran-field, a widower in his mid-forties, rich and suitable for promotion to higher offices, was just the husband for her handsome but penniless cousin, Anne Brett. Cranfield's own inclination was towards the widow of Not-tingham's eldest son, even though the Howard connection, now that the family was out of favour at court, would do him more harm than good. For a while he avoided the Villiers alliance. Then ambition won out. On December 29, 1619, he went to the altar with Anne Brett. He did not have to wait long for the first of his rewards—on January 4, 1620, he was made a Privy Councillor. It was in 1621, however, that he received his real dividends. On July 9th of that year he was created Baron Cranfield, on September 30th he was appointed Lord Treasurer, and in November Anne presented him with a son.

Cranfield's predecessor as Lord Treasurer was Sir Henry Montagu, a former Chief Justice of King's Bench, who in December 1620 had invested £20,000 in the purchase of the treasurership, vacant since Suffolk's dis-missal. Montagu, created Viscount Mandeville, had incurred Bucking-ham's displeasure during his nine months in office, but when he was eased out to make way for Cranfield he was promised repayment of his money and consoled with an appointment as Lord President of the Council.

At last Cranfield had in his hands the direction of the whole of the King's finances. Like Cecil he began his administration with a com-prehensive survey, and found that things were in a bad way indeed. His predecessor had left him a debt of £900,000. Writing to Buckingham he declared, 'The more I look into the King's estate the greater cause I have to be troubled.' He affirmed that the mismanagement which he found was such that '. . . until your lordship see it you will not believe any men should be so careless and unfaithful'.[23]

Working to the point of actual breakdown, Cranfield tried to clean up the mess. He instituted a policy of conserving the royal forests, stopping the alienation of crown lands, and calling a halt to further borrowing. At his insistence persons who had owed the Crown money for years and never been called to a reckoning were now required to pay up. In view of the critical condition of the Exchequer, he suspended payment on all pensions, amid cries of anguish from the Court. Later, to strengthen his hand, he got a letter from Buckingham declaring that when suitors came with letters of support obtained from him Cranfield need attach no more importance to their suits than he himself saw fit. A significant postscript declared, 'This letter was contrived by the King, the Prince, and myself, all three.'[24]

At first Cranfield was hopeful of success. Writing to Buckingham a few months after he had become Treasurer he declared:

> . . . if God bless me, and his Majesty, the Prince, and your Lordship continue constant, and will back me, I will perfect the work, and the King shall live with honor upon his own in despite of all the world.[25]

In 1622, by way of encouragement, Cranfield was given the title of Earl of Middlesex.

In the end, however, Cranfield failed. The King and Buckingham cooled towards him when his economies ran counter to their own desires. During their Spanish visit of 1623 both Buckingham and Prince Charles grew angry at the Lord Treasurer's attempts to cut down on their lavish expenditures. In May 1623, when the King learned that Cranfield was holding up a payment which His Majesty wished made to Sir Francis Stewart, he had one of his Secretaries of State write a letter pointing out that, while His Majesty appreciated Cranfield's 'oppressive loads and spiritful endeavours', the latter should remember that 'when a gracious king is earnest and a worthy gentleman's wants are pressing, it becomes a great treasurer to do his utmost. . . .'[26] When the letter failed to have any effect James, not for the only time, intervened with a direct order to make payment.

The showdown came in 1624. The year opened with Buckingham and Prince Charles demanding war with Spain. Cranfield knew that, even with parliamentary assistance, the royal treasury was facing its greatest crisis of the reign because of the diplomatic and military expenses being incurred in attempts to get Spain's allies out of the Palatinate of the Rhine, the patrimony of James's son-in-law, the Elector Frederick. To Cranfield, Buckingham's policy of all-out war meant bankruptcy. Grimly he set himself to frustrating the war party's plans. The result was that the now all-powerful favourite demanded that Cranfield be broken. The King knew how much he owed to his Treasurer but, old and worn out, he made only fitful attempts to defend him. In the end he consented to his ruin.

Cranfield had not been altogether clear in his great office. Charges of corruption were now brought against him. On May 13, 1624, the House of Lords found him guilty, ordered him stripped of his offices, fined £50,000 and sent to the Tower for imprisonment during His Majesty's pleasure.

The King released him within a few weeks and greatly reduced his fine. In his place as Lord Treasurer, James appointed Sir James Ley. But the King now had only a few more months to live and the story of Ley's treasurership really belongs to the succeeding reign. The debt which Cranfield had left him was £1,000,000.[27]

CHAPTER X

The Fox of Hatfield Chase

ON MAY 22, 1607, to the accompaniment of banqueting and a suitably allegorical 'entertainment' from the pen of Ben Jonson, Robert Cecil, Earl of Salisbury, presented King James with Theobalds, the great house which he had inherited from his father. It was a magnificent gift, one calculated to make yet closer the friendly relations which, by a thousand little attentions, Cecil had maintained between himself and his sovereign.

The giver was not left uncompensated, for five days later the King formally transferred to Cecil the old royal palace at Hatfield. A month or so earlier, when the exchange of the two properties was being arranged, Cecil had visited Hatfield in company with three of his fellow earls, surveyed the estate, and decided where he would build his own great house.

This was the time when the aristocracy of England began dotting the shires with enormous country houses, 'magnificent buildings, wherein the nobleness of spirit is much discerned'. The building of these 'prodigy houses' had begun under Elizabeth with Longleat, Wollaton Hall, and Worksop Manor, Kirby, Holdenby and Theobalds itself. Now, in the reign of her successor, the Earl of Suffolk was building his fantastically expensive mansion at Audley End as a monument to the greatness of the Howards. Lord Zouch was busy on an enormous house at Bramshill, and other noble lords were poring over plans with their master builders. Too often their desire for ostentation outran the resources of their purses.

With his acquisition of Hatfield, Cecil began building what was, perhaps, the greatest of all the private palaces of the reign. He had already remodelled Beaufort House in Chelsea, rebuilt Cranborne Manor in Dorset, and raised for himself a splendid London residence, Cecil House. Now at Hatfield he began his most ambitious project. It was vastly expensive, but Cecil, with the fees and profits of his numerous offices, and the rents from the many estates he had either inherited or purchased, was a very wealthy man. Hatfield House was planned on a magnificent scale and every care went into laying out its spacious gardens. Master Tradescant travelled about France and the Low Countries securing fruit trees and flowers. From the Netherlands Cecil's military kinsman, Sir Edward Cecil, sent

four hundred sycamore trees. From M. de la Boderie, the French ambassador, came thirty thousand vines for the vineyard. Since King James
was interested in starting an English silk industry, five hundred mulberry
trees were ordered for Hatfield. Meanwhile the carpenters, the wood
carvers, the bricklayers, the plasterers, the limners, the glaziers, toiled
mightily raising and decorating the fabric of the mansion.

Among the stream of notes of instructions, queries and memoranda,
which Cecil sent down from London to his agents at Hatfield, one dated
November 1, 1609, seizes the eye:

> Mr. Steward,
> This bearer, Mr. Colt, having this morning brought my Lord a model of
> his tomb and demanded fifty pounds in imprest towards his workmanship
> of the three chimney-pieces at Hatfield, his Lordship commanded that you
> should deliver him so much money.[1]

Before his new home was anything like complete, Cecil had commissioned
Maximilian Colt, the King's Master Sculptor, to design for him another
home, his tomb in Hatfield Church. Was it just the usual strange foresight
of Cecil, anticipating every mischance and contingency, or did he already
feel in himself the seeds of decay and half suspect that he would never
survive to see Hatfield completed in its final glory? Whether there was any
premonition or not, he had in fact less than three years longer to live.

The truth was that his titles and offices, riches and lands, had been
bought at the price of appalling overwork. His health never had been
robust. An injury which he had sustained as a babe in a fall from his
nurse's arms had left him not only hunch-backed but dwarfed, a mere five
foot two or three inches in later life. In boyhood his delicate health had
worried his father, who had needed to be constantly reassured of his
younger son's health when young Robert Cecil went abroad on a diplomatic mission in 1588. The father William Cecil, Lord Burghley, was
aware of the brilliance of his son's mind and had ambitions for him. Carefully he educated him for the duties of statecraft even, Polonius-like,
drawing up maxims full of worldly wisdom for his guidance. He saw to it
that, at the earliest possible moment, the young man secured membership
in the House of Commons; and he brought him early into the negotiations
of foreign diplomacy. When Robert Cecil was only twenty-nine his father
secured for him a seat in the Privy Council. Finally on July 5, 1596,
Burghley had the satisfaction of seeing him, at the age of thirty-three,
appointed Principal Secretary of State. Burghley's own health was already
giving way, and the succeeding months saw the son taking over more and
more of the duties, responsibilities and burdens of the father. It was
Robert Cecil who was the Queen's chief minister during her final years.

King James up in Scotland had been aware of the power wielded by

Cecil when he urged his emissaries in London to make every effort to reach an understanding with Master Secretary to ease his coming to the English throne. He rejoiced accordingly to receive Cecil's promise that when Elizabeth died 'your shippe shalbe steered into the right harbour, without cross of wave or tyde'.[2]

Arrived in England as England's King, James had no disposition to conceal his gratitude to the man who had secured his uncontested accession to the throne. He had, too, the good sense to realize that in Secretary Cecil, Lord Treasurer Dorset, and Lord Keeper Egerton, he had inherited from Queen Elizabeth devoted and highly skilled servants whom he would be a fool to replace with unproven men. Cecil's brother Thomas, second Lord Burghley, after meeting with the new king, was able to write to Cecil, 'He said he heard you were but a little man, but he would shortly load your shoulders with business.'[3] The words were only too true. In Cecil, King James found the indispensable man, the ever available servant, the councillor never without an acceptable suggestion, the minister to whom to refer any inconvenient complaint or petition. He indeed loaded his shoulders with business. Within a month of James's coming, Cecil was writing with a rueful weariness to Sir John Harington, who had been importuning him for a post at Court:

> You know all my former steps, good Knight, rest content and give heed to one that hath sorrowed in the bright lustre of a Court and gone heavily even on the best-seeming fair ground. 'Tis a great task to prove one's honesty, and yet not spoil one's fortune. You have tasted a little hereof in our blessed Queen's time. . . . I wish I waited now in her presence–chamber with ease at my food and rest in my bed. I am pushed from the shore of comfort and know not where the winds and waves of a Court will bear me. I know it bringeth little comfort on earth; and he is, I reckon, no wise man that looketh this way to Heaven.[4]

Whatever the demands made upon him, Cecil persevered: serving on commissions, hearing delegations, meeting foreign emissaries, writing to the English ambassadors abroad, attending at the council board, placating Parliament, superintending the secret service, attending to the querulous complaints and greedy suits of influential courtiers, and keeping up the steady stream of flattery needed to lubricate his relations with the King. If the load of all his manifold duties was heavy before, it became heavier in 1608 when, after Dorset's death, Cecil assumed the post of Lord Treasurer. He had indeed become 'that great Engin of the State, by whom all Wheels moved',[5] but the weight upon the 'little great Lord' was killing. He lacked the gift of delegating power and duties. With only a few devoted servants such as Levinus Munck, he tried to carry the whole crushing load himself. The King sported and jested while his 'little beagle',

E*

as he termed Cecil, ran his errands and tried to keep the finances and the
government of the realm in working order. A vivid picture of the endless
labour that was Cecil's life shows itself in two letters from John Chamberlain. Chamberlain, just back from a visit to his friend Sir Dudley Carleton,
the English ambassador at Venice, had brought with him despatches for
Cecil. On November 6, 1611, he wrote despairingly to Venice:

> . . . I have waited now three dayes and cannot get accesse; yet have I all
> the furtherance that Sir Walter Cope, Master Kirkham and Master Finet
> can affoord.

Finally, on the fourth day, he managed to see Cecil:

> . . . at last an honest doore keeper offered me the curtesie to bring me to
> my Lords presence. . . . My audience was short and sweet with inquirie
> after your health and my Ladies, and remembrance of acquaintance, and
> that we were both growne gray, and that he wold confer with me at more
> leysure and so forth. There is a world of suitors continually attending. . . .[6]

One has it all there: what Archbishop Mathew has so well described as
'his strange pacific courtesy'.[7] The man himself always poised, always
soberly attentive, and with the same unfailing politeness and appearance
of personal interest for all comers. He had, said Sir Henry Wotton, 'a
sweet and a grave presence'.[8] And there is the other part, the merciless un-
ceasing burden of business—*There is a world of suitors continually attending.*

What was it that kept Cecil for ever immersed in business and the
intrigues of the court? It cannot have been the titles—the barony, the
viscountcy, and finally the earldom—these brought jeers as well as congratulations:

> Lord Robert in ye Law is a medlar
> Twas neever his fathers trade.
> For he and his dad were both Pedlars,
> And for money a Lord he was made.[9]

To the older aristocracy the Cecils were upstarts. It cannot have been the
money. Playing the court game entailed expenditures as great as the
rewards. It was not love for King James. Cecil must have sensed that
James valued him only because he was useful and saved him trouble. He
winced under the heavy humour of his royal master's jokes about his
dwarfish size, just as he had when Queen Elizabeth gave him 'her sporting
name of Pigmy'. His cousin Sir Francis Bacon obviously believed that it
was what, in the psychological jargon of our own day, would be called
'compensation' for his physical defects. Less than a year after Cecil's
death Bacon published in his essay 'On Deformity', a passage which
everybody took to point directly at the dead man:

> Whosoever hath any thing fixed in his person that doth induce contempt,
> hath also a perpetual spur in himself to rescue and deliver himself from

scorn. Therefore all deformed persons are extreme bold: first, as in their own defence, as being exposed to scorn; but in process of time, by a general habit. Also, it stirreth in them industry, and especially of this kind to watch and observe the weakness of others, that they may have something to repay.

Cecil had, of course, his relaxations. Apparently he enjoyed the excitement of the gaming table, though in any case it would not have been advisable to cut himself off from one of his master's amusements. He took an interest in hawking. He was not the kind of man to have intimate friends but his relations with his political allies the Howards, especially Suffolk, appear to have been cordial. Women seem to have been necessary to him. His own marriage with Elizabeth Brooke, sister of the ill-fated Lord Cobham, was a very happy one. When early in 1597 she died unexpectedly in giving birth to their third child, he seems to have been prostrated with grief. He never remarried. Instead he entered into various irregular relationships. Scandal linked his name with various ladies of the court. Lady Anne Clifford mentions Lady Suffolk, Lady Derby, and Lady Walsingham as 'great favourites' of his. King James in a letter that has been preserved for us teases Cecil directly with the reports in circulation about him and the wife of the Lord Chamberlain:

> Well, I know *Suffolke is married*, and hath also his handis full now in harbouring that great littell proude man that comes in his chaire. . . .[10]

There were other tales. Cecil took notice of one of these when he wrote to the Master of Gray protesting against the latter's spreading so 'strange and unworthy an invention' as his tale that he had first made Cecil's acquaintance when patronizing the same brothel. Cecil's reputation, however, was sufficiently bad that after his death an anonymous writer recorded:

> He was Lavish in his Lust; the caus that this amongst others of like nature
> were sprinkled upon his Grave
> Here lies Robert Cicil
> Compos'd of back & Pisle.[11]

When he died most of London believed, incorrectly, that it was the ravages of venereal disease that had killed him.

By the midsummer of 1611 Cecil's health was causing genuine concern to those about him. The King had recently secured as permanent physician to the royal family a very distinguished French practitioner, Dr. Theodore Turquet de Mayerne. In August Mayerne made a detailed examination of Cecil, taking notes that survive for us in his *Opera Medica*. The chief result of this examination was the discovery of a large abdominal tumour (presumably cancerous) which Mayerne thought might be looked after through careful regulation of the diet. This hope was not realized. The succeeding months saw the Lord Treasurer visibly weakening while his spirits gave way at times to a settled depression. Writing in February 1612 to Winwood, the English ambassador at The Hague, Master John More declared:

> ... it is on all hands concluded that his Lordship must shortly leave this World, or at least disburden himself of a great part of his Affairs. In this short time of his Lordship's Weaknesse, almost all our great Affairs are come to a Stand, and his Hand is already shrewdly missed.[12]

A few weeks later Cecil was sufficiently recovered to take daily walks in his garden at Cecil House, but the improvement did not last. Renewed weakness and a recurrence of his symptoms sent him again to his doctors, who decided that the waters at Bath might perhaps help the stricken man. On April 28th Cecil started out on the long and painful journey. With the great man travelled three physicians, three surgeons, and sixty other attendants.

At Bath he appeared to benefit for a while from bathing in the waters, but the sickness returned. Cecil's mind became clouded at times and a scorbutic rash broke out on his body. More and more his thoughts turned to religion. After one of his worst attacks his chaplain, to comfort him with the assurance of God's mercy, told him the parable of the Good Shepherd and the lost sheep. This so moved the dying grandee that he cried again and again, 'That sheep am I. That sheep am I.' The next day the Lord Treasurer was calling, 'My auditt is made, let me come nowe, O Jesus, in the strength of my understanding! in the acte of my memorye!'[13]

Death, however, was not yet ready to give Cecil his release. He rallied, and on one of his better days was visited by his old friend Sir John Harington, now himself half-paralysed. Cecil greeted him sadly:

> Sir John, nowe doth one cripple come to see & visite another. This it is. Death is the center to whome wee all doe move. Some diameter-wise; some circulerly; but all men must fall downe to the center. I knowe not, Sir John, which of us two is neerest, but I thinke my selfe. ... Yet God, by his visitation, hath sweetned death unto me; because he hath given me the light of his grace. ... I doe not dispaire of life; & I doe not feare death: Godes will be done, I am prepared for it. And nowe, Sir John, let me ask yow, what good have yow founde by the Bath?[14]

Three days later, ignoring his father's command to the contrary, Cecil's heir, Lord Cranborne, arrived in Bath. Cecil had a great affection for his son, a good-natured simple lad, completely without the mental brilliance of his line. Asked by his chaplain, Master John Bowles, if it would give him comfort to see his son, Cecil in his agony exclaimed, 'the greatest comfort in the world', whereupon the young man was brought in. Father and son greeted each other in tears.

National Portrait Gallery

ROBERT CECIL, EARL OF SALISBURY

Attributed to John De Critz

LADY ARBELLA STUART

Shortly after, into this sombre world of physical agony, religious meditation and penitence, like the ultimate irrelevance, arrived King James's expensive Scottish favourite Lord Hay with tidings from the Court and, as a gift from the King, a fair diamond set in a golden ring. With the ring came a message for Cecil from James that 'the favour and affection he bore him was, and should ever be, as the form and matter of the ring, endless, pure, and most perfect'. With Lord Hay came Sir John Holles with a gift from the Queen.

Perhaps in consequence of these new arrivals, Cecil was seized by a sudden desire to return to London. Next morning the horses were saddled, the great lord's coach, litter and portative chair brought out, and the company set forth. Cecil's mind wandered on the way, as fit after fit shook his weakened frame. Travelling by slow stages the entourage reached Marlborough. Here on Sunday, May 24th, the long torment ended. Late in the afternoon while his chaplain was praying with him, 'he was cleane gone, & noe breath nor motion in him'. He was only forty-nine years old. The news of the death of his chief minister was brought to the King next morning. Postponing his departure by only a few hours, he went ahead with a planned hunting trip, leaving that afternoon for Eltham.

The Lord Treasurer's body was conveyed to Hatfield where his great house was still incomplete. In the nearby church he was buried within the ornate tomb he had commissioned from Master Colt three years before. There it may be seen today. Kneeling white marble figures of the four Virtues support on their shoulders the black marble slab upon which Cecil rests in effigy in his robes of office, the very rod of office which he bore in life resting in the carved hand. Beneath, on a lower level, in the best medieval *memento mori* tradition, lies a skeleton sculptured in the same white marble as the other figures.

Cecil was hardly cold in his grave when there burst a storm of revulsion and spite against him. Men who had been afraid of him and his spies while he lived now spoke freely. He was painted as the 'proud and terrible hunchback', the very personification of Machiavellian duplicity, an evil-cankered soul possessed utterly by envy, greed and distrust. 'I never knew so great a man so soone and so generally censured,' wrote John Chamberlain three days after Cecil's departure from this life. Six weeks later he was writing:

> The memorie of the late Lord Treasurer growes dayly worse and worse and more libells come as yt were continually, whether yt be that practises and juglings come more and more to light, or that men love to follow the sway of the multitude: but yt is certain that those who may best maintain yt, have not forborn to say that he jugled with religion, with the King, Quene, theyre children, with nobilitie, Parlement, with frends, foes, and generally with all.[15]

The truth is that Cecil had left too many enemies: friends of Essex's who blamed their hero's death on the 'malice' of Cecil; admirers of Raleigh (and they were growing in number) who believed Cecil the author of his ruin; disappointed courtiers who had failed to loot the king's exchequer because of the vigilance of Cecil. His own great fortune was made a prime argument against him. His enclosure of Hatfield Chase was made a chief instance of his insatiable greed. His reserve and poise were interpreted, perhaps with reason, as coldness. Witness apparently was borne against him here by his own kinsman, Bacon, in an essay already referred to:

> Deformed persons are commonly even with nature: for as nature hath done ill by them, so do they by nature; being for the most part (as the Scripture saith) *void of natural affection*; and so do they have their revenge of nature.

Many years later Lord Stanhope reading in Cresacre More's *Life and Death of Sir Thomas More* that Henry VIII:

> ... loved none but to serve his owne turne; and no longer was anie in his favour but as long as they applyed themselves to his humours. . . .

scrawled in the margin, 'Noe more did my Lord Treasurer Salsburye'.[16] Two anonymous libels are typical of the abuse heaped upon the dead magnifico. The first reads:

> Here lies thrown, for the Worms to eat,
> Little Bossive *Robin*, that was so Great.
> Not Robin Good-fellow, nor Robin Hood,
> But *Robin* th'Encloser of *Hatfield* Wood.
> Who seem'd as sent from Ugly Fate
> To spoil the Prince and rob the State.
> Owning a Mind of dismal ends,
> As Traps for Foes, and Tricks for Friends.
> But now in *Hatfield* lies the [Fox]
> Who stank while he liv'd and died of the [pox].[17]

To which may be added the even more pithy:

> Here lyes little Crookbacke
> Who justly was reckon'd
> Richard the 3rd and Judas the second,
> In life they agreed,
> But in death they did alter
> Great pitty the pox prevented the halter.[18]

Cecil was not without his defenders. Shortly after his death Sir Walter Cope, who as Chamberlain of the Exchequer had worked closely with him, appalled at the coarse abuse being heaped upon the late Lord Treasurer, wrote for him an *Apology* affirming, 'The heart of man was never more free from baseness or bribes; he hated the bribe and the taker.'[19] Earlier

the Earl of Dorset, drafting his will, had gone out of his way to pay tribute
to the man who was to succeed him as Treasurer. Noting 'what infinite
cares, crosses, labours, and travails both of body and mind' Cecil was
undergoing, Dorset offered a prayer 'that he sink not under the weight of
so heavy a burden'. At the end of this passage of his testament, Dorset
wrote:

> Thus I have faithfully set down in some sort the noble parts of this
> honourable Earl who, besides such his worthiness and sufficiency for the
> public service of his sovereign and country, is also framed of so sweet a
> nature, so full of mildness, courtesy, honest mirth, bounty, kindness, grati-
> tude, and good discourse, so easily reconciled to his foe and enemies, so
> true unto his friends, that I may justly say it were one of the choicest
> felicities that in this world we can possess to live, converse, and spend our
> whole life in mutual love and friendship with such a one.[20]

Men do not put hypocritical panegyrics into the wills which are to be read
when they are dead. It would seem that Dorset, aware of the slanders
already beginning to surround Cecil, felt so much for the man that he put
this refutation in the place where its sincerity would least be suspect.

With such accusers and such defenders, where does the truth lie?
Certain things seem beyond dispute. Plainly Cecil was a diligent if not a
great statesman. 'His ideas on all important subjects,' says Gardiner,
'were the ideas which had been prevalent at the Court of Elizabeth at the
time when he first grew up to manhood under his father's care'.[21] Bacon
probably had much the same view when he remarked to King James, 'I do
think he was no fit counsellor to make your affairs better, but yet he was fit
to have kept them from getting worse.' On the other hand, within limits,
his intellectual powers were very considerable, exhibiting 'a full mynd in
an imperfecte bodye'. No one has questioned that England owed Cecil a
debt of gratitude for the manner in which he secured the accession of King
James, or that James himself owed him a further debt for his skilful, if not
very imaginative, management of his affairs after he came to the throne.
But beyond this lies the debatable ground.

One recalls the charges of bribery and corruption. But one remembers
too that the first year Cecil was Lord Treasurer, he refused 'a world of
new yeares gifts', hoping to avoid any suspicion that he was permitting
himself to be bribed. One recalls the quiet dignity of his letter to the Earl
of Northumberland in 1600 pointing out just why it was improper to offer
him so expensive a gift as a coach and horses; yet one remembers too that
he accepted Northumberland's present. One recalls Cecil's fulsome pro-
testations of loyalty to his King, yet one cannot forget that he accepted
from the King of Spain a pension of £1,000 (which he contrived to get
increased to £1,500). On the other hand, one notes that James himself was

a Spanish pensioner, and the two may have felt free to trick the Spaniard while taking his money. Certainly the Spanish ambassador was disgusted with the returns he got from Cecil. And then there is the case of Raleigh. A nice pathos surrounds the picture Cecil painted of himself at Winchester, a friend anguished at having to abandon a friend because of a higher loyalty to King and country. But pathos gives way to other feelings when one remembers those damning letters Cecil and Howard sent to James before 1603, seeking to set him against Raleigh.

It is the task of the historian to try to reach a verdict in cases such as Cecil's. The evidence is incomplete and contradictory. The witnesses cannot be called for cross-examination, and the man himself cannot be heard in his own defence. Turning to Cecil as he survives in a score of contemporary portraits, one looks at the small bent frame decently clad in black, at the pale anxious face, the pursed mouth, and the eyes through which looks out the sharp, incisive, guarded mind within. One's glance travels to the exquisite, thin, sensitive hands of which any woman might have been proud. What was he really like? Feelings of pity, admiration, and distrust swirl confusedly within one. It is impossible to give the man a clean acquittal. He cannot be proven guilty. All that remains is the old Scots verdict of 'Not proven'. Certainly, as Cecil himself wrote to Harington of the life of the Court, 'no wise man looketh this way to Heaven'.

CHAPTER XI

The Languishing Lady

SOON AFTER King James arrived in England he met a lady who had been much on his mind in recent years, though he had never seen her before. She was an attractive blonde with large intent blue eyes and the demure manner (not to say slightly hangdog look) of a girl who throughout her formative years had endured the loving tyranny of a domineering old female. Beneath her quiet exterior lurked a streak of wilfulness and self-indulgence, the product of the spoiling which had alternated with the bullying. James must have regarded the young woman with considerable interest. Had he succumbed to one of the illnesses of his infancy, or perished from an assassin's blow in Scotland, she would have become Queen Regnant of England, and now be ruling in his place. He had, indeed, been frequently aware of her as a possible rival who might yet snatch the English crown from his grasp. This young woman, who now was presented to the King, was Lady Arabella Stuart, or 'Arbella' as she signed herself and was known to her contemporaries. She and King James were cousins on their fathers' side; but whereas James hitherto had never been in England, Arbella had never been out of it.

The two derived their English royal blood from their great-grandmother Margaret, elder daughter of Henry VII. James enjoyed priority, having descended from Margaret's first marriage, that with James IV of Scotland; whereas Arbella was Margaret's sole surviving descendant by her second marriage, that to Archibald Douglas, Earl of Angus. Although Arbella's claim to the English throne (not that she ever advanced it) was thus subordinate to that of James, she enjoyed one qualification which her cousin lacked—English birth. For years James was haunted by the fear that his enemies would exclude him from the English succession by invoking the statute of 25 Edward III which barred anyone born outside England from inheriting land within the realm.

One disqualification applied to both James and Arbella. Henry VIII, using the power Parliament had given him to determine the royal succession, had directed in his will that, should his own issue fail, the descendants of Margaret, his elder sister, were to be passed over and the succession to devolve upon the descendants of his younger sister, Mary. If in 1603 the English had chosen to abide by the will of Henry VIII rather than by common sense, neither James nor Arbella would have come to the throne. Instead, Elizabeth would have been succeeded by Edward Seymour, Lord Beauchamp, elder son of the old Earl of Hertford by his first wife, a granddaughter of Princess Mary. Hertford, however, knew that it would be absurd for his son to advance any pretensions against James and persuaded him to join in proclaiming the King of Scotland as King of England.

During the reign of Queen Elizabeth, Arbella's life was not a very happy one. Her father, Charles Stuart, Earl of Lennox, died when she was a babe of eighteen months and her mother, Elizabeth Cavendish, followed him to the grave a few years later, leaving their only child to be raised by her maternal grandmother, the formidable old 'Bess of Hardwick' who, by the fourth of her marriages to wealthy husbands, had both augmented her own great wealth up and become Countess of Shrewsbury. Arbella was brought at Hardwick by the ambitious old woman who hoped some day to see her grandchild ascend the throne of England. Queen Elizabeth herself, when annoyed with James up in Scotland, occasionally gave some slight grounds for this hope, but only to destroy them when, in turn, she was out of temper with the Shrewsburys.

The years passed, Arbella advanced to womanhood, and various marriages were proposed for her. Elizabeth mentioned Arbella and the Danish princess Anne as equally satisfactory choices when writing to James in the days of his bachelorhood. James subsequently suggested that Arbella be married to Ludovic Stuart, Duke of Lennox. There was talk too of a match with either the Duke of Nevers or the Prince of Condé. For a while some of the English Catholics hoped that she could be converted and then married to the son of the Duke of Parma, who had a remote claim to the throne in his own right. Nothing came of any of these schemes and Arbella remained both Protestant and single, living on a pittance from Queen Elizabeth in the great house at Hardwick with her old dragon of a grandmother. Only occasionally was she summoned to the royal presence in London.

As Arbella saw the best years of her life drifting away in attendance upon the crotchety old Dowager Countess of Shrewsbury, the fires of resentment began to smoulder beneath her protective humility. Hers was not the courage for open revolt. Instead, she followed the sort of tortuous indirect course which the cowed and defeated resort to when they become desperate. It seemed clear to Arbella that her only chance of escape from Hardwick and the old woman lay through marriage—but marriage to whom? It happened that the summer of 1602 had brought mounting speculation as to who would succeed the failing Queen Elizabeth. One of the wilder stories going around was that a grandson of the Earl of Hertford was to be married to Arbella and the succession settled upon him through this coalescence of claims. Something of this tale probably reached Arbella at Hardwick. Later, she declared that the Earl of Hertford had made overtures to a Shrewsbury servant through a lawyer. This is hard to believe for old Hertford, who had already suffered much because of his unhappy mingling with the royal blood, went in fear and trembling of Elizabeth and would hardly have dared to embark on any course bearing so closely upon the royal succession. However, with the folly of desperation, Arbella at Christmas 1602 sent a servant to the old Earl intimating that he would do well to negotiate for a marriage between herself and one of his family.

She could not have taken a more foolish step. Hertford at once locked up her messenger and tremulously informed the Privy Council of Arbella's overture. His one concern was to clear himself and his house of any complicity in a matter so likely to enrage the Queen. Actually Elizabeth (now within three months of her death) behaved with surprising restraint. She could not help but be worried by this ominous conjunction of possible claimants to her throne, for behind it might lie political machinations which would bring disastrous consequences. She contented herself, however, with letting Cecil send Sir Henry Brounker to Hardwick to investigate the whole matter.

Finding herself with her fantastic little scheme suddenly out in the open and the two old women, her grandmother and the Queen, angry with her, Arbella had a nervous breakdown. Sir Henry, when he arrived at Hardwick Hall, found her far from lucid and reported as much to Cecil. After he left, Arbella began indulging in fantasies about a secret lover and insisted that she had great secrets to divulge, but only to the Queen. On March 17th, one of Arbella's uncles and a Roman Catholic friend raised a troop of forty men and made an ineffectual attempt to force the Countess to release Arbella. Nothing came of their attempt except some final worries for the dying Queen.

After Elizabeth's death, everything cleared up very quickly. The Privy Council, with delayed common sense, removed Arbella from her irksome grandmother into the care of the old Earl of Kent whose nephew had recently married one of her cousins. In the Earl's house at Wrest, Arbella speedily recovered her mental balance and lost no time in seeking an interview with King James.

This crucial interview with the new king seems to have gone well. James was probably relieved to find his cousin so shy and diffident a young lady. Certainly he need no longer fear her as a competitor for the English throne. Moreover, there were ties of family. Writing from Scotland a year earlier, he had declared that '. . . nature enforces me to love her as the creature living nearest kin to me, next to my own children'.[1] The fears which he had earlier that she might turn Catholic were now removed. Despite the Catholicism of some of her Shrewsbury relatives, she was herself unshakably Protestant, something of a Puritan indeed, in her religion. King James's goodwill towards his newly met cousin was shown by the alacrity with which he presented her to Queen Anne when the latter arrived at Windsor from Scotland.

Had there been any doubt about Arbella's place in the new court it was speedily resolved by Anne. The Queen was of Arbella's own age, and she took her up with enthusiasm. The royal children, too, were delighted with her. With James's agreement his cousin was made one of the family. The formerly lonely prisoner at Hardwick was now to be a person of consequence in the royal court.

The next seven years were the happiest of Arbella's life. She had her own apartment and small establishment at Whitehall. The King, in September 1603, quadrupled the £200 a year which Elizabeth had allowed her, and a year later he increased this to an even £1,000.[2] When James and Anne made their delayed coronation procession through London, Arbella's status, in the absence of the seven-year-old Princess Elizabeth, as second lady of the court was recognized by a position immediately after the Queen and ahead of the countesses. The next year Arbella was one of the godmothers of Princess Mary, the first royal child to be born in England in seventy years. As the older royal children advanced in years they practised their penmanship in little letters of courtesy to Arbella. She replied to each in letters whose handwriting was so exquisite that it might have been taken from one of the engraved manuals of calligraphy of the time.

It is not surprising that various foreign princes began to think that they might make a useful alliance by marrying a kinswoman who so manifestly enjoyed the esteem of the English king. Once more report linked various names romantically with Arbella's. For a time it was thought she would marry Queen Anne's brother, the Duke Ulric, who paid a good deal of attention to her during an extended visit to England. Others reported to be seeking Arbella's hand were the Prince of Anhalt, the Count Maurice, and the King of Poland. In the end nothing came of any of these courtings, real or rumoured. To some offers, Arbella was herself averse. To others the King was opposed, his old sense of insecurity making him feel that it was better to keep one so close to the succession at his own court rather than let her marry a foreign prince who might one day advance claims to the English throne on behalf of her or their children, to the embarrassment of James or his heirs.

Not everything at the English court was pure enjoyment for Arbella. Queen Anne's demands for her company were not always pleasing. At times she had to accompany the King and Queen to the dank confined quarters at the royal hunting-lodges. Her own tastes were literary and she resented being called from her books to take part in the children's games 'Rise, pig, and go' and 'One penny, follow me', which were among the recreations of Anne and her ladies. Dutifully, however, Arbella allowed herself to be 'persuaded by the princely example I saw to play the child again'.[3]

A greater trial to Arbella was her difficulty with finances. Her total annual income was probably in excess of £2,000 a year, but this proved insufficient to maintain her, caught as she was in the extravagances of the Jacobean court. Court weddings, court christenings, court festivals, called for expensive gifts. She had a weakness for fine clothes, and sought to be as resplendent as any in jewels and tissue of gold and silver at the court masques. In any event, she was expected to maintain a style befitting the King's kinswoman. For all this her income proved insufficient. Again and again she had to appeal to the King for help. In 1609, seeking financial independence, she asked him for a 21-year monopoly of the sale of wine and whiskey in Ireland. Cecil was her friend, and by the end of the year it appeared that with his good offices this highly lucrative grant would be passed to her. Then unexpectedly she put before Cecil a whole set of new proposals about her tangled finances. She asked first that the King, instead of giving her the Irish monopoly out of which to pay her debts, pay these debts directly himself; secondly, that her annual allowance be increased to a figure that would permit her to live 'in such honour and countenance hereafter as may stand with His Majesty's honour and my own comfort';[4] and finally that in lieu of her present diet at court she be granted an additional £1,000 annually. This last item suggests a reason behind these proposals—that Arbella was intending to withdraw from the gaudy extravagance of court life. Probably she wanted to marry, and find in retired domestic life the peace and quiet which by now she knew would never be found in the Court.

At this juncture Arbella was suddenly arrested by Viscount Fenton, the Captain of the Guard, and brought before the King and Privy Council for questioning. Apparently a report had been received that Arbella was intending to cross beyond the seas and there to marry. The Council now held a critical series of meetings at which the lady's causes for discontent, financial and otherwise, were thoroughly threshed out. Arbella pleased the King by voluntarily promising never to make a marriage abroad without his consent. James, for his part, seems to have assured her that she could marry any man who was a loyal subject to himself. If he had stopped to think and had tempered his impulsive good nature towards his gentle cousin, the King would undoubtedly have added a proviso. One match would have to be ruled out on political grounds if Arbella ever sought an

English husband. Marriage with a possible heir of the Earl of Hertford would need to be precluded, for the children of such a match would have a twofold claim to the English succession, one which might some day be advanced against King James's own line. What James did not for a moment suspect was that Arbella had already fallen in love with William Seymour, grandson of the Earl of Hertford, and was resolved to marry him.

The early days of 1610 saw James blissfully unaware of Arbella's love and in fine good humour towards her. She was released from her arrest. To help her with her finances, James gave her a valuable New Year's gift of plate. He followed this up with a special grant of 1,000 marks to assist her with her debts, and he increased her pension.

On February 2nd young William Seymour (he was twenty-three, and Arbella now thirty-five) visited the lady in her chambers and proposed marriage. Despite their disparity in age, much could be said for their match apart from its political aspects. In the years which lay ahead, after he had succeeded to the Hertford title, Seymour was to prove himself a valiant and noble friend to Charles I amid the disaster of the Civil War. He was at this time a young man of good breeding, gentle manners, and literary inclinations, which made him a singularly attractive husband for Arbella who was herself very much a bluestocking. Other meetings between Seymour and Arbella followed. Apparently no great effort was made to keep them secret. After all, the King had said that his cousin could marry any loyal subject, and was not William Seymour loyal and a subject? The King however was not prepared to sanction such a match, even though through oversight he had neglected to forbid it. Learning of the love in his cousin's bosom, he lost no time in ordering the imprisonment of both her and her young man.

On February 20th William Seymour wrote a not undignified letter of submission to the Privy Council. It read in part:

> I doe therefore humblie confesse that when I conceaived that noble Ladie might with his Majesties good favor and without offence make her choise of any subject within this kingdome, which conceipte was begotten in mee upon a generall report after her Ladyships last beinge called before your Lordships that it might bee my selfe beinge but a younger brother, and sensible of myne owne goode, unknowne to the worlde, of meane estate, not borne to challenge any thinge by my birthright and therefore my fortunes to be raysed by myne owne endevor, and shee a Lady of great honor and vertue and as I thought of great means: I did playnlie and honestly endevor lawfully to gayne her in marriage, which is gods ordinance common to all, assuringe my selfe if I coulde effect the same with his Majesties most gratious favor and likinge (without which I resolved never to proceede) that thence woolde growe the first beginninge of all my happines, and therfore I bowldlie intruded my selfe into her Ladyships chamber in the Court on Candelmas day last, at what time I imparted my desire unto her,

which was entertayned, but with this caution on eyther parte, that bothe of us resolved not to proceede to any finale conclusion without his Majesties most gracious favor and likinge first obteyned. . . .[5]

Placated by this apparently complete submission to his wishes, James was forgiving. After all, he had told Arbella she could marry any of his subjects, and the whole troublesome affair did appear to be the consequence of his own carelessness. Accordingly, he ordered that Arbella and Seymour be given their freedom. Relieved at seeing Arbella still obedient, he continued his favour towards her. The monopoly of Irish wines and whiskey was passed to her and two associates, with considerable profit to herself.

Young William Seymour proceeded as gracefully as possible to ask Arbella to release him from his commitments. Arbella, however, would not relinquish love. Just before midnight on June 21st, William Seymour slipped into her chambers at Queen Anne's palace at Greenwich and there, after sitting up most of the night with the lady, he was married to her, without licence, in the presence of a small group of friends and servants by a clergyman named Blagew, a son of the Dean of Rochester.

Seventeen days later the secret marriage was known to everybody, and bride and groom were under arrest—Seymour in the Tower and Arbella in the custody of Sir Thomas Parry at his house in Lambeth. There was a good deal of sympathy for the lovers in the Court, and the King's severity towards them was not expected to continue long. Weeks and months passed, however, with no sign of royal forgiveness. Not that Arbella or her husband suffered greatly. Arbella's quiet dignity and charm soon won Sir Thomas for a friend. She had her own servants with her, and found ways of corresponding secretly with her husband. As for Seymour in the Tower, he was comfortable in an apartment which he furnished rather expensively. With the King's consent his grandfather, Hertford, paid him an allowance of £50 a quarter. It is not impossible that, with some discreet greasing of palms, Seymour was able to slip away from the Tower for an occasional secret meeting with Arbella.

The lady meanwhile was busy getting friends to intercede for her with the King. The Queen herself was moved to speak on Arbella's behalf, but King James's only response was to mutter that the lady had eaten of the forbidden tree. It is easy to blame James for his severity, especially in view of the tragedy to which it would lead, but much can be said to defend the King's attitude. Contested successions were notorious causes of civil war, and it did seem a matter of simple prudence to keep Arbella and the Hertford line from uniting. Hitherto James had consistently treated Arbella with kindness. Instead of following Elizabeth's example of banishing her to Derbyshire, he had treated her as one of his own family and made her a principal person in his court. When he had learned of her money troubles he had assisted her. And he had been prepared to let her marry any man in England outside of the Hertford line. On the other hand, she and Seymour had deliberately deceived him and broken their word by marrying when they had promised not to. James had every reason for feeling that Arbella had shown herself both ungrateful and unreliable. Her clinging to Seymour when she had all the rest of England to choose from must have seemed to James the blindest pigheadedness.

If Arbella felt sorry for herself in the indulgent care of Sir Thomas Parry, she was shortly to look back on her time in his house as halcyon days. James became aware of the laxity with which she and Seymour were guarded and, at the beginning of 1611, he arranged for her transfer to the keeping of the Bishop of Durham. With Arbella in Durham and Seymour in London there should be no chance of surreptitious encounters and the possible begetting of a child. Arbella's reaction to the King's decision was piteous to behold. There were tears, hysteria, and fainting fits. Frantically she wrote to the Lord Chief Justice of England and the Lord Chief Justice of Common Pleas asking for a writ of habeas corpus. On strictly legal grounds she was certainly entitled to one. James had not a shadow of legal right to keep her a prisoner. It was, however, pathetically naïve of poor Arbella to think that the judges would bring upon themselves the fury of the King by interfering with his disciplining of a member of the royal family. No writ of release came to Arbella, only a most unhappy bishop, who on March 16th started on the journey northward with her. By the time he had travelled the few miles to Highgate he was only too glad to call a halt at the house of Sir William Bond. The lady had fainted three times on the way, and gave every sign of imminent collapse. On March 21st actual force had to be used to get her to Barnet, where Arbella wrote a desperate letter to the Privy Council imploring time for the recovery of her health. A month's delay was granted and, returned to Highgate, she settled in a house close to Hampstead Heath. Attended by her devoted Dr. Mountford and an ever loyal serving-woman Mrs. Bradshaw, Arbella kept to her bed. James thought she was shamming and said as much, but when he sent Dr. Hammond, a royal physician, to examine her, Hammond agreed with Mountford that the lady's health would not permit the arduous journey north. The month's grace was extended. Finally, the King and Council wearied of the delay. June 5th was peremptorily fixed as the day by which Arbella must resume the journey to her northern banishment.

It was at this point that poor Arbella, with the help of various devoted friends and servants, made her last desperate bid for freedom and happiness. On June 3rd she asked her attendant, Mistress Adam, to secure for her male apparel, alleging that she needed it to slip away for a final meeting with her Seymour. Between three and four o'clock that afternoon, 'disguising her selfe by drawing a pair of great French-fashioned Hose over her Petticotes, putting on a Man's Doublet, a man-lyke Perruque with long Locks over her Hair, a blacke Hat, black Cloake, russet Bootes with red Tops, and a Rapier by her Syde',[6] Arbella assisted by her gentleman Markham walked the mile or so to an inn where Hugh Crompton, her trusted steward, was waiting with horses. The short walk so exhausted her that she had hardly the strength to mount. She managed, however, to get into the saddle and, partly reviving with the ride, reached the Thames at Blackwall about six o'clock. Here she found Mistress Bradshaw and another servant waiting for her with her own baggage and Seymour's. Small boats were in readiness to row them down the river. All that was missing was Seymour. At the anguished implorings of Arbella, the party postponed its setting out for two more hours. Finally at eight o'clock, just when Seymour was sauntering out of the Tower disguised as a carter, Arbella's party started down the river. What absurd misunderstanding about the time made Seymour so late we shall never know. In any event, when Seymour and his friend Edward Rodney did reach Blackwall, they found to their consternation that Arbella and her servants had left about an hour before. Hiring a waterman, Seymour and Rodney hurried down the Thames after them.

It was four o'clock in the morning of June 4th when Arbella's party reached Leigh at the mouth of the Thames, where they expected to find a French ship waiting to take her and Seymour to France. Arbella's arrival would have been earlier had it not been for trouble with her boatmen. These disliked having to take their boats down the Thames by night, and had to be placated with drinks ashore at Gravesend. The delay, however, was not sufficient for Seymour to overtake her. Arrived at Leigh, she and her party at first could find no sign of the French ship. Hailing a brig commanded by one John Bright, they tried to hire him to take them to Calais. Bright refused, but during subsequent conversation it came out that he had seen a strange ship some two miles further out. Arbella's party rowed to the stranger and to their delight found it flying the agreed signal flag. Once aboard, Arbella frantically implored the captain, Corvé, to await her husband. He and Crompton ignored her commands. Pursuit was to be expected, and the wind was such that their journey to Calais would not be a swift one. They insisted upon hoisting sail. When Seymour arrived a little later, he found that his wife had already left. Fortunately he managed to hire a collier for £40 to take him to Calais.

The escape of the two prisoners was not discovered until some time after their flight. Mistress Adam, believing Arbella's fiction, had assured her that no one would be permitted to enter her chamber until she returned. In the Tower, Seymour's man, under the impression that his master similarly was away on a visit to Arbella, was telling everybody that Seymour was confined to his chamber with a raging toothache and could see nobody. With their flight thus masked, it is hard to say how long the escape of the prisoners might have gone unknown had it not been for Seymour's younger brother Francis. Those plotting the escape had decided that though Francis was undoubtedly attached to his brother it would be well, if only for his own sake, that he should know nothing about it. Rodney, who shared quarters with young Francis, left a letter to be delivered to him on the morning of June 4th, when they would all presumably be safely embarked for France. In his letter he excused his own sudden departure and suggested, in the most general way, that Seymour had made good his escape. Upon receiving this letter, Francis headed at once for the Tower and insisted upon being admitted to his brother's empty room. His hubbub made known the flight of Seymour. Sir William Wade, the Lieutenant of the Tower, forthwith took Francis to Greenwich where the flight of the lovers was made known to an appalled King and his Privy Council. It was idle for Arbella's friends to try to persuade James that he was well rid of the pair. The flight of the lady represented a political danger of the first magnitude. Since the execution of Mary Queen of Scots there had been no real Catholic claimant to the throne about whom religious malcontents at home or exiles abroad might rally. If Arbella were to change her religion, she could provide the English Catholics with just the counter-claimant which hitherto they had lacked. James was torn between fury and fear. Which of his enemies on the Continent might not harbour Arbella, persuade her to change her religion and to claim his crown? It was useless to tell him that such fears were groundless. The King knew better. Ships of the Royal Navy were ordered in pursuit.

Half-way across the Straits of Dover, His Majesty's Ship *Adventure* overtook the French vessel bearing Arbella to Calais. After thirteen shots had been fired, the French captain Corvé struck his flag. Arbella, surrendering herself to Griffin Cockett, the captain of the *Adventure*, declared that her husband's escape would entirely console her for her own misfortune. Seymour was, in fact, about this time landing at Ostend.

Back in England and lodged in the Tower of London, Arbella found her situation grim indeed. Earlier, when she had been committed to the custody of the Bishop of Durham, that prelate had confided, 'My own poor opinion is that if she wrong not herself, God in time will move his Majesty's heart to have compassion upon her.'[7] But Arbella had wronged herself and now could hardly hope for royal mercy. Nevertheless she did what she could, appealing vainly by letter to all whom she thought might help her with the King.

Early in 1613 James's only surviving daughter, Princess Elizabeth, was married to Frederick, the Elector Palatine of the Rhine. Arbella seems to have persuaded herself that she would be released to attend the wedding. Indulging her old extravagance in costume, she ordered four dresses, one costing £1,500, but the wedding came and passed, with Arbella still in prison even though the King's new son-in-law petitioned directly on her behalf. At this, Arbella gave way to despair. Gradually she drifted into mental and physical decline. After weeks of final agonizing suffering, she died in the Tower on September 25, 1615.

The royal physicians examined poor Arbella's emaciated corpse to set to rest the wild rumours that had arisen as to how she had met her death. Then the remains were handed over to her people for burial. Perhaps as a sign of ultimate forgiveness by James, she was given burial in Westminster Abbey, in the same vault as the King's mother and his son. For her final epitaph one may well quote the kindly praises of Dr. Goodman, Bishop of Rochester:

> She was very virtuous and a good-natured lady, and of great intellectuals harmless, and gave no offense.[8]

Even while Arbella was still alive in the Tower, there had been an understanding between the absent Seymour and the Privy Council that as long as he lived quietly in Paris on the pension allowed him by his grandfather he need have nothing to fear. After his wife's death, he waited a decent interval of a few months before writing a letter of profuse apology and submission to the King. In reply he was informed that he could return to England without fear of punishment. In February 1616 William Seymour was back in England. Subsequently he was received at court. In November he was knighted. The next year he remarried (later he named one of his daughters Arbella). Upon the death of his elder brother he became Lord Beauchamp and finally, in 1621, he succeeded his grandfather as Earl of Hertford. James seems to have forgiven him completely his escapade with Arbella. In the next reign he was to prove a loyal supporter of Charles I. After the Restoration, Charles II rewarded him with the Dukedom of Somerset, the dignity lost by his great-grandfather in 1552.

Less happy than Seymour was Arbella's aunt, Mary Talbot, Countess of Shrewsbury, a daughter of the formidable Old Bess, now dead. The double escape had of course required outside help and undoubtedly the Countess had been a principal abettor. Under the guise of buying various pieces of embroidery from Arbella and lending her money to pay her debts before leaving for Durham, the Countess had supplied her niece with much of the money she had with her when overtaken by the *Adventure*. The Countess's ardent Catholicism made the government suspect that she had had the worst of motives in trying to get Arbella to France. Summoned before the Court of Star Chamber, the Countess was sentenced to a fine of £20,000 and imprisonment during the royal pleasure. In 1616 she was allowed temporary freedom to nurse her husband during his final sickness, but six years later she was still in the Tower begging for release, even while Seymour basked in the glory of his earldom and the King's favour. James evidently had decided to put all the blame on the women.

CHAPTER XII

Tears for Prince Henry

IN 1610 King James decided that the time had come for his elder son, Henry, to be created Prince of Wales. His decision was not unattended by problems, for there had not been a Prince of Wales since the accession of Edward VI in 1547 and nobody around the Court was at all sure what ceremonies were involved or how they should be conducted. The archives were searched, however, and the investiture of Prince Arthur, elder son of Henry VII, was found to supply a suitable model. The notorious parsimony of Henry VII was taken as a guarantee that his way of doing the thing would be economical and save King James needless expense.

Aged sixteen, Henry was a gallant and handsome prince. Tall by Jacobean standards (five feet eight inches when he reached his full height), he was broad-shouldered and slim-waisted. Dark auburn hair set off his rather long face, generally tanned from his outdoor life. A habitual sobriety and dignity of manner set him off from other men. He stood out when on May 30th, attended by 'divers young Lords and Gentlemen of speciall marke', he arrived at Richmond to prepare for the morrow's journey down the Thames for his investiture at Whitehall.

Rising early on May 31st, Prince Henry and his company began their leisurely progress down the river. At Barn-Elms the water was so low that they landed on the banks and lunched while waiting for the rising tide. About four o'clock in the afternoon they arrived at Chelsea. Here, since nine o'clock in the morning, the Lord Mayor of London, the aldermen and the livery companies, had been waiting in a fleet of richly decorated barges to greet the Prince with drum, trumpet and fife. Also awaiting him were two 'artificial sea-monsters', a whale and a dolphin, provided at the expense of the City. From the whale's back Corinea, Queen of Cornwall (personated by John Rice, a lad who played female parts for Shakespeare's company the King's Men), greeted Henry as Duke of Cornwall. Then, escorted by whale, dolphin, and all the civic barges, the young prince journeyed on to Whitehall. Here, from the dolphin's back, Richard Burbage disguised as Amphion (for some reason identified as the Genius of Wales) made a speech of farewell. The water-progress, chosen as less expensive than a state procession through the streets of London, was ended.

At Whitehall Stairs Prince Henry was received with the fantastically elaborate protocol reserved for high state occasions. While cannon thundered salutes from the Lambeth shore, the young prince was greeted at the watergate by the Knight Marshal and the Sergeant Porter. These conducted him to the Great Hall where he was received by Lord Knollys, Treasurer of the Household, and Lord Wotton, the Comptroller. The latter conducted Henry into the Guard Chamber where Viscount Fenton, Captain of the Guard, saluted him and brought him finally into the Presence Chamber. From here the Lord Chamberlain conducted him into the Privy Chamber where his royal parents awaited him.

Just as when Shakespeare's Duncan invested Malcolm with the title of Prince of Cumberland, so when James advanced Henry to the dignity of Prince of Wales it was felt:

> . . . honour must
> Not, unaccompanied, invest him only,
> But signs of nobleness, like stars, shall shine
> On all deservers.

As accompaniment to Henry's investiture as Prince of Wales, twenty-five young men of noble birth were made Knights of the Bath.

Two days were required for the ceremonies of the Order of the Bath. On June 2nd, the candidates came in procession from Durham House to Whitehall, where they attended divine service in the Chapel Royal and dined in the Guard Chamber. After supper they withdrew to an adjacent chamber for the ceremonial bath, each having his own tub lined inside and out with white cloth and canopied with red. They slept that night on pallets in the Guard Chamber. The next day, attired in 'heremeticall weedes' (grey gowns and hoods, with russet girdles from which their handkerchiefs hung down), the initiates went once more to the Chapel Royal. Here they swore their oaths before the altar, then retired to change into their robes of crimson taffeta and white sarsenet before returning to Durham House. The climax of the whole ceremony came next with the twenty-five riding in procession back to Whitehall, trumpeters sounding before them, until they came into the King's presence and were formally knighted. Finally there was one last service in the Chapel Royal with each of the new Knights of the Bath pledging his sword at the altar. As they left the chapel precincts, they were each confronted by the King's Master Cook with white apron and gilded chopping knife who, according to custom, 'challenged' their golden spurs. When they each had redeemed their spurs with payment of a noble (six shillings eight pence) they departed with the Master Cook's admonition ringing in their ears:

> Sir Knight, looke that you bee true and loyall to the King my master: or else I must hew these Spurres from your heeles.[1]

The next day, June 4th, was that set aside for the creation of the new Prince of Wales in the Parliament House at Westminster. After the lords had assembled and the King was on his throne, the Prince's procession, which had formed up in Westminster Hall, entered with due state. At its head walked the heralds followed by the brand new Knights of the Bath. Behind them came Garter King at Arms bearing the Prince's letters patent, the Earl of Sussex with the purple robes, the Earl of Huntingdon with the train, the Earl of Cumberland with the sword, the Earl of Rutland with the ring, the Earl of Derby with the rod, and the Earl of Shrewsbury with the cap and gown. Last of all came the young prince flanked by the Earls of Nottingham and Northampton. After three deep bows before his father, Henry knelt while the Earl of Salisbury, Lord Treasurer Cecil, read his letters patent. As the words of investiture were spoken, King James put on his son the robe of office, girded him with his sword, handed him his rod and ring, and set the cap and coronet upon his head. Finally, taking him by the hands, he kissed him. Then the Earls of Worcester and Suffolk led the new Prince of Wales to his place on the King's left hand. The ceremony thus concluded, the whole assembly arose and, still in their parliament robes, went to Westminster Stairs where the royal barge waited to take the King and Prince back to Whitehall.

The most punctilious ceremony was observed that evening when the Prince dined in state with the new Knights of the Bath and the lords who had attended his creation. No one was allowed to sit within half a table-length of the Prince. The Earl of Pembroke was Henry's sewer, the Earl of Southampton his carver, and the Earl of Montgomery his cup-bearer. While the young man enjoyed his great moment in the Hall, King James had his own supper served him privately in the Privy Chamber.

The next few days were given over to merry-making and sport. On the evening of June 5th there was a masque, Samuel Daniel's *Tethys' Festival*, in honour of the new Prince of Wales. Henry's ten-year-old brother, Charles, Duke of York, appeared in the antimasque, attended by 'two great Sea Slaves' and 'twelve little Ladies, all of them the daughters of earls or barons'. The little girls danced to the admiration of all and were packed off to bed, being replaced in the masque proper by more mature ladies of the court who kept up the dancing until half an hour before dawn.

June 6th brought entertainments calculated to delight a young prince whose taste for arms and martial exercise was already becoming widely known. In the afternoon there was tilting. The noble participants in Jacobean tournaments were as concerned to display their wealth and luxury as their prowess in arms. History, instead of immortalizing the tilter who most distinguished himself that day with his spear, informs us that the Earl of Pembroke excited particular admiration with his two caparisons of peach-coloured velvet embroidered all over with fair orient pearl. That evening there was a mock sea-battle between two merchant ships and a Turkish pirate on the Thames opposite Whitehall, with the storming of a Turkish castle built on the Lambeth shore. After the pirate ship had been captured and the castle blown up, the evening was concluded with a wonderful display of fireworks.

Invested as Prince of Wales, Henry found much uncertainty surrounding the powers and prerogatives that went with his new title. What form of signature should he use ? If he and his mother were both signing a document, who should sign first ? What procedures should he follow in the government of his principality ? Henry applied to the great antiquary, Sir Robert Cotton, for answers to these questions.

The people of Great Britain were justly proud of their new Prince of Wales. Serious and courageous, candid and high-minded, loyal to his friends and devoted to honour, Prince Henry seemed to epitomize the princely ideal. He was indeed the 'expectancy and rose of the fair state', a seeming nonpareil among princes. His education for kingship had been carefully planned by his father who, in the years before he came into his English kingdom, had penned for his guidance the famous *Basilikon Doron* laying down precepts and principles to guide his son when he came to reign. Nor did King James's concern with the Prince's education slacken after the royal family's remove to England. Setting up a household for Henry in the royal country house of Oatlands, James declared, 'the Princes house shold rather imitate a Colledg then a Court'.[2] Here, and at the Prince's other house of St. James's, the scholarly Sir Thomas Chaloner had presided as 'governor' over the Prince's establishment with Adam Newton, Henry's tutor in Scotland, still superintending his studies. Numerous reports had kept King James informed of his heir's progress in learning. On his ninth birthday, Henry himself wrote to his father that he had been reading Terence's *Hecyra*, Phaedrus's *Fables*, and the *Select Epistles* of Cicero. Every New Year he submitted to him a Latin composition of his own inditing. That which he delivered at the beginning of 1609 must have been particularly acceptable to King James, for its subject was that learning is more needful to kings and princes than to men of lesser station.

Others besides his father encouraged the young prince with his studies. Bancroft, the Archbishop of Canterbury, began collecting subscriptions for the purchase of a library for the Prince. Perhaps in consequence of his endeavours, the eccentric old Lord Lumley, when he died in 1609, left his books to Henry. Rich in manuscripts which had come from monasteries suppressed in the previous century and in books once owned by Archbishop Cranmer, the Lumley Library was the finest in private hands in England at this time.

It was in this same year of 1609 that Prince Henry, impressed by the learned Thomas Lydiat's *Emendatio Temporum*, 'took the author into his family to read to him and appointed him Chronographer and Cosmographer'.[3] His action was typical. Prince Henry liked to surround himself with men of parts. A clergyman who preached to the Prince's admiration, or a writer who won his regard, was likely to find himself brought into the Prince's circle. Henry's taste was, of course, the unformed taste of a boy. He extended his patronage indiscriminately to both George Chapman, the translator of Homer, and the pedestrian Joshua Sylvester. His interests in fact ranged far. He began to collect pictures, coins, medals. Oddly enough, in a family with a strong inclination for the theatre, Prince Henry had no great taste for the drama, even though the nominal patron of a company of players.

The qualities which most endeared the young Prince of Wales to the nation were those which he did not share with his father. Whereas James was a mass of neurotic fears, Prince Henry even as a child exhibited courage and fortitude. James was above all a man of peace; *Rex Pacificus* was the title he cherished. His son, on the contrary, early evinced a taste for martial exercise and military glory. We are assured that even when he was a little boy he showed:

> a *Noble and Heroick Spirit*, no musick being so pleasant in his eares, as the sounding of the Trumpet, the beating of the Drumme, the roaring of the Canon, no sight so acceptable as that of Pieces, Pistols, or any sort of Armour. . . .[4]

As he grew older, Henry delighted to have military men about him and to discourse with them of 'Wars, Battailes, Furniture, Armes by Sea and Land, Disciplines, Orders, Marches, Alarmes, Watches, Stratagems, Ambuscadoes, Approaches, Scalings, Fortifications, Incampings.' On a long table he ranged lead soldiers in military formations and practised tactics and manœuvres. He practised making long marches to fit himself for the wars. Word passed among the captains and old soldiers that here was a prince of the old heroic breed, another Black Prince or Henry V.

The young prince's enthusiasm for the arts of war caused, indeed, one curious incident. This was in 1607 when the Prince de Joinville returned to France after being magnificently entertained in England. Prince Henry sent back in his company a military engineer who was one of his own servants. This man the French found busy investigating the fortifications of Calais. They were not a little perturbed by the discovery, but finally put it down to extreme naïvety on the part of the young prince.

A favourite pastime of the Jacobean court was the martial exercise

F

known as 'Barriers'. In this the opponents, not horsed as in the tilt but on foot, thrust at each other with pikes from opposite sides of a waist-high barrier. Prince Henry's first public participation in this sport was taken to mark the opening of his career in manly arms. Accordingly, 'Prince Henry's Barriers' held at Whitehall on January 6, 1610, became a great court occasion, celebrated with pomp and ceremony and invested with an aura of chivalry befitting a prince ardent for military glory.

The preliminaries came at Christmastide 1609. From an old romantic tale Henry borrowed for himself the name of Meliades. Then on December 29th, when King, Queen and court were assembled in the Presence Chamber at Whitehall, the Prince's followers entered in strange attire with trumpets and drums and loudly cried that Meliades, their young master, 'boyling with an earnest desire to trie the Valour of his young yeares in foraigne Countreyes', had sent them to visit all lands, but that they had found nowhere such courage as here in 'the Fortunate Isle of Great Britain'. For this reason, they said, they had now come to this Court to issue the challenge of Meliades, who longed to lay at the feet of King James 'the first fruits of his Chivalrie'.[5]

The day appointed for young Meliades came, but before the combatants entered the lists marked off for them within the Banqueting-House, there was a little allegorical play from the pen of Ben Jonson. First appeared the Lady of the Lake, who deplored the decay of Chivalry. Then, as the spirit of King Arthur looked down from a star and Merlin arose from his tomb, she hailed the young Meliades, Lord of the Isles, as 'glory of knights, and hope of all the earth'.[6] At Meliades' name, Chivalry awakened from the cave where she had long slept and called for the knights to take the field. With this the fighting began. Aiding the Prince as challenger were the Duke of Lennox, the Earls of Arundel and Southampton, Lord Hay, Sir Thomas Somerset and Sir Richard Preston. After the seven challengers had encountered the first seven defendants, with pike and then with sword, the barriers were raised for an interval of rest before the challengers met the next seven to come against them. In this manner the contest continued until the challengers had been matched with fifty-six defendants. The young prince, still more than a month short of his sixteenth birthday, conducted himself to the admiration of all. The next day he banqueted the combatants at St. James's and gave rich prizes to the 'best deservers defendants', these being the Earl of Montgomery, Master Thomas Darcy and Sir Robert Gordon. It was five months later that Henry, having thus proved himself in arms, received the dignity of Prince of Wales.

Part of the young prince's martial side was his interest in the Royal Navy. This began early. He was only ten years old when the Lord Admiral Nottingham instructed the great shipwright Phineas Pett to build for him a little pinnace, twenty-five feet along the keel. Once completed, she was anchored in the Thames opposite Whitehall from where Prince Henry sailed her on her maiden voyage down the river to Paul's Wharf. Here, with a great bowl of wine, he christened her *Disdain*. Afterwards, in the cabin of the little craft, Prince Henry had Pett sworn into his personal service. Pett found the Prince a good patron in the years that followed, ardent and eager in his love for the navy and ready to stand by him in his battles for the rebuilding of the fleet. Many times Henry journeyed to Woolwich or Chatham to inspect the fleet. In September 1610 Prince Henry, accommodating himself to the tides, came down to Woolwich in the midst of a gale at two o'clock in the morning to launch Pett's new warship the *Prince Royal*. He was down again in September to inspect the ship after her rigging had been completed. The following May he went from ship to ship making notes of the state of every vessel in the fleet. On one of these tours of inspection he delighted his hearers by declaring that, should it ever please the King his father to end his peace with Spain, he would personally lead a fleet against the Spaniards in the West Indies.

Henry differed from his father in more than his interest in arms and war. James was often devious and indirect. The Prince was open and frank. James enjoyed the 'court holy water' of extravagant praise and adulation, the son despised flatterers. When a nobleman wrote a letter to him concluding 'Yours before all the world', young Henry, offended by the fulsome lip-service from one whom he was convinced had 'untruly and unfaithfully dealt with him', ordered Sir Charles Cornwallis in drafting his reply not to use any of the customary closing words of formal regard, declaring, 'that his hand should never affirm what his heart thought not'.[7]

Some historians have been inclined to label Prince Henry as a self-righteous young prig, but it is unfair to stigmatize thus his fierce, uncompromising, youthful idealism. Rather he deserves the admiration which his contemporaries gave him for making his house a centre of sobriety and good manners in contrast to the lax, loose court of his father. The differences here were startling. One example may suffice: whereas King James was notorious for his profanity, Prince Henry not only did not swear himself, but had boxes kept in which all who swore in his presence were required to pay fines, the money going to the poor. As far as adventures with women were concerned, scandal had it that Lady Frances Howard had initiated the Prince into that world, only to be dropped contemptuously when the Prince learned of her connection with Somerset. No real evidence supports this story, though the Prince was certainly susceptible to women. On the other hand, there can be no doubt of his general sobriety and piety. Three times a day he withdrew for private devotions, and every member of his household was required to attend prayers daily.

Creation as Prince of Wales meant the beginning of a new era for the young man. He was now regarded as of age. Earlier he had had several hundred servants and attendants assigned to his service. Now he was given a remodelled and enlarged household, organized like that of the King his father, and the lesser one of the Queen his mother. He had his own Chamberlain(Sir Thomas Chaloner), Treasurer (Sir Charles Cornwallis), Comptroller (Sir John Holles), Cofferer (Sir David Foulis), Groom of the Stole (Sir David Murray), Chancellor (Sir Edward Phelips), Secretary (Adam Newton), Receiver-General (Sir George More) and Surveyor-General (Sir William Fleetwood), as well as all the requisite lesser officers and servants. This establishment included almost five hundred persons, though many of these gave only part-time attendance. To finance the Prince's court various sources of revenue were made over to him, some by right as belonging to the Prince of Wales and Duke of Cornwall, others through the generosity of the King. From manors, lands and tenements in the Duchy of Cornwall came an estimated £1,713; from the Cornish coinage and customs £2,000; from the pre-emption of Cornish tin £8,000; from the Principality of Wales £11,713; from the lands in the earldom of Chester £282. These and lesser sources gave Prince Henry an assigned income, as of May 9, 1610, of about £25,000 per annum, or £200,000 in modern values.[8] Actually, His Highness's total income ran far beyond this, amounting several years later to £80,746.[9] In his management of his money, the Prince was again in marked contrast to his father. While the King got mired deeper and deeper in debt, the young Prince of Wales not only kept within his means, but achieved a surplus of receipts over expenditures.

It might have been better if Prince Henry had not handled his affairs so very well, for his success made him arrogantly confident of his own virtues and abilities. Over-eager to participate in the government of the realm, he began to infringe upon his father's prerogatives. With more disquiet than amusement, the King's ministers learned that the sixteen-year-old Prince of Wales was encouraging subordinates in various royal offices to report to him upon defects in their administration. Perhaps because of what he learned by these enquiries, the Prince became openly critical of various of his father's officers.

The Prince's temper is seen in an imbroglio in which he became involved with Sir Thomas Edmondes, King James's ambassador to France. Edmondes' despatches were addressed, as a matter of course, to Cecil who had retained with his Treasurership the post of Principal Secretary. Apparently Cecil passed various of these along to the Prince of Wales, probably feeling it part of his duty to contribute thus to the education of the heir in matters of international politics and diplomacy. His action was not sufficient for the impetuous Henry, who tried to get Edmondes to send reports directly to him. When the ambassador declined and pointed out the impropriety of such a course Adam Newton, replying for the Prince, indicated to Edmondes the very considerable displeasure of the Prince. It took some time to make His Highness see the justice of Edmondes' position.

Henry did not hesitate to remonstrate directly with his father about the conduct of the latter's affairs. In 1611 when King James named as governor for young Prince Charles not Sir James Fullerton, Prince Henry's candidate, but Sir Robert Carey who had been recommended by Lord Chamberlain Suffolk, Prince Henry hastened to Whitehall and made his discontent plain both to Suffolk and the King. Getting no satisfaction, he argued with Carey himself, vainly trying to induce him to take the prince's surveyorship instead.

According to one rather unreliable chronicler,[10] in 1611 the young Prince of Wales sought to have King James appoint him President of the Privy Council. Taken with what else we know of the Prince, the story is not unlikely. Certainly one way and another, Henry gave his father reason enough for his muttered observation that the Prince wanted to bury him before he was dead.

In one area, however, Henry played completely the role of the faithful and obedient son. This was in the negotiations begun in 1612 with a view to marrying him either to a daughter of the Duke of Savoy, or to Christine, the second sister of Louis XIII of France. Here the Prince's behaviour was scrupulously correct. He kept his own views to himself until the King invited him to express his opinions. Then he drafted a careful statement of the political advantages and disadvantages of either match, but concluded that it was better for King James to make the decision. 'Your Majesty,' he observed, 'may think, that my part to play, which is to be in love with any of them, is not yet at hand.'[11] Since Princess Christina was only nine years old, the comment was decidedly apposite. Prince Henry's filial acquiescence may have been a blind to cover a resolution not to make a Catholic match but to tour Protestant Germany and seek in one of the courts there a bride of his own choosing. Whatever Prince Henry's real intentions, they really mattered little; within a month of writing the letter just quoted he was on his deathbed.

It was during the spring of 1612 that Prince Henry's health began to cause concern. His spirits flagged, his face became pale and thin, and he complained of 'a giddy lumpish heavinesse in his forehead'. In June the Prince took up residence at Richmond. Here he drove his body to the limits of its endurance, hunting or playing tennis all day, and then in the evening either swimming in the Thames or walking pensively along the river bank in the moonlight, listening to the music of trumpets from the farther shore. His health did not improve, but he kept up his Spartan regime, as if hoping through sheer exertion to overcome his weakness. In August he insisted on riding in two days, through one of the hottest summers England had ever known, the ninety-six miles from Richmond to Belvoir where he joined King James on his summer progress.

By late autumn the Prince's continual headache and listlessness had so increased that he could no longer make himself get up to take his customary early-morning walks through the fields, but lay late in bed complaining of his own indolence. By the middle of the month he was suffering fits of fever and violent diarrhœa. On October 24th, however, he was able to muster enough strength for a match of tennis with Count Henry of Nassau. His appearance really worried the spectators. The next day was that subsequently taken as marking the onset of his fatal illness. In the morning he was well enough to hear a sermon preached prophetically on the text:

> Man that is born of a woman is of few days and full of trouble.
> He cometh forth like a flower, and is cut down: he fleeth also as a shadow and continueth not. (Job xiv. 1–2.)

Three o'clock that afternoon, despite his indomitable will, he was seized with such weakness that he had to be put to bed.

The process of Henry's last agony has been preserved for us in gruesome detail in *The Relation of the Sicknes and Death of the most Illustrious Henry, Prince of Wales* by an unknown Master W.H., in Sir Charles Cornwallis's *The Short Life and Much Lamented Death of that Most Magnanimous Prince Henry, Prince of Wales*, and in the notes of the chief of his physicians, Sir Thomas Mayerne, preserved in his *Opera Medica*. Here will be found the chronicle of the next few weeks after Mayerne found Henry 'in a feaver, with a red visage, with troubled eyes, that could not endure the light of the candle, his lippes blacke, his tongue drie'.[12] Here are recorded the 'lenitive glysters', the bleedings, and the 'gentle medicine of boiled Sene and Rhubarbe' which caused the Prince 'incredible pain' and brought away 'great store of putrified choler'. Even unicorn's horn, powdered with pearl and the 'bone of the Stagges heart' and administered in a julep, helped not at all. As the Prince became more and more subject to delirium and convulsions, every expedient of medical science was employed. Deciding that the trouble lay in the head, the doctors ordered it shaved and applied to it the still warm bodies of pigeons and roosters newly killed. All was in vain.

On November 5th advantage was taken of a lucid period to bring to the Prince's bedside the Archbishop of Canterbury, who that day ordered prayers throughout the kingdom for his recovery. Next day the physicians finally abandoned all hope. King James, with his neurotic terror of death, had already fled from Whitehall to Theobalds. Queen Anne, who much preferred her younger son Charles, had withdrawn into seclusion in Denmark House. In the parents' absence the Prince's attendants summoned the Archbishop of Canterbury to the deathbed. In a loud voice he reminded the Prince of what he had said on the previous day and then,

> . . . calling more loud then ever, thrice together in his eare, Sir heare you mee, heare you mee, heare you mee; If you heare mee, in certaine signe of your faith, and hope of the blessed resurrection, give us for our comfort a signe, by lifting up of your hands, which hee did, lifting up both his hands together: Againe hee desired him yet to give him another signe, by lifting up his eyes; which having done, they left him alone.[13]

The end in truth was not far off. Sir Charles Cornwallis, who has given us the indignant account of how the Archbishop clamoured for signs from the dying prince, tells us too how the end came:

> . . . his Highnesse, quietly, gently, and patiently, halfe a quarter, or thereabouts, before eight a clocke at night, yeelded up his Spirit unto his Immortall Maker.[14]

The shock of Prince Henry's death brought home to the English how much they had built their expectations upon him. Those who wanted an active policy of war and expansion abroad had of course long since pinned their hopes upon Henry. The Puritans, bitterly disappointed by King James's enthusiastic championship of the bishops, had persuaded themselves that the pious young prince would be their champion and they had circulated verses:

> Henry the 8. pulld down abbeys and cells,
> But Henry the 9. shall pull down Bishops and bells.[15]

But it was not just the soldiers and Puritans who had looked to the heir. As the court of his father became more and more recognized for the lax spendthrift ill-disciplined thing that it was, the English had increasingly either looked back nostalgically to the great days under Queen Elizabeth or had promised themselves future greatness under King Henry. In the high idealism of the young prince had been something that appealed to all that was good in the age. When he died, the grief of the nation was commensurate with its sense of loss. In the following months more than thirty works were published celebrating his virtues and lamenting his death. A passage from one may serve for all:

> For hee that was the worlds admired Lampe,
> The life of Peace, of War, of Court, of Campe,
> Th'expected hope of blest ensuing time,
> Fell in his spring, and died in golden prime.

So John Taylor, the Water Poet, in *Great Britaine All in Blacke*, and so a score of other petty poets of the time. More moving than their flourishes and conceits are the phrases of the men who had known Prince Henry personally. Sir Walter Raleigh in his long imprisonment in the Tower had found a friend in the son of his persecutor. 'What man but my father,' Prince Henry had exclaimed, 'would keep such a bird in a cage?'[16] Raleigh had been writing a treatise for Prince Henry 'Of the Art of Warre by Sea', but with Henry's death he laid it by uncompleted.

> God hath spared me the labour of finishing it by his losse; by the losse of that brave Prince; of which, like an Eclypse of the Sunne, wee shall finde the effects hereafter. Impossible it is to equall wordes and sorrowes.[17]

Phineas Pett, who had built for Henry his little ship *Disdain* and later found him so good a master, came to St. James's when the Prince was dying and wrote this account:

> I found a house turned to the very map of true sorrow, every man with the character of grief written in his dejected countenance, all places flowing with tears and bitter lamentations; and . . . the same evening, the most renowned Prince of the world, our royal and most loving master, departed this life, not only to the loss and utter undoing of his poor servants, but the general loss of all Christendom of the protestant religion.[18]

The young Earl of Dorset used the same sun image that Raleigh had employed: 'our rising sun is set ere scarcely he had shone, and . . . with him all our glory lies buried'.[19] One could list many such phrases, ones which lie far beyond the usual empty adulation lavished on Jacobean royalty. Perhaps they were all summed up best by the devoted Sir Charles Cornwallis when he said very simply of Henry, '. . . hee had a certaine kind of extraordinary unspeakable excellency'.[20]

The day after Prince Henry's death an autopsy was conducted by six doctors in the presence of many of the court, among them the Elector Palatine of the Rhine who had recently arrived from Heidelberg to marry Princess Elizabeth. Using Dr. Mayerne's notes on the Prince's illness and the findings of the autopsy, Dr. Norman Moore in 1882 arrived at the conclusion that the evidence all boiled down to 'a case of typhoid fever . . . very clearly described'.[21]

There remained the costly and complicated funeral ceremonies. The room in St. James's Palace in which Henry had died was hung from top to bottom with black velvet. His body, embalmed and in its coffin, was placed in the centre of the room and covered with a black pall under a tent-like canopy of black taffeta. The adjoining rooms, too, were hung with black from ceiling to floor. Here the dead prince remained for four weeks, attended ten at a time by the seventy gentlemen of his household. It was during this period that a young lunatic, stark naked, burst in upon the mourners at St. James's and announced that he was the Prince's ghost come from heaven with a message for the King. After the ghost had been lashed and exposed in his nakedness for twenty-four hours at the porter's lodge, King James ordered him turned loose.

On December 3rd the coffin was carried from the Prince's bedchamber to his privy chamber, where it remained for the next twenty-four hours. Then it was moved to his great chamber, where his guard were in attendance, together with all his servants and officers. In procession, they carried the coffin into the chapel. Here on Sunday, December 6th, the Prince's household attended a service of mourning for their master. This was their private farewell before the great state funeral of the following day. That evening a waxen effigy of the Prince was brought into the chapel and apparelled in the robes which Henry had worn when he was created Prince of Wales. The cap and crown were set on its head, the collar of the Order of the Garter placed about its neck, and the golden staff put in its hand. Thus decked out, the effigy was fastened firmly on top of the coffin.

Next morning the long funeral procession to Westminster Abbey began its slow march. First came 140 poor men in gowns, recipients of funeral charity, followed by 300 servants of various gentlemen and nobles among the mourners. Two drums covered in black and a fife preceded the great standard of Prince Henry borne by Sir John Win. Upon it was embroidered the motto which Henry had chosen for himself years earlier, *Fax mentis honestae gloria*[22]—'Glory is the torch which leads on the honourable mind.' Behind their master's banner marched over 300 of Prince Henry's own servants. Then, preceded by three trumpeters, came Sir Roger Dallison bearing the coronet of the Prince of Wales. He was followed by 360 servants of the principal noblemen of the court. Similarly preceded by trumpeters, Sir David Foulis advanced with Henry's banner as Earl of Carrick. An equerry led a horse with the Prince's escutcheon of Carrick embroidered upon black cloth.

Eighty mourning servants of the Archbishop of Canterbury, of the Elector Palatine and of the new heir, Prince Charles, walked ahead of Lord Howard of Effingham who carried Henry's banner as Earl of Chester and was followed by a horse bearing the escutcheon of Chester. Sixty members of the Chapel Royal and the Prince's twenty-four chaplains followed. Then, conducted by another herald, came Lord Bruce bearing Henry's banner as Duke of Rothesay, and a horse with the escutcheon. Next were the pages and gentlemen of the Prince's household, his solicitor and counsel at law, groom porter and grooms of the privy chamber and bedchamber, followed by Lord Clifford bearing Henry's banner as Duke of Cornwall, and still another horse shrouded in black with the appropriate

F*

escutcheon. The gentlemen of Count Henry of Nassau, of the Elector Palatine and of Prince Charles walked next, followed by the gentlemen extraordinary of Prince Henry's privy chamber, his sewers, carvers, cup-bearers, secretary, the treasurer of his household, the treasurer of his revenues, and the comptroller of his household. These last three high officers bore their white rods of office.

Preceded by a herald, Viscount Fenton bore the banner of Prince Henry as Prince of Scotland, followed by a steed with the arms of Scotland. Then, following a phalanx of baronets and the younger sons of barons, came Sir Edward Phelips, the Prince's chancellor, and after him the Privy Council and barons' eldest sons. Three trumpeters advanced, followed by Lancaster Herald and Viscount Lisle with a banner with the arms of England, France and Ireland quartered with those of Wales, and Sir William Webb leading a steed whose black cloth exhibited the plume insignia of a Prince of Wales. In due order walked the younger sons of earls followed by the eldest sons of viscounts, and the barons, first of Scotland and then of England.

At this point came the climax of the whole vast procession: the coffin and its immediate attendants. Five bishops walked abreast followed by the chamberlain of the Prince's household, Sir Thomas Chaloner, who was followed by Lord Chancellor Ellesmere, Count Henry of Nassau, and the Archbishop of Canterbury. Bearing the 'Banner of the Union' came the Earls of Montgomery and Argyle, followed by a steed caparisoned in black velvet. Windsor Herald followed with Prince Henry's spurs, Somerset Herald with his gauntlets, Richmond Herald with his helmet and breast-plate. York Herald carried his shield, Norroy King of Arms his sword, and Clarenceux King of Arms his coat. Then came the hearse, an open carriage covered with black velvet and set off with black plumes. Face up, on top of the coffin containing the actual remains, was the prone waxwork effigy of the Prince in his robes of state. By the coffin sat a solitary mourner, Sir David Murray, one of the oldest servants of the Prince and his closest friend, he to whom Henry in his long agony had cried again and again with an anguished 'David, David, David!' Six baronets carried the black velvet canopy over the hearse. Ten baronets carried banneroles beside it. Four lords held up the corners of the long black pall. Following the hearse came Garter King of Arms leading the twelve-year-old Prince Charles, who as his brother's chief mourner was supported by the Earl of Northampton and the Duke of Lennox. The Elector Palatine came next with twelve English earls and his own foreign counts. These were succeeded by the Prince's Master of Horse leading the Horse of Estate, the Elector's privy council, and Prince Henry's grooms of the stable. Bringing up the rear were the guard, the Knight Marshal, and twenty servants.

For four hours the immense procession with its two thousand mourners passed along the way to Westminster Abbey. Here, after the Archbishop of Canterbury had conducted the funeral service, the coffin still surmounted by the strikingly lifelike effigy of the Prince was left to be viewed by the public until the 19th of December. Then at last Henry's remains were transferred to the vault of his grandmother, Mary Queen of Scots. A year later there still was owing £16,000 for the expenses of the sumptuous obsequies.

One last thing remained to be done. The members of Prince Henry's household, his 'family' as the old term was, returned to St. James's and remained there until the last day of the year when the household was formally dissolved. For many this dissolution meant personal disaster. Since Prince Charles already had his establishment, and posts about the King were hard to obtain, not a few of Prince Henry's people would now lack places at court. Had their master lived, they might have hoped for high and powerful office when he became king. Now their bright prospects had faded. On the day of the dissolution of the household Joseph Hall, one of the chaplains of the late prince, preached a sermon to Prince Henry's officers and retainers for the last time in the chapel at St. James's. He reminded them of the nobility of the master whom they had served, 'the Glory of the nation, ornament of mankind, hope of posterity, a glorious saint, a Prince, whose countenance was able to put life into any beholder', and recalled for them how he, 'compounded of all loveliness, had infused an harmony into his whole family . . . the most loving and entire fellowship that ever met in the court of any Prince'. He concluded with the exhortation:

> Go in peace, and live as those that have lost such a master; and those that serve a master whom they cannot lose.[23]

What had the English lost in Prince Henry? It is interesting to speculate. Admittedly he was, as Francis Osborn declared, 'an active, generous and Noble Cavalier'. But Osborn was probably right also in declaring that the hopes built upon him were extravagant:

> . . . it may be doubted, whether it ever lay in the power of any Prince meerly humane, to bring so much felicity into a Nation, as they did all his life propose to themselves at the Death of King James.[24]

Certainly if Henry, instead of the vacillating Charles, had come to the throne there would never have been any conquest of the Crown by Parliament. Far more probably, Henry would have built a strong central monarchy on the French model. With his eager passion for war and arms, his 'many straunge and vast conceits and projects' of which men found record in his papers after his death, it seems quite likely that in Henry England lost its Louis XIV, a sun monarch who would have ruined his country through the grandiosity of his ideas. Fine and admirable as he was in so many ways, it may have been for the best that he never came to the throne.

CHAPTER XIII

The Marriage of Thames and Rhine

KING JAMES was not very fortunate in his daughters. Princess Mary, born in 1605, was a delicate little girl who died in 1607 of some 'Dissease in the Lunges'. Princess Sophia, born on June 22, 1606, died the next day. Her tiny corpse was borne on a barge covered in black velvet to Westminster Abbey, there to be buried, in the presence of the great lords of the court, close to Queen Elizabeth. Subsequently a 'small neat monument' was erected to the baby's memory. Of King James's daughters only Princess Elizabeth lived to maturity.

Elizabeth was the one member of the royal family whom the Gunpowder Plotters of 1606 meant to spare. Ten years old at the time, she was being brought up in the loving care of Lord and Lady Harington at their home, Combe Abbey in Warwickshire. Combe Abbey was only ten miles from Dunsmore Heath where Catesby and Digby called in vain upon the Catholic gentry of the shire to take up arms. The conspirators' plan was to abduct Elizabeth from the keeping of the Haringtons, to declare her Queen of England in consequence of the death of her parents and brothers, and to rule in her name. Fortunately, with the refusal of the Catholic squires to join in his rebellion, Catesby had to abandon his intended raid on Combe Abbey, and Elizabeth was spared the horror of just that sort of political kidnapping which her father had experienced during his youth. After the failure of the Gunpowder Plot, Elizabeth was told of what the conspirators had intended. Lord Harington recorded her reaction in a letter to one of his kinsmen:

> Her Highness doth often say, 'What a Queen shoud I have been by this means? I had rather have been with my royal father in the Parliament-House, than wear his crown on such condition.' This poor Lady hath not yet recovered the surprize, and is very ill and troubled.[1]

A queen, in time, Elizabeth would become. For a few months in 1619–20 she would reign in Prague as Queen of Bohemia, the Protestant faction in that unhappy country having invited her husband to succeed to its throne. In short space, however, invading Catholic armies occupied all Bohemia, leaving Elizabeth only her name of 'The Winter Queen' to commemorate her brief glory. The marriage which brought Elizabeth this subsequent adventure in Central Europe was contracted on St. Valentine's Day 1613, when she wedded Count Frederick V, Elector Palatine of the Rhine or, as the English usually called him, the Palsgrave.

She might have married somebody else and had a happier life. Inevitably, in that age of dynastic marriages, she had hardly been out of the cradle before possible matches were being considered for her. In 1607 there was a scheme to marry her to the heir of the Duke of Savoy, provided that her Catholic bridegroom would allow her free practice of her Protestant faith. Later in 1610 two Protestant princelings, Otto, heir of the Landgrave of Hesse, and Christian, Prince of Anhalt, drawn perhaps by report of the beauty of the young English princess, presented themselves successively as suitors. Neither was successful, and in 1611 the talk once again was of a Savoy match, a double one this time with Elizabeth marrying the Duke's eldest son and Prince Henry the Duke's daughter. In October of that same year another match came into prospect when Sir Thomas Edmondes, the English ambassador in Paris, reported that the Duc de Bouillon, leader of the French Calvinists, had informed him of a decision made in Heidelberg to seek Elizabeth as the bride for the young Elector Palatine. Finding this a more attractive offer, James rejected the Savoyard proposal for a double match. In April 1612 the Duc de Bouillon arrived in England to treat for the marriage, and a little later Count Hanau arrived as a special ambassador from the Elector. In the negotiations which followed, Hanau found a spirited supporter in the young Prince of Wales. Suitable terms were agreed upon without much difficulty and by the end of July another of Frederick's ambassadors, Schomberg, received permission for his master to come to England and claim his bride.

Suitable ceremony greeted the Palsgrave when, late on the night of October 16, 1612, he disembarked at Gravesend after a quick crossing from Holland. King James had earlier sent his Master of Ceremonies, Sir Lewis Lewkenor, to Gravesend to await the Palsgrave. The day after the latter's arrival, Lord Hay appeared with a personal message of welcome from the King. Then on October 18th the Duke of Lennox arrived with a glittering retinue of lords and knights to fetch him to London. When the Palsgrave's barge approached the Tower of London, eighty great pieces of ordnance volleyed in salute. At the watergate of Whitehall Palace, Frederick found the frail young Duke of York waiting to conduct him to the Banqueting House where the rest of the royal family awaited him. There, after presenting his compliments to the King, kissing the hand of the Queen, and exchanging 'certaine Passages of Courtesy' with the Prince of Wales,

> . . . he ended (where his Desires could not but begin) with the *Princess*, (who was noted till then not to turn so much as a corner of an Eye towards him,) and stooping low to take up the lowest part of her Garment to kiss it,

shee most gracefully courtesying lower than accustomed, and with her
Hand staying him from that humblest Reverence, *gave him at his rising a
fair Advantage (which he took) of kissing her*.[2]

His reception thus ended, Frederick was carried off by his future father-
in-law for a private talk in the royal bedchamber. Afterwards the young
man left for Essex House where he was to be lodged at the King's expense.

The next few weeks found the court busy sizing up the young German.
By and large, he created a favourable enough impression. Master John
Finett who, as an assistant in the Office of the Ceremonies, probably had
as good chance as any to observe Frederick, wrote of him in a letter:

> He is *straight* and *well shaped* for his growing Years: His Complexion is
> brown, with *a Countenance pleasing*, and promising both *Witt, Courage and
> Judgment*.[3]

More qualified approval was given by John Chamberlain in a letter some
while later:

> . . . I thincke but only this, that he owes his mistres nothing yf he were a
> Kings sonne as she is a Kings daughter. The worst is mee thincks he is much
> too young and small timbred to undertake such a taske.[4]

Generally, however, Frederick won sufficiently high regard. His skill in
horsemanship, his studied politeness, his desire to be agreeable, won him
acceptance enough in a court which had awaited him without any notable
enthusiasm. Certainly the King gave every sign of approval. The person
who most obviously did not approve was the Queen. Secretly Catholic,
Anne had entertained visions of her daughter marrying into a Catholic
court and, as a queen or a duchess, being converted to her mother's faith.
Confronted with the prospect of Elizabeth being bound for life to the
Lutheran prince of a petty German state, Anne gave way to petulance and
mortification, feelings which she took out partly on Frederick and partly
on Elizabeth herself. To nettle her daughter she began referring to her as
'Goodwife Palsgrave' and, according to the talk going around Whitehall,
was rewarded with a retort from Elizabeth that she 'would rather be the
Palsgrave's Wife, than the greatest Papist Queene in Christendom'.[5] The
whole marriage in fact became embroiled in the religious hopes and fears
of the time. A wild story went around London that the Catholics were
ready to stop the marriage by killing Frederick and to that end had smuggled in a whole shipload of pistols from Spain.

If the open and crypto-Catholics at court from the Queen down were
Frederick's enemies, he had his friends in the solidly Protestant element.
Chief among these was the Archbishop of Canterbury, Dr. George Abbot,
whose 'entertainment and kind usage' Frederick went out of his way to
acknowledge shortly before the day of his marriage. On October 29th

Frederick was given a state welcome by the zealously Protestant City of London. Other festivities were to have followed in the succeeding weeks, but these were either cancelled or deferred because of first the sickness and then the death of Prince Henry.

At Christmas the Court came out of mourning, and the festivities traditional to the season merged with those preceding Elizabeth's marriage. Among the plays which received command performance was *The Tempest* by William Shakespeare. This had been performed at court several years earlier. Some scholars, however, believe that *The Tempest* as we know it dates from 1612 and comes to us as revised by Shakespeare for presentation before Frederick and Elizabeth.[6] They find a special interest in the wedding masque which Duke Prospero (a learned ruler to King James's own taste) offers his daughter Miranda and her betrothed, young Ferdinand. In it, they think, lies evidence that Juno and Ceres in their song of marriage blessing turned from the young lovers on the stage to the other young lovers seated in a place of honour in the audience:

> *Juno :* Honour, riches, marriage blessing,
> Long continuance, and increasing,
> Hourly joys be still upon you!
> Juno sings her blessings on you.
>
> *Ceres :* Earth's increase, foison plenty,
> Barns and garners never empty,
> Vines with clustering bunches growing,
> Plants with goodly burden bowing,
> Spring come to you at the farthest
> In the very end of harvest!
> Scarcity and want shall shun you,
> Ceres' blessing so is on you.
>
> (IV, i, 106–117.)

Counting the months from her marriage in mid-February, learned men have concluded that Elizabeth could indeed have hoped for a child 'by the very end of harvest', allowing poetic licence to extend the harvesting a couple of weeks later than might be expected.

We do not know on what particular day *The Tempest* received its performance. A very suitable occasion would have been the evening of St. John's Day, December 27, 1612, for it was earlier that day that Frederick and Elizabeth, appearing before King James seated in state in the Banqueting House, pledged their troth.

A few days earlier Frederick had been created a Knight of the Garter. The offhand and bungled fashion in which the honour had been conferred was typical of the strange mixture of sloppiness and magnificence that prevailed in the English court under King James. Since the court was

settled at Whitehall, it was decided to convene a chapter meeting of the
Order there rather than at Windsor. Accordingly, the available Knights of
the Garter met with the essential officers and elected both Frederick and
Count Maurice of Nassau. Summoning Frederick, they led him to the
royal bedchamber where King James, sitting up in bed, addressed a few
words to the new member of the most distinguished order of chivalry in
his realm, and proceeded to put the George around his neck. The senior
K.G. present, the Earl of Nottingham, put the Garter itself about Frederick's leg. At this point somebody remembered that Frederick had never
been dubbed a knight and that the statutes of the Order declared that the
Garter could only be conferred on knights. After some consultation it was
decided to get Frederick knighted some other time, before he was formally
installed in the Chapel of the Order at Windsor. And thus, hugger-mugger,
Frederick became a Knight of the Most Noble Order of the Garter. *Honi
soit qui mal y pense.*

The early weeks of 1613 brought mounting excitement as the wedding
day approached. On New Year's Day Frederick created a highly favourable impression by his princely generosity in the traditional gift-giving of
the day. To Prince Charles he gave a rapier and spurs set with diamonds,
to the King a bottle (holding two quarts) cut out of one entire agate
'esteemed a very fayre and rich jewell', and to the Queen an agate cup and
jewel. It was for his Elizabeth, however, that he had his most dazzling
gifts:

> a rich chaine of diamonds, a tire for her head all of diamonds, two very
> rich pendent diamonds for her eares, and above all two perles, for bignes,
> fashion and bewtie esteemed the rarest that are to be found in Christen-
> dome: insomuch that the jewells bestowed only on her are valued by men
> of skill above 35000[li].[7]

On January 31st and February 2nd the banns were read at Whitehall, and
on February 7th, for the third and last time, at Windsor, where Frederick
was formally installed as a Knight of the Garter.

Chief of the 'triumphs, pastimes, and sundry devices' of the week preceding the wedding were a fireworks display and a mock naval battle. The
fireworks, presenting the story of St. George's delivery of Lucida, Queen
of the Amazons, from Mango the necromancer, consisted of set pieces
representing 'fantasticke or enchanted Castles, Rocks, Bowers, Forrests'.
These were set up on barges on the Thames opposite Whitehall but, because of technical difficulties, proved only a very moderate success.

The climactic celebration, in any case, was to be the naval battle between the Turks and the Venetians, with the storming of Algiers, scheduled
for the night before the wedding. This was planned on a really grand scale.
An earlier mock battle at the time of Henry's creation as Prince of Wales

had been a decided success, hence the decision to do the same thing, only bigger and better, for his sister's nuptials. On the Lambeth shore opposite Whitehall there had been built a representation of the fort, town and haven of Algiers. Up from Rochester and Chatham came every longboat, barge and armed pinnace the Navy could muster. Booms were laid across the river above and below Whitehall while this fleet of small boats was outfitted to look like galleons, galleasses, carricks and argosies. Pressed into service were 500 Thames watermen and 1,000 musketeers from the London militia companies. In charge of the whole affair was Sir Robert Mansell, Treasurer of the Admiralty.

The night of February 13th arrived and with it the long-awaited battle. A sorry fiasco it proved to be. The first engagements were so protracted that the 'Venetians' never did get around to storming the fortress. 'The King and indeed all the companie tooke . . . litle delight to see no other activitie but shooting and potting of gunnes'[8] and were soon bored. They had no idea of the scenes of actual horror occurring in the mimic war. As hundreds of cannon let off their volleys of gunpowder, mishaps began to happen left and right. One man lost both his hands, another both his eyes, and a host of others were burned and maimed. Phineas Pett had been persuaded by the Lord Admiral to serve in the fight as commander of an old pinnace named the *Spry*, mounting nine pieces of brass ordnance. Of his experience in the mock battle he subsequently declared, 'I ran more danger than if it had been a sea service in good earnest.'[9] There was talk of resuming the battle another day and storming the fortress then, but when a count had been made of the casualties nobody had any stomach for going on with the business and the King ordered the fortress dismantled and the companies disbanded. As for the blinded and the maimed, one can only hope that they were granted at least the recompense accorded those who suffered their injuries in actual war—a licence to beg for the rest of their days without molestation by constables, headboroughs or other officers of the law.

The next day was that of the wedding. Since the Chapel Royal at Whitehall was very limited in its accommodation, it was ruled that no one under the rank of baron would be admitted except for the three Lord Chief Justices. To give those excluded an opportunity to see the bride and her groom, the wedding processions followed a circuitous route through the palace from the King's Presence Chamber to the Chapel. First to pass along this route was the Palsgrave, attired in cloth of silver and accompanied by sixteen noble bachelors, symbolic of his age of sixteen. A railed platform had been erected in the centre of the Chapel, open at both ends, with cloth of gold draped about the railings. Mounting this with his party, the bridegroom took his place at one side.

Next to enter was the bride with her attendants. Before her walked Lord Harington, the devoted friend and mentor in whose house she had been raised. Flanking her were her bridesmen (two bachelors), her brother Prince Charles on her right, and the old Earl of Northampton, Lord Privy Seal, on her left. Elizabeth like her groom was dressed in cloth of silver. It was traditional that a virgin bride should wear her hair hanging down in tresses, and for that reason Elizabeth wore 'her hayre hanginge downe at length dressed with ropes of pearle'.[10] On her head she wore a coronet 'richly dect with precious stones'. Being like her bridegroom sixteen, she had sixteen bridesmaids. After Elizabeth had taken her place on the platform opposite Frederick, the King and Queen entered with the chief lords and ladies attending upon them. James, splendid in jewels which court talk valued at £600,000, seated himself on his throne. Close beside him was Frederick's stool. Queen Anne, in a white satin gown, wearing jewels valued at £400,000,[11] took her place beside her daughter.

The ceremony began. The Gentlemen of the Chapel sang an anthem. Then the Dean of the Chapel Royal (the Bishop of Bath and Wells) entered the pulpit to preach on the marriage of Cana in Galilee. During a second anthem the Bishop and the Archbishop of Canterbury retired to the vestry to put on their rich copes. Returning, they proceeded to the communion table where the actual ceremony was performed. King James gave his daughter away, and Frederick proved to have mastered enough English to speak his part creditably. After the Archbishop's benediction, the principals returned from the communion table while the Gentlemen of the Chapel sang a special anthem composed for the occasion by the famous Dr. Bull. Versicles, prayers, and another anthem followed, then Garter King of Arms advanced to declare the style and titles of the newly married couple. Various lords brought wine and wafers from the vestry and, after receiving the communion, the wedding party withdrew. The newly-married Elizabeth was now escorted by two married men, the Duke of Lennox and the Earl of Nottingham. In the Great Chamber the party broke up, James and his queen slipping away to their private suites and leaving the bride and bridegroom, their attendants and guests, to dine in state in a specially built new room of the palace.

The marriage of the King's only daughter was not allowed to go unsaluted in verse. In resolute doggerel the poetic Thames waterman, John Taylor, complimented Frederick:

> Most mighty, all-beloved lovely Lord,
> Warrs patterne, and a Patrone unto Schollers:
> Great Brittaine doth a Jewell thee afford,
> More rich in price then all the German Dollers,
>> Live ever happy with thy joyfull Gem
>> In Earth, and in the new Jerusalem.[12]

Henry Peacham expressed his hopes in a smoothly mediocre epithalamion:

> . . . pass ye many an happy night,
> Untill *Lucina* brings to light,
> An hopefull Prince who may restore,
> In part, the losse we had before.
> Io Hymen Hymenaeus.
>
> That one day we may live to see,
> A *Frederick Henry* on her knee,
> Who mought to *Europe* give her law,
> And keepe encroaching Hell in awe.
> Io Hymen Hymenaeus.[13]

Master Peacham's hopes were to be realized. Elizabeth proved to be notably prolific. In time she provided England with Prince Rupert and ultimately, through descent, with her Hanoverian kings.

The arts contributed more to the wedding of Princess Elizabeth than such dutiful versifying as that just quoted, and more than the anthem specially written by Dr. Bull. On the wedding night and two nights following there were masques at court honouring the newly married couple.

Part masquerade ball, part drama, and part pure pageantry, the court masque was the supreme artistic expression of the Jacobean court. Behind it lay the old medieval court mumming in which a band of courtiers came unannounced, diced in silence with their hosts, and departed. Behind this in turn (like the humbler visits of village mummers taking their Christmas play from cottage to cottage) lay the ritual good-luck visits of pre-Christian times. For the process by which the court mumming borrowed spectacle and allegory from the intermezzi, masquerades, and triumphs of Renaissance Italy and the fantastic banquet displays of the Burgundian court to produce the early Tudor 'disguising', and for the further process in the time of Henry VIII by which the 'disguising' joined with the flirtatious Italian *masquerie* to produce the first English masque, the interested reader may consult the definitive study of Miss Enid Welsford.[14] Let it suffice here to say that in the reign of James I the masque achieved its real flowering in England, and became a setting of exquisite beauty for an evening of dancing and music at court.

Ben Jonson and Inigo Jones were the men who brought the masque to its perfection. Jonson, the 'king's poet',[15] wrote the librettos and secured a unity of incident, theme and mood before unknown. Jones, the painter and architect, full of first hand-knowledge of the sumptuous staging of the court theatres in Italy, designed the sets and achieved stage effects which were the wonder of the court. During the time of King James these two difficult and domineering men worked together in uneasy compromise, and script, scene and music were held in an ideal balance. (Later, in the reign of Charles, Jones was to cast off Jonson, secure complete ascendancy, and subordinate everything else to the spectacle of his sets.)

Jonson and Jones began their collaboration with *The Masque of Blackness*, played at Whitehall on Twelfth Night 1605. Right off, Jones made a sweeping reform. The medieval use of multiple stages, long abandoned in the theatres, had lingered on in the court, with pieces of scenery dispersed all about the hall: here a mountain, there a castle, and somewhere else a hermit's cave, a ship, or whatever else was required. When the courtiers streamed into the Banqueting House to see *The Masque of Blackness*, they found all the scenery set within a proscenium arch stage at the lower end of the hall where, for the moment, a painted curtain concealed it from their sight. Before the stage stood an open space to be used for dancing later in the evening. In the forefront of that part of the hall available for the spectators was the 'state', the canopied platform from which King James, protected by palisades, could watch the masque without being jostled by the courtiers thronging about him.

The masque began. The painted curtain dropped to the floor of the stage and revealed 'an artificiall sea . . . raysed with waves, which seemed to move, and in some places the billow to break'. In the foreground stood Tritons, their hair dyed blue, sounding music on wreathed horns. Behind them were seamaids and, borne on the backs of great sea-horses, Oceanus and Niger. Addressing his black son, the River Niger, Oceanus asked why he had flowed as far as Britain, keeping his fresh billow unmixed with Ocean's 'brackish streame'. Speaking like his sire in rhymed couplets, Niger replied that it was because of his daughters. These negro ladies had believed their colour beautiful until they had learned otherwise from 'poore braine-sicke men, stil'd Poets'. At this, Niger's daughters had wept until the moon, shining upon a lake, had revealed a message on its waters —in a land whose name ends in 'TANIA' they would find one 'who formes all beauty with his sight'. So far they had unavailingly visited Mauritania, Lusitania and Aquitania. Once Niger had finished this explanation, the Moon was revealed seated on a silver throne in a heaven vaulted with blue silk. She explained that the journey of Niger and his daughters was at an end for they had reached Albion, now, since the union of England and Scotland, to be known as 'Britania', and:

> . . . were the world, with all his wealth, a ring,
> Britania (whose new name makes all tongues sing)
> Might be a Diamant worthy to inchase it,
> Rul'd by a Sunne, that to this height doth grace it:
> Whose beames shine day and night, and are of force
> To blanch an Æthiope, and revive a *Cor's*.
> His light scientiall is, and (past mere nature)
> Can salve the rude defects of every creature.[16]

After this heavily buttered compliment to the onlooking King James, the Moon instructed Niger to invite his daughters to set foot on this happy British shore.

Thus far the lady masquers, the twelve daughters of Niger, had remained seated within a huge concave shell, seemingly of mother of pearl and illuminated by lights in its upper part, set far back on the artificial sea and rising and falling with its motion. Attended by the daughters of Ocean, dressed in sea-green, gold and silver, and having garlands of sea-grass and coral in their hair, the lady masquers now advanced two by two. All had darkened skins and wore the same costume:

> ... *azure* and *silver*; (their hayre thicke, and curled upright in tresses, lyke *Pyramids*,) but returned on the top with a scroll and antique dressing of feathers, and jewells interlaced with ropes of pearle. And, for the front, eare, neck, and wrists, the ornament was of the most choise and orient pearle; best setting off from the black.

Having once come ashore and offered dances of their own, the lady masquers chose partners from the courtly audience and danced with them in the open space in front of the stage. Measure followed measure, and coranto succeeded coranto, until the evening ended with the ladies' returning to their great mother of pearl shell and taking their departure.

It had been Queen Anne's idea to appear in a masque as a negress and Ben Jonson had done his best to gratify her. Not everybody was impressed by the results. Dudley Carleton, who saw the performance, was candid about its deficiencies:

> At Night we had the Queen's Maske in the Banquetting-House, or rather her Pagent. There was a great Engine at the lower end of the Room, which had Motion, and in it were Images of Sea-Horses with other terrible Fishes, which were ridden by Moors: The Indecorum was that there was all Fish and no Water. At the further end was a great Shell in form of a Skallop, wherein were four Seats; on the lowest sat the Queen with my Lady *Bedford*; on the rest were placed the Ladies *Suffolk, Darby, Rich, Effingham, Ann Herbert, Susan Herbert, Elizabeth Howard, Walsingham* and *Bevil*. Their Apparell was rich, but too light and Curtizan-like for such great ones. Instead of Vizzards, their Faces and Arms up to the Elbows were painted black, which was Disguise sufficient, for they were hard to be known; *but it became them nothing so well as their red and white, and you cannot imagine a more ugly Sight, then a Troop of lean-cheek'd Moors.* The *Spanish* and *Venetian* Ambassadors were both present. . . . [The Spanish ambassador] took out the Queen, and forgot not to kiss her Hand, though there was Danger it would have left a Mark on his Lips. The Night's Work was concluded with a Banquet in the great Chamber, which was so curiously assaulted, that down went Table and Tresses before one bit was touched.[17]

Despite the carping of the literal-minded Carleton, Ben Jonson and Inigo

Jones emerged with considerable prestige from *The Masque of Blackness*. A masque, usually by these two, became a feature of any great festive occasion at court.

Since King James had a taste for spectacle (in his younger years he had tried his hand at writing a masque himself), and the Queen loved masquerading, it is not surprising that the Jacobean masque soon exhibited a complexity and magnificence undreamt of in the parsimonious days of Queen Elizabeth. 'Double masques' were introduced, with not one but two companies of masquers. To the simple form of the basic masque with its 'entry' (presentation of the masquers), 'main' (dance among the masquers), 'revels' (dances with the spectators), and final 'going-out', Jonson added a prefatory 'antimasque' offered by grotesque characters as a foil for the elegance of the masque proper. *The Masque of Queens* in 1609 was the first to be so supplied. In this a dance by witches preceded the appearance of the masquers.

Jones meanwhile was experimenting with placing scenes in depth so that each opened to reveal another hitherto concealed behind it. In *The Hue and Cry after Cupid*, presented at Lord Haddington's marriage early in 1608, Jones introduced from Italy the *scena ductilis* when, to a sudden burst of music, the rocky cliff which had supplied the earlier scene parted to reveal a silver astronomical globe, eighteen feet in diameter. This, as it revolved, bore within it the twelve gentlemen masquers, each beneath a golden sign of the Zodiac.

Increasing elaboration meant increasing expense. Queen Anne had been granted £3,000 from the Exchequer for *The Masque of Blackness*. The Haddington masque cost about £3,600. By 1618 King James was laying out £4,000 annually (about £32,000 in modern values) for the Christmas masque, which was traditionally paid for out of the Exchequer. Such expense for a single night of revelry becomes explicable when one thinks not only of the costliness of the materials but of the scores of carpenters, gilders, painters, sempstresses, jewellers, stage hands and artisans required.

When court lords, either singly or collectively, footed the bills for a masque, they knew that its very expensiveness made it a culminating compliment to those whom they chose to honour. The greater the charges, the more the devotion. Sir Francis Bacon rejected the offer of Solicitor-General Yelverton to contribute £500 towards the masque Bacon was about to present at the marriage of the King's favourite, Somerset. Bacon knew that to diminish the cost to himself would be to reduce his credit with Somerset. To Bacon the whole thing was an investment to secure the favourite's favour.

Because of the time needed for their preparation, let alone their cost, rarely more than two of these entertainments were produced at court in a single year. Entirely exceptional were the three masques planned for the nights immediately following the marriage of Princess Elizabeth. Ben Jonson was at the time touring the Continent in somewhat debauched fashion as the tutor of young Carey Raleigh, whose father was still in the Tower. In the absence of the supreme master of the form, Thomas Campion, George Chapman and Francis Beaumont were called upon to produce scripts.

Campion's *The Lords' Masque* was given pride of place on the wedding night. In this Inigo Jones outdid himself, doubling his scope by dividing the stage into two levels, each curtained independently. When a double consort of music opened the evening's entertainment, the curtain masking the lower stage dropped to reveal a woodland scene. Forth stepped Orpheus to summon the goddess of madness, Mania, from her cave and deliver Jove's command to release from her company of madmen Entheus, the spirit of 'Poeticke furie'. At this cue, twelve 'Franticks' entered for the antimasque. When these had withdrawn, the curtain veiling the upper stage dropped to reveal Prometheus standing against a background of glittering stars. To him, Entheus explained the business of the evening:

> Patron of mankinde, powerfull, and bounteous,
> Rich in thy flames, reverend *Prometheus*,
> In *Hymens* place aide us to solempnize
> These royal Nuptials; fill the lookers eyes
> With admiration of thy fire and light,
> And from thy hand let wonders flow tonight.[18]

The requested wonders followed. While a choir sang one of Campion's loveliest songs,

> Advance your Chorall motions now,
> You musick-loving lights:
> This night concludes the nuptiall vow,
> Make this the best of nights,

the stars behind Prometheus moved in 'an exceeding strange and delight-full maner', eliciting from Campion when he published the masque the tribute, 'I suppose fewe have ever seene more neate artifice, then Master *Innigoe Jones* shewed in contriving their Motion'.[19]

When the singers invited the spirits of the stars to appear in human form and to grace the nuptials with dance, clouds engulfed the glittering lights and in their place stood the eight lord masquers:

The ground of their attires was massie Cloth of Silver, embossed with flames of Embroidery; on their heads, they had Crownes, Flames made all of Gold-plate Enameled, and on the top a Feather of Silke representing a cloude of smoake.

Sixteen pages performed a torch dance on the lower stage, then the lord masquers came down from the upper level in a bright transparent cloud. Their descent completed, the cloud 'brake in twaine, and one part of it (as with a winde) was blowne overthwart the Scæne'.

While the cloud was vanishing, the lower stage underwent a sudden change. The woodland disappeared, and in its place appeared various 'Noble women-statues of silver' standing between 'Pillasters all of gold, set with Rubies, Saphyrs, Emeralds, Opals and such like'. To the accompaniment of song these statues were transformed into living ladies. The two sets of masquers, lords and ladies, then danced together before choosing partners from among the onlookers. Elizabeth and Frederick were the first to be brought on the dancing-floor. Measures and corantos followed until a new song brought them all to a halt:

> Cease, cease you Revels, rest a space;
> New pleasures presse into this place,
> Full of beautie and of grace.

All this while Jones's artisans had been working mightily to contrive a fresh spectacle. There was now revealed on the stage:

> ... a prospective with Porticoes on each side, which seemed to go in a great way; in the middle was erected an Obeliske, all of Silver, and in it lights of severall colours; on the side of this Obeliske, standing on Pedestals, were the statues of Bridegroome and Bride, all of gold in gratious postures. This Obeliske was of that height, that the toppe thereof touched the highest cloudes, and yet *Sybilla* did draw it forth with a thread of gold.

When the sibyl (no doubt with mechanical aids) had worked this wonder, there was a 'dance triumphant of the Maskers' accompanied by the song, 'Dance, dance, and visit now the shadowes of our joy'. Then the sibyl, observing decorum and speaking in Latin, blessed the bride and groom, and the masquers had their going-out dance.

The Banqueting House at Whitehall where *The Lords' Masque* was performed was not an enormous building. It measured, in fact, only 120 feet by 53 feet. Much of this space must have been taken up by the deep stage required for the complicated sets, and a fair proportion of what was left had to be kept clear for the dancing. A consequence was that the spectator area was decidedly limited. For this reason it was ruled that no lady or gentlewoman would be admitted to watch the wedding masques if she was wearing a farthingale. Farthingales would mean that even fewer people could get in to see the show.

The next night saw the gentlemen of the Middle Temple and of Lincoln's Inn marching through the streets of London in a torchlight procession as they went to present their masque at Whitehall. In the tiltyard gallery there the King, Elizabeth, Frederick, the Privy Council and the chief of the nobility watched their arrival. Fifty gentlemen 'richly attired, and as gallantly mounted' provided the vanguard. Then came the players of the antimasque—twelve little boys made up as 'baboons, attired like fantastical travellers in Neapolitan suits and great ruffs'—a topical gibe at Italianate Englishmen with their affectations. Two elaborately decorated 'cars triumphal' carried musicians dressed like the sun-worshipping priests among the Indians of Virginia. Then came the masquers themselves riding in single file.

> [They were attired] in Indian habits all of a resemblance: the ground-cloth of silver richly embroidered with golden suns, and about every sun ran a trail of gold imitating Indian work; their bases of the same stuff and work, but betwixt every pane of embroidery went a row of white estridge feathers, mingled with sprigs of gold plate; under their breasts they wore bawdricks of gold, embroidered high with pearl, and about their necks ruffs of feathers spangled with pearl and silver. On their heads high sprigged feathers, compassed in coronets, like the Virginian princes they presented. Betwixt every set of feathers, and about their brows, in the under-part of their coronets shined suns of gold plate, sprinkled with pearl; from whence sprung rays of the like plate, that mixing with the motion of the feathers, showed exceedingly delightful and gracious. Their legs were adorned with close long white silk stockings, curiously embroidered with gold to the mid-leg. . . . In their hands (set in several postures as they rode) they brandished cane darts of the finest gold.[20]

Before each masquer rode a torchbearer in Indian garb, with a waxen torch in a great gilded cane. Beside them marched Moors attired like Indian slaves. The culminating spectacle was a great chariot 'with paintings and glittering scarfings of silver, over which was cast a canopy of gold borne up with antic figures'. Driven by Capriccio, wearing on his head a pair of golden bellows, the chariot bore the goddess Honour and Pluto, god of Riches. Behind it marched two hundred halberdiers. At Whitehall, this glittering procession made the full circuit of the tiltyard for 'the more full satisfaction of his Majesty's view', then dispersed to prepare for the masque.

The gentlemen of the Middle Temple and Lincoln's Inn had not been well advised in commissioning the translator of Homer to write their masque. Chapman's humour in his prose antimasque was heavy-handed and prolix, and his poetry in the masque proper quite unexceptional. Fortunately the spectacle, contrived in part at least by the indispensable Inigo Jones, achieved a triumph for the piece.

The next night was set aside for a third and concluding masque presented jointly by Gray's Inn and the Inner Temple. Alas for the gentlemen of Gray's Inn and the Inner Temple! Nothing went wright. The masquers of the previous night having made their journey to Whitehall by land, these decided to come by water, an especially apt choice since the theme of their masque was 'The Marriage of Thames and Rhine'. The lights on their galleys made a nice show as they came towards Whitehall, but somebody had miscalculated the timing of the tide and the masquers had a lot of trouble getting ashore. Worse still, when they arrived at the Hall they found it so full that there was no room left for them. Moreover, noble ladies of the court who had thronged to the riverside windows to see the masquers come ashore found that they too could not get in. Nobody could figure out how to get the wrong people out of the Hall and the right people in. As occasionally happened, the palace arrangements had broken down completely. Then came the final blow. King James announced that he was utterly worn out after three late nights and did not want to see the masque anyway. Sir Francis Bacon, a principal contriver of the piece, pleaded with the King that to disgrace the masquers by dismissing them thus unseen would be 'to bury them quick' (i.e. alive). His Majesty had just enough energy left to retort with a pun—one more masque, said James, and they would have to bury him quick. However, he gave the gentlemen good words and promised to see their masque if they would bring it four nights later. Dutifully they returned on the night of February 20th. Beaumont had supplied them with a pleasant, skilfully written script which won the applause of a sympathetic audience.[21]

The next night King James, Queen Anne, Elizabeth and Frederick banqueted the great court lords and ladies and the chief participants in the wedding masques, about eighty persons in all. Fortunately for James the feast cost him nothing. A well-placed bet with the Palsgrave and nine of his supporters had left them paying the expenses. Lady Rich was particularly annoyed that her husband, one of the losing betters, was among those allowed only to look on, not to sit at the board. As her ladyship put it, he got not even a drink for his money.

This banquet concluded the marriage festivities. The next day King James left for Theobalds, en route to his hunting lodge at Royston. Behind him he left an exchequer drained to the very lees by the wedding expenses, and instructions to cut costs as quickly as possible. The Palsgrave's household was speedily broken up and most of his company dismissed, all of which his new wife took very grievously but, as John Chamberlain philosophically observed, 'necessitie hath no law'.

On April 21st the Palsgrave and his bride boarded at Margate the *Prince Royal*, flagship of the squadron which was to conduct them beyond the seas. Foul weather kept the ships from sailing until the 25th. Three days later the fleet anchored off Sluys where the Prince of Orange came aboard for a complimentary visit. Next day the Palsgrave and Elizabeth landed at

Flushing and started for Elizabeth's new home in the Palatinate. Among
the English lords accompanying her was her old guardian, Lord Harington.

Back in England James, like many another father after the wedding of a
daughter, looked at the cost after all the bills had come in. To pay off the
£30,000 which he owed Lord Harington for bringing up Elizabeth, he had
had to grant him the right to coin brass farthings. Elizabeth's dowry had
cost £40,000, paid over to the Palsgrave's agent in hard cash. Frederick's
household during his stay in England had cost the King £6,000. One way
and another his installation as a Knight of the Garter had cost £4,000. The
bride's wardrobe had cost £6,252, and the furnishing of her chamber
£3,023. Jewels and apparel for her servants had run up another £3,914.
The naval fight and fireworks had cost £4,800. When everything was
added up, the grand total came to £93,200.[22] Against this, the feudal aid
which James was entitled to collect upon the occasion of his eldest daughter's marriage had brought in only £20,000. James may have felt for a
moment that it was not entirely unfortunate that his other daughters had
not reached marriageable years.

CHAPTER XIV

The Courtier's Life

FROM HIS FRAME in the Long Gallery he surveys the tourists who straggle through the great house on 'open days'. Unenthusiastically a guide declaims, 'Painted by Mytens, considered very fine.' Here, standing in the middle of the twentieth century, is the Jacobean Courtier.

The visitors regard him. Their eyes travel from the fantastic lace 'roses' which conceal his shoe buckles to the golden clocks which reach almost to the knees of his white silk stockings. They observe his immense pleated breeches with their intricate embroidery of flowers and foliage. They glance from the doublet converging on the wasp-like waist to the heavy brocade of the cape weighing down one shoulder. For an instant they regard the face framed in the incredible ruff which radiates wired and starched salients in all directions. Few notice his tasselled earring. Fewer recognize the fantastically decorated object by his shoulder as the hat he once wore at Whitehall.

For half a minute, over three and a half centuries, courtier and tourist confront each other. Then the sightseers move on. But what if through some chink in Time they could slip through into the courtier's world? What would they find there?

At ten o'clock our courtier awakened and began his day. The time was late, for most people had been up since six when they had eaten their breakfasts of meat stew, rabbit or chicken, washed down with beer. Our courtier, however, had been up late the night before, and blenched at such early hours. Arisen, he began the ritual of 'apparelling himselfe, with frizling and curling his haire with his curling pin, with poudring and turning up the same, this way and that way, about his eares, continuing thus in his bed-chamber, even till noone at least. . . .'[1] Noon brought him to his table for dinner, the chief meal of the day, joined perhaps by friends, or eating with the waiting gentleman who was his paid companion and sycophant. After dinner, if the day was fine, he may have had a waterman row him and his friends to the south bank of the Thames to watch the baiting of bears or bulls in the rings there, or to go to a playhouse. If he went to a theatre, his wish to see the play was no stronger than his desire to display his fine attire:

To see one of your gender either shew himselfe (in the midst of his pride or riches) at a Play house, or publique assembly how: (before he dare enter) with the Jacobs-Staffe of his owne eyes and his Pages, hee takes a full survay of himselfe, from the highest sprig in his feathers, to the lowest spangle that shines in his Shoo-string.[2]

He was known to the players and, should he decide to see their play, they set out stools for him and his friends beside other dandies along the edge of the high platform stage. Their presence was an obstruction which irked the 'groundlings' standing in the open pit of the theatre, and they hooted their farewell when the courtier, bored by the play, maliciously chose a point of high drama to arise and make his ostentatious departure.

If the day was a rainy one, our courtier and his friends were likely to go not to a playhouse but to Whitehall Palace. Here, after mingling with the throng in the Presence Chamber, ready to make their bow to King James should the monarch choose to make an appearance, they were likely to slip away to the recreational area in the western part of the palace grounds. Here they may have watched the birds fighting in the high-roofed Cockpit, engaged in the old game of court tennis in covered quarters, or bowled in the long indoor alley. His sport concluded, our courtier probably repaired to the chambers of a friend who enjoyed some post in the court and would obligingly carry him off for supper at his mess. Supper was served about half past five. Afterwards there was gaming, with the groom porter keeping the record of the wagers.

At nine o'clock began the elaborate procedure known as the 'Order of All Night' with the King going to bed, the doors to the Privy Chamber being locked, the guard being mounted in the Great Chamber, and the password being given for the night. Now was the time for our courtier to take his departure before the locking of the gates. Leaving Whitehall he made his way, perhaps to his own lodgings in Westminster, perhaps to the rooms where he had installed his expensive mistress. Here they amused themselves with the pet monkey he had recently presented to her, before turning to more intimate matters. Perhaps, desiring variety, our courtier headed for a bagnio for sport with the whores. Then homeward he went at last, with his page holding a flaming link before him as he staggered through the dark echoing streets, the night air cold in his face.

Over the year, the courtier's life was governed by the cycle of the court's migrations. Whitehall was the home of the court, but King James disliked the noisome city of London, 'that filthie toune' he called it,[3] and spent as little time as he could, barely one-third of the year, in his kingdom's capital. One season, however, was sure to see the court at Whitehall—the Yuletide days extending from Christmas to Twelfth Night. Important here was the festival New Year, kept on January 1st according to the old

By permission of the Countess of Suffolk and Berkshire

RICHARD SACKVILLE, 3RD EARL OF DORSET

Roman practice, even though the calendar new year did not begin until Lady Day (the Feast of the Annunciation), so that the day after March 24, 1603 was March 25, 1604.

New Year was a most important day at court for it, not Christmas, was the time for gift-giving. This was the time to cement alliances with handsome gifts of gilt cups or pieces of plate, and buy the favour of the 'great men' of the court with expensive presents. The Lord Treasurer reputedly received about £17,000 each New Year from the officers serving under him. A chief concern for a nobleman such as our courtier was to find a suitable present for the King himself. While humble commoners could come to court with pots of green ginger, marchpane, embroidered mittens, or bottles of hartshorn or 'ypocras', noblemen were expected to give gifts of real worth. Our courtier probably thought hard to find a gift which either through its cost or novelty would catch the royal eye. The King for his part seems to have used a rather standardized scale in giving his gifts. A list for January 1606[4] shows that twenty-one earls each received £20 in gold, and twenty-five barons each £10, besides pieces of gilt plate of varying worth.

Once Twelfth Day was past, King James could hardly wait to get away from Whitehall and head north to his favourite hunting lodges at Royston and Newmarket on the borders of Cambridgeshire. James devoted about a third of each year to hunting the hare and the deer (gentlemen scorned the fox), or such allied sports as catching larks and hawking. His devotion to his sport meant much inconvenience for his ministers. Foreign ambassadors had to be kept waiting, and necessary public business held in abeyance, until the King would reluctantly come back to Whitehall for a few days and meet with his Privy Council.

There were other unfortunate consequences. The farmers over whose fields the King and his courtiers rode were furious at the damage done, while the savagery with which James enforced the laws against poachers made men say that His Majesty dealt worse with a deer-killer than a man-killer. Inevitably expostulations reached the King. In December 1604 the Archbishop of York wrote to Cecil:

> . . . as one that honoureth and loveth his most excellent Majesty with all my heart, I wish less wastening of the treasure of the realm, and more moderation in the lawful exercise of hunting, both that poor men's corn may be less spoiled, and other his Majesty's subjects more spared.[5]

The Earl of Worcester, being Master of the Horse, was given the delicate task of delivering the archiepiscopal letter to the King. We have his report of how James received it:

> He was merry at the first, till as I guessed he came to the wasting of treasure, and the immoderate exercise of hunting. He began then to alter

countenance, and, in the end, said it was the foolishest letter that he ever read.[6]

Other protests reached the King through less formal channels. One day a favourite hound of the King's, Jowler, was missing when the dogs were whipped in. During the morrow's hunting he rejoined the pack. About his neck was tied a paper on which was written:

> Good Mr. Jowler, we pray you speak to the King (for he hears you every day, and so doth he not us) that it will please his Majesty to go back to London, for else the country will be undone; all our provision is spent already, and we are not able to entertain him longer.[7]

Another time, a set of doggerel verses was found in the hand of Queen Elizabeth's effigy on her tomb in the Abbey:

> Roman and Joller, Ringwood and his mate
> Comparde to us are in a better State;
> They can be heard and they can be Regarded
> Where we are curst, slighted, and unregarded.
> Is there a people, Heavens, full a degree
> Below the condition of a Dogg but wee?[8]

To all protests James had the same reply—the open-air life of the hunting field was essential to his health, and it was the patriotic duty of the English to put up with the consequences:

> The Kinge . . . findes such felicitie in that hunting life, that he hath written to the counsaile [Privy Council], that yt is the only meanes to maintain his health, (which being the health and welfare of us all) he desires them to undertake the charge and burden of affaires, and to foresee that he be not interrupted nor troubled with too much busines.[9]

What was life like for our Jacobean courtier when he headed northward with the King on one of his innumerable hunting expeditions? Expense and discomfort were involved. Lodgings were costly and hard to come by in the little towns of Newmarket and Royston. The courtiers' wives, if they accompanied them, must often have been bitter about the lack of room, the dirt, the squalor, and the boredom when their men were in the field with the King. Admittedly the ladies joined in the sport when the deer were chased past screened ambushes from which the courtiers, male and female alike, shot at them with the cross-bow. The ladies, however, were left behind when the hunters took to horse and pursued their quarry until it was finally brought to bay by the dogs and despatched.

Sometimes King James and his lords rode forth falconing. There would be hawking 'at the high mountee', with the bird soaring from its master's wrist to bring down some heron or bittern passing overhead. Sometimes another method was used: the hawk would circle high in the central blue

above its master then, when dogs flushed wild ducks and similar fowl
from the marshes below, it would plummet earthward with such stunning
impact as to knock the victim bodily out of the air.

Added interest was found in bets on favourite falcons or dogs. Our
Jacobean courtier was a quick man with a bet and could turn almost anything into a wager. (When Cecil died, large sums were laid out as men
backed their fancy as to who would succeed him as Secretary of State.)
Certainly all sport was hedged about with betting. Gaming gave half the
attraction to the Cockpit at Whitehall, and almost as much to the bowling
alleys. In a single day in 1623 Lord Howard de Walden lost over £1,500
betting at bowls. Two days earlier he had lost £500 in the same way.

Wagers were often placed on races between 'running footmen' serving
various of the court. In her diary Lady Anne Clifford ruefully relates how
her husband, the Earl of Dorset, dropped £200 when his footman was
beaten in a race by the Earl of Salisbury's footman. This match was a
minor one compared with the race from St. Albans to Clerkenwell in
1618 between an English footman belonging to the Countess of Bedford
and an Irishman serving a son of the Earl of Suffolk. An enormous crowd
turned out for this event. Even King James was present, despite the foul
weather. When the race was over, the King's favourite, Buckingham, collected some £3,000 from those who had backed the Irishman. At Newmarket, where practically everybody had good mounts in his stable for the
hunting, another pastime developed, betting on the horses. The Newmarket
races of today began in the time of James.

Early February usually saw the court back in Whitehall for a week or
so while the King attended to the arrears of state business that had piled
up in his absence. Even with frequent couriers arriving from the Privy
Council and a specially detailed Clerk of the Signet attending James
during his hunting, there were matters which required extended conference between the King and his ministers. Courtiers whose addiction to the
chase was more moderate than their master's must have looked forward to
the respite of these returns to Whitehall. Even his Master of Horse complained at times about the strenuousness of life in the field with James:

> . . . in the morning we are on horseback by eight, and so continue in full
> career from the death of one hare to another, until four at night; then for
> the most part, we are five miles from home. . . .[10]

March and April followed the same pattern as February, with intervals
at Theobalds or in Cambridgeshire alternating with spells at Whitehall.
Almost invariably the court was back at Whitehall on March 24th, the
'King's Day', as the anniversary of James's accession to the English throne
was known. This was one of the high occasions of the year. Salvos of

G

artillery fired from the Tower and bells ringing from the churches made all London aware of its importance. At Whitehall a select group of courtiers, clad cap-à-pie in plate armour, rode in tournament in the tiltyard.

Skill in horsemanship was greatly admired in the English court. Hence the courtier spent as much or more time with his French riding-master as with his Italian master of fencing. To have a stable of fine high-spirited horses and to manage their curvetting with an easy negligent grace, was an ambition of every young aspirant at the court. Nowhere was a man's skill in the saddle more evident than in the sport of 'running at the ring'. For this, two high posts were erected with a crossbeam at the top from which a small ring dangled at the end of a string. Each contestant took his turn in charging between the posts and trying to carry away the ring on his lance. Sometimes teams would ride at the ring, with the losers bound to some such forfeit as paying for a supper for the winners.

Running at the ring was a means of training for jousting in the tiltyard. To the modern historian of arms, an Elizabethan or Jacobean tilting with all its irrelevant spectacle and by-play was a mere decadent survival of the great joustings of medieval chivalry. To the Jacobeans, a tournament such as that held annually on King's Day was a splendid and magnificent state performance.

Often the tilting was cast in a semi-dramatic setting, with triumphal chariots first entering, from which allegorical characters delivered speeches of compliment to the King and wove some fanciful myth of chivalry to account for the jousting and to introduce the contestants. Each of the latter sought to surpass his fellows in richness and display. Dudley Carleton sardonically records the efforts of the tilters on King's Day, 1609, to outdo each other:

> The Duke of Lennox exceeded all in feathers; the Lord Walden in followers; and Sir Richard Preston in a pageant, which was an elephant with a castle on his back; and it proved a right *partus elephantis*, for it was long a coming, till the running was well entered into, and was then as long a creeping about the tilt-yard, all which time the running was intermitted.[11]

Although the tilters used blunted spears as they charged towards each other alongside the separating railing which prevented head-on collision, there was danger of real injury. In June 1603 one of the two Alexander brothers, who were among the most expert jousters in the court, was almost killed by the Earl of Cumberland. In a practice joust before the King's Day in 1612, Lord North had the flesh and sinews of his arm badly torn when the spear of the Earl of Montgomery splintered and penetrated his armour. The risks involved may have accounted for the curious behaviour of Lord Hay who, on King's Day 1618, availed himself of the privilege of naming a substitute (permissible when a man could not himself attend) and then committed the unheard-of folly of coming and sitting among the spectators. Learning that the noble lord was present, his substitute, a French rider named Beauclaire, 'peremptorily refused to runne in the place and according to the degree of the Lord Hay'.

Eastertide also usually saw the court at Whitehall. On Maundy Thursday the King performed his ritual washing of the feet of the poor and distributed the Maundy money. Easter Day itself, along with Whit Sunday, Allhallows, Christmas Day and its three holy days, New Year's Day and Twelfth Day, comprised the festival days when the Household Ordinances provided for feasting and a special allowance of Gascon wine out of the Cellar. Not that the courtiers fared badly on ordinary days. The lists of diet approved for the usual consumption of the court are staggering in their prodigal plenty. When the King and Queen sat down to their meal, twenty-four dishes were served, unless they were dining in state, when a minimum of thirty dishes was in order. The great officers of the court lived almost as well as Their Majesties. When the Privy Councillors dined together once every week in the Star Chamber, they had plenty to choose from. The expenses for their dinner on January 30, 1605,[12] were:

Bread	38/		10 Teals	10/
Beer	12/		12 tame Pigeons	8/
Ale	5/		24 Rabbits	16/
Flour	6/		36 Blackbirds	9/
Oysters	12/		6 doz. Larks	7/
4 Stone of Beef	£4/13/6		1 fresh Salmon	30/
6 Neat's Tongues	8/		pounded Butter	16/
7 joints of Veal	27/6		Cream	
Suet	4/		Eggs	
Marrow Bones	2/		Herbs	
9 joints of Mutton	23/		Apples and Pears	
2 Lambs	28/		Oranges and Lemons	
3 Turkeys	21/		Berberries	
7 Capons	21/		Rosewater	
9 Pulletts	28/			
2 Pheasants	26/8		Gascoigne wine	
10 Partridges	20/		Sack	
18 Woodcocks	27/		Red and white wine	
12 Widgeons	16/			

When a court lord entertained King James or others whom he wished to honour, the surplus beyond what could possibly be consumed was staggering. Particularly noteworthy were the endeavours of Lord Hay, who brought into fashion the 'ante-supper':

The manner of which was, to have the board covered at the first entrance of the Ghests with dishes as high as a tall man could well reach, filled with the choicest and dearest viands Sea or Land could afford: And all this once

seen, and having feasted the eyes of the Invited, was in a manner thrown
away, and fresh set on to the same height, having only this advantage of
the other, that it was hot.[13]

The lesser civil servants at Whitehall did not dine in the same style as
their superiors but, on paper at least, they did not do badly. Seven dishes
a day were served in the mess of the Clerks of the Signet and of the Privy
Council. True, the quality of their food was not always beyond reproach.
Collusion between the royal purveyors and the victuallers resulted often,
despite the surveillance of the clerk comptrollers, in spoiled or inferior
produce being delivered to the court. Moreover, since the purveyors
exercised their prerogative of requisitioning supplies at less than the market
price, and even then often bought on credit, dealers usually withheld their
best stocks for those who paid promptly and well. The consequence was
that 'for varietie and dressing of meate yt cannot be denied but the forme
of a Noblemans howse is better then the Court'.[14] However, for the King's
own table, the Lord Steward's department probably managed to secure
the best of everything.

Of particular note was the feast of the Order of the Garter, held annually
on St. George's Day. Great magnificence attended this. The Knights of
the Order wore their blue mantles and garters, while the gentlemen who
were in attendance at the court honoured the Order that day by wearing
blue coats and golden chains, and bearing on their caps the colours of the
member whom they wished to compliment. The banquet with its ceremonies and its plenitude of dishes lasted about four hours.

May and June saw a notable change in the life of the court. The hunting-
boxes in Cambridgeshire were shut up, to remain unvisited until the
autumn, while the King established a 'standing court' (a comparatively
fixed one) at the riverside manor at Greenwich to which its first builder
had given the name of 'Placentia' or 'Pleasance'. The name was well
chosen. Here, amid green parkland and beside the still unsullied waters of
the lower Thames, James and his courtiers spent the lovely days of spring.
Trips to Whitehall were kept to an absolute minimum and London saw
the King hardly at all. Occasionally James and his courtiers rode over to
another royal house near by to spend a few days there. This was Eltham
where the Dutch engineer Cornelius Drebbel built for King James his
famous perpetual motion machine, a brass globe which not only recorded
the day and the month, but showed the course of the sun, the moon and
the planets. Surrounding this globe was a vertical glass ring containing
water which fell and rose with the ebb and flow of the tides in the vicinity.
Another mechanical wonder said to have been on view at Eltham was a
mechanical maiden which sang when the sun shone upon it but went
silent when clouds obscured the light.[15]

Late in the spring came the publication of the 'gests', the itinerary for the King's summer progress through the shires. Once these were out, knights and lords who found they were to have the expensive pleasure of entertaining the King on his travels hastily sent letters to their stewards to begin preparations. Cities and towns along the route received notification, and aldermen hurriedly convened to decide how to welcome His Majesty.

Late June and early July found the court on the move. This was the time for brief visits to the royal 'houses of attendance' at Richmond, Nonsuch and Oatlands. Usually there was a week or so at Windsor. By the end of the third week in July the King's summer tour or 'progress' was under way. Sometimes he was accompanied on this by the Queen and his heir, but often these made smaller independent progresses of their own, taking in parts of the kingdom unvisited by the King.

The English court on the move afforded a notable spectacle. The King and his courtiers travelled on horseback escorted by the liveried 'running footmen' who enjoyed such a vogue at this time. Sometimes riding with the gentlemen, but often seated in the large square springless coaches that had first come into use in the previous reign, were the ladies of the court. Then came a vast train of hundreds of great two-wheeled carts, drawn by six-horse teams and loaded with tents, baggage, and all the other *impedimenta* of the court. Riding on top of these, or walking alongside, were a host of menials. So vast a procession could travel neither far nor fast. Accordingly, a day's journey seldom exceeded twelve miles, with a midday pause for dinner at some conveniently placed country-house or inn. Failing these, a temporary 'dining-house' was erected along the route.

Being so slow and cumbersome, the royal progress could not in its six or seven weeks extend to such remote parts of the kingdom as Cornwall, Devon, Wales, or the northern counties. Indeed, the royal progress was usually limited to one or the other of two areas. The first was that encompassed by a southern circuit into Surrey, Hampshire and Wiltshire. A southern progress usually included a week or so at the home of the Earl of Southampton at Beaulieu Abbey, conveniently close for hunting in the New Forest. More frequently, however, King James's progress took him into the second of these areas—a Midlands circuit including Bedfordshire, Northamptonshire, Leicestershire and Nottinghamshire. Here a series of vast 'prodigy houses', built by their noble masters with a view to entertaining the sovereign upon just such visits, afforded ideal halting-places.

Typical of this midland circuit is the itinerary set forth in the 'gests' for 1612. This year the progress began on July 20th when the court set out from Theobalds for St. Albans. The next day James and his entourage travelled to Wrest where they were the guests of the Earl of Kent. On

July 24th the King and his company arrived at Bletsoe, the Bedfordshire home of Lord St. John. After three nights here they continued on to Castle Ashby where their host was Lord Compton. From there, on July 30th, they moved to the ornate grandeur of Kirby Hall and the hospitality of Sir Christopher Hatton. On August 3rd the court moved on to Apethorpe, the home of the Mildmay family. Here on August 5th the King celebrated his preservation from the Gowrie conspirators. On August 6th there was an overnight stop at Brooke, the modest home of Sir Edward Noel, and the next day the court arrived at Belvoir (or Bever) Castle for a few days with the Earl of Rutland. The night of August 10th was spent in the little town of Newark. On the 11th the court moved on to Rufford Abbey where they were received by Sir George Saville, and on the 14th to Newstead Abbey, the home of Sir John Byron, ancestor of the poet. There were civic receptions at Nottingham on August 17th and Leicester on the 18th.

Civic preparations were always much the same. Houses along the royal route were repaired and freshly painted. The streets themselves were newly paved or sanded. If judged too narrow, the city gates would be enlarged. The city's recorder prepared a welcoming oration. Gentlemen ushers from the court arrived well in advance to check over the plans to receive their master. Gratuities were paid to the Knight Marshal, the royal harbingers, the King's way-maker, and the other royal officials whose co-operation the city needed. Finally all was ready for the great day. When the King entered the city, the civic mace or sword, freshly gilded, was delivered to him. He touched it and returned it. Then, preceded by a magnate of the county bearing the Sword of Estate before him, His Majesty passed through the streets. That evening the burgesses would feast the King and his courtiers at a civic banquet.

With the visits to Nottingham and Leicester, the progress of 1612 was almost at its close. On August 21st James was at Dingley, stopping overnight with Sir Thomas Griffin. The next day he arrived at one of his favourite stopping-places, Holdenby (shortened colloquially to Holmby), the enormous mansion built by Sir Christopher Hatton in the previous reign but bought by Queen Anne and eventually her gift to Prince Charles. Here the progress ended, with James going on to another of his manors, that of Woodstock (where Blenheim Palace now stands).

The fact that King James visited his favourite stopping-places summer after summer, occasionally staying for a week or more, meant a decided drain on the finances of the owners of such favoured places as Castle Ashby, Burghley, Grafton, Bletsoe, and Belvoir Castle. King James expected to be entertained royally, and his annoyance was plain when he felt that the hospitality was niggardly. Even when James was at pains to limit the number of his retinue so as to spare charges for his host, the expenses were considerable. When Bishop Lancelot Andrewes of Winchester entertained James with notable magnificence at Farnham Castle for three days in 1620, the cost exceeded 2,400 Jacobean pounds (£19,200 at least in modern values). All things considered, it is not surprising that some Englishmen were just as pleased not to receive the honour of a royal visit. In July 1615, those living in the counties which James proposed to visit petitioned:

> ... to be spared this yeare in respect of the hard winter, and hitherto extreme hot and drie summer, wherby cattell are exceding poore and like to perish every where.[16]

The petition gives an interesting indication of just what a drain the gargantuan Jacobean court could be on the local food supply.

Early September saw the court at Windsor for a week or ten days. Towards the end of the month a standing court was established at Hampton Court. This was a time for reassembling. Lords and ladies who had spent the summer months in the privacy of their own estates now rejoined the King. Hundreds of servants in the departments of the Lord Steward and Lord Chamberlain, whose services had not been needed during the summer progress, again took up their duties. There was not room for everybody in Hampton Court and rows of tents lined the approaches to the palace. Some of the tents provided quarters for menials serving in the royal kitchens and stables. Others were occupied by the parasitic 'hang-bys' who, despite the searches made by the royal avenors, were forever infesting the court with their presence, cutting purses or filching whenever they saw the chance, and insinuating themselves with the connivance of the lower servants into their messes where they could eat at the royal expense. In their own malodorous and dirty persons and those of their companion whores, the 'hang-bys' were a major threat to the health of the court. It was generally in the tents that the plague first began its ravages.

October saw the court once more established at Whitehall but with protracted periods during which the King was off hunting at Royston, Newmarket and the other favoured places in the same region, such as Hinchingbrooke and Thetford. As in January, James took with him only a selected company of courtiers, and Sir Richard Wigmore, Marshal of the Field, was charged to see that His Majesty 'be not attended by any but his owne followers, nor interrupted and hindered in his sports, by straungers and ydle lookers-on'. Once more for the courtier it was in the saddle at eight in the morning, hard hunting until four, and then a five-mile ride home. Fair weather or foul, the King was afield. Only when the day was utterly atrocious did the courtiers keep indoors, whiling away the time at dicing, shuffleboard, backgammon or prickpenny. In the lengthening winter evenings there was hard drinking in the royal quarters, crude horse-play, bawdy jesting, and ponderous practical jokes organized by Sir George Goring, unofficial 'Master of the game for Fooleries'. This was the time when Archie Armstrong, the King's Fool, was on his mettle to dispel the King's morose mood. It paid to be on the right side of Archie. Olivares was well advised when he rewarded Archie with 'an extraordinarie rich suit' when he came to Spain with Prince Charles, and the city of York knew what it was doing when it presented him with a reward when he accompanied the King there in 1621. Archie's wit could be devastating. We still remember how he evened the score with the future Archbishop Laud. Laud's small stature was notable. Receiving King James's permission to say grace one night at supper, Archie said his piece: 'All thanks to God, and little laud to the Devil.'

Each royal return to Whitehall saw more and more of the gentry coming up from the country and thronging to the court. Blenching at the prospect of winter in the shires—the isolation, the foul roads, the grim tedium of life with only some poor relatives and the parson for company—many a squire, urged on by his lady, closed up house and came to London for the diversions of the town and the festivities of the court. Their appearance in the corridors at Whitehall gave no pleasure to the Privy Council or the officers of the household. Here were still more persons to importune the King for favours and grants. They and their servants were so many more mouths that could become chargeable to the King's hospitality. In the view of the Council, the right place for these people was in the country, serving usefully as Justices of the Peace and maintaining their own houses, both strengthening the rural economy by providing employment and helping support the poor through the charity given at their buttery door.

Not surprisingly, this was a likely time for a royal order sending all the country gentry back to their homes in the shires, even though there would be an agonized outcry from the City merchants who saw a profitable set of moneyed customers suddenly thrust from their stalls. A typical proclamation is that issued on November 20, 1622. This bears the explanatory title:

> A Proclamation commanding Noblemen, Knights, and Gentlemen of quality, to repayre to their Mansion houses in the Country, to attend their services, and keepe hospitality, according to the ancient and laudable custome of England.[17]

This proclamation apparently failed to do what was desired, for a little later John Chamberlain reported:

. . . even upon Christmas eve came foorth another proclamation, for their
wives and families and widowes to be gon likewise, and that henceforward
gentlemen should remain here during termes [while the law courts were
sitting] only or other busines, without bringing their wives and families,
which is *durus sermo* to the women. . . .[18]

The next winter saw the issuance of a new proclamation. This had real
teeth, for it instructed the authorities in London and Westminster to make
a speedy certificate to the Privy Council of all the noblemen and gentlemen residing within their jurisdiction, and it declared that those on the list
would be subject to trial in the Star Chamber for failure to obey the earlier
proclamations. It would be interesting to know how many of those offending had 'a friend at court' to see that no action was taken against them.

Christmas invariably saw the King and his court at Whitehall for the
splendid festivities of the season. The Master of the Revels and his staff
would have the King's Men and other professional companies of actors
ready with plays, and a glittering court masque would be in prospect. This
was the season, too, for 'Golden Play' at the gaming tables at court, when
no gamester was admitted unless he brought his £300 with him, and the
King watched while a favourite played his money for him, with the hope
that if he fared well His Majesty would make him a gift of the winnings.
And so the year came to its close, bringing our courtier once more the old
question: what to give to whom for a New Year's gift.

The annual cycle of the courtier's year took its place within the larger
cycle that was his life. In youth, he conned his lessons with his tutor, often
the family chaplain. A few years might follow at one of the universities.
If he were of noble blood, he secured his degree in one year less than his
more plebeian fellow students, the university presumably feeling it took a
little longer to make a silk purse out of a sow's ear. From the university
he went to London to 'cast his academic skin'. Here he might reside in
one of the Inns of Court, though his study of the law was apt to be purely
nominal. Then came entry into the life of the court with the winning of a
post of some kind, however trifling or honorific. Marriage came next.
First the protracted negotiations over his bride's dowry, then the nuptials
themselves with

> . . . marriage sweetly honoured in gorged stomachs
> And overflowing cups.[19]

The babies began to arrive, each christening calling for careful choice of
godparents who were, or would prove to be, useful allies. There was an
elaborate baptismal banquet for all the guests. Gifts were presented to the
babe and its mother, who received her visitors amid the luxury of her
expensive lying-in chamber.

The years passed. Sometimes the courtier was at court attending the

G*

King; sometimes he was at the fashionable resorts of Bath and Salisbury.
(Epsom and Tunbridge Wells were just beginning to become popular with
the discovery of their medicinal waters.) Sometimes he visited the great
country houses of his friends; more often he maintained the old custom of
hospitable 'housekeeping' in his own family seat. Months, seasons, years
passed by, until he found himself arranging marriages for his own sons and
daughters. Then finally came the summons which drew the courtier to
attend not the King in the halls of Whitehall but the King of Kings in the
halls of heaven. To his grave he went with all the costly panoply of a noble
funeral: the superintending herald, the long train of paid mourners in
their black gowns, the poor men bearing baskets of food given in ritual
charity, and finally the coffin, covered with black and tied with bunches of
yew and rosemary, in which our courtier made his last journey to church.
Here he would lie through the centuries under his great 'half-acre tomb'
loaded with sculpture and obelisks.

What drew young men of good family to embark upon 'this turgent and
turbulent Sea of the Court'? Several answers may be given. There was the
old tradition that the aristocrat's place was by his royal master, serving him
cheerfully. Bishop Joseph Hall puts it nicely in his 'Description of a Good
and Faithfull Courtier':

> He is a good husband of his houres; equally detesting idlenesse and base
> disports; and placing all his free time upon ingenuous studies, or generous
> delights; such as may make either his body or mind, more fit for noble
> service. . . . His life is his owne willing servant, and his Princes free vassall;
> which he accounts lent to him, that he may give it for his Master: the
> intercepting of whose harmes, he holds both his duty and honour. . . .[20]

Probably more men were drawn by a desire to be at the centre of things
and participate in the excitement and bustle of court life, than were
inspired by this kind of old-fashioned idealism. Certainly, the motive of
most was self-interest. Many served the King only as a means of serving
themselves.

Most of King James's courtiers were office-seekers pure and simple.
Some sought offices for themselves, others for sale to their fellows. Like
commissions in the British Army in the next century, appointments at the
Jacobean court were highly vendible. Unless ignominiously dismissed, a
man holding an office had to receive his price before relinquishing it to his
successor. When Sir George Calvert was replaced as Secretary of State in
1625, Sir Albertus Morton, whom the King had designated to succeed
him, had to pay him £3,000. The price was considered very low and James
compensated Calvert further by throwing in an Irish barony which Calvert
could either claim for himself or sell to somebody who wanted to become
a lord and would pay him for the title. When Sir Edward Zouch became

Knight Marshal in 1618, the King was reported to have paid personally half the asking price (£3,000) of his predecessor, Sir Thomas Vavasour. After it was decided that the Navy could no longer be left rotting in the corruption of the Earl of Nottingham's administration, Buckingham still had to buy out Nottingham with a lump sum and a pension.

There never were enough posts in the court to go around. To satisfy the demands of aspirants, 'extraordinary' appointments were made over and above the normal establishment, and entirely new offices created. The use of 'quarter waiters' quadrupled certain positions. (A quarter waiter discharged his duties for three months each year, then made way for another quarter waiter.) But still there were not enough posts for all who sought them. Accordingly, the King sometimes mortgaged against the future and promised not an office, since this was already filled, but the reversion of the office. Reversions, long a feature of the English court, were as vendible as offices themselves. Moreover, they appreciated in value, since each year brought nearer the death of the incumbent and the moment when the reversion took effect. Reversions were considered first-rate investments by the courtiers who traded in them. Persons who could not afford an entire reversion often bought a share in one.

The rewards at court extended far beyond profitable offices and the rights to their succession. An impressive list could be compiled of the other spoils available for the fortunate courtier. There were, for instance, the parasitic 'monopolies' attached to so many of the nation's trades and industries. A typical monopoly was that enjoyed first by the Earl of Northampton and then by Lord Hay on the manufacture of starch. The monopoly on the retail sale of wine was shared by the Earl of Nottingham and his heir, and that on the manufacture of glass by the Earl of Montgomery and Sir Robert Mansell. A monopoly on gold and silver thread enriched Sir Edward and Christopher Villiers. The original purpose of monopolies, to encourage and protect native industries, was forgotten in the scramble to secure them. Everybody of any consequence at court tried to procure one. Even Archie Armstrong, the King's Fool, had his—that of clay for making tobacco pipes. Issuance of a monopoly meant that everyone engaged in the trade concerned had either to buy his licence from the agent of the fortunate patentee or lose his livelihood. The royal proclamation of August 1619 conferring upon Henry Heron, gentleman, at the petition of William, Earl of Tullibardine, the monopoly of salting fish, not only declared that no one was to salt or pack fish without licence from Heron, but gave him power of search and entry, and authorized him to keep foreigners from fishing in the adjacent seas. Inevitably these monopolies were a great grievance to King James's subjects. Speaking in the House of Commons in 1621, Sir Edward Coke estimated that some 2,000 monopolies were in force, worth £400,000 annually to their owners.

In arriving at his figures, Coke may have included the farm of various profitable import and export taxes. Early in the reign Suffolk secured the farm of the import duty on currants, Cecil that on silk, and Southampton that on sweet wine. All were received at very favourable rates. In 1613 Suffolk made a profit of £5,000 over and above what he was bound to transmit to the Crown. Sometimes the entire receipts of certain duties were handed over to courtiers. Thus in 1607, for a nominal rent of £10 paid jointly, Sir Fulke Greville was granted £400 annually out of a new levy on Rhenish wine, and Sir David Murray the rest of its proceeds. In 1615 Sir Richard Coningsby was given the right to collect and retain the entire import duty on playing-cards brought into the kingdom.

The ingenuity of the courtiers in finding ways of fixing their blood-sucking grip upon the national economy was almost without limit. There was, for instance, the matter of 'alnage', the official inspection and measurement of woollen cloth. This was granted to the Duke of Lennox, who must have found it a source of considerable wealth since this cloth accounted for something like 85 per cent of the nation's export trade. Even the building of lighthouses was turned into a source of profit for courtiers. In 1618, it being decided that the seas about Wintertonness were dangerous, Sir William Erskine and John Meldrum were given leave to erect lights there and to charge a penny a ton on all shipping passing that way.

There remained many other ways in which a courtier could enrich himself. He might secure the collection of debts due to the Crown—Sir Richard Preston, one of the King's Scots, was awarded £2,317 in this manner in 1606. He might be granted the goods or estates of persons attainted on charges of treason, felony or murder. He might be given a first call on the fines levied by one or other of the King's courts—William Shaw, in 1605, was awarded 'out of the fines in the King's Bench £800'. He might be awarded the patronage of ecclesiastical benefices in the royal gift—Sir Oliver Cromwell was granted '200li a yeare in parsonages in regard to his service'. He might be given the fines levied against some wealthy Catholic recusant—'John Gib, out of Recusants' lands and goods £3,000'. He might secure such a profitable right as 'to sell all the under-woods in his majesty's own tenure' and keep half of the proceeds for himself, a grant which was reported to have been worth £20,000 to the Earl of Somerset. He might receive lands out of the royal holdings. He might secure from the King, as Lord Kinloss did, the dowry for his daughter.

There was, in fact, no limit to the ways in which the courtier could prosper. The best and simplest, however, was an order upon the royal exchequer for payment in cash. Among such royal 'benevolences' paid during the year ending at Michaelmas 1611 were these:

Earl of Montgomery	£8000
Earl of Essex	£3000
Viscount Fenton	£8000
Lord Hay	£5000
Viscount Rochester	£5000[21]

Real prizes were the annuities which King James granted with remarkable generosity. Unfortunately, the royal exchequer was sometimes too exhausted to pay them. Persons in a position to do so, therefore, got the King to make their pensions 'assignments', i.e. first charges against the revenues of such reliable sources as the Court of Wards or the Duchy of Lancaster. Pensions payable by assignment were, as Professor Tawney has observed, the gilt-edged securities of the Jacobean court.

At times of acute financial embarrassment, the King might find that the only rewards he could give were titles of honour. Even these could be made a source of profit by the courtier who petitioned not for a title for himself but one to sell to someone else. In 1619 the Earl of Huntingdon made £2,500 when he sold Sir Richard Wingfield the title of Viscount Powerscourt. Perhaps the most gratifying reward of all for a courtier, however, was when he received from the King not only a title for himself but a grant of estates to allow him to live on the scale his new dignity demanded. When Sir John Ramsay was created Viscount Haddington, he received lands worth £1,000 per annum to support the title.

Not everybody prospered at court. Some made the wrong alliances and secured powerful enemies. Some bankrupted themselves trying to keep up with the senseless extravagance of the court, and had to retire at last, impoverished. Some incurred the dire fate of the King's active displeasure. There was, for instance, the luckless soul who was so intent upon begging a suit that he neglected to admire the King's handsome new saddle. When his friends asked the King why he had not granted the man's petition, James snorted, 'Shall a King give heed to a dirty paper, when a beggar noteth not his gilt stirrups?'[22]

The courtier who had exhausted his means and become distasteful to the King was faced with the grim prospect of life as a 'cast-courtier' languishing in poverty on the Continent. Indeed, if he were a person of sufficient importance and his faults flagrant enough in the royal eye, he might not escape with exile either compelled or self-imposed, but find himself like Lord Grey, Raleigh, the Earl of Northumberland and poor Lady Arbella, confined to the Tower while the offices and monopolies, pensions and lands he had earlier secured were rapaciously sought by his more fortunate fellows. In his eclipse, the courtier could only reflect that 'courtly hopes they are the aires atomes, a sun-shine engenders them, and a frost kills them'.[23] He could only hope that, his disgrace being final, he would henceforth be free of 'the court fever of hope and feare that continually torments those that depend upon great men and theyre promises'.[24] And he could find a final rough consolation that for him and all his kind it had been a sort of gamble: 'The Court being a kind of Lottery where men that venture much may draw a Blank; and such as have little may get the Prize.'[25]

What did the common Englishman think of our Jacobean courtier with his garish extravagance, untidy morals, and insatiable thirst for the royal bounty? For answer we have a ballad of the time, comparing him with his predecessor, the courtier who had been held more strictly to his duties by Queen Elizabeth.

The Old Courtier of the Queen's

With an old song made by an old aged pate
Of an old gentleman that had an old wealthy estate,
Who kept an old house, at an old bountiful rate,
With an old porter to relieve poor people at his gate;
    Like an old Courtier of the Queen's,
    And the Queen's old Courtier.

With an old lady whose anger one word assuages,
Which every quarter pays her servants their wages,
Who never knew what belonged to footmen or pages,
But kept fifty stout fellows with blue coats and badges;
    Like an old Courtier, etc.

With an old study filled full of old learned books,
And an old reverend parson you may judge by his old looks,
And an old buttery hatch worn off the old hooks,
And an old kitchen that maintained half a dozen old cooks;
    Like an old Courtier, etc

With an old hall hung round with pikes, guns, and bows,
And old blades and bucklers that have bidden many old blows,
And an old frisadoe coat, to cover his worship's trunk hose,
And a cup of old sack to burnish out his honourable nose;
    Like an old Courtier, etc.

With an old fashion when Christmas is come,
To call out his old neighbours, with old bagpipe and drum,
And meat enough to furnish out every old room,
And old beer that will make a cat speak and a wise man dumb;
    Like an old Courtier, etc.

With an old falconer and huntsman and a kennel of hounds,
Who never hawked but in his grandfather's old grounds,
Who like a wise man kept yearly within his old bounds,
And when he died gave each child a thousand old pounds;
    Like an old Courtier, etc.

But to his son and heir his house and land he assigned,
With an old will and charge to hold the same bountiful mind,
To be good to his neighbours and to his tenants kind,
But in the ensuing ditty you shall hear how he was inclined;
    Like a new Courtier of the King's,
    And the King's new Courtier.

With a new flourishing gallant, new come to his land,
Who kept a brace of new painted creatures to be at his hand,
And could take up a thousand readily upon his own new bond,
And be drunk in a new tavern till he be not able to go or stand;
    Like a new Courtier, etc.

With a new Lady whose face is beautiful and fair,
Who never knew what belongs to housekeeping or care,
But purchased seven new fans to play with the air,
And seventy new dressings of other women's hair;
    Like a new Courtier, etc.

With a new study stuffed full of pamphlets and plays,
And a new pedagogue chaplain that swears faster than he prays,
And a new buttery hatch that opens once in five or six days,
And a new French cook to devise kickshaws and toys;
    Like a new Courtier, etc.

With a new hall where the old hall stood,
And a new chimney that burns neither coals nor wood,
And a new shovel-a-bord table whereon meat never stood,
Hung round with pictures that do the poor no good;
    Like a new Courtier, etc.

With a new fashion when Christmas is coming on,
With a new journey to London they must all be gone,
Leaving none to keep in the country but his new man John,
Who relieves the poor people with a new thump of a stone;
    Like a new Courtier, etc.

With a new gentleman usher whose carriage is complete,
With a new coachman and two footmen to carry up his meat,
With a new waiting gentlewoman whose dressing is very neat,
Who, when her lady and master hath dined, leaves her fellows
                         little to eat;
    Like a new Courtier, etc.

With new titles purchased with his father's old gold,
For which many of his grandfather's old manors newly are sold,
And hath a new reason why housekeeping is grown so cold,
That is the new course that most of our new gallants do hold;
    Like a new Courtier of the King's,
    And the King's new Courtier.[26]

CHAPTER XV

The Rising Star of Somerset

TO SEE HOW a young man with nothing more than good looks and good luck could achieve a dazzling career at the court of King James, one need only turn to Robert Ker. Ker, the penniless fifth son of an obscure Scottish knight, became, next to the King, the most powerful man in all Britain. If we stop short of his final disaster, his is one of the great success stories of the Jacobean Court, his the climb which less fortunate courtiers only dreamed of making. It all began when he had the good fortune to break his leg.

This auspicious accident happened on King's Day 1607. There was the tilting customary to the occasion at Whitehall, with each of the contestants having a shield bearing his device borne before him as he entered the lists. When the page of Lord Hay came to dismount and present his master's device to the King, the young man's horse threw him as he was alighting and broke his leg. Out of a kindly impulse, the King visited the young man when he was recovering from his injury. He found a handsome flaxen-haired Scot of some twenty years of age, not tall in stature but compact and well-proportioned. His complexion was fair, his full oval face good-looking in a bland unintelligent fashion. He was, it transpired, not unknown to King James, for a few years earlier he had been one of his Pages of Honour in Scotland. Out of a job after he had accompanied King James to England, he had crossed to France and had only recently reappeared at court in the service of Lord Hay. Repeating his visit, James found himself powerfully attracted to young Ker. Although no evidence has ever been produced to prove the charges that King James was a homosexual, there can be no doubt that he had a notable weakness for handsome young men. Young Ker had more than good looks in his favour. His father, Sir Thomas Ker of Ferniehurst, had been a close friend of King James's boyhood hero Esmé, Duke of Lennox, and so the innate clannishness of the Scots drew James closer to young Robert Ker (or Carr, as his name was anglicized).

Shortly after his accession to the English throne, King James had installed as his favourite Philip Herbert, whom he created Earl of Montgomery. Although Montgomery had the requisite good looks, he had shown himself an unappreciative boor, interested only in hunting, wenching and drinking. King James, despite a coarse streak in him, was an educated man with an interest in ideas. Montgomery had proved a disappointment; Carr seemed much more promising. Residence in France had given polish to his manners and he listened politely and appreciatively to the King. Soon it was arranged for His Majesty to visit him every morning to teach him Latin. English courtiers snickered that the young man's accent was so thick that it would be more to the point if the King were to teach him English, but James was oblivious of such gibes. He was by nature a Scottish dominie, a schoolmaster rather than a king, and a wonderful project was stirring in his mind. He would take this highly attractive young man, so docile and so grateful; he would himself instruct him in the mysteries of statecraft, and educate him into a minister to serve under him. To Cecil he confided something of his scheme, declaring that he had chosen his man with care, having 'bred him in his youth', a sanguine recollection of the days when Carr had been one of his pages in Scotland.

Soon all the court was aware that the King had a new favourite. Lord Thomas Howard, writing to Sir John Harington, told him with some bitterness how the young Scot had won the royal favour 'wondrously in a little time', and remarked nastily how James 'leaneth on his arm, pinches his cheek, smoothes his ruffled garment'. He gave Harington some pointed advice on how to succeed at court—'You must see Carr before you go to the King, as he was with him a boy in Scotland, and knoweth his tastle and what pleaseth.' Towards the last of his letter, Howard gave a little word-picture of the new favourite on whom all attention had so suddenly fallen:

> . . . I tell you, good knight, this fellow is straight-limbed, well-favourede, strong-shoulderd and smooth-faced, with some sort of cunning and show of modesty; tho' God wot, he well knoweth when to shew his impudence.[1]

Years later Sir Anthony Weldon was to exclaim, in retrospect, at the way in which the courtiers had flocked to the chamber where Carr lay while his leg mended:

> Lord! how the great men flocked then to see him, and to offer to his Shrine in such abundance, that the King was forced to lay a restraint, least it might retard his recovery by spending his spirits. . . .[2]

It is hard for a twentieth-century historian to assess the merits of a seventeenth-century royal favourite. He has to guard against a prejudice in himself against favourites *per se* and to remember that he is dealing with an age when all sovereigns had their minions (a derivation from *mignon*) and when both their existence and the rich rewards yielded to them were taken as inevitable and right. The testimony of contemporaries about these favourites is usually hopelessly at odds. On one hand, we have the unctuous flattery of those who sought favours from them; on the other, the slanders spread by defeated rivals and rejected suitors. Dealing with Carr, the historian hardly knows whom to believe. On one side stands Sir Edward Peyton assuring him that Carr 'furnished his library onely with twenty play-books and wanton romances, and had no other in his study'.[3] On the other stands Sir Anthony Weldon declaring he 'was observed to spend his time in serious studies, and did accompany himselfe with none but men of such eminencies as by whom he might be bettered'. Seeking a way out, he may turn to Bishop Goodman who earnestly assures him:

> Now for the favourite Sir Robert Carr: truly he was a wise, discreet gentleman; and as Sir Robert Cotton, the great antiquary, told me, he did very often send unto him for precedents, when as things were to be done in the State which he doubted whether they were lawful and expedient, and therefore did desire to have the example of former times for his warrant.[4]

Our historian would do well, however, to recall that Bishop Goodman was a dear old gentleman incapable of thinking badly of anyone, and to remember that Carr was Cotton's special patron. All things considered, it is not surprising that modern historians range in their appraisal of Carr from the magisterial S. R. Gardiner's contemptuous summation, 'His weak brain was turned by his rapid elevation,'[5] to T. F. Henderson's protesting declaration:

> Carr was in fact both strong willed and clear sighted; and for many years he was a thoroughly trustworthy and exceptionally proficient public servant.[6]

Seeking to be just to Carr, we may say that, while he was certainly no fool, he gave no evidence of any real mental acuity, that he was on the whole loyal to King James and, according to the standards of his time, honest. He did not deprive other men of their posts and emoluments, though ready enough to benefit from those which happened to be available. He took bribes, as almost everyone at court did, but he was always scrupulous to inform the King and secure his approval before taking proffered money. Apparently he persuaded himself that money thus accepted did not constitute a bribe. Certainly, if James had to have a favourite, he could have done worse than choose Carr. In the end, like all royal favourites who have been pampered too long, he became overweening, forgetful of his dependence upon the King, and invited disaster.

In 1607 this fate lay well in the future. Young Carr was mounting the ladder and not yet scornful of the base means by which he did ascend. Progressively the vista of honours opened before him. In the closing days of 1607 he was appointed a Gentleman of the Bedchamber and knighted. Early in 1608 he received the King's portrait mounted in gold and diamonds. In January 1609 King James, taking advantage of a scribe's omission of a phrase from a legal document, deprived Sir Walter Raleigh of his estate of Sherborne in Dorset and gave it to his young Scot. Feeling ran high against his act. Lady Raleigh went on her knees before the King and begged to be spared this much out of her husband's ruin, but James, muttering 'I maun have the land, I maun have it for Carr', refused her. In 1610 Carr benefited from another man's ruin and received the forfeited Scottish estates of Lord Maxwell.

A golden year for the young favourite was 1611. On March 25th he was given the title of Viscount Rochester, which carried with it a seat in the English House of Lords—something which James had not granted before to any of his Scots. A few months later came the grant of Rochester Castle to support the dignity. In April Carr was elected a Knight of the Garter. In June he was appointed keeper for life of Westminster Palace. The succeeding years yielded fresh honours. In 1612 he was named to the English Privy Council. In 1613 he was appointed Lord Treasurer of Scotland, succeeding the Earl of Dunbar, King James's trusted adviser on Scottish affairs, who had died almost three years earlier.

Carr's advancement was not without its rubs. Prince Henry did not conceal his dislike for his father's favourite, and Cecil skilfully contrived to keep real political power out of his hands. It is significant that only when Cecil was a dying man, preparing to take his last hopeless journey to Bath, did Carr secure his place on the Privy Council. The death in 1612 of both Cecil and Prince Henry removed the two men who might have done most to limit Carr's powers. Ironically, it was in this year that he made the fatal error which was to bring ruin after two more years of power and influence—he fell in love with the Countess of Essex.

Lady Frances Howard, who had become Countess of Essex, was a bad lot. A daughter of King James's Lord Chamberlain, Thomas Howard, Earl of Suffolk, and that avaricious virago his wife, she had been brought up in an atmosphere of self-interest and self-indulgence, and of intrigue sexual and political. In January 1606, at the age of thirteen, she had been married at Whitehall to the fourteen-year-old Robert Devereux, third Earl of Essex. King James had rejoiced at their union. His favourite role was that of *rex pacificus*, the kingly peacemaker. Abroad, he had secured peace between England and Spain; at home, by this marriage, he terminated a feud which had begun when the Howards had helped bring the bridegroom's father, Queen Elizabeth's Essex, to the scaffold. The youthfulness of the principals seemed no reason for postponing their nuptials. After the ceremonies were over, the bride returned to her father's house while her young groom left to mature during two years of travel on the Continent.

In 1609 the Earl, a solid, humourless young man, was back in England.

ROBERT CARR, EARL OF SOMERSET

FRANCES, COUNTESS OF SOMERSET

Collecting his bride from her parents, he carried her off to his country home at Chartley for the consummation of their marriage. That consummation never was achieved. Later, witness after witness was to testify that the two had repeatedly gone to bed together, and the Countess to depose that she had done all that she could 'that shee might be made a lawfull mother',[7] but whatever was done was of no avail. Whether the Earl's impotence was natural from the beginning, or whether it was the consequence of the drugs which, years later, it transpired the young countess had secretly procured from quacks and ministered to him, it is idle to speculate. Whatever the truth, things went from bad to worse at Chartley. The Countess felt a mounting aversion for her husband. At times she hid herself from him and sent despairing messages to her kin and friends. After the first year the Earl, according to his own subsequent testimony, continued at times to bed with her but 'felt no motion or provocation, and therefore attempted nothing'.[8] Thus things dragged on for three years, sometimes at Chartley, sometimes in London, sometimes at the houses of friends, until the compulsory period of 'triennial probation' should be completed, after which the marriage could be nullified and the two given the release for which both longed.

By early 1613 it was common talk at court that the young Essexes wanted a divorce. It was also becoming common talk that the royal favourite Carr was in love with the Countess. Some said that she was his mistress. Other scandalous tales were heard in the corridors. Some said that Lady Frances had relieved Prince Henry of his virginity and that jealousy over her had been the real cause of his hostility to Carr.

The Howards were delighted to see Lady Frances make such a useful conquest as the King's favourite. Earlier they had possessed a key ally in Cecil, but now Cecil was dead. Carr had hitherto been against them, siding with Lord Chancellor Ellesmere and his strongly Protestant court faction. Lady Frances's great-uncle, the devious Northampton, set himself to bring about a marriage that would signally strengthen the power of his house, but he found himself confronted by an implacable enemy to this design.

Favourites have their favourites, and the favourite of Carr was Sir Thomas Overbury, the poet and 'character' writer, whose name is still to be found in the histories of English literature. Clever, able, and intolerably arrogant, Overbury had plenty of enemies. His ascendancy over Carr, however, had made him a real power in the court. As the favourite's political adviser as well as his personal mentor, Overbury unsealed and read the reports from the English ambassadors abroad, before passing them on to Carr with his notations. Some claimed that Overbury knew more secrets of state than the Privy Council itself and declared that, while Carr ruled the King, Overbury ruled Carr. The latter quip reached King James, who was not in the least amused.

Overbury was quite clear about Lady Frances: he did not trust her an inch. A look at her picture now preserved in the National Portrait Gallery helps to explain his view. The descending curve of her dress takes advantage of contemporary fashion to display her breasts. An amused sensuality lurks about her mouth. A coldly appraising stare marks the eyes.

At first, thinking Carr aimed only at an affair, Overbury let him indulge himself. He even helped him with his love letters. When he discovered that Carr actually wanted to marry the lady, Overbury set himself to end the connection. Prophetically he warned Carr. The woman, he said, would ruin him. The violence of Carr's infatuation defeated Overbury, and finally there came the inevitable head-on collision. Returning to his chambers at Whitehall at one o'clock one morning, after visiting the lady, Carr found Overbury waiting for him in the Privy Gallery:

> *How now*, said my Lord, *are you up yet? Nay*, answers Sir Thomas Overbury, *what do you here at this time of Night? Will you never leave the Company of that base Woman? And seeing you do so neglect my Advice, I desire that to-morrow Morning we may part; and that you will let me have that Portion you know is due to me; and then I will leave you free to your self, to stand on your own Legs.* My Lord of Somerset answer'd, *His Legs were strong enough to bear himself;* and so departed in great displeasure.[9]

This quarrel was overheard by a servant of Overbury's, Henry Payton, in an adjoining room, and his is the account just quoted. Subsequently Payton testified that he had certain knowledge that after this incident 'they were never perfectly reconcil'd again'.

A stage had been reached where just about everybody wanted to see Overbury leave the court. Carr was tired of his insolence in other matters besides his attacks on his inamorata. The Howards knew that he had always 'professed Hatred and Opposition' against them. The Queen had never forgiven what she regarded as a personal insult, and had already once secured his temporary banishment. The King had a rooted aversion to him, being involved in a complicated psychological jealousy over Carr. Everybody, in short, wanted Overbury off the scene. Carr suggested that a good way to get rid of the obstreperous fellow would be to send him on a long journey—in fact, to appoint him ambassador to Russia. Overbury was summoned to Lambeth where the Archbishop of Canterbury broached the project to him. Overbury, of course, saw the move for what it was: an endeavour to remove him from the court. Recrossing the Thames after his visit, he revealed his discontent to Sir Dudley Digges. When Digges subsequently came to him from the Privy Council to know whether or not he would accept the embassy, he replied evasively that he would be governed in this by Carr since 'My precious Chief knows the King's Mind better than any, and I the Mind of my precious Chief.'[10]

Not suspecting how little he really knew of the mind of his 'precious Chief,' Overbury sought him out and made it plain both that he did not mean to give up his place at court and that he expected Carr to save him from the exile of the foreign embassy. Carr masked his annoyance at finding Overbury unwilling to be eliminated so easily. His own situation was a bit difficult. With the ticklish business of Lady Frances's divorce coming up, he could not risk any of the damaging disclosures that Overbury might make if he found himself discarded. Just what passed between the two men we do not know, but Overbury left satisfied that he could refuse the embassy and count on his patron to prevent any unfortunate consequences. Thus deceived, he walked into a trap which was now prepared for him.

The trap was sprung on April 21, 1613. At six o'clock that evening Lord Chancellor Ellesmere and the Earl of Pembroke met with Sir Thomas and informed him officially that it was the King's pleasure to send him on an embassy abroad. (In an attempt to make the offer more acceptable to him, the destination had been changed from Russia to either the Low Countries or France.) This was the moment of supreme crisis for Overbury. He could throw in his hand, abandon his place at the favourite's side, accept the face-saving form of his banishment, and begin the overtures of surrender to the Howards which might reopen doors in the future, or he could fight. Unaware that the deeply offended Carr was now against him, he decided to fight, and ensured his ruin and death. He told Ellesmere and Pembroke 'that he was not capable of such Imployment for want of Language, nor able to undergoe it by reason of his Weakness, being so exceedingly troubled with the Spleen that if he had a long Letter to write he was feign to give it over'.[11]

Overbury's refusal was reported to the King. Pembroke was forthwith despatched to meet with the Privy Council. Here Overbury's refusal of 'an honourable Imployment' was presented as a direct insult to the King. It was ordered that, for his contempt of his sovereign, Overbury be imprisoned in the Tower.

The trap had been sprung. The time had been skilfully chosen. A minor indisposition had given Carr an excuse for absenting himself from the Council board, where failure to come to the rescue of his man would have made it obvious to all, including Overbury, that Carr was no longer his friend. With Overbury's imprisonment ordered, Pembroke repaired to Carr's quarters to inform him of the Council's action and to persuade him there would be 'no hurt to his friend' and he should not press for his release. How little persuading Carr needed, only the very few in the secret realized.

When one considers the skill with which Overbury's downfall was achieved, one cannot help speculating as to who was responsible for the artistry of the manœuvre. The job bears the mark of a much more skilful practitioner than Carr ever showed himself to be. It is hard not to suspect the fine Italian hand of the arch-schemer Northampton, who had contributed so much to the ruin of the man whom Overbury in many ways resembled, Sir Walter Raleigh. If Northampton was the architect of the scheme, it must be admitted that he had been successful in keeping the Howards completely uninvolved in the actual workings of the plot. The men with whom Overbury had to deal, Canterbury, Ellesmere and Pembroke, were all of the strongly anti-Howard Protestant party. (Perhaps they had been chosen to make it plain to Overbury that both factions at court were against him.) Once Overbury was in the Tower, however, Northampton moved directly into the scene. Within a few weeks he had a nominee of his own, Sir Gervase Elwes or Helwys, appointed Lieutenant of the Tower, and charged him to keep Overbury incommunicado.

With the obstreperous Overbury safely out of the way, and Carr eager for marriage with Lady Frances, there was no reason for not proceeding swiftly with her divorce. King James was now as eager to marry her to Carr as he once had been to yoke her to Essex.

In June 1613 a commission heard the petition for divorce. It consisted of the Archbishop of Canterbury, the Bishops of London, Ely, and Coventry (Lichfield), Sir Thomas Parry and Sir Julius Caesar, and four doctors of law. It was soon apparent that, though both parties agreed that their marriage had never been consummated, a long and complicated set of hearings lay ahead, for both husband and wife were determined to establish their fitness to remarry. The consequence was that the next few months brought a welter of sensational charges and intimate details, all mixed with prurient gossip, which had all London by the ears.

Lady Frances maintained she had done her full duty by the Earl and it was no fault of hers that she was still a virgin wife. This brought up a very important question of fact for the commissioners. Was she really a virgin? A jury of twelve matrons was asked to determine by examination the virginity of Lady Frances. They certified her a virgin. Since the repeated assignations between the Countess and Carr were already becoming known, there were doubts about this verdict. Some said that the jury had been bribed; others that Lady Frances, for reasons of modesty, had been allowed to wear a veil during the examination and that the veiled woman who presented herself was not really Lady Frances. People who claimed inside knowledge even had the name of the true virgin who had personated the pseudo-one. Some said she was Lady Frances's cousin Katherine

Fiennes, daughter of Lord Clinton; others that she was a daughter of Sir Thomas Monson, a chief of the Howard faction.[12]

Essex, while admitting impotence, insisted that this existed only where Lady Frances was concerned and that he found in himself 'an hability to know any other woman'. To complicate matters, there were suggestions that the Earl's difficulties were due to witchcraft. All of these matters invited cross-examination; but sober, respectable men were disgusted by the spectacle of bishops trying to establish the exact extent and nature of the Earl's sexual achievements and failures.

In midsummer King James received a nasty surprise: the divorce he so ardently wished to see granted would apparently not be forthcoming. From the Archbishop of Canterbury came a letter in which the prelate revealed very serious misgivings about the whole matter. There had been a lot of talk about witchcraft, said the Archbishop, but reading the Church Fathers he could find nothing there about 'maleficium' causing impotence in marriage. Moreover, there were other objections. Surely the remedy in such cases of impotence due to witchcraft, supposing them to exist, lay in the spiritual medicine of prayer and fasting, but the Earl and Countess had not sought such aid:

> Now admitt the Earle of Essex might be imagined to be troubled with *Maleficium versus hanc*: I demaund what Almes hath been given? What fasting hath been used? What Prayers have been powred out to appease the indignation of God towards him and his wife?[13]

The Archbishop thought it would be a very dangerous precedent to grant a nullity in this case.

King James was furious. In a long letter he set the Archbishop right in his theology. His Grace's insistence upon judging everything according to Holy Writ he found Puritan. If the Archbishop did not think the Devil had invented plenty of new tricks since the time of the Church Fathers, let him consult the book which James had written himself, his *Daemonologie*. Surely it was significant that the member wherein Essex had been bewitched was that 'wherin the devill hath his principall operacon'.[14] How did the Archbishop know that Essex and Lady Frances had not resorted to alms and prayer, but privately and secretly as befitted true Christians? Let the Archbishop consider all this with his brothers, James concluded, and they would be convinced of the weakness of the objections. Just to help things along, James added to the commission two more of the Archbishop's brothers, carefully chosen to vote properly, the Bishop of Winchester and the Bishop of Rochester.

On September 25th the commission announced its decision. By a vote of seven to five it ruled that by reason of nullity Essex and Lady Frances were not man and wife. Essex was ordered to repay the lady's dowry. The minority against the divorce was headed by the Archbishop of Canterbury, who had been left unpersuaded by the King's arguments. The majority of two which established the decision consisted of the King's two nominees added when the divorce seemed in danger. A short while later the son of one of them, Bishop Bilson of Winchester, was knighted. It became a joke around the court to refer to him as 'Sir Nullity Bilson'. The death of Sir Thomas Overbury in the Tower a few weeks after the commission brought in its verdict went almost unnoticed.

All eyes turned now to the great wedding in prospect for Robert Carr, Viscount Rochester, and Frances Howard. Expressing a kindly wish not to see the lady reduced from a countess to a mere viscountess, King James on November 4th obligingly advanced Carr to the dignity of Earl of Somerset, and it is as 'Somerset' that we shall refer to him hereafter. Due to a typical piece of carelessness, James had neglected to make his favourite a baron before creating him a viscount, so the opportunity was now seized to make him, belatedly, Baron of Brancepeth in the bishopric of Durham.

On St. Stephen's Day (December 26) 1613, Somerset and Lady Frances were married in the Chapel Royal at Whitehall. The joyful King James bore all the expenses except those for apparel. There was some comment upon the tactless choice not only of the same place but the same priest (the Bishop of Bath and Wells who was Dean of the Chapel) that had been chosen for Lady Frances's disastrous first marriage. One interesting speculation lurked in the minds of the glittering guests as they took their places. How would the bride wear her hair? Would she be wearing it un-bound, hanging down over her shoulders, the prerogative of a virgin bride? They had their answer when she appeared, conducted by her bridesmen, the visiting Duke of Saxony and her great-uncle, Northampton. Lady Frances was wearing her hair 'pendant almost to her feet'.

From all sides gifts came in for the newly married pair. There were silver dishes curiously enamelled from Queen Anne, a rich jewel from the Spanish ambassador, a golden ewer and basin from the agent of the Dutch. All sorts of people who wanted the favourite's favour came up with presents: the City of London, the farmers of the customs, the East India Company. The bride's kinsman, the Lord Admiral, made a gift of the gold plate which he had received when ambassador in Spain for the peace treaty of 1604, though rumour had it that this did not 'prove pure metall now yt comes to the touch'. Sir Arthur Ingram, a creature of the Howards who was to join the bride's mother in looting the royal exchequer during the treasurership of the bride's father, presented a whole set of kitchen implements made of silver. Sir Robert Carey hit upon the happy thought of a set of fire-irons, tongs and shovel and 'all the furniture of a chimney' of silver, only to find his gift duplicated by Sir Robert Mansfield. In came more and more gifts. The goldsmiths of London estimated that the plate and jewels alone were worth about £12,000 (about £100,000 in modern values).

The inevitable round of masques and entertainments followed. On the wedding night there was a masque by Thomas Campion with enchanters and enchantresses and gentlemen masquers who played the parts of knights freed from enchantment when Queen Anne plucked a branch from a golden tree. There were the usual dazzling sets: one of a sea flanked by promontories each with a pillar of gold, another of 'London with the Thames . . . very artificially presented'. December 29th brought Ben Jonson's *Irish Masque*, which no doubt convulsed the court when the anti-masquers with suitably heavy accents complimented 'King Yamish' and explained that they were here to attend the nuptials of 'ty man Robyne' (Robert, Earl of Somerset) and the daughter of 'Toumaish o'Shuffolke' (Thomas, Earl of Suffolk). On January 4th Somerset, his bride, and a company of court lords were banqueted by the Lord Mayor and aldermen of London in the Merchant Tailors' Hall, the tables being waited on by the choicest citizens picked from the twelve major livery companies. Afterwards there were 'two pleasant Masques, a Play and Dancing' followed by further banqueting. Little wonder that Somerset and his wife did not get home to Whitehall until three in the morning. Scarcely was this 'Surfeit of pleasure and Excess . . . well digested' than it was Twelfth Night, and the gentlemen of Gray's Inn were at court to congratulate the two with their *Masque of Flowers*, the cost of £2,000 being defrayed by Sir Francis Bacon.

This masque concluded the special ceremonies and entertainments for Somerset's marriage, but not the round of nuptial celebrations for the court. Another wedding was due in a few weeks time. By a curious coincidence it was that of another Robert Ker, this one Lord Roxburgh, who on Candlemas (February 2) 1614 wedded Jane Drummond, one of Queen Anne's maids of honour.

Somerset reached the peak of his fortunes in 1614. Since the death of Cecil he had exercised many of the functions normally discharged by the Secretary of State, and he continued to do so even after the belated appointment, in March of this year, of Sir Ralph Winwood. The death of another of King James's chief councillors, old Northampton, the Lord Privy Seal, made King James turn increasingly to Somerset for advice. Finally in July, when Suffolk began his disastrous regime as Lord Treasurer, it was Somerset who succeeded him as Lord Chamberlain, the King declaring 'that no man shold marvayle that he bestowed a place so neere himself upon his frend, whom he loved above all men living'.[15]

Suddenly it seemed that all the sources of power, even all access to the King, were passing to Somerset and the Howards. Their enemies, among whom were the leaders of the strongly Protestant faction, held anxious consultations. Apparently the only way of dealing with Somerset was to supplant him with a new favourite. They looked about for a suitable candidate, and found him in twenty-two-year-old George Villiers, the personable but penniless younger son of a Leicestershire squire. In August 1614 Villiers was presented to the King at Apethorpe during the summer progress. In November James appointed him one of his cup-bearers. A clash with Somerset's friends was not long in coming. Over-ambitiously thrusting ahead of one of Somerset's clique who was also serving at the royal table, Villiers got involved in an ugly little scene which reached its climax when Villiers struck the other man a box on the ear. The penalty for a blow struck in the royal presence was amputation of the offender's hand. James, however, immediately pardoned Villiers and by doing so 'without any satisfaction to the other party, made him suspected a budding Favourite'.

The opening months of 1615 saw increasing friction between Somerset and the King. Instead of the old pleasant frankness which had made Somerset so attractive to him, James found querulous suspicions and bad temper. It was the King and not the subject who tried to get things back on the old footing. Somerset, however, behaved like a fool, neither heeding the King's warnings nor responding to his overtures. Too long enjoyment of a favourite's prerogatives had left him thinking he could bully James into giving him whatever he wanted. Significantly, on April 23rd Villiers received the two signs of royal favour which had marked Somerset's own emergence as a royal favourite—knighthood, and appointment as a Gentle-man of the Bedchamber. By May John Chamberlain was speaking of 'Sir George Villiers, the new favourite', and remarking thoughtfully of Somer-set '. . . he makes more shew now the world thincks him in the waine then ever heretofore'.

The summer progress of 1615 was made miserable for everybody by constant wrangling between the followers of the rising and the falling favourites. James, sick of the bad feeling, tried to stop the feud by sending Sir Humphrey May to Somerset to inform him that Sir George Villiers would call to offer his services and that Somerset should accept them. When Somerset declared his unwillingness, May revealed that it was the King himself who had instructed Villiers thus to subordinate himself. Sir Anthony Weldon, who is generally favourable to Somerset, tells us that Villiers made his submission in these words:

> My Lord I desire to be your servant, and your creature, and shall desire to take my Court preferment under your favour and your Lordship, and your Lordship shal finde me as faithfull a servant unto you, as ever did serve you

To this Somerset replied:

> I will none of your service, and you shall none of my favour.
> I will, if I can, break your necke, and of that be confident.[16]

The reply, as Weldon observed, 'savoured more of spirit then wisdome'.

Seeing his eclipse drawing near, Somerset prepared to defend himself against his enemies. Summoning the famous Sir Robert Cotton, who knew more than any other man of legal precedents and the history of the English law, Somerset asked him to draw up a comprehensive pardon which, once signed with the Great Seal of England, would protect him from any charges his enemies could bring. Cotton prepared the pardon. Unfortunately for Somerset, in the days of his waning power men were prepared to fight him openly. Solicitor-General Yelverton, who owed his advancement to the Howards and Somerset, declared that he could not certify the pardon fit for the seal. If his scruples were honest, we must admire Yelverton; if they sprang only from a desire to ingratiate himself with the rising Villiers, we can only note with gratification that a few years later, ruined by the new favourite, he was a prisoner in the Tower on a trumped-up charge of having improperly extended the liberties of the City of London when renewing its charter. Angered at Yelverton's opposition, Somerset had a new and even more comprehensive pardon drawn up. But this the old Lord Chancellor, Ellesmere, flatly refused to seal. On July 20th the whole matter was threshed over at a meeting of the Privy Council. At the end of the meeting James ordered Ellesmere to sign Somerset's pardon. The knives were out for Somerset however. After James left the council board, he was persuaded not to force Ellesmere to go against his conscience. The blanket pardon which Somerset wanted as his bulwark against his enemies went unsigned.

It was not long before Somerset needed the pardon which he had sought in vain. In mid-October London was electrified by the news that Sir Thomas Overbury's death in the Tower had been due to poisoning, and that the Earl and Countess of Somerset were under house arrest for complicity in the crime.

CHAPTER XVI

Murder in the Tower

IN THE SUMMER of 1615 William Trumbull, King James's ambassador at Brussels, arrived home on leave. With him he brought news that he had not dared to transmit in any of his despatches, knowing how often these were either intercepted by foreign spies or viewed by unauthorized persons about the English court. Seeking out Sir Ralph Winwood, the Secretary of State, Trumbull acquainted him with his information. Some little while before a young Englishman from his sickbed had sent for some of Trumbull's servants to hear secrets which he could no longer keep to himself if he were to die in peace. The conscience-stricken young Englishman was William Reeve, formerly an apprentice to the London apothecary William de Loubell. The disclosure which he made was that in September 1613, having been sent by his master to administer a 'clyster' [enema] to Sir Thomas Overbury, then a prisoner in the Tower of London, he had introduced into it a poison, mercury sublimate, and so had procured his death the next day. Further, said Reeve, the person who had paid him £20 for the murder was the then Countess of Essex, since her remarriage Countess of Somerset, daughter of the Lord Treasurer of England and wife of the King's Lord Chamberlain.

Sir Ralph Winwood, the recipient of Trumbull's revelations, was a somewhat anomalous figure to enjoy high office in a court increasingly dominated by the pro-Spanish and pro-Catholic Howards and their allies. An uncompromising Protestant, almost a Puritan, he longed for renewal of war with Spain. Like Trumbull, he was one of the select group whom Cecil had trained for the diplomatic service, and he had served with considerable credit when stationed at The Hague as English agent to the United Provinces. Harsh and austere in manner, he was a notable exception among the facile courtiers who held so many of the key posts at court. There had been surprise when King James, after an interval of muddling through the duties of the secretaryship with Somerset, had appointed him Secretary. Installed in his new office, Winwood had speedily joined Archbishop Abbot and Lord Chancellor Ellesmere in striving to limit the power of the Somerset-Howard coalition. One step in that opposition, the advancing of a counter-favourite in young George Villiers, has already been noted.

Trumbull's news did not come entirely as a surprise to Winwood. As Sir Francis Bacon later admitted at Somerset's trial, Sir Thomas had hardly been in the grave before there was 'a certain Rumour and Muttering . . . that *Overbury* came strangely to his Death'. Winwood in fact had had the Countess of Shrewsbury, a prisoner in the Tower since her involvement in Lady Arbella's tragedy, collect for him all the rumours circulating there about Overbury's end. Trumbull's report offered Winwood something a good deal more usable than rumour. But it also presented great risk. If Winwood advanced charges based upon it and could not substantiate them, he would inevitably ruin himself. Accordingly he moved with the greatest circumspection.

Somerset apparently became aware of danger threatening him. Not only did he desperately try to secure his general pardon despite Ellesmere's refusal to attach the Great Seal to it, but he also sent one of his people to seek out Lawrence Davis, formerly Overbury's trusted servant, and secure from him all the originals and copies he had of letters which Somerset had written to Overbury. For these he paid Davis £30 and then destroyed them.

Winwood decided upon a crucial move. Arranging to meet the Lieutenant of the Tower, Sir Gervase Helwys, at the home of the Earl of Shrewsbury, he told Helwys that he was glad to meet him but wished that Helwys would clear himself of 'a kind of heavy Imputation on him about Overbury's Death'. In coming out so bluntly, Winwood gambled on his ability to crack the Lieutenant. Fortunately Helwys was only too anxious to unburden himself. He talked and all unconsciously sent himself to the gallows.

Reviewing his story, one finds it almost impossible not to feel sorry for Helwys. When he took over command of the Tower of London he was a soldier, approaching late middle age, who had served in the wars on the Continent but had won no fortune. People who knew him liked him, but he was not widely known at court and his appointment had been something of a surprise. In youth he had been pretty wild and had kept himself poor at the gaming tables, but all that was past. Sober John Chamberlain, who was well acquainted with him, spoke favourably of his appointment in a letter to Sir Dudley Carleton, English ambassador at Venice, even while thinking that he was 'of too mild and gentle a disposition for such an office'. As for Sir Gervase, concerned to find some place of security and profit for himself and his family in his declining years, the offer of the lieutenancy must have seemed a great piece of good fortune, even though Sir Thomas Monson, who looked after the business for Northampton, bluntly told him 'that if he succeeded Sir *William Wade* he must bleed, that is, give £2,000'. With the help of a London alderman to whom he was related, Helwys raised the money and on May 6th, a couple of weeks after Overbury's committal, he was installed as His Majesty's Lieutenant of the Tower. The very next day, acting on the request of Northampton and Monson, he gave the post of underkeeper in charge of Sir Thomas Overbury to an elderly serving-man named Richard Weston, previously unknown to him.

Two days after engaging Weston, Helwys received a nasty shock. Walking about the Tower, still in the first pride of his fine post, Helwys met his new underkeeper. In one hand he was carrying food for Overbury's supper, in the other he held a glass vial. 'Sir, shall I give it him now?' he asked. Sir Gervase then discovered that by 'it' Weston referred to the contents of the vial, poison which had just been delivered to him from the Countess of Essex. Rallying from the shock, Sir Gervase sought to dissuade Weston from the murder. He was successful and Weston, deeply moved, declared that he thanked God upon his knees that he had met with him and been saved from the deed.

If Weston rejoiced at the meeting, Helwys certainly did not. His world lay about him in ruins. Now he saw why he, a good easy man, pretty much an unknown with hardly a friend at court, had been chosen for the lieutenancy. Who on earth would believe him if he went to Whitehall with this fantastic story about the daughter of the Earl of Suffolk, the great-niece of the Earl of Northampton, the wife of the Earl of Essex and, as most people suspected, the future wife of the King's own favourite? He would probably become a prisoner in the Tower himself. The £2,000 which he had invested in his office would be lost irrevocably. Profoundly shaken, he decided to keep his discovery to himself while doing all he could to frustrate the other attempts to murder Sir Thomas which he divined would follow. When tarts and jelly arrived from Lady Frances as gifts for Sir Thomas, Sir Gervase found that they turned black and foul and were of 'strange colours'. He concluded quite rightly that they were poisoned, destroyed them, and had his own cook prepare others in their place. By such stratagems, he assured Winwood, he had done all he could to save Sir Thomas from his enemies. At the end of his interview with Helwys, Winwood felt he had sufficient evidence to go to the King. He met with the monarch, who immediately ordered Helwys to make a written statement of everything he knew.

King James was terribly upset by the Lieutenant's disclosures. The crime was unpardonable—the more so since the King's own honour was directly involved. As a prisoner in the Tower, Sir Thomas had, as the lawyers put it, passed out of his own protection and into that of the King. Moreover, Helwys's story, if substantiated, showed appalling moral corruption in the royal court of England. On the other hand, the charges might not be true. King James had not spent a lifetime surrounded by courtiers without knowing how merciless and Machiavellian their intrigues could become. The whole thing might have been cooked up by enemies who were out to get Somerset. One thing was certain—a sweeping investigation would have to be made. James gave a commission to Lord Zouch, Sir Thomas Parry, Sir Fulke Greville, and Winwood to see what truth lay in the Lieutenant's allegations. Apparently it was to these commissioners that King James gave the directions in his own hand which were later read at Somerset's trial:

> There be two things in this Cause to be try'd, and the Verity can be but in one of them: First, Whether my Lord of *Somerset* and my Lady were the Procurers of *Overbury's* Death; or, That this Imputation hath been by some practised to cast an Aspersion upon them. I would first have you diligently enquire of the first; and if you find them clear, then I would have you as carefully look after the other, to the intent such Practices may be discover'd and not suffered to pass with Impunity.[1]

Examined on September 29th, the underkeeper Weston made a confession incriminating the Countess of Somerset. The commissioners submitted their findings to the King: the charges made against the Somersets appeared to be true, further investigation must be pursued, and the criminals brought to trial in the proper courts of law. Grimly King James summoned the most persistent and relentless prosecutor he could have found—Sir Edward Coke. Since the days when he had harried Raleigh at Winchester, Coke had advanced to the dignity of Chief Justice of King's Bench.

A son of Coke's has left a vivid account of the haste with which the King sent for the Lord Chief Justice to acquaint him with the work he must take in hand. It was one o'clock in the morning when the royal courier arrived from Royston and knocked at the door of Coke's apartments in the Temple. Following his usual routine, Coke had retired at nine to sleep until he began his man-killing day at three o'clock in the morning. Brusquely addressing the son, the messenger said, 'I come from the King, and must immediately speak with your Father.' To this young Coke retorted: 'If you come from ten Kings, you shall not, for I know my Father's disposition to be such that if he be disturbed in his Sleep, he will not be fit for any business; but if you will do as we doe, you shall be welcome, and about two hours hence my Father will rise, and you then may do as you please.'[2] Right on schedule, at three o'clock, Coke awoke and rang the little bell by his bedside. The royal post entered and presented the King's letter.

Coke flung himself into his task with his usual intense energy. In all he held between two and three hundred examinations of persons who might

H

throw light on the Overbury business. Carefully he fitted together the jig-saw pieces of evidence, and gradually the picture emerged. Lady Frances, it appeared, had a marked inclination towards murder. Even before Over-bury had been sent to the Tower, she had tried to incite Sir David Wood, 'an ill-looked red-bearded Scot' who had a private quarrel with Overbury, to murder him, offering £1,000 and protection from his enemies if he would attend to the assassination. Sir David had had the good sense to tell her 'He would be loth to hazard going to Tyburn upon a Woman's Word',[3] but she had not easily given up her attempts to persuade him to murder. About the same time, apparently to avoid the tiresome processes of a divorce, she had asked an unsavoury character, Mary Woods alias 'Cunning Mary', to supply her with poison which would kill Essex. As far as the poisoning of Overbury was concerned, she was deeply involved. The whole plot originated with her, though she was aided by her confi-dante Mrs. Anne Turner.

Mistress Turner was a key person being, as Bacon declared, 'the Lay-mistress of the Poisons'. A small, rather good-looking blonde, she was a gentlewoman by birth and had been brought up with Lady Frances before leaving the service of the Howards to marry a Dr. Turner. Widowed early, she had wasted her means and ended by making her living ostensibly as a dressmaker but really as one of the parasites who ministered to the vices of the court, dealing in love charms, procuring aphrodisiacs, and running houses of assignation. It was under her roof that Carr and the Countess of Essex had held many of their meetings. Her own lover was Sir Arthur Mainwaring, who had fathered several children by her. It was Mistress Turner who found for Lady Frances the man Weston who would adminis-ter the poison for her. The latter was Mistress Turner's servant both before and after his service in the Tower as Overbury's keeper.

Having arranged for Weston's employment, Lady Frances and Mistress Turner looked for an apothecary to supply them with poison. They found him in James Franklin, a crooked-shouldered, swarthy Yorkshireman. When Mrs. Turner told him that the Countess of Essex wished him to procure the strongest poison he possibly could, he supplied her, according to his subsequent confession, with no less than seven: 'Aquafortis, White Arsenick, Mercury, Powder of Diamonds, Lapis Costitus, great Spiders, and Cantharides.' Tests were made on various animals to determine their effectiveness. Dealing sometimes directly with the Countess and Mrs. Turner, at other times through their servants, Franklin kept the poisoners supplied with the essential ingredients. The remarkable carelessness that attended the whole operation is apparent not only in the number of people involved, but also in the somewhat haphazard methods of delivery. One batch of poisoned tarts was sent over to the Tower by a certain Simon

Merston who, unaware of their lethal content, helped himself with his finger to some of the syrup overflowing from them. He was lucky to escape with nothing worse than the loss of his nails and hair.

As the months passed with Overbury still preserved through Helwys's secret precautions, Franklin, if we may believe his later confession, vainly tried to get the Countess to abandon her attempts:

> She afterwards wrote unto me to buy her more Poisons. I went unto her, and told her I was weary of it; and I besought her upon my Knees that she would use me no more in those Matters: But she importuned me, bad me go, and enticed me with fair Speeches and Rewards; so she overcame me, and did bewitch me.[4]

Finally the Countess hit upon a device which Helwys had not anticipated, the poisoned enema. With the end of Sir Thomas, Franklin's usefulness was over. He had to wait some time for his reward. At last, on the day of her marriage to Somerset, Lady Frances sent him £20 by Mrs. Turner. Reeve, the apothecary's boy who had administered the fatal clyster, was paid the same amount and shipped out of the country.

First of the conspirators to stand trial was old Weston, on October 19, 1615. Weston's case was the crucial one. Before the others could be charged with being accessories to Overbury's poisoning, the Crown had to establish that he had been poisoned. In the absence of Reeve, Weston was the only person who could be charged with actually administering poison. If he could not be convicted, everyone else involved might escape punishment. Right off the Crown ran into difficulties with Weston. Although he had freely confessed during earlier examinations, he had since been secretly persuaded by an adherent of the Howards—some said Solicitor-General Yelverton—to refuse to enter a plea when indicted in court. According to the law of the time, a defendant could not be tried until after he had entered a plea of either 'Guilty' or 'Not Guilty'.

Coke was furious at the obstruction. Grimly he enumerated for Weston the tortures of weight, cold and hunger inflicted upon those who refused to submit their cases to the law of the land:

> For the first, he was to receive his Punishment by the Law, to be extended, and then to have Weights laid upon him, no more than he was able to bear, which were by little and little to be increased.
> For the second, that he was to be exposed in an open Place, near to the Prison, in the open Air, being naked. And lastly, That he was to be preserved with the coarsest Bread that could be got, and Water out of the next Sink or Puddle to the Place of Execution, and that Day he had Water he should have no Bread, and that Day he had Bread he should have no Water; and in this Torment he was to linger as long as Nature could linger out, so that oftentimes Men lived in that Extremity eight or nine Days.[5]

Men had been known to die under the torments of this *peine forte et dure* rather than enter their plea. Their motive nearly always had been to preserve for their wives and children their estates, which would have been confiscated had they stood trial and been found guilty. Weston had no such motive to sustain him. After the case had been adjourned, he was visited in his cell by one of the sheriffs of London who persuaded him to enter his plea in the form prescribed. Capitulating, Weston said he hoped that the consequence would not be to 'make a Net to catch the little Birds, and let the great ones go'. When his trial resumed, it became clear that there could be only one end for Weston: the jury convicted him, and on November 10th he was taken to Tyburn for execution. As he stood on the scaffold, some courtiers of the Somerset-Howard faction came riding through the crowd, calling upon him to deny that Overbury had been poisoned. If they hoped by so foolhardy a manœuvre to save the falling favourite, they were greatly mistaken. Weston gave no answer and a few days later two of their number, Sir John Holles and Sir John Wentworth, were brought before the Star Chamber to answer for their conduct.

After Weston's conviction, the trials of Turner, Helwys and Franklin swiftly followed. The most sensational was that of Anne Turner on November 7th. Although entirely irrelevant to the manner of Overbury's death, a mass of lurid evidence was produced to show how she and Lady Frances had resorted to Dr. Forman and Dr. Gresham, practisers of arts inhibited and out of warrant, to make sure of the affections of their lovers. Dr. Forman's widow testified that Turner had brought in customers for her husband. Dr. Forman's register of ladies and their lovers was produced in court, but Lord Chief Justice Coke forbade the reading of the names (because, said report, the first name in it was that of his own wife). Various exhibits were produced from the apparatus of mumbo-jumbo with which Forman had played upon human lust and cupidity. Obscene leaden figures were shown along with the moulds for casting them. Cabalistic manuscripts were exhibited, and the Lord Chief Justice assured the court that some of the incantations had been written in blood. When a parchment was produced, bound in human skin and marked with crosses and sacred names, there was a most ominous and dramatic happening:

> At the shewing of these, and inchanted Papers and other Pictures in Court, there was heard a crack from the Scaffolds, which caused great Fear, Tumult, and Confusion among the Spectators, and throughout the Hall, every one fearing Hurt, as if the Devil had been present, and grown angry to have his Workmanship shewed, by such as were not his owne Scholars.[6]

Equally irrelevant to the poisoning of Overbury but titillating for the audience was the evidence of assignations, at Mrs. Turner's house and elsewhere, between Lady Frances and Carr in the days before the Essex divorce. Letters were produced: one from Lady Frances to 'sweet Turner' lamenting her parents' harshness in wanting her to consummate her marriage with Essex, and another to the quack Forman, in which the Countess greeted him as 'sweet Father' and signed herself 'Your affectionate loving daughter'. In the second of these letters, Lady Frances reported her husband 'lusty and merry' and was urgent that Forman remember to send her 'the Galls', apparently the medicine to keep him impotent. Along with such highly irrelevant materials, there was plenty of evidence to justify the jury's verdict that Anne Turner was guilty of assisting Richard Weston in the poisoning of Sir Thomas Overbury.

When she came to die, Anne Turner wore with her dress, cuffs and a ruff which had been treated with yellow starch. As a dress designer she had been responsible for introducing this fashion into England. It was one which, for some reason, had incurred a good deal of hostility and scorn, and there were those who hoped that with her death 'yellow Starch, which so much disfigured our Nation, and rendered them so ridiculous and fantastic, will receive its Funeral'.[7] Many of the court came in their coaches to Tyburn to see Mrs. Turner die. She did not meet her end unpitied. After it was all over, a certain John Castle wrote to a friend:

> Since I saw you, I saw Mrs. Turner die. If detestation of painted pride, lust, malice, powdered hair, yellow bands, and the rest of the wardrobe of court vanities; if deep sighs, tears, confessions, ejaculations of the soul, admonitions of all sorts of people to make God and an unspotted conscience always our friends; if the protestation of faith and hope to be washed by the same Savior and by the like mercies that Mary Magdalene was, be signs and demonstrations of a blessed penitent, then I will tell you that this poor broken woman went *a cruce ad gloriam*, and now enjoys the presence of her and our Redeemer. Her body being taken down by her brother, one Norton, servant to the Prince, was in a coach conveyed to St. Martin's of the Fields, where in the evening of the same day she had an honest and decent burial.[8]

As far as Mrs. Turner was concerned, there never had been any real doubt about her guilt and the verdict of the court. Such was not the case when Sir Gervase Helwys, dismissed from his post of Lieutenant of the Tower, stood trial. It seemed a strong presupposition of Helwys's innocence that he had, by his voluntary disclosures to Winwood, brought the whole matter into the open. Surely, if a party to the murder, he would never have revealed any part of his knowledge of it. In court Helwys created a good impression with his frank and sensible defence and the expectation grew that he would win his acquittal. Unfortunately for Helwys the Crown was able to produce letters written by him which clearly showed that he had led the poisoners to consider him one of themselves. Coke in his summing up put the worst possible interpretation upon these, and the jury found Helwys guilty.

In the light of all that we know of Helwys, his decent, kindly good nature and his piety, it is hard to see him as one of Lady Frances's creatures. He had, however, allowed himself to drift into a situation where appearances were hopelessly against him. When he confessed his guilt on the scaffold, he did not speak of having joined the plotters in their crime but rather lamented that 'when it was in his power to have hindered the proceedings of the poisonings, he suffered them to go on to the murthering of an honest Gentleman'.

Next to stand trial were Franklin and Sir Thomas Monson. Franklin went to the gallows like the others. With Monson it was different. However discreditable his part in securing Helwys his lieutenancy, there was no evidence to implicate him in the poisoning. Seeing Monson about to escape, Chief Justice Coke began speaking of ramifications still to be discovered. Darkly recalling the slanderous rumours that Prince Henry had been poisoned, Coke seemed to suggest that there was some truth in them and that the poisoning of Overbury was related to an earlier poisoning.[9] The consequence was twofold. The proceedings against Monson were suddenly suspended, never to be resumed; while the King, angered by Coke's references to the death of his son, gave him a stinging rebuke. When the Earl and Countess of Somerset were arraigned, it was not Coke but Sir Francis Bacon who presented the case against them.

Although Lady Frances and her husband had been under arrest since October, and the others involved in the plot had all been tried and executed by December, it was not until late May that the Somersets went on trial before the Lord High Steward's Court with its jury of twenty-two peers. The delay was due in part to the health of Lady Frances. Pregnant at the time of her arrest, she was delivered in December of a daughter whom she named Anne in an attempt to win the Queen's favour. The main reason for the delay, however, was the time consumed in attempts to persuade the Earl and Countess to plead guilty when they were arraigned. King James wanted such pleas for they would make unnecessary extended hearings at which his own reputation and that of his badly tarnished court might be further darkened. Moreover, pleas of 'Guilty' could be construed as evidence of contrition and justify the leniency James wished to exercise in the punishment of the Somersets. Much time was spent trying to get the two to see the wisdom of meeting the King's wishes and summarily admitting their guilt.

On May 24th Lady Frances stood her trial, clad entirely in black except for the delicate lawn of her cuffs and ruff. While her indictment was read she stood pale and trembling, shedding some tears. When Weston's name was mentioned she put her fan before her face and held it there until the rest of the indictment had been read. She then entered a plea of guilty.

Probably no murderess has ever been treated with greater solicitude at her trial than Lady Frances was. The prosecutor went out of his way to compliment her on her noble family, her natural endowments, and her penitence. Coupled with this went a heavy emphasis on the merciful nature of King James who reigned 'in a white Roabe not besprinkled with bloud' and had never yet shed noble blood, not even that of the traitors Grey and Cobham. As for Lord Ellesmere who, as Lord High Steward, presided over the trial, he was almost apologetic when he came to pass sentence:

> Since my Lords have heard with what Humility and Grief you have con-
> fessed the Fact, I do not doubt they will signify so much to the King, and
> mediate for his Grace towards you: but in the mean time, according to the
> Law, the Sentence must be this, That thou shalt be carried from hence to
> the *Tower of London*, and from thence to the place of Execution, where you
> are to be hang'd by the Neck till you be dead; and the Lord have Mercy
> upon your Soul.[10]

It seems unlikely that anybody in the hall was so naïve as to think that the sentence would be carried out.

Next day saw the arraignment of Somerset. Although under the greatest pressure to follow his lady's course, plead guilty, and throw himself upon the mercy of King James, he absolutely refused to do so. Defiantly he entered his plea, 'Not Guilty'. It is hard not to sympathize with Somerset for he seems to have been innocent of the charge of murder brought against him. His crime was that of an accessory after the fact. Apparently some little while after Overbury's death Somerset learned the real truth about it. In the summer of 1615 when the case began to break, Somerset, possibly out of devotion to his wife, did everything in his power to destroy evidence and frustrate the investigators. After his arrest, Somerset failed completely to realize how profoundly the King had been shocked by Overbury's murder. (James had, in fact, been so appalled that he had gone to the Council table and 'kneeling down there, desired God to lay a Curse upon him and his posterity for ever, if he were consenting to Overburies death'.[11]) Somerset apparently believed that King James, because of his earlier love, would not let him stand trial in jeopardy of his life. He would have thought otherwise had he known what followed his last leave-taking from His Majesty. Carefully concealing from Somerset any intimation of his imminent arrest, James had said good-bye to him at Royston with his usual unpleasantly affectionate gestures. Once Somerset was off on the

London road, however, the King had exclaimed, 'Now the de'il go with
thee, for I shall never see thy face again.'

Gradually it dawned on the ex-favourite that the King, determined to
clear himself of complicity in the wrong done to Overbury, had removed
his protection from all involved in his death. When Somerset realized that
James actually intended to have him arraigned on the charge of murder,
he turned ugly. He sought to blackmail the King into dropping the charges
against him. Just what Somerset's threatened disclosures were, it is impossible to determine. The King, in a highly confidential letter sent in his
own writing to Sir George More, the new Lieutenant of the Tower, spoke
of Somerset 'laying an aspersion upon me of being in some sorte accessorie
to his crime'. It may be that James, who had loathed Overbury, had in one
of his furies spoken somewhat after the fashion of an earlier king who had
cried for someone to rid him of a pestilent priest. It may be that Somerset's
threatened disclosures would have dealt with something quite different.
Whatever they may have been, they had the King badly worried, but to
his credit James refused to be intimidated. His letters to More make his
position entirely clear. Satisfied that Somerset was guilty, he felt that the
only sensible course for the latter to take was 'by confessing the trewthe
to honoure god & me & leave some place for my mercie to worke upon'.[12]
He was ready to stretch that mercy to the utmost, and he wanted Somerset
to know as much, but on one point he was adamant—Somerset must either
admit guilt or stand the full course of his trial.

King James was a physical coward, but he had a conscience; and that
conscience would not allow him to take the easy way with Somerset.
Sending him, despite his threats, to stand trial in an open court was perhaps
the most courageous thing that James ever did. On the day when Somerset's trial began, the King's extreme tension was apparent to everyone:

> But who had seen the Kings restlesse motion all that day, sending to every
> boat he sees landing at the Bridge, cursing all that came without tidings,
> would have easily judged all was not right, and there had been some grounds
> for his fears of Somersets boldness. . . .[13]

While King James was thus on tenterhooks at Whitehall, a great throng
jammed Westminster Hall, less than a mile away, to watch Somerset's
trial. So many had sought entry that men paid up to £5 for a place of
vantage. Few of the onlookers came with any pity for Somerset. Significant
of public feeling was a little punning jingle which had been going the
rounds:

I.C.U.R. [1 see you are]
Good Monsieur Carr,
About to fall.

U.R.A.K. [You are a K—]
As most men say;
        But that's not all.

U.O.Q.P. [You occupy]
With your annulity
        That naughtie packe.

S.X.Y.F. [Essex' wife]
Whose wicked life,
        Hath broke your backe.[14]

As for Somerset, laying aside his earlier projects of malingering or of resisting by force, he made his appearance readily enough, 'his Hair curl'd, his Visage pale, his Beard long, his Eyes sunk in his Head'. He was clad in a plain black velvet suit, and about his neck he wore his George as a Knight of the Garter.

After the accused had entered his plea of 'Not Guilty', the day's long proceedings got under way. Somerset's shameful double-crossing which had resulted in Overbury's imprisonment was laid bare. The testimony of the victim's father, of various of his servants and friends, of his own desperate letters to Somerset and the latter's bland replies, made it plain that while Somerset had pretended to be working for Overbury's release he had in fact consistently blocked it. Sir Francis Bacon, acting as prosecutor, maintained that Somerset had sent Overbury to the Tower in order to facilitate his murder. Somerset was prompt with the reply:

. . . in respect I consented to, and endeavour'd the Imprisonment of Sir *Thomas Overbury* (. . . I design'd it for his Reformation, not his Ruin).[15]

It was mere allegation and counter-allegation: neither side could prove a thing. In other ways it was a stand-off. Bacon established that food for Sir Thomas had come from Somerset as well as from Lady Frances. Somerset rejoined that the poison must all have come in his wife's offerings. Evidence was produced that Lady Frances had made free use of Somerset's name in dealing with her accomplices. In her eagerness to impress her creatures with the protection she could offer, she might well have done so without any warrant.

The evidence really damaging to Somerset concerned his actions after Overbury's death. It was shown that in the summer of 1615 he had paid handsomely to regain letters which he had sent Overbury in the Tower. It was also shown that he had misused his authority as a privy councillor in an attempt to recover various papers in the custody of a sister of Mrs. Turner. Most serious of all was the revelation that after Weston's arraignment Somerset and Sir Robert Cotton had attached false dates to various

H*

of Overbury's letters from the Tower. Then there was the curious matter
of the pardon. The previous September, after Winwood had launched his
investigation, Somerset had made a final desperate attempt to secure a
blanket pardon from the King. He had claimed to need this because in the
days of his greatness he had attended to 'many things of Trust under the
King, and the Custody of both the Seals, without particular warrant'.
What was remarkable, according to the prosecution, was that the pardon
which Somerset had sought from the King, while ostensibly based on that
which Henry VIII had granted to Cardinal Wolsey, differed from it in that
murder had been slipped in among the offences pardoned.

The Crown's evidence showed that Somerset had been utterly conscienceless in duping Overbury and that he had both destroyed and forged
evidence. It did not show that Somerset had sought Overbury's death, the
charge on which he was being tried. Somerset, however, had been
manœuvred into having to prove his innocence. As was customary, he had
no legal counsel to aid him in this formidable task. (It was considered a
notable privilege that during the testimony against him he was allowed to
take notes to aid in his defence.) When he did arise to defend himself,
Somerset could not prove that he had not been one of the poisoners.
Bacon, on the other hand, had shown Somerset in such a bad light that,
when it came to the vote, the peers were unanimous in their verdict of
guilty.

The strongest evidence that when Overbury died Somerset had no
knowledge that murder had been committed is supplied by letters written
at the time by Northampton. The latter seems to have been fully aware
of his grand-niece's venture in murder. He was lucky that death carried
him off before the exposure of the whole affair, for the letters he wrote
when informed of Overbury's demise would have called for more explaining than perhaps even that wily old brain could have invented. In his
letter to Somerset informing him of Overbury's death, Northampton reported that the prisoner's end had been unexpected, described his last
hours, and concluded, 'The Lieutenant sent for the Coroner to view the
body as the manner is of dealing with close prisoners to satisfy the world
and clear himself.' In the whole of this letter there is not the slightest
suggestion that Overbury's end was other than natural, even though
Northampton thoughtfully added, 'This is the whole course of this mans
drawing to his end.'[16]

Northampton's letter brought from Somerset the entirely natural response
that now that Overbury was dead he would like to see him given a decent
funeral. Northampton obviously found this request highly unwelcome.
As far as he was concerned, the sooner Overbury was underground the
better. However, he was more or less bound to communicate the request

to Helwys, and did so in a letter[17] in which he mentioned that Somerset had intended to petition the King for Overbury's release had the latter lived. He hinted strongly in this letter that Helwys would be well advised to bury Overbury as quickly as possible himself and so have an excuse for not turning over the body to Somerset. In case Helwys was stupid enough not to perceive the hints with which this letter was laden, Northampton sent him a second letter. This was concerned not at all with Somerset and his wishes, but only with the threat represented by Overbury's kinsman Sir John Lidcote.

> Worthy Mr Lieutenant
> Let me entreat you to call Lidcot and 3 or 4 of his frindes if so many come to vewe the body if they have not already don it and so soone as it is vewed without stayinge the cominge of a messenger from the court in any case see it interred in the body of the chappel within the Tower instantly.
> If they have vewed then bury it by and by for it is time consideringe the humors of this damned crewe that only desire meanes to move pity and raise scandales. Let no mans instance move you to make stay in any case and bring theas letters when I next see you.
> Faile not a jote herin as you love your frendes not after Lidcot and his frends have vewed stay one minute but let the jurye be ready and if Lidcot be not thear send for him spedely pretendinge that the body will not tarry.
> In post hast at 12
>
> Yrs own[18]

This last letter went unsigned but the original, in Northampton's own hand, survives to this day.

Helwys dutifully saw to it that Overbury was buried with the expedition his patron required. It then remained only for Northampton to write again to Somerset, explaining the hasty burial and assuring him that all was really for the best:

> He stunk intolerably, in so much that he was cast into the Coffin with a loose Sheet over him. God is gracious in cutting off ill instruments from off the factious Crew: If he had come forth, they would have made use of him. Thus, Sweet Lord, wishing you all Increase of Happiness and Honour, I end,
> Your Lordship's, more than any man,
>
> Henry Northampton[19]

In view of these letters, it is hard not to conclude that at this stage Northampton was in the plot quite as deeply as Lady Frances, that Helwys's compliance, real or pretended, had got him hopelessly involved, and that Somerset while wanting Overbury off the scene did not desire his murder and knew nothing of it. Indeed, reading the letters closely, one gathers that Somerset may at last have relented and really meant to have the King release Overbury. Such a development would explain the renewed attempt at poisoning at this time.

After the conviction of the Somersets, things went pretty much as Weston had suspected when he spoke of the net catching the little birds and letting the big ones go. The death sentences passed on the Earl and the Countess were commuted, and they settled down to live comfortably in their apartments in the Tower. Somerset's estates were confiscated, but enough was restored to allow him £4,000 a year for life. Drawing on this money, Somerset rebuilt his quarters in the Tower more to his own taste. Even those who knew how hard it was for James to deal harshly with one whom he had loved were surprised at the King's decision to allow Somerset, a convicted felon, to remain a member of the Order of the Garter.

Perhaps the most distasteful thing about life in the Tower for the Somersets was that they had to endure each other's company. There were bickerings and ugly flare-ups. Somerset saw now that Overbury had been right—the lady had indeed been his ruin. In January 1622 the two were released from the Tower to take up residence at Grays, a country house in Oxfordshire, upon condition that they never go more than three miles from the house. On October 7, 1624, Somerset's pardon was passed under the King's privy seal. His wife had received hers years earlier. People wryly recalled that His Majesty had once sworn he would never pardon anyone concerned in Overbury's death. Those who saw God's judgment in the disastrous conclusion to the next reign recalled King James's oath: if ever he spared any that were guilty, he wished the curse of God might light on him, and his posterity.

CHAPTER XVII

The Great Villiers

WITH SOMERSET in the Tower, young Sir George Villiers moved smoothly to the centre of the great stage of the court, the undisputed new favourite. In many ways he was an improvement. There had been an effeminate almost flaccid fulness to the bland good looks of Somerset. Young Villiers had an aristocratic handsomeness, grace and charm far beyond Somerset. He was, moreover, a person of real intelligence, and could display a certain talent for government and administration. Bishop Goodman of Gloucester, writing after Villiers's death, has described for us his notable good looks:

> . . . he had a very lovely complexion; he was the handsomest bodied man in England, his limbs were so well compacted, and his conversation so pleasing, and of so sweet a disposition.[1]

For his inner qualities we have the account left in the time of Charles II by the great Earl of Clarendon, who had known him in his youth:

> . . . this great man was a person of a noble nature and generous disposition, and of such other endowments as made him very capable of being a great favourite to a great King. He understood the arts and artifices of a court, and all the learning that is professed there, exactly well. . . . He had obtained a quick conception and apprehension of business, and had the habit of speaking very gracefully and pertinently. He was of a most flowing courtesy and affability to all men who made any address to him; and so desirous to oblige them, that he did not enough consider the value of the obligation or the merit of the person he chose to oblige. . . . He was of a courage not to be daunted.[2]

His faults—his sensitive egotism which demanded the breaking of all who went against him, his obstinacy which won him the nickname of the 'white mule', his promiscuous wenching, his adulation of the King which he took as part of his job—these things must not blind us to his undoubted gifts. He was the best as well as the last of King James's favourites, and he secured an ascendancy over him more complete than that of any of his predecessors.

After Somerset's disappearance from the court, Villiers's ascent was rapid. At the beginning of 1616 James appointed him Master of the Horse. In April he created him a Knight of the Garter. In August, at the end of his summer progress, he made him Baron of Whaddon in the

County of Buckingham, and Viscount Villiers. Five months later, in
January 1617, King James advanced him to the dignity of Earl of Buckingham. In a little over two years Villiers had made the ascent from esquire
to earl which had taken Carr seven. One month later Buckingham, as we
shall henceforth know him, was admitted to the Privy Council, 'beeing
(they say) the youngest that hath ben seen sit at that boord'. On New
Year's Day 1618, within a year of obtaining his earldom, Buckingham was
advanced to the dignity of marquess. His ascendancy over James was
already complete. John Chamberlain noted of the King, 'he is never so
out of Tune but the very sight of my Lord of Buckingham doth settle and
quiet all'. Only one further promotion in the nobility was possible—that
to a dukedom. This would have followed shortly had there not been a
number of attendant difficulties.

England had had no dukes, outside the royal family, since the last Duke
of Norfolk had died on the scaffold back in Elizabeth's time, and the
Howards for years had been urging King James to restore the title of Duke
of Norfolk to the head of their house, the Earl of Arundel. While James
was not ready to meet their wishes, it would be hard to make a duke of
the mushroom Villiers and pass over Arundel. The King's cousin, the
Scottish Duke of Lennox, presented a further problem. Villiers as an
English duke would outrank the royal kinsman. The consequence was
that for a long time the King did nothing. Finally, in May 1623 when
Buckingham and Prince Charles were in Madrid, King James, wanting
his favourite to receive all possible recognition from the haughty Spanish
court, made him Duke of Buckingham. The previous day he had given
Lennox the title of Duke of Richmond in the English nobility, thus pre-
serving his precedence. As for the Howards, they had to wait until the
restoration of the monarchy itself in 1660 for the restoration of their dukedom. In the interval, to keep his claim alive, Arundel had his men wear
on their livery a ducal coronet surmounting the white horse emblem of
his house.

Buckingham was attended by golden opinions during his rise. James was
enamoured with him. Once more there awoke the old schoolmasterly
dream which had so excited him when he had given Latin lessons to the
young Carr. Now it was Villiers who was to be the creation of the royal
Pygmalion:

> [James] taking him into his regard taught him more and more to please
> himselfe, and moulded him, (as it were) Platonically to his owne *Idea*,
> delighting first in the choyse of the Materialls: (because he found him
> susceptible of good forme) and afterwards by degrees as great Architects
> use to doe in the workmanship of his Regall Hand. . . .[3]

When King James, as a New Year's gift in 1619, dedicated to Buckingham

GEORGE VILLIERS, DUKE OF BUCKINGHAM

after Daniel Mytens

CHARLES, PRINCE OF WALES

by Daniel Mytens

the *Meditation upon the Lord's Prayer* which he had written 'for the benefit of all his subjects, especially such as follow the Court', he affectionately pointed out to his favourite, 'I dayly take care to better your understanding to enable you the more for my service.'

If James was delighted with his new protégé, most of the court found him a much easier man to get along with than Somerset.

> In the beginning of Mr. *Villiers* coming into Favour he was Affable and Courteous, and seemed to Court all Men as they Courted him, he promoted Mens Suits to the King *gratis*, which *Somerset* would not do, but for great Sums of Money, and hereby *Villiers* stole all the Hearts of the Courtiers and Petitioners to the King from *Somerset*, who was now wholly forsaken by God and all Men.[4]

Even the Howards found the new man apparently quite prepared to accept them and allow them their positions of power and honour in the court. Indeed, the gratification of the Howards can only have been matched by the chagrin of Buckingham's original backers when in the summer of 1616 the new favourite decided to support the Howards' pet project, a marriage between Prince Charles and the Spanish Infanta.

Of course not everybody was enthusiastic about the new man. Queen Anne took a dislike to him at first, and her coolness threatened his whole career. Perhaps as a means of keeping peace in the family, James had a set rule that he 'would receive none into Favour, but who was first recommended to him by the Queen'. The Queen was reluctant to recommend the newcomer, explaining 'if he became a Favourite, he would become more Intollerable than any that were before him'. In the end she gave way to Archbishop Abbot's importunings, even though assuring him 'he among the rest would live to repent it'. Apparently the young man's charm had finally melted her, and she was ready enough to take a part in the little play which preceded the knighting of her husband's new find. This occurred on St. George's Day 1615, when, with Prince Charles's sword in her hand, Queen Anne entered his Majesty's bedchamber and asked him 'that special favour as to knight this noble gentleman, whose name was George, for the honour of St. George'. Report had it that James needed a while to recover from the scare of seeing his wife coming at him with a drawn sword, but he joyfully conferred the accolade on the said George who was waiting just outside.

Less easy to win was the favour of the King's son. Just as Prince Henry had resented Somerset, so Prince Charles was offended to see Buckingham securing more and more of his father's affection. Charles, the sickly child who had never been expected to survive infancy, whose legs had been so weak that at the age of almost five he had been carried in the arms of Nottingham when created Duke of York, had grown into a shy, sensitive young man, completely unsure of himself. Perhaps his inner weakness was the consequence of growing up in the shade of the splendid Prince Henry, who 'would often taunt till he made him weep, telling him that he should be a Bishop, a gown being fittest to hide his legs'. Created Prince of Wales in November 1616 with 'not half so great a pomp as was the creation of Prince Henry', he continued to be 'Baby Charles' to his father. The pathetically unsure, priggish young prince was bound to regard the gorgeous virile Buckingham with either agonizing jealousy or all-admiring dependence. For a while it appeared that it would be the former. King James, who hated personal bitterness among those close to him, was obviously worried by the coolness with which Charles treated his new favourite. Buckingham, if only out of self-interest, wanted to make a friend of the rather unprepossessing young man who was only a heart-beat away from being king. It was with Charles that the difficulty lay. In the end the Prince, faced with semi-isolation from the court if he persisted in keeping aloof from Buckingham, agreed to the entente sought by his father.

To signal their new understanding to all the court, Buckingham entertained Prince Charles at a sumptuous banquet in June 1618. King James attended 'though the end whereunto it was designed, of reconciling His Highness, gave it the name of the Prince's Feast'. At the end of the banquet King James left his table and came over to that at which Buckingham's kin were seated. Here, after drinking a toast to the family, he swore that he and his descendants would 'advance that House above all others whatsoever'. The extravagance of the King's statement may have sprung from earlier draughts of wine, but the basic impulse was sincere.

'The Prince's Feast' was followed by an era of cordiality between Charles and Buckingham which lasted ten years and ended with a griefstricken King Charles I weeping over the murdered Buckingham. Indicative of the new relationship is a letter from Charles begging Buckingham to mediate between himself and his father, who had taken offence at the Prince's attempts to get Queen Anne to make a will. In this letter Prince Charles addressed Buckingham as 'Steenie', using the nickname reeking of Scottish croniness which James had attached to his favourite. (Apparently a supposed resemblance between Buckingham and a portrait of St. Stephen had given rise to the name, though there may also have been a jest about Buckingham being ready to die as a martyr for King James.) Prince Charles ended his letter thus:

> . . . To conclude, I pray you to commend my most humble service to his Majestie, and tel him that I am verri sorri that I have done anie thing may offend him, and that I will be content to have anie pennance inflicted upon me, so he may forgive me, although I had never a thought nor never shall have to displease him, yet I deserve to be punniched for my ill-fortune. So

hoping never to have occasion to wryt to you of so ill a subject againe, but of manie better, I rest, your treu constant loving friend,

Charles P.[5]

His position with the King and the Prince unassailable, the newly created Marquess of Buckingham proceeded to destroy the Howards as a power in the court. His action was perhaps inevitable. Buckingham could be generous to those who put themselves under his protection, but he was ruthless to any who would not submit and derive their position in the court from him. How long he would have tolerated the Howards as an independent power bloc it is hard to say. Sooner or later they would have had to make the submission which Buckingham's ego and policy demanded. Probably they realized this and decided to strike first, for it was they who made the move which ended the era of peaceful co-existence between themselves and the man who had supplanted their ally, Somerset. Their plan was remarkably unsubtle. Following the lead of those who had used Villiers to supplant Somerset, they sought to transfer the King's favour to a candidate of their own, a good-looking nephew of that Sir Thomas Monson who had been involved in the Overbury business. Their attempt was a hopeless failure. For one thing, they neglected the elementary first step of getting their man a post about the court which would give him a pretext for coming a good deal into the royal presence. For another, they were all wrong in their timing. Instead of waiting until the King was out of sorts with Buckingham, they advanced their man in the opening weeks of 1618 when James, having just created his new favourite a marquess, was obviously still enchanted with him and had little interest for even the most handsome of newcomers. King James realized quite clearly what the Howards were up to, and made his annoyance plain:

> . . . the day before the Kings going to Tiballs, the Lord Chamberlain (by expresse order) told yonge Mounson that the King did not like of his forwardnes, and presenting himself continually about him: that his father and uncle were not long since called in question for matters of no small moment [the Overbury business], that his own education had ben in such places and with such persons, as was not to be allowed of, wherfore his Majestie willed him from henceforth to forbeare his presence, and yf he wold follow his advise he shold likewise forbeare the court. This was a shrewde reprimende and crosse-blow to some who (they say) made account to raise and recover theyre fortunes by setting up this new idoll, and tooke great paines in tricking and prancking him up, besides washing his face every day with posset-curd.[6]

Looking for a reason for this rebuff, young Monson and his backers concluded that it was probably suspicion that he bore the Howard taint of Catholicism. Accordingly, the young hopeful made a point of attending

the Anglican services, and at Easter received communion from the Archbishop of Canterbury himself. The renewed endeavours of the Monson
group won only one small success—Monson, applying to the King for a
licence to travel abroad on the grounds that he could find no content in
England while barred from the royal presence, was told that the Lord
Chamberlain had gone beyond the King's intent in forbidding him the
presence. The victory was a very minor one, and could not be exploited.
Young Monson disappeared into obscurity. Buckingham remembered him
however when preparing for his Spanish trip in 1623. Thoughtfully
removing a temptation from the King, who might grow lonely while he
himself was beyond the seas, he arranged for Master Monson to take an
extended journey abroad at the same time as himself. To make Monson's
temporary banishment the more palatable, he secured him a knighthood.

After this fiasco, it was only a matter of time before Buckingham would
launch his counter-offensive. He drew first blood when a timely case in the
Star Chamber helped him to secure the dismissal of Sir Thomas Lake, a
key member of the Howard faction, from his post as Secretary of State.
Sir Thomas was 'a Fellow of meane birth and meaner breeding'. As a
Clerk of the Signet during the early years of the reign, he had attended the
King to secure his signature for necessary state documents during the
latter's extended hunting trips. Lake had used this opportunity of close
association with the court to ingratiate himself with the new king's Scots
and to form a mutually advantageous alliance with the Howards. In
January 1616 he was appointed as an additional secretary of state, serving
jointly with Winwood, Cecil's successor. Whereas Winwood was a militant
Protestant, Lake like his patrons the Howards was both pro-Catholic and
pro-Spanish. He was also the secret recipient of a Spanish pension.

One of the reasons for Lake being passed over originally for the secretaryship was that the City heiress, Mary Ryder, whom he had married
years earlier, had turned out to be a domineering virago who kept Sir
Thomas pretty much under her thumb. It was to her folly that Sir
Thomas owed the troubles which came upon him in the opening months
of 1618.

One of the Lakes' numerous children was Anne, who had married the
highly erratic William Cecil, Lord Roos, grandson of the Earl of Exeter.
This 'aged, gouty, diseased, but noble Earl' had taken as his second wife
a youthful widow. In August 1617 Lord Roos suddenly fled from England, leaving his affairs in great disorder and his brother-in-law, Sir
Arthur Lake, with no answer to a challenge to a duel. From the Continent
he defied a Privy Council order to return home and travelled on to Naples,
'his earthly Paradise'. Back in England Lady Lake, eager to excuse the
failure of her daughter's marriage, began circulating a story that Lord Roos

and the pretty young wife of his grandfather had been lovers. The Countess of Exeter at once insisted that this was a malicious slander and in January 1618 the old earl, her husband, petitioned the Court of Star Chamber to examine the whole matter.

The requested hearing did not occur until almost a year later, partly because of the interval necessary while one of the King's sergeants-at-arms went to Rome and returned with depositions from Lord Roos and his servant Diego clearing the Countess, partly because Lake had offered £15,000 if Buckingham would take him under his protection. In the end Buckingham spurned the offer and abandoned Sir Thomas to his fate, but for a while things were left in abeyance.

The hearing of the Exeter slander case began on February 3, 1619. King James had become so interested in the matter that for the first time in his reign he presided in person at a Star Chamber hearing. He made a little opening speech 'in which among other thinges he compared himself to Salomon that was to judge between two women . . . and to find out the true mother of the childe, (that is veritie)'. And he took the opportunity to urge brevity upon the lawyers who had managed to fill over nine thousand sheets with 'examinations, exemplifications and such other stuff'.

Called upon to prove their charges, Lady Lake and her daughter had no real evidence. They had, however, a forged 'confession' which they claimed the Countess had signed when seated one day by a window in the great chamber of the Earl of Exeter's mansion at Wimbledon. To establish the genuineness of this confession the Lakes, mother and daughter, produced a servant, Sarah Swarton, who testified that she had stood concealed behind an arras and had heard the Countess of Exeter read aloud her confession after she had written it.

At this point King James switched his role from Solomon to Sherlock Holmes and adjourned the hearing to Wimbledon for an inspection of the scene of the alleged confession. Here His Majesty stood behind the hangings where Sarah Swarton was supposed to have been, and demonstrated that no one standing there could possibly have overhead what was said at the window. He pointed out, moreover, that since the hangings were several feet short of the floor, Sarah Swarton could not have stood behind them undetected. As for the letter of confession, James declared it an evident forgery. One thing more completed the King's triumphant exposure of the fraud of the Lakes. Among their forgeries was a confession, supposedly signed by a Luke Hutton, to the effect that the Countess of Exeter had paid him £40 to poison Lady Roos. Royal officers managed to find Hutton and King James, interviewing him privately, secured a complete repudiation of the document.

Their charges revealed to be a tissue of forgery and perjury, the Lakes were found guilty of slander. The penalties were heavy. Sir Thomas Lake, who had stood by the charges made by his women, was fined £5,000 and ordered to pay the Countess £3,000 damages. Lady Lake was fined another £5,000 and Lady Roos 10,000 marks. All three were ordered to make public apology to the Countess and sentenced to imprisonment for life, at their own expense, in the Tower. Lake's post of Secretary of State was taken from him immediately after his conviction. King James seems to have felt rather sorry for Sir Thomas, who had been involved in all this trouble by his turbulent and unscrupulous womenfolk. Summing up the case, His Majesty compared the crimes of the Lakes 'to the first Plot of the first sin in Paradise, the Lady to the Serpent, her Daughter to Eve, and Sir Thomas to poor Adam, whose love of his Wife (the old sin of our Father) had beguiled him'. After a few months Sir Thomas was released into the custody of his brother, the Bishop of Bath and Wells. A year later he was permitted to kiss the royal hand as a token of forgiveness, but despite the strenuous efforts of the Spanish ambassador Gondomar, Lake never regained office.

Lake's ruin came within a few months of a greater downfall, that of his friend and patron the Earl of Suffolk. The disaster which overtook Suffolk was not merely part of Buckingham's revenge after the ill-starred Monson venture; it was also a necessary part of the energetic reform of the royal administration being undertaken by the new favourite. Of course, even if the Howards had been never so clear in the discharge of their offices, Buckingham would have broken them.

It happened that their record was far from good. The Earl of Suffolk, intent upon building his palatial country seat of Audley End 'laden with carvings and sculptured panels and debts', had got hopelessly out of his depth, committing himself to expenditures of about £200,000, a fantastic sum in Jacobean values. Left to himself, Queen Elizabeth's 'Honest Thomas' probably would never have stooped to peculation. Unfortunately his second wife, Katherine Knyvet, like Buckingham's mother and Lady Lake, was one of the unscrupulous domineering matrons who bedevilled the court at this time. It was she who arranged with Sir John Bingley, Remembrancer of the Exchequer, the schemes for extortion and bribery which got under way shortly after Suffolk in July 1614 became Lord Treasurer of England.

For a remarkably long time the depredations of Suffolk's treasurership went undetected, though it became a wry jest that while other court officers received their gifts on New Year's Day, the Lord Treasurer received his all the year round. The Overbury trials came and went, leaving Suffolk unscathed. After a tactful retreat to the country he reappeared at court and, within a month of the conviction of his daughter and son-in-law, served as fellow godfather with the King at the christening of the son born to another of his daughters, Katherine, wife of young William Cecil, second Earl of Salisbury. However, reports of the Suffolks' peculations became more and more widespread. Finally, in the summer of 1618 Buckingham felt he had enough evidence to go before the King. On July 19th Suffolk was summarily dismissed and a commission of Buckingham's nominees went to work trying to restore some sort of order in the treasury.

For a while it seemed that Suffolk, protected by a release passed under the Great Seal, would escape all punishment other than loss of office and acknowledgment of guilt, but in the end it was decided to make a Star Chamber matter out of Suffolk's malfeasance. The hearing in November 1619 saw Coke fulminating against Suffolk, and demanding an unprecedented fine of £100,000, as well as imprisonment in the Tower. Most of the court, however, sided with Sir Henry Hobart when he declared that 'the institution of that court was not to ruine men and theyre families'. There was indeed a fair amount of sympathy for Suffolk. Most people realized that his wife was chiefly to blame, 'The Lady keeping the Shop, and Sir John Binglie, her Officer, crying, What d'ye lack?' 'The Countis,' it was said, 'made use of her husband but as a seale-Ring, with a man's headd upon it, to confirm what before she had resolved to do.'[7] The consequence was that the fine fixed by the court was £30,000, not Coke's £100,000, and even this was later reduced to £7,000 which Suffolk was instructed to pay to one of King James's Scots. Suffolk might have had his fine still further reduced if King James had not learned that the Earl, distrustful of his mercy, had stripped his house of furniture and transferred his lands to trustees so that seizures could not be made.

In addition to the fine, the Star Chamber court ordered imprisonment in the Tower for Suffolk. This was reduced by James to a nominal ten days in custody, during which time the quip ran around London that a Privy Council meeting could be held at any time in the Tower, for they had there a Lord Chamberlain (Somerset), a Lord Treasurer (Suffolk), a Secretary of State (Lake), and a Captain of the Gentlemen Pensioners (Suffolk's eldest son Theophilus Howard, Lord Howard de Walden, who had been sent to share his father's imprisonment). It was made a condition of Suffolk's release that his sons resign all their posts at court. Nor did the royal displeasure against the Howards, whetted by Buckingham, stop at Suffolk's sons. His eldest daughter had married old William Knollys, Viscount Wallingford, who because of his own complicity in the Monson affair and his wife's industry in circulating anti-Buckingham lampoons, was required to surrender his highly lucrative post of Master of the Wards.

King James expressed his sympathy to Wallingford when the latter came to surrender his patent. He assured him that he had given good and faithful service both to Queen Elizabeth and himself but 'he had one fault common to him with divers others of his frends and fellowes, which could not stand with his service nor of the state, that he was altogether guided and over-ruled by an arch-wife'.[8]

It was while Suffolk was vainly striving to avoid trial that his brother, the old Earl of Nottingham, lost his post of Lord High Admiral. In his younger days as Lord Howard of Effingham, Nottingham had commanded the fleet which had routed the Spanish Armada. Perhaps because of the lingering prestige of that great victory, he was dealt with very gently. His marriage to a distant kinswoman to the King may have helped him also. In any case, after Cranfield's revelations of the appalling state of the navy, he was permitted to retire gracefully on grounds of age. Buckingham, when he succeeded him in February 1619, recompensed him with £3,000 cash, plus a pension of £1,000 per annum payable first to him, then to his widow, and then to one of his children. Moreover, as a sop to the old man's vanity, he was allowed for his earldom 'the Antiquitie, Place and Preceedence of John Lord Mowbray, his Predecessor whome King Richard the Second . . . created Earle of Nottingham'. Thus he was given precedence above all earls of later creation.

One can feel little regret at the way in which Buckingham dealt with the Howards. It is hard to know which to stigmatize the more strongly—their sheer incompetence and stupidity, or their conscienceless graft and cupidity. Their dismissal was indispensable for any real reform; and reform, not personal ends, may have been Buckingham's prime purpose in purging them from the King's service. Only one of the Howards had the intelligence and the skill in intrigue which might have saved them. This was Northampton. Unluckily for his family, Northampton had departed this life in 1614, dying on June 14th in his great house at Charing Cross. On his deathbed he finally declared himself a Catholic. One of his dying wishes was that neither the Earl of Pembroke nor Viscount Lisle, who were his enemies, should succeed to his office of Warden of the Cinque Ports, which had proved so useful to him in allowing priests to slip in and out of England.

After 1619 only one of the Howards remained a person of consequence at Whitehall. This was Thomas Howard, Earl of Arundel. Although much younger than Suffolk or Nottingham, he was the head of the house. A friendless boy of seventeen at the time of King James's accession, he had had to stand by helplessly while the rapacious Northampton, Suffolk and Nottingham secured from the King the estates forefeited to the Crown by his father, which certainly should have gone to him. He never for-

got how these kinsmen had pillaged him, and pointedly supported
Buckingham when they intrigued against the favourite. His own interests,
it happened, were artistic, not political. Realizing this, Buckingham accepted his friendship. He was perhaps glad to have his position countenanced by the man who, among the mushroom creations in James's
court, stood forth as the epitome of the old nobility.

Arundel's alliance was not without its rewards. Through Buckingham's
help he was able to achieve one of his life's ambitions in 1621 when he was
created Earl Marshal, regaining for his family a hereditary honour lost by
his grandfather, the attainted Duke of Norfolk. A further reward was the
pension of £2,000 per annum allowed him a little later.

Suffolk came to realize the wisdom of his nephew's course. In November
1623 he married one of his sons, Sir Edward Howard, to a daughter of
Buckingham's half-sister, Elizabeth Villiers, and thus belatedly allied himself with the all-powerful favourite. As for Nottingham, the prodigal old
man died in poverty in December 1624.

As the family of Howard moved to the wings, that of Villiers advanced
to centre stage. Buckingham was abundantly furnished with family connections and seemed determined to advance them all. Should he prove
forgetful and overlook this cousin or that, he received a torrent of re-
minders from his mother whose vulgarity, cupidity, and arrogance made
her perhaps the most objectionable of the whole set of female dragons
pestering the court at this time. Born Mary Beaumont, she came of good
family though she had served almost as a menial in the home of her kinswoman, Lady Beaumont of Coleorton. A widowed Leicestershire squire,
Sir George Villiers, had been struck by her beauty while visiting Lady
Beaumont and proceeded to marry her. Of the children she bore her elderly
husband her favourite was George, the future duke. Carefully she brought
him up for the brilliant career she wanted him to achieve at court—
though the actuality must have surpassed her most ardent dreams. It was
she who encouraged him to spend the two years' residence in Paris which
brought him back with the polished manners of a French chevalier.
Though his father left George Villiers only £50 a year, his mother saw to
it that he was more generously endowed with less tangible assets.

When Villiers began his splendid court career, his father had long been
dead and his mother had remarried twice. Buckingham's second step-
father was a Sir Thomas Compton, younger brother of William, second
Lord Compton, with whom he shared a tendency towards mental derange-
ment. Compton was a soft-spirited man, and Buckingham's mother never
pretended to have married him for anything other than the money which
he expected to inherit. She gave signal expression to her contempt for
Compton in July 1618 when it was arranged that, her son now being a

marquess, she should enjoy the title of Countess of Buckingham for life. The new countess insisted that her husband be left a bare knight.

Exercising to the utmost her influence with her son, the Countess of Buckingham set herself to becoming a power in the English court. So successful was she in advancing her favourites and blocking the suits of those whom she disliked, that the Spanish ambassador ventured the quip that England was ripe for conversion to Catholicism since more persons there worshipped the mother than the son. By the autumn of 1616 she had become such a nuisance that, to keep her meddling within bounds, Buckingham sent her away from the court for a while.

The Villiers matriarch was out to provide for her family. Her concern extended beyond her own children and step-children to an abundant circle of more remote connections—Beaumonts, Botelers, Bretts, Hills and Sheltons. Following the Countess's success in marrying one of her nieces to young Sir Thomas Lake in February 1621, it was ironically observed:

> In truth she is to be commended for having such care to preferre [advance] her poore kindred and frends, and a speciall worke of charitie yt is to provide for younge maides, whereof there be sixe or seven more (they say) come lately to towne for the same purpose.[9]

The chief of the Countess's endeavours were devoted to Buckingham's brothers, John and Christopher, though her exertions on their behalf were not really needed for King James himself was determined to reward and advance them. Despite, or perhaps because of, the very mediocrity of Buckingham's kin, His Majesty extended to all of them the fatherly benevolence in which his favourite basked. He meant every word when, at 'The Prince's Feast', he proclaimed his intent to advance all the Villiers.

Entirely lacking Buckingham's charm and talent, his brothers were poor material for James to work with, but their deficiencies did not deter the resolutely benevolent monarch. For John, weak in body and head who finally ended up insane, there was early knighthood and appointment as Master of the Robes in the household of Prince Charles. What his mother most wanted for John was a handsome wife with a very large dowry. The bride-to-be was found in the daughter of Sir Edward Coke. Coke, out of royal favour at the time, agreed eagerly to the offered alliance with Buckingham, though his skinflint haggling over the dowry lost him much of the favourite's good will. In the end he promised a dowry of £10,000 in return for resumption of the King's favour, and restoration to his place on the Privy Council. When Coke found that his wife, whom he had married when she was the young and very wealthy widow of Sir William Hatton, would not consent to the match, he coolly abducted the girl from her keeping, smashing down doors to get at her, and departing with Lady Coke and her followers in hot pursuit. Outpacing his lady, he handed the prospective bride over to the care of her future mother-in-law. When Lady Coke regained custody of her daughter through an appeal to the Privy Council, King James sent his personal order that the girl be delivered to her father to be disposed of as he found best. The marriage came with a rush. On Saturday, September 27, 1617, the banns were read for the first time. On Sunday the 28th they were read for the second time and the father-in-law-elect restored to the Privy Council. On Monday the 29th they were read for the third time and the marriage celebrated at Hampton Court with the King giving away the bride.

After the marriage every effort was made to placate Lady Coke. Buckingham himself with a group of the court lords went to the house of Sir William Craven where she had been committed to keep her from preventing the marriage, and brought her back to Whitehall. James exerted all his charm, and everyone rejoiced when the lady swore in his presence that she loved her daughter as dearly as ever. Touching though the scene proved to be, such kind attentions had not been lavished on Lady Coke only for this. It was hoped that she would not only forgive her daughter but add to her dowry out of the very extensive property she possessed in her own right. In this James and the Villiers were disappointed. True, Lady Coke entertained them all to a magnificent banquet from which she pointedly excluded her husband, but she would not present lands to her daughter and her disappointing groom. Whereas the Villiers were particularly pressing that Lady Coke transfer to the newly married couple the Island of Purbeck, the most that she would do was to talk of letting them have it some time in the future. Finally an offer was made to create Lady Coke Countess of Purbeck, and her son-in-law Viscount Purbeck, if only she would make the transfer. She still declined. A threat to make Coke a baron to spite her proved equally ineffective. Among the strong-minded women who were present in over-plus at this time, Lady Coke was by no means the least. Finally in June 1619 James went ahead and gave John Villiers the title of Viscount Purbeck anyway, even though he had not got the island.

The next year Buckingham tried to make an assistant out of Purbeck, referring to his brother some of the crowd of suitors who haunted him. The strain proved more than poor John could stand. His wits began to wander and he slipped into the first of his attacks of madness. In June 1622 the passers-by in a London street were shocked to see Purbeck shattering with his bare hands the glass windows in Wallingford House and crying from the room within that he was a Catholic who would shed his blood for the Faith.

For his wife poor Purbeck had a dog-like devotion. When she was sick with smallpox late in 1624 he would not move from the foot of her bed.

Ironically, a few months later all London was talking about a charge the Villiers family had brought against Viscountess Purbeck that the son she had recently borne had been begotten by Sir Robert Howard, a son of the Earl of Suffolk. As for Coke, his sale of his daughter advantaged him little. A few years after the marriage he was more than ever out of the King's favour, a prisoner in the Tower for his temerity in opposing the royal wishes in the House of Commons.

Somewhat happier than John Villiers was Buckingham's other brother Christopher, the shallow, feckless 'Kit' whose amiable inanity seems to have been his chief asset. Kit made his first appearance at court about the beginning of 1617 when Buckingham got him a position as a groom of the Bedchamber, and a malicious little jingle was passed around:

> Above in the skies, shall Gemini rise,
> And Twins the court shall pester,
> George shall call up his brother Jacke
> And Jacke his brother Kester.[10]

The next few years saw Kit busy lining his pockets. He was granted a share in the highly lucrative patent to license alehouses; given an annual pension of £800 by the King; and made heir to lands worth £500 per annum by Sir Robert Naunton. Naunton, one of his mother's allies, thus assured for himself the post of Secretary of State left vacant by the death of Winwood.

For Kit as for John it was necessary to secure a wife, preferably pretty but indispensably rich. Surveying the scene in 1619, his mother decided upon the daughter of Sir Sebastian Harvey, an extremely rich merchant who had become Lord Mayor of London. Informed of the intended honour, the Lord Mayor lamented that he would rather have both himself and his daughter dead than endure such a marriage. He added that, since his daughter was not past fourteen and small of growth, he was not minded to marry her off for another four or five years anyway. The consequence was a series of messages from the King of England, alternately cajoling and threatening, urging Harvey to accept the match. As a warning of the danger of incurring the King's displeasure, Sir Sebastian was summoned before the Star Chamber and fined £2,000 for a small error committed ten years earlier when he had been an under-sheriff. This manœuvre failing, King James summoned the Lord Mayor, the Lady Mayoress, and their daughter into his presence and undertook himself to plead Kit's case to them. The Lord Mayor was a man and stood by his child. To the amazement of the court he refused to be moved by even the pleadings of the King.

Baffled, the Countess of Buckingham had to look elsewhere for a mate for her son. In 1622 she thought she had found her in Lady Norris, the only child and heiress of the Earl of Berkshire, who had recently accomplished the difficult feat of committing suicide with a cross-bow. Kit's mother was not deterred by the fact that her boy had recently shown himself less amiable than was generally supposed by almost killing with his spurs one of the Earl of Southampton's gentlemen in an assault launched by himself and Sir Robert Dalyall. His Majesty had stepped in to see that Kit did not have to face the gentleman in a duel after the latter had regained his health. Now he exerted himself to secure the Norris heiress for Kit. Although the estates of a suicide were forfeited to the Crown, King James agreed that the coroner investigating Berkshire's death should be tipped off not to urge the manner of his demise. The lady's inheritance thus preserved for her, the King let it be known that Kit, when he married her, would himself be created Earl of Berkshire. Unfortunately Elizabeth Norris turned out to be much more subtle than any one had suspected and suddenly eluded Kit by marrying Master Wray of the King's Bedchamber, 'not so much . . . for the love of the one as to be rid of the other'. Wray was forthwith dismissed from his post and ordered never to come within the twelve-mile radius of the verge of the court.

As for Kit, further wife hunting proved unnecessary. While his family had been busy looking for a lucrative match for him, he had become involved in a liaison with his cousin Bess Sheldon and given her 'such earnest that he cannot well forsake the bargain'. (Bess was one of the needy female relations Kit's mother had brought to court to catch husbands.) All thoughts of lucrative matches were put aside and the two were married. Kit's indiscretion entailed no loss of favour with His Majesty. About this time he was promoted from groom to gentleman of the King's Bedchamber. Better things were in store for him. On April 18, 1623, James writing to Buckingham during the latter's visit to the Spanish Court informed him:

> Kitte is now an earle & hath also the patent of his lande [a royal grant of estates sufficient to maintain him in the state the title required], thus was thow borne in a happie howre for all thy kinne.[11]

James, in fact, had created the witless Kit Baron of Daventry and Earl of Anglesey.

Much might be said of others who had the good fortune to share in the Villiers blood, or at least to be married to it. There was Buckingham's half-brother, Sir Edward Villiers, rather better qualified than most of them, who served as an ambassador to Bohemia and later as President of Munster. There was the entirely unexceptional Sir William Fielding who, having married Buckingham's sister in the days of the family's obscurity, found himself sucked up in the roaring up-draught of royal favour and became first Viscount Fielding, then Earl of Denbigh, and Master of the

Wardrobe, and was enriched by a good proportion of the import duty on the French and Rhenish wines.

It is time, however, to pass from minor members of his family to the great Buckingham himself. Amid all the negotiations for good marriages for his brothers, the finding of a bride for Buckingham was not overlooked. Few women, of course, could aspire to become the wife of the King's great favourite. To qualify, a girl needed more than beauty and station—she had to have great wealth. Pending discovery of a lady so endowed, Buckingham, according to scandal, 'by his greatness vitiated many gentile and noble virgins in birth, though vitious for yeelding to his lust; whose greatness opened the door to allure them more'.[12] In the spring of 1620, however, the court learned that a match was in prospect between Buckingham and Lady Katherine Manners, only daughter of the Earl of Rutland, perhaps the wealthiest nobleman in England.

The course of true love (for such it certainly proved on the lady's part) did not run smooth. There were a number of difficulties: the attitude of her father who seemed not to appreciate the greatness of the honour to his house; the sad truth that Lady Manners had a brother who would inherit most of the Rutland fortune; and the unfortunate fact of her own Catholicism. Rutland's unfriendliness was quite unconcealed. He regarded as exorbitant Buckingham's demand for a dowry of £20,000 ready money and lands worth £4,000 per annum. When Buckingham's mother kept Lady Katherine overnight without his permission, he proclaimed that the honour of his house had been blemished. The consequence was a letter from Buckingham coldly declaring that he no longer sought the match. Probably it was at this time that Buckingham addressed a semi-jocular petition to the King, one which even allowing for the eccentricities of Jacobean spelling supports Sir Henry Wotton's blunt description of the royal favourite as 'illiterate':

> To the kings most excelent Maj
>   The humble peticion of yeet your
> not antient-enough servant and bacheler
>   G. Buckingham
>   Maye it please your maj That you have bine and is still a good master to me the world by your actions is well satisfied but how to give them as greate satisfaction of my thankefullnes if I should marie [marry] before the runing out of my prentiship I knowe not, and therefore I most humbli beseech your maj: That for presarving me from the foule blemich of inthankefullnes you would lay a straight charge upon my lord of ruttland to caule whom [call home] his daughter againe or att least I may be secured that in case I should marie her, I may have so much respitt of time given me as I may see some one act of wisdome in the foresayde lord as may put me in hope that of his stocke I may some time begett one able to serve you in some meane imployment.[13]

The difficulties with Rutland were substantially lessened when, in March 1620, the death of the Earl's only son left Lady Katherine his sole heir. There remained the matter of religion. The Manners were a family remarkable for their unswerving devotion to Catholicism. Fortunately Lady Katherine consented to receive instruction in the doctrines of the Church of England. How much she grasped of the finer points in theology remains open to doubt, but converted she was, and received the Anglican communion at Easter 1620. Her marriage, on May 16th, was celebrated so quietly that the usually well-informed John Chamberlain, writing eleven days later, could only speak of it as a matter of uncertain report. In fact, only the King himself and the Earl of Rutland had been present to witness the nuptials.

Lady Katherine, infatuated with her handsome glittering lord, became a completely doting wife. The letters she wrote to Buckingham three years later during his absence in Spain with Prince Charles are touching in their outpourings of adoration:

> ... I thinke ther was never such a man borne as you ar and how much am I bound to god that I must be that hapye womane to injoy you from all outher wemen and the unworthiest of all to have so great a blesing only this I can say for my self you could never a had one that could love you better then your poore true loving katte [Kate] doth, poore now in your absencs but els the hapyest and richest woman in the world.[14]
>
> ... You [might] have a finer and handsomer, but never a lovinger wife than your poor Kate is. . . .
>
> ... there was never woman loved man as I do you. . . .[15]

It is part of an old old story that the recipient of these loving epistles was making himself objectionable to the Dons by scandalous overtures to their women. His adventures in Spain were not surprising after the freedom he had enjoyed in the English court:

> For the Marquess himself, as he was a man of excellent *symmetry*, and proportion of *parts*, so he affected *beauty*, where he found it; and yet he looks upon the whole race of *Women* as inferior things, and uses them as if the *Sex* were one, best pleased with all.[16]

Buckingham was like a magnificent animal let out to stud. To the worth of his blood line a study in heredity published only recently gives remarkable testimony.[17] Kate herself was aware of her husband's proclivities, but out of her great love could extenuate them:

> ... for truly you are so good a man, that, but for one sin, you are not so great an offender, only your loving women so well. But I hope God has forgiven you. . . .[18]

One other thing Kate's letters to Spain reveal. She may have been a very nice girl, but she was not very bright. Partly this is shown in her naïve belief that her husband had become a reformed character in Spain:

> Everybody tels me how hapy I am in a husband, and how chast you ar; that you will not looke at a woman, and yett how thay woo you.

More amusingly, Kate's humourless credulity emerges in the matter of the telescope. Buckingham had mentioned in one of his letters the difficulty that Prince Charles was encountering in getting close to the Infanta whom he had come to woo, and had quipped that the Prince needed a telescope to see her. Kate's response was a model of wifely alacrity and helpfulness:

> . . . I have sent you some perspective glasses, the best I could get. I am sorry the Prince is kept at such a distance that he needs them to see her.[19]

If marriage for Kate meant the beginning of eight years of bliss to be shattered only when an assassin's knife ended her husband's life, for Buckingham too it brought in a new era. No longer did his fortunes rest entirely upon the favour of the King. Marriage to the Manners heiress had given him a measure of independence, and he was the prospective founder of a family. In the latter role, he had either to purchase or build one of those enormous mansions which the magnates of the kingdom maintained as their family seats. After considerable negotiation, Buckingham bought New Hall in Essex from Robert Radcliffe, Earl of Sussex. An impoverished member of the old aristocracy, Sussex was glad to sell his house to King James's upstart. Hoping to ingratiate himself with both Buckingham and the King, he let him have it cheap. Buckingham at once began a costly programme of enlarging and modernizing the mansion.

New Hall was not Buckingham's only acquisition. A town house was required as well as a family seat in the shires. Not satisfied with Wallingford House, his usual London residence, Buckingham secured from Bacon York House, a fine riverside mansion on the Strand. Bacon had fitted out York House in considerable style during his greatness as Lord Chancellor, but Buckingham rebuilt it with greater magnificence. To fill its galleries he bought paintings.

The collecting of the masterpieces of Renaissance art had only recently become fashionable in England. Through prodigal expenditure Buckingham took his place in the forefront of the Whitehall group of collectors. The contemporary Duveen who secured most of his pictures for him was the painter Balthasar Gerbier. Writing from Paris in the fall of 1624, Gerbier supplied a list of possible purchases calculated to make the mouth of any collector water. In the house of the Bishop of Paris he had discovered and could buy 'three of the most rare pictures that can be'. One of these, a crucifixion by Michaelangelo, 'should be seen kneeling . . . the most divine thing in the world'. Other pieces that Gerbier had discovered were somewhat less divine in their inspiration. He positively drooled as he wrote of 'a most beautiful piece by Tintoret of a Danae, a naked figure the most beautiful, that flint as cold as ice might fall in love with it'. He had put down a deposit to hold this last item. There were other things: a head by Titian, and 'the most beautiful statues that can be spoken of' in the possession of Monsieur de Montmorency who was ready to sell. At the end of his list Gerbier made an eloquent plea to Buckingham to spare no expense in furnishing York House bravely:

> ... for the love of Paul Veronese, be pleased to dress the walls of the gallery: poor blank walls, they will die of cold this winter.[20]

Buckingham had little inclination to spare. Should his own means ever prove insufficient, he could count on King James for assistance. Writing to Lord Treasurer Cranfield in January 1622, James declared that he must have £33,000 for Buckingham (the sum including the costs of Kate's recent lying-in). Anticipating any possible expostulations, James vowed that until Buckingham was extricated from his financial difficulties, 'I proteste I can have no joye in the going well of my owin busienesse.'[21]

James's involvement in Buckingham's life and his dependence upon him and his family was complete. To analyse the relationship between King James and his favourite is a matter of some complexity. There was the attraction, tinged at least with homoseuxality, of the young man's good looks and virility. There was the teacher-disciple relationship always so dear to the pedagogical James. And there was also the role that Buckingham played as an entertainer, supplying the crude humour and buffoonery the King enjoyed, and skilfully keeping ennui away from the royal presence. At times Buckingham was reduced to such expedients as the burlesque christening of a pig in his attempts to arouse James out of melancholy moodiness. A Venetian, Horatio Busino, describing a masque in 1618, indicates what Buckingham and the court had to endure when the King was out of temper:

> Last of all they danced the Spanish dance, one at a time, each with his lady, and being well nigh tired they began to lag, whereupon the king, who is naturally choleric, got impatient and shouted aloud Why don't they dance? What did they make me come here for? Devil take you all, dance. Upon this, the Marquis of Buckingham, his Majesty's favourite, immediately sprang forward, cutting a score of lofty and very minute capers, with so much grace and agility that he not only appeased the ire of his angry lord, but rendered himself the admiration and delight of everybody.[22]

The real secret of Buckingham's hold on the King, however, lay in the fact that he and his family gave him persons upon whom to lavish love and affection. Without them James would have been a very lonely old man in his final years. His own family had disappeared from about him. Queen Anne had joined Prince Henry in death in 1619, ending James's loveless marriage. Princess Elizabeth was as good as dead, lost to her father in Germany. Only the shy undemonstrative 'Baby Charles' remained. The King found himself returning to the condition of his early years when he had spoken so poignantly of his solitariness, without mother or father, wife, sister, brother or child. In his isolation, the King rejoiced to find himself drawn into the warm bustling circle of the Villiers. The role of the King as one of the family becomes particularly evident after Buckingham's marriage, when the doting Kate began to reward her lord with a series of babies. The King delighted in having the little Villiers girl Mary (or 'Mall') brought to his bedchamber, where he would play with her by the hour. He was a sort of honorary grandfather, more than filling the place of the long defunct Sir George Villiers. When plans were made for New Hall or York House, they were discussed with James. When rebuilding was in progress, James came around with Buckingham and Kate to see how things were getting on. When cousins or other relatives needed help, King James was applied to. During Kate's pregnancies, His Majesty wrote to Buckingham, laying down rules for her care:

> My onlie sweete & deare chylde the lorde of heaven blesse thee this morn-ing, & thy thing my daughter & the sweete litle thing that is in her bellie, I pray thee, as thow loves me, make her praeciselie observe these rewlis, let her never goe in a coache upon the streete, nor never goe fast in it, lette youre mother keepe all haistie newis from comming to her eares, lette her not eate too much fruite, & hasten her owte of London. . . .[23]

When it was time to wean the little girl Mall and Buckingham was absent in Spain, it was to the King that Kate wrote in anxious consultation:

> I hope, my Lord Anan has tould your Majestie, that I ded mean to wene Mall very shortly. I wood not by any mens a don it, till I had furst mad your Majestie acquainted with it. And by reason my Cusen Brets boy has binne ill of latt, for fere shee should greeve and spyle her milke, makes me very desiorous to wene her: and I thinke shee is ould enufe, and I hope will endure her wening very well; for I thinke there was never child card les for the brest then she does. I do entend to make triall this night, how shee will endure it.

After Mall had safely passed through this momentous stage, the King him-self acquainted Buckingham with the safe conclusion of the operation. Writing from Whitehall to his 'sweete boys', Buckingham and Prince Charles in Madrid, he informed the Duke:

> Kate & thy sister supped with me on Satterdaye night last & yesterdaye both dyned & supped with me, & so shall doe still with godds grace, as

long as I am heere, & my litle grandchylde with her fowre teethe is, god be thanked, well wained.

The letters just quoted are a few of many between the King, Buckingham, and Buckingham's kin, dating from the final years of James's reign, preserved in the Harleian collection in the British Museum. They cast a most interesting light on the relationship between the monarch and his favourite. Buckingham's letters almost invariably begin with the jocular formula 'Dere Dad and Gossop' and close with an equally formuarly 'Your Majesty's humble slave and dogge, Steenie.' Running throughout is the mixture of adulation, professions of love, and privileged impertinence and familiarity which Buckingham found best for winning and holding the King. Typical of their sportive element is a note about King James's recurrent gout:

> My dere dad, Gossope, and steward
> I know not whether first to express my thanks for your innumerable favours and cares of me, or greefe I have to here you keepe your bed, but my comfort is that no other indisposition of helth accompanies your lamenes, and the time of the yere serves so luckilie in oure absence that by the next I hope to receave this news, that you are marching upon your well shaped legs againe. This sweet Jesus grant.

Part of the sportive note was an unpleasantly scatalogical humour which included Buckingham's use of an anatomical obscenity as a synonym for his womenfolk.

Another and more important element in the correspondence was flattery. The King had to be supplied with comforting reassurances that Buckingham loved him. He had to be kept filled with a joyous sense that this wonderful young man was his own particular creation and creature. Buckingham was careful to lard his letters with the declarations which the King craved. Acknowledging one of James's letters, Buckingham expatiated on the goodness of His Majesty in writing in a style 'of more tendernes than fathers have of children, of more frendship then between equalls, and more affection then betwene lovers in the best kind man and wife'. Continuing, he declared that he must address James as 'My pourvier [purveyor], my goodfellow, my phesition, my maker, my frend, my Father, my all.' No extravagance was too gross for Buckingham in this constant eulogizing of the King:

> All and the least I can say is this: that I naturallie so love your person, and upon so good experience and knowledge adore all your other parts, which are more than ever one man had, that were not onelie all your people but all the world besids sett together on one side, and you alone on the other, I should, to obey and pleas you, displeas, nay dispise all them.

In a letter from Paris Buckingham really outdid himself, declaring, 'I ame

I

now goeing to give my redemer thankes for my maker.' He meant, presumably, that he was about to go to chapel where he would thank God for
having sent him so bountiful a patron. The conceit would commend itself
to James who always had a bit of a tendency to equate himself with the
Deity.

James's own letters are even more illuminating. Writing to Buckingham
in Spain, he puns on his own family name as he happily assures Buckingham how good a steward he has been in looking after his interests. Proudly
he tells how he has persuaded the East India Company to pay £2,000 to
secure Buckingham's favour. Along with mention of favours done or
intended, the King again and again declares his love for Buckingham.
These declarations are not the shallow rhetorical avowals of the favourite;
they spring with a disturbing ardour right from the warped but living
heart of the King. They include disarming revelations such as 'I weare
Steenie's picture in a blew ribbon under my wastcoate, next my hairte.'
Again and again the King exhorts Buckingham to return from Spain to his
disconsolate old dad. Sometimes the King's involvement with his favourite shows itself indirectly in half-ludicrous fussing about his health:

> . . . remember now to take the aire discreitlie . . . & for gods saike & myne,
> keepe thy selfe verrie warme, especiallie thy heade & thy showlders. . . .

Sometimes it shows itself in a torrential pouring forth of love for Steenie:

> My onlie sweete & deare chylde blessing blessing blessing on thy hairte
> rootes & all thyne.

There was something terrible in the old King's yearning.

In the end Buckingham, like Somerset, came to be so confident of the
King's dependence upon him that he began to domineer. He rudely up-
braided James with being false to his word when the latter tried to prevent
his Spanish journey. He went counter to his sovereign's known wishes
when dealing with Parliament. He coerced him into ruining faithful servants like Digby and Cranfield because they had incurred his own enmity.
The King swore at Buckingham and had black moods; but he did not
break with him. Buckingham could indulge in such conduct because, un-
like Somerset, he was right in thinking he was indispensable. James came
around every time. He had to have Buckingham. Old and weary, he lacked
the energy to build a new relationship with a new favourite. The reign
ended with Villiers still all-powerful, 'conferring all the honours and all
the offices of the three kingdoms, without a rival; in dispensing whereof he
was guided more by the rules of appetite than of judgement'.[24]

CHAPTER XVIII

Titles, Money and Morals

WHEN KING JAMES'S SUBJECTS looked at their sovereign and his court, they could not but note a painful discrepancy between theory and practice. The ideal against which they measured the court was an exalted one, and it was one which James had accepted in his book on the kingly office, his *Basilikon Doron*. In the centre was to be the King, attended by the state and pomp befitting God's steward in the management of things temporal. About him were to be the bravest, wisest and noblest of the kingdom, to serve, counsel, and defend. From the royal court rays of light and goodness were to illumine the entire land. By his bestowal of offices and titles, the King was to make known to all beholders those of his subjects pre-eminent for valour or virtue.

A most eloquent description of the ideal court was supplied by John Webster in the opening scene of *The Duchess of Malfi*, written about 1614. Antonio, speaking of his travels in France, declares what a court should be:

> In seeking to reduce both State, and People
> To a fix'd Order, their juditious King
> Begins at home: Quits first his Royall Pallace
> Of flattring Sicophants, of dissolute,
> And infamous persons—which he sweetely termes
> His Masters Master-peece (the worke of Heaven)
> Considring duely, that a Princes Court
> Is like a common Fountaine, whence should flow
> Pure silver-droppes in generall: But if't chance
> Some curs'd example poyson't neere the head,
> Death and diseases through the whole land spread.
> And what is't makes this blessed government,
> But a most provident Councell, who dare freely
> Informe him the corruption of the times?
>
> (I, i, 6–19.)

Indicative of Webster's view of the realities of court life is the fact that in the rest of his play he uses 'court', like many another Englishman, as a term of angry opprobrium, speaking contemptuously of 'Court-honestie', 'Court teares', 'Court promises', and:

> court calumney
> A pestilent ayre, which Princes pallaces
> Are seldome purg'd of.
>
> (III, i, 59–61.)

227

Antonio, who began the play with the encomium of the ideal court, gasps
as he dies:

> . . . let my Sonne flie the Courts of Princes.
>
> (V, iv, 84.)

In his satirical bitterness concerning the realities of court life, Webster
expressed the view of most of his contemporaries. Most took it as axiomatic
that 'envie is . . . the common pestilence and infection of a Court', that
'the Court is the flatterers stage or *Theatre* wherein he still doth practise',[1]
that at the court 'men live *injurias ferendo, gracias agendo*' [inflicting
injuries while expressing thanks].

The blame for the enormous distance separating the Jacobean court
from the ideal accepted by both King James and his subjects must be laid
upon the King himself, his unsuitable choice of officers, his own laxity,
and his indulgence towards offenders. The responsibility to maintain
stand rds and discipline was his.

Looking back at the Jacobean court the modern observer must be impressed by its extravagant luxury, its unruliness, its sycophancy, and its
all-pervasive graft and corruption. Of the first of these, its *nouveau riche*
extravagance, something has been said already. After every possible allowance has been made for the Jacobeans' conviction that court magnificence
was a matter of national prestige, the fact remains that the senseless display
with which too many of the courtiers bankrupted themselves passed all
measure of taste or sanity. There was little point in King James declaring
it part of a king's duties 'by his and his Courts moderatenesse in Apparell,
to make us ashamed of our prodigalitie',[2] when he countenanced ladies
of his court appearing in gowns which cost fifty Jacobean pounds to the
yard for the embroidering. The trouble was that the pullulating egotism
and ambition of the courtiers made such expenditure of money mandatory
as a means of securing prestige. The prodigality of the Jacobean lords and
ladies is only intelligible in this light. Fourteen thousand pounds were
spent in hanging the lying-in chamber of the Countess of Salisbury with
white satin embroidered with gold or silver and pearl. This was not done
because the family wanted to spend the money, or thought that aesthetic
delight would lighten the pangs of childbirth. It was done to signalize the
greatness of the House of Cecil which could expend such a sum to usher
into the world a possible son and heir. As it turned out, the Countess had
a daughter.

Many courtiers, playing the court game of ostentation and prodigality,
got hopelessly in debt. For them the court offered one final comfort,
however. No pursuing bailiff could arrest for debt within the royal precincts of Whitehall. Slinking about the corridors of the palace was the
occasional unfortunate gentleman who dared not stir beyond the gates for

fear that the bailiffs of Holborn, set on by his tailor, would carry him off to
debtors' prison. Persons belonging to the nobility were protected by their
titles. In an important case in the Star Chamber, it was argued how far
'noble men and women are priviledged in theyre persons from arrest'. The
judgment went finally against Richard Millard, goldsmith of London,
Thomas Stephenson, sergeant-at-mace, John Fermor his yeoman, John
Stone, secondary of the Counter in the Poultery, and others who had had
the effrontery to arrest Elizabeth, Countess of Rutland, because she had
not paid her bills.

The disorder that prevailed at the Jacobean court was at times hardly
credible. Lady Arbella, arriving at court, was so disgusted by what she
saw that in a letter to the Earl of Shrewsbury she could not help exclaiming:

> But if ever there were such a virtue as courtesy at the Court, I marvel what
> is become of it, for I protest I see little or none of it but in the Queen.[3]

It would be interesting to hear Lady Arbella's comments on the debacle
which followed the performance of *The Masque of Blackness*, on Twelfth
Night 1605. Some details of this are preserved for us in a letter of Dudley
Carleton's:

> The confusion in getting in was so great that some Ladies lie by it and
> complaine of the fury of the white stafes [ushers]. In the passages through
> the galleries they were shutt up in several heapes betwixt dores and there
> stayed til all was ended, and in the cuming out a banquet which was pre-
> pared for the king in the great chamber was overturned table and all before
> it was skarce touched. It were infinit to tell you what loses there were of
> chaynes, Jewels, purces and such like loose ware.[4]

Things had improved hardly at all, years later, at a banquet served after
the masque *Pleasure Reconciled to Virtue*. The Venetian Busino, describes
the scene thus:

> The repast was served upon glass plates or dishes and at the first assault
> they upset the table and the crash of glass platters reminded me precisely
> of a severe hail storm at Midsummer smashing the window glass. The story
> ended at half past two in the morning and half disgusted and weary we
> returned home.[5]

Members of the court could be guilty of discourtesy even to the King
himself. An amusing example is provided by the Marquess of Hamilton's
curiosity when the King received letters from Buckingham and Prince
Charles in Spain. Writing to the latter, James explained why it was hard
for him to keep confidential what they had written to him:

> . . . I have bene trowbled with hammilton, quho being present by chawnce,
> at my ressaving both of youre first & seconde pacquette out of madrid,

wolde needs peere over my showlder quhen I was reading thaime, ofring ever to helpe me to reade any harde wordis.[6]

Worse offenders were the Countess of Dorset who, clamorous about some suit, forced her way into the Privy Chamber; and Arthur Brett who had the effrontery to lay his hand on the King's bridle to compel his attention during a day's riding in Waltham Forest.

Generally, elaborate etiquette saved the King from this sort of thing. Accomplished courtiers made much of such fine points as not actually touching with their lips the royal hand when given it to kiss, and found guilty of 'low absurdity' those uncouth enough to do so.

Testimony abounds as to the savage boorishness of various of the Jacobean courtiers. There were all too many like Sir Edward Bellingham, who struck and spurred Anthony Byott in Westminster Hall 'in the face of the Courts of Justice then setting'. The citizenry of London provided a frequent butt for the rudeness of gallants of the Bellingham breed. If feeling in the City was often hostile to the court, it was the consequence of much provocation. The citizens of London did not forget quickly indignities such as certain courtiers put upon them when the Lord Mayor banqueted the new Knights of the Bath created when Charles was made Prince of Wales:

> On Saterday the Knights of the Bath were entertained by the Lord Mayor at Drapers Hall with a supper and a play, where some of them were so rude and unruly and caried themselves so insolently divers wayes but specially in putting citizens wives to the squeake, so far foorth that one of the sheriffes brake open a doore upon Sir Edward Sackvile, which gave such occasion of scandall, that they went away without the banket though it were redy and prepared for them. Neither did they forbeare these disorders among themselves, for there were divers picques and quarrells at their severall meetings, but specially at the Miter in Fleetstreet.[7]

Sometimes the 'roaring boys' from the court had their blood tamed by the City watch. Little quarter appears to have been given by either side in these encounters. One such clash resulted in the death of perhaps the first of the innumerable 'remittance men' sent to the New World:

> An unruly sonne of the Lady Finches (whom she sent to Virginia to be tamed) within five or six dayes after his return fell into a drunken quarrell with the watch where he was so hurt that he died the next morning, and a brother of Sir Gilbert Haughtens his companion is almost in the same case yf he be not dead alredy.[8]

Even earls had to take their punishment if they provoked the sturdy cudgels of the watch. In 1620 John Chamberlain reported:

> . . . on Goode Friday night the earle of Oxford and Sir Harry Parker (the Lord Mounteagles sonne) for some yll rule therabout were well battered and beaten by the watch, specially the earle that is scant well yet.[9]

Within the precincts of the court (and under certain circumstances the area within a twelve-mile radius of it known as the 'Verge'), law and order were maintained by the Knight Marshal and his men. Those whom they arrested were locked up in the Porter's Lodge pending hearing before the Court of Marshalsea, commonly known as 'The Marshal's Court'.[10] Here the Knight Marshal and the Lord Steward jointly presided. Those guilty of minor offences were committed either to the Marshalsea or the Fleet prison. Major offenders were hanged at the palace gate. Sir Thomas Vavasour and his successor as Knight Marshal, Sir Edward Zouch, had plenty of work for the staff of twenty or so who served under them. This ranged from nailing up 'mandates at the court gate for annoying the palace with filth or making water' to 'expelling the dangerous number of master-lesse men, boyes, and rogues serveing in every office and lodgeing in our Court ready to committ any disorders or outrages'.

Despite the responsibility of both the clerk comptrollers within the palace and the porters at the gates to keep unauthorized persons out of the precincts, a constant company of 'hang-bys' managed to circulate through Whitehall. Some of these 'infantry that follow the court' were vouched for as servants, others found pretexts of one kind or another to slip past the gates. They were responsible for constant pilfering. Dudley Carleton in a letter to Winwood gives a picture of their depredations:

> Sir Henry Goodier had his Chamber broken up at Court, and £120 stollen. Sir Adolphus Cary was robb'd at the last remove from Whitehall of £50 and three Suites of Apparell . . . and at the same time my Lady Dorothy Hastings (who lay in the Chamber above him), was spoyl'd of all that ever God had sent her, save that she had on her Back and her Belly.

Even Somerset had his quarters entered and ransacked. Cutpurses as well as burglars found their way about the court. The throng of spectators at a court masque gave these a great opportunity, but they found other occasions too. On Christmas Day 1611, one was captured in the Chapel Royal, close to the King's elbow as he was going up to receive communion.

Much of the thievery at court was done by royal servants. By no means exceptional was the case of one Henry Alred, dismissed as a yeoman 'for many disorders, and for suspicion of stealing 3 coapes out of his Majesty's Vestry at Greenwich'. Thefts by dishonest officers and underlings plagued the court from the beginning of the reign to the end. In 1604, in con-sequence of 'the daily losse of our silver vesselles', a rule was passed that food was to be brought to and from the kitchen on pewter dishes and transferred to silver only at the door to the Presence Chamber where the King was dining. In 1624 a royal proclamation was issued in a desperate attempt to recover two silver basins taken from the communion table in the Chapel Royal at Whitehall, and a 'great quantity of plate' stolen from the King. Goldsmiths and others in possession of filched silver were ordered to return it to the Jewel House.

The royal household was riddled with dishonesty. When its consumption of wood, coal, butter, fruit and other commodities was investigated, it was found that 'a greate deale of the same is secretlie conveyed out of the howse'. Everywhere there was peculation. When the Dutch merchant Sir Peter Van Lore was asked to lend King James £20,000 on the security of jewels which had been bought from him for £27,000, he refused, declaring: 'Though the king paid twenty-seven thousand pounds, yet the money was not paid to me, but others did share in the price of my jewels'. This thievery and fraud, as noted earlier, was partly due to the King's servants often being months, if not years, in arrears in their salaries and having to depend upon illegal profits for their livelihood. Mere financial reforms, however, would not have rooted out these abuses; the whole atmosphere of the court had become too deeply tainted.

King James, in his own way, was as guilty of peculation as any in his court. His unabashed sale of titles of honour became one of the scandals of the time. Theoretically, all such titles were given as rewards for services and in recognition of persons who were the ornaments of the kingdom and whose presence at the royal court would add to its magnificence or enhance its prestige. But under King James everything boiled down to money. Just about every title and every office was available for a price—King James's honours were nothing if not vendible.

Queen Elizabeth had been cautious in conferring knighthoods, and even more so in creating peerages. In consequence, the number of titled subjects she left at her death was far below what might have been expected. As Lucy Aikin observed in her study of the Jacobean court more than a century ago:

> James, at his entrance into England, found a nobility neither numerous, recent, nor necessarily dependent on the crown; and a gentry very numerous, extremely wealthy, and abounding with individuals eagerly pressing for admission into the order of knighthood or into the peerage, the dignity of which they could well support and had long in vain aspired to. This consideration ought somewhat to modify the censure generally passed upon James for the lavish distribution of titles by which the first years of his reign were distinguished; he found in fact many subjects ripe for honours.[11]

While admitting that King James found the nobility unduly depleted in numbers, one cannot ignore the fact that his pouring forth of titles went far beyond what was justifiable. The matter of knighthoods provides a good illustration. Queen Elizabeth had created so few knights that when she died hardly a shire in England could muster enough knights to make a jury. Perhaps one of the reasons for this shortage of knights was that Elizabeth, like most of her subjects, had thought primarily in terms of medieval knighthood, which represented military distinction and rank. Not for nothing was the Latin equivalent for 'knight' often taken to be *miles*. When Elizabeth sent Essex to the Irish wars, she gave him permission to create knights. The derogatory term 'carpet knight' was in use for the man who won his spurs not in the field but in the sheltered confines of the court.

King James, who had no intention of going to war, had no reluctance about creating knights by the hundreds during peacetime. During his first six weeks in England he created at least 237 knights. If this left his subjects gasping, they were in for further shocks. By the end of his first year the new king had created 838 new knights. In the beginning, this wholesale extension of the honour may have been due to the euphoria which possessed James as he advanced southward into his new kingdom, and a genial wish to emblazon his way with honours generously bestowed. If such was the original impulse, it soon gave way to one considerably less magnanimous. The King found the £30 fee each new knight had to pay very useful in replenishing his purse. It was decided to forget about knighthood as a mark of royal favour and make it an impost on any subject who could afford it. On July 17, 1603, the new king issued a summons to all of his English subjects possessing land yielding £40 a year or better to come and be knighted, or else to make a payment in lieu of taking the title. With knighthoods thus deprived of any relationship to merit, James was heedless as to who received them. There was some raising of eyebrows, however, when the King knighted William Herrick, goldsmith of Cheapside, uncle of the poet, 'for making a Hole in a great Diamond the King doth wear'. Eyebrows went up even further when Adam Hill, who had been the Earl of Montgomery's barber, and a certain Greene, married to one of the Queen's laundresses, became knights.

Not surprisingly, the 'a Jeammy a Jemmy knights of the new edition' became the butts of disrespectful humour, and it was a well-worn quip that one enjoyed more distinction as an undubbed gentleman now there was 'scant left an esquire to uphold the race'. The King's new knights were ridiculed even in the public playhouses. In one of his comedies John Webster produced Sir Fabian Scarecrow, a poor thing who had borrowed the price of his title from his landlady. Not the least amusing sidelight on James's wholesale creation of knights is cast by a royal proclamation issued in April 1623. This admits that the College of Arms has lost track of James's new creations, and orders that future knights submit a certificate to the Earl of Arundel, the newly created Earl Marshal, within three months of their creation or lose their precedence.

About the beginning of 1611 Lord Treasurer Cecil became interested

I*

in a possible new source of income. Since knighthoods had proved useful
in bringing in money, let the King invent a new honour, a sort of super-
knighthood, carrying the same title of 'Sir', but inheritable and carrying
higher precedence, and therefore a higher price. Out of this suggestion,
which may have originated in the fertile mind of Sir Robert Cotton the
antiquary, emerged the order of knights baronet.

To give at least the shadow of military distinction to the new order, the
money qualification—the one that really mattered—was defined in terms
of maintaining 'the number of thirtie foote-Souldiers in Ireland, for three
yeeres, after the rate of eight pence sterling Money of England by the
day'.[12] This worked out at £36 10s. for each hypothetical soldier in
Ireland. Thus, the asking price for a baronetcy was £1,095. One-third of
the sum had to be paid in cash and the rest secured by a bond before
letters patent were issued conferring the title. To protect the investment
of the new baronets, the King promised that their number would not
exceed two hundred.

To screen applicants for the new title and make sure that each had an
income of £1,000 to sustain the dignity, King James appointed a commission of eighteen noble lords and Privy Councillors headed by Lord
Chancellor Ellesmere. Meeting in the Council Chamber at Whitehall, the
commissioners interviewed the 'divers principall Knights and Esquires of
sundry parts of this Our Realme, mooved with zeale and affection to further the Plantation of Ulster, and other like Services in Our Realme of
Ireland' for whom the new order was ostensibly intended. By May 1611
the commissioners had processed the first applicants and letters patent
were sealed creating eighteen baronets, the first of their order England
ever had seen. These were followed in June by a further batch of fifty-four.
The new order was off to a flying and lucrative start.

During the years that followed, King James's baronetcies proved subject
to the law of supply and demand. Originally overpriced at £1,095, they
could be picked up towards the end of the reign for a quarter of that
amount. The scheme to colonize Ulster did not benefit much from the
money raised by their sale. Generally the King had more pressing uses for
the money. Not infrequently it went to reward some servant, officer, or
favourite to whom he had turned over the right of sale. Phineas Pett, the
naval architect, tells how he was thus rewarded in 1619:

> The 20th day of November, attending at Theobalds to deliver his Majesty
> a petition, his Majesty of his princely care of me, by the means of the
> honourable Lord High Admiral [Buckingham], had before my coming
> bestowed on me for the supply of my present relief the making of a knight
> baronet, which I afterwards passed under the broad seal of England to one
> Francis Radclyffe of Northumberland, a great recusant, for which I was to

have £700, but by reason that Sir Arnold Herbert (that brought him to me) played not fair play with me, I lost some £50 of my bargain.[13]

The creation of a new rank in the aristocracy was attended by problems in the very sensitive matter of precedence. No sooner had the first baronets received their titles than there was a first-class row between them and the younger sons of viscounts and barons as to priority. Moreover, there was a rift within the ranks between those who had been knights before their elevation and those who were baronets but not knights. To settle these matters the King issued a 'Decree and Establishment' for the order. In it he declared that he would at once knight any baronet who was not already a knight, and that the male heirs of baronets would be knighted automatically upon reaching the age of twenty-one. Baronets would have to yield place to the younger sons of viscounts and barons, but for their consolation the King granted some additional privileges: the bloody hand of Ulster on their coats of arms, a place near the royal standard in battle, and the right to have 'two assistants of the bodie to support the Pall, a principall mourner, and foure assistants to him at their funerals, being the meane betwixt a Baron and a Knight'.

Generally considered, the 'project of baronets' was a success. A contemporary estimate that it brought in £120,000 (Jacobean values) for the King and his courtiers is probably correct enough. James showed his satisfaction with the venture by extending the baronetcy first to Ireland and then to Scotland. The first baronets of the Kingdom of Ireland were created in 1619. For ambitious and well-to-do Scots, the Order of Knights Baronet of Nova Scotia was instituted in the closing months of the reign. To save candidates the inconvenience of visiting the New World (they were supposed to establish settlements there), a small area within the precincts of Edinburgh Castle was declared part of Nova Scotia. Although the creation of baronets of this order ceased in 1707, the royal edict was never revoked; and Canadian tourists today may stand on Canadian soil when visiting Edinburgh Castle.

If payment was essential for a baronetcy, it often entered also into the attainment of a peerage. According to John Nichols' count, apart from numerous creations in the nobility of Ireland and Scotland, King James created in England three dukes, one marquess, thirty-two earls, nineteen viscounts and fifty-six barons, 'in all 111 Peerages—about seven times as many in a reign of twenty-two years as his Predecessor had created in a reign of twice that duration'.[14] While many of these titles were conferred free of price by the King, a good many were purchased. The price for a peerage depended upon the degree of favour with which the King regarded the man, the usefulness of his connections, and the amount the court thought could be screwed out of him. Men were known to have paid as little as £5,000 for a baronage. In 1615 when there was talk of creating fifty barons, the suggested price was £6,000. In 1616, however, Sir John Roper and Sir John Holles had each to pay £10,000 to become Lord Teynham and Lord Houghton respectively. Roper's title was converted into a pun and he became known as Lord 10M. Ten thousand pounds was the sum collected from both Lord Cavendish and Lord Rich when they acquired their earldoms of Devonshire and Warwick.

For light on the lucrative trade in honours carried on in the inner circle at court, we have a letter from Buckingham to King James dealing with the proposed elevation of Sir Francis Fane to the dignity of Baron Burghersh and Earl of Westmorland:

> Dere Dad and Gossope,
> Watt Steward hath bine withe me this morning to tell me your Majesty was well inclined to make Sir Francis Vaine an Erle for hime. I answered, that I could hardlie beleeve it, but if he would be contented that Sir Frances Steward might share with him [in the money Fane would pay], I would be suter to your Majesty for them in that for the present, and here-after, as occasion would serve, for somthing else; but with this condition, that he would perswade my Lord Hauton to give five or six thousand to be another [earl], which monie I tould him I desired to make use of myself. . . .
> Your most humble slave and doge,
>
> Stinie[15]

King James's court comprised members of not one but three aristoc-racies, those of England, Scotland and Ireland. The general rule was that a man took his title from the country to which he belonged by birth. Thus James, particularly at the beginning of his reign, was careful to confer Scottish, not English, titles upon his Scottish followers. In England the English lords of any particular rank took precedence over all persons of the same rank in the Scottish or Irish nobility, but the latter had place before all English lords of lower rank. An English viscount outranked any Scottish or Irish viscount, no matter how ancient his title; but an Irish or Scottish viscount outranked any English baron, even if his title went back to the Conquest.

Things went along fairly well on this basis until King James took to conferring titles of one nationality upon persons of another. Feeling ran particularly high in 1621 when English barons found themselves forced to yield precedence to Englishmen who had secured Irish viscountcies at cut-rate prices, far below what was asked for an English barony. A number of English earls and barons drew up a petition asking that all English peers enjoy precedence over compatriots holding Scottish or Irish titles, regard-less of rank. James was so furious when he learned about this petition that he refused to accept it. When it finally reached him through Prince Charles, he summoned the English lords who had signed it and gave them a tongue-lashing. If he thought this ended the matter he was badly mistaken. In 1624 when Oliver St. John, whom King James had created Viscount Grandison in the Irish peerage despite his English birth, sought precedence over Lords Carew and Brooke in the English baronage, the fat was in the fire all over again. In high dudgeon the English lords pointed out that 'the waight of an English baron was 10000^{li} whereas an Irish vicount was valued and might be had for 1500^{li}'.[16]

Despite all the sordid trafficking when wealthy landowners satisfied their egos by buying the King's honours, the pretence was kept up that titles were won through merit and attended by responsibilities. Knights of the Bath continued to be charged to 'defend wydows, maydens and Orphines as far forth as ye may'.

Once at least (in the case of Sir Francis Michell) the reign saw a formal dishonouring in which knighthood was taken away from the offender. Narrowly escaping execution of the same sentence was Sir Giles Mompesson, a kinsman of Buckingham, who was out to get rich through his connection with the King's favourite. In 1617 Mompesson contrived to make 'a vast waste in the spoil of his Majesty's timber' in the New Forest. Later he went on to bigger things, securing a patent for himself and two fellow commissioners to license all inns. In his exercise of this patent, Mompesson proved utterly exorbitant and brought no less than 3,401 charges against innkeepers whom he considered delinquent. So detested did he become that in 1621, when Parliament met full of anger against the courtiers who by their monopolies and licensing powers kept a leech-like hold on the economic life of the nation, the King's advisers decided to sacrifice Mompesson. On March 26th sentence was passed on him. He was to be degraded from his order of knighthood, made a perpetual outlaw incapable of benefiting from any general pardon, deprived of his property and fined £10,000. Mompesson, however, had slipped away from the sergeant who had him in custody and was safely abroad when the sentence was passed.

Not so fortunate was his confederate, Sir Francis Michell, who had similarly been sentenced to degradation from the knighthood. On the afternoon of June 20th, Michell was brought to Westminster Hall for the ceremony of degradation. Here the sentence of Parliament was read by one of the pursuivants. Then the gilded spurs of knighthood were hacked off his heels, the sword was taken from his side and broken over his head, and the heralds proclaimed that from henceforth he must be known not as Sir Francis Michell, Knight, but Francis Michell, Knave. With papers on his front and back declaring his fault, he was mounted on a horse with his face towards its tail, and led through the hooting mob to Finsbury gaol. As for Mompesson, he stayed abroad until the excitement had died down.

When he returned in 1623 he received a pardon 'for all ffynes received of Innholders' and began trying to enforce once more his patents to licence the inns and alehouses, maintaining 'they were not then abrogated and damned by act of parliament when he was driven to so fowle a retreat. . . .'

Among those most aware of the thriving trade that the King and his favourites carried on in the disposal of titles were the Heralds. Not surprisingly they concluded that, since the King was selling titles left and right, they themselves need not be too particular about selling the much less important honour of a coat of arms and the name of 'gentleman'. Installed with wives and domestics in their official residence, Derby House, the thirteen members of the College of Arms received handsome incomes far beyond their annual stipends from the Crown. For every coat of arms they granted they received their fee. When they superintended the heraldic pomp at the funerals of nobles or gentry, they received further emoluments, and their searching of pedigrees brought in useful returns. The College fought a running war with 'painters of coaches, marblers, Glasiers, Embrotherers, and gravers of sealls' who usurped their function of issuing or blazoning arms. Particularly annoying to them were the 'pseudo-heralds' in the provincial capitals of York, Chester and Exeter. These were unauthorized persons who executed the heralds' duties for local notables who wanted to avoid the expense of bringing in the royal heralds from London. It was a major grievance with the College of Arms that 'There is never a shyre towne in England, which hath not a paynter or two, that playeth the herold',[17] and that these 'counterfeit heralds' would bury a lowly knight with 'viii banerolles as if he had byn a duke'. Unfortunately, some of the offenders were able to claim a shadow of legality, having secured letters of deputation from Garter King of Arms to the great annoyance of his colleagues.

The heralds themselves were split into violently contending factions, constantly fighting over the allocation of duties and the division of fees. Back in 1599 William Smith, Rouge Dragon pursuivant, had written of 'ye dissensions & brablements of this troublesome office, consisting only of xiii persons: a monster wth iii heads [the Kings of Arms: Garter, Clarenceux and Norroy], vi bodies [the heralds proper: York, Richmond, Somerset, Lancaster, Chester, Windsor] and iiii legges [the pursuivants: Rouge Dragon, Blue Mantle, Portcullis, and Rouge Croix]'. Much of the trouble was due to the overbearing character of Sir William Dethick, Garter King of Arms, who was heartily detested by the rest of the College. A man with a furious temper, Dethick once wounded his own brother when the two were at Windsor with the court. While superintending the funeral of the Countess of Sussex in Westminster Abbey, he attacked with his dagger two men who had aroused his anger. His removal in 1605 and the appointment of Sir William Segar, Norroy King, as his successor did not bring the hoped-for peace.

Another trouble-maker was Ralph Brooke, the arrogant and opinionated York Herald, who considered most of his colleagues incompetent and made no secret of his feelings. In Dethick's time he had circulated a little treatise charging Dethick not only with fabricating pedigrees but with granting arms to persons not of fit station. Among the latter were: Tay, a hosier living in Fish Street; Dungayn the plasterer; Parr the embroider-er, the son of a pedlar (to whom Garter King had sold for £10 the arms of Parr, the last Marquess of Northampton); Robert Young, a soapmaker; William Sanderson, a fishmonger; and 'Shakespear ye Player'.[18] After Dethick's removal, Brooke found time not only to continue a feud with William Camden, Clarenceux King of Arms (to whom he had endeared himself by publishing a list of all the errors to be found in the latter's *magnum opus*, his *Britannia*), but to clash repeatedly with Segar, Dethick's successor as Garter King.

December 27, 1616, is a date memorable in the history of the College of Arms. It was then that Brooke scored his great coup against Sir William Segar. On that day the Earl of Arundel showed King James a most in-teresting document which had been turned over to him by Brooke: 'an attestacon and a confirmacon under the hand and seale of Sr Willm Segar Garter of these Armes viz: Or three pales Gueles on a Canton Sable a Lyon rampant of the first and for the Creast a feather Azure in a Crowne murall Gueles as the Armes of Gregorye Brandon of London Gent'. The scandal was that the arms so described were those of the kingdom of Aragon, the canton that of the duchy of Brabant, and Gregory Brandon, gentleman, to whom Segar had assigned them for a price, the common hangman of London.

King James exploded with anger. He swore he would take away Segar's office and proceed against him personally in the Star Chamber. Fortu-nately for Segar, the Lord Chamberlain persuaded James to do nothing until the entire matter had been investigated by the commissioners for the Office of the Earl Marshal. Hurriedly convened that same afternoon, these dignitaries heard Segar's lame excuse that he had issued the certificate to an unknown person who had appeared before him with the arms all tricked out and had offered 22s. for immediate approval so that they could be despatched to Spain in a ship that was waiting to sail. Segar entered a counter-charge that the whole matter had been 'a subornacon by Yorke to draw him into danger'. Brooke readily admitted his complicity, but declared he had arranged it all to 'detect unto the Lords the ignorance and greedy covetuosnes of Garter'. When these discoveries were made, 'the Lords mervailed muche and not without Laughter condemned both the ignorant covetuosnes of the one and the malitious complott of the other'.[19] Having received their report, King James vented his annoyance by ordering both Garter King of Arms and York Herald locked up in the Marshalsea prison. Meanwhile, the commissioners were told to reform the College of Arms. Descending on Derby House, they ordered the heralds to find other quarters for their wives and children, and to suppress their other abuses.

The troubles in the College of Arms emphasized the need for an Earl Marshal to exercise surveillance over its members. In 1621 King James finally heeded the pleas of the Howards and gave the office, claimed through hereditary right, to the Earl of Arundel, the head of their house. In November 1623, Arundel convened a Court of Chivalry in the Painted Chamber at Westminster. All matters pertaining to the jurisdiction and rights of the College of Arms were scrutinized, and an attempt was made to restore peace among the warring heralds. Whatever Arundel was unable to do, death attended to in 1625 when it ended Brooke's forty-five irascible years in the College.

The gap between the ideal and the actual was nowhere more apparent than in the sexual morals of the Jacobean court. The ideal was hopefully proclaimed by Samuel Daniel in a poem written at the beginning of the reign:

> What a great check will this chaste Court be now
> To wanton Courts debauch'd with Luxury. . . .

The actuality was admitted by an anonymous A.D.B., in his *Court of the Most Illustrious and Most Magnificent James the First*, when he wrote of the 'licencious life, which for the most part, Courtiers doe enjoy in a Court'. There was plenty to offend the Puritan in the untidy private lives of most of King James's courtiers, whether it was the Earl of Sussex's precipitant marriage to his mistress the day after his countess died, or the Earl of Oxford's comprehensive career in drinking and wenching, which inspired the following lampoon when he went to the wars under the generalship of Vere:

> Some say Sir Edward Cecill can
> Do as much [as a general] as any man.
> But I say no, for Sir Horace Vere
> Hath caried the earle of Oxford where
> He neither shall have wine nor whore,
> Now Hercules himself could do no more.[20]

Offensive as the conduct of these court lords might be in the view of the bourgeois morality of the City, it was palliated among their own class as 'the necessary consequence of witt & valour'. Most of the aristocracy accepted their bastards with no more shame than Shakespeare's Gloucester did his Edmund. 'Natural children' held their place on the periphery of the family circle, and if a legitimate heir was lacking, a legal procedure known as 'rehabilitation' could legitimize one of the deceased's by-blows. Lady Anne Clifford, herself a person of impeccable respectability, provided generously for the illegitimate daughters left by her husband, the Earl of Dorset. Lady Anne accepted her husband's infidelities. What she could not forgive him was the shameless way in which he brought his mistress, Lady Peniston, into their house. Jacobean society had its own standards and Lady Anne, recording her husband's action in her autobiography, could note that it was 'much talked of abroad and my Lord was condemned for it'.

The most unsavoury side of Jacobean court life was that of the pimps and procuresses who lived by the vices of the court—persons such as Lady Grisby 'a Dame of Pleasure heretofore, but now declined . . . and turned House-keeper to such like as herself had been'. Here were panders and charlatans such as Dr. Forman and Mrs. Turner, whose services meant so much to Lady Frances Howard, and the infamous Dr. Lamb who finally had his brains knocked out by a furious London mob. Creatures of this kind arranged assignations at Ware or Brainford. They dealt in aphrodisiacs more potent than the customary 'eringoes, artichokes, potatoes and your buttered crab', and for the women they had 'those excellent receipts . . . to keep yourselves from bearing children'.

The women who gratified the lusts of the court were a mixed lot. They ranged from the 'younge mignon of Sir Pexall Brockas . . . whom he had entertained and abused since she was twelve years old' to old hands who could not remember when they had been virgin. They ranged from court laundresses ready to earn sixpence, the minimum rate, in a dark corner, to highly expensive courtesans such as Venetia Stanley, one of the most beautiful women of the age. The latter was married finally by Sir Kenelm Digby who declared that 'a wise man, and lusty, could make an honest woman out of a Brothell-house'. Less fortunate but more typical in her end was Elizabeth Broughton. 'She was,' said old John Aubrey, 'a most exquisite beautie, as finely shaped as Nature could frame, had a delicate Witt.' For a time she was one of Dorset's women. In the end, grown cheap and infamous, she died of venereal disease but only after she had become a byword for her profession. One of Ben Jonson's curses against Vulcan when his apartment burned down was 'Thy Wives pox on thee, and Bess Broughtons too.' A mock litany of the time had a verse:

> From the Watch at Twelve a Clock,
> And from Bess Broughton's buttond smock,
> Libera nos Domine.

What concerned contemporaries was not so much the number of kept women about the court—after all, theirs was the oldest profession—as the increasing sexual freedom some of the ladies of the court were permitting themselves. The licence of their husbands was one thing but, in an age that completely believed in the double standard, the frequency with which their ladies got embroiled with lovers seemed a matter of real scandal.

If King James, alternately lax and irascible, was unable to keep his courtiers under proper discipline, Queen Anne with her rather lackadaisical self-indulgence did no better with their ladies. Lady Anne Clifford recorded how, even during the first year of the reign, 'there was much talk . . . how all the ladies about the Court had gotten such ill names that it was grown a scandalous place'. The scandal grew with such spectacles as that of the countesses and viscountesses staggering drunk at the prolonged binge at Theobalds during King Christian's visit. Particularly notorious was the new fashion for the ladies to wear extremely low necklines with only the most transparent of lawn across the bosom:

> To burn men's souls in sensual hot desires,
> Upon whose naked paps a lecher's thought
> Acts sin in fouler shapes than can be wrought.[21]

The scandals involving Lady Frances Howard and Viscountess Purbeck have been noted earlier. Plenty of other noblewomen had their names blackened. There was Lady Lettice Lake, a daughter of the Earl of Warwick, who after her death from 'pox' (the ubiquitous venereal disease which plagued the Jacobeans in consequence of their pleasant vices), was found to have an illegitimate daughter—'Dicke Martins, or rather a greater mans.' There was Sir Michael Stanhope's lady who died soon after 'her late disgrace of having a daughter (as is saide) by Sir Eustace Hart'. There was the Countess of Suffolk, mother of Lady Frances Howard, whose intimacies with Cecil were a matter of heavy-handed humour on the part of the King. There was the lovely Countess of Hertford, who many maintained was the mistress of the Duke of Lennox before the death of the eccentric old earl her husband left them free to marry. One of the more surprising centres of scandal in the court, however, was Mrs. Overall, wife of the Bishop of Coventry and Lichfield. In her time she was reputed one of the most beautiful women in England. Overall, who married her when he was Dean of St. Paul's, doted on her and forgave her infidelities. Her escapade in running away briefly with one of her lovers gave rise in 1608 to a little jingle:

> The Deane of Paule's did search for his wife,
>   And where d'ee thinke he found her?
> Even upon Sir John Selbye's bed,
>   As flatte as any Flounder.[22]

Not all lovers could count upon such tolerant and forgiving husbands. The common course for the husband who found his wife had given him a cuckold's horns was either to challenge the lover to a duel or, more contemptuously, to hire some bullies to beat him within an inch of his life. In 1618 Sir Humphrey Tufton and his men were fined £4,000 in the Star Chamber for bastinadoing Master Christopher Neville, whom he suspected of making love to his wife.

As good a sidelight as any on the morals of the court is cast by the plays written for its entertainment. The theatre chiefly patronized by the Jacobean courtiers was the Blackfriars. This was the expensive indoor playhouse where the King's Men gave evening performances after playing in the afternoon in the open arena of the Globe. The plays written for the Blackfriars reflect the morals of its audience. Taste increasingly favoured a strained, artificial species of tragi-comedy, such as Beaumont and Fletcher's *Philaster*, which evaded all real criticism of life and dealt instead in empty rhetoric about honour and chastity. For anyone concerned with real morality, these sentimentalizings were ludicrously theatrical, but they passed for the real thing with the debauchees from King James's court.

In comedy, the Blackfriars audience favoured such productions as John Fletcher's *The Humorous Lieutenant*. Fletcher knew that highly spiced stuff was wanted, and he gave it in good measure. This play is ostensibly set in 'ancient Greece', but this is an ancient Greece which, with its gentlemen ushers who keep the citizens from pressing too close to visiting ambassadors, strangely resembles Whitehall. The second act presents Leucippe, the court procuress, who is shown with two assistants as she reviews her ventures:

> *Leucippe.* What have you dispatcht there?
> *Second Maid.* A letter to the Country maid, and't please ye.
> *Leu.* A pretty girle, but peevish, plaguy peevish:
> Have ye bought the embroydered gloves, and that purse for her,
> And the new Curle?
> 2 *Ma.* They are ready packt up Madam.
> *Leu.* Her maiden-head will yield me; let me see now;
> [*She hunts through her records*]
> *Cloe, Cloe, Cloe*, here I have her,
> *Cloe*, the Daughter of a Country Gentleman;
> Her age upon fifteen: now her complexion,
> A lovely brown; here 'tis; eyes black and rolling,
> The body neatly built: she strikes a Lute well,
> Sings most inticingly, these helps consider'd,
> Her maiden-head will amount to some three hundred,
> Or three hundred and fifty Crowns, 'twill bear it handsomly.
> Her Father's poor, some little share deducted,

To buy him a hunting Nag; I, 'twill be pretty.
Who takes care of the Merchants Wife?
First Maid. I have wrought her.
Leu. You know for whom she is?
1 *Ma.* Very well, Madam,
Though very much ado I had to make her
Apprehend that happiness.
Leu. These Kind are subtile;
Did she not cry and blubber when you urg'd her?
1 *Ma.* O most extreamly, and swore she would rather perish.
Leu. Good signs, very good signs,
Symptoms of easie nature,
Had she the Plate?
1 *Ma.* She lookt upon't, and left it,
And turn'd again, and view'd it.
Leu. Very well still.
1 *Ma.* At length she was content to let it lye there,
Till I call'd for't, or so.
Leu. She will come?
1 *Ma.* Do you take me
For such a Fool, I would part without that promise?
Leu. The Chamber's next the Park.
1 *Ma.* The Widow, Madam,
You bad me look upon.
Leu. Hang her, she is musty:
She is no mans meat; besides, she's poor and sluttish;
Where lyes old *Thisbe* now, you are so long now—
2 *Ma.* [*Searching the records*] *Thisbe, Thisbe, Thisbe,* agent
Thisbe, O I have her,
She lyes now in *Nicopolis.*
Leu. Dispatch a Packet.
And tell her, her Superiour here commands her
The next month not to fail, but see deliver'd
Here to our use, some twenty young and handsom,
As also able Maids, for the Court service,
As she will answer it: we are out of beauty,
Utterly out, and rub the time away here
With such blown stuff, I am asham'd to send it.
[*Knock within*]
Who's that? look out, to your business, Maid.
There's nothing got by idleness: there is a Lady
Which if I can but buckle with, *Altea*
[*She hunts through her records*]
A, A, A, A, Altea young and married,
And a great lover of her husband, well,
Not to be brought to Court! say ye so? I am sorry,
The Court shall be brought to you then.

At this point Leucippe is interrupted by the entry of an old woman with
a pretty young thing named Phoebe. Leucippe examines Phoebe and

though she finds her 'low i' the pasterns', concludes by buying her for ten crowns. After this the play goes on with the main plot which had been held in abeyance all through this scene. To appreciate the difference between the English court under Elizabeth and under James, one need only compare Elizabeth's courtiers listening to the delicate art of Lyly's *Endymion* with those of King James's attending this stuff.

The court vice which most alarmed the Jacobeans was not sexual laxity but sycophancy. The former affected only the individual and his immediate circle; the latter could threaten the well-being of the nation. In an age when almost everything was determined ultimately by the decisions of the King, men held it axiomatic that the health of the commonwealth depended upon the worth of the sovereign. It was not enough for the King himself to be wise and virtuous; he had to have honest councillors who would inform him of abuses in the state and recommend beneficial courses. A good and honourable monarch might be led astray and perverted by flattering sycophants who would conceal unpleasant truths and give counsel tainted with self-interest. The Jacobeans saw sycophantic courtiers as destroyers of kingdoms, and stigmatized flattery as 'that most filthy and slavish sinne'. They agreed with Castiglione that those who give ill counsel in order to ingratiate themselves with a prince 'do infect with deadlie poyson, not one vessel wherof one man alone drinketh, but the commune fountain that all the people resorteth to'.

King James not only enjoyed admiration but poured forth his bounty upon those he found appreciative of his good qualities. This compulsive generosity tempted all, except men of the highest integrity, to ingratiate themselves with him; while the theory that he ruled as God's deputy made inevitable a mode of address which could slip only too easily from fitting respect to gross flattery. Flattery of the King became the orthodoxy of the court.

From all sides adulation was heaped upon King James:

> This most Religious, Learned, Gracious *Prince*,
> This Parragon of Kings, this Matchlesse Mirror,
> This *Faiths-defending* Antichristian Terror,
> This Royall al-beloved King of *Harts*,
> This Patterne, and this Patron of good Arts.[23]

Cecil, addressing Parliament, admonished the members:

> Remember what a king you have. Not only the wisest of kings (well I may say of men) but the very image of an angel, that doth both bring good tidings and puts us in the fruition of all good things.[24]

Passing an act to make the anniversary of the detection of the Gunpowder Plot a perpetual day of thanksgiving, Parliament proclaimed:

. . . no nation of the earth hath been blessed with greater benefits than this nation now enjoyeth, having the true and free possession of the Gospel under our most gracious Sovereign Lord King James, the most great, learned and religious king that ever reigned therein. . . .

No praise was too extravagant. Attending Jonson's masque of *Oberon*, James found himself eulogized thus:

> He is a god, o're kings; yet stoupes he then
> Neerest a man, when he doth governe men;
> To teach them by the sweetnesse of his sway,
> And not by force. He's such a king, as thay,
> Who are tyrannes' subjects, or ne'er tasted peace,
> Would, in their wishes, forme for their release.
> 'Tis he that stayes the time from turning old,
> And keepes the age up in a head of gold.
> That in his owne true circle, still doth runne;
> And holds his course, as certayne as the sunne.
> He makes it ever day, and ever spring,
> Where he doth shine, and quicken every thing,
> Like a new nature: so that true to call
> Him, by his title, is to say, Hee's all.

John Savile, wishing to outstrip others in his expression of joy at seeing King James's first entry into London, likened his own bliss to that of the Virgin at the Annunciation, and implied a comparison between the expectations England had for James and those Mary held for the fruit of her womb.

There were refinements of sycophancy. One of the Howards, who had a talent for this kind of thing, had advice for Sir John Harington who intended to visit the court:

> Do not of yourself say, 'This is good or bad'; but, 'If it were your Majesties good opinion, I myself should think so and so.'[25]

Reading the masses of eulogy and panegyric heaped on King James, one needs to recall the reality. All this went to bolster the ego of an irascible opinionated Scot who drank too much, neglected his duties for his pleasures, and exchanged filthy jests with debauched favourites. True, he had good qualities; but they got lost under the heaping of promiscuous praises for every conceivable virtue. The marvel is that in this atmosphere King James managed to keep as much good common sense and awareness of realities as he did.

Adulation was not limited to the King. The court lords were all served up with the same shameless flattery. Abraham Darcie, writing in 1624 of the death of the Duke of Lennox, could ask:

> What accident falne in a 1000 yeares
> Hath from his friends drawne forth more store of teares.

> Since the first man that in the world was borne,
> A fuller number was not knowne to mourne.[26]

The next year, seeking to ingratiate himself with the Howards, he could speak of:

> ... the Princely Lady *Frances Howard* ... second daughter to *Tho :
> Howard* Earle of *Suffolk*, &c, and Grandchild to *Tho : Howard* late Duke of
> *Norfolke*, to whose immortall goodnesse and greatnesse, these my poore
> endeavours are by me humbly consecrated.[27]

In view of the fact that the lady so lauded was a convicted murderess, it is easy to see why honest men spoke with contempt of 'court holy water' and vowed 'He that thryvethe in a courte muste put halfe his honestie under his bonnet.'

For all its colour, richness and magnificence, the Jacobean court was deeply tainted. Almost everyone was motivated by self-interest. Each clawed for as much as he could get of the spoils. It was a place filled with 'persons betraying and betrayed'. The Earl of Worcester, speaking particularly of the Queen's ladies, could declare, 'the plotting and malice amongst them is such, that I think envy hath tied an invisible snake about most of their necks to sting one another to death'.[28] Little wonder if the advice given the aspirant courtier was *Nulli fidere*, 'To trust none', and that many an honest English gentleman escaped with relief from the stratagems, envy, and treachery of the court to the quiet of his country place and returned no more to the corridors of Whitehall, Hampton or Windsor.

CHAPTER XIX

Duels and Affrays

THE JACOBEAN COURTIER'S concern for honour was obsessive and irrational. It made him pathologically sensitive to any imagined slight, and it could cost him his life.

Theoretically, devotion to honour was a fine and ennobling thing, with a philosophy behind it derived from the ancient Greeks and Romans. Aristotle in his *Nicomachean Ethics* had defined honour as the recognition which men of worth accord to virtue, and he had declared that the winning of honour was the particular purpose of the magnanimous or great-minded man. Renaissance courtiers accepted this coupling of honour with virtue. 'Virtue' for them, however, was not the slightly anaemic term it is today. The word still lay close to the old Roman *virtus*, that which makes a man. The 'virtue' of the Renaissance was a quality compounded of self-sufficiency, integrity, valour, and generosity of spirit.

Jacobean writers frequently mentioned the link between honour and virtue. According to Sir Francis Bacon, 'the winning of honour is but the revealing of a man's virtue and worth'. John Webster in a splendid passage in one of his plays declared:

> Vertue is ever sowing of her seedes:
> In the Trenches for the Souldier; in the wakefull study
> For the Scholler; in the furrowes of the sea
> For men of our Profession—of all which
> Arise and spring up Honor.[1]

During his life, the man who was truly noble achieved honour through virtue. If he had won it in sufficient degree, he did not lose it when he died, for it was transmuted into immortal fame. Honour and Fame! By these two stars the great-minded man steered his course. This philosophy, or rather secular religion, of Honour was perfectly attuned to the Renaissance cult of the individual. Within its limits it was fine and admirable, producing and sustaining in persons such as Sir Philip Sidney some of the finest spirits of the age.

Unfortunately, honour did not rest entirely upon this single ground of virtue. Entangled with it was the aristocrat's pride in family. It was argued that when a great-souled man had won honour, he bequeathed it with his blood to his descendants. It was in vain that thinking men protested against the absurdity of this notion of inheritable honour. A Sir Thomas More might expostulate, 'For never the more noble be we for their [our ancestors'] nobleness, if ourselves lack those things for which they were noble.'[2] Almost all the Jacobeans accepted the fiction of noble blood. A lord might be a cowardly drunken debauchee, but he expected to be treated with honour because of his ancestors.

A number of questions could be posed concerning honour. What of the King? Where did he enter in? The orthodox view was that:

> The fountaine of honour is the King and his aspect, and the accesse to his person continueth honour in life, and to be banished from his presence is one of the greatest eclipses of honour that can bee. . . .[3]

But what if a man of virtue were banished from court because he had refused to perform a wicked deed, though commanded to it by a legitimate though immoral king? Did he then lose honour? Or what if a king conferred a title of honour upon a vicious parasite? Did he then, *ipso facto*, become honourable? And what of Christ and His Church? What connection had all this matter of courtly honour with God, the sole source of all good? How were these pagan doctrines of fame and honour to be related to the tenets of Christianity? What of Christian humility? In 1610 Thomas Milles in his *Catalogue of Honour, or The Treasury of True Nobility* endeavoured to categorize these conflicting concepts of honour:

> Nobilitie . . . is of three sorts: And is devided into Nobilitie *Coelestiall* which consisteth in Religion; Nobility *Philosophicall* which is got by *Morall vertues*; and Nobilitie *Politicall*, whereof this present Treatise is. Out of the two first sortes of Nobilitie no man can come Noble, except that he the same be a *Good man* also. But out of this third sort, a Man, although he be never so wicked and ungracious, may yet excell the rest of men, even in the highest degree of Nobilitie: so as did *Caligula*, *Nero*, and such others like.[4]

Involved in his intriguing at court, his gaming, his wenching and hunting, the average Jacobean courtier did not concern himself with distinctions such as Milles's. He assumed that his birth, or his place at court, or what he took to be his own achievements, (or a combination of all three which he never bothered to analyse), made him a person of honour. For him honour had lost all that attachment to virtue which might give it a moral sanction. It had become a mechanistic matter of title, office, or birth, plus whatever deference the world could be bullied into according the personal pretensions of the individual.

Beneath the gleaming cloak of 'Honour' lay the naked realities of egotism, irrational and provocative, anti-social and corrosive. At times honour could turn ludicrous as when Anthony, Viscount Montague, instructed his Clerk of the Kitchen to see that no servant insulted his lordship by turning his back upon the joint being roasted for his table. At times it could turn criminal, as when Lord Sanquhar had the fencing-master Turner murdered because he had dishonoured him by accidentally blinding him in one eye.

Sanquhar's venture in murder was only one of the criminal attacks and affrays which arose when courtiers regarded their honour as affronted. An 'affray' was a more or less spontaneous outbreak of fighting. Often both the principals had been heated by drinking, and were accompanied by friends and partisans whom they felt bound to impress with their mettle. Little provocation was needed, especially if the two were old enemies. If they once drew their swords, the fighting could soon become general. John Chamberlain's letters are studded with references to affrays of this kind:

> Sir Thomas Cornwallis the Groome porters sonne having a quarrell with a brother of the Lord Haye drew upon him in companie of other Scotts, and was sore hurt and indaungered by Ramsey.

> I was told yesterday of an untoward accident happened [during Queen Anne's visit to Bath] in the renewing of an old quarrell twixt the Lord Willoughby and the Lord Norris wherin the Lord Willoughby (overlayde with number) shold be sore hurt and one of his men slaine.

One of the nastiest types of affray arose when some young hothead caught an enemy in a position of unreadiness and suddenly launched an assault against him:

> Here was an odde fray fell out the last weeke twixt one Huchinson of Grayes Inn and Sir German Poole, who assaulting the other upon advantage, hurt him in three or fowre places, and cut off three of his fingers before he could draw his weapon, whereupon inraged he flew upon him and getting him downe bit off a goode part of his nose and caried yt away in his pocket.

So John Chamberlain writing at the end of February 1613. In a subsequent letter he was able to add the detail that Sir Jermyn Poole had with his teeth torn away one of Hutchinson's eyebrows.

So disturbed was the court by these outbreaks that the Lord Chamberlain and the principal officers of the court issued a proclamation declaring that the following rules were going to be enforced:

> (1) Anybody using 'anie woorde of reprouche whereby a quarrell may arise' was to be fined by the Privy Council, imprisoned for four months, and banished from the court for eight. Moreover, if the word was spoken in the Presence Chamber or any other of His Majesty's chambers or lodgings, the imprisonment was to be for eight months and the banishment from the court for a year.
> (2) Anybody present when a reproach was uttered or fighting arranged was to notify the Privy Council, or be himself subject to four months in prison and eight months of banishment from the court.

(3) Any person carrying a challenge to a duel, or passing on tales or reproaches apt to cause fighting, was to be imprisoned for two years and not allowed within the court gates for three years.

(4) Anybody, other than an officer reasonably correcting an inferior, who should within His Majesty's houses, including gardens, tennis courts, bowling alleys, or tiltyards, or within two hundred feet of the outward gates 'malitiouslie strike and maim wherebie bloud is or shalbe shed' was to have his right hand stricken off, be imprisoned for life, and pay whatever fine was set at the King's pleasure.[5]

The article dealing with challenges involved a very sensitive matter among the courtiers—the right to duel. The duel, with its rules and formalities, had only recently come to England. Commenting upon its increasing use during the time of Queen Elizabeth, G. M. Trevelyan has properly observed that it was

> . . . a step in the direction of humanity and law, for it took the place of the 'killing fray'. . . . It was the new code of honour, which insisted that man should stand up alone against man, with equal weapons, that was now superseding that odious power of the grandee to set upon a poor neighbor with a host of bullies and retainers.[6]

The question, however, was not whether the duel or affray was preferable, but whether they did not both offend the law. To men like Sir Francis Bacon, both were forms of private revenge, which 'putteth the law out of office'. Those who stood by the right of a gentleman to defend his honour in a duel argued that, far from encroaching upon the law, the duel was its complement, necessary for the remedy of those injuries to honour for which the law provided no satisfaction.

George Chapman, in *Bussy D'Ambois* written in 1604, presents the arguments for and against the duel. Early in Act II, Bussy is the sole survivor of a triple duel which he and his two seconds have fought with three opponents. His patron, the King's brother, intercedes for Bussy with Henri III. There follows some interesting dialogue in which the French king takes the same view of the duel as murder that King James always maintained in the English court:

> *Henry :* Brother, I know your suit; these wilful murders
>   Are ever past our pardon.
> *Monsieur :*   Manly slaughter
>   Should never bear th'account of wilful murder;
>   It being a spice of justice, where with life
>   Offending past law, equal life is laid
>   In equal balance, to scourge that offence
>   By law of reputation, which to men
>   Exceeds all positive law. . . .
> *Henry :* This would make every man that thinks him wrong'd
>   Or is offended, or in wrong or right,

Lay on this violence, and all vaunt themselves
Law-menders and suppliers, though mere butchers;
Should this fact (though justice) be forgiven?
Monsieur : Oh, no, my lord; it would make cowards fear
To touch the reputations of true men
When only they are left to imp [reinforce] the law.
   Justice will soon distinguish murderous minds
   From just revengers.

The king, apparently won over, proceeds to pardon Bussy. Probably most of the courtiers in the audience felt that the latter was in the right and merited his pardon. Certainly in the court of King James there were plenty of men who claimed for themselves, as Bussy did, the right to 'do a justice that exceeds the law'.

Despite King James's known determination to end duelling, each year brought its challenges, meetings and deaths. A particularly bad year was 1610, when a single week in April saw a duel between the Earls of Southampton and Montgomery narrowly averted by the King's intervention, and two duels actually fought. In one of these the eldest son of Sir John Egerton was slain by his opponent, Morgan. Only a few weeks later, Sir John Gray and Sir Henry Hastings left for the Low Countries to fight outside the jurisdiction of the King's courts.

Apart from legal considerations, the trouble with the duel was that it gave no guarantee that the aggrieved party would prove the victor. On the contrary, too often it allowed a bravo who was expert with his rapier an opportunity to extend his injuries. A quiet decent gentleman, seeing his wife insulted by such a gallant, might feel compelled by the code of honour to issue a challenge, with the melancholy consequence that the lady, having been wronged by the insulter's tongue, might be widowed by his sword.

The basic injustice of the duel is exemplified in the Dutton-Cheke encounter, another of the many duels fought in 1610. During the war over the succession of Cleves, the English contingent at the siege of Juliers was joined by Sir Thomas Dutton, who arrived with a letter of recommendation from Prince Henry. Dutton proceeded to make himself such a nuisance through his insolent insubordination that the English commander, the veteran Sir Edward Cecil, had to write to the Prince begging to be relieved of Dutton as one who 'dare contest with me, and be content, upon any terms, to murder his commander'.[7] In fact, Dutton's colonel, Sir Hatton Cheke, was so insulted that at the conclusion of the siege he felt impelled to call Dutton to account.

> Some small time after the taking of Juliers *Cheek* fell sick; and his *distemper* was the greater, because he had heard *Dutton* strove to defame him, both in Court and City: for being full with *passion*, he vented it with

freedom enough in every place. *Cheek* being recovered, and heart-whole, would not give time to his decayed limbs to suck in their old vigor, but sends to *Dutton* that threatned him, to give an account of the large expence of his tongue against him; *Dutton*, that waited for such a reckoning, willingly accepted the Summons: *Cheek* took *Pigot*, one of his Captains, to be his second; *Dutton* took Captain *Gosnald*, both Men of well-spread fame; and they four met on *Calais* Sands: On which dreadful Stage, at first meeting, *Dutton* began to expostulate his *injuries*, as if a Tongue-Combate might decide the *Controversie*; but *Cheek* would dispute it otherwise. Then their Seconds searching, and stripping them to their Shirts in a cold morning, they ran with that fury on each others Sword, as if they did not mean to kill each other, but strive who should first die. Their Weapons were *Rapier* and *Dagger*, a fit Banquet for *Death*. At first course, *Cheek* ran *Dutton* into the neck with his *Rapier*, and stab'd him in the neck backward with his *Dagger*, miraculously missing his windpipe; And at the same instant, like one *motion*, *Dutton* ran *Cheek* through the Body, and stab'd him into the back with his left hand, locking themselves together thus with four bloody *keys*, which the Seconds fairly opened, and would fain have closed up the bleeding *difference*: but *Cheeks* wounds were deadly, which he finding, grew the *violenter* against his *Enemy*; and *Dutton* seeing him begin to stagger, went back from his *fury*, only defending himself, till the others *rage* weakened with loss of *blood*, without any more hurt, fell at his feet. *Dutton*, with much difficulty recovered his *dangerous* wounds, but *Cheek* by his Servants had a sad *Funeral*, which is the *bitter fruit* of fiery passions.[8]

Great as its notoriety was, the Cheke-Dutton fight was eclipsed by what was certainly the most notable duel fought during the reign of King James, that in 1613 between Edward Sackville, in time to become Earl of Dorset, and Lord Bruce of Kinloss. The cause of their quarrel was never made known. Apparently it concerned a lady whose name the two gentlemen had sufficient taste not to divulge. Feeling between Sackville and Bruce was running so high in January 1613 that they agreed to cross to the Continent to settle matters with a duel. This scheme was frustrated by the vigilance of the King's officers who stopped Bruce at his place of embarkation. James set himself to make peace between the angry pair, but his success was of short duration. In April there was a very nasty flare-up at Canterbury when the two men were accompanying Princess Elizabeth and the Palsgrave to their port of depature. Sackville, at the moment unarmed, showed his anger by giving the Scot 'two or three goode buffets on the face'. Bruce, determined not to be intercepted this time, left almost immediately for France. From here he wrote to Sackville:

I that am in ffraunce heare how much you attribute to yourselfe in this tyme that I have given the world leave to ringe your praises ... And if you call to memorie when I gave my hande last I told you I reserved the hart for a truer reconciliacon. Nowe bee that noble gentleman my Love once spoke and come and doe hym reason, that could recite the tryalle you owe your birth and countrey, were I not confident your owne honor gives you the same Courage to doe me right that it did to doe me wrong. Be master of your owne weapons and tyme; the place wheresoever I will waite on you, by doeinge this you shall shorten revenge and clere the idle opinion the world hath of both our Worthes.

E. Bruce

Receiving this letter at his father-in-law's house in Derbyshire, Sackville despatched his high-spirited reply:

A monsieur le baron de Kinlosse,
    As it shalbe allwaies far from me to seeke a quarrell, soe will I allwaies be readie to meete any that desire to make triall of my valor by soe faire a course as you requier. A witnes whereof your selfe shalbe who within a month shall receave a strict accompt of tyme place and weapon by him that shall Conduct you thether where yow shall finde me disposed to give you honorable satisfaccon. In the meane tyme be as secret of the appoyntment as it seemes you are desirous of it.

E. Sackvile

Two weeks later, having arrived on the Continent, Sackville sent the promised second letter:

I am readie at Torgose a Towne in Zeland to give you what satisfaccon your sword can render you, accompanied with a worthie gentleman for my second, in degree a Knight; and for your comynge I will not lymyt you a peremptorie daie but desire you to make it definite and speedie for your owne honor and feare of prevencon, untill which tyme you shall find me there.

E. Sackvile

Bruce's reply was short and to the point:

I have receaved your Letter by your man and acknowledge you have dealt noblie with me, and nowe I come with all possible hast to meet you.

E. Bruce[9]

A letter, written by Sackville while he was in Louvain recovering from his wounds after the duel, gives us a vivid picture of what subsequently happened at Torgose.[10] Bruce upon his arrival had with him an English gentleman named Crawford who was to be his second, a surgeon, and a man-servant. Sir John Heydon, Sackville's own second, and Crawford decided to transfer the scene of the duel to Bergen-op-Zoom. Here they would be almost on the border of territory under the rule of the Hapsburg Archdukes, to which the survivor might speedily retire to avoid punishment by the Dutch. Accordingly it was at Bergen-op-Zoom, or Bruceland as the English knew it for long afterwards, that the duel was fought.

During the negotiations within the town as to weapons to be used,

Bruce insisted that the seconds be absent from the actual combat. When Heydon protested, Bruce became so angry that Sackville decided to fight without any further delay, and on Bruce's terms, even though he himself had just finished a large meal and 'Surgeons hold a wound upon a full stomach much more dangerous then otherwise'. Accordingly lots were drawn which determined that they should fight beyond the Lille gate. The seconds searched the two men for concealed weapons or armour and then, attended only by their two unarmed surgeons, Sackville and Bruce rode forth some two English miles to what seemed a suitable place.

In a meadow, which turned out to be ankle-deep in water, the fight began. At the outset things went badly for Sackville, who sustained both a wound in the arm and one in his right breast with the blade almost passing through his body. Catching hold of each other's swords, the two men wrestled together furiously. Without seconds to part them, they tried to agree how to break their clutch but neither dared trust the other sufficiently to release him. Finally, with a kick and a wrench, Sackville got his sword free. Holding it at Bruce's throat, he called on him to submit. Bruce refused and Sackville, finding his strength ebbing away (by this time one of his fingers was hanging by a mere shred of skin), seized his opportunity and ran him through twice. Bruce fell from his wounds and cried that he was slain. At this point Sackville could not, he testified, 'finde in my hart to offer him any more violence', and allowed Bruce's surgeon to minister to him. He did not take his adversary's sword from him, however, 'accompting it unhumane to robb a dead man; for soe I held him to bee'. In fact, Sackville fainted at this point and needed his own surgeon's help. When he revived he found that Bruce's surgeon had picked up his master's sword and was coming for him even though the dying Lord Bruce cried, 'Rascall, hould thy hande.' Fortunately Sackville's own sword, now wielded by his surgeon, gave him sufficient protection.

In England the court was still buzzing over the Sackville-Bruce encounter when, in September, there were reports of more duels in prospect. Lord Chandos and Lord Hay were said to be ready to meet, and it was known that a challenge had been sent from the Earl of Essex to a kinsman of his ex-wife, Lady Frances Howard. Nothing came of the Chandos-Hay quarrel, but Essex and Master Henry Howard both arrived on the Continent with their seconds, only to be overtaken by Master Gibb of the King's Bedchamber, with orders to return and submit their differences to arbitration.

There was fresh trouble early in November. Two gentlemen, Skevington and Bray, who had a case in the Court of Chancery, happened to meet in the court of Gray's Inn. They drew their rapiers and killed each other on the spot.

King James loathed physical violence of any kind. Again and again he had intervened when duels were in prospect, and now it seemed that everybody was taking to the sword. Utterly sick and tired of these murderous encounters, he resolved on an all-out campaign to stop duelling. His chosen instrument was Sir Francis Bacon, the Attorney-General Bacon himself had lost 'two of his choise men that dispatcht one another in the feild' some six years earlier.

Bacon's first move was to summon before the Star Chamber two nonentities (chosen perhaps because of their lack of friends at court): William Priest, who had sent a letter of challenge, and Richard Wright, who had delivered it for him. Priest was fined £500 and Wright 500 marks. Both were sent to Fleet Prison and ordered to make public admission of guilt at the next Surrey assizes. More important than the exemplary sentences passed on Priest and Wright was the ultimatum which Bacon delivered in court, that from now on he was going to make a Star Chamber matter of all challenges and all duels. Strongly supporting Bacon, the court drafted a decree which all assize judges were ordered to read when next they went on circuit. Furthermore, the court ordered the printing of both their decree and Bacon's charge in the case.

Bacon's *Charge* showed a clear comprehension of the real issues and a sensible practicality in suggesting remedies. Noting that duelling had become 'a mischeefe that groweth every day', Bacon pointed out that what was wrong was the entire climate of opinion, not just a few individuals:

> . . . we have not to doe, in this case, so much with perticuler persons, as with unsound and depraved opinions, like the dominations and spirits of the ayre, which the Scripture speaketh of.[11]

Accordingly Bacon directed his attack not so much against the hapless Priest and Wright but the 'false and erronious imagination of honour and credit', and 'this fond and false disguise or puppetrey of honor' involved in duelling. Dealing with 'the lie', which so often provoked duels, Bacon pointed out the absurdity of attaching such importance to mere words. In true Renaissance style, he noted that the ancient Greeks and Romans had found verbal retorts sufficient. He declared that a gentleman's honour should be 'of a good strong warppe or webbe, that every little thing should not catch in it, when as now it seemes they are but of copwebbe lawne, or such light stuffe'.

There were, according to Bacon, three main evil consequences of duelling. One was that a private duel might lead to a family feud, and this in time to a national quarrel. Another was that all duels were an affront to law, setting up a wild law of reputation against the decencies of 'Gowne-law'. The third was that duels robbed the king of the services of some of the best of his subjects, hopeful young men at the threshold of their best years.

King James allowed an interval for Bacon's *Charge* to be circulated and have its effect. Then he backed it up with two royal proclamations. The first, issued in February 1614, simply set a day, forty days hence, after which nobody was 'to send or accept any Challenge or seeke satisfaction otherwyse then by lawe, or by the Marshalls Court'. For the rest, it denounced duelling as a thing unworthy of Britons, and a root producing daily 'fruits of very bitter taste, and desperate effect, depriving the State of the Kingdome of strong limmes, Our selves of worthy Subjects, and great houses of great hopes'. It declared that those who thought there was any grain of worth, of reputation, or true honour in a duel must have drunk the 'very dregges of Circes Cup'.[12]

King James's second proclamation, 'His Majesties Edict against Private Combats',[13] set forth a list of penalties which would henceforth be enforced. Anyone publishing an account of a duel or quarrel in which he was involved would be banished from the court for seven years. Anyone issuing a challenge, or voluntarily accepting a challenge, would be banished from the court for seven years, be denied all office for the same period, and be deprived of all the grants which the King had formerly given him. (He would also be kept in prison until he had confessed his gross error.) In the future, the bishops and archbishops would be asked to excommunicate duellers. A man killed in a duel would not be interred in any church, chapel, or churchyard unless witnesses could testify that he had died contritely, forgiving his enemy. Seconds were to share in the punishments passed on the principals.

As the edict pointed out, persons who conceived themselves 'to be behinde in the least respect or point of Honour' did not lack their remedy. If they dwelt within the verge of the court or the City of London, they should 'discreetly and advisedly' repair to the court provided by the Commissioners for the Office of Earl Marshal. Otherwise, they might seek out the Lord Lieutenant of their shire. Finally, the edict took cognizance of those who fled abroad to fight on Calais Sands or other places outside the jurisdiction of the English courts. For these persons there was to be created a Constable or Marshal of England in whose court they might be condemned to death.

It would be pleasant to relate that this fierce proclamation ended duelling in England. Unfortunately the practice was too deeply bred into the national tradition and, for almost two and a half centuries more, murders continued to be committed in the name of honour. Within a few months of King James's edict, two army captains met in the field and one was slain. Nevertheless, something was effected. Persons of real position avoided

K

giving or receiving challenges, and there was a marked decline in the number of duels that were fought. The King kept men mindful of his determination by such actions as appearing personally in the Star Chamber in February 1617 and making a speech against duels when two young law students, Bellingham and Christmas, were each fined £1,000 for the passing of a challenge.

More might have been effected if King James himself had not in the end weakened in his resolve to punish implacably. Early in 1620 two Scottish courtiers took the field. One, Maxwell, was killed. Twice before he had slain men in duels and King James allowed himself the quip that he had pardoned Maxwell his first offence and the King of France his second, but it seemed that the King of Heaven had not pardoned his third. When Prince Charles, the Duke of Lennox, and the Marquess of Hamilton all interceded for the survivor saying that the duel had been forced upon him, King James let him off lightly.

The consequence was predictable. Once more challenges were sent and exchanged by noble lords. In 1621 Lord Gerard was slain by Lord St. John. In 1623 the Earl of Warwick and Lord Cavendish headed beyond the seas to settle matters with swords, leaving behind their wives, who were observed to 'forget not their old familiaritie but meet daylie to lament this misfortune'. Fortunately, Lord Cavendish was stopped by a royal officer in Sussex before he could embark.

The last duel of any importance in the reign was a very curious affair. Will Murray, one of Prince Charles's gentlemen, had summoned Sir Humphrey Tufton to a meeting in St. George's Fields. When they met, the two could not agree about the use of seconds and decided to postpone their duel until this point had been decided. After Tufton had left, Murray's second, a Scot named Gibson, told Murray that he had disgraced Scotland. The two drew, and Murray killed Gibson.

CHAPTER XX

Home to Scotland

IN JUNE 1616, King James had his fiftieth birthday. For the Jacobeans, with a life expectancy of some forty-eight years, fifty was a more advanced age than it is today. King James, his half century completed, turned to thoughts of rounding out his life and labours. Early the next year his collected literary works, except for his poetry and a few ephemeral pieces, were published in a volume edited by James Montagu, Bishop of Winchester.

Indicative of the King's inner feeling was his resolution to travel up to Scotland and revisit the scenes of his youth. Plans were laid for the court to spend the summer of 1617 in King James's northern kingdom.

In a revealing letter to the Scottish Privy Council, His Majesty set forth the reasons for his journey. They arose out of psychological tensions deep within the aging king:

> First, wee ar not achamed to confesse that we have had theise many yeirs a great and naturall longing to see our native soyle and place of our birth and breeding, and this salmonlyke instinct of ours hes restleslie, both when wee wer awake and manie tymes in our sleip, so stirred up our thoghtis and bended our desyris to make a Jornay thither that wee can never rest satisfied till it sall pleas God that wee may accomplish it. . . .[1]

The image of the salmon was revealing—it returns to die in the stream that gave it birth.

The court was not happy at His Majesty's determination to travel to Scotland. The Queen had no wish to revisit the bleak land to which she had come as a bride, and hastened to disassociate herself from the enterprise. (Some said that she held a hope, a vain one indeed, that she might be regent in England during her husband's absence.) As for the courtiers, they were completely unenthusiastic about the long tiresome journey. The Scottish lords in the English court were observed to be particularly reluctant to make the trip, finding little to attract them to their half-barbarous homeland. A month after the King had started it was noted in London that 'the greatest part of the prime Scotts are here still and make no great haste homeward'.

A major problem was the financing of the trip. King James felt that, if he was to revisit Scotland for the first time in fourteen years, he must

259

come attended by sufficient state. Scotland must be impressed with the wealth and magnificence that his realm of England had yielded him. Moreover, James was determined that those who travelled north with him should be received with a lavish hospitality becoming the honour of their king's native land. All this meant spending a very large amount of money. 'Yt is like to prove a very costly viage every way,' noted the prescient John Chamberlain; and he thoughtfully added, 'I never knew a journy so generally misliked both here and there.' However, James was bent on going and the money was raised. The merchants of London lent £100,000 on the security of the King's jewels, and the farmers of the customs advanced £50,000.

On March 14, 1617, King James set forth on the journey which meant so much to him. At Hyde Park the Lord Mayor of London, who had recently been knighted for pushing through the loan from the City, presented a highly suitable farewell gift, a purse containing five hundred pieces of gold. By very gradual stages the royal procession took its way north. Theobalds, Royston, Huntingdon, Hinchingbrooke, Apethorpe, all were visited. At each stop more of the court lords found excuses for leaving, often with a promise to rejoin later. At one point in Northamptonshire, according to the Earl of Dorset, James had only a single lord left in attendance. Undeterred, the King went on with his hundreds of officers, gentlemen, grooms, ushers, yeomen, harbingers, purveyors, clerks. From Burghley he went on to Grantham and Lincoln. The Sheriffs of Lincolnshire had gone to meet him at the border of the shire, but in vain they awaited him. James, intent on his day's hunting, had left the highway and, cutting across the heath with his hounds, had by-passed them completely.

Northward still the procession went, to Newark, Worksop, Doncaster, Pontefract, York. At the gates of York, the Lord Mayor on his knees presented James with the keys to the gates and posterns, a cup of silver double gilt, and a purse containing one hundred double sovereigns. Four days later James was again on the road with his retinue. Stopping at Ripon, Aske Hall, Bishop Auckland, Durham, Newcastle-upon-Tyne, Bothal Castle, Alnwick Abbey, and Chillingham, he arrived at last at Berwick. Here on May 13th, practically two months after his setting out, King James crossed the Tweed into Scotland. By now he had been joined by a notable company of English peers, among them the Earls of Southampton and Pembroke, and the newly created Earl of Buckingham. Three days later King James entered Edinburgh, scene of his birth and capital of his northern realm.

Edinburgh had laboured long and hard to receive its King. A note of 'direction' from the Privy Council of Scotland had warned the provost and baillies to survey their city and its suburbs so as to find good lodgings for the five thousand men with their five thousand horses which were expected to arrive with the King. Exhorting the provost and his brothers to clean the streets and banish the beggars, the Privy Council had pointed out that the Sassenachs coming with His Majesty would be looking at the city critically, ready to spread either good report or reproaches according to the entertainment they received.

James had made arrangements of his own for his sojourn in Edinburgh. Determined that his Scots should see religious services conducted as they ought to be, he had ordered a contingent of choristers from the Chapel Royal at Whitehall despatched ahead of him so that the services at Holyrood could be conducted in the seemly Anglican manner. Religious figures and paintings had also been sent up from England to ornament the chapel, and an organ installed to help with the music. All this badly upset the Presbyterians, who darkly observed, 'The organs are come before, and after comes the Mass.'[2]

Despite whatever doubts they may have had about James's attachment to the Kirk, the burgesses turned out in great numbers to welcome him as he entered the old city by the West Port. After receiving from the Provost the city's gift of a purse containing five hundred double angels, laid in a silver basin with double gilt, His Majesty proceeded to St. Giles's, where he heard a sermon delivered by the Archbishop of St. Andrews. Then, after knighting the provost at St. John's Cross, James proceeded to Holyrood House.

Although the King's retinue numbered substantially less than the expected five thousand, the quarters provided proved neither adequate nor satisfactory. The English courtiers found the houses along the Royal Mile cramped and dingy in comparison with the splendid mansions along the Strand. They were less than enchanted by the royal burgh of Edinburgh.

Just as King James had stood by his Scots in England, so he stood by his English in Scotland. A correspondent delightedly informed Sir Francis Bacon that:

> . . . his Majesty was pleased to do England and Englishmen much honour and grace; and that he studied nothing so much, sleeping and waking, as to reduce the barbarity (I have warrant to use the King's word) of this Country unto the sweet civility of ours. . . .[3]

Pleasant though these sentiments were to the English, they could hardly have sounded sweet to Scottish ears.

Leaving Edinburgh on May 19th, King James made a tour up to Dundee. Back in Edinburgh by June 19th, he lingered there until the end of the month, when he set out on a second more extended tour, first by way of Stirling, Perth and Falkland to St. Andrews, then over to Glasgow, Paisley, Hamilton, Sanquhar Castle, Drumlanrig and Dumfries, crossing

back into England on August 4th, when he arrived in Carlisle. The reception of King James at these various Scottish towns was very similar.
Typical of the various speeches of welcome was that delivered at Stirling
by 'Master Robert Murray Commissar there':

> Most Sacred Soveraine, Amongst the manie comforts wee enjoy under this
> your calme and most glorious reigne, this is not the least that your Majestie
> deignes to heare your owne Welcomes, and disdaines not the humble
> applause of your meanest Subjects, no more than *Augustus Caesar* did when
> in name of the Senate and People of *Rome*, *Valerius Messala* welcomed and
> saluted him, PATREM PATRIAE [father of his country], which (as hee answered)
> was the hight of his desires, and beyond which hee had nothing more to
> sollicite the Gods for; Provyding onlie that That harmonie could continue
> and be the last sound should strick his dying eare.
>   I your Majesties most humble Subject in name of the Magistrats and
> indwellers of this your ancient Towne, in all reverence most hartlie and
> justlie Welcome and salute your Majestie, PATREM PATRIAE after this your
> happie returne to your late languishing bot now fullie contented Cuntrie.[4]

Perhaps revisiting Stirling, where he had seen his grandfather killed,
and Perth, where he himself had narrowly escaped death at the hands of
the Gowries, revived old fears in the mind of the *Patrem Patriae*. In any
event, a highly embarrassing incident occurred at Culross up in Fifeshire
when James was shown the workings of a mine there. One of the shafts
went underground and re-emerged on a small island. Thinking to give
the King a surprise, his guide led him thither. The King's response
when he emerged to find himself not where he had started but alone
with his conductor and entirely surrounded by water was most unexpected. Suddenly imagining that it was all a plot to murder him, King
James dissolved in panic and began screaming 'Treason' at the top of his
voice. Fortunately the somewhat shattered guide managed to calm his fears
and reassure him.

Travelling by way of Carlisle, Brougham Castle, Appleby, Wharton
Hall, Kendal, Hornby Castle, Ashton, Myerscough Lodge, Hoghton
Tower (where undaunted by his experience at Culross, he went down an
alum mine), Lathom, Bewsey Hall, Vale Royal, Nantwich, Gerards
Bromley, Tixall, Hoar Cross, Ashby-de-la-Zouch, Coventry (where the
city presented him with a superb gold cup), Warwick, Compton Wynyates,
Woodstock, Rycote and Bisham, King James arrived back in Windsor on
September 12th, six months after first setting out.

The English courtiers who had accompanied King James on his expedition had little to say in praise of Scotland. Among them was Anthony
Weldon, Clerk of the Green Cloth, whom James had knighted at Berwick
just a day or two before he and his train crossed into Scotland. Back in
England, Weldon had with him a nasty satiric account of the Scots.[5]

Unfortunately, he was careless enough to let this get mixed with some of the records of the Board of Green Cloth. Discovered there, and its authorship betrayed by Weldon's handwriting, this *jeu d'esprit* cost the recently created Sir Anthony his job. True, the King softened the blow by granting a small pension in partial compensation. Weldon, however, came of a family which for generations had provided officers in the royal household, and he never forgave King James the injury. He did not go unrevenged, for his bitterly hostile *Court and Character of King James*, published during the Commonwealth, greatly helped the Whig historians of the eighteenth century to paint the unfair and unflattering portrait of King James which still lingers in the minds of most people.

Chapter XXI

Death Beckons

A COMET SHONE in the skies over England from mid-November to mid-December 1618. The superstition of the age viewed such phenomena as auguries of coming disaster, particularly the death of royalty:

> When beggars die, there are no comets seen.
> The heavens themselves blaze forth the death of princes.

It was taken as the fulfilment of an omen when several months later, on March 2, 1619, death came for Anne of Denmark, Queen of England.

Poor Anne's life in England had not been a particularly happy one. True, in many ways King James had dealt kindly with her. After her arrival from Scotland he had assigned for her use not only Greenwich Palace, but Somerset (renamed Denmark) House in London, Hatfield Place, Pontefract Castle, Nonsuch and Havering-at-Bower. To her Scottish jointure he had added £5,000 from English lands, and this sum he had later increased repeatedly. When Anne died, her total jointure was £24,000 annually, to which was added £13,000 from the sugar and cloth duties. The King, moreover, had paid all the expenses of her household and stable, other than the wages of her servants and the cost of her own apparel. Since Anne, because of her heedless prodigality, had been unable to live within her means, the King had repeatedly assisted her with her debts. At all times James had insisted that Anne should be treated with the respect due to a queen. When the termagant Lady Coke had been rude to Anne, she was banished not only from the Queen's court but from the King's also.

The root of the Queen's discontent lay deeper than real financial difficulties or imagined slights. It lay probably in the curious sexual abnormalities of the King. As part of his duty to his realm, James bred children by her, but he was psychologically incapable of the fulness of married love. The love that he might have found and given in marriage he sought in ambiguous relationships with his handsome male favourites. Little wonder if Anne became a discontented and frustrated woman.

It is by no means certain that another woman, one with a stronger personality, greater intelligence, and more sexual attraction than Anne possessed after her first prettiness had worn off, could have established a happy marriage with James. Anne, however, would probably have been a much happier woman (though never a model of stability and good sense) had she been married to a more normal husband. The Queen's irresponsibility and petulance, her ineffectual meddling which alternated with languid indifference, were more the consequence than the cause of the unsatisfactory relationship between herself and her husband.

The story of the royal couple's early years in England is one of an appearance of affection dutifully maintained by the King, punctuated by clashes and decisions to dwell apart as much as they decently could. There were repeated rows. One, concerning the custody of Prince Henry, attended her first arrival in England. Soon after there was another, this time as to who should be her chamberlain. King James threatened to break the white staff of office over the head of the unfortunate Kennedy whom Queen Anne preferred to her husband's own candidate, Sir George Carew. Later we find James angered because the Queen had not been sufficiently solicitous in writing when he had been afflicted with gout at Royston. And we find Anne disloyally assuring Prince Henry that learning, to which his father attached such importance, was really unworthy of a person of great rank. Perhaps out of some obscure impulse to be revenged on the sexually disappointing James, she encouraged the young prince to indulge in amorous adventuring.

In their later years, as the sexual causes of tension grew less important, James and Anne became better friends. A pleasant little story illustrates the cordiality that existed between them in the summer of 1613:

> . . . at theyre last beeing at Tiballs which was about a fortnight since, the Quene shooting at a deere mistooke her marke and killed Jewell the Kings most principall and speciall hound, at which he stormed exceedingly a while, but after knew who did yt, he was soone pacified, and with much kindnes wisht her not to be troubled with yt, for he shold love her never the worse, and the next day sent her a diamond worth 2000li as a legacie from his dead dogge. Love and kindnes increases dayly between them, and yt is thought they were never in better termes.[1]

It is too bad that there was not always this love and kindness, for Anne seems to have had a rather kindly and affectionate nature. Holding her own court at Greenwich while the King was at his hunting at Royston or Newmarket, 'Rina', as her ladies familiarly called her (an abridging of the Latin *Regina*), showed herself friendly and accessible. She had a talent for assembling about her rather pleasant people like her favourite Lucy, Countess of Bedford. Again and again we get little glimpses of Anne putting aside her too frequent lethargy and doing or saying something nice, even if in a rather feather-brained sort of way. We see her visiting the

K*

University of Oxford with King James and, at the end of the speech delivered by the university Greek orator, thanking him very nicely, explaining that she had never heard Greek before. We find that when Captain John Smith presented Pocahontas to her, Anne made the friendly gesture of inviting the dusky princess to the coming Twelfth Night masque.

This basic kindness in Anne emerges in her befriending of Lady Anne Clifford. In February 1609 Lady Anne, the sole child and heiress of the third Earl of Cumberland, married Richard Sackville, Lord Buckhurst. Two days later her bridegroom, through the death of his father, became Earl of Dorset. This Dorset was one of the dashing handsome courtiers on whom King James lavished his favours. In the spring of 1616, badly in need of money, Dorset subjected his wife to every kind of pressure in vain attempts to make her sell some of the lands inherited from her father. King James made it clear that he wanted her to agree, and the Archbishop of Canterbury, the Bishop of St. David's, Lord Roos, and a host of others tried to argue her into complying with the wishes of her profligate lord. Finally, in January 1617, His Majesty said that he would speak to her himself. Lady Anne's heart almost failed her. Fortunately she found a friend in the Queen. One evening the Countess of Derby conducted the diminutive but high-spirited young wife (she was only four feet ten inches in height) to a meeting with Queen Anne in her withdrawing chamber:

> Lady Derby told the Queen how my business stood and that I was to go to the King so she promised me she would do all the good in it she could.[2]

Moreover, according to Lady Anne, 'The Queen gave me warning not to trust my matters absolutely to the King lest he should deceive me.'

The Queen understood her husband. Sure enough, when the little countess had her interview with His Majesty, the line he took was that of a domestic mediator: let Dorset and his wife put the whole matter into his hands, accept his decision, and maintain the family peace. Dorset rejoiced and agreed; but Lady Anne, forewarned by the Queen, 'beseech'd His Majesty to pardon me for that I would never part from Westmoreland while I lived upon any condition whatsoever'. James fretted and fumed. He arranged another meeting, this time with the Lord Chief Justice and the Solicitor-General attending, but the lady, strengthened by Anne's support, still refused to give way. In the end she kept her lands. Outliving Dorset and subsequent noble husbands, she died one of the greatest land-owners in all England.

Queen Anne was not without influence with her husband. As noted earlier, James always required his favourites to secure the Queen's commendation before he would advance them. But there were strict limits on

Anne's powers. She could secure for Sir Robert Carey the post of chamberlain to Prince Charles after the latter's creation as Prince of Wales, even though James secretly had promised the position to the Earl of Roxburgh; but her intercessions during her final months could not save the life of Raleigh. Where major political decisions were concerned, she counted not at all. Her lack of influence here was one of her causes of discontent. She never realized that her own indiscretion and inconsistencies disqualified her as a political adviser. Instead, she felt frustrated and unappreciated.

The Queen's feelings showed themselves clearly when she visited Bristol in June 1613. Anne, who had been at Bath for some weeks taking the waters, had decided to make a progress, unattended by the King, into the West Country. Bristol, the second largest city in the kingdom, traditionally enjoyed the title of the 'Chamber of the Queen', just as London did that of the 'Chamber of the King'; and it put on a great show for Her Majesty. A civic poetaster described in resolute doggerel the scene when the mayor and aldermen greeted her:

> The grave and auncient Counsell first, in gownes of Scarlet dye,
> Attended on (each by a Page) did ride triumphantly,
> With foot-cloaths were their Horses deckt; no cost they thought too much
> For to expresse their willing hearts, their love to her was such.[3]

The city militia were mustered for her inspection. The Recorder delivered a speech and the Mayor made a presentation:

> A rich imbrodered Purse it was, most sumptuous to behold
> In outward shew, the inside was cramm'd full of massie gold.[4]

When Anne reached her lodgings, sixty pieces of ordnance volleyed a salute. On Sunday she attended divine service at the cathedral. Monday brought a spectacle, presented for her entertainment but watched by forty thousand other spectators, a sea-fight between a Bristol merchantman and two Turkish galleys. The Turks boarded the English ship with fife and drum, but in the end they were captured and made to crave, on bended knees, mercy from Queen Anne, who graciously pardoned them all. The next day Anne took her leave of Bristol. The citizenry fervently cried 'The Lord preserve Your Grace', and the train-bands fired off farewell volleys. At the city boundary the mayor knelt to say farewell. It was all too much for poor Anne. With tears in her eyes, she declared that she had never known that she was a queen until she came to Bristol.

A decline in Her Majesty's health became evident in the spring of 1615 with the appearance of the first symptoms of dropsy. A visit to Bath to take the cure that summer did nothing to help her. The next year she made a fair recovery, but when James came back from Scotland in the autumn of

1617, he found her once more laid up. Though she herself clung to the idea her circulatory trouble was gout, her doctors realized that there was 'an yll habit or disposition thorough her whole body'.

The next year was one of diminishing health and strength. In January she could hardly muster the strength to move from Whitehall, but she rallied and went to Oatlands where she became increasingly dependent upon Catholic priests smuggled in to attend to her spiritual needs. In October she had a bad heart attack during her sleep, and her physicians were summoned in great haste. November and December found her sick at Hampton Court, with King James riding over from Whitehall for occasional visits. At Christmas she was too ill to come to Whitehall for the seasonal festivities which usually so delighted her. The new year began with word that her doctors were giving up hope.

A sudden turn for the worse came at the end of February. On March 1st the Archbishop of Canterbury, the Lord Privy Seal and the Bishop of London came into her presence and advised her to prepare herself for death and to set all things in order. Poor Anne could not believe that she was going to die. Making a childish excuse that this was Childermas or 'dismal day' and so inauspicious, she declared that these things must be left until the morrow. When Prince Charles arrived, she spoke a few bantering words with him but still put off making her will. The morrow did not afford the time she had so confidently reckoned on. At two o'clock in the morning, when no one was with her except her maid, Danish Anna, her sight suddenly failed. When the Prince and various court dignitaries were hastily summoned to her bed she was sinking fast. Within an hour she was dead.

There followed one of the more bizarre interludes in the history of English royalty. On March 6th the Queen's body was eviscerated and the entrails, except for the heart, buried in the Henry VII Chapel of Westminster Abbey. The precaution was a sensible one. Royal corpses not so treated had been known, in their putrefaction during the lengthy period of the lying in state, to break the lead in which they were wrapped. On March 9th the corpse was conveyed by night to Anne's residence of Denmark House, where her privy chambers had all been hung from ceiling to floor with funeral black. There she was laid in state for the extended period of mourning preceding her funeral.

Day succeeded day, week succeeded week, and finally month succeeded month. All the time, right around the clock, the court ladies presented themselves in relays to sit as mourners by the body and to wonder when on earth 'Rina' would be interred. The players in the theatres grew clamorous at losing their livelihood while their theatres remained closed through this unconscionably long period of public mourning. The public swung between jocosity and indignation as the period of Anne's lying in state went on and on, far beyond that for the great Queen Elizabeth.

Various reasons lay behind the delay in getting Queen Anne into her grave. One may have been the serious illness of the King during part of the period. This was probably not too important. James, with his dread of death and hatred of funerals, was no more inclined to attend Queen Anne's funeral than Prince Henry's. Another cause for postponement was a most unseemly squabble as to who should be the chief mourner. This post was claimed by the Countess of Arundel, but the Countess of Nottingham pointed out that the agreement under which her husband had surrendered his post of Lord Admiral had accorded him first place among the earls. Surely she, then, enjoyed precedence over all other countesses, including the Countess of Arundel, even if Arundel was the head of the family of Howard to which Nottingham belonged. Another claimant was the Countess of Northumberland who, though her husband was a prisoner in the Tower, felt that, as a Percy, she must concede nothing where ancient nobility of family was concerned. In this situation somebody remembered that there was one lady who outranked all the combative countesses. This was the ancient Marchioness of Northampton (the Marquess had died in 1571). Fortunately it did not prove necessary to bring the old lady up from the country. Somehow it was agreed that the Countess of Arundel should be chief mourner after all. The countesses were not the only difficult females with whom the heralds had to deal as they struggled to arrange the funeral. Various Catholic ladies who were asked to serve as mourners objected to attending a heretic service in a heretic church.

What really held up the funeral and caused the repeated postponements was an old embarrassment—lack of money. It was unthinkable that the daughter of a king of Denmark, and the consort of the King of England, Ireland and Scotland should go to her grave without all the pomp and circumstance that the occasion demanded. Unfortunately, pomp and circumstance were very expensive and the royal exchequer was going through one of its recurrent crises. All sorts of shifts were contemplated to raise the wherewithal to bury Anne. There was talk of melting down the gold plate she had left and pawning her jewels—until the unpleasant discovery was made that the Queen's French gentleman Piero, and her maid Danish Anna, had seized the opportunity afforded by Her Majesty's death to embezzle some £30,000 worth of her jewels and an indeterminable amount of ready cash.

Finally enough money was procured for Anne to be buried. On May 13th, ten weeks after her death, the Queen's funeral procession filed through the railed streets of London on its way to the Abbey. Prince Charles preceded the hearse and the Countess of Arundel, the triumphant

chief mourner, followed. Within the Abbey the Archbishop of Canterbury, his eyes upon the Queen's effigy and coffin set under an elaborate
multi-storeyed heraldic catafalque designed by Maximilian Colt, delivered
the funeral sermon. At seven o'clock that evening, when all the company
had left and the doors had been closed, the Dean of Westminster, the
prebends, and Sir Edward Zouch, the Knight Marshal, entered the Abbey
by a side door and buried the Queen in the east end of the Henry VII
Chapel.

On June 1st twenty-four persons clad all in black arrived in London.
Despatched by the Duke of Lorraine, they were the first of various embassies sent by foreign princes to condole with King James on the loss of
his wife. They must have been sorely puzzled by what they saw. Everywhere there was an air of festivity. No mourning black other than their
own was to be seen. King James was coming back that day from Theobalds
and the aldermen were gorgeous in scarlet as they went to greet him. The
'fayre troupe' of mounted citizens who accompanied them were resplendent in chains of gold, pearl or diamonds. As for the King, when he
appeared riding across the fields to meet the welcoming Londoners, he
was attired in blue and silver, so gay 'that all the companie was glad to see
him so gallant and more like a wooer than a mourner'.

A ready reply awaited any of the Duke of Lorraine's people who might
express amazement at such scandalous disregard of the decencies. A most
serious illness had brought the King himself close to death, and joy at his
recovery had left no room for continued mourning for his Queen.

After James's return from Scotland in the autumn of 1617, his spirits
had not been improved in the slightest by satisfying his yearning to revisit
his old kingdom. On the contrary, everyone noticed how morose the King
had become. Part of the trouble may have been the gout which now
plagued him, a possible consequence of his addiction to sweet Greek
wines. The word 'gout', in fact, became anathema in the court. Each time
His Majesty was seized by a new attack, the fiction was maintained for as
long as possible that it was the result of a twist or a sprain, or some name-
less 'defluxion in his knees'. In February 1619 James had something worse
than gout to contend with—gallstones. When Anne died on March 2nd,
the King was recovering at Newmarket from 'a shrewde fit of the stone'.
At the end of the month his attacks reached a harrowing crisis with the
passing of three stones. Prince Charles was called for and all the chief of
the nobility. To the Prince, James delivered a speech in anticipation of
his death, recommending various of his lords by name, and charging his
successor to rely on the advice of his bishops as wise and prudent men.
Fortunately the King's health began to mend after the passage of the
stones, and on April 11th the Bishop of London, preaching at Paul's

Cross one of those sermons which served almost as government communiqués, was able to give thanks for the King's recovery, while divulging that at one point the physicians had abandoned hope of their royal patient's survival.

By April 20th the King was sufficiently recovered to travel from Royston to Ware in a Neapolitan 'portative chair' lent by Lady Coke. Going on to Theobalds the next day, he was in such discomfort that he had to be taken from his litter and carried part of the way by his guards. The setback proved temporary. May saw the King rapidly regaining good health, though his legs remained so enfeebled that men feared he would be reduced to a sedentary regimen for the rest of his life.

It was at this time that James had an unnerving experience when a madman confronted him in Theobalds Park and declared that God had sent him to tell the King that, since he had perverted justice, He was going to take his kingdom from him. After the Knight Marshal had locked the fellow up in the porter's lodge, the Bishop of Durham questioned him to discover if he was a Puritan. Since the prisoner declared that the Spirit of God had appeared to him in the form of a bishop, it was concluded that he was not a Puritan. The only alternative was that he was a lunatic, and accordingly he was packed off to Bedlam. As for James, it became apparent that God was not minded to take him from his kingdom for some time yet. Bathing the King's feet and legs in the bellies of stags slain in his hunting was found to be 'an excellent remedie to strengthen and restore the sinewes'. Writing at the end of June, the Reverend Samuel Lorkin reported, 'The King, God be thanked, was never in his life in better health than at this present.'[5]

In a way, it was unfortunate for King James that he did not follow Anne in death in 1619. Had he done so, he would have left a fairer fame behind him. He was ready for retirement, if not death. Burned out nervously and weakened physically, he was not the man to cope with the crises which lay ahead. But retirement was not a relief afforded seventeenth-century kings; and the last six years of his reign were to bring ignominious failures which would discredit James in the eyes of foreign observers and of his own subjects.

CHAPTER XXII

The Whitehall Connoisseurs

THE EFFECT of the Italian Renaissance on the arts in England was belated. Even in the reign of Elizabeth I, though literature and music owed much to Italy, in architecture, painting and sculpture, the stream of Renaissance influence was surprisingly thin. The 'surveyors' who designed the great country houses of the Elizabethan grandees produced pastiches of native Gothic and contemporary French or Flemish design, taking from Italy only bits of detail lifted from the design books of Serlio. True, Zuccaro was briefly in England in the 1570's to paint the Queen and Leicester, but he was the only major Italian artist to visit England during Elizabeth's long reign. Visitors to the galleries in Elizabeth's palaces were shown genealogical tables, trick mirrors, mechanical novelties and mediocre semi-medieval portraiture—not Titians or Leonardos. Shakespeare, through his associations with the Earls of Southampton and Essex, was in touch with the centres of Elizabethan taste and culture; yet when he wanted to signify the ultimate in Italian painting, the name he came up with was that of the second-rate Julio Romano. As far as Elizabethan England was concerned, Raphael and Titian, Leonardo and Michaelangelo might never have existed. Only in the middle years of the reign of King James did Englishmen begin to receive their real heritage from the visual arts of the Italian Renaissance.

This lag in England between the literary and visual influences of the Italian Renaissance is not hard to explain. Nothing is more portable than a book, and little money is needed for its purchase. But paintings are both bulky and expensive. Elizabethan Catholic exiles, government spies, or the travelling younger sons of noble houses could bring back books from Italy in their bags. It was less easy to fetch home sculptures by Donatello or canvases by Veronese. What was needed was for Englishmen of real position and wealth to come into direct contact with the art of the Italian Renaissance, and then have both the desire and means to bring that art home with them. Only in the reign of James I did this process really begin.

Various developments encouraged Italian travel by wealthy and titled Englishmen during the reign of King James. One was a change in attitude taken by the papacy. Whereas his predecessors had sought to keep Protestants from visiting Rome, Pope Clement VIII, hoping to win converts, sent out 'invitation and allurement of all nations and religions promiscuously'. Important too was the establishment of diplomatic relations between England and certain of the Italian states, particularly Venice.

After the first years of her reign Elizabeth had maintained no representatives in Italy. With the accession of James, however, Venice, most tolerant of all the Italian states (so tolerant that some felt it had 'slipped into a neutrality of religion') despatched a resident ambassador to London. One of James's early decisions was to reciprocate by sending Sir Henry Wotton as English ambassador to Venice. The choice was an excellent one. Wotton, with years of residence in Germany, Austria and Italy behind him, combined suave cosmopolitanism with unshakable Protestantism, a taste for the arts with a talent for political intrigue. Facile, ingratiating, imaginative, though flawed by the over-subtlety so common to his breed, he served James well during his three terms as English ambassador to Venice (1604-9, 1616-19 and 1621-3). He had first come to the King's attention in 1601 when he had arrived in Scotland with a highly confidential letter to James from Ferdinand I, Grand Duke of Tuscany, warning him of a Catholic plot to poison him and bringing a casket of antidotes for his better protection.

After Wotton had been stationed at Venice, accredited to the republic but expected to keep all Italy under his surveillance, English representatives were sent to other Italian states. In 1608 Sir Stephen Le Sieur took up his post at Florence, already becoming noted for 'a great confluence of English', while first Albertus Morton and then Isaac Wake served as English agent at Turin.

Because of these developments, an increasing number of Englishmen of family and means visited Italy. Among those whom Wotton presented to the Doge in 1608 were the Marquess of Hamilton, Lord Roos, Lord St. John, Lord Wentworth, Lord Cranborne (Cecil's heir), Sir John Harington (Prince Henry's close friend), and Henry Howard, son of the Earl of Suffolk.

There were still some hazards for the itinerant Englishman in Italy. In May 1609, when Lord Wentworth and three companions stopped for the night at Bologna, two Dominican friars and the local police seized Edward Lichfield, his lordship's tutor, and put him in the prison of the Inquisition. A little earlier there had been the remarkably similar case of Master John Mole. Mole was an earnest Church of England clergyman who made the mistake of travelling to Italy as the tutor of the vicious and erratic young William Cecil, Lord Roos. Roos, against the advice of Wotton and Mole, decided to visit Rome. Mole accompanied him, but was arrested by the Inquisition, probably with the connivance of Roos himself, who shortly turned Catholic. For thirty years Mole languished in the papal dungeons.

Contemporaries were quick to spot the significance of the arrests of Lich-field and Mole—while the papacy was glad to welcome to Italy young milords whom its blandishments might convert, it did not desire to have them accompanied by tutors who would endeavour to keep them Protestant.

Sometimes the over-zealousness of the Inquisition extended to persons of more consequence than chaplains and tutors. In 1617 Henry Bertie, brother of Lord Willoughby d'Eresby and cousin of the Earl of Oxford, found himself imprisoned at Ancona. Such events however were rare, and English gentlemen who showed reasonable tact and an intelligent awareness of local conditions could get around Italy without too much trouble. In fact, the grand tour was already in the making and Ben Jonson, writing *Volpone*, could include a comic sub-plot dealing with English tourists in Venice.

The most important single visit made by an Englishman to Italy during the reign of King James was that undertaken in 1613 by Thomas Howard, Earl of Arundel. Accompanied by Inigo Jones, he began in that year an extended tour of Italy which was to alter the whole cast of English culture.

Head of the house of Howard and premier earl of England, married to Alethea Talbot, one of the great heiresses of the age, Arundel was a major figure in the English court. In his appearance he was tall and thin, in his nature sensitive, reserved, and fastidious. Proudly conscious of his lineage amid the upstarts of King James's own creation, he epitomized the 'old aristocracy'. It was the Scot James Hay, whom James had created Earl of Carlisle, who once remarked, 'Here comes the earl of Arundel in his plain stuff and trunk hose, and his beard in his teeth, that looks more like a nobleman than any of us.'[1] Arundel was respected for his dignity and integrity rather than liked for any endearing qualities. He was, in fact, an arrogant and difficult man. Perhaps much of Arundel's touchiness was due to recollections of his poverty-haunted youth, when his widowed mother had brought him up in the shadow of Queen Elizabeth's disfavour. Even after prosperity came to him under the beneficent friendship of King James, he remained rather cold and aloof.

It is impossible to fix the date of Arundel's first visit to Italy. He was apparently on the Continent, as the youthful Lord Maltravers, in Queen Elizabeth's time. He may have made a short Italian trip in 1609. The first certain information we have is that in the summer of 1612, being threatened with consumption, he went to Spa for the cure and ended up by spending a couple of months at the baths of San Cassiano, near Padua. He returned to England determined to make a really extended tour of Italy. He did not long delay this journey. In April 1613, when Princess Elizabeth and her bridegroom sailed for Germany, Arundel and his countess accompanied

By permission of the College of Arms

THE HEARSE OF QUEEN ANNE

By permission of the Duke of Norfolk

THOMAS HOWARD, EARL OF ARUNDEL
with his gallery of sculptures.

by Daniel Mytens

them to Heidelberg on what was the first stage of the Earl's momentous Italian journey.

Arundel did not travel light. A personal suite of thirty-six accompanied the noble lord as he journeyed to Strasbourg, to Basle, to Milan, and to Padua where he settled a while in a pleasant country villa. He was, as Archbishop Mathew has observed, 'the very first of what was to become a familiar English species, the rich travelling *milord*'.[2] As if cognizant of this, the Republic of Venice entertained him sumptuously upon his arrival there.

By far the most interesting of those who accompanied Arundel on his tour was the court painter, architect, and stage designer Inigo Jones, whom the Earl had engaged as a species of *cicerone* to inform and advise him during his travels about the peninsula. A tempestuous self-willed man, who under all his bluster and vehemence possessed a delicacy of taste and ingenuity of approach to the visual arts which almost amounted to genius, Jones was singularly well qualified to serve as Arundel's mentor. The son of a Smithfield joiner, Jones had spent his early adult years in Italy, probably under the patronage of the Earl of Rutland, 'designing many works and discovering many antiquities before unknown, until Christianus the Fourth, King of Denmark, first engrossed him to himself'. His service in Denmark did not last very long. By the end of 1604 he was home in England from his Danish stay, designing for Ben Jonson's *Masque of Blackness* the first of those dazzling pieces of stage spectacle which he supplied for the court. It was probably through the masques that Jones and Arundel became acquainted, since the Earl was a participant in the second of the Jonson-Jones masques, *Hymenaei* (1606), and in various others that followed.

In Italy, Arundel and Jones set about an energetic programme of reconnaissance and discovery. While the Countess relaxed in the villa at Padua (though less energetic than the men, she loved Italy and on a subsequent trip brought back to England a gondola), Arundel and Jones made a sweep through Vicenza, Bologna and Florence, ending up at Siena where the Countess rejoined them. During the winter of 1613–14 the Arundels were in Rome, and here the Earl secured permission to excavate. To his delight his diggers unearthed some antique statues which were sent back to England. He and Jones then moved on to the South. Back from Naples in the late spring of 1614, they paused for a while at Rome before heading north to Genoa where the Arundels spent the summer.

In September they started for England. Jones's notebooks were full of sketches and observations made during the year and a half of their tour. Even so, they might have stayed longer if the death in June of Arundel's great-uncle, the Earl of Northampton, had not given a rather pressing reason for returning to England. Northampton, dying without issue, had left Arundel all his lands as well as his magnificent house at Greenwich.

Back in London in his own sumptuous riverside mansion, Arundel House, the Earl could look about him with satisfaction. To the picture collection which he had inherited in 1609 from Lord Lumley (chiefly historical and iconographical but rich in Arundel's favourite, Holbein), he had added the acquisitions yielded by his Italian journey. The statues dug up in Italy he set out in the gardens of Arundel House. The effect was somewhat surprising. The English were accustomed to painted effigies and Bacon, seeing for the first time the gleaming white shapes of the Arundel marbles, cast up his hands in mock amazement, started back, and exclaimed 'The resurrection!'[3]

The succeeding years saw Arundel consolidating his position as a collector. When Somerset came to disaster in 1616, it was to Arundel that King James transferred his fallen favourite's valuable collection of pictures. In this same year he received another gift when Lord Roos sent him a number of statues from Italy.

With Arundel setting the lead, art collecting became fashionable, and an important Whitehall group of patrons and collectors came into being. One of the most important of these was Buckingham. By profligate expenditure the King's favourite set himself to go far beyond what Arundel had been able to accomplish by taste joined to very considerable wealth. The ambassadors at Venice and The Hague were recruited as purchasing agents for Buckingham, a role they had already discharged on a less extensive scale for others of the King's courtiers. Experts such as Balthasar Gerbier in France and Daniel Nys in Italy ferreted out Veroneses and Tintorettos for the great duke.[4]

Breathtaking though Buckingham's programme of acquisition was, it was eclipsed by that of Prince Charles. The latter's interest in pictures had begun in 1612 with the inheritance of a small collection already begun by Prince Henry. Charles had added to this and was already winning a reputation for his sensitive and discerning taste when he made his trip to Spain in 1623 to court the Infanta. The treasures of the Spanish royal collections came as a revelation to Charles. For Titian especially, he developed an almost obsessive admiration. The Spanish king, perceiving this, presented him with the great Venetian's *Venus of the Prado*. Charles also brought back with him from Spain Titian's *Charles V with a Dog*. Back in England Charles embarked upon an extended programme of acquisition. One of his first purchases was the Raphael cartoons, which are now the pride of the Victoria and Albert Museum. His greatest acquisition, however, the greater part of the collection of the Gonzaga dukes of Mantua, fell

THE QUEEN'S HOUSE, GREENWICH, THE NORTH FRONT

within the early years of his own reign and lies beyond the limits of this study.

It was the purpose of both Arundel and Prince Charles 'to align and marry the tradition of art in Britain to the European tradition'.[5] Their collections by their very existence refined taste and bred discontent with the half-medieval two-dimensional painting of the English artists of the time. But more than this was needed to jolt the complacent members of the Painters and Stainers Company. Left to themselves, these were quite content to go on painting in the old stiff Elizabethan fashion. Accordingly, Arundel and Charles encouraged Continental artists of real excellence to practise in England. First Paul van Somer and Daniel Mytens arrived from Holland and then, towards the end of King James's reign, Van Dyke on his brief first English visit.

The artist who received the most serious and sustained encouragement from the Whitehall connoisseurs, however, was Inigo Jones. On April 27, 1613, just a few days after he and Arundel had left for Italy, Inigo Jones was given in reversion the post of Surveyor of the King's Works. This office was an important one, the surveyor being the architect in charge of the building and repair of all the King's houses and palaces. In more ways than one, Jones was the logical man for the post—a few years earlier he had been surveyor in the household of Prince Henry. He did not have to wait long for his reversion to take effect. In September 1615 Simon Basil died, and a month later Jones was installed as his successor. He could not have obtained a better position from which to initiate the reforms which he felt were overdue in English architecture. To Jones the vast houses built in the ramshackle Elizabethan fashion were semi-barbarous piles destined to give way to the cool elegance of neo-classical design. Palladio was the god of his idolatry. His copy of the master's *Quattro libri dell' architettura* survives today, crammed with annotations made during his pilgrimages to view the masterpieces of Palladian design.

Jones soon had an opportunity to introduce the new architecture. The pleasant riverside mansion of Placentia at Greenwich had long been a favourite residence of Queen Anne and in 1616 King James decided to build here a little palace as a gift to his queen. Inigo Jones was commissioned to draw up plans. Of the two which he submitted, the one accepted was for a little masterpiece of Palladian design. His building still stands for those who will to visit. In its compactness, its admirably functional design, and above all in its quiet and charming elegance, the Queen's House is an authentic masterpiece. Unfortunately Queen Anne died while it was still abuilding and King James left it unfinished. Not until 1637 did Jones see the Queen's House completed, now the gift of Charles I to his adored Henrietta Maria.

Fortunately for Jones, suspension in 1619 of the work on the Queen's House did not leave him without an outlet for his architectural genius now, in his late forties, ready for belated fulfilment. In this same year fire destroyed the Banqueting House at Whitehall. Commissioned to replace it with one of his own design, Jones began planning the building by which he is now chiefly remembered. Filled with such military bric-à-brac as the skeleton of Napoleon's horse, it is familiar today as the United Services Museum to all who pass between Trafalgar Square and the Houses of Parliament.

CHAPTER XXIII

Inigo Jones Builds at Whitehall

OF THE MANY establishments maintained by King James, only one was officially a palace—'Whitehall alias the new Pallace of Westminster.' Windsor, properly speaking, was a castle, Hampton Court an 'honour', Greenwich and St. James's 'manors'. The other royal residences were simply known as 'His Majesties houses of attendance'. Despite its proudly unique designation, Whitehall was hardly palatial. A vast rookery of undistinguished buildings trailing along the Thames, Whitehall signally failed to impress foreign visitors as a palace worthy of the King of England.

Topographically, the master fact about Whitehall was that it was a palace bisected by a public thoroughfare. How this came to be was a matter of history. In 1529 Henry VIII had eagerly transferred himself and his court from the dilapidated 'Old Palace' of Westminster to adjacent York Place, which Cardinal Wolsey had been sumptuously rebuilding in the years before his fall. Wolsey's York Place had lain entirely between the Thames and the highway linking Westminster with London, but once King Henry had moved into the 'new palace' (or 'Whitehall' as it came to be known, first informally but gradually officially) and begun his own programme of building, he found that he needed some of the land which lay beyond 'The Street'. A problem arose. Even so autocratic a monarch as Henry could hardly deny a centuries-old right of way and close a major highway. On the other hand, it was unthinkable to have the general public streaming through the palace grounds. The solution was to retain The Street but to line it on both sides with high brick walls, while linking the two parts of the palace grounds at either end by bridges which constituted the upper storeys of large gatehouses.

Now for a swift survey of King James's Whitehall (for a diagram, turn to the end of the book). Heading north from Westminster, the traveller was first aware of Whitehall as he passed under the arches of the King Street Gate. Once beyond it, the traveller found himself flanked by the two high walls just referred to. Beyond the wall on his right lay the Privy Garden much frequented by the court lords and ladies. Beyond the wall on his left lay the recreational area of the palace. In this section was the 'Brake' or 'Balloon Court'. Large and unroofed, it was devoted to the old game of court tennis. Here on a hot summer's day, the ill-fated Prince Henry might have been seen working himself into a lather of sweat as he relentlessly played game after game after game, striving to punish the physical weakness within him. Beyond lay a long double-storeyed edifice housing the indoor bowling alleys. On rainy days, forsaking the greens in adjacent St. James's Park, the courtiers rolled their bowls instead in the alleys on the upper floor. The alleys on the floor below were apparently for the lesser officers and servants of the court. West of the Bowls-house rose the Cockpit, connected with The Street by Cockpit Lane. Octagonal in shape, with galleries and staircases, the Cockpit rather resembled in design the public playhouses on the Bankside shore. It was, in fact, used both for cockfights and plays in King James's time, and his successor converted it into a private court theatre. Adjacent were the Cockpit Lodgings. Here Princess Elizabeth, before her marriage, lived in quarters subsequently occupied by Somerset and his bride.

Just north of where Cockpit Lane debouched into The Street, there rose a lofty building with steep pitched roof and gable ends set between high angular towers. This was the Chief Close Tennis Court, the larger of two roofed halls where tennis could be played indoors when bad weather made unattractive the open Brake across the way and the Little Open Tennis Court beside the Tiltyard. Having passed the Chief Close Tennis Court, our traveller along The Street soon found himself under the arches of the second of the two gatehouses, the misnamed Holbein Gate. Almost twice the height of the other, this, with its sculptured roundels, chequered pattern of stone and flint, and elaborate bay window over the central arch, was much the more impressive and ornate. Once through the Holbein Gate, our traveller entered a species of plaza. Facing it on his right were the Banqueting House and the cavernous mouth of the Court Gate. Beside the latter stood the substantial building which was the Porter's Lodge. There was usually a crowd around the Court Gate, partly of courtiers and their ladies taking or leaving horse or carriage, partly of serving-men who, lacking the Green Cloth officers' permission to enter the precincts, had to await here their masters' return. During the Commonwealth the scene at the Court Gate was nostalgically remembered:

> ... where there had wont to be a continual throng, either of Gallants stand-ing to ravish themselves with the sight of Ladies hansome Legs and Insteps as they tooke Coach; Or of the tribe of guarded Liveries [servants in their masters' liveries], by whom you could scarce passe without a jeare or a saucy answer to your question.[1]

Supposing our hypothetical traveller to be a very privileged person indeed, he could win admittance to Whitehall not by making his way through the crowd at the Court Gate but by cutting across the plaza to the

Tiltyard, which occupied its opposite side. At the south-west corner of the Tiltyard he could mount an elaborate set of wooden stairs going up from St. James's Park and giving access to the galleries where annually, on King's Day, James, his favoured courtiers, and foreign ambassadors watched the jousting below. Threading his way along these galleries, an exceptionally privileged traveller might conceivably be permitted by the Yeoman of the Guard on duty to pass across the Holbein Gate on the level just above the arched roadway.

Our traveller would now enter, on the second storey, a long range of buildings which constituted the very heart of the palace. Before him extended the broad width of the ornate Privy Gallery where the King occasionally received ambassadors and where, in 1611, he created Robert Carr Viscount Rochester. Opening off this gallery on the left was the Council Chamber. In the time of Edward VI this had been the royal bedchamber and it occasionally reverted to similar use. On the wedding night of the Earl of Montgomery and his bride, King James bedded them there so that he could saunter over from his own nearby bedchamber to greet them next morning. The Privy Council regularly met in this chamber until after the death of Queen Anne, when it moved into what had been her Presence Chamber. The King's cousin, the Duke of Lennox, then moved into this room, surrendering his chambers in the Holbein Gate. Flanking the Council Chamber were two ante-rooms, the Stone Table Room and the Chamber of Ordinary Audience, where foreign ambassadors cooled their heels while awaiting royal interviews. On the right hand side of the Privy Gallery, looking onto the Privy Garden, were the King's Cabinet (or study), the Horn Room (his lesser withdrawing room) and other of his private rooms, as well as the Adam and Eve Room, from which stairs led to the floor below where the chief of His Majesty's officers, such as the Lord Treasurer and the Secretaries of State, had their chambers.

At the end of the Privy Gallery stood the Vane Room, named for the weathercock set above it. The Vane Room was, in fact, the King's Withdrawing Room,[2] through which one had to pass to reach the adjoining King's Bedchamber. Nearby were the King's Back Stairs which permitted unobtrusive access to the royal quarters. (Not for nothing has the term 'backstairs intrigue' entered our language.) Should our sightseeing traveller continue east after passing through the Vane Room, he would end up at the Shield Gallery, so called since at the end of a day of tilting the contestants' shields were hung up here as trophies. The end of the Shield Gallery projected out over the Thames on the palace's second level. Below were the Privy Stairs, the private landing-stage from which the King set forth on the royal barge.

Let us deal now with the probable rather than the barely possible, and take it that our traveller was not one of the very few persons permitted access to the inner parts of the palace by way of the Tiltyard Gallery Stairs. In this case, he would have to present himself at the Court Gate. If the Porter there permitted his entry, he could step into the Great Court of the palace. This was known also as the Whale-bone Court because of some curios on display there. It was used at times for bear-baitings and bull-baitings. This courtyard was bounded on the right by a high brick wall and on the left by one of the ranges of buildings which centred around Scotland Yard—a warren of kitchens, storehouses, woodyards, servants' quarters, and miscellaneous 'offices'. On the east side of the Great Court stood the Great Hall, the scene of state banquets and the most usual place for the command performances of plays. Beyond it a narrow alley, flanked on the right by the Chapel Royal and its vestries and on the left by the Office of the Green Cloth, led to Whitehall Stairs, where a constant stream of rivermen landed or took on passengers. Between Whitehall Stairs and the Privy Stairs extended the block of buildings where Queen Anne had her suite of privy chambers.

If, after entering the Great Court, our traveller had wished to view the inner rather than the peripheral parts of the palace, he would have ascended a broad flight of stone stairs in the south-east corner of that courtyard. These would have led him into the Guard Chamber, commonly known also as the Great Chamber. Here he would find 'His Majesties great Beefe-eaters . . . in attendance on their places, which was nothing but to tell Tales, devour the beaverage, keepe a great fire, and carry up Dishes, wherein their fingers would bee sometimes before they came to the King's Table.'[3] Leaving the Guard Chamber by a door on the west, he would come out on 'The Terrace', the balustraded wooden roof of a ground-level cloister which extended along two sides of the larger inner courtyard known as the Preaching Place. This took its name from the outdoor pulpit in its centre from which sermons were at times delivered. By means of the Terrace, it was possible to route people having business with the Privy Council to the Council Chamber without letting them use the Privy Gallery or other areas more or less reserved for the monarch and his intimates. The Terrace became, in consequence:

> . . . that Exchange of Projectors [persons with projects] . . . where th'Atten-dants upon the Councell Table had wont to coole their toes, and by their whispering consultations digest every trade into the forme of monopolies.[4]

The Terrace served also to connect the royal quarters with the Banqueting House, which rose on the west side of the Preaching Place.

Various tales could be told concerning the Terrace. It was here one December night in 1604 when a masque was being put on at court that 'one woman among the rest lost her honesty, for which she was carried to the porters lodge, being surprised at her busines on the top of the Taras'.[5] During the later years of King James, the Terrace was in a pretty rotten condition. In March 1620 part of it collapsed as Gondomar, the Spanish ambassador, was being escorted from a meeting in the Council Chamber. Among those hurt in the collapse were the Earl of Arundel, Lord Gerard, and Lord Grey. Fortunately for Gondomar, he was saved by two of the Yeomen of the Guard who caught him and pulled him to safety.

A visiting dignitary receiving a state reception at Whitehall did not, as a rule, pass along the Terrace. Instead, he was conducted from the Guard Chamber by the Captain of the Guard to the door of the adjacent Presence Chamber. Here he was received by the Lord Chamberlain, who took him to the King. The Presence Chamber was open to all who were entitled to appear at court. In fact, it was considered a matter of royal prestige that it should never appear deserted. Admission to the Privy Chamber, which lay beyond, was confined to those close to the King who had his specific permission to enter. An interloper here was liable to a year's banishment from the court. Beyond it lay the King's Withdrawing Room (the Vane Room) which, as earlier noted, might also be reached by way of the Privy Gallery from the west. Southward beyond the Vane Room extended the Long or Matted Gallery. Like the loggia of the Stone Gallery directly beneath it, this looked out on the Privy Garden on the one hand, and gave access on the other to suites of apartments where Prince Charles and various court lords had their quarters. Broad and roomy, these galleries were popular places of concourse for the courtiers on rainy winter days.

Such then was Whitehall Palace, sprawling over twenty-three acres, vast, complicated, and shapeless. Its irregular passageways and unexpected tiny courtyards gave access to over two thousand rooms. Its skyline was a hodge-podge of towers and chimney-pots. To anyone acquainted, like Inigo Jones, with the ordered façades of the 'new architecture' on the Continent, Whitehall must have seemed both monstrous and archaic.

In 1619 the Banqueting House burned down. Built only eleven years before, it was architecturally one of the more presentable parts of the palace. Accounts differed as to just how the fire started, but everybody agreed that the oiled paper of some masque sets stored in the hall gave a special fury to the fire. Despite the august direction of the fire-fighters given by the Duke of Lennox and the Earls of Arundel and Pembroke, not only was the hall itself lost, but all the archives stored in the Signet and Privy Seal offices in the basement below. Moreover, some of the terrace and the adjacent lodgings were destroyed and part of the Privy Gallery block was severely damaged.

Ordinarily, the rebuilding of the Banqueting House might have been delayed. The nation had entered an economic depression which was making the shaky royal finances even more insecure than usual. There was, however, an overriding reason why the Banqueting House should be rebuilt at once and with the greatest possible magnificence. Negotiations were already well advanced for the marriage of Prince Charles and the Spanish Infanta, and national honour required that the marriage be solemnized with all possible magnificence. There was, however, the unfortunate architectural inadequacy of Whitehall. To supercilious Spaniards who knew the palaces of Italy and the sombre majesty of the Escorial, the buildings at Whitehall would seem old-fashioned and mean. The obvious thing was to build, without loss of time, a new Banqueting House architecturally as contemporary and as impressive as anything of its kind to be found in Europe. Accordingly, King James at once appointed a commission comprised of the Lord Steward (the Duke of Lennox), the Lord Chamberlain (the Earl of Pembroke), the Under-Treasurer of the Exchequer (Sir Fulke Greville), the Earl of Arundel and Lord Digby. The commissioners were for the most part chosen because of the offices they held but, as Per Palme has noted, 'Had the selection been dictated by the historians of English connoisseurship it could hardly have been better.'[6] Within three months of the fire the commissioners had approved the model of a new building submitted by Inigo Jones. Within six months work had begun upon construction.

By Jacobean standards the work proceeded with remarkable expedition. True, there were delays. Although a special wharf was built at Portland for the shipment of stone, Luke Wilson, the purveyor and stone farmer there, failed to get the barges loaded. Only after the commissioners had invoked the powers of the Privy Council did stone begin to arrive. There was trouble securing wages for the masons. When the latter found themselves unpaid, they showed little sympathy for the difficulties of the Exchequer, and deserted to more lucrative private employment. But despite all difficulties, the work was pushed ahead.

By the end of March 1622 the new building was officially complete even though some incidental decorating had still to be finished. Not until 1623, in fact, did Isaac de Caux finish transforming the basement, designated as the King's Privy Cellar, into the semblance of a grotto. This was intended for His Majesty's boozing parties with his cronies. For its dedication Ben Jonson came up with some suitable doggerel, of which a brief sample may suffice:

> Since, Bacchus, thou art father
> Of Wines, to thee the rather
> We dedicate this Cellar,
> Where now thou art made Dweller.[7]

Perhaps King James could forget in his cups how much the new Banqueting House had cost him. According to the accounts of the Paymaster of the Works, the expenses totalled in 1622 not the estimated £9,850 but £14,940. But whatever the cost, the new Banqueting House was a dazzling addition to the royal palace.

What Inigo Jones had built for his king was a masterpiece of Palladian design. Aware of King James's aversion to pillars which might disrupt his view, Jones had abandoned his early plan for a species of basilica and instead had come up with a marvellously spacious and unencumbered hall proportioned according to the famous 'double cube'. Seen from the outside, its two ranges of windows, one pedimented on the floor level, the other unpedimented on that of the gallery, were perfectly set off by the verticals of intervening pilasters or columns, and by the horizontals of the bold cornices and frieze. In his first drafts, Jones had provided a central pediment above the side of the hall, with a pitched roof beyond, but these he scrapped to produce a building which is a pure study in horizontals and verticals, relieved just sufficiently by the occasional minor curve or oblique line to confer courtly elegance. In fact, mounted on the rusticated stone base of its cellar, and capped by a sky-line balustrade, the building exemplifies perfectly those principles of the 'masculine, sollid, simpell' in architecture to which Jones had long since sworn his allegiance.

The brilliance of Inigo Jones's achievement was recognized at once. The complaint, if any, was that Jones had been too brilliant. Beside the Banqueting House the rest of Whitehall looked hopelessly dowdy and passé. But a revolution had been effected in English architecture. For the next two centuries, when the English aristocracy built, their style would be Palladian, and a long line of major architects descending from Jones—Webb, Wren, Vanbrugh, Kent—would be ready with plans for them.

The way in which the Banqueting House eclipsed the rest of Whitehall may not have been entirely unintended. Nothing would have pleased Jones better than to have razed all the old Tudor buildings and have built in their place a whole new palace, symmetrical, integrated, and monumental, in the splendid Palladian style. In the reign of Charles I he actually drew the plans for such a palace. Had it been built, England would have had something to match the Escorial and Versailles. But King James could never have afforded it. And as for Charles, Destiny was to take him through one of the Banqueting House windows to a platform beyond, and the headsman's axe.

CHAPTER XXIV

Lord Chancellor Bacon

FOR TWENTY YEARS Francis Bacon's father was Queen Elizabeth's Lord Keeper of the Great Seal, and Elizabeth, amused by the precocity of the son, took to calling him her 'young Lord Keeper'. The boy never forgot the phrase. It whetted his ambition to match his father's achievement.

The memory of his father dominated Bacon's life. Gross-bodied, domineering, and yet not unkindly, Sir Nicholas Bacon bred into his son an instinct for compliance with authority, and a nervous eagerness to please. He also gave the boy an abiding sense that safety was afforded by paternal authority. Perhaps out of this came Bacon's intense feeling in later years that a parental discipline exercised by the monarchy was essential to the well-being of the state. Again and again the father affords the key to Bacon's actions.[1] Whatever he could identify with him became precious and gave a sense of reassurance and security. In the days of his greatness, Bacon had to secure for his London residence York House, which had been his father's dwelling; and he agonized when he was forced to relinquish it. In his downfall, it was his comfort to declare that he had been the justest Lord Keeper that England had known since his father's time.

It took Bacon a long time to satisfy his compulsion to equal his father's achievement. Born in 1561, he had to wait until 1617 to become Lord Keeper. When at last he did obtain his life's ambition, he had years of frustration behind him.

He had started well. Residence at Cambridge had been followed by admission to Gray's Inn to study law, and to round out his education by foreign travel he had gone abroad in the train of Sir Amias Paulet, the English ambassador to France. Then, just before his return to England, Francis Bacon lost his father. Sir Nicholas's death at this time was doubly unfortunate. For one thing, it meant that he did not live long enough for his son to see him with the critical eyes of maturity, so that throughout life Francis Bacon carried with him the magnified father image of his younger years. For another, it meant that young Francis Bacon, not yet appointed to any of the offices which his father might have secured for him, was confronted with a difficult climb up the ladder at court.

Serious as was the setback to his career, it was not necessarily disastrous. Francis Bacon had his own superb talents, and he still possessed powerful family connections. William Cecil, Lord Burghley, Queen Elizabeth's chief minister and most trusted adviser, was married to Bacon's aunt, and this was an age when it was taken for granted that men helped their kinsmen to secure office. Burghley, however, did little or nothing for his wife's nephew. Perhaps both he and the Queen, out of long experience, suspected the smooth obsequiousness of Bacon, an obsequiousness which though it may have warmed the heart of old Sir Nicholas was not to everybody's liking. Perhaps they sensed the subtle unsoundness of the man. In any event, no doors were opened to Bacon at court and, cursing the Cecils in his heart, he had to make a livelihood as a lawyer while his crook-backed cousin, Robert Cecil, entered upon the career for which Bacon was convinced he himself was much better fitted.

Denied a place at court, Bacon turned to Parliament. Here his eloquence and address soon brought him to the fore, but in the process he lost what was left of the Queen's favour. Convinced that heavy taxes would make a breach between the sovereign and her subjects, he opposed in the Parliament of 1593 the Crown's plan of collecting three subsidies during the coming four years. Furious at his temerity, Queen Elizabeth exclaimed that in her father's time a lesser offence would have banished a man from the royal presence for the rest of his life. After an interval, she permitted Bacon to present himself before her again, but she never really forgave him.

Bacon's talents were so manifest that the Queen and her ministers, while not deeming him a man to be trusted in great affairs, used him in lesser matters. He was sworn as a Queen's Counsel extraordinary and used by the Privy Council to examine prisoners, sometimes under torture. It was not work that would commend itself to every man, but Bacon was ambitious.

In 1601 when Elizabeth's Essex stood his trial for treason, Bacon found a place among the Crown's prosecutors. There was every reason why he should not have done so. Essex had been his friend and patron. In 1594 Essex had done his utmost to secure the post of attorney-general for Bacon. When this went to Edward Coke, the man whom nature and destiny had singled out as the great adversary of Bacon's life, Essex strove to get him the lesser appointment of solicitor-general. Denied this suit also, Essex had humanely sought to soften Bacon's disappointment by a generous gift, out of his own estates, of land worth £1,800. In the face of such obligations, Bacon might have been expected to keep clear of any part in the proceedings against Essex. No office held by Bacon required that he appear in court against his former friend, and every decent feeling must have urged refusal of the employment. Bacon, however, was a cold man; and feeling was never his long suit. Not for nothing did John Aubrey later report that he had the 'Eie of a viper'. Francis Bacon decided to act for the prosecution, and was as effective as any in sending Essex to his death. He could remind himself that when he had accepted Essex's gift he had written to him, half jestingly but half presciently, that while he must now do homage to Essex, it must always be with a reservation of loyalty to the monarch. But human feelings transcend quibbles and technicalities, something that Bacon never fully realized.

Elizabeth's death and James's accession brought new hope to Bacon. A new monarch meant a new chance. Within a couple of days of the passing of Queen Elizabeth, Bacon wrote letters to Scotland. They were addressed to the Lord of Kinloss, to Sir Thomas Chaloner, to Dr. Morrison (the King's physician) and to Mr. David Foulis. All extended the same unabashed offer. Let the recipients speak well of Bacon to the King, and they would find the favour requited when they arrived in England. Also Bacon wrote, with infinite care, a letter to His Majesty offering his services.

Bacon's prospects did, in fact, improve with the arrival of King James. His manner, which hovered between being ingratiating and toadying, was not unacceptable to the new monarch. Himself an intellectual, James could appreciate the enormous range of Bacon's mental horizons. Temperamentally the two were congenial, and King James could see a fair bit of himself in Bacon. Significantly, when somebody drew the King's attention to Bacon's prodigality in grossly over-rewarding the servant who had brought him His Majesty's gift of some venison, King James simply replied, 'I and he shall both die beggars.'[2]

Bacon received his first advancement when King James knighted him on his coronation day, July 23, 1603. True, the fact that Bacon was one of a mob of three hundred knighted that day took away half the sweetness from what Sir Francis called 'this almost prostituted title', but it was a step forward. In 1604 Bacon was appointed King's Counsel and given a pension of £60 per annum for life. In the same year he was appointed one of the English commissioners to negotiate a union of England and Scotland. In 1606 he fought mightily in Parliament for acceptance of the terms arrived at by the commissioners. It was not his fault that the narrow commercialism of the Commons precluded acceptance of the proposed customs union of the two kingdoms—what Bacon could do he did, and he received his reward the next year when King James made him Solicitor-General. But there, apart from a few minor offices acquired in the next few years, Bacon's career halted. At the King's shoulder was Robert Cecil, now Earl of Salisbury, and Cecil had long since taken Bacon's measure. It would be so far and no farther for Bacon so long as Cecil lived. In May 1612, how-

THE BANQUETING HOUSE, WHITEHALL

FRANCIS BACON, VISCOUNT ST. ALBAN

Studio of Paul van Somer

ever, Cecil died. Within a week Bacon had written to the King reassuring him of his services. Quite truthfully he identified himself as 'a perfect and peremptory royalist'.

The forward march to honours and great office did not begin at once, but in a little more than a year Bacon was on his way. A typical piece of intrigue was involved. Sir Edward Coke, who had snatched the Attorney-Generalship from Bacon in Elizabeth's time, and had followed up this triumph by marrying the rich young widow, Lady Hatton, whom Bacon had likewise sought, had become in 1606 Chief Justice of the Court of Common Pleas. Masterful, fearless, resourceful, and cantankerous, Coke as Chief Justice had used his enormous knowledge of the law to curtail the powers of the Church of England's Court of High Commission, to limit the royal prerogative and to maintain the supremacy of the common law, and to set forth a novel theory that the King himself ruled under the law. From the bench Chief Justice Coke declared, 'The King cannot change any part of the common law, nor create any offence by his proclamation, without Parliament, which was not an offence before.'

Despite the reluctant concessions which he made to English custom, King James was at heart an absolutist. He was gratified to find that the more conservative of his advisers, Lord Chancellor Ellesmere and Solicitor-General Bacon, regarded Coke's rulings as wilful invasions of the royal prerogative. It was Bacon who came up with a solution for the King's difficulties. The Lord Chief Justice of the Court of King's Bench had died. Why not reduce Coke's capacity for mischief by promoting him to the higher court? As Chief Justice there, Coke would enjoy more prestige, having the title of Chief Justice of England. On the other hand, dealing chiefly with criminal cases between subjects and the Crown, he would find less opportunity for infringement upon the royal prerogative. As for the position vacated by Coke, that could go to Hobart, the Attorney-General, a timid man who would never go against the King's wishes. There remained only the matter of finding a new Attorney-General. Bacon was at no loss for a candidate here. Setting forth an earlier scheme to the King (he was full of schemes), Bacon had already mentioned his own claims for promotion:

> I have served your Majesty above a prenticehood, full seven years and more as your solicitor. . . . God hath brought mine own years to fifty-two, which I think is older than ever any solicitor continued unpreferred.[3]

Such was Bacon's triple play. In his eyes it had everything to commend it. Close on the heels of his letter outlining the plan to the King came a memorandum: 'Reasons for the Remove of Coke.' The sinuous plausible reasoning set forth within it won the King's consent. Weeping, Coke walked from the end of Westminster Hall where the Common Pleas were

L

heard to the opposite end, where sat the Court of King's Bench. Hobart took his vacated place and Bacon was sworn in as Attorney-General. Before him, he could almost persuade himself, lay the road to the Lord Keepership, his father's great office.

Adroitly Bacon cleared the way before him. The good will of the royal favourite, Somerset, was indispensable. As a means of keeping it, Bacon insisted upon paying the entire cost of the marriage masque offered by the gentlemen of Gray's Inn when Somerset married Lady Frances Howard. Two years passed and Somerset was confronted with disaster because of his wife's crimes. In Somerset's ruin also, Bacon found a means to strengthen his own position. Prosecuting the Earl, he secured his conviction in the manner least likely to embarrass the King and won an abundant measure of royal gratitude.

Coke still remained a danger. With his enormous knowledge of the law and great personal prestige, he might yet succeed the aging Ellesmere as Lord Chancellor and so rob Bacon of his ultimate ambition. Coke, however, had learned nothing from his transfer from the Court of Common Pleas. Still obstreperous, he not only continued to 'disesteem and weaken the power of the King in the ancient use of his Prerogative', but encroached increasingly upon the jurisdiction of other courts. In so doing he supplied the means for his own removal. When Bacon judged the time ripe, he drafted a list of the Chief Justice's 'Innovations Introduced into the Laws and Government', and sent it forward to the King. Suave, reasonable, unassailable in his logic, Bacon urged the enormity of Coke's offences in perverting the law to serve his own ends, especially in his use of writs of *praemunire* against the Court of Chancery. A few days later he drew up a form for the dismissal of Coke, and a blank warrant for the appointment of his successor. On November 15, 1616, the King used these documents and Coke was a ruined man.

Bacon, meanwhile, was within sight of his goal. In June of this year he had become a member of the Privy Council. Other honours followed as he became High Steward of St. Albans, Chancellor and Keeper of the Great Seal of the Prince of Wales, and High Steward of Cambridge. Sinecures or archaisms though some of these dignities might be, each marked a small move upwards in the royal esteem. But more than royal esteem was necessary if Bacon was to win the post of Lord Keeper. A new royal favourite had arisen; and nothing could be hoped for unless Buckingham gave his nod. Applying all his genius to the art of pleasing, Bacon addressed himself to Buckingham. He did not have to wait long for his reward.

As 1616 ended, it became obvious that the Lord Chancellor, Thomas Egerton, Baron Ellesmere, the last of the councillors whom King James had inherited from Queen Elizabeth, was near his end. A passionate champion of the royal prerogative, so venerably handsome and impressive a figure when seated in Chancery that men had gone thither only to see him, Ellesmere had been a tower of strength to King James. While the old man visibly faltered, James sought by worldly titles to encourage him to prolong his lease on life and office. In November he created him Viscount Brackley. The promotion was of no avail. In February Ellesmere wrote a singularly moving letter asking for release from his high office. On March 5, 1617, he delivered from his sickbed the Great Seal into the hands of a weeping king. Two days later Bacon was summoned to Whitehall and received the seal from His Majesty's hands. Jubilantly he returned to his lodgings. At last he stood where his father had stood. He had proved, or thought he had proved, something to himself. Taking a piece of paper, he wrote to the Earl of Buckingham. Fluently the empty, insincere eulogies flowed. Bacon was thanking him for the Lord Keepership.

One of Bacon's first tasks was to call upon his dying predecessor. With him he brought a message from the King. His Majesty had decided to bestow upon his old and faithful servant the Earldom of Bridgewater, to invest him with the presidency of the Privy Council, and to bestow upon him a pension of £3,000 annually. It was a princely offer to come to one who had been born the bastard son of a Cheshire squire, but it came too late:

> . . . he was so far past that no wordes or worldly comforts could worke with him, but only thancking his Majestie for his gracious favor, saide these thinges were all to him but vanities.[4]

Half an hour later he was dead. In his will he had ordered that he be given no solemn funeral or monument, but be buried in oblivion.

Within ten days of Bacon's installation as Lord Keeper, the King, accompanied by Buckingham, was off on his six months' Scottish journey. In his absence it was Bacon who exercised the real government of England, convened meetings of the Privy Council, dealt with foreign ambassadors, and passed on the King's business. After his years of waiting, Bacon revelled in the power and the magnificence. Nobody believed more than Bacon in gorgeous ceremony. He had a whole *mystique* of statecraft which required magnificence as a necessary adjunct of power. At times he seemed almost to confuse the two.

Bacon's great opportunity for pomp and circumstance came with the Easter law term, when he went for the first time to preside over his Court of Chancery. John Chamberlain, learning in advance of the preparations, came to London earlier than he had intended 'to see the new Lord Keper ride in pompe to Westminster'. The display was impressive indeed, befitting a minor coronation. The clerks and officers of the Chancery marched in procession. Behind them came the Inns of Court men, wearing all their finery in honour of Sir Francis Bacon, who for so long had been one of their number. The servants and officers of Bacon's own household followed. Next walked the serjeants-at-arms and Bacon's seal-bearer, carrying before him on a cushion the embroidered purse which contained the Great Seal of England. Behind, on horseback, rode the great Lord Keeper himself, gorgeous in a gown of purple satin. He was flanked on the one side by the Earl of Suffolk, the Lord Treasurer of England, and on the other by the Earl of Worcester, the Lord Privy Seal. Behind them rode other earls, various barons, the Privy Councillors, and the judges. To compliment Bacon, both Queen Anne and Prince Charles had sent their people to join in his procession.

Display on this scale and Bacon's lordly direction of the realm were hardly likely to go without nasty comments. There were gibes enough about 'King Bacon', and malicious exaggerated accounts of the Lord Keeper's presumption travelled up to Scotland. In London, Sir Ralph Winwood became so infuriated with the airs that Bacon was giving himself that he was ready to refuse to carry on as Secretary of State. Peacemakers patched things up after a fashion, but the friction continued. Later when Queen Anne asked Bacon why he and Winwood so constantly jarred, all that Bacon replied was, 'Madame, I can say no more but he is prowde and I am prowde.'

In the late spring Bacon heard disquieting news. A match was in prospect between Buckingham's brother, the brainsick Sir John Villiers, and Frances Coke, the only child of his old enemy by his second wife, the tempestuous Lady Hatton. If Coke were allied to Buckingham through marriage, he could hope to resume his career. The thought made Bacon apprehensive.

On July 12th a clamorous intruder awakened Bacon from an afternoon nap. It was Coke's wife, full of indignation that her husband had abducted the beautiful Frances from the home of Sir Edmund and Lady Withipole, where she had sought to hide her in an attempt to prevent the marriage. Bacon heard the lady out, then told her to appear before the Privy Council and relate to it the wrongs done to her. Meanwhile he himself wrote to Buckingham, urgently arguing that Coke should not be encouraged in his presumptuous plan to marry into the Villiers family.

While Bacon's letter was on its way to Scotland, the Privy Council met to thrash out the Coke-Villiers business. Lining up with Bacon, the Councillors decided that the Attorney-General should prosecute Coke in the Star Chamber 'for the force and riot used by him upon the house of Sir Edmund Withipole'. And they informed Winwood that he had exceeded his authority in issuing the search warrant Coke had used to give a colour of legality to his raid. When the Council rebuked Winwood for encouraging

Coke to seek this marriage, he was ready with his defence. Dipping into his pocket, he produced a letter from King James giving his approval to the match.

Suddenly Bacon saw the noose into which he had thrust his head. Coke and Winwood had deliberately kept him ignorant of the consent of Buckingham and the King, and in his ignorance Bacon had done exactly what his enemies had wanted—he had set himself against the wishes of Buckingham. Caught in this trap, Bacon had to decide whether to capitulate or still to oppose the Villiers-Coke alliance. Despite the risks of the latter course, he decided upon it. Grimly he wrote to King James. If Coke were permitted to regain favour, he argued, all the malcontents and turbulent spirits which had been tamed through the example of his disgrace would once more plague His Majesty. Seeking to by-pass Buckingham, he asked that this matter be settled between the King and himself. It was utter folly for Bacon to proceed thus. Buckingham was furious at the Lord Keeper's audacity in seeking to deal directly with the King instead of through himself, and James eagerly showed his devotion to his favourite by outdoing him in finding fault with the hapless Bacon.

It took the latter some time to learn these things. For a while Buckingham contemptuously left his letters unanswered, but finally he sent a curt note:

> My Lord,
>   If your man [who had carried Bacon's letters to the King and Buckingham] had been addressed only to me, I should have been careful to have procured him a more speedy dispatch: but now you have found another way of address, I am excused; and since you are grown weary of employing me, I can be no otherwise in being employed. In this business of my brother's that you overtrouble yourself with, I understand from London by some of my friends that you have carried yourself with much scorn and neglect both toward myself and friends; which if it prove true, I blame not you but myself, who was ever
>   Your Lordship's assured friend,
>   G. Buckingham[5]

'Who *was* ever Your Lordship's assured friend.' Bacon must have reeled as he read that ominous past tense. Suddenly he saw that he stood on the very brink of disaster. Only complete ignominious submission could save him now. When he next wrote to Buckingham, it was to report that he had informed the interested parties that he was now resolved to further the match upon the most advantageous terms that he could procure for the favourite's brother.

As Buckingham and King James drew homeward from Scotland, an agonized Bacon awaited his fate. From Nantwich the King sent him a terrible letter in which he made a further offence of every attempt that

Bacon had made to explain away his earlier actions. When the royal party reached Coventry, Sir Henry Yelverton sent an ominous warning that Coke had arrived and was as close to Buckingham as his shirt. Buckingham, he reported, was saying openly that he regretted ever having made Bacon Lord Keeper.

Finally the day came for Bacon and Buckingham to meet. Buckingham had probably already decided to spare Bacon. Perhaps it had been Bacon who had persuaded Lady Coke to agree finally to the marriage and to double the dowry offered by Coke—if so, he had certainly done something substantial to mollify Buckingham's anger. Perhaps Buckingham realized that Bacon had been unfairly trapped by his enemies and was too useful to be sacrificed out of mere pique. At any rate, he had decided to give him a second chance. Writing to Bacon from Warwick on September 5th, Buckingham intimated that he and the King would give him a fair hearing. About two weeks later Bacon was given his audience.

After all his pomp and magnificence, Bacon was to be humbled. The price for regaining Buckingham's patronage was a submission that would convince the royal favourite that Bacon would never cross him again. The story of the Lord Keeper's humiliation loses nothing as recounted by Weldon:

> . . . he attended two dayes at *Buckinghams* Chamber, being not admitted to any better place, then the roome where trencher-scrapers and Laquies attended, there sitting upon an old wooden chest, (amongst such as for his basenesse were only fit for his companions, although the Honour of his place did merit farre more respect) with his Purse and Seal lying by him, on that chest; My selfe told a servant of my Lord of *Buckinghams*, it was a shame to see the Purse and Seale of so little value, or esteeme, in his Chamber, though the Carryer without it merited nothing but scorne, being worst among the basest. Hee told me they had command it must be so; after two dayes hee had admittance: at first entrance, fell down flat on his face at the Dukes foot, kissing it, vowing never to rise till hee had his pardon, then was hee againe reconciled, and since that time so very a slave to the Duke and all that Family, that he durst not deny the command of the meanest of the kindred. . . .[6]

Placated, Buckingham agreed to intercede for Bacon with the King. According to his subsequent letter, Buckingham found 'so deep conceived an indignation' in the King that he had to go on his knees to persuade him not to disgrace the Lord Keeper.

In January 1618, fully restored to royal favour, Bacon was given the title, which his father had never enjoyed, of Lord Chancellor.[7] On July 12th he entered the peerage as Baron of Verulam.

Writing to Burghley some time around 1592, Bacon had observed, touching on his disappointment in politics, 'I confess that I have as vast contemplative ends, as I have moderate civil ends: for I have taken all knowledge to be my province.' The years of toiling up the ladder of political advancement had seen no suspension of those labours which would finally win Bacon a name in literature and philosophy far transcending the shoddy transitory brilliance of his political career. In 1597 he had published the first edition of his famous *Essays*. In 1605 had come the *Proficience and Advancement of Learning Divine and Humane*, in 1609 *De Sapientia Veterum*, in 1612 the augmented second edition of the *Essays*. Now, in 1620, he published in stately Latin his greatest work, the *Novum Organum*. Intended, as the title indicates, to supersede Aristotle's *Organum* after two thousand years of acceptance, it was Bacon's attempt to define the nature and provinces of human learning and to formulate a truly scientific technique of experiment and induction through which objective knowledge could be infallibly obtained. Proudly he presented a copy to King James. Within a few months King James was ready with his verdict on Bacon's book. Blasphemously he observed that, like the peace of God, 'it passeth all understanding'.[8] However, the British Solomon was probably in his heart rather proud of having so profound a philosopher for his Lord Chancellor, and about the time that he indulged in this quip he created Bacon Viscount St. Alban. Knowing the philosopher's love of pomp, he ceremoniously invested him with his robes and coronet, though other noblemen newly created or promoted at this time had to be content with merely receiving their patents.

When the new Viscount St. Alban returned home from his investiture on January 27, 1621, he stood at the highest point of his fortunes. Always owing money (he had even been briefly under arrest for debt in Elizabeth's time), he nevertheless enjoyed a very large income and spent it prodigally. Besides the splendours of York House in London, he maintained at St. Albans not one house but two. Gorhambury House, inherited from his father, he used as his winter house. A mile from it, connected by three parallel roads, stood Verulam House, a second great mansion which Bacon had built himself and used as his summer residence. Such, he felt, was true magnificence. It signified nothing that out of his hearing men spoke of the two great houses collectively as 'Bacon's Folly'. About the Lord Chancellor's mansions moved a host of servants wearing his livery and his boar crest. To him flocked suitors and clients.

> When his Lordship was at his Country-house at Gorhambery, St. Albans seemed as if the Court was there, so Nobly did He live.[9]

A favourite image that the Jacobeans had for life with its vicissitudes was the old figure, inherited from the Middle Ages, of Fortune and her wheel. At her whim the goddess turns her wheel, raising on its rim the fortunate man until he rejoices in prosperity and felicity at the top. Then caprice seizes Fortune again and, giving her wheel a further turn, she casts him down to disaster. The day when Fortune flicked her wheel to ruin Bacon was Thursday, March 15, 1621.

Disaster never struck out of a bluer sky. Bacon was secure in the favour of the King and Buckingham. His glittering new viscountcy was barely two months old. Beyond, an earldom seemed to beckon. True, Parliament was sitting and Parliament was no friend of Bacon, who consistently championed the royal prerogative at the cost of its own claims. True, Bacon had plenty of enemies in this parliament, among them Coke and Cranfield. True, aggressive capitalists, conspicuous among the M.P.s, were angry at the protection afforded bankrupts by Bacon's Court of Chancery. True, this parliament was in a nasty mood about the monopolists who hung like leeches on the nation's economy, and Bacon was conspicuous among the referees who had certified the desirability of various monopolies before the King had granted them. But seated in his Lord Chancellor's chair, with the King and Buckingham to support him, Bacon might well have regarded himself as parliament-proof. And so he should have been if he had exercised his great office with reasonable circumspection and caution. However, he had not, and on this fifteenth day of March, Sir Robert Phelips, rising to report for the Committee Appointed to Enquire into Abuses in the Courts of Justice, told a shocked House that his committee had received complaints of corruption against a person 'no less than the Lord Chancellor, a Man so endued with all Parts, both of Nature and Art, as that I will say no more of him; being not able to say enough'.[10] He then gave the gist of the charges that had been made against Bacon by two men, Christopher Aubrey and Edward Egerton, who claimed to have given him bribes. The House agreed that these charges should be investigated with 'as much Expedition as might be, because so great a Man's Honour is soiled', and called for a further report.

On March 17th the committee reported again. Nothing had been discovered to refute the charges. In fact, what further had been learned seemed only to confirm them. Rising after the committee's report had been received, one M.P. declared bitterly:

> Justice is the Fountain, the King the Head thereof, clear as the Waters of *Siloah*, pure as the River of *Damascus*: but there is a derivative Justice brought unto us by Channels, those are often muddy and more bitter than the Watters of Marah: Such Waters flow abundantly in Chancery.[11]

At the end of the debate, it was resolved to seek a conference with the Lords at which these charges might be forwarded 'without Prejudice or Opinion'. If the Lord Chancellor was to be tried for corruption, it was the House of Lords that would have to try him.

On March 20th the Commons learned that Lady Wharton had presented evidence that Bacon had accepted bribes from her. The next day brought further disclosures for John Churchill, whom Bacon had recently suspended as Registrar of the Court of Chancery because of malfeasance, had revenged himself by supplying the Commons committee with details of case after case in which the Lord Chancellor had improperly accepted money:

1. In the Cause betwixt *Hull* and *Holeman, Hull* gave or lent my Lord one thousand pound since the Suit began.
2. In the Cause between *Wroth* and *Manwaring*, there were one hundred Pieces given, of which *Hunt* had 20 *l.*
3. *Hoddy* gave a Jewel which was thought to be worth 500 *l.* but he himself said it was a Trifle of a hundred or two hundred Pound Price: It was presented to the Lord Chancellor by Sir *Thomas Peryn* and Sir *Henry Holmes.*
4. In the Cause between *Peacock* and *Reynell*, there was much Money given on both sides.
5. In the Cause of *Barker* and *Bill, Barker* said he was 800 *l.* out in Gifts since this Suit began.[12]

'Since this Suit began'—that was the damning phrase. The custom of the age permitted persons to give valuable gifts to the King's officers and justices in order to create a general atmosphere of good will, but even by the lax standards of the Jacobeans it was unforgivable for a judge, let alone the Lord Chancellor, to accept gifts from a person who was a party in a case either pending or actually before him. Yet this was what Bacon had done. There was enough evidence to convict him ten times over.

What was the hapless Bacon doing while these disclosures were being made? At first he attempted in half-hearted fashion to get Christopher Aubrey to withdraw his petition to the Commons which had started the whole investigation. He only made his own position worse by doing so. He got some comfort from visits by Buckingham and various court lords who appeared to be rallying to his support. To Gondomar, however, he wrote that he would rather not be visited, making the wry quip, 'he was now neerer to his [Gondomar's] religion then ever, for that he began to beleve and feele a purgatorie'. At times the Lord Chancellor rallied his spirits, but in the end he relapsed into one of his not infrequent psychosomatic illnesses. From his sickbed he wrote, on March 19th, to the Lords. In its way the letter was a masterpiece. Without ever saying he was innocent—conscience could not let him unequivocably say that—Bacon contrived to give the impression that this was the letter of an innocent man eager to defend himself. Actually it was a tissue of skilful ambiguities as consonant with guilt as with innocence—'I would be glad to preserve my

L*

Honour and Fame *as far as I am worthy*. . . . I shall not by the Grace of God *trick up* an Innocency.'[13]

In the end Bacon threw himself on the mercy of the Lords. Racked by fearful migraine headaches, he drafted a letter of submission which Prince Charles delivered to them on April 24th. It was a tortuous document, mingling citations from Livy with eulogies of King James, declaring that Bacon was ready to resign the Seal, and asking 'that my penitent Submission may be my Sentence, and the Loss of the Seal my Punishment'.[14]

If Bacon had really hoped to get off so lightly, he was badly mistaken. As their Lordships were quick to note, while Bacon had spoken expansively of making 'clear Submission and Confession', he had, in fact, confessed to no particular sin, least of all bribery and corruption. Moreover, their Lordships were affronted that a culprit, even if a Lord Chancellor, should presume to propose his own punishment. Sternly the Lords informed Bacon that they could not accept a 'doubtful answer', and that he must inform them 'directly and presently [immediately] whether his Lordship will make his Confession, or stand upon his Defence'.

The sands had run out for Bacon. The infinite subtlety, the fine art of saying one thing while seeming to say something else, the ambiguities and the evasions could serve him no longer. He faced the facts and wrote a second letter:

> I do plainly and ingenuously confess, that I am guilty of Corruption, and do renounce all Defence, and put my self upon the Grace and Mercy of your Lordships.[15]

There followed a lengthy statement in which Bacon dealt one by one with the particular cases of corruption with which he was charged. Some he admitted, others he sought to refute or extenuate.

Bacon's second submission proved acceptable to the Lords. They took the precaution, however, of despatching a delegation to York House to demand of Bacon whether it was his hand that had signed the letter and whether he would stand by it. To them the stricken man replied: 'My Lords, it is my Act, my Hand, my Heart; I beseech your Lordships to be merciful to a broken Reed.' His answer being reported to the House of Lords, it was resolved to ask the King to sequester the Seal. Accordingly on May 1st Bacon was visited by Pembroke, Lennox, Arundel, and Lord Treasurer Montagu. They had come from King James to demand the Great Seal of England. Handing it over, Bacon cried in his anguish a polished parallelism: *Deus dedit; culpa mea perdidit*.[16]

It remained only to pass sentence on the disgraced man. On May 3rd, the Commons were called to the bar of the House of Lords. From Sir James Ley, the Lord Chief Justice, they learned the verdict passed on Francis Bacon:

Upon Complaint of the Commons against the L: Vicount St. Alban this high Court hath proceded to a Judicall examinacon upon oath and hath thereby and by his owne confession found him guiltie of the Crimes and corruptions of like nature. And therefore this high court having warned him to attend, and having receyved his excuse of not attending by reason of infirmitie and sicknesse which he protested was not feined or else he would most willingly have attended doth nevertheless thincke fitt to pro-ceede to Judgement and therefore this high Court doth adjudge.

The L. Vicount St. Alban late Lord Chancellor shall undergo fine and Ransom of fortie thousand pounds.

That he shalbe imprisoned in the Tower during the Kings pleasure.

That he shalbe uncapable to beare any office, place or imployment in the state or commonwealth.

Never to sit in Parliament nor to come neere the verge of the Court.[17]

Had it not been for the votes of the bishops, and of Buckingham and his friends, there would have been one clause more, stripping Bacon of his titles of viscount, baron and knight.

Here, clear, unequivocal, and inevitable, is the verdict of Bacon's peers. But of course we want to know more. Was the man who wrote the *Essays*, the *New Atlantis*, the *Novum Organum*, one thing in his theories and another, completely despicable, in his practice? Away from his books was he only a corrupt politician? What really lay behind his conviction? How did Bacon come to accept these bribes? To these questions there are a number of answers.

Bacon's apologists have made much of his indolent carelessness where money was concerned. To him, constantly preoccupied with ideas, money in itself was of little interest. Anyone who has known a college professor to use the cheques which reach him in the mail as bookmarks instead of cashing them has had some acquaintance with Bacon's type. Frequently, of course, he had to have money. Impatiently he took it wherever he could get it, then forgot about it, immersed once more in his schemes, projects and intrigues. He seems at times to have had only the dimmest awareness of what was going on about him. An illuminating story tells how a gentle-man waiting in Bacon's study at Gorhambury for an interview saw first one and then another of his Lordship's people step in, pull out a drawer where a heap of money lay loose, fill their pockets, and depart. When he told Bacon what he had seen, the only response was a sad little shake of the head and, 'Sir, I cannot help myself.'[18] So it was that, while Bacon's mind was engaged with the interpretation of law, the niceties of government, or the articulation of the structure of human knowledge, his servants swindled him and the officers of the Chancery, lacking surveillance, grew rich through abuse of their positions. Probably many of the bribes paid to Bacon never reached him. At the hearings it came out that often it was some member of Bacon's household—Sir George Hastings particularly—

who suggested to litigants that they pay, through him, a gift that would make a friend of the Lord Chancellor. It seems highly probable that many a sum so accepted never reached the Lord Chancellor.

It would be nice if the whole matter of Bacon's 'corruption' could be explained away by these two things, his own habitual carelessness where money was concerned, and the deceptions practised by his servants. Unfortunately, the scandal cannot be disposed of so tidily. In one instance after another, Bacon must have known that gifts were coming to him from persons who were parties in cases before him in Chancery. At times the money was put directly into the Lord Chancellor's hand. Lady Wharton paid her money directly to Bacon and, to make sure that she got the ruling for which she was paying, she brought along with her Churchill, the Chancery Registrar.

Mention of Lady Wharton brings us to a remarkable feature of the whole business. Even when people had paid Bacon and paid him well, his decisions as a judge could still go against them. Having accepted Lady Wharton's purse, he gave Churchill the instructions that she wanted him to issue. After she had paid another £300, he entered a decree for her in the case. But in the end he reversed himself and she had nothing at all for her money. After Christopher Aubrey had borrowed £100 from a usurer to speed a case with the Chancellor, Bacon passed 'a murdering Order' against him. Sometimes Bacon did rule for the party which had paid him, but one finds oneself suspecting that his decision would have been the same if no money had been paid. In fact, it appears that when Bacon as Lord Chancellor finally rendered judgment, he took no account of money which he had received and delivered true justice. He could truthfully declare to the King, 'I had no bribe or reward in my eye or thought, when I pronounced any sentence or order.'[19] *He had accepted bribes but he had not been bribed*. It was a nice distinction, but a very real one. To Bacon it probably afforded satisfaction.

Significant in this connection is an incident which occurred during the transactions between Bacon and Edward Egerton. By mortgaging his estate, Egerton had got money for Bacon. When Sir George Hastings and Sir Richard Young presented it to the Lord Chancellor, they used the face-saving fiction that this was a gift to show Egerton's appreciation for what Bacon had done for him when he was Attorney-General. Bacon protested that the sum was too great. In the end he accepted it, however, and sent Egerton a message 'that he did not only enrich him, but laid a Tie on him to assist him in all just and lawful Business'.[20] 'In all *just and lawful* Business!' Egerton, when he received the message, no doubt thought that the Lord Chancellor was a hypocritical old fox. Very likely Bacon knew that Egerton would think that he was a hypocritical old fox. But

Bacon himself knew that he really meant what he had said and could rejoice in the preservation of his integrity. It seems doubtful that the moral aspects of such double dealing worried him. Probably he reasoned that if the fool Egerton thought he could buy a Lord Chancellor who was the son of Sir Nicholas Bacon, he deserved to be mulcted—certainly he himself, getting deeper and deeper into debt for all his magnificence, needed the money. Why not spoil the Egyptians?

Others could hardly be expected to divine the exquisite fineness of the Lord Chancellor's distinctions. When Bacon found Egerton's suit not 'just and lawful' and gave judgment against him, Egerton, instead of recalling what Bacon had said, felt double-crossed. Joining with Aubrey, who believed himself similarly bilked, he sent a petition of complaint to the House of Commons, where it was shortly joined by the petition of the outraged Lady Wharton. It is one of the ironies of the whole affair that if Bacon had really been corrupt and had given these people the unjust decrees for which they had paid, he might never have been brought to trial.

In the end Bacon's position was quite impossible. How could he convince a cynical House of Lords that he was essentially innocent, and that all that he had done was to let people who thought they could buy him delude themselves and waste their money. The clever tissue of rationalization with which he had protected himself broke, and he realized the truth. He had broken faith, even if with rascals, and he had misused his office for personal benefit. He deserved to lose the Seal. Summing up the whole matter in his commonplace book a few years later he wrote, 'I was the justest judge that was in England these fifty years. But it was the justest censure in parliament that was these two hundred years.'[21]

One at least among his contemporaries may have realized the truth about Bacon—his king. James had a mind which was almost as tortuous as that of his former Lord Chancellor. Perhaps, in consequence, he understood what had happened. He was, in any case, tolerant and merciful. (One feels that he had almost come to expect corruption in his ministers.) Whatever the reason, he proved singularly indulgent to Bacon. Within a few days of Bacon's commitment to the Tower, King James, heeding his desperate appeals, gave him his release. As for the fine levied against him, His Majesty turned this over to trustees who would administer it on Bacon's behalf, thus giving him unexpected protection from his creditors. Finally, within six months of Bacon's conviction, he granted him a pardon exempting him from all penalties except his exclusion from office. Early in 1622 he gave him a pension of £1,200 a year to make up, in part at least, for the income lost with his offices.

Resuming the elegance of his old mode of life, Bacon turned to literary activities to occupy his new-found leisure. Typically, he seized the opportunity for some skilful flattering of his sovereign. Writing to James, he expressed a hope that His Majesty would assign some task for his pen. In letters to Buckingham he used all the blandishments of his highly polished sycophancy, seeking to resume his career in politics. In vain the honeyed sentences. Bacon remained excluded from office. There was nothing left for him but literature, philosophy and science, until an ill-timed experiment in refrigerating a chicken brought him to his death in 1626.

The world very shortly was made aware of another failure in Bacon's life. In 1606 he had married, inevitably with enormous display, the rich City heiress Alice Barnham. Ten days after Bacon died she married her gentleman usher. Bacon's will reveals that some months earlier he had felt that she had offended unforgivably against him.

So ended Francis Bacon, the incredibly active and subtle mind stilled at last. Disliked and distrusted by many, though always clinging tenuously to principle, he had sought vainly in the company of catamites and in the empty glories of pomp and magnificence for the satisfactions which more normal and less gifted men find in the pattern of quite commonplace lives. For all its achievements, his had been a lonely and misguided life. A fitting epitaph could have been provided by a dramatist not to be born for almost three centuries: 'The man never knew who he was.' Bacon himself put it rather differently: 'I may truly say, my soul hath been a stranger in the course of my pilgrimage.'[22]

CHAPTER XXV

Clergy at Court

DIRECTLY ACROSS the Thames from Whitehall stood Lambeth Palace, chief of the houses of the Archbishop of Canterbury. It was fortunate that a medieval archbishop, seeking to escape from the meddling monks of Canterbury, had acquired Lambeth. Otherwise, it would have been necessary for the post-Reformation primates of the Church of England to secure some similarly located property where the spiritual head of the Church could have ready access to its political head, the monarch.

Whitehall was as important as Lambeth to many a rising Jacobean cleric. Matters of doctrine or the day-to-day running of the vast ecclesiastical machine might take a man to Lambeth, but if he were ambitious for a deanery or a bishopric, his shortest path was by way of Whitehall and a chaplaincy to some great lord, if not to the King himself.

The occupant of Lambeth when King James came to the English throne was John Whitgift, Elizabeth's 'little black husband'. Old and grey now, though still implacable in maintaining the claims of the Church, he depended more and more upon Richard Bancroft, the robust and energetic Bishop of London. Too few of the Church's dignitaries were of the calibre of Whitgift and Bancroft. Queen Elizabeth's spoilation of the Church through the sale of bishoprics and deaneries, one of the forgotten scandals of her reign, had seriously impaired the quality of the hierarchy. Indicative of how Elizabeth made her bishops pay for promotion by transferring episcopal estates to her or her favourites was the jest of the Bishop of Llandaff. That merry prelate liked to refer to himself as the Bishop of Aff, explaining to everybody that his diocese's land had long since been given away. When Elizabeth died, she left an episcopacy made up largely of mediocre careerists, 'court bishops' who would spend much of their time in obsequious attendance on King James, hoping for translation to richer sees.

Whitgift and his brother archbishop, Hutton of York, awaited with anxiety the coming of King James. Could the equipoise which had held the Church midway between Rome and Geneva be preserved? It was all very well to maintain that the new king would be only the political, not the spiritual, head of the Church. With an amateur theologian like James on the throne, the distinction would probably prove a nice one indeed. Catholics, Puritans and Anglicans, all were out to win the royal ear. Watson, the Catholic priest, had sought to negotiate with James while Elizabeth was still alive. A Puritan Northamptonshire squire was the third man out of England to reach James with news of her demise. Close on his heels arrived Dr. Thomas Neville, Dean of Canterbury.

It did not take long for the Church of England to find which way King James inclined. First to be laid to rest were their apprehensions about the Puritans. No sooner had James arrived in England than Puritan petitions began to pour in upon him. Chief of these was the 'Millenary Petition', supposedly representing the views of a thousand Church of England clergymen of mildly Puritan leanings. This was a moderate and reasonable document. It asked that the sign of the cross should no longer be used in baptism, that the ring be abolished from the marriage ceremony, and that the use of surplice and cap be made optional. The petitioners were chiefly concerned that there should be more preaching and fewer pluralists. After the Millenary Petition came others such as 'The Memorial of Abuses' and 'A Complaint in the Name of the Meaner Sort of the Laity', and one from that peculiar little sect, 'The Family of Love'. The result of all this activity was that King James decided to grant the conference on matters of religion requested in the 'Memorial of Abuses', and the Hampton Court Conference was accordingly convened.

To this conference came the King and his Privy Council, four representatives of the Puritans, and the Archbishop of Canterbury supported by eight bishops, eight deans, and two doctors of divinity. On the first day of the conference, January 14, 1604, James met with the bishops to propound his reasons for summoning the conference and to set forth its agenda. Three things, said the King, were to be considered: the objections being advanced against the Book of Common Prayer, the abuses alleged in the Church's practice of excommunication, and the problem of finding suitable clergy to serve in Ireland. His Majesty then announced that there were various things about which he himself required satisfaction. Searchingly he questioned the bishops. What did they mean by speaking of the service of 'confirmation'? Did they mean a 'confirming of baptism', implying that without confirmation baptism was of no validity? If they did, the very name was 'plainly blasphemous'. Then there was the matter of absolution. 'I know not how it is used in your church,' declared James, 'but have heard it likened to the pope's pardon'. (There must have been raised eyebrows when the titular head of the Church of England spoke of it as 'your church'.) Proceeding to the matter of baptism itself, King James made clear his objections to letting midwives and other lay persons perform the sacrament. The bishops, in their answers to the royal cross-examination, were able to reassure the King on some points and arrive at understandings with him on others. Nevertheless, they must have felt pretty badly bruised at the end of the day and could hardly have looked forward to the next session.

The conference resumed on January 16th. This time a Scottish divine, Patrick Galloway, minister of Perth, joined the deliberations, while young Prince Henry entered and sat on a stool by his father. For the first time the four Puritan delegates were admitted and their spokesman, Dr. Reynolds, Dean of Lincoln, began to set forth their position. It was a severe strain on the equanimity of the authoritarian Anglican prelates to have to listen to Reynolds calling into question their canons and proceedings. Was it for this that they had harried the Puritans these many years? When Reynolds declared that the twenty-fifth of the Thirty-nine Articles was self-contradictory, Bishop Bancroft could stand it no longer. Angrily he called the King's attention to the ancient canon, *Schismatici contra episcopos non sunt audiendi* (Schismatics are not to be heard when they speak against bishops). King James put Bancroft in his place, and Reynolds continued with the presentation of his case.

If the conference had not gone very well for the bishops so far, things shortly improved for them. Reynolds had brought up the question as to who should conduct the 'confirmation' or, as King James preferred to call it, the 'examination' of those who had reached years of discretion. Should it be left to the local parson or performed, as in the past, by the bishops? James took this as his cue for a statement which established once and for all his championship of episcopacy:

> I approve the calling and use of bishops in the church and it is my aphorism, 'No bishop, no king'; nor intend I to take confirmation from the bishops.[1]

From here on the Puritans fared worse and worse. Reynolds, who was falling far short of what had been expected of him, advanced one of those stupid little quibbles to which the Puritans were always so prone. It was not enough, he complained, that the Thirty-seventh Article declared 'The Bishop of Rome hath no authority in this land'—the statement should be enlarged to say 'nor ought to have any'. The response to this hair-splitting might have been anticipated: 'Here passed some pleasant discourse betwixt the king and the lords about puritans.'

As the day wore on the King more and more championed the Church of England. He was in his element. Surrounded by admiring lords and applauding bishops, he pleasantly bantered with the Puritans. When Reynolds protested against the line in the marriage service which read 'With my body I thee worship', James indulgently explained he too had once thought that 'worship' signified divine adoration but he had learned that in England, as in the phrase 'a gentleman of worship', the word meant nothing more than 'honour'.

> As for you, Dr. Reynolds, many men speak of Robin Hood, who never shot in his bow. If you had a good wife yourself, you would think all worship and honour you could do her were well bestowed on her.[2]

When another of the Puritans, Knewstubs, blurted out, 'I take exception at the wearing of the surplice, a kind of garment used by the priests of Isis', James pretended great interest. He said that he had understood the objection was that it was 'a rag of popery'. Since England did not border upon Egypt, he thought there was little danger of surpliced Anglican clergy being mistaken for priests of Isis and suggested that the surplice be kept 'for comeliness sake'.

It would have been well for the Puritans if the King could have been kept in this mood of amused good humour. In the end, though, disaster overtook them. Reynolds was dealing with the manner in which theological arguments should be settled among the clergy. He thought these matters could first be canvassed in 'prophesyings' in the rural deaneries, then referred to the archdeacons on their visitations and finally, if need be, 'to the episcopal synod, where the bishop with his presbytery shall determine such points'. By 'presbytery' the learned doctor meant only what the word means etymologically, an assembly of priests. For James, after his Scottish experience, 'presbytery' was a fighting word. Furiously he retorted, 'If you aim at a Scottish presbytery, it agreeth as well with monarchy as God and the Devil. Then Jack, and Tom, and Will, and Dick, shall meet and censure me and my council.' On and on the angry sentences followed. Turning to the surprised but delighted bishops he exclaimed: 'My lords . . . if once you were out, and they [the nonconformists] in, I know what would become of my supremacy; for *no bishop, no king.*' Coldly he asked Dr. Reynolds, 'Well, doctor, have you anything else to say?'

> *Dr. Reynolds :* No more, if it please your majesty.
> *His Majesty :* If this be all your party hath to say, I will make them conform themselves, or else I will harry them out of the land, or else do worse.[3]

On the final day of the conference, January 18th, the King conferred with the bishops and other divines representing conformity, and a group of ecclesiastical lawyers. It was agreed to make certain changes in the Prayer Book, in the powers of the bishops, and in the workings of the Church courts. In connection with this last, there was an extremely touchy matter—the *ex officio* oath, by which the ecclesiastical Court of High Commission forced those who appeared before it to answer all questions administered *ex officio* by the judge, quite apart from the formal charge. This oath, which often forced a man to testify against himself, had long been unpopular. Even Elizabeth's Burghley had declared that it savoured of the Roman Inquisition. At the final session of the Hampton Court Conference, King James gave his verdict on the *ex officio* oath. He said that its use was wise and profitable. At this, the cup of the bishops overflowed.

> *Archbishop of Canterbury :* Undoubtedly your majesty speaks by the special assistance of God's Spirit.
> *Bishop of London :* I protest my heart melteth with joy, that Almighty God, of his singular mercy, hath given us such a king, as since Christ's time, the like hath not been.[4]

Sir John Harington, subsequently commenting upon both the bishops' praises and the somewhat indelicate language that His Majesty had occasionally used at the conference, declared, 'I wist not what they mean; but the spirit was rather foule mouthede.'

At the end of the conference the four Puritan representatives were informed of the decisions which had been reached. They accepted them with the best grace they could, and Dr. Reynolds promised that they would all work for the quiet of the Church.

So ended the Hampton Court Conference. Its greatest achievement, almost incidental, was the undertaking of a new translation of the Bible. Out of this in 1611 came the famous King James Version. The most important of its other results was that, for once and for all, King James's relationship to the episcopacy and to English Puritanism had been defined. In the next few years the more irreconcilable of the Puritans were expelled from their livings in the Church. Their number was not great. Bancroft, who had succeeded Whitgift as Archbishop of Canterbury, agreed that moderate men were not to be goaded into defiance so long as they made some sort of compliance with the Prayer Book and the canons. From this time, the Puritans counted less and less as a force within the Church of England, and turned more and more to sects outside it. Realizing that they could hope for nothing more from the King, they proceeded to that alliance with Parliament which ultimately proved so disastrous to both King and Church.

The case of the Catholics was somewhat different. James had no use for popery, but did not wish to persecute papists for purely doctrinal differences. Although not proclaiming toleration, he did what he could to mitigate the harshness of the Elizabethan anti-recusant measures. The result was that Romanist priests streamed into the country and began to preach openly. In consternation, the Church of England, Parliament, and most of the Privy Council united to urge repressive policies upon the King. Reluctantly he gave way. With the subsequent tightening of measures against recusancy, the English Catholics saw the mirage of toleration fading before their eyes. Financial ruin, if nothing worse, seemed to confront them and their families. The more fanatic turned to the murderous Gunpowder Plot and succeeded only in uniting King and nation in one great wave of anti-Catholic feeling.

In the wake of the Gunpowder Plot came a mass of anti-Catholic legislation from Parliament. One of the new statutes provided an Oath of Allegiance as an instrument by which loyal Catholics could be distinguished from traitorous ones. It did not require papists to abjure the spiritual authority of the Pope. What they were required to swear was:

> ... That our Soveraigne Lord King JAMES, is lawfull King of this Realme, and of all other his Majesties Dominions and Countreyes: And that the *Pope* neither of himselfe, nor by any authority of the Church or Sea of *Rome*, or by any other meanes with any other, hath any power or authoritie to depose the King, or to dispose of any of his Majesties Kingdomes or Dominions, or to authorize any forreigne Prince to invade or annoy him or his Countreys, or to discharge any of his Subjects of their Allegiance.... [5]

Those taking the oath were required to swear also that the Pope had no power to absolve them from it, and that they themselves swore it freely, without any 'Equivocation, or mentall evasion, or secret reservation whatsoever'.

What made the Oath of Allegiance as unpalatable as it proved to be for the English Catholics was the violence of the language. There was a needless offensiveness when the oath read:

> And I doe further sweare, That I doe from my heart abhorre, detest and abjure as impious and Hereticall, this damnable doctrine and position, That Princes which be excommunicated or deprived by the *Pope*, may be deposed or murthered by their Subjects or any other whatsoever.

In spite of this clause a great many English Catholics, following the lead of Blackwell the arch-priest, took the oath. When there arrived a breve from Pope Paul V instructing them not to subscribe, they defended their action by alleging that the breve was a forgery. Angrily the Pope sent out a second breve reaffirming his ban on the oath. This arrived in England accompanied by an open letter from Cardinal Bellarmine to Blackwell declaring that, no matter how craftily the Oath of Allegiance might have been worded,

> ... it tends to this end, that the Authoritie of the head of the Church in *England*, may bee transferred from the successour of *S. Peter*, to the successour of King *Henry the eight*. [6]

Closing his letter, Bellarmine recalled how Bishop Fisher and Sir Thomas More had died for the faith, and urged Blackwell to crown his own life with martyrdom.

Within a few months Pope and Cardinal had their reply from the pen of

King James himself. His *Apologie for the Oath of Allegiance* was published anonymously, but its authorship was an open secret. In his retorts King James showed himself as usual both pithy and acute. Mockingly he invited Bellarmine to affirm the propositions counter to those in the oath: that James was not a lawful King, that 'the *Pope* may give leave to my Subjects to offer violence to my Person', 'that this Oath is to be taken with Equivocation, mentall evasion, or secret reservation'. Citing historical precedents left and right, King James declared the temporal rights of kings and recorded infringements by the Papacy. At one point, dropping the matter of the Oath of Allegiance, James launched a general attack against Bellarmine's integrity as a controversialist. Heaven only knows how many Anglican bishops, deans, professors of theology, and court chaplains had been set to combing through Bellarmine's works for discrepancies but, drawing upon their researches, His Majesty was able to come up triumphantly with a long list of passages in which the Cardinal had apparently been inconsistent in his writings.

In attacking Bellarmine, King James had crossed swords with the greatest Catholic controversialist of the day, the 'Goliath of the Roman Church'. The Cardinal was not a man to let the challenge go unheeded. In 1608 he published his *Responsio*. Since James's *Apologie* had been published anonymously, Bellarmine fathered his reply upon his chaplain, Matthew Tortus.

In 1609 came the English counter-attack, with King James bringing out a new edition of his *Apologie*, this time putting his name to it and prefacing it with a fresh piece of royal polemics: *A Premonition to all Christian Monarchies, Free Princes and States*. The 'Premonition' [advance warning] was intended to put all Christian rulers, Protestant or Catholic, on guard against the temporal encroachments of the popes. Sumptuously bound copies were sent abroad to the English ambassadors for presentation to the courts to which they were accredited. Those in Catholic countries found the 'King's book' an acute embarrassment. Henri IV accepted it but threw it down on a table, exclaiming, in the best aristocratic tradition, that the writing of books was no fit business for a king. The King of Spain, horrified by reports of what James had written, sent word to Sir Charles Cornwallis begging him not to put him to the necessity of refusing it. The Duke of Savoy refused his copy outright. In Milan the royal opus was cut to shreds, while in Florence the Grand Duke was reported to have burned his copy. The Venetian Senate decided after anxious deliberation that the Doge should accept a copy, which would then be immediately locked up. The book's circulation in Venice was flatly prohibited. Sir Henry Wotton, tired of his Venetian post and eager to get home to England, gladly seized the opportunity, declared his king insulted, and resigned on the spot.

It was beneath the dignity of the King of England to answer directly in his *Premonition* Bellarmine's *Responsio*, a work ostensibly written by a mere chaplain even though everyone knew it to be Bellarmine's own. Accordingly, someone else had to deal with the *Responsio*. The royal choice fell upon Lancelot Andrewes.

A gifted preacher, a profound scholar, and a great and good man, Bishop Andrewes was one of the lights of the Church of England. His learning was great. Even in the midst of his duties as a bishop and a privy councillor, he insisted that, apart from prayer, his mornings be devoted entirely to his books. The saintliness of his life shone forth amid the worldliness of most of his fellow churchmen. After twice refusing bishoprics which Queen Elizabeth had offered him with unworthy conditions of alienation of diocesan property, he had become in 1601 Dean of Westminster. His sermons in the Abbey were famous as much for their moving delivery as for their substance. To King James's credit, he early recognized the worth of Andrewes. In 1605 he not only made him Bishop of Chichester and his almoner, but established him as the chief preacher to himself and his court.

Set to his task by the King, 'the good and gentle Andrewes' drafted the reply to Bellarmine. Punning on the name of the chaplain Tortus, he called his work *Tortura Torti*. Published in 1609, it brought a prompt retort from Bellarmine in his *Apologia pro Responsio Sua*, in which he acknowledged the *Responsio* to be his own and replied to the King's *Premonition*. King James lost no time in setting Andrewes, aided by the famous Isaac Casaubon who had been brought over from France, compiling a *Responsio ad Apologiam Cardinalis Bellarmini*.

Meanwhile the uproar provoked by the King's writings had sent half the theologians in Europe to their ink-pots. In support of Bellarmine, Martin Becanus, another of the big guns of the Roman Church, thundered from Mainz his *Refutatio Torturae Torti*, which he followed up with treatise after treatise more. From Ingolstadt came a blast from the Jesuit Gretser. From Spain another Jesuit, Suarez, volleyed forth his *Defensio Fidei Catholicae*. Lessius and Scioppius added to the clamour against James. Eudaemon, Cofteteus, Peleterius, joined them. Meanwhile Protestant theologians were rallying to the support of the embattled king. From Thorn in Germany Professor Conrad Graser led off with his *Plaga Regia*. At Whitehall, or Theobalds, or Royston, there were comings and goings of clerics. Even amid his cherished hunting, James took time out for earnest conference with chaplains and bishops. Proofs, arguments, retorts were urgently debated. From the printing presses poured the Anglican replies. Battles developed within the battle. Barlow, Bishop of Lincoln, attacked the Jesuit Parsons in his *Answer to a Catholicke Englishman*, only to have Parsons come back at him in *A Discussion of the Answer of Mr.*

William Barlow. William Tooker, Dean of Lichfield, ardent to distinguish himself before the gaze of his king, took on the mighty Martin Becanus in his *Duellum . . . cum M.B.*, only to find himself confronted by M.B.'s *Duellum . . . cum Gulielmo Tooker*.

On and on the great debate continued, each side with its quibbles, its mockeries, and its acute turning of the other fellow's phrases while ignoring all that could not be refuted in his arguments. Today the old Latin books lie gathering dust in college libraries, the great fight forgotten which once was fought for the minds of men before blood arbitrated the issue in the Thirty Years War.

Not all of King James's polemical writings were directed against the pretensions of the Pope. In Holland the works of Arminius had been winning many persons away from the extreme Calvinist view of predestination and divine grace, and persuading them to adopt the position later to be taken by the English Methodists. King James, despite his alliance with the Anglican bishops, was at heart a Scottish Calvinist, and he considered Arminianism a shocking heresy. When Arminius died in October 1609, the King, through his ambassador at The Hague, tried to keep his disciple Conrad Vorstius from succeeding him as professor of theology at Leyden. When the Dutch pointed out that they could not dismiss the man after bringing him and his family from Germany, James was furious. In vain did Caron, the Dutch agent, try to soothe the King. Heading off to Royston, James relieved his feelings with his pen, composing in French a seventy-page treatise, *Declaration du Roy, touchant la faict de C. Vorstius*, which was published with Latin and English translations.

To give further emphasis to his disapproval of heretics, King James decided to let two English Unitarians be burned at the stake. These men, the last in England to die for their faith, were Legate and Wightman. Wightman was a poor ignorant creature. Legate, on the other hand, was a man of real intelligence whom the King had found a stimulating opponent when, closeted with him, he had tried to win him from his Arianism. However, because of his running battle with the Catholic theologians and his irritation concerning Vorstius, James was bent on a striking demonstration of his own orthodoxy. He allowed the old medieval writ of *de heretico comburendo* to be issued for the last time. On March 18, 1612, Legate died amid the flames at Smithfield. On April 11th Wightman met the same agonizing end at Lichfield. It was indicative of the changing temper of the age that there was some outcry at these burnings. James himself may have regretted his act. In the future he commuted death sentences for heresy to life imprisonment.

Some men attributed King James's vehemence against Vorstius and the Arminians to the influence of his new Archbishop of Canterbury. Bancroft, that harrier of the Puritans, had died in November 1610 and everybody had expected that Lancelot Andrewes would succeed him as primate. It was therefore with great surprise that the court learned that the new archbishop was to be Dr. Abbot, Bishop of Lincoln. Combining a certain easy familiarity of manner with a basic conscientiousness which at times shaded over into gloom, Abbot was a left-wing Protestant. His appointment may have been a deliberate move to keep moderate Puritans from leaving the Church and joining the more violent in sects opposed to it. No fanatic where the episcopacy was concerned, Abbot viewed the bishops as a set of superintendents from among the clergy. Holding these views and being basically Calvinist in his theology, he got on well with Scottish Presbyterian ministers. For this reason he had been signally successful in 1608 in reconciling the Scots to restoration of their episcopate. Abbot's patron was King James's old crony George Home, Earl of Dunbar. According to James, his reason for making Abbot archbishop was that Dunbar, just before his death in January 1611, had recommended him for the post.

Abbot proved to be a good, though not an outstanding, archbishop. Laud and the High Church group beginning to muster about him loathed Abbot as a latitudinarian, but the archbishop had courage where principles were concerned. When King James wanted to permit a group of his courtiers to use legal quibbles to divert into their own pockets the munificent bequests left by Thomas Sutton to found the Charterhouse school and almshouse, Abbot contrived to save the money for the intended charity. In doing so, he skilfully avoided direct conflict with the King. When direct conflict could not be avoided, as in his opposition to the Essex divorce, he had the courage to stand up to the King. His policies were stalwartly Protestant. More than anyone else, it was he who pushed through the marriage of Princess Elizabeth to the Palsgrave Frederick. The match between Prince Charles and the Spanish Infanta, so dear to James in his later years, was utterly repugnant to Abbot. In consequence he found himself more and more a lonely voice in an increasingly pro-Catholic court.

To increase his difficulties, Archbishop Abbot had the misfortune to kill a man. This disaster overtook him in July 1621. At the time he was staying with his friend Lord Zouch at the latter's country house at Bramshill in Hampshire. During the day's hunting, Abbot loosed an arrow from a crossbow just as a keeper ran forward to drive the deer towards him. The arrow severed an artery in the man's arms and he bled to death on the spot. Appalled, the Archbishop wrote to the King reporting what had happened. James sent a kindly reply that this kind of accident could happen to any man. He recalled that he himself had once killed a keeper's horse, and that Queen Anne had shot one of his dogs. The situations were not analogous, of course, and James was reported to have observed, 'I should think it a signe that God loved me not, if I killed a man by chance.'[7] On the whole, however, His Majesty was sympathetic and understanding. Abbot, after arranging for the care of the widow and children of his victim, retired for a while to the almshouse he had recently founded at his native Guildford.

The accident had come at a particularly bad time. Four bishops-elect were awaiting consecration. Three of them—Cary of Exeter, Williams of Lincoln, and Abbot's old enemy, Laud of St. David's—begged the King to spare them the imputations that might arise from consecration by an archbishop with blood on his hands. James accepted their petition and they were consecrated by other bishops.

A commission was appointed to investigate the status of the archbishop. The main point to be decided was whether or not he had any right to be hunting in the first place. St. Jerome, as Chaucer knew, had declared that 'hunters ben nat hooly men'. There was much quoting of Church fathers, councils and synods. In the end, the commission decided by a slender majority that the archbishop was not culpable, and Abbot was granted his pardon by the King. It later transpired that the man who had saved Abbot, deserting his fellow bishops to vote with the secular judges and lawyers to clear him, was Lancelot Andrewes. As for Abbot, the rest of his life he fasted monthly on the Tuesday of the keeper's death.

One of the most interesting events during Abbot's archiepiscopate was the arrival in England of Marco Antonio de Dominis, Archbishop of Spalato, who had defected from the Church of Rome to the Church of England. His coming created an enormous stir and was a source of much self-congratulation on the part of King James and his bishops, especially since His Majesty was able to persuade himself that his own *Apologie for the Oath of Allegiance* was responsible for the archbishop's conversion.

Marco Antonio de Dominis was a brilliant but somewhat naïve intellectual. Educated by the Jesuits, he lectured in mathematics at the University of Padua before becoming successively Professor of Rhetoric, of Logic, and of Philosophy at Brescia. Recruited for the episcopacy, De Dominis was shocked, upon leaving the rarefied atmosphere of the universities, to see how the Church dealt with the common people. He was disgusted at the Church's exploitation of the laity, and recoiled from the gross superstitions which he found it encouraging. Moreover, he soon became angered by what appeared to him to be papal infringements upon his own rights as primate of Dalmatia and Croatia. A Venetian himself, governing an arch-diocese within the territories ruled by Venice, he was furious when the Pope passed an interdict against Venice in 1606. Turning to the Church Fathers, he became convinced that the Bishop of Rome had originally enjoyed no more rights than any other bishop. Long interested in the reunification of Christendom, De Dominis decided that Rome itself, by its unwarranted claims and blind insistence upon orthodoxy in minor matters, was chiefly responsible for the schisms which had rent the Church. Leaving his archdiocese, he came to Venice to campaign for reforms within the Roman Church.

In Venice, De Dominis brought himself and the books which he had written to the attention of Sir Dudley Carleton, the English ambassador. To him he declared that he wished to live and die a member of the Church of England, which he was convinced represented the purest form of Christianity. All that he desired was sufficiency to live, one servant, and £200 per annum.

Carleton's despatch containing this information was received with excitement in England. The Church of England was less than a century old. Some men still regarded it as a shaky improvisation, and it suffered from the constant slur that it was merely the creature of Henry VIII's matrimonial necessities. So striking a confirmation of the validity of its theological position as the adherence of a Roman Catholic archbishop was joyfully received. When King James consulted with Archbishop Abbot about bringing De Dominis to England, the English primate was so eager that he proposed a levy on the English bishops for the Italian's support, and promised that he would supply him with lodging and diet in his own house.

In December 1616 Archbishop De Dominis arrived in England, where the Anglicans promptly accorded him place directly after the Archbishops of Canterbury and York. Thronging to meet him, Englishmen encountered a corpulent Italian churchman who looked all of his sixty years. Many were disappointed to discover that he was decidedly opinionated, if not downright arrogant. Though he was voluble in his admiration of the Church of England, he was obviously far from unaware of the distinction that he was conferring upon it.

Established in lodgings in Lambeth Palace, De Dominis wrote to Cyril, Patriarch of Alexandria, proposing union between the Greek and English churches, and began work on his *Manifestation*, declaring the motives which had led him to break with Rome. Efforts to secure him a suitable post were long unavailing, but in the end De Dominis received not one but two handsome appointments, becoming Master of the Savoy and Dean of Windsor. (The apartments in the 'Hospital' of the Savoy had for many years been rented out to courtiers who found the place conveniently close to Whitehall; but when De Dominis proposed to restore the Savoy to its original charitable use as a hostel for foreign travellers, James crustily advised him to leave things as he found them.)

As master and dean, the refugee archbishop began to reveal more and more the unpleasant side of his nature. Not only was he arrogant and over-bearing, he was grasping and greedy. Accustomed to the spoils system of the Italian pluralists, he engrossed unto himself everything that he could. The English themselves were far from innocent in these matters, but De Dominis as a foreigner should have been circumspect. Instead, he grabbed everything he could. Years later, presenting him on the London stage as the unnamed Fat Bishop in *A Game At Chesse*, Thomas Middleton had De Dominis declare:

> I am persuaded that this flesh would fill
> The biggest chair ecclesiastical,
> If it were put to trial.
> To be made master of an hospital
> Is but a kind of diseas'd bed-rid honour;
> Or dean of the poor alms-knights that wear badges:[8]
> There's but two lazy, beggarly preferments.
>
> . .   . .   . .
> My merit doth begin to be crop-sick
> For want of other titles.

Crop-sick for other titles and misled by a false report of the death of Tobie Mathew, Archbishop of York—a report quite possibly originated by that mischievous and eccentric prelate[9]—De Dominis requested the supposedly vacant archbishopric for himself. The move did nothing to improve his steadily declining reputation.

By 1621 the English were tired of the archbishop, and he of them. In his sermons he began to maintain that the Roman Church, though in need of reform, was guilty of no heresies. When exception was taken, he discontinued preaching. Meanwhile an old friend of his had become Pope, and De Dominis began to build hopes that the Roman Church would now be purged of its faults and errors. The Catholics were, of course, eager to end the scandal of De Dominis's apostasy; and the Spanish ambassador in England, judging the time opportune, sought to bring the lost shepherd back to the flock. Cautiously, through various intermediaries, Gondomar and De Dominis began to negotiate. The Pope, it seems, offered to confer the wealthy diocese of Salerno upon De Dominis if he would return.

In January 1622 De Dominis wrote to King James. Blandly he reported that his friend Gregory XV had invited him back to Italy 'to use my poor help to work the inward peace and tranquility of this your majesty's kingdom'. The diseases of old age and the severity of the English winters, said De Dominis, 'make my longer stay in this climate very offensive to my body'. Accordingly he was asking leave to depart, while thanking James for his many royal benefits and promising to become 'in all places a reporter and extoller of your majesty's praises'. The response of the angry monarch was to post a watch on De Dominis's house in Greenwich, to send a commission of ecclesiastics to interrogate him, and to demand an answer to the Star Chamber offence of entering into unauthorized correspondence with the Pope. On March 30th the Archbishop of Canterbury delivered a curt order from the King giving De Dominis twenty days in which to get out of England, and warning him that he would return at his peril. In mid-April he sailed in company with Swartzenberg, the imperial ambassador. Royal officers searched his trunks and impounded £1,700 which they found there but, at the suit of various ambassadors, this was later restored to him.

How far De Dominis had deceived himself with expectations that the new Pope would convene a general council for the reformation of the Roman Church, and how far Gondomar had 'inchaunted him into this fooles paradise', it is impossible to say. Certainly when De Dominis arrived in Italy, he was ceremoniously received back into the Church by Gregory XV. But then disaster struck. In July 1623 Gregory died and the new Pope handed De Dominis over to the Inquisition. Death from illness carried off the unfortunate man before he could be brought to trial, but a posthumous verdict convicted him of seventeen heresies and resulted in his body, picture and books being publicly burned in the Campo di Fiore.

During the last years of King James the greatest power in the Church of England was exercised, not by Archbishop Abbot, but by a fresh-faced little Welshman named John Williams. The latter straddled two worlds, the ecclesiastical and the secular, being both Bishop of Lincoln and Bacon's successor as Lord Keeper of the Great Seal.

Williams's career rested upon enormous industry and great shrewdness. His capacity for work was fantastic—during his student days at Cambridge he was sometimes at his books from six o'clock one morning until three o'clock on that following. However, while admiring Williams's prodigious industry, one cannot help but note also that he was one of those smooth men who never miss a trick in the game of getting ahead. As a fellow of St. John's, Williams adroitly used the opportunity of some college business to catch the attention of Archbishop Bancroft, and reaped the reward of becoming Archdeacon of Cardigan. Given the chore of showing a visiting German dignitary, the Duke of Wurtemberg, around Cambridge, Williams so captivated him with his charm that the Duke carried him off to Newmarket to meet the King. Presentation to His Majesty was Williams's big chance, and he made the most of it. One way or another, it was arranged that he should preach before James and Prince Henry. Writing to a relative, Williams made an illuminating comment upon the effect of his sermon: 'I had a great deal of court holy-water, if I can make myself any good thereby.'[10] Lord Chancellor Ellesmere had, in fact, some months earlier invited the personable young don to become his chaplain. Williams had asked that he be allowed to serve out his year as a proctor at the university, but he really needed little urging and in 1612 he accepted the offered chaplaincy.

A sure instinct leads the Williamses of this world to the sources of power and wealth. Lord Chancellor Ellesmere had both. Among other things Ellesmere was largely responsible for dispensing the ecclesiastical patronage of the Crown, and Williams, brisk, cheerful and invariably well informed, helped him as his chaplain with his decisions. To his credit, Williams used his position to help poor scholars to livings, but he also took care to feather his own nest very comfortably. Already rector of Honnington and Archdeacon of Cardigan, he became rector also of Grafton Underwood and of Walgrave, and a prebendary in the dioceses of Hereford, St. David's, Peterborough and Lincoln.

Partly under his patron's tutelage, Williams began to study law. Old Ellesmere enjoyed being with so agreeable and intelligent a companion, and he soon took to talking over with him cases that had been debated either in Chancery or in the Star Chamber. On his deathbed Ellesmere bestowed upon Williams his legal notes and papers. 'I know,' said he, 'you are an expert Workman; take these Tools to work with; they are the best I have.'[11]

When Bacon succeeded Ellesmere he invited Williams to remain as his chaplain, but he declined. Withdrawing to Walgrave, he actually devoted himself for a while to his duties as rector there. Not that all his time went to Walgrave. An ambitious man must keep in circulation, and it was important for Williams to be in touch with things at court. Through the influence of his friend James Montagu, Bishop of Winchester, he got himself appointed a chaplain to the King. Preaching before James at Theobalds in 1619, Williams so pleased His Majesty that he not only ordered the sermon printed, but shortly afterwards made Williams Dean of Salisbury even though Buckingham was pushing another candidate.

It does not seem to have worried Williams that he had crossed the wishes of the touchy Buckingham. Like Bacon, he was slow to realize the magnitude of the new favourite's power. James himself, however, did Williams the kindness of letting him know that further advancement would depend upon Buckingham's good will. Accordingly the new dean set himself to dissipate whatever ill-feeling might have resulted from his appointment. In the process he so ingratiated himself with that unpleasant old termagant, Buckingham's mother, that the court began to hear rumours that Williams had become her lover. It seems unlikely that such was the case—a boyhood accident had almost certainly left Williams sexually impotent.

By March 1620 Williams felt himself sufficiently established with Bucking-
ham to write to him asking 'to be by your happy Hand transplanted from
Salisbury to Westminster'. The petition was heeded and, in July 1620,
Williams became Dean of Westminster.

From this time on Williams kept the favour of both the King and his
favourite. With James there was never any difficulty. As Williams's latest
biographer has put it:

> Their minds chimed well together. They liked to wander in the tortuous
> by-ways of theology, and to exchange the quips and quibbles of pedantic
> wisdom. Often they conversed in Latin, an exercise which gave the chaplain
> plenty of opportunity to admire and applaud the royal learning, and to air
> his own.[12]

With Buckingham it was a bit different, for the two were not naturally
congenial. However, Williams made himself serviceable to Buckingham.
It was he who converted Lady Katherine Manners to Anglicanism so that
Buckingham could marry her. It was he chiefly who reconciled her father
to the match and secured a suitable jointure for the bride. It was he,
fittingly, who officiated at the marriage. Moreover, in the next year 1621,
it was his shrewd advice that saved Buckingham from becoming embroiled
with Parliament. Buckingham, appreciative of Williams's help at this time,
swore that he would 'use no other Counsellor to pluck him out of his
plunges'.

Reward was not long in coming. The impeachment of Bacon had left
James in need of a new Lord Keeper. For a little while the King dillied
and dallied, but finally, on July 7, 1621, he gave Williams the Great Seal.
Several weeks earlier, by way of preparation, Williams had been made a
member of the Privy Council and designated Bishop-elect of Lincoln. He
had by now become so notorious a pluralist that men observed that the
new bishop was a complete diocese in his own person.

There were good reasons why Williams should not have been appointed
Lord Keeper. He was not a lawyer, and the lawyers resented having one
not of their profession preside over the Court of Chancery. He was a
churchman, and the last clerics to hold the position had been Roman
Catholics, a fact which stirred some uneasy recollections. Finally, there
was his comparative youth. Bishop Williams was only thirty-nine.

Under the circumstances Williams conducted himself with skill and
understanding. He stipulated that his first eighteen months should be
probationary ones during which he would have the assistance of several
of the principal judges. Using these eighteen months to augment what he
had learned from Ellesmere, Williams made a concentrated study of the
law under the direction of Sir Henry Finch, one of the serjeants-at-law.
So hard did he drive himself that he was in danger of seriously undermin-

ing his health. Meanwhile, making it clear that Ellesmere was to be his model, he reassembled about himself all whom he could secure of those who had served his former patron. The consequence was that Williams filled his great post with distinction. At the end of his self-imposed period of probation, King James confirmed him in his office and he kept him there for the rest of his reign.

Tieing in as it does with the alliance between James and the bishops made at Hampton Court in 1604, Bishop Williams's appointment as Lord Keeper invites a review of the King's relations with the national church. James took very seriously his responsibilities to the Church of England. The trouble was that he persistently acted as if his political headship carried with it the spiritual direction of the Church. If a bishop's preaching displeased him, he could rudely interrupt and correct him. Even so experienced a time-server as Bishop George Mountain (or Montaigne) could not be sure of himself here:

> Somwhat in the bishop of Londons sermon on Christmas day gave the King so litle content that he grew lowde, and the Bishop was driven to end abruptly.[13]

Generally James liked to have his clergy about him at court. The Duke of Saxe-Weimar, who was at Theobalds with him in 1613, offers testimony on this point:

> As a bishop is required to wait during every meal, his Majesty generally converses with him at table, and occasionally with others, as it indeed happened on the following evening, when Isaac Casaubon, who is a very little man with a black beard, presented himself at dinner time, and laid before his Majesty a sheet of paper, on which he had written something against Cardinal Bellarmine at Rome; and this the King not only read, but during the whole meal-time discussed the merits of it with him, speaking in Latin and French.[14]

A man needed to be careful, however, during such theological discussion with the King. One news-letter writer tells how '. . . Dr. Baylie, bishop of Bangor, was committed to the Fleet [prison] for disputing (they say) somwhat malapertly with the King about the Sabbath.'[15]

It is impossible to muster any great enthusiasm for the Anglican episcopacy in the time of King James. As noted earlier, the bishops inherited from Queen Elizabeth's time were rarely outstanding. When it came to his own appointments, James, while occasionally going out of his way to reward merit, was more concerned with qualities of tolerance and good sense than fervour. The consequence was that James's appointees were usually 'court bishops', rather worldly, undistinguished, middle-of-the road-men who could be counted on not to cause any trouble. Most of them probably did their best according to their lights. No real scandals disgraced the bench of bishops during King James's time. (Dr. Theophilus Field had not yet become Bishop of Llandaff when he was serving as a broker transmitting bribes to Bacon.)

For certain things King James deserves more credit than he has usually been given. Whereas Queen Elizabeth fleeced the Church left and right through 'gifts' exacted from the bishops, King James approved a measure of his first parliament prohibiting any alienation of Church property to the Crown. Amid all the financial crises of his reign, he never sought to evade or repeal the provisions of this statute.

James did continue one bad practice of Elizabeth's, that of occasionally conferring ecclesiastical preferment upon laymen. In 1606, for example, he appointed Adam Newton, the tutor of Prince Henry, Dean of Durham. Such appointments were few, however, compared with those of Elizabeth who had used deaneries as a handy way of paying a good number of the men in her diplomatic service. James never promoted any of his Scots to an English bishopric.

CHAPTER XXVI

Gondomar

IN THE SPRING of 1613 a new Spanish ambassador, Don Diego
Sarmiento de Acuna, arrived in England. The character of the man
was shown by an incident which occurred immediately after his landing at Portsmouth. No sooner had Sarmiento gone ashore to receive a
welcome from the civic authorities, than the captain commanding the
English flagship called upon the Spanish captain to obey the custom which
required a foreign ship to strike its colours whenever it entered a harbour
of the Narrow Seas in which there was an English man-of-war. Foreigners
found the custom somewhat galling, but the Constable of Castile had
observed it when he arrived for the peace treaty of 1604, and so had King
Christian of Denmark upon his visits. On instructions from Sarmiento,
however, the Spanish captain refused to lower his flag. Dumbfounded at
the arrogance of the Spaniards, the English captain told them that they
would either strike their flag or be blown out of the water. At this point
the ambassador asked and received time to write directly to King James.
In his letter Sarmiento recounted what had happened and asked permission to return to his ship—if she were to be sunk by the guns of the English,
he meant to go down with her. On the basis of everything he had been
able to learn about King James, Sarmiento had already made a just appreciation of the character of the sovereign to whom he had been accredited.
The peace-loving James was not the man to risk a war over the formality
of a salute. Sarmiento travelled up to London with one notable blow
already struck for the prestige of Spain.

If the courtiers who thronged to see the new ambassador expected, in
consequence of his exploit at Portsmouth, to see a fire-eating monster of
Spanish arrogance, they were agreeably disappointed. Sarmiento was
gracious, charming and polite. He moved habitually in an atmosphere half
of jest, half of earnestness. Behind his easy wit lay, however, a piercing
mind. While he took his part with an easy carelessness in the frivolities of
the English court, he remained at heart utterly dedicated to Spain and the
advancement of Spanish interests. And whenever it suited him, the easy
wit and pleasantry could give way to chilling hauteur in the best Castilian
tradition.

Established in his new post, Sarmiento took stock of the situation. The

Treaty of 1604 had brought peace between England and Spain, and in
1609 the Treaty of Antwerp had begun a twelve-year truce between Spain
and Holland. Nobody, however, could count upon more than a few years'
lull before the Protestants and Catholics would once more take up arms
and renew their deadly struggle. In the interim—and an interim it proved
to be—diplomats of both sides sought to strengthen their nations' positions
as much as possible, consolidating their own alliances and securing defec-
tions from the opposite camp. For Spain the future course of English
policy was particularly important. Here was a Protestant country with a
native Catholic element still sufficiently large (so the Spaniards persuaded
themselves) to make possible national reconversion to Catholicism. Failing
such reconversion, the Spaniards could hope at least to detach England
from the Dutch and German Protestants and keep her neutral in any
coming war. Should England join wholeheartedly in any general Protestant
attack upon the Spanish alliance, the consequences might well be catastro-
phic for the latter.

Looking about him in 1613, Sarmiento could find little or nothing that
had been achieved by his predecessors in the years since the signing of the
peace treaty of 1604. The reconversion of England to Catholicism had
slipped farther and farther away. The unofficial tolerance which James had
conceded for a few months at the beginning of his reign had long since
ended, and the penal laws and the Oath of Allegiance which had followed
the Gunpowder Plot of 1605 had made the Catholics' lot increasingly hard
and had weakened their position. While commercial rivalry had brought
coolness between England and Holland, England was far from turning her
back on the Continental Protestants. In fact, the King had only a year
earlier married his only daughter to Frederick V of the Rhenish Palatinate,
one of the three Protestant Electors of the Empire. This marriage carried
with it dire possibilities of future English intervention on the Continent.
Meanwhile another marriage was being negotiated, that between Prince
Charles and the French princess Christina, a marriage which would ally
England to Spain's chief rival within the Catholic camp.

Such was the situation which confronted Sarmiento. What he needed
was a scheme which would simultaneously strengthen the position of the
English Catholics, counteract the Palatinate marriage, and prevent the
French match. Sarmiento found what he wanted in the 'Spanish match'.
Choosing the right moment, he asked King James why Prince Charles
should wed a French princess when he could make a much more illustrious match with the Spanish Infanta.

The idea of marrying the heir to the English throne to a Spanish princess
was not a new one. Queen Anne had broached the matter to the Constable
of Castile in 1604, almost certainly at the instigation of her husband.

Various motives could have led James to seek such a marriage. The title he sought beyond all others was that of *Rex Pacificus*; the role he cherished that of the peace-making king. The Treaty of 1604 had brought peace between England and Spain, but James knew that what was really needed was an end to all religious war in Europe. Why should not he and the King of Spain, united through a marriage of their children, become joint arbiters of Europe? Or why, indeed, should not he himself, through marriages of his children to both Catholic and Protestant houses, lay the foundation for a golden era of European peace? It was a noble dream. The only thing wrong was that it assumed qualities of tolerance, moderation and abnegation of which just about everybody concerned, except King James himself, was quite incapable. When the Constable of Castile left for Spain he told the Count of Villa Mediana, who remained behind as resident ambassador, that Prince Henry's conversion to Catholicism must be insisted upon as a condition for any match with Spain.

The succeeding years saw the Spanish match used again and again as a gambit by the Spaniards. In each case, some expert probing by the King's ministers soon revealed that the Spanish really had nothing to offer. Writing to Winwood in September 1611, Cecil was contemptuous of the Spanish manœuvrings. Ever since 1604, he said, there had been marriage overtures from the Spanish ambassadors but they had never been direct or official and always seemed intended to put the English royal family under the servitude of Rome.

In reviving the project of the Spanish match, Sarmiento had certain advantages denied his predecessors. Death had removed the fervently Protestant Prince Henry and it was the much more pliable Prince Charles who would now be the prospective bridegroom for the Infanta. Death had also removed the ever-vigilant Cecil who had effectively kept James from useless and time-wasting negotiations. Moreover, King James had a new reason for desiring the Spanish match: a breakdown in the financial bargaining with Parliament had prevented ratification of the Great Contract of 1612, and had left the King longing for the hundreds of thousands of pounds which the Spaniards could be expected to pay as the marriage portion for the Infanta.

By early 1614 the projected French match for Prince Charles was obviously losing favour both in London and Paris. In June Sarmiento, after discussions with James and his ministers, wrote to Philip III recommending approval of a marriage between Prince Charles and the Infanta Maria, on the condition that religious toleration be granted to the English Catholics. Philip III had, in fact, already written to Pope Paul V to determine his views on the proposed marriage. In July he received his reply. His Holiness expressed the strongest disapproval.

Since a papal dispensation was absolutely essential to the marriage, matters might reasonably have ended here. However, Philip and his ministers were not ready to give up so easily. Further negotiations, they reasoned, might produce English concessions which would make the match acceptable to Rome. In any event, the English would be kept occupied and an undesirable French or Protestant marriage be held in abeyance. Accordingly, Philip took the first steps which, with Sarmiento's skilful aid, led the luckless King James into the endless labyrinth of the Spanish marriage negotiations. Convening a junta of Spanish theologians, Philip carefully withheld from them the Pope's message, but communicated Sarmiento's views and asked them to draft terms for a possible marriage treaty.

Meanwhile, in England, Sarmiento began softening up King James. By now he realized that all real decisions in foreign policy were the King's own, and that personal friendship was the surest way of modifying the King's views. He used all his charm, wit and flattery to make a conquest of James. He studied the King's little foibles and crotchets. Finding that His Majesty liked to parade his learning by carrying on discussions in Latin, Sarmiento talked with him in that tongue, and when the ambassador committed a solecism he excused himself by saying that while James spoke Latin like a Master of Arts, he himself spoke it like a gentleman. Not one ambassador in a thousand would have had the insight to know that this remark, insulting to any other monarch, would be secretly pleasing to James.

The personal ascendancy that Sarmiento achieved over King James was a psychological *tour de force*. It was the key to all his subsequent successes, enabling him in time to make King James first betray and then execute Sir Walter Raleigh, to dissolve a parliament, and to alienate the vast majority of his subjects. In 1614 Sarmiento won the first of his triumphs when James decided to send Sir John Digby to Madrid to negotiate a match between Prince Charles and the Infanta.

Awaiting Digby in Madrid were the terms arrived at by the theologians. In May 1615, after a lengthy series of conferences, Digby sent these conditions to England. They came as a terrible shock to the King. All children of the proposed match were to be baptized by a Catholic priest. Their education was to be directed by their mother. If, when they came of age, they chose to adopt her religion, they might do so without losing their rights to the throne. All the Infanta's servants—including the wet-nurses for her children—were to be Catholics. Her chapel was to be a church open to the public. Her chaplains were to wear their ecclesiastical habits openly in the streets. One of them was to be the governor of the Infanta's household. Moreover, there was to be a complete suspension of the laws penalizing the English Catholics.

King James was furious. His first impulse was to break off the negotiations completely. Had he known that these exorbitant demands still carried no likelihood of a papal dispensation—that the Pope had already expressly condemned the match—he certainly would have ended the business then and there, and saved himself a world of trouble. As it was, he allowed Sarmiento to mollify his wrath, and drafted a moderate reply to the Spanish demands.

Back to Madrid went the royal answer. While Digby's time was wasted there in petty and wearying negotiations, Sarmiento in England contrived to keep King James cool to the French match, which still lingered as a fitful possibility. When Digby came back with a revised set of Spanish terms, these were found to offer only a few minor concessions. Digby, a man of cool common sense, was by now suspicious about the good faith of the Spaniards, and put his own views before the King. He reminded James that there could be no marriage without a papal dispensation and pointed out that, since there was no assurance that this would be forthcoming, the negotiations so far conducted were largely meaningless. His own feeling, he said, was that His Majesty should forget all about the Spanish match and marry his heir to some Protestant German princess. James was very nearly persuaded. Appreciative of Digby's services, he appointed him his vice-chamberlain. In May 1616 the Spaniards were told that King James would have to have assurance of the Pope's dispensation before proceeding farther.

At this point negotiations came to a standstill. The wonder is that they did not collapse completely. In September Sarmiento glumly reported that the great concessions demanded of James had choked him and taken away his breath, and that the King had told him that the Spanish terms 'contained terrible things'.[1] Philip III, for his part, was now inclined to let the whole business drop. However, Lerma, his chief minister, persuaded him that there were advantages to keeping King James negotiating. After all, there was no rush about getting the Infanta married—she was only ten years old—and every month that King James could be kept occupied was another month in which he was kept from an undesirable marriage alliance elsewhere. Sarmiento was instructed to revive King James's earlier hopes for a Spanish match. He began making skilfully noncommittal intimations of concessions still in prospect, and drew pleasant pictures of what James might yet win in prestige and dowry money.

Sarmiento was successful far beyond what Philip and Lerma had any right to expect. On March 2, 1617, King James convened a special commission of Privy Councillors. Utterly unaware that the Pope had recently informed the Spaniards that the conversion of Prince Charles and toleration for the English Catholics were essential conditions for any marriage dispensation, King James assured the commissioners that Sarmiento and Lerma 'had so far declared themselves, as they did neither expect alteration in religion in the Prince nor any liberty or toleration for His Majesty's subjects'. Pointedly he noted that his poverty gave him 'cause to make the best use of his son, thereby to get some good portion towards the payment of his debts'. Digby made a verbal report and submitted various documents. Then the commissioners were asked for their opinion—were the Spaniards sufficiently in earnest to warrant King James proceeding to negotiate a marriage treaty? The commissioners replied with words which, in their cryptic ambiguity, were worthy of the Delphic oracle—they found 'as much assurance of good success as in such a case could be had'.[2] This was enough for King James. Letters began to pass between London and Madrid. That autumn Digby was despatched to Spain as ambassador extraordinary to negotiate a marriage treaty. As for Sarmiento, King Philip recognized his achievement by conferring upon him the title of Count of Gondomar, giving him the name by which posterity remembers him, and by which we shall henceforth refer to him.

When Digby arrived in Madrid, he found that Aliaga, King Philip's chaplain, had been given charge of the Spanish negotiations. With him, and only with him, was Digby to conduct his discussions. The two began a process of feeling out, each trying to discover the real intentions of the other. Aliaga made the first move. Point-blank he asked Digby if King James was prepared to secure total repeal of the anti-Catholic statutes. Digby bluntly replied that he could discuss only the household and dowry arrangements for the Infanta and could make no commitments about the English Catholics. No doubt he hoped by so uncompromising a rejoinder to force a showdown. A showdown, however, was the last thing that Aliaga wanted. Had he desired one, he had his own means of securing it. A new junta of theologians, this one acquainted with the Pope's views, had recently drawn up a whole new set of conditions for the match: King James must undertake the repeal of the anti-Catholic laws; the Infanta must not be delivered before the end of a three-year period of probation during which the English Catholics should enjoy complete religious freedom; and Prince Charles must come in person to Spain to claim her (it was hoped that he would be converted while in the country). Knowing these new terms would be utterly unacceptable to the English and would end the negotiations for once and all, Aliaga never let Digby know of their existence, but blandly went on negotiating on the basis of the articles which Digby had brought over from England with him.

As the discussions proceeded, it emerged that King James was not prepared even to suspend the operation of the recusancy laws. Taken aback by this discovery, the Spaniards seemingly played a major card. The

English had already asked for a gigantic dowry of £600,000. The Spanish now announced that they would pay this sum if guaranteed that their English co-religionists would be given freedom from persecution. To Digby the bargain appeared neither unreasonable nor impossible. Unaware that the real Spanish conditions had not even been mentioned to him, he returned to England unexpectedly hopeful, his original twenty articles now augmented by five more which had been worked out by Aliaga and himself.

It is hard to determine the Spanish position at this point. Perhaps King Philip and his ministers hoped that, having brought James part way to their position, they would be able ultimately, by progressive revelation of their further requirements, to manœuvre him into giving everything that the theologians had stipulated in their junta. In any event, Gondomar was now instructed to tell King James plainly that he would have to agree to religious toleration for his Catholic subjects. James would agree to nothing of the sort. For a second time things had reached an impasse. In July 1618 Gondomar ended his ambassadorship. He and his masters could congratulate themselves that for five years he had completely immobilized England's foreign policy.

Gondomar's departure from England was accompanied by demonstrations of remarkably different feelings by the English and their King. Gondomar's ascendancy over the King, and his part in promoting the loathed Spanish match, had not gone unnoted by the Protestant English. The Londoners, especially, saw Gondomar as a real life representative of the diabolical Machiavellian villains whom they delighted to hoot on the playhouse stage. A minor incident gave them a chance to vent their feelings. Just before Gondomar left London, one of his gentlemen while galloping down Chancery Lane knocked over a little boy. The boy was not badly hurt, but within minutes a mob of thousands was storming the Spanish embassy. Only the timely arrival of Chief Justice Montagu and the Lord Mayor of London saved the terrified Spaniards from the fury of the mob. Gondomar himself was absent, dining with the Earl of Worcester, but next day Buckingham called upon him with the King's apologies.

King James, despite the breakdown in the marriage negotiations, was very sorry to see Gondomar depart. As Fuller later quaintly put it, the Spaniard,

> ... so carried himself in the twilight of jest-earnest, that with his jests he pleased his majesty of England, and with his earnest he pleasured his master of Spain. Having found out the length of king James's foot, he fitted him with so easy a shoe, which pained him not, (no, not when he was troubled with the gout,) this cunning don being able to please him in his greatest passion.[3]

To show his regard for the departing Gondomar, James released from prison a hundred or so Catholic priests who accompanied Gondomar as he travelled to Dover. Moreover, in one of his final interviews, he gave him satisfaction in the matter of Sir Walter Raleigh.

After his disaster at Winchester, Raleigh had lived a not unpleasant life in the Tower of London. Here he had his own apartments and, for his exercise, that stretch of the battlements still shown to tourists as Raleigh's Walk. He had entertained himself with his scientific and medical interests, indulged in the philosophical speculations which had long interested him, and written his great *History of the World*. He had indeed shown that 'hee could dooe his Majesty more service in a dungeon then in a grave'.[4] At various times his release seemed in prospect. Much was hoped for from Prince Henry, who was frank in his admiration for Raleigh and candid in his desire to see him freed; but Henry died, even though a cordial despatched by Raleigh from the Tower was credited with reviving momentarily his spark of life. At the end of the first part of his *History*, all that he ever completed, Raleigh put a brief eulogy of the dead prince, then concluded sadly, *Versa est in luctum cithara mea, et organum meum in vocem flentium* [my lyre is changed into the sound of mourning; and my song into the voices of people weeping]. Raleigh had confidently counted upon the *History* to win favour from the scholarly King James, but when it was finally published in 1614 it was 'called in by the Kinges commaundement, for divers exceptions, but specially for beeing too sawcie in censuring princes'.[5]

In 1616 Raleigh's luck seemingly improved. The fall of Somerset had removed the leader of the pro-Spanish faction at court, and for a brief while ascendancy seemed to be passing to an ardently Protestant party headed by Secretary of State Winwood, the Earl of Pembroke (the Lord Chamberlain), and Archbishop Abbot. Supporting the latter was their protégé Villiers, the new favourite, who had not yet switched to a pro-Spanish policy of his own. These men urged war with Spain. War, they maintained, would end the King's financial difficulties by securing the enormous booty of the Spanish plate fleets. Much more important, it would end the constant Catholic threat to the Protestant states on the Continent. Not surprisingly, this group urged King James to release Raleigh, the most consistent champion of their view that Spain was the national enemy.

Raleigh at this time was seeking release so that he could undertake a project which, he claimed, would be very beneficial to the King's bankrupt exchequer. Back in 1596 Captain Lawrence Keymis, sent by Raleigh on a voyage of discovery, had journeyed up the Orinoco River to a point which, the natives reported, was very close to a rich gold mine. Let King James release Raleigh, and he would outfit an expedition to find this mine and bring its riches back to England. Knowing the King's desire to remain on good terms with Spain, Raleigh promised that he would do all this without making any attack upon the Spaniards in the New World. Partly out of the desperation created by a new financial crisis, partly at the urging of Winwood and his friends, King James in March 1616 released Raleigh from the Tower.

Through the summer and winter of 1616 Sir Walter busied himself preparing for his voyage. In December his flagship *Destiny* was launched, built to Raleigh's orders by the master shipwright Phineas Pett. Meanwhile Gondomar was urgent in his objections. Guiana, he protested, was Spanish. In any case, Raleigh had no intention of mining, and the whole thing was a mask for piracy. According to the Spanish ambassador, Raleigh and his friends were out to embroil England in war with Spain. King James pointed to the promise which Raleigh had given him. To reassure Gondomar further, he secured from Raleigh full information about the forces he was taking with him and the course he meant to follow to the mine. Secretly His Majesty transmitted this information to the Spaniard, who lost no time in forwarding it to Madrid.

This is not the place to retell the tragic story of Raleigh's last voyage. Sufficient to say that it was dogged by misfortune from the outset. When he finally arrived off the Orinoco with his little squadron diminished through disease, desertion and shipwreck, the aging Raleigh was too enfeebled through sickness to accompany the party that went up the river to seek the mine. Instead he despatched it under the command of the faithful but not overly intelligent Keymis. Finding an unexpected Spanish settlement, San Thomé, alerted to expect the coming of the English and barring their way to the mine, Keymis committed the folly of a headlong assault upon the town. In the attack Raleigh's beloved elder son was slain. Amid the burned ruins of San Thomé Keymis found two ingots of gold. With these he returned to Raleigh, further passage to the mine being prevented by Spanish ambushes in the jungle. Belatedly realizing that he had brought ruin upon his master, Keymis slew himself. There followed some months of pointless forays in the waters of the New World, then Raleigh's mutinous crews forced him to sail back to England. When he landed at Plymouth in June 1618, he was taken under arrest by his kinsman Sir Lewis Stukely, Vice-Admiral of Devon.

As soon as Gondomar learned of Raleigh's return, he went to King James. He reminded James that he had warned him that Raleigh would not keep his promises. Now the man was back after an unprovoked attack upon a Spanish settlement. He told King James that he must either punish Raleigh himself or hand him over for trial in Spain.

M*

That Raleigh should be handed over to the Spaniards was of course unthinkable. He was King James's subject and his offence was quite as much against the King as against Spain. It would be an abnegation of James's own authority to hand him over to a foreign power. Raleigh, moreover, was no longer hated by the common people as he had been in the days of his arrogant prosperity. Men's sympathies had swung decisively towards him at the end of his trial at Winchester. With the passage of the years, and the growing nostalgia with which the English looked back to the stirring days of war with Spain, Raleigh's reputation had grown, not withered. He epitomized both the past heroic age and the traditional English hostility to Spain. For King James meekly to hand over such a man to die to the plaudits of a Spanish mob would be to send a shock of shame and rage throughout England and alienate most of his subjects for ever. It was unthinkable. Such had become Gondomar's ascendancy over the King, however, that he could make him do the unthinkable.

On June 22nd James went to the Privy Council and asked approval for surrendering Raleigh to Spain. When the King found that many of the councillors thought the proposal outrageous, he angrily dissolved the meeting. He could, he said, proceed as king without their advice. The next day he told Gondomar that he would surrender Raleigh unless King Philip himself preferred to have him hanged in England. It was with this promise that Gondomar left England a few weeks later. In September the King of Spain's decision was received in England. He had declined King James's magnanimous offer.

Meanwhile in England a commission of Privy Councillors was investigating the whole Raleigh affair. Penetrating Raleigh's lies and evasions, they discovered that from the moment of his release from the Tower he had entertained thoughts of looting the Spaniards in the New World in the Drake and Hawkins manner, and returning to England with a treasure so vast that the impecunious James would be unable to relinquish it, thus bringing on the war with Spain which Raleigh and the Winwood group so ardently desired. There was plenty of evidence to convict Raleigh of having regarded as empty words his undertaking to his king to avoid hostilities. Before he had sailed for Guiana, he had sought the assistance of a French squadron which could be used against the Spaniards without breaking the letter of his promise to King James, and he had secretly negotiated with Montmorency, the Admiral of France, for asylum in a French port should direct hostilities with the Spaniards make it dangerous for him to return to England. Again and again, both before and after his sailing, he had carelessly spoken of attacking the Mexico plate fleet.

Equally damaging was Raleigh's conduct after his return to England. While Stukely's prisoner in Devon, he almost effected an escape to France before reconsidering and returning to his captivity. En route to London in August, he first vainly tried to bribe Stukely to connive in his escape, and then sent one of his captains, King, ahead of him to London to secure a ship in which to escape to France. Only because of his confidence in King did he refuse an offer by Le Clerc, the French agent, to get him safely away in a French vessel. As it turned out, Stukely learned of all these schemes and revealed them to the King. Acting upon royal instructions, Stukely then pretended belated acquiescence in Raleigh's plots and tried to draw all his secrets out of him. While King James and Stukely were playing their little game with Raleigh, the deluded man was allowed to stay in his house on Bread Street, instead of the Tower, the better to facilitate his escape attempt. When Raleigh, accompanied by King and Stukely, finally made his break for freedom on August 9th, he was intercepted, as planned, at Woolwich and sent to the Tower.

The commissioners who investigated Raleigh's conduct (Bacon, Abbot, Worcester, Caesar, Coke and Naunton) gave him every opportunity to state his case before they reported adversely upon him. The main outlines of Raleigh's defence have been preserved in his *Apologie*. In it he conveniently omitted everything discreditable in his proceedings and spoke, in terms of the most fervent and thrilling patriotism, of the nation's epic struggle in the past with Spain. Proudly he advanced the English claims to sovereignty over Guiana. As for his failure to keep his promise to the King, Raleigh 'represented his own dereliction of duty as a high and noble deed'.[6]

With the Privy Council commissioners confirming Raleigh's guilt and King Philip leaving his fate in the hands of King James, questions at once arose as to what his punishment should be and how it should be imposed. On the first point James had little doubt. It must be death—nothing less would be acceptable to Spain. But in what fashion should the sentence be passed? Here the lawyers came in with their strange logic. Raleigh, they argued, had already been sentenced to death by the court at Winchester, even though the execution of that sentence had been suspended by royal clemency. Being sentenced to death, he could not be tried on any other charge since, as far as the law was concerned, he was already doomed to the ultimate punishment. Accordingly, said the lawyers, if Raleigh was to be executed, it would have to be in consequence of the verdict passed in 1604. Against this bizarre reasoning, Raleigh could only reply that the King, by releasing him from prison and giving him power of life and death over those of his subjects who had served on the Guiana expedition, had in effect pardoned his earlier offence.

The matter was settled when a privy seal writ was sent to the Court of King's Bench asking for execution of the original sentence of death passed upon Raleigh. On October 28th Raleigh, old and weak, appeared before the court and was told that, unless he could produce a document from the King explicitly pardoning his previous offence, he must suffer the sentence originally imposed. Raleigh could produce no such pardon. The Attorney-General, ending the Crown's case with characteristic Jacobean rhetoric, told Raleigh 'that he had lived like a star, and like a star must fall, when it troubled the firmament'.[7] A nicer way of saying that he had to be killed to prevent friction with Spain could hardly have been contrived. Chief Justice Montagu ordered execution of the old sentence of death. The morrow was thought suitable for Raleigh's execution. It was the day of the Lord Mayor's show, and the authorities hoped that this counter-attraction would reduce attendance at Raleigh's death and make less likely any popular demonstration against it.

Immortal in the memory of our race, the scene of Raleigh's death has come to us with its vividness undimmed by the centuries. Everything that had been mean, false, or petty in his life had somehow been sloughed off. The man who went to the block was the heroic Raleigh who all along had existed as Sir Walter's ideal and now was to become a national legend.

He had been lodged in the gatehouse at Westminster. At midnight his wife left him for the last time, and miraculously he lay down and slept for a few hours. Early in the morning the Dean of Westminster gave him his last communion. Afterwards he had his breakfast and enjoyed his last pipe of tobacco. At eight o'clock he started on his short journey to the scaffold erected in Old Palace Yard.

Raleigh, so completely a man of the Renaissance, was inevitably concerned at this time with thoughts of fame beyond death. In his speech from the scaffold he did what he could to protect that fame, assuring his hearers that he was a true Englishman who had never passed under allegiance to the King of France. He was concerned also that men should not believe the old slander that he had puffed tobacco smoke at Essex when the earl had come to die. At the end he concluded:

> And now I entreat that you all will join me in prayer to that Great God of Heaven whom I have so grievously offended, being a man full of all vanity, who has lived a sinful life in such callings as have been most inducing to it; for I have been a soldier, a sailor, and a courtier, which are courses of wickedness and vice; that His Almighty goodness will forgive me; that He will cast away my sins from me, and that He will receive me into everlasting life; so I take my leave of you all, making my peace with God.[8]

There followed the famous moment in which Raleigh asked to see the axe. The headsman was reluctant to show it. 'I prithee, let me see it,' said Raleigh, and he asked, 'Dost thou think that I am afraid of it?' Running his finger along the edge he mused, 'This is sharp medicine, but it is a sound cure for all diseases.' There was some fussing about the way he should have his head on the block. Somebody insisted that it should be towards the east. Changing his position, Raleigh uttered a last superb phrase—'What matter how the head lie, so the heart be right?' He prayed briefly, gave the signal to the headsman, and died.

The headsman needed two strokes to sever the head. After holding it up for the crowd to see, he put it in a red leather bag, covered it with Raleigh's wrought velvet gown, and despatched it in a mourning coach sent by Lady Raleigh. Finally both head and body were buried by her in St. Margaret's Church, Westminster.

The consequences of Raleigh's death might have been anticipated. In the popular imagination he became a martyr sacrificed to Spain. In vain King James published a *Declaration*, written partly by Bacon, making manifest Raleigh's duplicity and treachery. James was properly regarded as subservient to Gondomar and no arguments, however just, could exculpate him. True, the habit of reverence towards the sovereign saved James from any direct demonstrations of the popular feeling. The hapless Sir Lewis Stukely enjoyed no such protection. He became 'Sir Judas Stukely' and was greeted everywhere with loathing. Two years later he died mad, in self-imposed exile on the lonely Isle of Lundy.

Chapter XXVII

Disaster in Bohemia

MAY 1618 saw the resumption, after years of uneasy peace, of the wars of religion on the Continent. In that year began the Thirty Years War which ruined Spain, brought to an end the Holy Roman Empire, and reduced the population of Germany by one-third. The war began neither at the instance nor at the desire of any of the major powers. A chance spark started it, and the man as responsible as any for the conflagration that followed was King James's son-in-law, Frederick V, the Elector of the Palatinate of the Rhine.

The disastrous process started in 1617 when the aging and childless Emperor Matthias, who was also King of Bohemia, instructed the Bohemian Estates to designate his cousin, Ferdinand of Styria, as his successor to their throne. The Estates reluctantly complied, but within a year the Protestant Bohemian lords rose in revolt against this imposition of a man bred by the Jesuits and known as an inflexible Catholic. In May 1618, in the famous 'Defenestration of Prague', they hurled Matthias's deputies from the windows of the Hradschin palace. Soon the rebels possessed most of Bohemia. The Hapsburg rulers in Madrid and Brussels lost no time in sending soldiers and money to help their kinsman Ferdinand. They had more than dynastic reasons for wishing to help. Unless the fire kindled in Bohemia was put out quickly, the long dreaded general war between Catholics and Protestants might tear Europe asunder.

At this juncture everything depended upon the actions of the Protestant rulers who were receiving urgent appeals from the Bohemians. Particularly important were the three Protestant Electors of the Empire. Two of these, the Electors of Saxony and Brandenburg, were for allowing Matthias and Ferdinand to restore the *status quo*. The third, Frederick, the Elector of the Rhine, sent in forces which saved the rebels from two imperial armies and captured the Catholic stronghold of Pilsen.

The Bohemian struggle was about to broaden into a general war. For Spain nothing could be more undesirable. Her economic condition was steadily worsening. In a few years, when the Treaty of Antwerp expired, she would almost certainly be engaged in renewed hostilities with the Dutch. The last thing she wanted was to become involved in a war with the German Protestant princes and possibly with Frederick's father-in-law, the King of England. Yet the western branch of the house of Hapsburg could hardly stand by and see the eastern branch, and the Catholic cause in Central Europe, go down to defeat. Deciding to do what they could to stop the drift towards war, but hoping that in the interim Matthias and Ferdinand would regain control in Bohemia, the Spaniards endorsed a suggestion, already advanced indirectly by King James, that the differences between the Emperor and the Bohemian rebels be given to him for mediation. James was flattered and delighted by the Spanish action. Self-importantly he drafted despatches left and right. In May 1619 a resplendent embassy under James Hay, Viscount Doncaster, set out for the Continent to advance the good work of peace-making. Actually, neither Ferdinand nor his rebellious subjects had accepted the King of England as their mediator, and James soon began to look ridiculous as Doncaster and his gallants traipsed unavailingly about the courts of Central Europe.

Meanwhile, Matthias had died, and on August 18th, partly through the ineptness of Frederick and the other Protestant Electors, Ferdinand was chosen to succeed him as head of the Holy Roman Empire. The new emperor had problems enough confronting him. Nine days earlier the Bohemians had formally deposed him as their king, and they had offered the vacant throne to Frederick. Their choice was inspired not by any particular admiration for Frederick, a well-meaning but singularly colourless young man, but by the hope that he would bring them as allies the group of German princes known as the Protestant Union, and his father-in-law, the King of England. In England feeling was running high in favour of the Bohemians, and the Bohemian directors hoped that the accession of James's daughter as Queen of Bohemia would prove decisive in winning English support.

A month of fateful indecision followed while Frederick debated with himself whether or not to accept the offered crown. His mother and his council warned him to keep clear of further involvement with Bohemia. On the other hand, his wife was eager that he accept. Elizabeth swore that she would rather eat sauerkraut as the wife of a king than roast meat as the wife of an Elector.

In mid-September Frederick made his decision. Secretly he informed the Bohemians that he would accept. A little earlier he had despatched Baron Dohna to England to tell King James of the offered crown and to learn his views. When James learned that his son-in-law had made his decision without waiting for his answer, he was furious. Summoning Dohna, he told him that since Frederick had proceeded without his advice he could expect no help from him if he got into trouble. Bluntly he informed Dohna that his subjects were as dear to him as his children and he 'wold not embarke them in an unjust and needlesse quarrell'.

King James would almost certainly have advised Frederick to refuse the Bohemian offer. He knew the enormous hazards which attended the venture. Moreover, he felt that the whole principle of royal legitimacy was at stake. James had a feeling which was little less than pathological against rebellion. Ferdinand, as he saw it, was the lawful King of Bohemia and the Bohemians had no right to depose him. For Frederick to accept the crown belonging to Ferdinand meant conniving with rebels.

In the autumn of 1619 Frederick arrived in Prague for his coronation. With him came brave, frivolous Elizabeth who, despite her advanced pregnancy, was not one to stay quietly at home in Heidelberg and miss all the festivities and the excitement. Prague had long been without a court— Matthias had transferred his to Vienna—but now there was an intoxicating period of pride and gaiety as Frederick and his wife were crowned in two separate and magnificent ceremonies. The fountains flowed with the red wine and the white. Hangings of blue and silver lined the streets. The new King and Queen scattered as largesse silver coins minted with the legend 'God and the Estates gave me the Crown.' Frederick and Elizabeth were delighted with the Bohemians and the Bohemians were captivated by their attractive young sovereigns.

On December 8th Frederick's cup overflowed when Elizabeth presented him with a son. Proudly he invested him with the name and title of Rupert, Duke of Lusatia. History was to know him as Prince Rupert of the Rhine. In England, meanwhile, an angry King James had refused to allow Frederick the name of 'King', and forbade his ministers to use it.

While Frederick and Elizabeth were passing the few happy months which were to win them their name of the 'Winter King and Winter Queen', Ferdinand was preparing to regain Bohemia. Secretly negotiating with Spain, the Spanish governors of Flanders and the Duke of Bavaria, he laid very skilful plans for a double onslaught. He and the Duke of Bavaria would launch the main attack against Frederick in Bohemia while the famous Spanish general Spinola made a diversionary attack upon the Palatinate itself.

With this offensive in the offing, it was more than ever necessary to keep England neutralized while the military decision was being reached on the Continent. The game of letting King James amuse himself with the role of mediator had by now run its course. Something more was needed. Accordingly, the King of Spain sent Gondomar to sojourn for a second time at the English court. He, if anyone, would be able to hold King James inactive while his daughter and son-in-law went down to disaster on the Continent. The first thing that Gondomar did upon his arrival in March 1620 was to blow the dust off the proposals for the marriage of Prince Charles to the Infanta.

Gondomar found England infected with war fever but King James wanting nothing so much as peace. His illness of 1618 had marked James's climacteric; he was never the same man afterwards. His mental powers as well as his physical were in obvious decline. More and more he was paralysed by indecision. Tillières, the French ambassador, noted the change:

> It seems to me that the intelligence of this King has diminished. Not that he cannot act firmly and well at times and particularly when the peace of the kingdom is involved. But such efforts are not so continual as they once were. His mind uses its powers only for a short time, but in the long run he is cowardly. His timidity increases day by day as old age carries him into apprehensions and vices diminish his intelligence.[1]

Despite the King's own lassitude, feeling at court was running more and more strongly for open support for Frederick. Grimly James told Gondomar that, whereas before there had always been Winwood urging war with Spain, he now had three hundred Winwoods about him.

At an audience Gondomar had with James in March, the Spanish match was discussed. Gondomar must have rejoiced at the King's words:

> I give you my word, as a king, as a gentleman, as a Christian, and as an honest man, that I have no wish to marry my son to anyone except your master's daughter and that I desire no alliance but that of Spain.[2]

Revealing the stress under which he laboured, the King at the end of this speech took off his hat and mopped his brow with a handkerchief. At the end of April James gave Gondomar a letter promising that the future Princess of Wales would have freedom of worship within the palace walls, and that he himself would mitigate in practice those anti-Catholic laws which no parliament could be expected to repeal.

Meanwhile, more and more alarming reports were coming in from the Continent, together with appeals for help from Frederick and his friends. James fluctuated wildly. Sometimes he spoke of standing by the German and Bohemian Protestants in their hour of need. At other times he declared petulantly that they would have to look after themselves. Gondomar, listening to everything, decided that it would be safe to attack the Palatinate and he let Madrid know as much.

In September Gondomar received two letters from King Philip. One, highly confidential, informed him that the King of England's terms for the proposed marriage were entirely unacceptable, but told him he must keep James involved in further negotiations while a decision was reached by force of arms on the Continent. The other, a most disarming letter, declared that King James would soon receive a reply to his terms. The second letter was, of course, intended for King James's eyes, a useful piece of bait provided for Gondomar who well knew how to use it. James rose to the lure. He could hardly have guessed that Philip III was already negotiating with the imperial ambassador at Madrid for the marriage of the Infanta to Ferdinand's eldest son.

About the time that Gondomar received King Philip's Machiavellian pair of letters, communications filled with the direst news began to arrive from Germany. Spinola had stormed into the Palatinate. Kreuznach, Alzei and Oppenheim had fallen before him. Frederick, pinned down in Bohemia by threatened offensives by Ferdinand and the Duke of Bavaria, was helpless to come to the rescue of his homeland.

Spinola's invasion of the Palatinate threw the English court into an uproar. All along King James had sworn that the Palatinate was safe. Now he furiously denounced the King of Spain, his ministers, and Gondomar, and declared that he would take up arms to defend his son-in-law's heritage.

Gondomar let the storm blow itself out. Then he went to work. From King James he extorted a reluctant admission that Spain had never promised that the Palatinate would be inviolable. Then he explained that Spinola's attack was simply a manœuvre to get Frederick to relinquish his usurped Bohemian crown—once Frederick had returned Bohemia to its rightful king, the return of Kreuznach and the other captured towns in the Palatinate could be negotiated. Sulkily James sank into acquiescence. Next Gondomar went into a flurry of activity calculated to make James believe that agreement on the marriage terms was really imminent. He informed King James that Fray de Lafuente, who was currently in London, would very shortly be going to Rome to apply directly for the papal dispensation. Here, he pointed out, was real action being taken to expedite the long-delayed marriage.

On October 16th Lafuente left London on his mission, which actually meant little or nothing. On October 29th Frederick's army was decisively defeated by the Imperialists and the Bavarians in the Battle of the White Mountain, and the next day he and Elizabeth were in headlong flight. Only by destroying the bridges behind them and following obscure, little-known roads, did they and their little company of followers escape to the territories of Frederick's brother-in-law, the Elector of Brandenburg.

For King James 1620 ended disastrously. Hoodwinked by the Spaniards, he had let the whole Protestant position on the Continent slip into jeopardy. The Bohemian Protestants had been crushed. Spanish forces had established themselves within the Palatinate, and England had no regiments in readiness should she have to fight. Her King, instead of arming, was still following the *ignis fatuus* of the Spanish marriage, hopefully awaiting word from Rome where Lafuente was due any day.

On March 21, 1621, King Philip III of Spain died. On his deathbed he addressed the Infanta: 'Maria, I am sorry that I must die before I have married you; but your brother will take care of that.' Then he turned to his successor, the carefree young libertine who would rule as Philip IV, and addressed him: 'Prince, do not forsake her till you have made her an empress.'[3] The truth was out at last. Despite all his shadow negotiations with England, Philip had intended to marry his daughter elsewhere. Only a garbled version of his last words was allowed to reach English ears. Digby, the English ambassador, blissfully unaware of the truth, wrote home that Philip had given 'speciall charge to his sonne and the counsaile to go on with the match for our Prince'.[4]

The time had certainly not yet arrived for Spain to disabuse the English. In this same month of March hostilities had resumed between Spain and the United Provinces. More than ever it was necessary to keep England neutral. More than ever the marriage negotiations seemed the surest way of doing so. The scene of these negotiations had shifted now to Rome. Paul V had died about the time of Lafuente's arrival and it was a new pope, Gregory XV, who had to decide about granting a dispensation permitting the Infanta to wed the heretic Prince of Wales. Gregory appointed a special congregation of four cardinals to pass on the marriage articles so far agreed to by England and Spain. By October the cardinals were ready with their decision. It was one which the Spaniards must have known that the Vatican would reach: King James's undertakings to connive in evading the anti-recusancy laws were quite insufficient, and the English Catholics would have to be given complete liberty of worship, accompanied by iron-clad guarantees. Urgently the Spanish ambassador represented to the Pope that, in view of the very ticklish Palatinate situation, the cardinals' decision should not be made known at this time.

Things had gone from bad to worse for poor Frederick. In September fresh military disasters had come, with Duke Maximilian of Bavaria making a lightning conquest of the Upper Palatinate. The consequence in England was a general clamour for war. So inflamed was feeling that James kept Elizabeth from visiting England, fearful that her arrival would whip up a storm of national sympathy which would sweep him into war. In fact, more and more of his own advisers were becoming alarmed and telling James that he would have to bridle the strength of Spain and her allies. Writing from Venice about what the Spanish had achieved, Sir Henry Wotton gloomily observed:

> . . . they go forward, being now able to walk (while they keep a foot in the Lower Palatinat) from Milan to Dunkercke upon their own inheritances and purchases, a connexion of terrible moment in my opinion.[5]

In view of all the pressures upon King James to go to war, the Roman

Curia agreed with the Spaniards that the time was not ripe for informing him that his terms for the match with the Infanta were wholly unacceptable. Anger at such news might well drive him to the armed intervention which the Dutch, Frederick, other German princes, and his own parliament were urging upon him. Month after month passed without any divulging of the cardinals' decision. Blissfully ignorant, and hopeful as ever of the match, King James allowed Gondomar to talk him into dissolving parliament, which had been shouting for war and pressing upon him grants for military expenditure. The dissolution, Gondomar exclaimed, was the best thing that had happened to the Catholic cause since Luther had begun to preach.

Despite the precautions taken at Rome, Wotton at his post in Venice learned through his spies of the decision of the cardinals. Writing on February 11, 1622, he acquainted the King's Secretary of State with what he had discovered. Wotton's despatch had no appreciable effect upon the besotted king, who now regarded the Spanish match as the solution to all his difficulties. The enormous dowry to be brought by the Infanta would pay his debts, and restitution of the Palatinate would be one of the terms of the marriage treaty.

In April 1622 Don Carlos de Coloma arrived to take over from Gondomar as Spanish ambassador. Gondomar had achieved great things. Through his network of spies and sympathizers, he had kept Spain informed of every significant development in England. In the face of a mounting demand both in court and country for war with Spain, he had steadily drawn James closer and closer to that nation, even while Spanish forces under a Spanish general had occupied the territories of his son-in-law. He had obtained for the English Catholics such a measure of freedom through countenance and connivance that men wondered at 'the incredible increase of that faction'. He had secured the dismissal of an English parliament. All these things he had won at the cost of his own impoverishment. Again and again he had gone into his own pocket for expenditures in his king's service. One by one he had mortgaged his Spanish estates. He had done Spain greater service than many of her armies, and he had beggared himself in the process. To upbraid Gondomar with treachery and deceit, as the Protestant English did both then and later, is to show a naïve unawareness of the very nature of diplomacy. What must be said of Gondomar is that he played the game of concealment and manœuvre with consummate skill. Digby saw through him at times, but there was no English diplomat capable of forcing him to a showdown—least of all King James floundering in the pathetic weakness of his declining years.

The Protestant English were profoundly relieved as they watched Gondomar depart, escorted in honour from Portsmouth by two ships of the Royal Navy. All the pent-up national frustration vented itself in abuse against him:

> . . . the mightiest Machiavel-politician
> That e'er the devil hatch'd of a nun's egg.[6]

Presenting him on the stage as the Black Knight in *A Game At Chesse*, Thomas Middleton had him complacently compare his achievements in England with those of the Jesuits:

> I have bragg'd less,
> But have done more than all the conclave of 'em.
> Take their assistant fathers in all parts,
> Yea, and their Father General in to boot;
> And what I've done, I've done facetiously,
> With pleasant subtlety and bewitching courtship.
> Abus'd all my believers with delight,—
> They took a comfort to be cozen'd by me:
> To many a soul I've let in mortal poison,
> Whose cheeks have crack'd with laughter to receive it.
> I could so roll my pills in sugar'd syllables,
> And strew such kindly mirth o'er all my mischief,
> They took their bane in way of recreation,
> As pleasure steals corruption into youth.[7]

The picture was absurdly over-simplified. It left out too much—there was also the calculated insolence with which Gondomar demolished his enemies, and the carefully assumed righteous anger which could cow the King of England. But, by and large, charm had been Gondomar's long suit.

By June 1622 Rome could no longer postpone announcing some sort of decision on the marriage treaty. For over a year King James's unofficial emissary, George Gage, an English Catholic, had been buzzing around the Vatican trying to get action of some sort. Now he was summoned before the cardinals of the congregation and given the Pope's reply. King James, he was told, would have to give his Catholic subjects complete liberty of worship, and supply guarantees that this toleration would not be withdrawn after completion of the match with the Infanta. At the same meeting, Gage was given the Pope's amendments to the articles which England and Spain had already agreed to include in the marriage treaty. His Holiness's changes were extensive and important. For one thing, the Infanta's chaplains in England were to be under the direction of a bishop and exempt from all English jurisdiction. For another, the Infanta was to have the direction of the education of her daughters until they were twelve years old and of her sons until they were fourteen. Late in August 1622 Gage arrived in England with the Pope's demands.

Meanwhile further disasters had overtaken Frederick. Spinola's occupation of the Lower Palatinate had so far been limited to holding a few captured strongholds. Now he extended his occupation. In September, after an eleven-weeks' siege, Frederick's capital of Heidelberg surrendered. In October Sir Horace Vere, who had garrisoned Mannheim with English troops recruited in Frederick's name, surrendered that city. Vere's act left Frankenthal the only place in the Palatinate held for Frederick.

With these fresh acts of Spanish conquest coming on top of the Pope's requirement of 'new and impossible things' as prerequisite to the match with the Infanta, the time had obviously arrived for England to have things out with Spain. From September 29th to October 2nd the Privy Council was busy drafting an ultimatum. On November 1st it was delivered in Madrid by Endymion Porter, a follower of Buckingham, who had earlier spent years in Spain and was well acquainted with Olivares, the favourite of the new king. Porter's message gave Philip IV seventy days in which to secure the return of Heidelberg, as well as Mannheim and Frankenthal if the latter had fallen. Should the Emperor refuse to agree to their transfer, Philip was to pledge himself to join with the English in recovering them for Frederick by force of arms. Ten days were allowed the Spanish king in which to draft a favourable reply. Should he fail to do so, Digby, the English ambassador, was to leave Madrid and the marriage negotiations were to be broken off for once and all. King James had endeavoured to get his Privy Council to send a less uncompromising message but had failed. Even Prince Charles and Buckingham were now ready to break with Spain. Charles, in fact, had declared that he was ready to go in person to the aid of his sister. When Porter had left the royal Presence Chamber in England, the room had echoed to cries of 'Bring us war! Bring us war!'

Upon his arrival in Spain, Porter found that Digby, recently created Earl of Bristol, had already decided that the new developments in the Palatinate demanded a showdown. Acting on his own initiative, Digby had let the Spanish know that either they would help Frederick regain his lands or they would risk a war with England. Confronted with this choice, the Spanish had attempted to prevent further depredations in the Rhineland. It was, however, too late to leash the dogs of war. Informed that the King of Spain wished him to abandon the siege of Frankenthal, Tilly simply replied that he took his orders from the Duke of Bavaria. When Philip told his aunt, the Archduchess Isabella who governed the Spanish Netherlands, to use Spanish troops to break up Tilly's siege by force, she told her nephew that his order was impossible and she could not obey it.

Caught in this impasse, the Spanish looked around for other ways of placating the English and keeping them from the drastic steps threatened in Porter's ultimatum. Knowing that nothing they conceded was binding upon the Pope, whom the English would finally have to satisfy, they made what appeared to be generous concessions. They agreed that the Infanta's direction of her children's education should last only until they were nine years old, and that her chapel should not be open to the general public. As for the religious freedom which the Pope had required for the English Catholics, it was conceded that this would be sufficiently guaranteed by attaching to the marriage treaty a secret article in which King James and Prince Charles would grant the English Catholics freedom of worship within their own houses. The Palatinate problem was not so easily solved, but King Philip promised to do everything he could to regain for Frederick his territories. In a final move to convince Bristol that the Spaniards really wanted the marriage, Philip wrote a letter to his ambassador at Rome asking him to exert every effort to get the Pope to issue his dispensation. Actually, this letter was nothing more than a trick intended to impress Bristol.

The compromise to allow the English Catholics freedom of worship but only within their houses had proceeded from the mind of Gondomar, who had been active in the negotiations at Madrid. Gondomar's position becomes important at this juncture. During most of his time in England he had probably had little expectation that the marriage between Charles and the Infanta would ever take place, and had shared the view of Philip III and his ministers that the whole business was merely a useful exploitation of unrealistic dreams cherished by King James. During the later years of his second English embassy, however, Gondomar had himself succumbed to the bright vision with which he had so long bemused James. He envisaged the match actually coming into being with all its great benefits for Spain. He saw England restored to the Catholic Church and his own career crowned with the greatest possible achievement. And somehow he persuaded himself that the shy young Prince of Wales could be converted if once removed from his shielding Protestant environment. Let Charles come to Spain and be exposed both to the charm of the Infanta and the instruction of the Church, and his conversion would surely be effected. Before leaving England Gondomar had received from the Prince a promise that he would come to Madrid whenever Gondomar should advise such a visit. When Porter left for England on December 13th he carried with him not only an amended marriage treaty embodying the Spanish concessions but a message from Gondomar accepting Charles's offer to come to Spain.

When Porter arrived in England at the beginning of 1623 both James and Charles found the amended treaty articles acceptable and promptly signed them. To Bristol, who had declared himself satisfied that the

Spanish were proceeding in good faith, they sent the required letter guaranteeing the English Catholics freedom of worship in their own houses though they instructed him not to release it until the dispensation should arrive from Rome. Optimistically it was assumed that with the King of Spain urging the Pope to grant the dispensation (and had not Bristol seen Philip's letter to his ambassador at Rome?) the marriage was as good as completed.

Some people still had their doubts. Among them was John Chamberlain. On January 4th, writing to Sir Dudley Carleton at his post at The Hague, he reported:

> ... we are so forward that we looke for the Infanta in May, because there is order taken for making redy of ten of the Kings ships with all speed, and we say that the Lord Admirall Buckingham shall go to conduct her, and I have yt *di buona mano* (and under the rose) that the Prince himself goes in person: in the meane time Gondomar is to be sent into Germanie to see the Palatinat restored. You may beleve as much of this as you please. For my part I shalbe Didimus till I see yt.

Chapter XXVIII

With Prince Charles in Spain

ON FEBRUARY 18, 1623, two heavily disguised young men using the names of Jack and Tom Smith crossed the Thames by ferry at Gravesend. The two were obviously wearing false beards (one fell off to its owner's embarrassment), grossly overpaid the ferryman, and had him put them ashore just outside Gravesend instead of at the usual landing-place within the town. All these circumstances aroused the suspicion of the ferryman, who told the local magistrates that he feared he had met with two gallants who were slipping out of the country to fight a duel. The Gravesend authorities sent off a man to intercept the travellers at Rochester but they had left by the time he arrived there.

Travelling along the Dover Road, the two Smiths saw the King's carriage and an escort coming towards them. In the carriage was Boiscot, ambassador from the Spanish Netherlands, accompanied by Sir Lewis Lewkenor, Master of the Ceremonies, and Sir Henry Mainwaring, Lieutenant of Dover Castle. Fearful of recognition, the two travellers turned their horses off the highway and cantered away across the fields. Suspicious of their behaviour, Mainwaring sent orders to Canterbury for their detention. Accordingly, when the Smiths reached that city, they found the mayor ready to arrest them. At this point Tom, withdrawing with the mayor, shed his beard and identified himself as the Marquess of Buckingham, Lord Admiral of England. Declaring that he had taken this disguise to permit a secret inspection of the fleet, he swiftly secured the release of himself, his companion and his groom. Jack Smith was in fact Charles, Prince of Wales, and the groom was Sir Richard Graham, Buckingham's Master of the Horse.

At Dover the three travellers were greeted by Sir Francis Cottington and Master Endymion Porter who had arrived a few days earlier, and had arranged for a ship to carry all five of them to the Continent. When they made their crossing on the morning of February 19th their secret, had they known it, was already shared by half of London: the Prince was off to woo and win the Spanish Infanta and to bring her home to England.

King James's consent had not been easily won. When Charles, ardently supported by Buckingham, had first put the project before him some nine weeks earlier, he had not opposed it; but second thoughts had filled him

345

with misgivings. What would happen to his heir and his favourite once they were in the Spanish Court and out of his protection? When the two saw the King a second time about their scheme, they were greeted with outcries and exclamations. The old king 'fell into a great passion of tears, and told them that he was undone, and that it would break his heart if they pursued their resolution'.[1]

It was Buckingham's idea that they take as their guide Cottington who had served as English agent at Madrid and knew Spain well. At one of the sessions at which the project was being threshed over, the King had Cottington called in, swore him to secrecy and asked his opinion. 'Cottington,' said the King, 'here is Baby Charles and Steenie, who have a great mind to go by post into Spain to fetch home the Infanta, and will have but two more in their company, and have chosen you for one; what think you of the journey?' Cottington was caught in a bad spot. He realized at once that the proposed journey was wildly dangerous and foolish, but if he said as much he would probably make an enemy of the all-powerful Buckingham. Little wonder that, according to his own account, he fell into such a trembling that he could hardly speak. To his credit, he gave his king a true answer. He declared that he could not think well of such a journey and that the Spaniards, once they had the Prince in their hands, would make new and unlooked for demands on behalf of the English Catholics. At Cottington's reply King James flung himself upon his bed, cried, 'I told you this before', and lamented that he was undone and would lose Baby Charles. Buckingham, turning bitterly on Cottington, told him that he had been presumptuous to give such an answer when all that His Majesty had wanted to learn from him was the condition of the roads for such a journey. This was more than even James could stand, and he spoke up in defence of Cottington: 'Nay, by God, Steenie, you are much to blame to use him so. He answered me directly to the question I asked him, and very honestly and wisely: and yet you know he says no more than I told you before he was called in.'[2]

In the end James, so long accustomed to letting Buckingham have his way, gave in to him and Charles. On February 17th the pair took their leave of James at Theobalds. A little by-play was used to keep their journey secret from the onlookers:

> ... the King told them, 'See that you be with me upon Friday night'. Then Buckingham replied, 'Sir, if we should stay a day or two longer, I hope your majesty would pardon us'.—'Well, well,' quoth the King; and so they parted.[3]

Charles and Buckingham were wretchedly seasick on the crossing to Boulogne, but once ashore they lost no time in riding towards Paris. Tired and weary, they arrived there on February 21st, and remained until the

23rd. In a couple of joint letters to King James they told of their adventures since leaving England. The first is a light-hearted missive telling how, after visiting a periwig-maker for suitable disguises, they had gone to the French king's court where a Monsieur du Proes had arranged for them to see the King and the Queen Mother. In their second letter they told how on a subsequent visit they had seen the Queen and her ladies dancing while rehearsing for a masque. Charles declared that having seen the beauty of the Infanta's sister, the Queen of France, he was the more eager to see the lady herself.

In his reply to these letters, King James gamely tried at the outset to answer in the same high spirits: 'My sweete boyes & deare ventrouse Knights, worthie to be putt in a new romanse, I thanke you for youre comfortable lettres. . . .'⁴ But quickly the mood changed to worried foreboding. It had proved impossible, he reported, to keep secret their departure from England. True, he had ordered all the ports sealed, but there were many 'blind creekes' from which surreptitious messengers might leave for the Continent with word of the princely adventure. 'Thinke it not possible that ye can be manie howris undiscoverid,' the King warned them. He ended on a note of querulous self-pity about the royal gout. 'Youre poore olde dade is lamer than ever he was, both of his righte knee & foote & wryttes all this out of his naked bedde.' One thing that James did not mention in the letter was that all England was in an uproar over the departure of Prince Charles. Typical of public feeling was the prayer offered by a minister who 'desired God to be mercifull unto him now that he was going into the house of Rimmon'.

At eight o'clock on the evening of March 7th the Earl of Bristol, sitting in his study in the English embassy at Madrid, was told that a Mr. Smith had arrived and was demanding to see him, even though informed that his lordship was busy with important papers. Mr. Smith turned out to be Buckingham, so saddle-sore and weary that he could barely drag himself into the house. Waiting outside in the street were Prince Charles and a guide. The notoriously delicate Charles had completed the journey in much better condition than the well-nigh exhausted Buckingham.

Bristol had been warned from England to be prepared for their coming. Welcoming them to his house, he quickly sent word to Gondomar of the Prince's arrival. Gondomar hastened to the Count of Olivares, the chief minister of Philip IV. His manner revealed his elation. 'What has brought you here at this hour, looking as pleased as if you had got the King of England at Madrid?' asked Olivares. Gondomar told him that though he had not the King he had got the Prince. At once Olivares went into the royal apartments and told Philip IV the startling news. The King's response was significant. Addressing himself to the crucifix by his bed, he swore that he would not allow the coming of Prince Charles to draw him in any matter touching the holy Catholic religion beyond what the Vicar of Christ, the Roman Pontiff, should resolve.

Two days later the Prince and the Spanish royal family had their first sight of each other. It was considered impossible to introduce Charles at court since he had arrived incognito and was without the retinue needed for formal presentation. Accordingly, it was arranged that Charles and Buckingham should sit in their coach by the side of one of the streets and then, acting as if this coach and its occupants were invisible, the King and Queen of Spain, the Infanta and Don Carlos, should drive by, affording each party a view of the other. This amusing little comedy was played through. Three times the Spanish royal coach proceeded through the jammed street, past the officially non-existent Prince of Wales. Afterwards Olivares entered the coach of Charles and Buckingham and rode back to the embassy with them. He declared that King Philip 'longed and died' for want of a nearer sight of the princely wooer. Flattered, Charles agreed to meet him at a rendezvous outside his palace. Here the two sat in Philip's coach and had half an hour of friendly conversation, with Bristol as their interpreter.

Off to England went an exultant joint letter from Baby Charles and Steenie telling of their arrival and these first meetings. Everything was seen in the rosiest light. King Philip was full of 'kindnes and compliment'. In pleasant humour, Olivares had quipped that if the Pope would not let the Infanta marry Charles they would give her to him for his mistress! In fact, everything was proceeding wonderfully. Bristol, in his own despatch, was somewhat less exuberant:

> . . . I must confess, ingenuously, that if your Majesty had been pleased to ask my advice concerning the Prince his coming in this manner, I should rather have dissuaded than given any such counsel, especially before the coming of the dispensation.[5]

'Especially before the coming of the dispensation'—nothing really meant anything until the Pope agreed to the marriage, and as yet he had not done so.

In England April 1st was appointed as a day of public thanksgiving for Prince Charles's safe arrival in Spain. Bells were rung and fires lit though, according to the Reverend Joseph Mead, only because the Privy Council had ordered the ringing and had stipulated that a certain number of festive bonfires must be kindled. The latter, he said, were 'suffered to burn out without company'.

King James, meanwhile, was having a troublesome time. Once it was known that the Prince was en route to Spain, half the court clamoured for permission to follow him. The directions which Charles had left behind as to who and what should be sent after him proved neither clear nor adequate. Amid his perplexities, King James was sure of one thing—chaplains would have to be sent to keep the Prince strong in his Protestant faith. Two Church of England clergymen were packed off to Spain, together with everything necessary to fit out a chapel. 'Thaire behavioure & service shall, I hoape,' said the King, 'prove decent & agreable to the puretie of the primitive churche'. He might have spared the trouble. The Spaniards, having moved Prince Charles to apartments in the royal palace the better to work for his conversion to Catholicism, took care to exclude the heretic clergy from the precincts.

Along with the Prince's servants, chaplains and chapel furnishings, the King sent various jewels for Charles to present in the course of his wooing. Carefully he coached him in the flat-footed compliments he wanted him to address to the Infanta:

> ... for my babies presenting his mistresse, I sende him ... a goodlie looking glasse with my picture in it to be hung at her girdle, quhiche ye must tell her, ye have cawsed it so to be enchawnted by airte magike, as quhensoever she shall be pleased to looke in it, she shall see the fairest ladie that ather her brother or youre fathers dominions can affoorde. . . .[6]

Conservative estimates in London valued the jewels so despatched at £80,000. Rich as they were, they were not enough for Charles and Buckingham, who were bent on dazzling the Spaniards. Note after note clamoured for more and richer jewels.

In one of his letters Charles asked to have tilting equipment and horses sent to Spain. Replying, King James expressed his fright at the soaring expenses:

> ... but in earniste my babie ye muste be as spairing as ye can in youre spending thaire, for youre officers are allreaddie putte to the height of thaire speede, with provyding the fyve thowsande powndis by exchainge, & now youre tiltinge stuffe quhiche thaye knowe not how to provyde, will come to three more; and god knowis how my coffers are allreaddie drained.[7]

The only solution that King James could think of was to ask for an advance of £150,000 on the Infanta's dowry. As for Lord Treasurer Cranfield, pursing his lips he observed 'that the voyage was foolishly undertaken and now must be maintained with prodigality'.

Meanwhile Charles and Buckingham were living in a sort of euphoria. Everywhere there seemed to be pleasantness and joy. The Spanish King proclaimed an amnesty freeing from the galley benches the miserable Englishmen whom the Spanish had seized as pirates. The laws against excessive richness in apparel were suspended to permit the Spanish court to appear at its most dazzling. Through the streets of Madrid the populace went singing a new song by Lope de Vega of how the Prince had com-

from beyond the sea, drawn by that star the Infanta Maria. King Philip insisted upon riding beside Prince Charles when he moved from Bristol's house to the suite hurriedly prepared for him in the royal palace, and he presented Charles with two golden keys giving access to his own apartments. Everybody, in fact, appeared to be utterly charming, except for the papal nuncio who was said to be cold and bitter. As for the Infanta, she was utterly ravishing. Buckingham became lyrical when writing about her to King James:

> I thinke there is not a sweeter creature in the world babie Charles him selfe is so tuchd at the hart that he confesses all, he ever yett saw is nothinge to her, and swares if that he want her there shall be blose [a typically Buckinghamesque spelling for 'blows'].[8]

Of course there were inconveniences. The Prince's quarters in the palace turned out to be so confined that he could not use most of the servants sent him from England and had to order them home as soon as they landed at Santander. Then too he was permitted to see singularly little of his inamorata, having to wait an entire month for his first conversation with her. Probably the delay was occasioned not so much by the formalities of Spanish etiquette as by the fact that the Infanta loathed the thought of marrying him. Not in vain had her confessor pictured the horror of lying nightly with a heretic destined to burn in Hell. Prince Charles was entirely unaware of the Infanta's real feelings when, at Easter, he was conducted to the Queen's apartments and finally presented to his prospective bride. It had been agreed that only formal greetings should be exchanged. Unfortunately young Charles, swept away by ardour, launched upon a declaration of his feelings. The icy disapproval of those about him cut the Prince of Wales short. The Infanta spoke only the few conventional phrases which she had previously decided upon, and her wooer withdrew.

Despite this and other disappointments, Charles and Buckingham kept in high spirits. Writing to King James, they gaily assured him that they had never seen the negotiations proceeding better, and urged him to speed the readying of the fleet which was to bring the Infanta to England. Meanwhile they saw the sights, arranged with Philip IV for King James to receive 'five cameles . . . and one ellefant', and hunted in the park of the Prado while awaiting the coming of the dispensation.

They did not have very long to wait. Early in April reports began trickling in from Rome, first that the cardinals had recommended the dispensation, and then that it was being drawn up and would shortly arrive. On April 14th De Massimi, the papal nuncio at Madrid, received word from the Vatican that the dispensation would soon be in his hands. He passed on the good news to Olivares who at once told Prince Charles. Congratulations streamed in upon the excited young man. On April 24th a courier from Rome delivered to De Massimi not only the dispensation but also a set of conditions which must be fulfilled before it passed out of his keeping, and the marriage treaty as finally amended at Rome.

The arrival of the Pope's dispensation began a new era of conferences and negotiations. The changes which His Holiness and the cardinals had made in the marriage treaty proved serious and far-reaching. Once more the Infanta had been given custody of the education of her children until the age of twelve. The condition, already rejected by James, that her chapel in England be a church open to the public had been reinserted. Worse still, there was an added requirement: English Catholics were to be exempt from the Oath of Allegiance and subscribe instead to an oath drafted by the Pope.

At first Prince Charles did not realize the seriousness of the new situation. Writing to his father, he airily undertook to make the Spanish realize the impossibility of dispensing with the Oath of Allegiance. He soon learned that the conditions with which the dispensation had been clogged could not be dealt with so easily. Entering into anxious consultations with the Spaniards, he persuaded them to intercede with the Church for withdrawal of these conditions. When De Massimi insisted that Rome's terms must be met, Buckingham obtained a secret interview with him. For three hours he begged, persuaded, threatened and stormed. The nuncio refused to be browbeaten and remained adamant.

Meanwhile an appeal from Prince Charles for a *carte blanche* to negotiate in his father's name reached England. It found James already a prey to morbid cravings and incessant worries about his son and his favourite. In earlier letters he had vainly called upon Steenie to return, even if he had to leave Baby Charles alone behind him. Thoughts of the young men losing their health in the heat of the Spanish summer had thrown the old king into panic. Only with an effort could he fall back upon the old familiar bawdy humour. Reporting to Charles the foaling of one of his horses, he had expressed the pious hope, 'God sende my sweete babie the lyke lukke with his spanishe breede, before this tyme twellmonth, readdie to foale.'

All that James really wanted, and wanted from every corner of his aching heart, was the return of his boys. Hoping his action would accelerate that return, he sent Charles the warrant he had requested, declaring he would abide by whatever his son might promise. Buckingham's position, he decided, should be strengthened also. Off to Spain went a warrant creating him Duke of Buckingham. Then, persuading himself that the arrival of his son and his new daughter-in-law could not be long delayed, he ordered renewed speed in sending to Spain the ships which were to bring them home. At St. James's, he and the Spanish ambassador presided at the laying of the cornerstone for the chapel which Inigo Jones was building for the Infanta. The ambassador had already been over Queen Anne's old home, Denmark House, arranging the expensive remodelling needed to make it ready for the Infanta.

The Pope's dispensation had created problems for the Spanish king as well as the English. Since Philip had never had any real intention of marrying his sister to a heretical English prince, Charles's arrival in Madrid had been a hideous embarrassment to him. His only hope was that the Prince had come prepared for conversion to Catholicism. Thus no time had been lost in discovering if Charles was ready to embrace, not only the Infanta, but her church. By the end of March, Philip IV had become convinced that Prince Charles, despite his mild answers and temporizings, was not likely to abandon heresy. The result had been a highly secret message carried to the Pope by the Duke of Pastrana, asking His Holiness not to grant the dispensation.

As it turned out, Pastrana had arrived in Rome too late to influence the Pope's decision; but even if he had come earlier his mission would probably have been of no avail. For the Pope, the interests of the Catholic Church, not of Spain, were paramount. He knew that, if he bluntly refused a dispensation, he would provoke the wrath of the King of England and invite all manner of retaliation upon the English Catholics. The condition of the latter was already improving, and the proposed treaty offered them considerable further relief. Accordingly, Pope Gregory felt bound to issue the dispensation while tightening, as far as he dared, the provisions.

If the King of Spain really wanted to end the match, the Pope had left it easily within his power to do so. Attached to the dispensation was a provision that the King of Spain was to guarantee that the King of England would fulfil the terms of the treaty. All that Philip needed to do to nullify the dispensation was to refuse to guarantee the good faith of the King of England. Of course, so crude an insult would almost certainly embroil him in war with England, but that was his problem.

Caught in this dilemma, King Philip wavered for several weeks. Then he fell back upon the time-winning and face-saving device which had proved so useful in the past—he appointed a junta of theologians, and asked them to decide the conditions upon which, with a clear conscience, he could give the guarantee required by the Pope. Working with unusual despatch, the theologians recommended that at the present the marriage be merely one *per verba de praesente* (very little more than a betrothal) and that the marriage be consummated a year hence, but only if the English Catholics had received in the interim all the benefits promised them under the treaty. If the English would agree to this arrangement, they opined, King Philip might venture to give the oath of guarantee.

The junta's requirements were a terrible shock to Prince Charles. Moping about the palace, staring at the Infanta through windows, the young man had worked up a bad case of unrequited love. The prospect of having to wait an entire year to possess the delectable but distant lady made him frantic. Desperately he and Buckingham tried to extort a reversal of the junta's ruling. For weeks they had postponed writing to England, hoping for good news to send to King James. Now they were forced to despatch Cottington, not only with word that they had failed to modify the conditions attached to the Pope's dispensation, but with the further bad news of the ruling made by the Spanish theologians.

Ironically, Cottington landed in England to find the country expecting the arrival of Charles and the Infanta. A fleet, under the direction of the Earl of Rutland, Lord Mounteagle, and Lord Windsor, had finally sailed to bring the bridal couple home. The cabin provided for the Infanta on the flagship was so costly in its furnishings that men declared it worthy to enshrine a goddess. Unfortunately not everything was harmonious within the fleet. Pro-Catholic courtiers so angered the Protestant seamen by interrupting their prayers and psalm-singing that the latter could 'scarce be stayed from throwing them overboard to feed the haddocks'.

With the fleet on its way, a special reception committee had been sent to Southampton to welcome the heir and his bride when they stepped ashore. It was a resplendent company headed by the Duke of Lennox and including the Marquess of Hamilton, the Earls of Arundel and Carlisle, the Lord Chamberlain and the Lord Treasurer. With them, to entertain the Infanta with 'shewes and pageants', had gone Inigo Jones and the old actor Edward Alleyn.

Cottington's tidings came like a thunderbolt out of the blue. By good luck head winds had detained Rutland's ships within the Channel and it proved possible to recall them. Lennox and his glittering lords were told to return to court. And James, faced with the prospect of a year's separation from his darling boys, gave way to despair. The day that he received the news brought by Cottington he sat down and poured forth his loneliness in confused but agonizing phrases:

My sweete boyes, youre letre by cottington hath strukken me deade. I feare it shall verrie muche shorten my dayes. . . . Come speedilie awaye, if ye can gette leave, & give over all treattie, & this I speake, without respecte of anie securitie, thaye can offer you, excepte ye never looke to see youre olde dade againe, quhome I feare ye shall never see, if ye see him not before winter, alace I now repente me sore, that ever I sufferd you to goe awaye, I care for matche nor nothing, so I maye once have you in my armes agane, god grawnte it, god grawnte it, god grawnte it, amen, amen, amen, I

N

proteste ye shalbe as hairtelie wellcome, as if ye hadde done all thing ye
went for, so that I maye once have you in my armes againe & so god blesse
you both my onlie sweet sonne & my onlie best sweete servant, & lette me
heare from you quikelie with all speede, as ye love my lyfe, & so god sende
you a happie and joieful meeting in the armes of youre deere dade.

James R.[9]

The next day Secretary Conway wrote to Buckingham that the King
would sign the treaty articles. Should the junta continue to insist upon the
year's delay, the Prince was to accept their condition, arrange for completion of the marriage by a proxy, and immediately come home. 'His
Majesty,' Conway noted, 'desires your speedy return before all other
respects.'

Travelling at breakneck speed, Sir William Croft arrived in Madrid
eleven days after leaving London with the replies to Charles and Buckingham. Buckingham promptly informed Olivares that peremptory orders
had come for Charles and himself to return to England. The announcement
was followed by renewed attempts by the English to get the Spanish king
to set aside the recommendations of the junta. Philip let it be known that
he would reduce the period of probation to eight months but beyond this
he would not go. Charles then declared that he could not accept any delay,
that negotiations were at an end, and that he would now return to England.

Charles's leave-taking from King Philip and his court was arranged for
the evening of July 7th. When the young man appeared, however, his
words were not of farewell. Instead he announced his complete capitula-
tion. Everything that he had said about breaking off the match was a
bluff, his bluff had been called, and he was ready to meet all the Spanish
and papal conditions.

King Philip must have received the Prince of Wales's surrender with
mixed feelings. Neither he nor his sister desired the marriage, but since
the English had accepted the humiliating conditions thrust upon them,
there was no longer any way of avoiding it. The Spanish royal family took
the only course open to them and accepted the match as made. Night after
night the streets of Madrid were bright with illuminations celebrating the
successful negotiation of the marriage. Amid the cheers of the madrileños,
the Prince and the Infanta appeared in public together. Blissfully Charles
wrote to his father:

> I your babie have since this conclusion bine with my mistris, and shee sits
> publicklie with me at the playes, and within this tow or three dayes shall
> take place of the Queene as princes of England.[10]

While Charles was enjoying himself sitting next to the Infanta, and
while Buckingham was scandalizing the Spanish court by seeking a more
intimate relationship with the wives and daughters of some of the dons,

King James was leading a miserable life in England. Having sent word that he would accept the marriage articles as revised by the Pope, he was swept by misgivings. How could he with a clear conscience give his 'Faith in the Word of a King' to seek from Parliament toleration for the Catholics, when he knew full well that Parliament would never grant it? Charles in his letters might glibly rationalize that the King need only go through the motions of seeking parliamentary approval, but James was a good deal more honest than his son and he did not like such double-dealing. Plenty of other things in the treaty worried him. Never in the future would he be able to legislate against the English Catholics. He would have to allow the Infanta not only a chapel within her palace but 'a Publick and Capacious Church'[11] outside it. And he must prepare himself for the arrival in England of a Roman Catholic bishop and twenty-four priests who, as the Infanta's chaplains, would be completely outside his jurisdiction. Into these and similar concessions he had been drawn by the machinations of Rome and Spain, and the folly of himself, of his son and of his favourite. Left to his own wishes James would have torn the treaty into shreds, but he was terrified that, should he refuse to sign it, Charles would become a hostage and used by the Spaniards to extort even worse terms from him. Breaking into tears one night, he asked an old and trusted attendant if he thought he would ever see his son again.

For weeks James fluctuated between fear of betraying the Protestant cause and of risking the safety of his boys. To onlookers he seemed like a man in a stupor. Finally he summoned the chief members of the Privy Council to advise him whether or not to proceed with the signing of the treaty. Deciding that what James really wanted was an excuse for doing so, Bishop Williams expertly persuaded the councillors to assume the responsibility which the King himself was now shirking. He was advised to sign.

On Sunday, July 20th, the marriage treaty was ceremoniously ratified in the Chapel Royal at Whitehall. At the end of the customary morning sermon the Spanish representatives Coloma, the resident ambassador, and Inojosa, the ambassador extraordinary, came forward from screened compartments in the transepts and joined the King at a table in front of the altar. Secretary Calvert read the treaty aloud in Latin and King James gave his oath to maintain its provisions. The anthem which followed, an innocuous 'Hymn of Joy in Praise of Peace', had been chosen as free from offence to the Catholic susceptibilities of the Spanish visitors. The latter had maintained all along that since they had come to 'maintain and warrant the Catholick, Apostolical, and Roman Church' they could not countenance the use of any Anglican prayers. When, at the end of the anthem, the Bishop of London began the customary prayer for the King, one of the Spanish chaplains pointedly put on his hat.

After the ceremony had been concluded, King James dined in state with the two ambassadors in Inigo Jones's new Banqueting House. Eight cart-loads of plate had been brought from the Tower to burden the table and sideboards. The plate on the multi-tiered cupboard of state nearest the King was 'all of pure and perfect golde'; that on the enormous sideboard occupying the entire end of the hall was of silver gilt. While the ambassadors dined amid this splendour, their attendants feasted with various of the English in other chambers of the palace. It was noted as a sign of the general antipathy to the treaty that only two of the English wore the gay and costly apparel customary on such occasions. One was Gage, the English Catholic who had helped with the negotiations; the other, splendid in black taffeta and gold pearl, was the irrepressible James Hay, Earl of Carlisle. As Gardiner tartly observes, 'Carlisle would probably have decked himself with gold and jewels if he had been invited to a funeral.'

At the end of the banquet the English Privy Councillors withdrew and, as part of the agreement with Spain, swore to see that the articles of the treaty were 'kept, fulfilled and observed inviolably, firmly, well and faithfully, effectually, *Bona fide*, without all exception, and contradiction'.

Only one thing more was needed: the King's oath to the secret clauses, those which he had not dared to make public. Before the ambassadors left, King James withdrew with them to swear to four 'private articles'. It was well that this part of the proceedings was shrouded in secrecy. Civil war could have broken out if the Protestant English had heard their King swear that night:

 1. That particular Laws made against Roman Catholicks, under which other Vassals of our Realms are not comprehended . . . as likewise general Laws under which all are equally comprised, if so be they are such which are repugnant to the Romish religion, shall not at any time hereafter . . . be put in execution against the said Roman Catholicks. . . .

 2. That no other Laws shall hereafter be made anew against the said Roman Catholicks, but that there shall be a perpetual Toleration of the Roman Catholick Religion within private houses throughout all our Realms and Dominions, which we will have to be understood as well of our Kingdoms of *Scotland* and *Ireland* as in *England*. . . .

 3. That neither by us, nor by any other interposed person whatsoever, directly or indirectly, privately or publikely, will we treat (or attempt) anything with the most renowned Lady Infanta *Donna Maria*, which shall be repugnant to the Romish Catholick religion; Neither will we by any means perswade her that she should ever renounce or relinquish the same in substance or form. . . .

 4. That We and the Prince of *Wales* will interpose our authority, and will do as much as in us shall lie, that the Parliament shall approve, confirm and ratifie all and singular Articles in favor of the Roman Catholicks, capitulated between the most renowned Kings by reason of this Marriage;

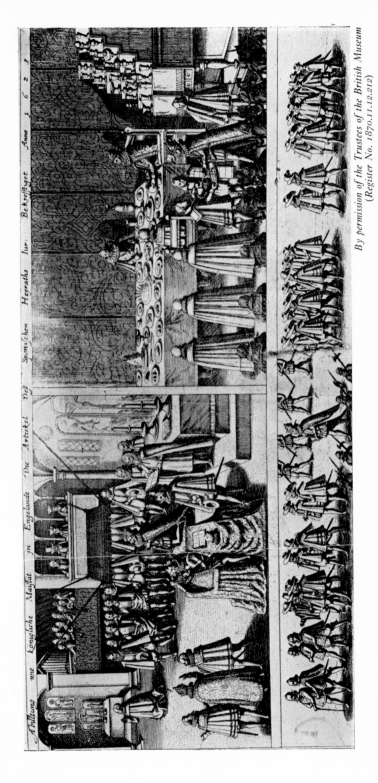

KING JAMES SWEARING TO THE SPANISH MARRIAGE TREATY

And that the said Parliament shall revoke and abrogate particular Laws made against the said Roman Catholicks. . . .[12]

The ceremonies at Whitehall once completed, no time was lost in sending Cottington off to Spain with the certificate that King James had ratified the treaty. When Cottington arrived in Spain, Prince Charles had already given his oath to articles even more sweeping than those signed by his father. James had sworn that he would forbid all attempts to convert the Infanta, but Charles had made a further pledge:

> That as often as the most illustrious Lady Infanta shall require that I should give ear to Divines or others whom her Highness shall be pleased to employ in matter of the Roman Catholick religion, I will hearken to them willingly without all difficulty, and laying aside all excuse.[13]

So amazed was Olivares when he learned that Charles had accepted the humiliation of this last proviso, that he cried out, 'Is it possible? I should have as soon expected my death.'[14]

The time was now approaching for Charles and Buckingham to return to England to wait out the probationary period until March when Charles could receive his bride. A few days after receiving King James's frantic summons home, the Prince had written to him setting August 29th as the day when they would leave for England, and new pleadings from their poor old Dad made it important that the date be kept.

The last weeks of Charles's stay saw a few final negotiations. King Philip, reconciled at last to the match, told the Prince that if he would remain in Spain until Christmas the marriage might be consummated then rather than in March. Charles declined, and once more asked Philip to set aside the whole of the probationary period recommended by the junta. The timing of his request was unfortunate for Philip's chaplains were growing increasingly suspicious about the good faith of the English. A Spanish gentleman passing through the Prince's apartments had been appalled to find a Spanish translation of a Protestant catechism contaminating the royal palace. It had, of course, been impounded. Various of the English were allowing themselves to show openly their contempt for the religion of their hosts, even behaving disrespectfully in the royal chapel. When one of Prince Charles's pages had been dying of fever, Sir Edmund Verney had used violence to keep a Jesuit father, summoned by the boy, from ministering to him. If the English dared behave thus in Spain, said the theologians, what would they not do once back in England? Assuredly King Philip could not dispense with the period in which the English must prove by deeds that they meant to give their Catholic compatriots the benefits promised in order to secure the Infanta.

On August 28th Prince Charles and King Philip swore jointly to the marriage contract, and the Prince presented his bride-elect with suitable jewels. The next day he took his public farewell of the Queen and Infanta. Buckingham did not accompany Charles on this last visit to the Infanta. James's favourite had by now made himself so objectionable to the Spaniards that a lengthy complaint against his arrogance and shamelessly loose morals was already on its way to England.

On August 30th Prince Charles began his journey home. Riding out of Madrid, he was escorted by King Philip and his two brothers to the Escorial, where they all stayed for the next few days. Here on September 2nd Charles signed forms authorizing either King Philip or Prince Carlos to stand as his proxy when the marriage should be performed. These documents he put into the hands of Bristol. Later that afternoon, taking his leave of the Spanish king, he rode forth with his company upon the road to Santander.

The next day Charles sent a trusted messenger back to Madrid with a message to the Earl of Bristol in effect cancelling the powers of proxy which the Prince had so recently signed.

No one can say when Charles first decided against proceeding with the marriage. Through all his months in Spain he had shown the shiftiness, evasiveness and deceit which were later to exasperate his English subjects. Whatever the time of his decision against the marriage, he had successfully masked his changed intentions. His secrecy is easily explained—King James almost certainly had infected his son with his own fear that the Spaniards would not let him return if they thought he did not mean to proceed with the marriage. As long as he remained on Spanish soil, Charles was at pains to conceal his altered feelings. From Segovia, from Olmeda, and from Carrion, he sent letters to Philip and the jilted Infanta declaring his loyalty and regard.

Various causes had contributed to the Prince of Wales's change of feeling. He had, apparently, recovered from his lovesickness for the Infanta. Buckingham seems to have effected the cure here. (Certainly the Spanish subsequently felt that it was he who had blighted the romance.) According to Buckingham himself, disagreement had arisen over the payment of the Infanta's dowry. The main reason, however, was neither of these. Everything in the end hinged upon the fate of the Palatinate. A chief motive behind Charles's journey had been to regain for his brother-in-law his dominions. The Spanish had promised much in the past—so much indeed that wits in London had taken to calling the Palatinate the Promised Land —but Charles had gone to Spain determined to get action, even armed Spanish intervention, to oust the Duke of Bavaria and the Emperor from the occupied territories. Amid all the fuss over the conditions attached to the Pope's dispensation and the junta's requirements, Charles had been able to do absolutely nothing for Frederick and Elizabeth. All that he had secured were polite Spanish explanations as to why one part of the house of Hapsburg could not be expected to attack the other, even at the wishes of King James. Prince Charles's last letter to his father from Spain was a confession of final failure. Possibly if the Spaniards had known that Charles was going to break off the match, they would have conceded something. As it was, the Prince masked his anger and headed back to England, there to raise his cry of a year earlier for war to aid Frederick.

Early on the morning of September 12th, Sir John Finett and Sir Thomas Somerset, having left Rutland's ships at Santander and ridden all the previous night 'over the mountains in most darke and tempestuous weather', met the Prince of Wales and his retinue on the last stage of their retreat from Madrid. They were greeted with raptures of delight. When Finett assured Charles that the English fleet was waiting only six leagues away to receive him, the Prince declared that he looked upon Finett as one that had the face of an angel.

At Santander, Prince Charles almost managed to climax his journey by getting drowned. After boarding the *Prince Royal*, His Highness decided to spend the night ashore since the Spanish had been at pains to arrange a final evening's entertainment. In high spirits Charles and his courtiers got into a barge, cast off the rope and headed for shore. Then they discovered that they had neither pilot nor mariner within the boat. A dangerous ebb tide was running and in no time the hapless gallants were being carried out to sea. Meanwhile there had arisen 'a very great tempest of rain and wind and darkness'. Luckily some officers on the warship *Defiance* noticed their plight. A rope held up by casks and lighted buoys was floated out towards them. The Prince's men managed to get hold of it, and their barge was pulled to safety.

Prince Charles landed at Portsmouth on Sunday, October 5th. The English, finding that he had been restored to them still both Protestant and single, went crazy with delight. There was feasting in the streets. Hogsheads of wine were rolled out and opened, and there were bonfires, bonfires everywhere. On Blackheath fourteen loads of wood went into the making of a single fire:

> . . . and the people were so mad with excesse of joy that yf they met with any cart loaden with woode they wold take out the horses and set cart and all on fire.[15]

At Cambridge the bells rang all Monday and all Tuesday. Patriotic speeches were delivered in the colleges, and bonfires lit in the quadrangles. On Wednesday the whole university assembled for a public oration and that night there were 'bonfires, drums, guns, fireworks, till past midnight, all the town about'.

As for Charles and Buckingham, they posted to Royston and encountered the King as he came down the stairs to meet them. They fell on their knees, he fell on their necks, and there was not a dry eye in the house.

A service of national thanksgiving was held in St. Paul's Cathedral. The words of the anthem were those of Psalm 114: 'When Israel came out of Egypt: and the house of Jacob from among the strange people.' The Spanish match was dead, though negotiations of a sort were to drag on for a few months more.

CHAPTER XXIX

The Pretensions of Parliament

THE PRIVY COUNCIL that took over the rule of England upon the death of Queen Elizabeth and proclaimed the accession of King James was one of the most powerful and highly respected bodies of its kind in Europe. Its twelve or so members, 'great lords' or 'great men' as the English habitually spoke of them, enjoyed such power that the Venetian ambassador could speak of them as so many kings. It was the Privy Council, and not Parliament, that under the sovereign ruled England.

King James confirmed in office Queen Elizabeth's Privy Councillors, added five of his Scots and six new English appointees. The resulting council of twenty-four members was really too large, as James soon realized. Nevertheless, the Privy Council continued to exercise most of the functions which it had performed earlier.

As its very name indicated, the primary task of the Privy Council was to advise the monarch. In theory at least, only distinguished statesmen were appointed to it, and these supplied a reservoir of experience and wisdom upon which the sovereign could draw when confronted with difficult decisions. Such indeed had been the nature and role of the Council under Elizabeth. Under James things were a little different. Some of the new King's appointees were hardly statesmen, and King James in any case preferred talking things over with a few bosom confidants to attending debates in the Council. His natural impatience made him restive at drawn-out sessions at the council board. The Privy Council registers for the early years of the reign have been lost, but when the records do begin, for the period May to September 1613, we find His Majesty attending only two of the thirty meetings held during these months. In 1616 the King attended only four meetings out of eighty-seven; in 1622 two out of seventy-four.[1] With the monarch so rarely present, the Council could hardly serve its original function as a body of royal advisers. King James might at times ask its opinion on matters of high policy, as he did at crucial points during the Spanish marriage negotiations, but if he did so it was usually to transfer to the Privy Council the odium of decisions which he knew would be unpopular with his subjects.

The second function of the Privy Council was to bring together at frequent intervals the ministers who directed the day-by-day government of the realm. Meeting together, they could agree on courses to be followed and means to be employed. It was in this area that the Jacobean Privy Council found its chief usefulness. Discovering that it functioned smoothly under Cecil's guidance, King James was only too glad to turn over to it all sorts of bothersome pieces of minor business. The volume of its transactions became enormous. It looked after the collection of the taxes authorized by Parliament and hunted down those who were delinquent in their payments. It busied itself with the import taxes and the 'benevolences' by which the Crown tried to make good the growing deficits in its finances. It enforced the recusancy laws, and attended to the country's military preparedness. From the council chamber poured forth letters of instructions to local authorities—town councils, sheriffs and lord lieutenants in the shires. At times it issued general proclamations. Nothing was too small for its attention. To Oxford it sent a ruling about a lane claimed by both city and university. To commissioners at Rye went a request for a report about the silting in the harbour. To the Justices of the Peace in Hertfordshire went orders to keep the highways in better repair, and to stop the Norwich and Cambridge carriers from using heavy wagons which would damage the same.

The flow of letters was not all in one direction. If the local authorities were constantly exhorted to further endeavours by the Council, they on their part looked to it for help whenever their own powers proved inadequate. Finding that colliers from London were dumping their ballast in the river before taking on coal, and so obstructing the channel, the authorities at Newcastle-upon-Tyne ordered the ships' masters to cease the practice. When the colliers failed to do so, the mayor and aldermen of Newcastle obtained a Privy Council order that the masters of the colliers must before sailing declare on oath where they had unloaded their ballast. Any who failed to do so would be guilty of contempt of the Council and this would be a Star Chamber matter.

Much of the Privy Council's business arose out of petitions. Some of these were made to the King, who then referred them to the Privy Council. Others were made directly to the Council. They dealt with an amazing range of subjects. There was a request from Mabel Griffith for a passport to travel abroad (the Council granted it though stipulating that she could not visit Rome). There was a petition from the Earl of Northumberland for relaxation of the terms of his imprisonment in the Tower, and one from Lady Parker that her husband be forced to pay the £200 per annum which the Council had earlier allowed her. Such was the press of people trying to get their petitions before the Council that some took to greasing the palms of the door-keepers of the council chamber. When the

Councillors became aware of this abuse, they issued strict orders that the keepers were not to demand gratuities from any persons having business with the Council, whether for admitting them to the council table or for delivering petitions. Sometimes the Councillors must have been overwhelmed by all the affairs over which they had to keep control. Fortunately they had a saving sense of humour, and at times this peeps out from their proceedings. After receiving an extremely lengthy letter alleging that persons of position had been accessary to a murder in the North but had escaped justice, the Privy Councillors sent their reply:

> We are sorry for the gentleman's death, and would have justice done upon the offenders: and desire that he that penned the letter may never pen more. Farewell.[2]

As earlier noted, failure to obey the commands of the Privy Council could become a Star Chamber matter. And here we come to the third function of the Jacobean Privy Council—the judicial. Each year when the law courts met at term time, the Council sat to hear cases which involved defiance or abuse of civil authority, subversion of the law, or breach of the peace. Since such cases required the punishment of offenders, the Privy Councillors added several of the judges to their number when hearing these cases. The augmented council usually met in the Star Chamber at Westminster instead of the council chamber at Whitehall, and hence it took the name of Court of Star Chamber when sitting in its judicial capacity. A succinct account of the Star Chamber Court is given by John Stow in his *Survey of London*:

> Then is there also the *Starre-Chamber*, where, in the Tearme time, every weeke once at the least, which is commonly on Fridaies and Wednesdaies, and on the next day after the Tearme endeth, the Lord Chancellor and the Lords, and other of the Privie-Councell, and the chiefe Justices of *England* from Nine of the Clocke, till it bee Eleven, doe sit.
>
> This place is called the *Starre-Chamber*, because the Roofe thereof is decked with the likenesse of Starres gilt: there be plaints heard, of Ryots, Rowts, and other misdemeanours, which if they be found by the Kings Councell, the party offender shall be censured by these persons, which speake one after another, and he shall bee both fined and commanded to prison.[3]

The range of cases heard in the Star Chamber is startling. Leafing through the index to its proceedings in the Public Record Office today, one finds it dealing among other things with perjury, assault, forcible entry, libel, rape, abuse of office, conspiracy, fraud, rescue of persons under arrest, packing of juries, destroying of enclosures, forging of affidavits, frivolous suits, seizures of goods, deer-stealing, abduction, breaking of church pews, malversion of funds, arrest without warrant, attempted poisoning and blasphemy.

In the time of King James the Court of Star Chamber had not acquired the odium which became attached to it under his son. Admittedly it had the reputation of 'beeing a court not to be dallied withall', but its record for dealing justly and expeditiously made most people look up to it. Towards the end of the reign, however, men began to realize the dangers inherent in such a tribunal, especially since its jurisdiction was being unwisely extended. Writing in July 1620 John Chamberlain observed:

> . . . indeed the world is now much terrified with the Star-chamber, there beeing not so litle an offence against any proclamation but is liable and subject to the censure of that court.

With its triple function, consultative, administrative and judicial, the Privy Council played so large a part, not only in the life of the court but of the entire nation, that some account must be given of its mode of meeting and operation. At the beginning of the reign, it met only once a week for its ordinary sessions. These meetings were held as a rule every Sunday, after the morning sermon. By 1605 it was obvious that these weekly sittings were not sufficient, and the King ordered the Council to meet on Wednesday afternoons also. Ordinarily all sessions were held in the council chamber at Whitehall. Meetings might, however, be convened at Royston, Theobalds, or anywhere else that the sovereign happened to be. When he was absent from his capital, a number of the Councillors usually remained behind and held meetings without him. Occasionally they might adapt themselves to the private convenience of one or more of their members. We hear of meetings at Suffolk House and at York House, but such use of the homes of Privy Councillors was quite exceptional.

The number of Councillors attending meetings was by no means constant. Full attendance was practically never to be expected, for some of the Privy Councillors regarded their membership as in part honorary and only occasionally bothered to attend. The actual membership of the Privy Council changed slightly, of course, from year to year. In 1613 it consisted of the following twenty-two members:

> The Archbishop of Canterbury (George Abbot)
> The Lord Chancellor (Lord Ellesmere)
> The Keeper of the Privy Seal (Earl of Northampton)
> The Duke of Lennox
> The Lord High Admiral (Earl of Nottingham)
> The Lord Chamberlain (Earl of Suffolk)
> The Earl of Shrewsbury
> The Master of the Horse (Earl of Worcester)
> The Earl of Pembroke
> The Earl of Exeter
> The Earl of Mar
> The Lord Chancellor of Scotland (Earl of Dunfermline)

Viscount Rochester
Viscount Fenton
Lord Zouch
Treasurer of the King's Household (Lord Knollys)
Comptroller of the King's Household (Lord Wotton)
Vice-chamberlain and Treasurer of the King's Chamber (Lord Stanhope)
Secretary of State (Sir Ralph Winwood)
Secretary of State (Sir John Herbert)
Chancellor of the Exchequer (Sir Julius Caesar)
Chancellor of the Duchy of Lancaster (Sir Thomas Parry)[4]

Checking this list against the attendance recorded for the thirty meetings held from the beginning of May until the end of September in this year, Professor E. R. Turner found that Northampton and Sir Julius Caesar missed only one meeting each, and that Archbishop Abbot missed only three. Ellesmere attended twenty-six meetings, Suffolk twenty-four, Parry twenty-two, Stanhope nineteen, Knollys seventeen, and Pembroke sixteen. The other members attended less than half the meetings. The frequent absence of the two secretaries of state occasions some surprise until we recall that the Privy Council really had comparatively little to do with foreign policy, which King James jealously kept under the management of himself and his favourites.

It was the custom of the Privy Council to dine together at Whitehall each council day, though probably with less magnificence and expense than attended their banquets when they were sitting at Westminster as the Court of Star Chamber. The practice must have helped to create a friendly sociable atmosphere within the Council, though at times there were inevitably clashes between the members. In June 1619 James, bent on keeping harmony among his Privy Councillors, ordered them to 'partake of the Sacrament of the Lord's Supper at Greenwich, in order to show mutual Charity one to another'.[5]

The Councillors had, of course, a clerical staff to help with their business. A clerkship to the Privy Council was a stepping-stone which led more than one man to distinguished office. Sir William Wade passed from one of these secretaryships to the Lieutenancy of the Tower of London. Sir Thomas Smith and Sir Thomas Edmondes, one-time clerks of the Council, became ambassadors to Russia and France respectively. The clerks had their own office adjacent to the council chamber and, like the Councillors themselves, were bound by an oath of secrecy.

During the early years of the reign the Archbishop of Canterbury presided over the Council whenever the King was absent. However, by 1616, probably because Abbot had lost the royal favour, the Lord Chancellor had taken over the presidency. In 1621, the long dormant office of Lord President of the Council was revived and conferred first upon Prince Charles and then upon Henry Montagu, Viscount Mandeville, as a sop to his feelings after he had been forced to resign the post of Lord Treasurer.

By Mandeville's time the Privy Council no longer enjoyed the prestige with which it had begun the reign. So long as Cecil had survived and the old Elizabethan way of doing things, the Council had retained its earlier importance. But after Cecil's death King James dealt more and more through his favourites, first Somerset and then Buckingham, rather than through the Privy Council. Matters of real importance were increasingly kept from the Council, which was left only thankless tasks of routine administration.

Paradoxically the decline of the Council was partly the consequence of a continued increase in its size. Beginning with about twelve members, it contained thirty-five by the end of the reign. Increasingly committees were formed out of it and special areas turned over to them:

> In 1623 there was a committee for the church—four members, a committee for revenue, trade, plantations, and courts—eighteen, a committee for patents, monopolies, fees and fines—eleven, and a committee for the army —thirteen.[6]

No doubt it was convenient to have business attended to in this way, but the Council became less important and less effective as an entity. Significantly there began to be references to a small inner group of Privy Councillors, 'a choise cabinet counsell to be selected out of the body of the whole table, to whom matters of most secrecie and importance are to be committed'[7]—the ancestor of the modern cabinet.

During the reign of King James there was a notable decline in the calibre of the Privy Councillors themselves. As early as 1613 Gondomar was discounting most of the Councillors as 'men of small property and little experience in affairs of state and of war'.[8] When Buckingham came to power he saw the Privy Council chiefly as an administrative tool to be used for his own convenience. The men whom he had the King add to its swelling membership were either abject creatures of his own (such as Conway, of whom even the complaisant James observed that Steenie had given him a secretary who could not write) or routine bureaucrats such as Calvert. Both types all too obviously lacked the ability and the personal prestige that would permit them to offer the advice in statecraft which Privy Councillors were originally intended to supply.

In any ultimate analysis it was King James himself who, through his negligence, was responsible for the decline of the Privy Council. He paid a price, for if ever there was a king who needed a strong Privy Council it was James. Had he had one and heeded its advice, he might have been saved from the shameful exhibition he made of himself both in the Palatinate negotiations and in the matter of the Spanish match. Certainly he needed all the help he could have secured from a strong Privy Council in the mounting struggle with Parliament.

James and his advisers regarded Parliament without enthusiasm or liking. The King, like every other monarch in Europe, was essentially an absolutist. To say this is not to imply that His Majesty was a hypocrite when he inscribed upon his coinage the motto *Salus populi suprema lex*. King James quite honestly believed that he himself, through his royal prerogative as well as his mastery of what he termed 'King craft', was the person best fitted to attend to the *salus populi*. James may have been mistaken in this belief, but nothing can be more unjust or unhistorical than to attack him because he did not have a set of nineteenth- or twentieth-century attitudes about the worth of parliamentary government. It is absurd to find reprehensible every attempt he made to keep power in his own hands, and meritorious every attempt of Parliament to impose its wishes upon him. Often it was Parliament and not the King that was unreasonable and unfair. We are concerned here not to commend or blame either side, but to see how King James and the court party which served him fared in their dealings with the various parliaments of his reign.

When King James arrived in England he found Parliament enjoying a position of considerable strength. His predecessors had conceded that they could not levy direct taxes without Parliament's consent, and had agreed that Parliament could seek satisfaction of grievances as a condition to voting supply. Moreover, Parliament had acquired a body of privileges intended to protect it from royal interference. One of these privileges, that of the lower house to determine the qualifications of its own members, King James violated in 1604 when he commanded the Commons to confer with the lords and judges after the right of Sir John Fortescue to hold his seat had been called into question.

If not often so overt in interference, King James was generally ungracious and suspicious when dealing with Parliament. He seemed to regard it as his right to be voted whatever money he wanted, and he was quick to abuse Parliament as perverse and malignant when it persisted in seeking reforms before granting him new taxes. He tried consistently to make its time-honoured privileges appear nothing more than favours, revocable at will, granted by himself and his predecessors. Had not a century of inflation and his own thriftlessness made it impossible for him to 'live of his own', James might have passed his reign without ever summoning a parliament. However, his financial position was such that either he had to seek supply from Parliament or, like his son later, outrage his subjects by securing needed extra income by means of dubious legality since lacking parliamentary consent. Deciding against the danger of the latter course, King James unwillingly summoned his parliaments. His distaste for doing so was no secret. Men remarked: 'That the king took physic and called parliament both alike, using both for mere need, and not caring for neither how little time they lasted.'⁹

In his endeavours to get money from Parliament without surrendering any of what he considered the rightful powers and prerogatives of his crown, King James had a number of cards in his favour. For one thing, it was he who determined when Parliament should be summoned, and drafted the proclamation declaring the purposes for which it was being called. For another, his ministers, many of whom would be elected to the coming parliament, could frame in advance the programme for the coming session, anticipate difficulties, and agree upon tactics. In any parliament the sovereign could expect to have a strong party working to advance his interests. About the Lords there was never any real worry; the peers almost invariably supported the King. But in the House of Commons, too, there was ordinarily a large group attached to the royal interest. The all-important core of this group was the cluster of Privy Councillors who, sitting close to the Speaker, formed almost a ministerial bench. Associated with them were a number of the King's legal advisers whose election could easily be arranged in boroughs or shires where the royal interest was strong. Moreover, a number of the rank-and-file members of the House either held or hoped to hold court offices and pensions, and so had a powerful motive for helping the King to get what he wanted. A somewhat cohesive and homogeneous group, these latter could be organized into a sort of 'court party' in the House of Commons. Finally, the Speaker, although theoretically the servant and spokesman of the House, was invariably nominated by one of the Privy Councillors and had been hand-picked to look after the sovereign's interests.

With Parliament in session, there were various ways by which the King could advance his wishes. Timely gestures and minor concessions could create an atmosphere of good will. Direct addresses, or messages despatched to the House, could make plain His Majesty's wishes. Should particular individuals let themselves emerge as leaders of opposition to the royal policies, the King could intimate through his servants the alarming consequences of royal displeasure, while offering the prospect of substantial rewards should they prove amenable to his wishes. If Parliament as a whole proved unco-operative, the King could adjourn or prorogue it whenever he pleased, or dissolve it altogether and rule without any parliament until such time as financial necessity compelled him to try again with a new one. The really surprising thing is that, with so many cards in their favour, James and his ministers fared so badly and failed so often in their dealings with Parliament. The fault lay chiefly in His Majesty's own negligence and impatience.

James's first parliament convened on March 19, 1604. Cecil and his assistants had carefully prepared for the occasion, not only by drafting memoranda on possible legislation but by seeing that a number of the right people got elected. When the House of Commons assembled it was found to contain a large contingent of M.P.s who were either royal officers or courtiers whose votes would support the King. They included Sir Roger Aston, one of the gentlemen of the King's bedchamber; Sir Richard Levison and Sir Edward Hoby, both gentlemen of the privy chamber; Sir Lewis Lewkenor, master of the ceremonies; Sir Thomas Vavasour, the knight marshal; Sir George Carew, vice-chamberlain to the Queen; John Corbett, clerk of the privy council; Sir Walter Cope and Sir William Killigrew, the chamberlains of the exchequer; Sir William Bowyer, a teller of the exchequer; Sir Robert Mansell, treasurer of the navy; Thomas Lake, clerk of the signet; Humphrey May, groom of the privy chamber; Sir William Fleetwood, receiver-general of the court of wards, and Robert Percival, remembrancer of the same court. Along with men such as these there sat in the Commons various junior members of the great families at court: Sir William Cecil and Sir Edward Cecil, Theophilus and Sir Thomas Howard, and Robert Sackville, heir to Lord Treasurer Dorset. Then there were others whose backgrounds were courtly—Sir Henry Rich, Sir Philip Herbert, Sir Robert Killigrew, Sir George More, Francis Clifford, Sir Robert Cotton, Sir Edward Denny, Sir John Egerton, Sir William Strode, Sir William Maynard, Sir Richard Warburton, and Tobie Mathew whose father was soon to become Archbishop of York.[10]

Despite the presence of this phalanx, which assumed something of the aspect of a court party during the next six years, serious weaknesses soon developed in the royal position. A notable deficiency was the lack of Privy Councillors in the House of Commons. In Elizabeth's time there had always been a strong group of Privy Councillors watching, and occasionally directing, the activities of the House. Since his accession King James had conferred peerages upon the most distinguished of these. Sir Robert Cecil, Sir William Knollys, Sir Edward Wotton and Sir Thomas Egerton had in consequence become incapable of serving the King in the House of Commons. No doubt it was nice for Cecil to sit in the House of Lords as Earl of Salisbury, but he could have done the King much better service in the Commons. Debarred from membership in the lower house, he attempted to act from the wings as the King's parliamentary manager. Keeping in very close touch with Sir Edward Phelips, the Speaker, he received reports, discussed tactics, and gave instructions. Nothing, however, could really take the place of Privy Councillors able to speak directly to the House of

Commons from a position of knowledge and prestige comparable to
Cecil's own. The two Privy Councillors in the Commons when the session
began in 1604, Sir John Herbert and Sir John Stanhope, were mediocrities
incapable of giving direction to the House.

When James prorogued the first session of his first parliament on
July 7, 1604, he made no secret of his disappointment in it. No funds had
been voted for his assistance. The title which he had assumed of 'King of
Great Britain' had not been ratified. And the Commons had annoyed the
King by the way in which they had concerned themselves with church
affairs. In his prorogation speech James could not keep from chiding
Parliament for its 'rashness' and lack of respect for himself.

Because of the Gunpowder Plot excitement which attended its opening,
the second session of this Parliament was marked by almost immediate
adjournment to January 21, 1606. In this second session the King and the
House of Commons got on together much better. Having shared together
the shock of discovering how near Fawkes had brought them to death,
they agreed well enough on new anti-recusancy laws. When the Commons
brought up, as they had in the earlier session, the abuse of purveyance,
they found the King and his ministers ready to give some satisfaction.

Purveyance was the right, long enjoyed by purchasing agents of the
King's household, to set the price at which suppliers must sell them their
commodities. In practice, the 'King's price' fell far short of the market
price. The Kent Purveyance Book for 1602 shows that the 'compounders'
for the supply of the court from Kent received only £947 10s. for supplies
worth £3,008 6s. 8d.[11] Suppliers had no escape from this form of exaction.

Purveyance was riddled with abuses. Not only did those supplying the
court receive less than a third of the real value of their produce, but they
were mulcted by purveyors who extorted from them at the 'King's price'
much more than the King's household ever used, and sold the surplus for
their own profit. Quite properly the Commons regarded purveyance as a
grievance which the King should remedy. In February 1606 a committee
of the Commons met with the Lords to deliver 'a complaint out of sorrow
and grief against the seed of the devil, namely, purveyors and officers of
the green cloth'. Nothing had been done in response to similar complaints
during the first session, but now the King issued a 'Proclamation for pre-
vention of future abuses in Purveyance' directed against such of his
officers as 'may make themselves (under colour of our prerogative royal)
the instruments of corruption and rapine'.

Partly because of the prospect of this proclamation, and partly because
of the skilful manœuvres of Bacon who, though no privy councillor, had
become Solicitor-General and so a leader of the court group of M.P.s,
Parliament was ready to help King James with money. Listening with

some sympathy to an account of his financial difficulties, it voted him three subsidies and six-fifteenths.[12]

There was little to please James about the work of the third session of this Parliament, which lasted from November 18, 1606 to November 10, 1607. The great issue this time was one of King James's fondest projects, the union of Scotland and England. Despite all the pressure that James's supporters could exert, the Commons resolutely refused to consent to this union. There was, in fact, a general weakening of the royal position at this time. One reason was a notable extension of the parliamentary committee system which had become established during the reign of Elizabeth. So great had the proliferation of committees now become that it was no longer possible to keep a Privy Councillor or some other reliable royal servant on each of them. The result was that the committees got more and more out of the control of the King's men. Moreover the Speaker, who had been a sheet-anchor where the royal interest was concerned, was steadily losing ground himself. By 1606–7 he no longer had the power of determining the order of the business before the House. Worse still, the Commons had found that they could by-pass him completely by sitting as a committee of the whole.

The device of having the House of Commons sit as a committee composed of all its members seems to have arisen, quite incidentally, from the use of an extremely large committee to report on the proposed union of England and Scotland. Apparently it was on May 7, 1607, that the House first took the revolutionary step of constituting itself as a committee of the whole.[13] The full beauty of the arrangement was not realized at first, but the M.P.s soon saw the advantages of getting the King's watchdog out of the Speaker's chair and replacing him with a chairman of their own choice. In 1621 a member quite frankly gave as his reason for moving that the House go into committee that they 'not be troubled this day with the Speaker'.[14]

This first Parliament of King James's reign convened for its fourth session in February 1609. The chief business before it was the Great Contract, Cecil's scheme for solving the King's financial difficulties by having Parliament vote him a very large annual sum in return for his relinquishing a whole series of feudal fees and prerogatives to which Parliament was opposed. The time was not altogether propitious for the submission of such a scheme. One of Archbishop Bancroft's protégés, a Cambridge don named Cowell, had published a book entitled *The Interpreter*, setting forth the doctrine that James was an absolute monarch and as such could make laws without consulting Parliament. So blatant an attack could not be ignored, and the M.P.s came to Westminster full of anger and suspicion. Fortunately, King James decided to give Parliament the reassurance it demanded. At a conference of the Commons and Lords, Cecil declared that the King 'did acknowledge that he had noe power to make lawes of himselfe, or to exact any subsidies *de jure* without the consent of his 3 Estates; and therefore he was soe farre from approvinge the opinyon that he did hate those that beleved yt'.[15]

Satisfied by this statement, the Commons proceeded to another grievance, the customs duties known as 'impositions'. In his herculean struggle to restore solvency to the royal finances, Cecil had introduced a new book of rates increasing many of these tariffs and introducing new ones. King and Parliament now clashed head on over the legality of Cecil's action. James maintained that it was his prerogative to set impositions. Various members of the Commons retorted that he had to have parliamentary authority to do so, and that Cecil's action circumvented the principle that parliamentary approval must be secured for taxation levied on the subject. In the end it was agreed, as part of the bargain embodied in the Great Contract that, though existing impositions should remain in force, the King would in the future levy impositions only after they had been approved by Parliament. The concession, as James saw it, was a notable one, and it left him the less inclined to permit the Commons to attach further conditions concerning church discipline and civil affairs. When the Commons persisted in seeking these, James decided upon prorogation.

Looking back over the session, Bacon felt that Cecil had weakened the whole royal position by proposing the Great Contract. Not only had he revealed to Parliament the economic weakness of the King and the extent of their own strength, but he had taught them a striking lesson in how to barter with the King. Bacon was convinced that this barter principle was dangerous to the King's prestige and authority. He himself envisaged a very different way of doing things: the King indulgently and sympathetically listening to the words of his Commons and then graciously, of his own volition, remedying the evils which they had drawn to his attention; the Commons faithfully advising the King and giving him, as a matter of course, whatever money was needed to sustain himself and his government in needful fashion and solemnity.

Bacon may have been dealing in old-fashioned romanticism about the relationship that should exist between the sovereign and Parliament. One thing, however, was undeniable—the protracted negotiations over the Great Contract had helped to bring into being something which was recognizably a 'country party', as distinguished from the court group in the Commons. The long life of this Parliament had allowed men of kindred views to get to know each other. Those who felt that they should stand up to the King and his ministers had now begun to consult together outside of Parliament and, matching Cecil's organizing of the King's friends, were making rudimentary attempts at co-ordinating their own endeavours. The development augured ill for future relations between James and the House of Commons.

The final session of this first of King James's parliaments began on October 16, 1610. It proved short and violent. James had by now decided that the Commons' terms for the Great Contract were exorbitant, and his small stock of patience soon gave way. Summoning thirty of the offending M.P.s to Whitehall, he attempted to browbeat them, declaring that it was their plain duty to give him the money that he needed. To Cecil, who urged patience, His Majesty wrote that for seven years he had shown patience and had received in return insults and ignominies. He would show patience but not 'asinine patience'. No house save the house of Hell, said the furious monarch, would have ventured to treat him as the House of Commons had done.

Young Robert Carr, who had reported to the King some anti-Scottish remarks passed in Parliament, may have been responsible for the violence of the King's feelings. Carr, too, was probably responsible for James's final burst of anger which resulted in him dissolving Parliament on February 9, 1611. James would not listen to a word spoken in defence of the Commons. With his pen he vented his frustration and anger:

> Wherein we have misbehaved ourselves we know not, but . . . our fame and actions have been tossed like tennis-balls among them, and all that spite and malice durst do to disgrace and inflame us hath been used. To be short, this Lower House by their behaviour have perilled and annoyed our health, wounded our reputation, emboldened all ill-natured people, encroached upon many of our privileges, and plagued our people with their delays.[16]

A little more than three years later, on April 5, 1614, King James met a new parliament. After his earlier experience he had been remarkably loath to summon it, and Northampton and the rest of the Howards had almost persuaded him against this second venture. On the other hand, James's financial position was desperate and parliamentary supply seemed the only hope. Moreover, Bacon had assured him that those whose opposition had tormented him earlier would trouble him no longer. Offices and money, discreetly bestowed, had helped to persuade many of the latter of the folly of their course. Indeed, one of the group, Sir Henry Neville, ambitious for the secretaryship of state left vacant upon Cecil's death, had come forward with certain 'propositions': let King James satisfy the Commons upon certain specified points and he 'dared undertake for most of them, that the king's majesty, proceeding in a gracious course towards his people, should find those gentlemen exceeding willing to do him service'. What Neville offered was a sort of reduced Great Contract, for which he was more or less guaranteeing parliamentary acceptance. The Privy Council listened with some scepticism to the plans of Neville and his fellow 'undertakers'. Most of the Councillors probably realized the presumption and folly Neville was showing in pledging a not yet existent parliament to any particular course. King James, however, was sufficiently reassured to summon a new parliament.

Many of the elections were bitterly contested. In various ridings the King's ministers intervened effectively to secure the election of members who would be responsive to their master's wishes. When two courtiers, Sir Julius Caesar and Sir Thomas Lake, were elected at Uxbridge as knights of the shire to represent Middlesex, one of Sir Francis Darcy's people 'getting up upon a table told the assemblie, that his master meant to have stoode, but was forbidden by the King'. How often such interference occurred it is impossible to say, but of the men recognizably oppositionist in the parliament of 1604–11, considerably less than half were present in that of 1614. On the other hand, the court faction was probably only a little larger numerically than before. Four Privy Councillors were present as members when the session opened. Over 65 per cent of the members of the House of Commons had never sat there before. Their votes would decide which way things would go.

If the King's ministers had hoped, partly by buying off opposition leaders and partly by exerting all the influence they could upon the electors, to secure a compliant parliament, they soon learned their mistake. The role of the 'undertakers' became known, and when they appeared in the House of Commons it was as discredited and vilified men. When, in accordance with Neville's scheme, concessions were offered to the House in the form of royal 'Bills of Grace', they were despised as crude bribes. New 'country' leaders took the place of those who had defected to the Crown, and from the outset the tone of this new parliament was belligerent. Ironically, Bacon, who had helped persuade James to call this parliament, found that now that he had become the King's Attorney-General the Commons were challenging his right to sit among them. To placate them James made a concession which would permanently weaken his position in the future—let Bacon remain in his place and no subsequent attorney-general would be allowed to sit in the Commons. The M.P.s accepted the King's offer. A few weeks later they were on the offensive again. Finding that one of the Privy Councillors, Sir Thomas Parry, had used corruption to secure the election of Sir Henry Wallop and Sir Walter Cope at Stockbridge, the Commons, brushing aside the King's request that Parry's punishment be left to him, expelled Parry along with Wallop and Cope.

As the session progressed, the majority of the Commons united in a determination not to vote the King any money until they had secured full satisfaction of their grievances. The matter of impositions, left unsettled with the failure of the Great Contract, was once more taken up. In vain Sir Ralph Winwood tried to get the House to discuss supply for the King. Ignoring all his pleas, the members continued to hammer away at their grievances. Winwood's position was unenviable. Appointed Secretary of State only seven days before the session had begun, he had not had time to organize his supporters or to lay his plans. In any case he was a blunt, tactless man with none of the smooth facility that characterizes an effective parliamentary manager. The King's friends in the House were soon hopelessly disorganized, with some courtiers urging one set of tactics, some another, and all of them achieving nothing.

King James, his worst fears realized, decided to take a hand. Writing to the warring Commons, he warned that either they would take up the matter of supply or he would dissolve them. The message failed to secure the desired effect. Instead young Christopher Neville, lashing out at those who had recommended such tactics to His Majesty, fulminated against various great persons at court as 'spaniells to the King and wolves to the people', while one John Hoskyns, delivering a vicious attack against the King's Scottish favourites, hinted darkly at another Sicilian Vespers.[17] Hoskyns's speech was the last straw. On June 7th King James dissolved parliament. It had lasted only two months. The next day a number of the members of the erstwhile House of Commons appeared, under orders, before the Privy Council. Those who had led the attack on impositions were required to hand over their notes on the subject, and these were burned on the spot. Young Neville and Hoskyns were sent off to the Tower of London, along with two others whose conduct the King had found particularly outrageous. A day or so later His Majesty tore up with his own royal hands the eight bills which this parliament had passed and which had been awaiting his approval.

In 1614 national opinion had not begun to get excited about conflicts between King and Parliament. As yet most of the English had little real sense of identity with the House of Commons, and foreign observers were impressed by the prestige enjoyed by 'the royal authority, which the English reverence above everything else'. The consequence was that when James abruptly dissolved parliament public opinion was on his side, not on that of the M.P.s who had opposed his wishes. No doubt an inexperienced House of Commons had been brash in their opposition to the King and had overestimated their power to extort concessions from him. No doubt members of the 'opposition', if it could be called that, had been rude, reckless and poorly led. The real fault lay however with the King, Somerset, and Bacon. First, there had been clumsy interference with the elections and the stupid attempt to commit parliament in advance to a particular course of action. In the face of the irritation and suspicion thus very naturally aroused in the Commons, the King and his councillors had failed completely to re-establish confidence in their own good faith or even to organize their supporters in the House. Having exacerbated the opposition, they attempted to bulldoze through a subsidy bill. When the Commons rebelled against passing it, their only response was dissolution followed by personal reprisals. The Jacobean man in the street failed however to realize all this. All that he knew was that Parliament had wrangled for weeks 'more like a cockpit then a grave counsaile', and that there were no new statutes to show. This Parliament had not served what was still considered its basic function, to vote needed supply for the King. Viewing matters thus, the mass of the English threw the blame on the Commons and labelled this the 'Addled Parliament'. As for King James, he had had enough of parliaments. For the next seven years he managed to do without one.

When a new parliament did meet, it owed its existence to developments on the Continent. The autumn of 1620 had seen the King's son-in-law, the Elector Frederick, going down to disaster. Spinola, doing what James had said he would never do, had invaded the Palatinate, and Frederick had lost his new kingdom of Bohemia in the Battle of the White Mountain. Swept by militant Protestant fervour, England called upon its king to declare war in aid of the Elector. James, torn between anger and mortification, was half inclined to do so. War, however, would require expenditures which only Parliament could provide. It was put to His Majesty that, with so grave a crisis abroad, a new parliament would surely support him with money while avoiding embroilment in controversial domestic issues. It was pointed out also that, even if he decided against war, the calling of a parliament might in itself be a move that would frighten Spain into aiding in the restoration of Frederick's lost territories. For these and a variety of other reasons, James decided once more to summon an English parliament.

Unusual care was shown by the royal ministers in their preparations for this third parliament. A commission composed of Bacon, the two Chief Justices, Sir Edward Coke, and Sir Randall Crew (who had been Speaker back in 1614) reviewed the grievances aired in the earlier parliament and considered what more recent suits might be added by the new one. They drafted an eloquent proclamation declaring that this time there would be no 'undertakers', and that the King's motive for summoning Parliament was his resolution to save the Palatinate at all costs. To complete their work they submitted a list of persons for whom it would be desirable, in the King's interest, to find seats in the new House of Commons. Their labours were not entirely acceptable to James. Reading the proposed proclamation, he was not so sure that he was determined to save the Palatinate at all costs. Accordingly he drafted a much less impressive statement of his own. When this was published in November 1620, its warning against the election of 'wrangling lawiers' was hardly considered a good omen.

With nine Privy Councillors seated in the Commons and Prince Charles in daily attendance in the House of Lords, this new parliament had a very distinguished membership. At the opening on January 20, 1621, King James delivered a conciliatory speech, jesting about a 'strange kind of beast called *undertaker*' which had caused much unhappiness in 1614. Parliament, for its part, had learned a lesson from the angry dissolution of its two predecessors. The new House of Commons was ready to do anything, short of surrendering its essential rights, to keep on good terms with the King. Within a few weeks, without awaiting redress of grievances, it unanimously voted the King two subsidies, not as a grant for the expected war but as a freewill gift to help him with his ordinary expenses. When the Commons came to consider grievances, they resolutely avoided questioning any of the King's powers and concentrated instead upon misuse of office by various of his servants. They were particularly concerned with the 'monopolies' by which a pack of worthless courtiers had fastened themselves parasitically upon the nation's economic life.

Before ever Parliament was summoned, there had been a mounting outcry against the monopolists. John Chamberlain, writing late in October 1620, noted the indignation against such monopolies as that which levied a toll of sixpence on every load of hay brought into London, and that 'for the probat of wills which raises a great clamor among the Proctors against Kit Villers who is to have the benefit'. The grant which received the particular scrutiny of Parliament was that for the licensing of inns and taverns. Ostensibly a measure for the reduction of drunkenness and the detection of bawdy-houses, this was found to amount to little more than a legalized 'shake-down' of innkeepers and tavern owners. One of the patentees, Sir Giles Mompesson, who was a kinsman of Buckingham's, fled the country to escape the wrath of the Commons. Buckingham himself took fright but John Williams, the future Lord Keeper, cannily advised him to swim with the tide and for the time he did so. Parliament, in fact, had no desire to antagonize the King by directly attacking his favourite. Leaving the big fish unpursued, it spread its net for the little ones. A parliamentary committee began zealously to investigate the patents conferring monopolies, their patentees, and the referees who had advised the King to make these grants. Grimly they reported that they found it a more than herculean labour to cleanse this Augean stable.

Parliament's zeal for discovering graft and malversation of office found other avenues. Lord Chancellor Bacon's peculiar ways were looked into. The King, deciding not to protect him, permitted Parliament for the first time since 1459 to impeach a royal minister. Almost unnoticed, Parliament had regained possession of an extremely dangerous weapon. King James professed himself delighted with the good intentions and energy of the Lords and Commons. If he had misgivings he concealed them. Appearing before the House of Lords on March 26th, His Majesty declared:

> This I professe, and take comfort in, that the House of Commons at this time have shewed greater love, and used me with more respect in all their proceedings, then ever any House of Commons have heeretofore done to mee.[18]

The Commons were receiving the rewards for their two subsidies.

Bacon was not the only royal officer that Parliament found guilty of corruption. Charges were successfully brought against Sir John Bennet, Judge of the Prerogative Court of Canterbury, and Sir Henry Yelverton, a former attorney-general. Largely because he had aroused the enmity of Buckingham, Yelverton had been deprived of office some months earlier and imprisoned in the Tower. His alleged offence was that he had exceeded his powers as attorney-general when drafting a new charter for the City of London. Everyone knew, however, that his real crime had been opposing the wishes of Buckingham. Now, in April 1621, he was brought from the Tower and charged before the House of Lords with scandalous compliance in the issuance of patents for the licensing of inns and for the manufacturing of gold and silver thread. Already a ruined man, Yelverton did not see why he should cover up for Buckingham. Angrily he divulged that only the threat of Buckingham's displeasure had made him support Mompesson's application. Then, losing all control over himself, he stormed against Buckingham and compared him with the royal favourites who had tyrannized over England in the time of Edward II. The implications of the parallel between James and the notoriously homosexual earlier monarch were not missed by Yelverton's scandalized hearers. Yelverton was speedily charged with slandering Buckingham and the King. The Lords made no attempt to get to the bottom of so perilous a case. Hurriedly they found Yelverton guilty, and Buckingham jubilantly declared himself 'parliament-proof'.

Despite the outcome of the Yelverton hearing, the King and his advisers were increasingly unhappy about Parliament. The latter's continued exposures of corruption in their administration hardly redounded to their credit. Moreover, after the initial two subsidies, Parliament was proving unresponsive to the King's requests for further grants. Decidedly disturbing was the emergence for the first time of a species of opposition party in the House of Lords. True, the latter, headed by the Earl of Southampton, was directed more against Buckingham than the King. But James considered opposition to his favourite as criminal as any directed against himself. In the Commons, too, trouble was threatening. Despite the presence of nine Privy Councillors, not one of them had emerged as a successful organizer of what might be regarded as the 'King's party'. In fact, one of the Privy Councillors, Sir Edward Coke, had defected and joined with those critical of the King and his favourite. The tactics of Coke and his associates were much more subtle than those of their predecessors in the Parliament of 1614, but for this very reason harder to detect and frustrate. In June, to the anger of the M.P.s, King James suddenly adjourned Parliament until November.

During the recess the King and his ministers followed a twofold policy. One part of it was to show the country that the government was capable of cleaning house without the aid of Parliament. Hence there appeared a royal proclamation cancelling a great many of the monopolies which had been the subject of complaint. The other part was to discourage through intimidation any future mustering of opposition to the royal wishes. Within a fortnight of the adjournment of Parliament, the Earl of Southampton was imprisoned in the Tower of London, not to be released for two months. Later that summer Sir Edwin Sandys, who during the session had been threatened by Cranfield with the consequences of opposing the King's wishes, was placed under arrest.

Parliament reconvened in November in an atmosphere of extreme tension. Bitterness, suspicion, and anger were all that the Crown had won by the sudden adjournment in June and the arrests of Southampton and Sandys. The explosion was not long in coming. Although King James had made it clear that the Commons were not to debate foreign policy—a matter which he declared lay wholly within his royal prerogative—the members felt that they could no longer remain silent while the King followed his fatuous scheme of the Spanish match and the last of the Palatinate was lost to Catholic armies. Accordingly, the House of Commons petitioned King James to rally about him the German Protestant princes, to redeem the Palatinate by force of arms, and to marry Prince Charles to a Protestant. Before Parliament had this petition ready to submit to the King, Gondomar gave him foreknowledge of it. Stirred on by the Spaniard, James was livid with anger. In a furious letter to the Speaker he forbade the Commons to meddle in matters of state or ever again to presume to speak about the marriage of his son.

In his letter the King took cognizance also of the concern expressed in the Commons at the arrest of Sandys during the summer recess. His arrest, said James, had not been the consequence of what he had said in Parliament. On the other hand, added His Majesty:

We thinke our Selfe very free and able to punish any mans misdemeanours in Parliament, as well during their sitting as after; which We meane not to spare hereafter, upon any occasion of any mans insolent behaviour there, that shalbe ministred unto Us.[19]

Queen Elizabeth had disciplined M.P.s by sending them to the Tower, but she had never challenged thus the whole principle that was gradually emerging of parliamentary immunity. The Commons, appalled by the King's letter, decided to lay aside all other business until their essential freedom had been fully established.

On December 11th a delegation from the lower house waited on James at Newmarket where, out of touch with Parliament but receiving the reports of Buckingham and Gondomar, His Majesty had been devoting himself to his hunting. With ponderous humour James greeted the Commons spokesmen as delegates from another sovereign state—when they entered he called for stools for the ambassadors. The petition now tendered to him renounced all claims to discuss foreign policy or the Prince's marriage. It declared, however, that there was one point which Parliament could not abandon, the 'Antient Liberty of Parliament for Freedom of Speech, Jurisdiction, and Just Censure'. This liberty was described as 'our antient and undoubted Right, and an Inheritance received from our Ancestors'.

Three days later the King's reply was read to the House. The rights which the Commons had claimed, said His Majesty, were actually not rights but only privileges 'derived from the grace and permission of our Ancestors and Us'. The Commons were in consternation. No time should be lost, they decided, in making a categorical declaration of their *rights*. When James learned that they had appointed a committee to draft such a manifesto, he despatched two further letters which he intended to be conciliatory. His efforts were in vain. Only explicit guarantees would now satisfy the aroused Commons, and these the King would not give. Racing to act before the King either prorogued or dissolved Parliament, the Commons on December 17, 1621, read into their journal a solemn 'protestation' of their liberties which affirmed:

That the Liberties, Franchises, Priviledges and Jurisdictions of Parliament, are the antient and undoubted Birthright and Inheritance of the Subjects of *England*; And that the arduous and urgent affairs concerning the King, State, and Defence of the Realm, and of the Church of *England*, and the maintenance and making of Lawes, and redress of mischiefs and grievances which daily happen within this Realm, are proper subjects and matter of Councel and Debate in Parliament; And that in the handling and proceeding of those businesses, every Member of the House of Parliament hath, and of right ought to have freedom of speech, to propound, treat, reason and bring to conclusion the same; And that the Commons in Parliament have like liberty and freedom to treat of these matters in such order as in their judgments shall seem fittest; And that every Member of the said House hath like freedom from all Impeachment, Imprisonment and molestation (other then by Censure of the House itself). . . .[20]

On purely historical grounds there was more justification for the King's view that parliamentary immunity was a special privilege granted by the Crown, but Coke had easily persuaded the Commons that history supported their own more extensive claims.

At the urging of those members who most feared a break with the King, it had been agreed that the Commons' protestation, though entered in their own journal, should not be sent as a petition to the King. James, however, was in no mood for evasions. Two weeks later he sent for the journal of the House and with his own hands tore out the offending pages, just as earlier he had ripped up the bills of the Parliament of 1614. On January 6, 1622, the inevitable further step was taken. To the delight of Buckingham and Gondomar, King James proclaimed the dissolution of his third parliament.

On February 12, 1624, James for the fourth and last time opened a parliament. There had been a startling reversal of situation since 1621. Prince Charles and Buckingham, hungering for revenge after the humiliations of their Spanish adventure, had now taken up the position held earlier by Parliament and were crying for war with Spain as the only way of regaining the Palatinate. Caught between their wishes and his own deep desire to keep the peace, the old king threw open to the Commons the long-forbidden field of foreign policy and, in his opening speech, asked for their counsel. James must have known that an English parliament would give him only one answer. However, before that answer was given, the Lords and Commons were summoned to the great hall at Whitehall jointly to hear Buckingham report on what had happened in Spain. Ignoring all that was shameful to Charles and himself, Buckingham gave an extended account of the perfidy of the Spaniards in the negotiations which had now been terminated. At times he turned to the Prince, who with a prompt 'Aye' confirmed his narration.

At the end of the Duke's speech, he and the Prince emerged as the idols of Parliament. Now at last English arms would punish Spanish treachery and make King Philip restore the Palatinate to Frederick and Protestantism! A few days later Lords and Commons concurred in advising the King to abrogate the Spanish treaty. When the idealistic Sir John Eliot brought up the still unresolved matter of royal recognition of the liberties of Parliament, the matter was hurriedly referred to committee and allowed to perish there. Zealously the Commons turned their attention to drafting new and stricter laws against the English Catholics, stripped now of the protection they had enjoyed during the marriage negotiations with Spain.

King James viewed with intense dislike Parliament's crusades against Spain and his Catholic subjects. Neither crusade, he knew, would do much to secure the restoration of the Palatinate. It was not the King of Spain but the Emperor Ferdinand and Duke Maximilian of Bavaria who chiefly stood between Frederick and his birthright—a fact which Parliament was largely ignoring. In vain the King tried to expostulate. The combined pressure of his son, his favourite, and Parliament was too strong for him to resist. When he wanted to reject a bellicose parliamentary petition, Buckingham immediately urged that he accept it and 'make a right under-standing between you and your people'. Buckingham and Charles, in fact, were rapidly taking control of things. When they disagreed with what James said in a message to Parliament, they blandly explained that His Majesty had really meant to say something quite different. James had neither the strength nor the courage to discipline them. His emotional dependence upon Steenie and Baby Charles was far too great. To break with them now, amid the weakness and desolation of old age, was unthink-able.

James's impotence was shown strikingly in the impeachment of Lionel Cranfield. If ever there was a man who had served King James well, it was Cranfield. With his dogged industry he had done as much as any man could to restore the King to solvency. He had been well rewarded with money, and had become Earl of Middlesex and Lord Treasurer, but inevitably he had made enemies. His economies, coupled with his all-too-obvious contempt for the greed and financial incompetence of the courtiers, had made most of the latter hostile to him. On the other hand, in the Commons in 1621 he had emerged as one of the strongest champions of the royal prerogative, and had infuriated the popular party by his ruthless bullying. Disliked by court and country factions alike, he needed a strong ally. For a time, after his marriage to Ann Brett, it appeared that he had the necessary support in Buckingham. By 1624, however, the two men had become estranged—perhaps because Cranfield had tried to curb Buckingham's extravagance in Spain, perhaps because in the latter's absence he had tried to advance young Arthur Brett as a new royal favour-ite. In any case, Cranfield now opposed Buckingham's war policy as financially ruinous. Tactlessly he declared that, even if Prince Charles no longer loved the Infanta, he owed it to the nation to marry her and salvage what benefits he could from the match. Knowing how closely Cranfield's opinions chimed with those still held secretly by King James, Buckingham and Charles decided that he was too dangerous a counsellor to leave near the wavering monarch. It became harder and harder for

Cranfield to secure access to James. Then, on April 15, 1624, charges of corruption were laid against him in the House of Commons. Tried by the Lords, Cranfield was found guilty, and was sentenced to loss of office, a fine of £50,000 and imprisonment in the Tower during the King's pleasure.

The King was sick at heart at what had happened. Like everybody else, he knew that while Cranfield had been guilty of some malfeasance, he would never have been brought to trial had he not opposed the wishes of Buckingham and Prince Charles. James had even made a few half-hearted attempts to save his servant. Sending for Lord Keeper Williams, he had asked him to use his influence to prevent the impeachment. Williams had answered him plainly that more than this was needed: Buckingham and Charles were seeking Cranfield's conviction and the King would have to dishonour either them or his Lord Treasurer. A week or so before the verdict was brought in against Cranfield, James in a speech before the Lords had offered a timorous extenuation of Cranfield's fault, but the gesture had been too weak and too late.

At times fits of his old anger still swept the King, and he vented his feelings privately to Buckingham and to Charles. He expatiated upon the folly and danger of letting Parliament pass judgment on royal ministers. (Apparently there had been second thoughts since he had permitted Parliament to impeach Bacon.) 'You are a fool,' he growled at Steenie, 'you are making a rod with which you will be scourged yourself.' And turning to Charles, who in his eagerness to be revenged on Spain was letting Parliament invade areas which James had always kept within the royal prerogative, he spoke even more prophetically. 'You will live,' said King James, 'to have your bellyful of Parliaments.'[21]

The impeachment of Cranfield was incidental to the main business of the Parliament of 1624, the intricate manœuvring by which a reluctant King James was brought to abrogate the treaties with Spain in return for a vote of supply considerably smaller than he wanted. On April 20th the Commons were notified by Secretary Conway that the hated treaties were now null and void. On May 14th they gave third reading to a bill voting the King three subsidies and six fifteenths. To make sure that the money would be spent on the purpose for which it had been voted, war to recover the Palatinate, Parliament stipulated that a commission of its own members should superintend the expenditure of the sums so raised—a gratuitous insult to the King's good faith and a remarkable further encroachment upon the royal prerogative.

In his speech proroguing Parliament, King James made no secret of his misgivings about its actions, and created a sensation by declaring that he would alter the wording of the preamble to the Subsidy Bill. As for impeachments, he said that if in the future Parliament had any grievances about his ministers, it was to send its complaints to him and he would see that the matter was 'redrest according to right'. There was an irony to the statement. James, had he known it, was taking leave of Parliament for good. The king who would have to cope with it next would be Charles I.

CHAPTER XXX

Last Scene of All

IN 1621 an unknown engraver portrayed King James mounted, like a colossus, upon a giant charger against a background view of London. The horse proudly turns his head, the monarch holds a sceptre in one hand and the reins in the other. The ribboned ends of the sash about his cuirass stream in the breeze. Despite much that is wooden in the draughtsmanship, the first impression is unmistakable—it is one of strength and kingly dignity. But then the gaze rests upon the monarch's features. The tired old face is filled with unutterable weakness and misery. The eyes stare bleakly. The once full cheeks, now sunken, lie in flat folds beside the ill-kept, thinning moustache and beard. The mouth hangs loosely. It is the face of a man who is utterly burnt out. Then one looks downward to the booted leg extending to the stirrup. How bloated and awkward it is! One recalls that in this year of 1621 the King had become so weak in the legs that he had to be carried in a chair to open Parliament, and men doubted if he would ever walk again. One notices the hands. How feebly the twisted fingers hold the sceptre; how awkwardly the bunched arthritic left hand clutches at the reins! Gradually the full irony of the portrait becomes apparent. For all the heroic dimensions of the King on his magnificent horse, the engraver had realized what everybody about the court during James's last years knew only too well—physically, emotionally and mentally, the King was in decay. The portrait bears its own testimony to the ever-increasing timidity, the maudlin dependence on Steenie and Baby Charles, the tantrums when they crossed his will, the tearful capitulations when the old man finally gave way.

There were repeated rumours during these last years of the reign that, melancholic and debilitated, James was about to abdicate, or at least to make a formal transfer of his powers to the Prince, and devote the rest of his life to his studies and to the hunting which was still his pleasure even when he had to be borne on a litter to see his deer. Charles and Buckingham would have been delighted had the King adopted such a course. James, however, was determined to keep a hold on the reins of government. When he discovered that Lord Evers was spreading reports of his imminent retirement, he forced him to sue for pardon for high treason before he let him go unpunished.

o

There can be no doubt that Charles and Buckingham, seeing the prema-
ture onset of senility in the King, intended to take the royal power almost
completely into their own hands. Some twisted version of their plans may
have lain behind the charges, submitted to King James by the Spanish
ambassador Inojosa in 1624, that Buckingham was plotting to dethrone
him and have Charles crowned in his stead. Inojosa was acting out of
desperation engendered by the losing fight that he had been waging to
keep Buckingham and Charles from detaching James from his Spanish
alliance. The Privy Council, to whom James referred the Spaniard's
charges, exonerated Buckingham completely.

Since their journey to Spain, both Charles and Buckingham had realized
that the King of Spain had no intention of forcing his allies to restore to
Frederick his lost territories. Another solution had to be found for the
Palatinate problem. Together the two young men evolved a dazzling new
programme. Let the Palatinate be regained through war, and let that war
take the form of a great crusade against both the Spanish and Austrian
Hapsburgs and their allies. Let Parliament be called forthwith, both to
supply a war chest and to rally the English to the cause. Let England
prepare for a maritime war against Spain and, while avoiding too great
involvement in a land war in the heart of Europe, form a grand alliance
with the Dutch and the Danes, the German princes, Venice, Savoy and
France, for a great onslaught upon the dynasty whose predominance
threatened them all. The scheme was grandiose but not impossible. Had
Buckingham possessed the infinite patience and skill of a Richelieu, he
might conceivably have made it work. Then one single concerted endeavour would have done in a year what it took the Thirty Years War to
accomplish. Unfortunately, Buckingham and Charles were not the men to
conduct successfully so complex a set of manœuvres.

The first obstacle was King James himself. Instead of appreciating the
greatness of the new plan, the old man clung with childish obstinacy to the
idea of marrying Charles to the Infanta, even though his son had made it
plain that he was 'irreconcilably disgusted' with the Spaniards. However,
by cajolery and bullying, James's heir and his favourite got him to call a
parliament and to abrogate the Spanish treaties. Not that they did not have
their anxious moments while steering the difficult old man along the course
they had plotted. Always there was the risk that the unhappy James would
rebel. To minimize this danger, they systematically isolated him from all
who might encourage his pro-Spanish hankerings. Ambassadors from
Spain found that they could never speak to the King without Charles or
Buckingham being present. The Venetian ambassador drily observed to
his government that the two were watching the King 'with great jealousy'
and that 'as though he were in a state of siege they keep away from him

IACOBUS D.G. MAGNÆ, BRITANNIÆ, FRANCIÆ
SCOTIÆ, ET HYBERNIÆ, REX, ANNO MDCXXI.

KING JAMES I IN 1621

those whom they consider suspect'.[1] He noted that when Charles was busy with Parliament in London, Buckingham stayed 'like a sentinel' with the King at Newmarket. The ruin of Cranfield was only part of a larger programme. Charles and Buckingham wanted Cranfield's impeachment to be a warning to everybody else in the court not to encourage the King in any lingering inclination to patch things up with Spain.

For their grand design, Charles and Buckingham needed the support not only of King James and the English parliament but of various foreign powers. Buckingham might be over-optimistic in his plans and negligent in details, but he was not a fool. He knew that England could never regain the Palatinate by her own military resources, chiefly directed by sea against Spain. She had to have allies. He realized, moreover, that to hearten these allies she would have to put some troops on the Continent. An obvious alliance to make was with the Dutch who were already at war with Spain and the Spanish Netherlands. Accordingly on June 5, 1624, a treaty was signed with the States-General, and under its provisions regiments of English soldiers under the Earls of Oxford, Essex and Southampton, and Lord Willoughby, sailed to serve under the Dutch command.

Quite as important to Buckingham and Charles were the French. Normally the Catholic King of France could not be expected to join the English in an action against his co-religionist the King of Spain. By 1624, however, the French were taking alarm at the Spanish encirclement of their country. If the English were concerned about the Palatinate, France was equally concerned about the Valtelline. In 1620 the latter territory—the valley extending northward from Lake Como—had been seized by the Spanish from the Protestant Grison Leagues. France, Venice and Savoy had all endeavoured to negotiate a Spanish withdrawal from this highly strategic area, but Spanish garrisons still remained there in 1624, and the French had decided to expel them by force. Nothing was more logical than a concerted Anglo-French endeavour to free both the Palatinate and the Valtelline. Buckingham and Charles received encouraging responses from Paris when they suggested an alliance against Spain.

The late spring of 1624 saw England, to the evident distress of King James, steadily moving closer to war with Spain. Parliament, as expected, had voted funds for the recovery of the Palatinate, and a Council of War had been appointed to direct their expenditure. Overtures were being made to Savoy and Venice as well as Holland and France. Moreover, Mansfeld had arrived in England.

Count Ernest of Mansfeld was one of those utterly unprincipled mercenary generals whose armies ravaged Central Europe during the Thirty Years War. Plausible, unreliable and brutal, he had been employed earlier by both Frederick and the Dutch. Now he was made the hinge of the contemplated Anglo-French alliance. Arriving in London from France in April, he was greeted rapturously by crowds infected with war fever. As the guest of Prince Charles, he was installed in the room in St. James's Palace which had been prepared for the Spanish Infanta, a savage irony which delighted the English. Days of exuberant planning followed, with the old King being constantly reassured that all that was intended was the expulsion of the imperialist and Bavarian troops from the Palatinate—not any English hostilities against Spain herself. With matters represented thus, James agreed tentatively to supply Mansfeld with 13,000 troops if France would raise a corresponding contingent. The two forces, it was planned, would be used to regain both the Palatinate and the Valtelline.

The negotiations with France in the spring, summer and autumn of 1624 were not limited to military matters. Charles was once more a-wooing. The lady sought this time was the fourteen-year-old princess Henrietta Maria, sister of Louis XIII. A match with her, Charles and Buckingham were convinced, would make unbreakable the bond with France which was now regarded as an indispensable ally.

The Prince had seen Henrietta during his brief stopover incognito in Paris on his trip to Spain. At the time he had had eyes only for Henrietta's sister-in-law the French Queen, sister of the Infanta whom he was going to woo. What he thought of Henrietta, if he was aware of the child as he watched the French court ladies rehearsing their masque, we do not know. Henrietta herself was reported to have observed that if the Prince of Wales wanted a bride there was no need for him to travel farther.

The first that the French knew of the interest in their princess being taken in the English court came in February 1624 when Henry Rich, Lord Kensington, arrived in Paris. An affable, ingratiating lightweight, Kensington was the ideal person to circulate about the French court, discreetly enquiring what plans, if any, had been made for the young lady and what sort of reception would greet an English proposal. His mission was completely informal, for officially Charles was still bound by a treaty of marriage to the Infanta. Kensington's letters home were enthusiastic. Henrietta was free of previous commitments and the Queen Mother would be delighted to see her wed the Prince of Wales. As for the girl herself, she was 'a lovely sweet young Creature'. True, she was not completely grown but, gushed Kensington, 'her Shape is perfect'.[2]

In April King James repudiated the Spanish treaty and left Prince Charles free to seek Henrietta Maria openly. On May 17th the royal family's trusty old friend and adviser, James Hay, Earl of Carlisle, set off for Paris to join in formal negotiations for a marriage. He, and not the butterfly Kensington, was charged with the main direction of the treaty-making.

The English were pained to discover that arranging a French match was 'not so fair, smooth and plausible in the progress, as in the entrance'. Right off, there was the old difficulty about religion. Henrietta, like the Infanta, was a Catholic and the French did not see why in matters of religion the English should deny them the terms which they had granted to Spain. It was hard for the English to reply that King James had allowed the Spaniards to manœuvre him into concessions which he had deeply regretted and now would not renew. They could, however, point out that only a few months earlier James had solemnly promised Parliament that no future marriage alliance would give the English Catholics the immunity promised them by the Spanish treaty.

In August a crisis was reached. Richelieu insisted not only that the English Catholics be given all the privileges extended under the Spanish treaty but that the English king formally guarantee as much. To permit James to keep the letter of his promise to Parliament, Richelieu was willing to keep his undertaking separate from the treaty, but 'baptize it by what name you will,' said the Cardinal, the guarantee would have to be given. James was ready to give a letter declaring benevolent intentions towards his Catholic subjects, but this demand was too much. He ordered the negotiations terminated.

When the King and the Prince of Wales concurred in sending a despatch to France declaring that there could be no match, the dismayed French ambassador knew that there was only one way of saving the situation. Post-haste he headed for Wellingborough where the Duke of Buckingham was taking the cure at the spa. Buckingham had committed himself completely to the French alliance. In his view either the marriage went through or the whole glittering structure of his foreign policy would dissolve into nothingness. Setting forth with Effiat, the French envoy, he intercepted the King's messenger who was bearing the fateful despatch to Paris. He broke the seals and read the royal letters. Then taking them into his own keeping, he rode to Derby to see the King.

For once Buckingham found James adamant. He would soften the language in his letters to Paris, but he would not give the undertaking required by France. When the despatches went off in less uncompromising form, Buckingham could reflect that he had at least won time in which to negotiate. The real showdown came in September. During three days of argument, James held out against giving the guarantee which the French still demanded. Now, however, Charles had joined with Buckingham in urging the King to meet the French terms. Finally James gave in and accepted the face-saving formula proposed by Richelieu of a letter not included among the treaty articles.

News of the King's surrender was soon all over the court. Under the circumstances it was impossible to reconvene Parliament as had been intended. The Commons would be outraged at learning that the King, through a technicality, had evaded his promise to them. The parliamentary session scheduled for November was put off until 1625.

On November 10th the marriage treaty was signed in Paris. News of the signing was passed on to the English people along with 'publike commaundment' to rejoice. For two hours the organ at St. Paul's volleyed forth its loudest music. The artillery at the Tower thundered a salute. The bells of all the churches clashed in jubilation. The populace dutifully kindled bonfires in the streets. What nobody in England knew was that the French, having just launched a successful invasion of the Valtelline, were preparing to disassociate themselves from Mansfeld's expedition.

On December 12th King James, whose hands had become so arthritic that he had taken to signing documents with a stamp, ratified the marriage treaty at Cambridge. To it Prince Charles added a private engagement that he, having seen the promise of his father, would extend 'to all the Roman Catholic subjects of the Crown of Great Britain the utmost of liberty and franchise in everything regarding their religion which they would have had in virtue of any articles which were agreed upon by the treaty of marriage with Spain'.[3]

While James and his son were ratifying the treaty, a portion of their kingdom of England was experiencing for the first time in the reign one of the horrors of seventeenth-century war—the ravages inflicted by an army in transit. Mansfeld's levies were finally on the move. On October 29th orders had gone out to conscript 12,000 men to fight for the recovery of the Palatinate. Later Mansfeld, back in England, had received a commission giving him command of these levies.

The bands of conscripts which travelled southward that December to their rendezvous at Dover were indeed the 'cankers of a calm world and a long peace'. The bellicosity of the Protestant English middle class had stopped short of going in person to fight for Frederick under Mansfeld. Consequently this army had been raised by press gangs which had invaded by night the ill-reputed 'suburbs' of London, and by beadles and constables who had seized upon vagrants and masterless men in the shires. The efforts of some of the 'raw and poore rascalls' to escape were pitiful. One drowned himself in the Thames after vainly seeking his release. Another hanged himself. One man in desperation blinded himself, another amputated the fingers on one hand. Persons who travelled in the wake of these bands, as their 'conductors' led them to Dover where their officers would meet them and assign them their regiments, reported the country-side so looted and ravished that it seemed as if an enemy army had despoiled the land.

Mansfeld no sooner got his mutinous and untrained levies on shipboard than the French cancelled his privilege to disembark at Calais and march overland through France to the Rhineland. Denied landing in France, Mansfeld sailed to Flushing where, while the Dutch and English quarrelled over the use to be made of the army, the undernourished and ill-clothed troops remained aboard ship. Plague broke out and spread like wildfire through the fleet. Every day a multitude of corpses were thrown to the fishes. When at last the survivors were put ashore, they suffered further hardships from cold and famine. Of the 12,000 men who had left England, less than 4,000 finally landed in Holland, and these survivors so mouldered away there that in the end no army was left. The one substantial military venture of the reign of James I had ended in utter disaster, without a single blow being struck in the cause of the Palatinate.

In England Mansfeld and his army were forgotten amid the excitement at court as preparations were made to receive the bride of the Prince of Wales. In March Buckingham outfitted a magnificent embassy with which to bring the future Queen of England across the seas to meet her husband. However, his departure was suddenly postponed. On March 27, 1625, King James died.

The King's death was hardly unexpected. Each year had seen greater physical decay and nervous debility. Arms, legs and feet were wracked by gout and arthritis. In 1622 a sudden accident had almost cost the King his life. Riding beside the New River, he had been thrown through the ice when his horse stumbled. For a moment all that could be seen of the monarch was his boots sticking out of the water. Then Sir Richard Young had dashed to the rescue and pulled James to the surface, the water streaming out of his mouth. Taken back to Theobalds and put into a warm bed, the King had recovered but the escape was a close one.

Christmas 1624 saw the King in bad shape. Keeping to his bedchamber, he attended neither the services in the chapel nor the plays offered in the Great Hall. But when the weather cleared, he had himself carried out on a litter to watch the falconers with their birds—a sad pleasure for the suffering monarch, his body bloated and wracked with pain, to watch the effortless flight of his birds.

At the beginning of March James was well enough to move to Theobalds in the hope of some hunting. It was here that he received the news of the death of one of his old cronies, the Marquess of Hamilton. The King took the news hard. He saw himself and his generation disappearing into the grave. Only the year before he had lost his cousin Lennox. A fine figure of a man, Lennox had 'shared his pleasur with many Ladis' before becoming the constant 'servant' of that imperious beauty, the Countess of Hertford. When her husband, a curious old eccentric, had died in 1621, Lennox had lost no time in marrying her. Retiring to bed in perfect health one might in February 1624, he had been found dead in the morning—the consequence, according to court gossip, of an overdose of an aphrodisiac His duchess had lamented mightily; some said because of the end of her short reign as first lady in the queenless court. Lennox's death had been a profound shock for King James. To his place of Lord Steward he had appointed Hamilton, and now Hamilton was dead. The King told his courtiers that he himself would be the next to go.

The royal prophecy was fulfilled more swiftly than even the lugubrious James might have imagined. On March 6th the King was attacked by a 'tertian ague'. Despite its recurrent attacks, he seemed 'without any manner of daunger yf he wold suffer himself to be ordered and governed by phisicall rules'. Within the week he was considered convalescent and plans were made to move him to Hampton Court. Impatient to speed his recovery, the King on March 14th drank a posset prepared by a country doctor named Remington, who had been enthusiastically recommended by Buckingham and his mother. Whether this potion had anything to do with the intensity of the attacks which now resumed, it is impossible to say. (The vast quantities of beer which the patient had insisted upon drinking were probably more to blame.) However, the King's physicians were furious at what had happened and refused to touch the case until both Remington's medicine and some plasters applied as a home remedy by Buckingham's mother were discontinued. According to one account, there was a very nasty scene when the royal physicians discovered what had been going on. Some of them said outright that the King was being poisoned and were driven from the sick-chamber by a furious Buckingham. His mother, meanwhile, frantically begged the King to clear her and her son from such slanders. But James, hearing the fearful word 'poison', had fainted from the shock.[4]

The King's condition was now recognized as serious. Reportedly his tertian fits were lasting as long as ten hours, but under regular medical care James seemed to improve. Within the week he once more demanded the Countess of Buckingham's remedies. Buckingham himself, no doubt apprehensive of future charges that he had poisoned the King, seems to have tried to dissuade James, but with his usual obstinacy the monarch insisted upon receiving the nostrums. Again there was a tense unpleasant scene with the royal doctors, who by now were really alarmed by the severity of their patient's attacks.

The long-drawn-out final agony began for King James on March 24th. In his distress he had called for saintly Lancelot Andrewes to come to comfort him. Andrewes, however, was a sick man himself and could not come. Instead Lord Keeper Williams came posting down from London, ready as Bishop of Lincoln to serve as priest. After conferring with the physicians and Prince Charles, Williams told the King to prepare himself for death. James, so often terrified of shadows, took the news with surprising courage. After receiving Communion from Williams, he sent for the Prince. When Charles entered, however, he found his father too exhausted to give him the intended message.

Death spared James nothing during the terrible next three days. A stroke left his jaw hanging weak and uncontrolled. His throat was choked with suffocating phlegm. Finally an appalling dysentery wracked the unwieldy old body. Shortly before noon on Sunday, March 27th, James died.

He had lived fifty-eight years, and for fifty-seven years he had been a king.

O*

Epilogue

'A ROYAL MAJESTY is not privilege against death.' After the autopsy —the heart and brain were said to be twice the size of those of ordinary men—the body of King James lay in state in Denmark House, where once his queen had lain so long while funds were sought for her burial. On May 7th the funeral cortège set forth for Westminster Abbey. The cavalcade was enormous (black cloth had been issued to nine thousand persons), as court lords, privy councillors, clerics, foreign ambassadors, and all the officers, gentlemen, grooms, esquires, sergeants, yeomen, and pages of the vast court went to pay their final tribute to King James. Behind the hearse walked King Charles as chief mourner. It took hours for the enormous procession to make the journey to the Abbey.

Bishop Williams preached the funeral sermon. It was a grandiose baroque composition and required two hours for its delivery. Taking for his text I Kings, 11: 41–3, especially the final verse, 'And Solomon slept with his fathers, and was buried in the city of David his father', Williams developed with loving artistry and some skilful juggling of text the parallels between the Jewish and the British Solomons. He extolled James as 'a Miracle of Kings and a King of Miracles'. He praised him for his eloquence, observing that if all the other books in the world were to be lost, 'yet could a man finde some footing, and impressions of all *Arts*, and *Sciences*, of all kindes of *Divinitie*, *Moralitie*, and *Humanitie* whatsoever, within the Workes of our late Soveraigne'.[1] He praised King James for maintaining the doctrine and discipline of the Church of England. He eulogized him as a monarch who never once had failed in justice. Borne on the full tide of his rhetoric, he even praised him for his warlike achievements, startling his hearers by recalling James's success when he took the field in person against the rebellious Earl of Argyle in 1594. Nearing his conclusion, the bishop declared of the deceased that 'as he lived like a *King*, so he died like a *Saint*'. Discreetly omitting all the horrible circumstances of the deathbed which he had attended, he portrayed the exemplary way in which James had died, hearing and repeating pious ejaculations until, with his lords and servants on one side of his bed and the clergy on the other, 'without any *pangs* or *Convulsion* at all, *Dormivit Salomon, Salomon slept*'.

Bishop Williams's text that 'Solomon slept with his fathers' proved to have an unexpected literalness. At the end of the obsequies, the magnificent tomb of James's great-great-grandfather, Henry VII, was opened, the coffins of Henry and his consort Elizabeth were pushed aside, and that of King James thrust in. Today not one in ten thousand of those visiting Westminster Abbey and glancing at the gigantic tomb raised a few years later by the widow of the assassinated Buckingham, knows that his master, King James, lies near by without an epitaph in another man's sepulchre.

James was a king who died six years too late. The verdict that posterity passed upon him would have been much more favourable had he been carried off during one of his gallstone attacks in 1619, before the great crises of his reign, those of the Palatinate and the Spanish match, could come upon him and find him prematurely aged and exhausted.

Had James died in 1619 certain things would, of course, have been remembered to his discredit. There was the prodigality of which so much has already been noted—'all Kings cast away Money the day of their Enthronement, but King James did it all his life'. There were the undignified outbursts of anger and profanity. Men would remember how he had furiously torn up the bills passed by an offending parliament or how, pestered by the suits of his grasping courtiers, he could shout: 'You will never leave me alone. I would to God you had, first, my doublet, and then my shirt; and, when I were naked, I think you would give me leave to be quiet.'[2] There was the King's tortuous indirectness—when he decided not to grant a suit he would not plainly say as much, but instead would darkly hint to the petitioner that he had 'very heavy enemies at court'. There was the King's notorious neglect of state affairs because of his addiction to hunting.

On the other hand, King James had a number of virtues. There was his shrewdness and good common sense, his wit and readiness of speech, and the intellectual curiosity which made him 'ever apt to search into secrets, to try conclusions'. His choice of his chief officers was on the whole good. He strove to advance deserving men. It was Bishop Goodman who testified, 'Let me . . . say so much for my old master King James, now with God; no man living did ever love an honest man more than he did.' Other things were to his credit. If quick to anger, he was quick to forgive. He kicked his faithful servant John Gibb for supposedly mislaying important papers, but knelt before Gibb for pardon when he learned that he was not to blame. He tried to be both just and merciful. Even the censorious S. R. Gardiner conceded:

> . . . to do James justice, during the whole course of his reign he never allowed personal favour to shield anyone whom he had reason to believe guilty of actual crime.[3]

As for mercy, James himself declared, 'In giving pardons, I doe allways suppose my selfe in the offender, and then judge how far the like occasion might have tempted me.'[4] One at least of James's virtues, his tolerance, extended beyond the moral horizons of his time. He was a king who, speaking to Parliament, could declare of recusants, 'I would bee sorry to punish their bodies for the error of their mindes.'[5]

Thus we find King James a man with many faults, enough psychological oddities to engage a corps of psychiatrists, and a surprising range of virtues. The more we study his record (setting aside the pitiful final years), the more we come to realize why Sir Robert Cotton declared that he would be content if England should never have a better king, provided it should never have a worse.

King James has fared ill at the hands of History. Even during his lifetime the pitiful failures of his final years overshadowed the not inconsiderable achievements of his maturity. When Charles had brought the monarchy to disaster and England was a republic, the slanderous stories that had circulated earlier about James, instead of dying with the generation that had conceived them, were put into print by Puritan booksellers. Few bothered to defend King James during the Commonwealth. The royalists who had stood by Charles were glad to exculpate their master by throwing the blame for his troubles upon his father. Only a few loyal old men like Bishop Goodman and William Sanderson took up pen in defence of their former king.

The eighteenth century saw Parliament triumphant; and the Whig historians of the age attributed the worst of tyrannical motives to King James's resistance to what he regarded, often quite justifiably, as infringements by Parliament upon his inherited rights. In the nineteenth century James began to find defenders, but it was Macaulay with his caricature who won the popular mind.

James has received greater justice from twentieth-century historians who see the political and economic problems of his age in truer perspective, but the verdict is still predominantly unfavourable. Perhaps it ought to be. Let us recall however that in 1619, when death had spared the King, John Chamberlain could write:

> I am glad to see the world so tenderly affected toward him, for I assure you all men apprehend what a losse we shold have yf God shold take him from us. . . .

The ignominy of the old King's final years must not be allowed to rob him of his earlier achievements.

And what of the court itself with its extravagance, its shady morals, and its murderous factions? Before permitting oneself the censorious comments of a Cromwellian Independent viewing its sexual misdemeanours, or those of a twentieth-century accountant examining its financial improvisations, one would do well to remember some simple truths. A

Renaissance court was bound to be addicted to costly display. In any court where great power and wealth were to be won, the struggle would at times be deadly. Only a man who was utterly exceptional could make a seventeenth-century court chaste and sober, its courtiers disciplined and useful to the state, its finances conducted with the regularity of a modern governmental budget. King James was an exceptional man, but his exceptional qualities were not along these lines. He did, however, keep some reasonable appearance of order in his court. One way or another he did stave off bankruptcy. He did, by and large, see that justice was done. Looking at his court, one may see much that was shameful, petty, and mean. But one sees too Shakespeare and the King's Men coming to play in the Great Hall, Inigo Jones building the Banqueting House, Queen Anne and her ladies amid all the brilliance of their masques, Bishop Andrewes preaching to the court, and John Donne advancing to the pulpit of St. Paul's. One calls to mind the phrase with which John Chamberlain described the funeral of King James: 'All was performed with great magnificence, but the order was very confused and disorderly.' One looks at the phrase a second time. Somehow it seems an epitaph for the whole court. Great magnificence . . . but the order very confused and disorderly.

A Note on the Plan of Whitehall

SINCE WHITEHALL was almost entirely destroyed by fire in 1698, all that can be offered the reader is a reconstruction based upon various sixteenth- and seventeenth-century views of the palace, eked out by such details as can be gleaned from the household regulations, the accounts for repairs of the Paymaster of the Works, and various minor sources. Particularly useful is a curious little book, *Finetti Philoxensis*, by Sir John Finett, Master of the Ceremonies under King James. In this he scrupulously notes the routes through the palace by which he conducted visiting notables. In the last analysis, one depends chiefly upon the only surviving survey of the entire palace, that made of the ground level by John Fisher shortly before 1670 and published by Vertue in 1747. Unfortunately, when Fisher's plan is compared with that of the Preaching Place to be found in the Smythson drawings (*v.* L.C.C., *Survey of London*, XIII: 119) and with the plan of the Guard Chamber, Hall and Chapel, based upon their ruins, by Stukeley in 1718 (ibid., XIII: 47), serious discrepancies appear. I have, however, taken Fisher's plan as giving us essentially the Whitehall known to King James I, modified it where I have seen strong reason, and deleted buildings which I felt must have been added after 1625.

The interested reader may compare my placing of the King's apartments with that of Per Palme in *Triumph of Peace*, his book on the Banqueting House. I have indulged in conjecture in my placing of the King's Bedchamber. We know that this opened off the Vane Room, and it seems obvious that it would have enjoyed a view of the Privy Garden. Accordingly, it had to be either at the north end of the Long Gallery (above the Stone Gallery) or off the Privy Gallery, where I have placed it. I think it would have been a matter of common convenience to have had the Vane Room connect directly with the Long Gallery, in which case the King's Bedchamber, like his cabinet and lesser withdrawing-room, would have been in the Privy Gallery block.

WHITEHALL PALACE

ST. JAMES'S PARK

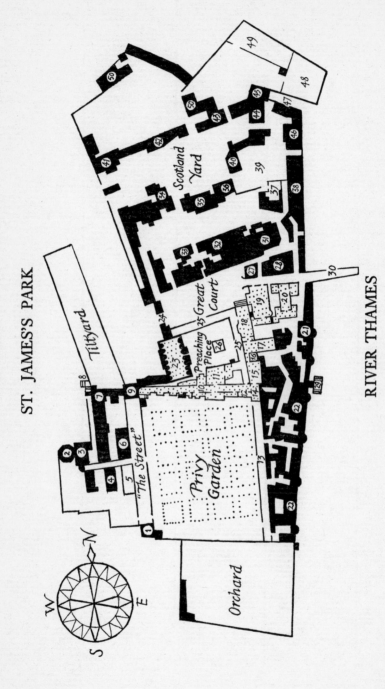

RIVER THAMES

Tiltyard

"The Street"

Privy Garden

Scotland Yard

Great Court

Preaching Place

Orchard

N · E · S · W

Key to the Plan of Whitehall Palace

1. King Street Gate
2. Cockpit
3. Cockpit Lodgings
4. Bowls House
5. The Brake
6. Chief Close Tennis Court
7. Tiltyard Gallery
8. Tiltyard Gallery Stairs
9. Holbein Gate
10. Privy Gallery
11. Council Chamber
12. King's Bedchamber
13. Stone Gallery
14. Vane Room (King's Withdrawing Room)
15. King's Privy Chamber
16. King's Oratory
17. King's Presence Chamber
18. Guard Chamber
19. Hall
20. Chapel
21. Queen's Apartments
22. Courtiers' Lodgings
23. Banqueting House
24. Court Gate and Porter's Lodge
25. Terrace
26. Pulpit
27. Pantry
28. Green Cloth Office
29. Privy Stairs
30. Whitehall Stairs
31. Kitchen
32. Pastery
33. Guard House
34. Lord Chamberlain's Office
35. Comptroller's Office
36. Scalding House
37. Coal Yard
38. Small Beer Buttery
39. Woodyard
40. Charcoal House
41. Surveyor's Office
42. Carpenters and Masons

43. Coachhouse
44. Spicery
45. Cider House
46. Great Bake House
47. Scotland Dock
48. Wharf
49. Deal Yard
50. Stables

NOTES

The following abbreviations have been used for the books most frequently cited:

Aikin: Aikin, Lucy. *Memoirs of the Court of King James the First*, 2 vols., London, 1823.

B.M.: Manuscripts in the British Museum Library.

Birch: Birch, Thomas. *The Court and Times of James the First*, 2 vols., London, 1849.

Cal. S.P. (Dom.): *Calendar of State Papers (Domestic)*.

Cal. S.P. (Ven.): *Calendar of State Papers (Venetian)*.

Cecil: Cecil, Algernon. *A Life of Robert Cecil, First Earl of Salisbury*, London, 1915.

Chamberlain: *The Letters of John Chamberlain*, ed. N. E. McClure, 2 vols., Philadelphia, 1939.

Clarendon: Edward, Earl of Clarendon. *The History of the Rebellion and Civil Wars in England Begun in the Year 1641*, 3 vols., Oxford, 1888.

Coke: Coke, Roger. *A Detection of the Court and State of England during the Four Last Reigns and the Inter-Regnum*, London, 1694.

Dietz: Dietz, Frederick. *English Public Finance 1558–1641*, New York, 1932.

Finett: Finett, Sir John. *Finetti Philoxensis; Som choice observations of Sr. John Finett Knight, And Master of the Ceremonies to the two last Kings, Touching the Reception, and Precedence, the Treatment and Audience, the Puntillios and Contests of Forren Ambassadors in England*, London, 1656.

Folger: Manuscripts in the possession of the Folger Shakespeare Library, Washington, D.C., U.S.A.

Fuller: Fuller, Thomas. *The Church History of Britain*, Oxford, 1845.

Gardiner: Gardiner, S. R. *History of England from the Accession of James I to the Outbreak of the Civil War 1603–1642*, 10 vols., London, 1883–4.

Goodman: Goodman, Godfrey. *The Court of King James the First*, 2 vols., London, 1839.

H.M.C.: Publications of the Historical Manuscripts Commission.

Harington: Harington, Sir John. *Nugae Antiquae*, 2 vols., London, 1804.

Herford and Simpson: *Ben Jonson*, ed. C. H. Herford, Percy and Evelyn Simpson, 11 vols., Oxford, 1925–52.

Lodge: Lodge, Edmund. *Illustrations of British History, Biography, and Manners in the Reigns of Henry VIII, Edward VI, Mary, Elizabeth and James I, Exhibited in a Series of Original Papers Selected from the Mss. of the Noble Families of Howard, Talbot, and Cecil*, 3 vols., London, 1838.

Nichols: Nichols, John. *The Progresses, Processions, and Magnificent Festivities of King James the First*, 4 vols., London, 1828.

Osborn: *The Works of Francis Osborn*, London, 1673.

P.R.O.: Manuscripts in the Public Record Office, London.

Pett: *The Autobiography of Phineas Pett*, ed. W. G. Perrin, Navy Records Society, 1918.

Rushworth: Rushworth, John. *Historical Collections*, London, 1659.

Rye: Rye, W. B. *England as Seen by Foreigners in the Days of Elizabeth and James the First*, London, 1865.

Sanderson: Sanderson, William. *A Compleat History of the Lives and Reigns of Mary Queen of Scotland, and of Her Son and Successor, James*, London, 1656.

Spedding: Spedding, James. *The Letters and the Life of Francis Bacon, Including All His Occasional Works*, 7 vols., London, 1862–74.

State Trials: *A Complete Collection of State Trials and Proceedings for High Treason and Other Misdemeanours*, 11 vols., London, 1776.

Stow: Stow, John. *Annales, or A General Chronicle of England*, continued by Edmund Howes, London, 1631.

Tawney: Tawney, R. H. *Business and Politics under James I : Lionel Cranfield as Merchant and Minister*, Cambridge, 1958.

Weldon: Weldon, Sir Anthony. *The Court and Character of King James*, London, 1650.

Wilson: Wilson, Arthur. *The History of Great Britain, Being the Life and Reign of King James the First*, London, 1653.

Winwood: *Memorials of Affairs of State in the Reigns of Q. Elizabeth and K. James I collected (chiefly) from the original papers of the Right Honourable Sir Ralph Winwood, Kt.*, 3 vols., London, 1725.

Wotton: *The Life and Letters of Sir Henry Wotton*, ed. Logan Pearsall Smith, 2 vols., Oxford, 1907.

CHAPTER REFERENCES

PROLOGUE

1. Birch, I: 232.
2. *Memoirs of the Life of Robert Cary, Baron of Leppington and Earl of Monmouth* (London, 1759), p. 147.
3. Ibid., p. 140.
4. Ibid., pp. 152–3. S. R. Gardiner (I: 86) believed it probable that James first received the news of Elizabeth's death from a certain George Marshall, but in view of James's own statement in a letter to Cecil, 'Sir Robert Carie, who did first acquaint us with the Queen's death. . . .' (H.M.C., *MSS. of the Marquess of Salisbury*, XV: 9), it is hard to deny Carey's claim. Marshall may have been a palace attendant at Holyrood, who brought Carey, and so the news, to the King.

I. THE NEW KING

1. Sir James Melville, *Memoirs* (Edinburgh, 1827), pp. 158–9.
2. Weldon, p. 179.
3. loc. cit.
4. Wilson, p. 289.
5. Aikin, I: 20.
6. Birch, II: 301.
7. D. Calderwood, *History of the Kirk of Scotland*, Wodrow Society (Edinburgh, 1842–9), III: 637.
8. Aikin, I: 20.
9. *Newes from Scotland*, ed. G. B. Harrison (London, 1924), p. 15.
10. Henry N. Paul, *The Royal Play of Macbeth* (New York, 1950), pp. 75–130.

II. THE JOURNEY SOUTH

1. For Thomas Wilson's list, made in 1600, of '12 Competitors that gape for the death of that good old Princess the now Queen', see *Camden Miscellany*, vol. XVI (1936), p. 2.
2. Nichols, I: 30.
3. *Folger MS. 1779.2*, p. 35.
4. H.M.C., *Salisbury MSS.*, XV: 20.
5. Ibid., XV: 11.
6. Thomas Dekker, *The Magnificent Entertainment Given to King James upon His Passage through London* (London, 1604), sig. A3^r.
7. Harington, I: 334.
8. Chamberlain, I: 189.
9. Goodman, I: 96–7.
10. John Fenton, *King James His Welcome to London* (London, 1603), sig. B4^v.
11. H.M.C., *Salisbury MSS.*, XV: 28.

12. *The True Narration of the Entertainment of His Royal Majestie, from the Departure from Edenbrough; till his Receiving at London* (London, 1603), sigs. El[v] and E2[r].

13. Wilson, p. 3.

14. John Savile, *King James His Entertainment at Theobalds* (London, 1603), sig. A4[v].

15. *v.* John Summerson, 'Theobalds: a Lost Elizabethan Palace', *The Listener* (March 31, 1955), pp. 567–8.

16. Rye, p. 44.

17. Stow, p. 823.

18. Nichols, I: 153–4.

19. Herford and Simpson, VII: 128

III. THE NEW COURT IS FORMED

1. The difficulty of arriving at figures for the court's establishment may be indicated by the fact that while *Folger MS. 1232.2* (a 'Book of Offices' dated 1607, but almost certainly obsolete in its figures) give 18 Gentlemen of the Privy Chamber, P.R.O. MS. *L.C. 2/6* shows that at King James's funeral black cloth was issued to 82. Carlisle in his *Inquiry into the Place and Quality of the Gentlemen of His Majesty's Most Honourable Privy Chamber* (London, 1829), pp. 95–104, gives the names of 48 Gentlemen of the Privy Chamber in 1608. Writing in 1610, Dudley Carleton reported that the 48 had been reduced to 32 (Birch, I: 130). Pegge in his *Curalia* (London, 1791), I, i: 60–1, speaks of 48 Gentlemen, 12 of whom were in attendance each quarter.

2. Stephen Harrison, *Arches of Triumph Erected in Honor of the High and Mighty Prince, James . . . at his Majesties Entrance and Passage through his Honorable Citty and Chamber of London* (London, 1604), sig. Cl[r].

3. Herford and Simpson, VII: 90.

4. Ibid., VII: 97.

IV. A DAY'S BUSINESS AT WINCHESTER

1. Algernon Cecil (*Life of Robert Cecil*, pp. 187–8) tried to clear Cecil of involvement in Howard's attacks against Raleigh. The view that is forced upon one after any complete examination of the evidence is that of Helen Georgia Stafford in her very useful book *James VI of Scotland and the Throne of England* (New York, 1940), p. 267: 'Lord Henry Howard seemed to be the evil genius in the affair, although Cecil must bear some share of the responsibility.'

2. Gardiner, II: 259.

3. Weldon, p. 22.

4. *The Secret Correspondence of Sir Robert Cecil with James VI, King of Scotland* (London, 1766), p. 6.

5. *v. Correspondence of King James I with Sir Robert Cecil and Others in England*, ed. John Bruce, Camden Society (London, 1861), pp. 4–8.

6. *Secret Correspondence*, p. 52.

7. *State Trials*, I: 220.

8. Verses scrawled by Charles, 2nd Lord Stanhope, in the margin of his copy of Raleigh's *Historie of the World* (London, 1634), sig. Al[r]. The book is now in the Folger Library.

9. *State Trials*, I: 212.
10. Ibid., I: 215–16.
11. Ibid., I: 223.
12. Ibid., I: 219.
13. Ibid., I: 218.
14. Ibid., I: 224.
15. Birch, I: 14.
16. *State Trials*, I: 225–6.
17. Birch, I: 20.
18. Ibid., I: 21.
19. Milton Waldman, *Sir Walter Raleigh* (London, 1928), p. 175.

V. THE HUNGRY SCOTS

1. Weldon, p. 343.
2. Ibid., p. 6.
3. Osborn, p. 470.
4. *Oxford Jests Refined and Enlarged* (London, 1684), cited in John Ashton, *Humour, Wit, and Satire of the Seventeenth Century* (London, 1883), p. 434.
5. Osborn, p. 505.
6. Ibid., p. 504.
7. Goodman, I: 215.

VI. AMBASSADORS FROM BEYOND THE SEAS

1. Finett, p. 140.
2. Ibid., p. 39.
3. Birch, II: 306.
4. Chamberlain, I: 214.
5. *State Papers Savoy* cited in Wotton, II: 95.
6. Garrett Mattingly, *Renaissance Diplomacy* (London, 1955), p. 211.
7. Chamberlain, II: 353–4.
8. Mattingly, pp. 260–1.
9. Finett, pp. 97–8.

VII. GUNPOWDER, TREASON AND PLOT

1. P.R.O., *S.P. 14/216*, no. 17.
2. *The Sermon Preached at Paules Crosse, the tenth day of November* (London, 1606).
3. *His Majesties Speach in This Last Session of Parliament, etc.* (London, 1605).
4. In view of the fact that Mounteagle had not been to his house at Hoxton for an entire year previous to this night, historians have almost unanimously agreed that the whole letter episode had been carefully prearranged.
5. *H.M. Speach in This Last Session*, sig. F3ᵛ.
6. Hugh Ross Williamson, *The Gunpowder Plot* (London, 1951), pp. 206–7.
7. Winwood, II: 171.
8. *Father Gerard's Narrative of the Gunpowder Plot* in John Morris, *The Condition of Catholics under James I* (London, 1872), p. 293.
9. *v.* Cecil, p. 61.

10. *Truth Brought to Light and Discovered by Time* (London, 1651), p. 11.

11. F. C. Dietz, 'The Receipts and Issues of the Exchequer During the Reigns of James I and Charles I', *Smith College Studies in History* (Northampton, Mass., 1928), XIII: 4: 136–45.

12. According to the official account, the government on November 5th knew nothing of the identity of the conspirators since Guy Fawkes was still refusing to name his accomplices. In fact, one of Rookwood's servants was already being examined, as well as the landlady of the house where Rookwood, Keyes and Christopher Wright had been staying. Both that day and the next Chief Justice Popham was furnishing Cecil with details of what he had been able to learn about Christopher Wright, Robert Winter, Rookwood, Keyes and Father Garnet (P.R.O., *S.P. 14/210*; for summaries see *Cal. S.P.* (*Dom.*) 1603–1610, p. 240 (XVI: 10–16).

VIII. THE ROYAL BROTHER-IN-LAW

1. Harington, I: 348–51.

2. *Folger MS. 6972*, pp. 284–5.

3. Henry Roberts, *The Most Royall and Honourable Entertainement of Christiern the Fourth* (London, 1606), sig. Dl^r.

4. *v.* Paul, *The Royal Play of Macbeth*, pp. 40–1 and *passim*.

5. Henry Roberts, *England's Farewell to Christian the fourth, famous King of Denmarke* (London, 1606), sig. C2^v.

IX. THE EMPTY EXCHEQUER

1. P.R.O., *L.S. 13/280*, f. 307^r.

2. B.M., *Harl. 642*, f. 236^r.

3. Dietz, p. 111.

4. Ibid., p. 113.

5. Tawney, p. 110.

6. P.R.O., *L.S. 13/280*, f. 194^v.

7. Dietz, 'Exchequer Receipts and Issues', pp. 158–9.

8. Nichols, II: 43–4.

9. B.M., *Titus CVII*, f. 175.

10. P.R.O., *L.S. 13/280*, ff. 58–9.

11. Goodman, I: 308–9.

12. Osborn, p. 537.

13. P.R.O., *L.S. 13/280*, ff. 302–4.

14. Ibid., Letter dated September 1608.

15. Osborn, p. 512.

16. *A Declaration of His Majesties Royall Pleasure in the matter of bountie* (London, 1610), sig. A4.

17. B.M., *Lansdowne MS. 165*, f. 213, cited in Dietz, p. 151.

18. Gardiner, II: 228.

19. Dietz, p. 161.

20. Ibid., p. 168.

21. *Folger MS. 1101.1*, pp. 100–1 (see also Gardiner III: 198).

22. Goodman, II: 165.

23. Ibid., II: 207.

24. *Sackville MS. 22* cited by Dietz, p. 192.
25. Goodman, II: 215.
26. Dietz, p. 193.
27. Tawney, p. 298.

X. THE FOX OF HATFIELD CHASE

1. Cecil, p. 329.
2. *Correspondence of King James I with Sir Robert Cecil and Others in England,* ed. John Bruce, Camden Society (London, 1861), p. 23.
3. H.M.C., *Salisbury MSS.* XV: 31.
4. Harington, II: 263.
5. Wilson, p. 55.
6. Chamberlain, I: 311–12.
7. David Mathew, *The Jacobean Age* (London, 1938), p. 55.
8. Wotton, II: 487 ('Character of Robert late Earl of Salisbury').
9. Marginalia of Charles, 2nd Lord Stanhope, in his copy of Cresacre More's *Life and Death of Sir Thomas More* (1642), sig. F3ᵛ (Folger Library).
10. Nichols, II: 204.
11. B.M., *Add. MS. 25348* (*The True Tragi-Comedie Formerly Acted at Court and Now Recived by Ane Eie Witnes*), f. 9ʳ.
12. Winwood, III: 338.
13. Francis Peck, *Desiderata Curiosa* (London, 1797), Lib. VI, p. 208.
14. Ibid., Lib. VI, p. 209.
15. Chamberlain, I: 364–5.
16. sig. K2.
17. Osborn, p. 513.
18. *Folger MS. 452.1.*
19. Printed in Gutch, *Collectanea Curiosa* (Oxford, 1781).
20. Quoted Cecil, p. 375.
21. I: 90.
22. Spedding, IV: 278.

XI. THE LANGUISHING LADY

1. *The Secret Correspondence of Sir Robert Cecil with James VI, King of Scotland* (Edinburgh, 1766), p. 118.
2. P. M. Handover, *Arbella Stuart, Royal Lady of Hardwick and Cousin to King James* (London, 1957), p. 212.
3. E. T. Bradley, *Life of Lady Arabella Stuart* (London, 1889), II: 190.
4. Ibid., II: 226–7.
5. B.M., *Harl. 7003,* f. 59.
6. Winwood, III: 279.
7. Handover, p. 272.
8. Goodman, I: 209.

XII. TEARS FOR PRINCE HENRY

1. Stow, sig. Ffff 6ʳ.
2. P.R.O., *L.S. 13/280,* f. 304ʳ.

3. Thomas Birch, *The Life of Henry Prince of Wales* (London, 1760), p. 148.

4. Sir Charles Cornwallis, *The Short Life and Much Lamented Death of That Most Magnanimous Prince, Henry, Prince of Wales* (1644), sig. A5ᵛ.

5. Ibid., sig. B1.

6. Herford and Simpson, VII: 328.

7. Sir Charles Cornwallis, 'A Discourse of the Most Illustrious Prince Henry, Late Prince of Wales', in *Harleian Miscellany* (London, 1809), III: 526.

8. B.M., *Harl. 642*, ff. 246–8.

9. P.R.O., *L.S. 13/280*, f. 200ʳ.

10. Robert Johnston, see Birch, *Life of Henry Prince of Wales*, pp. 253–4.

11. B.M., *Harl. 6986*, f. 180ᵛ.

12. W.H., *The True Picture of Prince Henry*, sig. E2.

13. Cornwallis, *Short Life of Prince Henry*, sigs. E6ᵛ and E7ʳ.

14. Ibid., E8ʳ.

15. Harington, II: 3.

16. Coke, I: 61.

17. Raleigh, *History of the World* (London, 1614), Ggggg2ʳ.

18. Pett, p. 100.

19. Birch, *Court of James the First*, I: 210.

20. *Short Life of Prince Henry*, sig. G5ʳ.

21. *The Illness and Death of Henry Prince of Wales in 1612 : A Historical Case of Typhoid Fever* (London, 1882), p. 5.

22. *The Funeralls of the High and Mighty Prince Henry* (London, 1613), sig. A4ʳ.

23. Birch, *Life of Henry Prince of Wales*, p. 369.

24. Osborn, p. 527.

XIII. THE MARRIAGE OF THAMES AND RHINE

1. Harington, I: 373–4.

2. Winwood, III: 403.

3. Ibid., III: 404.

4. Chamberlain, I: 416

5. Coke, I: 64.

6. *v. The Tempest*, ed. Sir Arthur Quiller-Couch and John Dover Wilson ('The New Shakespeare' ed.), (Cambridge, 1921), pp. xlvi–xlviii, p. 80.

7. Chamberlain, I: 403–4.

8. Ibid., I: 433.

9. Pett, p. 103.

10. Edward F. Rimbault, *The Old Cheque-Book or Book of Remembrance of the Chapel Royal*, Camden Society (London, 1872), p. 164.

11. Ibid., p. 165.

12. *Great Britaine All in Blacke*, sig. A4ʳ.

13. *The Period of Mourning ; Disposed into Six Visions, Together with Nuptiall Hymnes* (London, 1613), sig. F2.

14. *The Court Masque* (Cambridge, 1927).

15. Nichols, III: 62.

16. Herford and Simpson, VII: 177, ll. 250–7.

17. Winwood, II: 44.

18. 'The Lords' Masque', *Campion's Works*, ed. Percival Vivian (Oxford, 1909), p. 92.

19. Ibid., p. 93.

20. *The Plays and Poems of George Chapman*, ed. T. M. Parrott (London, 1914), II: 439–40.

21. For this 'Masque of Gray's Inn and the Inner Temple', see *The Works of Francis Beaumont and John Fletcher*, ed. A. R. Waller (Cambridge, 1912), vol. X, and E. K. Chambers, *The Elizabethan Stage*, III: 233–5.

22. Sanderson, p. 405.

XIV. THE COURTIER'S LIFE

1. *The Court of the Most Illustrious and Most Magnificent James the First* (London, 1619), sig. Y1ᵛ.

2. *Haec-Vir or The Womanish Man* (London, 1620), sig. C2.

3. B.M., *Harl. 6987*, f. 203.

4. Nichols, I: 593–600.

5. Lodge, III: 116.

6. Ibid., III: 131.

7. Ibid., III: 108.

8. *Folger MS. 1027.2*, p. 6.

9. Chamberlain, I: 201.

10. Lodge, III: 110.

11. Birch, I: 92.

12. *Folger MS. 697.4*.

13. Osborn, p. 533.

14. P.R.O., *L.S. 13/280*, f. 308ʳ.

15. On these mechanical wonders see Rye, p. 61 and p. 232 *et seq.*; also the travel journal of Baron G. von Schwartzstat, *Huntington Library Quarterly*, XIV (1950), pp. 92–3.

16. Chamberlain, I: 610.

17. Robert Steele, *A Bibliography of the Royal Proclamations of the Tudor and Stuart Sovereigns* (Oxford, 1910), No. 1342, I: 159.

18. Chamberlain, II: 475.

19. Thomas Middleton, *The Witch*, I, i.

20. *Heaven upon Earth and Characters of Vertues and Vices*, ed. Rudolf Kirk (New Brunswick, Rutgers U.P., 1948), pp. 202–3.

21. Dietz, 'Exchequer Receipts and Issues', p. 168.

22. Harington, I: 393.

23. Daniel Price, *Spiritual Odours to the Memory of Prince Henry* (London, 1613), sig. B3ʳ.

24. Chamberlain, II: 392.

25. Wilson, p. 3.

26. *Shakespeare's England* (Oxford, 1916), I: 40–2.

XV. THE RISING STAR OF SOMERSET

1. Harington, I: 395.

2. Weldon, p. 63.

3. Sir Edward Peyton, *Divine Catastrophe of the House of Stuarts* in *Secret History of the Court of James the First* (Edinburgh, 1811), II: 353.

4. Goodman, I: 215.
5. Gardiner, II: 212.
6. T. F. Henderson, *James I and VI* (London, 1904), p. 224.
7. B.M., *Titus CVII*, ff. 99–100.
8. loc. cit.
9. *State Trials*, I: 356.
10. Ibid., I: 328.
11. Winwood, III: 447.
12. *v.* Weldon, p. 80, and *Truth Brought to Light*, p. 31. B.M. *Add. MS. 25348* (*The True Tragi-Comedie*) identifies a 'Mrs. Shurley' as the countess's substitute.
13. B.M., *Titus CVII*, f. 101.
14. Ibid., f. 104ʳ.
15. Chamberlain, I: 548.
16. Weldon, p. 98.

XVI. MURDER IN THE TOWER

1. *State Trials*, I: 350.
2. Coke, I: 82–4.
3. *State Trials*, I: 330.
4. Ibid., I: 344.
5. Ibid., I: 325–6.
6. Ibid., I: 339.
7. *The Familiar Letters of James Howell*, ed. Joseph Jacobs (London, 1892), I: 20–1.
8. Goodman, II: 146–7.
9. For Coke's charges and the reasons for considering them groundless, see Spedding, V: 339–42.
10. *State Trials*, I: 352.
11. Wilson, pp. 89–90.
12. James's letters to More were printed in A. J. Kempe, *Loseley Manuscripts* (1836), pp. 400–5. The originals are now in the Folger Library.
13. Weldon, pp. 118–19.
14. G. F. Northall, *English Folk-Rhymes* (London, 1892), p. 542.
15. *State Trials*, I: 358.
16. B.M., *Harl. 7003*.
17. B.M., *Titus B VII*, f. 478.
18. Ibid., f. 480.
19. *State Trials*, I: 341.

XVII. THE GREAT VILLIERS

1. Goodman, I: 225–6.
2. Clarendon, I: 38–9.
3. Sir Henry Wotton, *A Parallell betweene Robert late Earle of Essex, and George late Duke of Buckingham* (London, 1641), sig. A2ᵛ.
4. Coke, I: 79.
5. Nichols, III: 484–5.
6. Chamberlain, II: 144.
7. B.M., *Add. MS. 25348* (*The True Tragi-Comedie*), f. 15ᵛ.

8. Chamberlain, II: 207.

9. Ibid., II: 338.

10. Ibid., II: 52.

11. B.M., *Harl. 6987*, f. 69.

12. Peyton, *Divine Catastrophe of the House of Stuarts* in *Secret History of the Court of James I*, II: 353.

13. B.M., *Harl. 6986*, f. 199ʳ.

14. B.M., *Harl. 6987*, f. 117.

15. Goodman, II: 310–12.

16. Wilson, p. 149.

17. *v.* Paul Bloomfield, *Uncommon People* (London, 1955).

18. Goodman, II: 311.

19. B.M., *Harl. 6987*, f. 119.

20. Goodman, II: 345.

21. B.M., *Harl. 6987*, f. 2.

22. *Cal. S.P. (Ven.) (1617–1619)*, pp. 113–14.

23. B.M., *Harl. 6987*, f. 178. (The succeeding letters are all from this volume.)

24. Clarendon, I: 12.

XVIII. TITLES, MONEY AND MORALS

1. A.D.B., *The Court of the Most Illustrious James the First* (London, 1619), sig. 12ʳ.

2. *A Counter-Blaste to Tobacco* (London, 1954), p. 8.

3. Lodge, III: 27.

4. P.R.O., *S.P. 14/12/6*.

5. *Cal. S.P. (Ven.) (1617–1619)*, p. 114.

6. B.M. *Harl. 6987*, f. 50.

7. Chamberlain, II: 35.

8. Ibid., II: 502.

9. Ibid., II: 302.

10. In June 1611 King James, taking cognizance of various complaints, ordered reforms made in the Court of Marshalsea and created a new Court of the Verge, 'for personal actions which concern persons not being or which hereafter shall not be of our household, to be before the Knight Marshal and some fit person learned in the law' (*v.* Spedding, IV: 264).

11. Aikin, p. 82.

12. *His Maiesties Commission Touching the Creation of Baronets* (London, 1611), sig. C3ʳ.

13. Pett, p. 121.

14. Nichols, I: xxxii.

15. Goodman, II: 362.

16. Chamberlain, II: 559.

17. *Folger MS. 423.2*, p. 15.

18. *Folger MS. 423.3*.

19. B.M., *Harl. 5176*, f. 226ᵛ.

20. Chamberlain, II: 315.

21. Thomas Dekker and John Ford, *The Witch of Edmonton*, Act IV, scene i.

22. *Aubrey's Brief Lives*, ed. O. L. Dick (London, 1949), p. 226.

23. John Taylor, *A Living Sadness, in Duty Consecrated to the Memory of Our Late Soveraigne James* (London, 1625), sig. B1ʳ.

24. Cecil, p. 299.

25. Harington, I: 393.

26. Abraham Darcie, *A Monumental Pyramide Erected to the Honour of Lodowick, late Duke of Richmond* (London, 1624), sig. B3ʳ.

27. *Honors True Arbor; or The Princely Nobilitie of the Howards*, sig. a5ʳ.

28. Lodge, III: 88–9.

XIX. DUELS AND AFFRAYS

1. *The Devil's Law-Case*, I, i, 73–7.

2. *The English Works of Sir Thomas More*, ed. W. E. Campbell (London, 1931), I: 349.

3. *The Charge of Sir Francis Bacon, His Majesties Attourney generall, Touching Duells* (London, 1614), sig. C1ʳ.

4. T. Milles, *Catalogue of Honour* (London, 1610), sig. B1.

5. P.R.O., *L.S. 13/280*, f. 78.

6. G. M. Trevelyan, *England Under the Stuarts* (London, 1930), p. 10.

7. Birch, p. 200.

8. Wilson, p. 50.

9. *Folger MS. 1054.4.*

10. The text of this letter as preserved in *Folger MS. 6972* agrees fairly well with that given by Charles Phillips in his *History of the Sackville Family* (London, 1930), I: 294–303, and reprinted by Vera Sackville-West in *Knole and the Sackvilles* (London, 1948), pp. 85–8.

11. Bacon, *Charge Touching Duells*, sig. B3ʳ.

12. *A Proclamation against Private Challenges and Combats* (London, 1614).

13. *A Publication of His Majesties Edict and Severe Censure against Private Combats and Combatants* (London, 1614).

XX. HOME TO SCOTLAND

1. Nichols, III: 309.

2. Sanderson, p. 451.

3. Nichols, III: 345.

4. John Adamson, *The Muses Welcome To The High and Mightie Prince James . . . at His Majesties Happie Returne to his Old and Native Kingdome of Scotland* (Edinburgh, 1618), sig. Ff6ʳ.

5. For Weldon's views on Scotland, see p. 48 above.

XXI. DEATH BECKONS

1. Chamberlain, I: 469.

2. *The Diary of Lady Anne Clifford* (London, 1923), p. 48.

3. Robert Naile, *A Relation of the Royall Entertainement Given to the High and Mighty Princesse, Queen Anne, at the Renowned Citie of Bristoll* (1613), sig. B1ʳ.

4. Ibid., sig. B2ᵛ.

5. Birch, II: 178.

XXII. THE WHITEHALL CONNOISSEURS

1. Aikin, I: 298.
2. *The Jacobean Age*, p. 132.
3. Aikin, I: 300.
4. See Chapter XVII, p. 222–3 *supra*. For an extended account of Buckingham's collecting, see C. R. Cammell, *The Great Duke of Buckingham* (London, 1939), Chapter XXVII.
5. E. K. Waterhouse, *Painting in England : 1530 to 1790*, p. 35.

XXIII. INIGO JONES BUILDS AT WHITEHALL

1. *A Deep Sigh Breath'd Through the Lodgings at Whitehall* (London, 1642), sig. A2ʳ.
2. London County Council, *Survey of London*, ed. M. H. Cox and P. Norman, vol. XIII: 'Parish of St. Margaret, Westminster' (London, 1930), pp. 97–8.
3. *A Deep Sigh*, sig. A2ᵛ.
4. Ibid., sig. A3ʳ.
5. P.R.O., *S.P. 14/12/6*.
6. *Triumph of Peace : A Study of the Whitehall Banqueting House* (Stockholm, 1956), p. 53.
7. Herford and Simpson, VIII: 220.

XXIV. LORD CHANCELLOR BACON

1. At the time of writing this chapter I had not seen Paul H. Kocher's admirable article, 'Francis Bacon and His Father', *Huntington Library Quarterly*, XXI (1957–8), pp. 133–58. Kocher's views coincide with my own. The article contains some fascinating examples of how the father's influence manifests itself in Bacon's political and philosophical writings, as well as in his life.
2. Fuller, V: 493.
3. Spedding, IV: 379.
4. Chamberlain, II: 65.
5. Spedding, VI: 237.
6. Weldon, pp. 132–3. Spedding rejects Weldon's account as a malicious fiction. On the other hand, it seems entirely in keeping with Buckingham's character to make Bacon go through a form of abject submission. Accordingly, with some misgivings, I have used Weldon's account, in the absence of any other, of Bacon's meeting with Buckingham.
7. '. . . the Lord Chancelor and Keeper of the Great Seale of England have all one power, yet differ in this, that the Lord Keeper is but at the pleasure of the Prince, the other alwaies during life.'—John Minsheu, *The Guide into Tongues* (London, 1617), sig. F4.
8. Chamberlain, II: 339.
9. *Aubrey's Brief Lives*, p. 9.
10. *State Trials*, I: 375.
11. Ibid., I: 377.
12. Ibid., I: 379–80. (The italics are mine.)
13. Ibid., I: 380.
14. Ibid., I: 383.

15. loc. cit.

16. Birch, II: 252. Elsing (*Notes of the Debates in the House of Lords A.D. 1621*, Camden Society, 1870, p. 54), gives a somewhat different version: 'By the Kinge's greate favour I received the great Seale; by my owne greate faulte I have lost yt.'

17. *Folger MS. 1617.1*, also in Spedding.

18. Spedding, VII: 563–4.

19. Ibid., VII: 238.

20. *State Trials*, I: 375.

21. Spedding, VII: 560.

22. Ibid., VII: 230–1.

XXV. CLERGY AT COURT

1. Fuller, V: 280.

2. Ibid., V: 294–5.

3. Ibid., V: 298.

4. Ibid., V: 300.

5. *The Political Works of James I*, ed. C. H. McIlwain (Cambridge, Mass., 1918), pp. 73–4.

6. Ibid., pp. 82–3.

7. *Crumms Fal'n From King James's Table* in *The Miscellaneous Works of Sir Thomas Overbury*, ed. E. F. Rimbault (London, 1890), p. 260.

8. The Knights of Windsor.

9. *v.* John Hacket, *Scrinia Reserata : A Memorial Offered to the Great Deservings of John Williams*, D.D. (London, 1693), pp. 98–9.

10. T. Pennant, *Tours in Wales* (London, 1781), II: 473–4, cited in Dew Roberts, *Mitre and Musket : John Williams, Lord Keeper, Archbishop of York 1582–1650* (London, 1938), p. 18.

11. Hacket, *Scrinia Reserata*, p. 30.

12. Roberts, *Mitre and Musket*, p. 563.

13. Chamberlain, II: 470.

14. Rye, p. 153.

15. Chamberlain, II: 387.

XXVI. GONDOMAR

1. Francisco de Jesus, *Narrative of the Spanish Marriage Treaty*, ed. S. R. Gardiner, Camden Society (1869), p. 130.

2. Gardiner, III: 59–60.

3. Fuller, V: 532–3.

4. Marginalia of Charles, 2nd Lord Stanhope, in his copy of Raleigh's *Historie of the World* (London, 1634), sig. Ssss6ᵛ. The book is now in the Folger Library.

5. Chamberlain, I: 568.

6. Gardiner, III: 141.

7. Birch, II: 99.

8. Gardiner, III: 151.

XXVII. DISASTER IN BOHEMIA

1. Tillières to Pusieux, July 3, 1620, cited by D. H. Willson, *King James VI and I* (London, 1956), p. 412.
2. Gardiner, III: 338.
3. Ibid., IV: 190.
4. Chamberlain, II: 366.
5. Wotton, II: 221.
6. Thomas Middleton, *A Game at Chesse*, V, iii.
7. Ibid., I, i, 253–66.

XXVIII. WITH PRINCE CHARLES IN SPAIN

1. Clarendon, I: 18.
2. Ibid., I: 21–2.
3. Goodman, I: 368.
4. B.M., *Harl. MS. 6987*, f. 15.
5. Hailes, *Memorials and Letters*, p. 153.
6. B.M., *Harl. MS. 6987*, ff. 29–31.
7. Ibid., f. 51.
8. Ibid., f. 23.
9. Ibid., f. 115.
10. Ibid., f. 116.
11. John Rushworth, *Historical Collections* (London, 1659), p. 86. Rushworth gives the full text of the marriage treaty.
12. Ibid., p. 89.
13. Ibid., p. 90.
14. Gardiner, V: 91.
15. Chamberlain, II: 515–16.

XXIX. THE PRETENSIONS OF PARLIAMENT

1. E. R. Turner, *The Privy Council of England in the Seventeenth and Eighteenth Centuries 1603–1784* (Baltimore, 1927), I :101–2.
2. Birch, II: 79.
3. Stow, p. 523.
4. *Acts of the Privy Council of England 1613–1614* (London, 1921), pp. 3–4. (This list has had added to it the name of Sir Thomas Lake, who did not become a P.C. until the next year.)
5. William Camden, *The Annals of James I*, in White Kennett, *A Complete History of England* (London, 1719), II: 652.
6. Turner, I: 15.
7. Chamberlain, II: 438.
8. *Spanish Transcripts*, II, iii, cited in Turner, I: 82.
9. Fuller, V: 565–6.
10. *v.* D. H. Willson, *The Privy Councillors in the House of Commons 1604–1629* (Minneapolis, 1940), pp. 107–8.
11. *Folger MS. 506.1.*
12. A subsidy was an income tax levied at the rate of 4s. on the pound upon land worth £20 a year, and at a rate of 2s. 8d. upon personal property worth £3 and up. Tenths and fifteenths were levied upon counties and boroughs according

to valuations made in the reign of Edward III. In actual practice, neither of these taxes yielded the Crown anything like the returns it should have. *v.* Tawney, p. 135, p. 146.

13. W. M. Mitchell, *The Rise of the Revolutionary Party in the English House of Commons 1603–1629* (New York, 1957), p. 36.

14. Willson, op. cit., p. 225.

15. S. R. Gardiner, *Parliamentary Debates in 1610*, Camden Society (London, 1862), p. 24.

16. Murdin, *State Papers*, cited in G. B. Smith, *History of the English Parliament* (London, 1894), I: 369.

17. Hoskyns apparently was all unconsciously acting the part of an *agent provocateur*, two of Northampton's creatures having supplied him with the inflammatory part of his speech in the hope that it would so anger the King as to move him to dissolve Parliament. *v.* T. L. Moir, *The Addled Parliament of 1614* (Oxford, 1958), p. 140.

18. *His Majesties Speach in the Upper House of Parliament, on Munday the 26 of March 1621* (London, 1621), sig. B1ᵛ.

19. *His Majesties Declaration, Touching His Proceedings in the Late Assemblie and Convention of Parliament* (London, 1621), sig. B3.

20. Rushworth, *Collections*, p. 53.

21. Clarendon, I: 28.

XXX. LAST SCENE OF ALL

1. *Cal. S.P. (Ven.) 1623–1625*, p. 201.

2. *Cabala, Sive Scrinia Sacra : Mysteries of State and Government in Letters of Illustrious Persons* (London, 1691), p. 290.

3. B.M., *Harl. 4596*, f. 144, printed in Gardiner V: 277–8.

4. George Englishman, *The Fore-Runner of Revenge*, 1642.

EPILOGUE

1. John Williams, *Great Britains Salomon : A Sermon Preached at the Magnificent Funerall of the Most High and Mighty King, James* . . . (London, 1625), sig. H3ʳ.

2. Goodman, II: 268.

3. Gardiner, IV: 84.

4. *Crumms Fal'n From King James's Table* in *The Miscellaneous Works of Sir Thomas Overbury*, ed. E. F. Rimbault (London, 1890), p. 272.

5. Stow, p. 841.

INDEX

Abbot, George, Archbishop of Canterbury, 95, 97, 134, 135, 138, 139, 143, 147, 182, 184, 185, 186, 190, 207, 266, 268, 270; character, 312; kills game-keeper, 312–13; 314, 316, 328, 331, 364, 365
Abington, Thomas, 74
Accatery, The, 26
Acuna, Diego Sarmiento de, Conde de Gondomar, 64, 65, 66, 67, 212, 283, 297, 315; first embassy to England, 321–8; ascendancy over King James, 324, 329, 330; second embassy, 336–41; English hatred for, 327, 341; his view of the Spanish match, 343, 347, 366; and parliament, 379–81
Adam, Mrs., 120, 121
Admiralty, The, 99–100
Adventure (ship), 122
Affrays, 250
'Aid' (feudal levy), 92, 156
Aikin, Lucy, 232
Albert, Archduke, Regent of the Spanish Netherlands, 40
Alexander, Henry, 162
Alexander, Sir Sigismund, 162
Aliaga, Luis de, 326
Alleyn, Edward, 353
Alnwick Abbey, 260
Alnwick Castle, 69
Alred, Henry, 231
Althorp, 23
Ambassadors, 56–68; special ambassadors, 56–7; lieger ambassadors, 63–4, 95, 96, 270, 273, 276, 316
Ancona, 274
Andrewes, Lancelot, Bishop of Chichester, Ely and Winchester, 167, 184, 310, 312, 313, 392
Anhalt, 142
Anne, Queen of England, marriage, 12–13; appearance and character, 21–2, 79, 264–6; travels to England, 23, 28, 30, 31, 32, 54, 56, 61, 62, 65; visited by brother, King of Denmark, 79, 83–4, 88, 114, 116, 135; opposes daughter's marriage, 143, 147, 150, 155, 166, 186, 187; and Buckingham, 207, 208, 242, 259; visits Bristol, 267; death, 268; funeral, 269–70, 277, 281, 282, 292, 312, 322
Annuities, 173
Ante-suppers, 163–4
Antimasques, 151, 187
Apethorpe, 166, 188, 260
Aphrodisiacs, 241
Appleby, 262

Architecture, 272, 277–85
Aremberg, Charles, Count of, 40, 61
Argyll (title). *See* Campbell
Aristotle, 248
Arminius, Jacobus, 311
Armoury, The, 25
Armstrong, Archie, 168, 171
Army, 129, 390
Arran (title). *See* Stewart
Arrest, courtiers' immunity from, 229
Art collecting, 222–3, 272–7
Arundel (title). *See* Howard
Arundel House, 276
Ashby-de-la-Zouch, 262
Ashton, 262
Aske Hall, 260
Aston, Sir Roger, 45, 49, 369
Astronomer Royal, 25
Atholl (title). *See* Stewart
Aubrey, Christopher, 296, 297, 300, 301
Aubrey, John, 241, 288
Audley End, 96, 103, 212
Avenors, 89

Babington, Gervase, Bishop of Llandaff, 303
Bacon, Lady Alice, 302
Bacon, Sir Francis, Lord Verulam, Viscount St. Alban; his opinion of Cecil, 106, 110, 111, 151, 155, 187, 191; prosecutor at Somerset's trial, 198, 201, 222, 248, 251; campaign against duelling, 256–7, 261, 276, 286–302; and Essex, 287–8; becomes Lord Keeper, 291; angers Buckingham, 292–4; regains his favour, 294; literary works, 295; character, 286–95, 299–301; impeachment, 296–9, 302, 317, 331, 333, 370; and Parliament, 372, 373, 374, 375, 376, 378
Bacon, Sir Nicholas, 286
Bake-House, The, 26, 89
Bancroft, Richard, Bishop of London and Archbishop of Canterbury, 128, 303, 305, 307, 311, 316, 371
Banqueting House. *See under* Whitehall
Banquets, 59, 83, 127, 155, 356
Barlow, William, Bishop of Rochester, and Lincoln, 72, 310
Barn-Elms, 125
Barnet, 120
Baronetcies, 233–5
Barons of the Cinque Ports, 30
Barons of the Exchequer, 88
'Barriers' (military sport), 130
Basil, Simon, 277
Basing, 81
Bate's Case, 92